On Burton Raffel's translation of

THE CANTERBURY TALES

" 'Wine can rot your mind,' warns Chaucer's Summoner, yet two tales earlier, a converse lament trickles from the same poet's Wife of Bath: 'Alas, alas, that ever love was sin.' Every kind of sentiment, of story; every form of speech, of speaker—no wonder *The Canterbury Tales* were 'unfinished'! Yet as they stand, they are complete, and now (not for the first time, but with a particular distinction, an emphasis on speed and the spur of the moment) the caracole from anxiety to lust, and back again, has been 'translated' into the kind of eager lection we managed to neologize for Shakespeare but had lost for the aberrance of an earlier language. This once we can sink into the narrative quicksand without *stalling for time* (and time's obstacular accents). The greatest *comédie humaine* in English herewith no longer barred from immediate consumption but rather urging its various tempers upon us, a gift from the poet and scholar (in that order) Burton Raffel, to whom many other vivications are owed. May I be among the first to thank him for this grandest fantasia in our literature on themes of reality and ... the other thing. As the insatiable Wife of Bath (who can escape her?) observes: 'Now lift the curtain, see just how it is.' "

—RICHARD HOWARD, *winner of the Pulitzer Prize for poetry*

GEOFFREY CHAUCER

THE CANTERBURY TALES

*A new unabridged translation
by Burton Raffel*

Introduction by John Miles Foley

THE MODERN LIBRARY

NEW YORK

LIBRARY OF CONGRESS CATALOGING-IN-PUBLICATION DATA
Chaucer, Geoffrey, d. 1400.
The Canterbury tales / Geoffrey Chaucer; a new translation by
Burton Raffel.—2008 Modern Library ed.
p.   cm.
ISBN 978-0-679-64355-5
1. Christian pilgrims and pilgrimages—Poetry.   2. Canterbury
(England)—Poetry.   3. Storytelling—Poetry.   4. Tales, Medieval.
I. Raffel, Burton.   II. Title.
PR1870.A1R34   2008   821'.1—dc22   2007049703

Printed in the United States of America on acid-free paper

www.modernlibrary.com

2 4 6 8 9 7 5 3 1

GEOFFREY CHAUCER

Geoffrey Chaucer, the preeminent English poet of the Middle Ages, is thought to have been born between 1340 and 1345 in London to parents John Chaucer, a prosperous wine merchant, and his wife, Agnes. Although little biographical information is confirmed, official royal service records have provided central facts. Chaucer was a public servant for much of his life, from about 1357 when he became a page, or personal servant, in the royal household of the Countess of Ulster, the wife of one of Edward III's sons. This position promised social mobility and afforded him an education in French, Latin, and Italian. Within a few years, he was promoted to the position of yeoman (higher than a sergeant, lower than a groom) under Prince Lionel and fought in the siege of Reims.

Few documents regarding Chaucer's life survive from the period 1360–67; however, it is known that he traveled extensively as a diplomatic messenger for the Crown, work that continued for many years and for which he was granted a lifetime annuity as a king's esquire. He married Philippa, daughter of Sir Payne Roet. During this time, Chaucer translated "Roman de la Rose," a popular secular poem, which in turn encouraged him to write poems and songs in both French and English.

The death of Blanche, Duchess of Lancaster, in 1368 is generally viewed as the impetus for Chaucer's first major poem, *The Book of the Duchess*. Running more than thirteen hundred lines, *The Book of the Duchess* is an elegiac and allegorical poem composed in the style of French court poetry. It employs a dream-vision framework, a French element that recurs throughout Chaucer's writing, with the narrator recounting a tale as if it had occurred in a dream.

In the early 1370s, Chaucer was again sent on trading and diplomatic missions. In Italy, he discovered the work of Dante, Petrarch, and Boccaccio, all of whom had a major influence on his poetry, especially in the use of vernacular language. In 1374, Chaucer was appointed controller of hides, skins, and wools in the port of London and was given small annuities and gifts from members of the royalty. His diplomatic work continued after the death of Edward III and the accession of Richard II in 1377. In addition to the short poem "Anelida and Arcite," his only major poetry from this period is an unfinished work of about two thousand lines titled *The House of Fame,* in which he reveals his skepticism of fame and possibly of his own reputation as a public poet.

But his fame increased. About 1380, he wrote *The Parliament of Fowls.* Heavily influenced by Boccaccio, this 699-line poem again uses the dream-vision to retell a mythical story about love and finding a mate, possibly alluding to the marriage negotiations of Richard II and Anne of Bohemia in 1380–81. During this decade, Chaucer also wrote *Troilus and Criseyde,* an eight thousand–line love poem about legendary Trojan War figures. It was modeled after both Boccaccio's *Il Frostrato* and Boethius's *The Consolation of Philosophy,* a classical work that Chaucer translated and retitled *Boece.* In 1385 Chaucer was appointed to a peace commission in Kent; in 1386, he served one session as a member of Parliament for Kent.

In the late 1380s, Chaucer produced an unfinished poem titled "The Legend of the Good Woman," written for Queen Anne. At this time, he resigned his posts and retired to Kent; his wife died in 1387; and he began work on the poem that would ensure his literary immortality, *The Canterbury Tales.* The frame for this poem is a pilgrimage during which thirty travelers must tell two tales each to pass the time. Many of the narratives would have been familiar to medieval readers, but Chaucer uses subtle satire to explore class issues, marriage, mortality, and religion. He worked at this poem for years but devoted more time to public service as the clerk of the king's works from 1389 to 1391 and, in the 1390s, as a deputy forester for the North Petherton Forest in Somerset. He also occupied himself with the composition of *A Treatise on the Astrolabe,* an essay on astronomy written for his son, Lewis, in 1391, and two short poems, "The Envoy to Bukton" and "The Envoy to Scogan."

Many of the individual tales that make up *The Canterbury Tales* had been circulated piecemeal among Chaucer's friends throughout the 1390s. With a prologue and twenty-four separate tales, however, the poem remained incomplete and without a finished ordering when Chaucer died on October 25, 1400 (according to his tomb at Westminster Abbey). Scholars have combined, arranged, and recopied the texts, helping to secure Chaucer's fame.

—THE MODERN LIBRARY

FOR JOSEF CHAIM PRIDE

Contents

THE CANTERBURY TALES

INTRODUCTION
John Miles Foley

A group of travelers of every sort
Arrived, who'd joined together as they walked
And rode. Turned good friends, they now proceeded
On as one, a band of pilgrims indeed,
Intending to worship Thomas at Canterbury.

—lines 23–27

THE WORLD OF *THE CANTERBURY TALES*

"Of every sort" indeed. Welcome to a world of characters you won't soon forget, of speeches and ideas and events that will stay with you long after you come to the end of the (supposedly) unfinished *Canterbury Tales*. For a start, consider the diverse and unlikely cross section of medieval society you'll be meeting. A Knight will begin by spinning a lofty narrative of romance and cosmology, which the lowly Miller will answer with a bawdy story of love and mistaken identity that reflects his view of the world, which in turn will so rankle the Reeve that he feels obliged to take his own tale-telling vengeance by featuring a doubly cuckolded miller. You'll encounter the infamous Wife of Bath, who never met a husband she couldn't tame—or almost never—and you'll hear some starkly conflicting ideas about marriage from such sources as the scholarly Clerk, for whom womanly patience is the highest virtue; the prosperous Merchant, who has "a wyf, the worste that may be" and recounts the perils of a January-to-May relationship; and the unabashedly epicurean Franklin, who through generosity of spirit charts a middle road between the medieval institutions of courtly love and the Christian Church.

Secular figures of all sorts appear, and religious orders, each with drastically different perspectives on the everyday world and the divine, abound as well. The lady Prioress sports a golden brooch with the inscription "Love conquers all," but her tale raises issues of anti-Semitism and moral rectitude. The Pardoner employs the bold gambit of first announcing his avarice and duplicitousness, then offering nothing less than a sermon on the seven deadly sins—before he once again drags out his facsimile relics and phony papal pardons to sell. The Parson may seem to provide a fit and satisfying closure to *The Canterbury Tales* by harmonizing the temporal and spiritual, at least until we remember that the original challenge (as formulated by the irrepressible Host, Harry Bailly) called for no fewer than four tales per pilgrim. If that's the plan, its actual implementation falls far short; some of the pilgrims fail to tell even a single tale, and none tells more than one. To make matters more confusing, Chaucer appends a short valedictory to the reader that seems to retract his major writings, among them *The Canterbury Tales,* as his final word.

So more than one question arises from the start. Are the *Tales* as we have them a fragment? Or is the original challenge a working fiction, that is, more a dynamic strategy than a set-in-stone blueprint? Is Chaucer truly distancing himself from his "translations and other writings, which deal only with worldly vanities," or hedging his religious bets, or simply adding another layer of operative fiction to his enterprise? On these points and on many others, just how realistically are we to understand this most diverse of storytelling communities? Just how do we grasp Chaucer's rich and wonderful portrayal of humanity?

CHAUCER'S INIMITABLE ART

One answer to the question of how to understand *The Canterbury Tales* lies in the nature of Chaucer's art, which presents a much more varied, traditional, and yet innovative landscape than we find in the modern and contemporary literature with which most of us are much more familiar. By "varied" I mean to emphasize not only the wide range of characters but in particular the many different kinds or genres of verbal art we find in the *Tales*. Writing over the last decades of the fourteenth century and deeply acquainted with Latin, French, and Italian as well as both classic and folklore-based English literature, Chaucer could choose from among many expressive color systems on his personal artistic palette. And his selections show extraordinary range.

What's more—and here is what I mean by "traditional"—these myriad choices already carried with them a host of expectations, of built-in, active associations and implications. In other words, the genres or types of poetry and prose from which Chaucer drew were in many ways idiomatic: They came complete with established plotlines, character types, stereotypical scenes, philosophical underpinnings, religious themes and clichés, and portraits of morality and immorality, as well as grounded, real-world attitudes and convictions. His tales thus appeal on many levels, and speak to hearers and readers with different life experiences about fundamental human concerns, bedrock issues that are as real and pressing in the twenty-first as in the fourteenth century. Audiences who grasp the highly varied nature and highly traditional background of the tales help create a reverberative context for their reception. At the same time, however, and much like Shakespeare's universally appealing creations, these same stories and characters and events can be deeply appreciated and enjoyed outside that frame of reference—that is, on their own terms. More than with any other author of his time (and most other eras as well), Chaucer's audience is everyone.

And why? Because alongside the inherent diversity and traditional origins of *The Canterbury Tales* stands perhaps their most impressive feature: Chaucer's innovative genius. For just as almost nothing in these *Tales* is wholly unprecedented in terms of prior literary or folkloric models, so no tale, character, genre, or scene escapes its author's singular, trademark stamp. At the most comprehensive level, consider the anthology-like system of the individual tales, the digest within which we read and react to separate but often interactive stories. Often called the "frame tale," this mega-structure goes back most immediately to Boccaccio's *Decameron* (completed about 1353) and ultimately at least to the medieval Arabic *Thousand and One Nights,* and probably much further.[1] But neither Boccaccio's nor any other frame story combines sequel tale-telling with such lively interchange across such a broad cross section of society; no other parallel or forebear raises such vital and timely questions for active and multifaceted debate among its constituency; and no other organizational fiction combines such a wealth of diverse tale types (suitably recast by the author) as an ever-evolving, many-sided narrative vehicle. As a whole and at its core, Chaucer's frame tale is both traditional and unprecedented—a judgment that applies equally to all of its contents as well.

VARIETY, TRADITION, AND INNOVATION IN THE *TALES*

And what about those contents? At one end of the spectrum lies the celebrated General Prologue, the extended dramatis personae that introduces the tale-tellers in swift, deft, and memorable fashion. Chaucer had no specific model for this lively set of portraits, which range from the august and honorific description of the Knight to tongue-in-cheek sketches of the irrepressibly merry Wife of Bath and the dour, scholarly Clerk to complex and contradictory portrayals like that of the unashamedly two-faced Pardoner. But there is more. So many of these unforgettable descriptions depend to some degree on contemporary rhetorical handbooks, the equivalent of medieval recipe books or manuals that contained inventories of conventional scenes, character-types, and rhetorical cues. But did that stereotypical background lead to stale formula writing or hackneyed characterization? Not in the capable hands of Chaucer, who never fails to mold a recognizable scene into something special, to turn stock figures into unique individuals, or to find fresh, suggestive ways to deploy standard rhetorical details in creating "new" characters. And if that weren't enough for the General Prologue to accomplish, he also uses this living frontispiece to introduce you to its fictional speaker— Chaucer the Pilgrim, who then serves as a naïve, delightful guide and narrative filter not just for the Prologue but for *The Canterbury Tales* as a whole, and not incidentally tells his own hilariously overblown and artistically negligible tale of "Sir Thopas."

This same blend of tradition and innovation across a varied set of story types appears everywhere in the separate tales that follow, but we must be content with a few examples. One of the best-established genres in medieval literature was the *fabliau,* the brief, bawdy, and comic French form that came to enjoy widespread currency in England.[2] But most non-Chaucerian *fabliaux* depended on relatively limited resources: They usually involved thinly drawn if highly recognizable character types such as promiscuous women with their betrayed mates, and priests with all sorts of moral failings, while the central action was, as many critics have noted, simple and single-stranded. The scene was set quickly, stock figures were deployed, and the inevitable climax ensued without much delay. Against this background of expectation Chaucer has his Miller tell a tale that delves into the psychology of a soon-to-be-cuckolded husband, a more than willing wife, her only too eager paramour, and a preening priest; and at the same time "quites" (revenges) what the Miller sees as the upper-class, over-serious, counter-worldly concerns of the Knight's tale that immediately precedes his own (just as the Reeve, who gives us another *fabliau* in the next story, will "quite" the Miller in different ways). Taken together, the first three tales after the General Prologue set a high standard for diversity of tales, tellers, issues, and perspectives. And if the characters, the basic actions, and the dénouement of the Miller's Tale are expectable enough, the virtuosity with which Chaucer moves far beyond the basic form is not.[3]

The Franklin's Tale offers cognate evidence of how the author of *The Canterbury Tales* manages to invoke familiar and resonant models in the process of creating something new and memorable for its uniqueness. In this case the foundation of the story is a *Breton lay*, another originally French genre, which typically concerns love-related adventures in a supernatural context of some sort. More precisely, scholars have traced this particular fable to an Italian source, Boccaccio's *Decameron*, but once again background is only part of the story. The tale opens with wife Dorigen and husband Arveragus happily married and devoted to each other, a situation threatened by the courtly lover Aurelius, the third leg in the triangle. When Dorigen foolishly agrees to allay his love pains if and only if he manages to remove all of the stones from the shores of Britain (ordinarily a safe bet!), Aurelius secures the assistance of a magician who uses his powers to create the illusion that he has done just that. Surprisingly to some, perhaps, the husband then insists his wife honor her ill-considered promise, and Aurelius responds in kind by releasing her from her verbal contract to become his lover. Typically, Chaucer's story is familiar in its cast of characters and general tale type (if markedly longer and more developed), and medieval audiences will have recognized the story map in its broad outlines. But Chaucer puts this idiomatic sequence of events into the hands of the Franklin, who responds to the ongoing theme of marital and extramarital relationships in the *Tales* by proposing his own solution to the often-posed problem of sovereignty in marriage. What matters most, he is saying through his tale, is not who's in charge but rather how partners can show each other selfless tolerance, goodwill, and generosity. And when the Franklin closes the proceedings with a more-than-rhetorical question addressed to the reader—"Which was the mooste fre, as thynketh you?"—our best response is not to affirm one or another hierarchy of authority but to recognize that an open-minded and trusting democracy "frees" both husband and wife.

CHAUCER AND MEDIEVAL LITERATURE

Because Chaucer's *Canterbury Tales* did not exist in a vacuum, it is important to glimpse what else was transpiring over the many centuries of medieval literature and especially during his own fourteenth century. The medieval period begins in England with the coming of the Angles, Saxons, and Jutes to the island, probably about 449 C.E., if we believe the seventh-century historian Bede's account. But since literacy was rare and narrowly employed for hundreds of years, most of the "literature" we call Old English or Anglo-Saxon stems directly or indirectly from oral tradition, with the major manuscripts dated only to the last third of the tenth century. This means that *Beowulf,* for example, presumably lived as a told and re-told story before being committed to writing, and that even after the establishment of textual technology, the poets of the Old English period continued to use specialized poetic language and forms that derived from oral tradition. Poems such as "The Seafarer," which Ezra Pound translated so memorably, or "The Dream of the Cross," which portrays a heroic Christ modeled on the Germanic warrior, constituted a tightly knit poetic tradition that depended on shared phrases and patterns for its structure and highly resonant art.[4]

Notwithstanding their historical relationship, Old English literature (roughly 450–1100 C.E.) is surprisingly discontinuous with Middle English literature (1100–1500 C.E.), leaving Chaucer and his contemporaries with much more of a debt to continental than to earlier "English" literature. The reasons for this discontinuity are primarily linguistic and cultural. At root, English belongs to the Germanic family of Indo-European languages, but it underwent enormous changes in the centuries immediately preceding Chaucer's time. What the Angles and Saxons brought to England looks and sounds much more like modern German than modern English. Conventionally called "Old English" or "Anglo-Saxon," it was already influenced to various degrees by Latin during the Roman occupation, and by Old Norse, the language of the Viking invaders. After William the Conqueror's victory over King Harold II at the Battle of Hastings in 1066, however, Norman French culture began to enter the picture as a major and continuous force, introducing French word stock, sounds, and literary forms.

As a result of the Norman Conquest and all that it engendered, the next stage of our language, called "Middle English" (1100–1500), looked and sounded very different from Anglo-Saxon. For one thing, it was more a collection of dialects than a single uniform language.[5] Five dialects arose, each of them supporting well-known literary works: Northern (e.g., John Barbour's *Bruce*), Southern (the anonymous *Owl and the Nightingale*), Kentish (the *Ayenbite of Inwyt*), West Midland (*Sir Gawain and the Green Knight, Pearl,* and William Langland's *Piers Plowman*), and East Midland (John Gower's *Confessio Amantis,* and, above all, the works of Geoffrey Chaucer). In time, the East Midland dialect eventually produced the London standard that was to become the basis of today's English. Chaucer's language is the direct ancestor of the English we speak.

CHAUCER'S OWN WORKS

As a well-informed literary person of his time and a well-traveled man of the world, Chaucer used his experience with Latin, French, Italian, and English literature to craft an extensive and heterogeneous body of work. Besides *The Canterbury Tales,* his other major achievement was the courtly romance entitled *Troilus and Criseyde,* the much-adapted tragic tale of the Trojan prince and his lover Criseyde that was also to become Shakespeare's *Troilus and Cressida.* As almost always, Chaucer's poem has a clear source: again Boccaccio, this time *Il Filostrato,* a so-called historical romance in its own right. But Chaucer tells the story not only at considerable length (five books totaling more than 8,000 lines arranged in rhyme royal stanzas, or ABABBCC), but more importantly in significant depth. His characterization of the two principals, Priam's honorable son Troilus and the much-beleaguered, noble Criseyde, as well as of the intermediary Pandarus (source of the pejorative verb "pander"), far outstrips his immediate source in Boccaccio or Benoît de Sainte-Maure's *Roman de Troie,* an even earlier French version of the story. And, in addition to summoning classical and medieval conventions appropriate to the genre, he instills in his characters—most especially Criseyde—a psychological texture and complexity unique in the medieval period. We wonder with her about the place of courtly love in society, about what loyalty and freedom mean in trying times, about the price of honor and trust within an unstable environment, and we agonize with Troilus on many of the same scores. In *Troilus and Criseyde* Chaucer presents us with a living digest of contemporary fourteenth-century issues clothed in classical garb, and not incidentally with a collection of universal, timeless human problems with which we can readily identify today.

Among Chaucer's other works, the most frequently read and written about are probably *The Book of the Duchess, The House of Fame,* and *The Parliament of Fowls,* which share the same story type but tackle quite different contemporary issues (that are once again universal human concerns as well). He also completed a partial translation of Jean de Meun's and

Guillaume de Lorris's hugely influential (and likewise unfinished) *Romance of the Rose*,[6] arguably the most important source work, across languages and cultures, of the later Middle Ages. *The Book of the Duchess* is a dream vision, one of the most common medieval story forms, that packs an allegorical punch, portraying a courtly love relationship between a black knight and his paramour, a lady named White. Also a dream vision, *The House of Fame* depends more on Latin and Italian precursors (principally Virgil, Ovid, and Dante) than on French models, though it uses the same framing strategy of a reader falling asleep while perusing a book. Apparently unfinished, this highly derivative and yet highly original poem discusses the nature of reputation and achievement through the dreamer's experience in the temple of Venus and houses of Fame and Rumor. *The Parliament of Fowls* presents yet another dream vision initiated by a reader nodding off, this time over the *Somnium Scipionis* (*The Dream of Scipio*) by the Roman author Cicero. Scipio Africanus, the celebrated Roman general who defeated Hannibal, then guides Chaucer's dreamer on a journey that culminates at a parliament in which competing birds choose their mates and argue their own worthiness. Using the well-known medieval strategy of imaging human actions and speech by referral to the animal world, Chaucer opts to let the upper-echelon competition end without any of the three competing tercel eagles (the males) winning the formel, but Nature intervenes and the lower-caste birds go ahead with their choices while spring erupts and the dreamer wakes. We're reminded of the General Prologue's time index for spring, fertility, and the start of the Canterbury pilgrimage: when "the sun, still young in the sky, / Compels small birds to sing their melodies, / Creatures who sleep at night with open eyes" (lines 7–9).

MAJOR CRITICAL TRENDS AND INTERPRETATIONS

As might be expected, an author as accomplished as Chaucer, with as broad and varied a repertoire as his, has inspired numerous different approaches to understanding and interpreting *The Canterbury Tales* and his other works. Two of the most basic address the double identity of the *Tales* as an oral performance and a medieval manuscript. Betsy Bowden's *Chaucer Aloud* is a unique guide to understanding the roots of the pilgrimage poem as a performed event, and includes recordings of thirty-two alternate performances of three passages from the poem, while Carl

Lindahl's *Earnest Games* lays bare some crucial folkloric patterns to counterbalance literary theories and return Chaucer to his composite medieval milieu. On the other side of the media divide, which was not as severe or exclusive in Chaucer's day as in our own, Ralph Hanna provides a readable introduction to what we can make of the Ellesmere and Hengwyrt manuscripts, the two principal textual sources for the editions of the *Tales* that have been assembled by scholars.[7]

Other perspectives on Chaucer and his art have included longstanding attention to philosophy,[8] especially Boethius's *Consolation of Philosophy* (dated about 524), and to the plethora of sources and analogues for his various works. Interested readers can consult Alastair Minnis's *Chaucer and Pagan Antiquity,* James Wimsatt's *Chaucer and His French Contemporaries,* and David Wallace's *Chaucer and the Early Writings of Boccaccio* to get some idea of the comparative context, and any first-rate edition of the *Tales* also includes apposite information on sources and analogues. But it is well to warn that, as noted above, models and correspondences are only half of the story: What Chaucer does with these shared traditions to make them his own remains a crucial aspect of the remarkable chemistry that characterizes his art.

In recent years the approach called "new historicism," pioneered by Lee Patterson,[9] has won wide acclaim and application. This perspective seeks to imagine how Chaucer's poetry can be understood from within its fourteenth-century historical context, yet without abandoning the tools of textual studies, linguistics, and even formalism. The challenge is "that if we can understand his poetry in something of the way in which he might have understood it himself, it can teach us more about ourselves than our immersion in our own modernity hides from us."[10] Toward that end, study of the late fourteenth century—not only its principal literary figures and works but also the network of real-life social concerns that served as their platform—can only enrich our reading of the *Tales.*

Another important strand of current critical thought is gender studies, which has sought to shake off conventional and unexamined notions about authors and their literary creations in favor of considering frequently ignored issues and problems associated with gender identity and interaction. Relatively early, Priscilla Martin's *Chaucer's Women* offered the first full-length consideration of women in a number of Chaucer's poems, and more recently Jill Mann's *Feminizing Chaucer* and Alcuin Blamires's *Chaucer, Ethics, and Gender* have more deeply theorized the discussion.

On the centuries-long history of reception, the grand and complex "tale" of Chaucer criticism from the medieval to the postmodern period, Stephanie Trigg's *Congenial Souls* provides an excellent guide. Companions to Chaucer in general or specifically on the *Tales* range from topic-oriented and thematic,[11] to broad-based and multi-focused,[12] to an A–Z dictionary of Chauceriana,[13] to a comprehensive collection of essays that includes information on Chaucer's reputation and influence in later centuries.[14] The *Wikipedia* article on *The Canterbury Tales* offers general information and links to many resources (including audio clips and external resources), and the continuously updated online bibliography published by the New Chaucer Society provides a searchable, annotated, and convenient resource.

RAFFEL'S *TALES*

For this reader, the genius of Chaucer has always resided most fundamentally in his thoroughgoing and delightful readability. Beyond the secondary activities of analysis, source hunting, critical interpretations, and the like, the *Canterbury Tales* presents a uniquely memorable experience rooted in their author's deft touch, lyric voice, human sensibility, citizen-of-the-world awareness, and unmatched sense of humor. To put it another way, no matter how weighty the superficial or underlying issues, no matter how complex the philosophy or religion or science associated with his subject, Chaucer has a knack for conveying his vision of humanity and how the world works, and for doing so with brilliant simplicity and grace. He doesn't keep us at arm's length, creating distance between reader and author; instead, he draws us in, speaks to us directly, and communicates sincerely (even when he's clearly pulling our leg).

To his great credit, that's just what Burton Raffel does with his and Chaucer's *Canterbury Tales*. Reflecting the quick, nimble movement of Chaucer's verse, the translator performs his own literary miracle by constructing an intelligible medieval world for the reader to explore. He uses modern English versions of Middle English words whenever and wherever he can, but doesn't shrink from updating or simply adjusting vocabulary and phrasing to keep his fictive universe linguistically whole and believable. Lavish descriptions are rendered lavishly but without resorting to artifice; sententious remarks sound appropriately hollow or arresting. At a fundamental level, the narrator's comments on the lively proceedings come across just as naïve and ironic (and many of Chaucer the pilgrim's comments are both at the same time) as in the original text, while the dueling interchanges among characters ring true to the Canterbury pilgrims' descriptions, diverse life experiences, and actual words. In short, Raffel's storytelling sounds like Chaucer's storytelling—so much so that *Tales* in this volume could and should be brought to life by reading them aloud, a practice to be strongly encouraged whether the audience is a literature class, one's friends or family, or even oneself.

So, then: Is reading this translation precisely the same experience as reading Chaucer inside his East Midlands dialect of Middle English and within the "indigenous" context of late fourteenth-century literature and culture? Of course not—that's a categorical impossibility. But Raffel has succeeded in creating a masterful facsimile, a crystal-clear window on the *Tales* world that allows us to appreciate its medieval character and context, its twenty-first century relevance, and thereby its timeless vitality. Unless and until you decide to make a personal pilgrimage through the original-language text, Burton Raffel's translation will provide far the best available realization of Chaucer's signature art.

BIBLIOGRAPHY

ORIGINAL-LANGUAGE EDITIONS
Larry Benson, ed., *The Canterbury Tales: Complete*. Boston: Houghton Mifflin, 2000.
John H. Fisher, ed., *The Complete Poetry and Prose of Geoffrey Chaucer*. New York: Wadsworth, 1989.
F. N. Robinson, ed., *The Works of Geoffrey Chaucer*, 2nd ed. Boston: Houghton Mifflin, 1961.

LITERARY HISTORY AND BACKGROUND
Thomas D. Cooke, *The Old French and Chaucerian Fabliaux: A Study of Their Comic Climax*. Columbia: University of Missouri Press, 1978.
Helen Cooper, *Oxford Guides to Chaucer: The Canterbury Tales*, 2nd ed. Oxford: Oxford University Press, 1996.
Steve Ellis, ed., *Chaucer: An Oxford Guide*. Oxford: Oxford University Press, 2005.
Douglas Gray, ed., *The Oxford Companion to Chaucer*. Oxford: Oxford University Press, 2003.
Robert L. Harrison, *Gallic Salt: Glimpses of the Hilarious Bawdy World of Old French Fabliaux*. Berkeley and Los Angeles: University of California Press, 1974.

Frances Horgan, trans., *The Romance of the Rose*. Oxford: Oxford University Press, 1999.

Bonnie D. Irwin. "What's in a Frame? The Medieval Textualization of Traditional Storytelling," *Oral Tradition*, 10 (1995): 27–53. Available online at http://journal.oraltradition.org/files/articles/10i/6_irwin.pdf

Norris J. Lacy, *Reading Fabliaux*. New York: Garland, 1993.

Seth Lerer, ed., *The Yale Companion to Chaucer*. New Haven: Yale University Press, 2006.

Lee Patterson, ed., *Geoffrey Chaucer's The Canterbury Tales: A Casebook*. New York: Oxford University Press, 2007.

David Wallace, ed., *Medieval English Literature*. Cambridge: Cambridge University Press, 1999.

CHAUCER AND THE ENGLISH LANGUAGE

Albert C. Baugh and Thomas Cable, *A History of the English Language*, 5th ed. Upper Saddle River, New Jersey: Prentice Hall, 2001.

Simon Horobin, *Chaucer's Language*. New York: Palgrave Macmillan, 2007.

Fernand Mossé, *A Handbook of Middle English*, trans. James A. Walker. 2nd ed. Baltimore: Johns Hopkins University Press, 2000.

CHAUCER'S CONTEMPORARIES

Russell A. Peck and Andrew Galloway, ed. and trans., *John Gower: Confessio Amantis*. Kalamazoo: Medieval Institute Publications, 2000.

Burton Raffel, trans., *Sir Gawain and the Green Knight*. New York: Signet, 2001.

Elizabeth Ann Robertson and Stephen H. A. Shepherd, eds., *Piers Plowman*. New York: Norton, 2000.

William Vantuono, ed. and trans., *Pearl: An Edition with Verse Translation*. Notre Dame: University of Notre Dame Press, 1995.

OLD ENGLISH LITERATURE

Robert D. Fulk and Christopher M. Cain, *A History of Old English Literature*. New York: Wiley-Blackwell, 2004.

Burton Raffel, trans., *Beowulf*. New York: Signet, 2008.

———, trans., *Poems and Prose from the Old English*. New Haven: Yale University Press, 1998.

APPROACHES TO CHAUCER

Alcuin Blamires, *Chaucer, Ethics, and Gender*. New York: Oxford University Press, 2006.

Betsy Bowden, *Chaucer Aloud*. Philadelphia: University of Pennsylvania Press, 1987.

Ralph Hanna, *Pursuing History: Middle English Manuscripts and Their Texts*. Stanford: Stanford University Press, 1996.

Carl Lindahl, *Earnest Games: Folkloric Patterns in the Canterbury Tales*. Bloomington: Indiana University Press, 1987.

Jill Mann, *Feminizing Chaucer.* Woodbridge and Rochester: D. S. Brewer, 2002.

Jill Mann and Piero Boitani, eds., *The Cambridge Companion to Chaucer.* Cambridge: Cambridge University Press, 2003.

Priscilla Martin, *Chaucer's Women: Nuns, Wives, and Amazons.* London: Macmillan, 1990.

Mark Miller, *Philosophical Chaucer: Love, Sex, and Agency in the Canterbury Tales.* Cambridge: Cambridge University Press, 2005.

Alastair Minnis, *Chaucer and Pagan Antiquity.* Cambridge: Cambridge University Press, 1982.

Lee Patterson, *Chaucer and the Subject of History.* Madison: University of Wisconsin Press, 1991.

————, *Temporal Circumstances: Form and History in the Canterbury Tales.* New York: Palgrave Macmillan, 2006.

Stephanie Trigg, *Congenial Souls: Reading Chaucer from Medieval to Postmodern.* Minneapolis: University of Minnesota Press, 2002.

David Wallace, *Chaucer and the Early Writings of Boccaccio.* London: D. S. Brewer, 1985.

James Wimsatt, *Chaucer and His French Contemporaries.* Toronto: University of Toronto Press, 1991.

ONLINE RESOURCES

Online bibliography of Chaucer criticism, New Chaucer Society: http://artsci.wustl.edu/~chaucer/bibliography.php

Wikipedia entry on *The Canterbury Tales:* http://en.wikipedia.org/wiki/Canterbury_Tales

NOTES

1. See Irwin, "What's in a Frame?"
2. See Harrison, *Gallic Salt.*
3. See Cooke, *The Old French and Chaucerian Fabliaux;* Lacy, *Reading Fabliaux.*
4. See Raffel, trans., *Beowulf* and *Poems and Prose from the Old English;* also Fulk and Cain, *A History of Old English Literature.*
5. See Baugh and Cable, *A History of the English Language;* also Horobin, *Chaucer's Language;* and, for background, Mossé, *A Handbook of Middle English.*
6. See Horgan, trans., *The Romance of the Rose.*
7. See Benson, Fisher, and Robinson for the three most commonly used original-language editions of *The Canterbury Tales.* The latter two also contain Chaucer's other works.
8. See, in general terms, Miller, *Philosophical Chaucer.*
9. See both *Chaucer and the Subject of History* and *Temporal Circumstances.*
10. Patterson, *Temporal Circumstances,* p. 18.
11. See Mann and Boitani, *The Cambridge Companion to Chaucer* and Patterson's *Geoffrey Chaucer's The Canterbury Tales.*
12. See Cooper, *Oxford Guides to Chaucer: The Canterbury Tales* and Lerer, *The Yale Companion to Chaucer.*
13. See Gray, *The Oxford Companion to Chaucer.*
14. See Ellis, *Chaucer: An Oxford Guide.*

Translator's Foreword

Literary classics do not change their language. But the languages in which they were composed are constantly changing. Homer's Greek, dating from about 800 BCE, remains Homer's Greek, but even a native speaker of modern Greek cannot read the classical form of his language without having studied it.

And the same thing is true of classical works written in English. The oldest surviving poem in our language, now titled "Caedmon's Hymn," looks like this:

> Nu scyuln herigean   heofonrices weard,
> meotodes meahte   and his modgethanc,
> weorc wuldorfæder,   swa he wundra gehwæs,
> ece drihten,   or onstealde.
> He ærest sceop   eaorthan bearnum
> heoofon to hrofe,   halig scyppend;
> tha middangeard   moncynnes weard,
> ece drihten,   æfter teode
> firum foldan,   frea ælmihtig.

This stage of our language is called Old English, and it might almost as well be Greek. I translated this poem in 1960:

Now sing the glory of God, the King
Of Heaven, our Father's power and His perfect
Labor, the world's conception, worked
In miracles as eternity's Lord made
The beginning. First the heavens were formed as a roof
For men, and then the holy Creator,

Eternal Lord and protector of souls,
Shaped our earth, prepared our home,
The almighty Master, our Prince, our God.

Old English evolved into Middle English, that evolution being quickened and changed by the Norman Conquest of 1066. Some Middle English poems looked like this:

Sithen the sege and the assaut watz sesed at Troye,
The borg brittened and brent to brondez and askez,
The tulk that the trammes of tresoun ther wrogt,
Watz tried for his treacherie, the trewest on erthe . . .

This is the opening of *Sir Gawain and the Green Knight* (*c*.1375–1500; the author is unknown). There is no need to translate it here. I offer it only as a language specimen, and plainly the language looks more like ours than Old English does but remains almost as hard to decipher.

In a somer sesun   whon softe was the sonne,
I schop me in-to a schroud   a scheep as I were;
In habite of an hermite   un-holy of werkes,
Wende I wydene in this world   wonders to here.

And this is the opening of *Piers Plowman,* by William Langland (the poem dates from *c*.1367–86; Langland lived from *c*.1330–86). Like *Sir Gawain and the Green Knight,* this is a poem that has long since been readable only by the learnèd, or in translation.

Yet as late as 1944, when I first read Chaucer (*c*.1343–1400), his language was not considered excessively difficult. A passage like the following, which my classmates and I were required to memorize, was certainly different from what we ordinarily read, but by no means impenetrable:

Whan that Aprill with his shoures soote
The droghte of March hath perced to the roote,
And bathed every veyne in swich licour
Of which vertu engendred is the flour;
Whan Zephirus eeke with his sweete breeth
Inspired hath in every holt and heeth
The tender croppes, and the yonge sonne

Hath in the Ram his halve cours yronne,
And smale foweles maken melodye,
That slepen al the nyght with open ye
(So priketh hem nature in his corages),
Thanne longen folk to goon on pilgrimages . . .

These are the opening lines of the long, unfinished poem here trans-
lated, Chaucer's *The Canterbury Tales*. There are unfamiliar words, and
the metrics—the poetic *movement*—are not at all clear. (Englishmen as
late as the seventeenth and eighteenth centuries could not follow
Chaucer's metrics, and thought him a brilliant but crude poet.) Still, na-
tive speakers of English, as recently as the first half of the twentieth cen-
tury, were not particularly uncomfortable with Chaucer's difficulties.
Time has, however, continued to move on, and our language has moved
with it. As is always the case, what was is now no more.

And that is why I have translated *The Canterbury Tales*.

I have tried to give as much of the *effect* of Chaucer's poetry as I could.
I have often borrowed Chaucer's words and even his rhymes. Indeed, I
have borrowed them whenever it was linguistically possible to do so. But
the *sound* of Chaucer is no more reproducible in modern English than is
the sound of Homer, or even the sound of Caedmon, whose language was
Old, not Modern, English. Chaucer's syntax—that is, the arrangement
and structure of his sentences—is sometimes like ours and sometimes it
is not. To insert the syntax of his Middle English into a Modern English
translation would destroy whatever poetic integrity and value the trans-
lation might have. This is equally a problem with Chaucer's grammar—
that is, the form and shape of his words—and I have been obliged to treat
this too as a line I cannot allow my translation to cross.

For as I have been saying, and writing, for half a century: *A translation
is not the original which it translates,* nor can it ever be. If you want and have
the opportunity to master Chaucer in the original, by all means do so. He
is by universal assent one of the three greatest poets in all of premodern
English poetry, the other two being Shakespeare, who is *the* greatest, and
Milton, who is either just behind or just ahead of Chaucer. But if you do
not have the opportunity, or the time, or the impulse to master Chaucer's
poetry in its original language, I think you can see and appreciate much
of his greatness in these pages. I am myself a poet—but Chaucer is far
better than I am. I have no desire to compete with him, or to rewrite his

poem. Here in these pages is as much as I have been able to bring out of Chaucer's fourteenth-century poem and into our language. I hope he is still well worth reading, even in translation.

ABOUT THIS TEXT

A translator is, almost by definition, in the position of an editor. But it is in his own language where he thus operates, not in the language of the author. There are many reliable editions of Chaucer's Middle English poetry. (I have here worked chiefly from F. N. Robinson, *The Works of Geoffrey Chaucer,* 2nd ed. Boston: Houghton Mifflin, 1961.; I have also, from time to time, consulted a variety of other editions, including the updated version of Robinson's text, a by-many-hands edition from the same publisher, edited in 2000 primarily by Larry D. Benson.) But none of the printed texts of *The Canterbury Tales* can truly be called "complete," because (a) Chaucer never finished the poem, and (b) Chaucer did not prepare a full, consecutive grouping of what he lived to finish. There are many manuscripts, written by many different hands; some manuscripts overlap with others, but some do not. (The best short overview of this is E. T. Donaldson, "The Manuscripts of Chaucer's Works and Their Use," in *Geoffrey Chaucer,* ed. by Derek Brewer. Ohio University Press, 1975, pp. 85–108.)

The scholarly consensus is that, when carefully collated and compared, there is a basic set of nine fundamental "fragments." Since this book is a translation *from* rather than an edition *of* the poem, I have not indicated where one fragment leaves off and another begins. Editions of the Middle English text often lineate from one fragment to the next— that is, numbering consecutively, straight through from the start of a fragment to the end of that fragment, repeating the process with each fragment. This is a somewhat risky business, since not all editors agree on the proper ordering of the fragments. Accordingly, I have lineated from the beginning of each tale to that tale's end and then started again with the tale that follows. Although I have been unable to match my translation, line by line, with the original—the syntax of Modern English does not always line up with that of Middle English—I have tried to match overall line length quite closely. The huge "Knight's Tale," e.g., is 2,248 lines as Chaucer wrote it, and 2,249 lines in this translation.

Translations do, however, present important editorial issues. The word "manciple," for example, is used by Chaucer fairly often; one of the tales belongs to the character thus named. But of a hundred native speakers of English, I doubt that even one will know the word's meaning. I have therefore changed "manciple" into "provisioner"—not exactly a thing of beauty, but unobnoxious as well as readily understandable. Comprehension by modern readers is the key. I have for the same reason changed "reeve" to "steward" and retitled Chaucer's Pardoner as "the Pardon-Peddler." Again, since virtually no one, today, understands what a "canon" is, or what he does, or even where he does it, and much the same may be said of a "yeoman," I have translated "The Canon's Yeoman's Prologue" and "The Canon's Yeoman's Tale" into "Prologue of the Cleric-Magician's Servant" and "Tale of the Cleric-Magician's Servant."

I use the word "cleric," here and elsewhere, rather than the Middle English "clerk," a word that is sprinkled all up and down Chaucer's pages (and pronounced to rhyme with "clark"), because (1) a "canon" was a cathedral official, and a priest, and (2) Middle English "clerk" has two basic meanings, only the secondary one of which has survived into our day. "Clerk," in Chaucer's work, is primarily used to mean someone who has studied to become a priest. This primary meaning, unfortunately, has sunk into the darkness of history, at least in common usage. Again, it is only the secondary meaning—someone who does secretarial and similar lower-level work—which the word "clerk" conveys, in our time.

In "The Miller's Tale," this happens to be Chaucer's meaning, too, and so in that tale, at least, a Middle English "clerk" can be allowed to remain a Modern English "clerk." But "the clerk of Oxenford" cannot, today, be so labeled—and thus he and all the other "clerks" like him have become, in these pages, "clerics."

Some larger issues in the translation of poetry, especially the handling of form (couplets, rime royal, etc.), are relatively simple to describe but exceedingly difficult to analyze. If I were asked, for example, why rime royal in "The Cleric's Tale" is in this translation rhymed more tightly, and thus more properly, than is the same form in "The Man of Law's Tale," I would have to say something like, "Well, 'The Cleric's Tale' is a better poem.'" But what does that *mean?* Shouldn't a less powerful, more loosely structured poem be easier, and not harder, to deal with, even in matters formal? I don't know the answer to that question. I would guess that somehow the translator, and thus the translation, has been influenced for the better by the taut rhetoric of "The Cleric's Tale," as well as by the Middle English poem's fuller and more fluent adherence to the demands of rime royal. (There is more poetic "cheating" in "The Man of Law's Tale"—but that is no subject for a brief foreword.) Talk about evasive generalities! Or, as my mother often used to say to me, "If you ask a silly question, don't be surprised when you get a silly answer."

Punctuation is a smaller and much more readily explained translation issue. Standards in such matters change, over time, and the blunt fact is that, frequently, punctuation does not exist, or is distinctly fragmentary, in older manuscripts like those of Chaucer's work. Modern editors of Chaucer have been obliged to supply most of the punctuation in their editions. I have frequently had to do the same thing, but for very different reasons. Punctuation is a set of signals, designed to enhance reader comprehension. But the *grammar* (the general rules of a language) of Chaucer's English is, not surprisingly, in significant ways unlike English grammar today. And the *syntax* (the arrangement of words in an utterance/sentence) has become perhaps even less similar. In this translation's punctuation and syntax, accordingly, I have had to set out acceptable ("readable") modern punctuation for a syntactically (as well as lexically) unmodern text. These are minor but knotty issues, and I want to do no more here than present the problems. I have solved them, to the extent that I have been successful, on the battlefield, not on a blackboard or in my study. That is to say, this translation has been punctuated by the particular needs of a specific sentence or phrase, and not by traditional principles—which are, in any case, extremely variable, there being *no* single standard principle for modern English punctuation.

I have tried, with some consistency, to quietly translate Latin phrases (and some Latin sentences) into English. The Latin items I did not so translate—for a considerable range of reasons—are not many, and they are available to the reader in the Notes section at the end of this book.

This being a translation from Middle English into our Modern language, I have not provided an elaborate guide to pronunciation—as editors of Chaucer's Middle English must do. For many words adapted from other languages, however, I have used a superscript sign (i.e., a mark placed over a vowel, as in Áve María) to indicate where stress should fall. I have sometimes used the same sign to indicate proper stress in less familiar words, as for example "márinér." I have employed the traditional sign used in "silent *e*" words, when a particular silent *e* is meant to be no longer silent (as in "cursèd"). This is a messy solution to a historically created situation: please take it simply on faith that I know what I'm doing.

TRANSLATING CHAUCER'S PROSE

Roughly a quarter of *The Canterbury Tales* is prose, not poetry. Prose is employed in two not entirely readable tales, "The Tale of Melibee" and—the longest segment of the entire volume—"The Parson's Tale."

Chaucer is a very great poet, the equal of every poet writing in our language, with the single exception of Shakespeare. But in the fourteenth century, English was just beginning to assert itself as the national tongue. After the Norman Conquest of 1066, although the common folk continued to speak English, no one else of consequence used anything but French. French was the language of the king's court; it was the language of all the law courts—a situation that lasted until the fifteenth century; it was the language of diplomacy, of high-order commerce, and certainly of high society.

In short, English had more or less gone underground. There are steadily increasing quantities of poetry, in English, which on the surviving record show continual progress toward standardization, particularly in the half century before Chaucer's time. Chaucer had a good deal to build on and to work with, in poetry. He did not, for example, invent the basic iambic pentameter metric, but he is surely its full and brilliant polisher, its shaper and standardizer. But there are only scattered scraps of prose, in English, mostly commercial and legal of nature. Latin, of course, had remained the language of the Church and of men of learning. However, in the thirteenth and, conclusively, in the fourteenth century, the English king and his lords were forced to choose between England and France. That is, the growing power of the hitherto weak French kings allowed him to make Englishmen choose either landownership and citizenship in France alone, or landownership and citizenship in England alone. Dual and simultaneous landownership and citizenship in both countries was now abolished, at least as to Englishmen's land and citizenship rights in France. After almost half a millennium of ever more comfortable rule and occupation, following on the Norman Conquest of 1066, the heirs of the Norman conquerors were without exception more "at home" in England than in France. They unanimously chose to retain their English holdings, though for many years they fought, ultimately without success, to regain their French lands and citizenship.

It would be an oversimplification to say that they then wholeheartedly embraced the English language as well as England. But by Chaucer's time (c.1342–1400), and especially under the rule of Chaucer's "patron," Richard II (king from 1377–1399), English had more or less inevitably become the language of choice. So familiar and powerfully entrenched were many French words, however, that over fifty thousand of them found their way into English. And so persistently ambivalent were the English that, although Chaucer wrote almost exclusively in English, his contemporary and friend John Gower (c.1330–1408) began his poetic career by writing in French, and then in Latin, and only toward the end of his long career did he finally turn to English.

Poetry is a universal form of utterance, existing in every culture of which we have knowledge, living or dead. Prose is not universal, since it comes into existence only when a culture and its language turn to *written* expression. (Poetry, in all the languages we know of, has begun as an oral form; we believe that Homer, one of the greatest of all the world's poets, the equal of Shakespeare and Dante, neither did nor could himself record his work on the written page.) Neither all cultures nor all languages have written forms—and when they do it takes time for those forms to stabilize, and even longer for them to excel. I do not refer simply to spelling issues, which are serious enough, but to the much larger and infinitely more difficult issues of grammar, syntax, and—at last— what we can loosely call "style and form." These stabilizations and standardizations had not yet occurred in Chaucer's time, and most of his prose is at best undistinguished, and sometimes plainly bad—that is, clumsy, ungraceful, and distinctly hard to follow. Nor does Chaucer as a writer of prose ever achieve anything like the brilliance of English's first great writer of prose, Thomas Malory, who died in 1471 (his dates, like his precise identity, are uncertain). The difference in time between the two writers is almost a century; the difference in prose quality—again, because of the very different cultural and linguistic matrix in which each of them worked—is enormous. English prose developed quickly, from a long-range perspective: those who followed Malory are legion. But the boat had left port before Chaucer ever had the chance to board it.

Translation is not supposed either to worsen or to improve what it tries to *re*-create. Change is obviously unavoidable, but quality—ideally—should be pretty much the same. Oddly, though it is frequently impossible for a translator to equal the author he translates, in the case of Chaucer's prose the difficulty lies in avoiding improvement. I have tried to be fair both to the modern reader and to my manifestly struggling fourteenth-century author. It may well be that, once upon a time, Chaucer's prose was as wholly readable, even pleasing, as literary prose tends to be today. I doubt that anyone truly knows. But all the same, *Caveat lector*—Reader be warned!

THE
CANTERBURY
TALES

General Prologue

When April arrives, and with his sweetened showers
Drenches dried-up roots, gives them power
To stir dead plants and sprout the living flowers
That spring has always spread across these fields,
And the God of Winds then blows his gentle seeds   5
In every wood and heath of England, feeding
Tender crops, as the sun, still young in the sky,
Compels small birds to sing their melodies,
Creatures who sleep at night with open eyes
(Exactly as Nature frames their lives' short ages).   10
Then people think of holy pilgrimages,
Pilgrims dream of setting foot on far-off
Lands, or worship at distant shrines, their thoughts
Reaching for grace, as holy teachers taught them.
And mostly, from everywhere in England, they hurry   15
To the blessèd ancient town of Canterbury,
To worship the martyred spirit of Thomas à Beckett,
Who'd helped so many, lying deadly sick.
     And as it happened, in that traveling time,
I came to Southwark, ready in heart and mind   20
To begin a lengthy journey. While awaiting
Morning, in Tabard Inn, anticipating
My day, a group of travelers of every sort
Arrived, who'd joined together as they walked
And rode. Turned good friends, they now proceeded   25
On as one, a band of pilgrims indeed,
Intending to worship Thomas at Canterbury.

The inn had rooms aplenty, and stable stalls
For all, and we were more than comfortable.
And soon, before the sun had gone to rest   30
I'd talked to each of them, and none I met
Took long to be my friend. We all agreed
To rise up early, next morning, knowing the need
To start out quickly, meaning to travel far.
   But while I still have time and space, before   35
I move along in my tale, it seems to me best
To tell you, now, just how my fellow guests
Appeared, to curious eyes, and what I took them
To be, what they wore and how they looked
And talked, both high and low, these twenty men   40
And women with whom I meant to travel. So then
I begin, which seems both proper and right, with our Knight.
He was a knight indeed, a worthy man,
Who from the very moment he first began
To ride, searching adventure, held chivalry   45
In his heart, and honor and truth, and courtesy
And grace. He fought a noble war for his lord,
Riding hard and far, wielding his sword
In Christian lands as well as pagan ground,
Honored as worthy, in every place he was found.   50
When Alexandria fell, he was there. How often
He sat at the table's head, most honored of men
From every nation, even in far-off Prussia!
He'd fought in Lithuania, and in Russia,
Harder and longer than any nobleman there.   55
He'd fought in Granada, and at the siege of Algecir,
He'd gone to Belmarin, on Moorish shores.
He'd ridden to Ayas, in distant Armenian wars,
And helped to win Attalia. His sword was raised
In Christian wars around the Mediterranean   60
Sea. He'd fought in fifteen deadly campaigns,
Fought fierce Muslims at Tlemcen, challenged thrice
And three times killed the bravest Arab knights.
This worthy man had once been known to fight
Side by side with Turkish Palatine lords   65
Against the armies of other heathen swords,

Everywhere known for noble spirit and worth.
But brave as he was, never free with his words,
Cautious and careful as any proper girl.
Never in all his life had he been churlish   70
Or mean to any creature on earth—a true,
A graceful, perfectly noble knight. But you
Should also know (speaking of how he looked)
Though his horse was good, not lame or crook-backed,
It was hardly showy. His long armored shirt   75
And cotton tunic were thoroughly spattered and dirty,
For he was not long home from another war:
Forgiveness for sin was what a pilgrim sought.
    Riding with him, his Squire, his bold young son,
Prepared for knighthood, but love had long since won him: 80
His hair lay curled, as if all ironed in place.
I guess he was twenty years old, from the look of his face.
Not either tall or short, somewhere between,
Agile, always in motion, strong as a beam.
He'd ridden with his father, on cavalry raids   85
In Flanders, Artois, and Picardy, and made
Himself useful, working hard to build a name
And have his lady think him already famous.
His clothes were embroidered up and down, and bright
As meadows full of fresh flowers, red and white.   90
He sang or played along on his flute all day,
As fresh to see as any month of May.
His flowing shirt was long, its sleeves were wide.
He sat like a practiced horseman, he knew how to ride.
He was quick at making songs, each matched with poems;   95
His sword hand was deft; he danced, and drew, and wrote.
His passion burned so hot that he closed his eyes
No more than a nightingale, and as hotly he cried.
Gracious and humble, his voice was soft, he was pleased
To serve. At table he carved his father's meat.   100
    A Yeoman also served the knight, but no
One more, for pilgrimages were not for show.
This yeoman's coat and hood were forest green.
Under his leather belt he wore a sheaf
Of peacock-feather arrows, and used them well: 105

Made by himself, they did not droop or melt
In heat or rain, standing stiff and ready.
He carried loose in his hand a mighty, heavy
Bow. His hair was cropped, his skin was brown.
He knew the forest just as he knew his home.   110
A bright protective guard was wrapped around
His arm, and a sword and shield were hung, both down
One side, a shining dagger hanging on
The other, sharp as a spear and beautifully mounted.
He wore a silver Christopher, saint   115
Of woodsmen, on his breast; his horn had a centure
Green as the trees. This was a hunter indeed.

      We had a Nun, a prioress, whose speech
And smile were mild and unpretentious. Her strongest
Exclamation was "Oh, by Saint Augústine!"   120
Her name was Madame Honeysuckle. Holy
Prayers and songs she sang most soulfully,
Chanting through her nose, in proper style,
Much like her full and flowing French, acquired
From English teachers at Stratford on the Bow,   125
For French as spoken in Paris she did not know.
Around the dinner table her manners were splendid:
Nothing she put in her mouth fell out, descended;
She never allowed a finger to sink in the sauce;
She knew how to pluck up food and carry morsels   130
So not a drop would fall upon her breast.
Courtesy was what she loved the best.
Before she drank she wiped her upper lip
So clean that food and grease could never stick
To her cup, where nothing but moisture could ever be seen.   135
She helped herself to meat with immense discretion.
And clearly she liked to laugh, and did so often,
With obvious pleasure, graceful, lady-like,
Working hard to appear amused, but of striking
Dignity and courtly importance, worthy   140
Of highest churchly reverence. Earthly
Sorrows pained her over-sensitive heart
So deeply that moved by pity, torn apart
By seeing a mouse caught in a trap, dead

Or bleeding, she barely controlled the tears she shed. 145
She kept a pack of tiny dogs, and fed them
Roasted meat, or milk and fine white bread.
How desperately she wept if one had died,
Or if some man had kicked it on the sly.
Her life was shaped by a sensitive, tender heart. 150
The wimple she wore was carefully ironed, and smart.
Her nose was straight, her eyes were green as glass,
Her mouth quite small, but soft, and red surpassing
Nature. And eyes to hair was a very long distance:
Her forehead a full nine inches, you could not miss it, 155
And no one could ever take her for thin and slender.
Her cloak, I saw, was truly rich, resplendent.
A pair of coral prayer beads was strung around
Her arm, great beads as green as anywhere found,
And hanging from them a brooch of the brightest gold, 160
Inscribed with a crownèd *A* and then a bold
Amor vincit omnia: Love Conquers All.
        Another Nun, her secretary, followed
Along. Her flock also included three priests.
        And then there was a Monk, a hunter in chief, 165
Daily riding out of his monastery,
A manly man, equipped with an equerry
Of fine, expensive horses, kept in his stable,
And when he rode out, all ears were easily able
To hear the bells on the bridle, ringing across 170
A whistling wind, like bells tolling on a house
Of prayer. This lordly monk was absolute head
Of a separate cell, and much preferred to let
The strict and ancient Benedictine Rule
Go sliding by; he favored the brand-new school, 175
Open to all that grew up high in this world.
He'd never give a well-plucked chicken for words
Declaring hunters were not holy men,
Nor that a monk ignoring rules of his Order
Was much like a fish that's taken out of water— 180
In short, a monk parading out of his cloister.
O that was a text, he said, not worth an oyster!
Which seems to me a very sane opinion.

Why should he study, bound by monkish dominion,
His nose forever in books, or like some minion   185
Of peasant stock, shoving a shovel in the dirt
As Saint Augústine commanded? The world must be served!
Let Aúgustine have the sweaty work he deserves.
Hunting on horseback was a monkish rule by right!
He owned greyhounds swift as birds in flight.   190
Tracking and running down a fleeing hare
Was everything he wanted, he'd never spare
Expense. His sleeves, I saw, were trimmed at the hand
With lovely gray fur, the finest in the land.
In order to fasten his hood beneath his chin   195
He'd made, of purest gold, a fine-worked pin,
And at the bottom he'd tied a love-knot. His head
Was bald, gleaming bright as glass and, whether
He oiled himself or not, he looked anointed.
He was a very fat lord, strong, well-jointed;   200
His large eyes rolled around, protruding, seeming
To steam like fire beneath a cauldron. The sheen
On his boots showed them supple, his horse was fantastic.
Now this was surely a first-rate ecclesiastic,
Not pale and wan, no deeply troubled ghost.   205
A swan sweltering in fat was his favorite roast.
The palfrey he rode was brown as any berry.
      There was a Friar, a sportive man, and merry,
A licensed beggar and a festive fellow.
No one in monastic orders was as mellow,   210
Fond of gossip and every form of perfumed
Speech. He set up many weddings, assuming
Costs, making marriage easy for girls
He'd been fond of. This was surely a shining pearl
Of a friar! Property owners, men of wealth,   215
Especially loved and entertained him well,
As did all proper matrons in the town,
For as he said himself, he was the crown
Of confessors, able to listen, then free from sin
Better than any mere priest, for he was in   220
A licensed order. He heard confessions sweetly,
His absolutions were soft and pleasant, meting out

Penance and gentle punishment, when he knew
Gifts and presents they'd give him were pleasant too.
Rewarding poor and faithful friars is a sign   225
Of good confession, a soul devoutly refined:
As the friar boasted, a man with open hands
Showed repentance had fallen upon a man,
For many are so hard of heart they cannot
Weep, even when body and mind are sore.   230
Behold, he said: this is what friars are for.
Why bother weeping and prayering when far, far more
Is accomplished by giving? He stuffed his cape with knives
And pins, generous presents for good-looking wives,
Offering gifts with a cheerful, tuneful voice,   235
For the man could carry a tune and pluck fine noise
From a lute. His stock of ballads was overflowing.
With a neck as white as fleur-de-lys, he could throw
Bullies to the ground, protecting the poor and weak.
He knew the taverns in every town, speaking   240
On intimate terms with barmaids and those who owned inns,
Better received than beggars or lepers had been.
And why should such a man as he, given
Position and powers like his, seek out such painful
And loathsome people? Wretches like that would stain   245
His reputation. And who could rise in this world,
Friendly with those who were only poor and worthless,
Rather than those who bought and sold good food?
Wherever profit seemed to grow from acquaintance,
He spoke most humbly, performed his courtesy dance.   250
No man alive could be so efficacious
And holy; no friar in his order had made
So much from so little. Exclusive license paid for,
No other friar intruded. A widow who hadn't a shoe
Never resisted his pleasant "How are you?"   255
And handed over a penny, before he left.
He gained much more than he would ever spend.
He dallied with women like boys playing with puppies.
And legal arbitration was a sport he played tough in.
This wasn't a penniless scholar, with threadbare cape: 260
He carried himself like a master, his manner papal.

His own short cape was woven of double twisted
Wool, round as a bell fresh from its fitted
Mold. He made himself lisp, to seem more lofty
And make his English words sing more softly.   265
Adding a few choice chords to a song he'd sung,
His eyes would twinkle, bright as stars hung
In the sky, across the darkness of a frosty night.
This excellent licensed beggar was called Huberd.

    There was a Merchant, wearing a forkèd beard.   270
Dressed in many colors, he sat high on his horse.
A beavered hat from Flanders sat across
His head, his boots were blessed with handsome buckles.
He mouthed opinions like men who do not truckle
With fools, careful to tell the world of his wealth.   275
He wished the sea were safe from pirates and stealth
From Holland over to the English shore.
He knew what foreign coins were worth, and more.
This was a man playing the game with his head:
No one knew how deep he stood in debt,   280
So dignified and stately he proceeded,
Bargaining, and always wheeling and dealing.
He was a worthy man, and worth his fame,
But truth to tell, I never knew his name.

    There also was a Cleric, a scholar at Oxford,   285
Steeped in philosophy's depths. His worthy horse
Resembled a rake, and the learned scholar himself
Was hardly fat, though rich in spirit, and healthy.
He seemed half hollow, which lent him a somber air.
The jacket he wore was old and long since threadbare,   290
For all his knowledge he'd won no scholar's reward,
His otherworldliness left him half-starved.
Clearly, he'd rather have beside his bed
Some twenty books, all bound in black and red,
Of Aristotle and his philosophy   295
Than velvet clothing, fiddles, or fine and sweet-
Tuned harps. Although he'd studied alchemy,
His money box contained no gold. Whatever
He got from friends he spent on books and never
Broke off reading, except to earnestly pray   300

For the souls of those providing him the way
To stay at Oxford, his heart so set on study
He could not waste much time on anybody
Or anything else. He didn't say much, although
His words were always courteous, not slow   305
At all, but full of good sense, which men most need.
Goodness and virtue were start and end of his speech.
And gladly would he learn and gladly teach.
  A Man of Law was there, a man of caution
And wisdom, often seen in halls and courts   310
Of London. Dignified and courteous, rich
In high good sense he seemed, not one to split
Fine hairs but balanced, careful, knowing, fair.
When courts would travel out of London, there
He was, judge on the bench by the king's commission.   315
Given his reputation and erudition,
Clients would shower this man with costly gifts.
He bought up all the land he could, swift
And silent, precise, and knowing how to draft
His deeds: they couldn't be questioned, now or after.   320
No one in England matched his bustling about,
But still, he wasn't so busy as he always made out.
He knew all legal jargon, and every case
Since William the Conqueror had taken his place
On the throne: his documentation and legal terms   325
Were perfectly aligned, no one could squirm
Around what he wrote. He'd memorized all laws
On the books. His clothes were modest, his coat was drawn
Around by a silken belt, brightly striped.
Of the rest of his clothing I've nothing more to write.   330
  A man who bought up land rode with him. His beard
Was white as any daisy, but his face was clearly
Sanguine, ruddier than simple red.
He supped, each morning, on rich and wine-soaked bread;
A life of pleasure was his constant passion,   335
For he was truly Epicurus' son,
Convinced at heart that endless days of delight
Made total happiness, and kept him righteous.
He'd bought up acres and acres of land, and his house

Was fairly bursting with ale, and bread, and carousing. 340
His bread and ale were always the height of perfection.
He'd made his cellar of wine a great collection.
Supplies of baked and roasted meat and fish
Flowed like rivers, tables heaped with delicious
Meat, and so much wine that under his roof 345
Food was almost snowing. As if in proof
Of his Epicurean passion, he had his table
Changed to suit each season. And he was able
To coop fat partridges in many pens,
And hordes of bream and pike in ponds. And then 350
Too bad for his cook if sauces were tame and flat
Or all his eating utensils not laid where he sat,
For here the table was never folded away,
But sat in his hall, covered and ready all day.
In local matters, lord and justice of the peace, 355
He often sat in a lofty Parliament seat.
A double-bladed dagger and purse of silk
Hung on his belt, white as morning milk.
He'd been a high-placed sheriff, and an auditor.
A vassal like this was sure to please his lord. 360
      We had a Hatter, a Dyer, and Weaver along,
A Haberdasher, a Tapestry Weaver—all strong,
United, wearing the standard uniform
Of their guild—a dignified and worthy order.
Every bit of equipment they had was new, 365
Knives not trimmed with brass, but shining silver,
Belts and purses a wonderful sight to view,
Fresh and clean as ever men could make them.
Each had clearly become a first-rate tradesman,
Ready for office at solemn guildhall sessions. 370
Each was wise enough, able, I guess,
To rise to alderman's robes, and some of the best.
They all owned plenty of land and had good incomes,
As surely their wives agreed. (They'd all be sinners
If not!) To be addressed as "madame" is very 375
Pleasant, just as it is to always be hurried
Up front, at feasts and celebrations, and to hand
Your cloak, like a royal queen, to some lesser man.

They had a Cook (something not unknown)
To boil up chickens with juicy marrow bones,   380
Sprinkling doses of spicy powder, and trace
Of something sweet. He knew good London ale,
And how to roast, and braise, and broil, and fry,
He made good stews and soup, and tasty pies.
It seemed a shame, I thought, to see on his shin   385
A festered ulcer, sore and red on his skin.
His blanc-mangé was one of the very best.
    A Shipman was there, coming from somewhere western.
For all I know he came from Devonshire.
His horse was a nag, he rode without skill or fear.   390
His coarse wool clothes came flapping onto his knees.
A string around his neck allowed him to keep
His dagger always ready, under his arm.
The boiling summer sun had tanned him dark.
A man to drink with, so long as he was watched: 395
Sailing from Bordeaux, he'd stolen draughts
From barrels of wine, when merchants were fast asleep.
Prissy correctness and conscience were not his meat.
Caught up in a fight, if he got the upper hand
He sent them home by water, to every land.   400
By knowledge and careful attention to swells and tides,
And rivers, and perils near his harbor, but hiding,
And how he measured the moon, and his pilotage—
In these he had no peer from Hull to Carthage.
Sturdy and rash, he knew what he was doing: 405
Tempests had shaken his beard, but none had ruined him.
He'd been in every harbor, no matter where,
From Gottland to the Cape of Finisterre,
And every creek in Brittany and Spain.
His ship now bore the name of "Madeleyne."   410
    We had with us a Doctor of Medicine.
No one in all the world could match this man
For knowledge of medical matters and surgery,
For he was grounded in astronomy.
He watched the stars intensely, knowing his patient   415
Must wait for the perfect magic time for treatment.
He knew exactly how to track the right

Ascendant, knowing the paths of astronomy's light.
He knew the cause of every ailment, spawned
In heat, or cold, or moist, or dry, born   420
Exactly where and how, and what was wanted.
He was a very perfect, practical man.
Knowing the cause and root of illness, he quickly
Gave each patient help for what the sick
Man suffered. He always had apothecaries   425
On hand, to make the drugs and remedies:
Doctors and druggists wash each other's hands—
And always have, exactly Nature's plan.
This doctor studied Aesculápius,
Dioscórides, and Trajan's doctor, Rufus,   430
Hippócrates, the Persian Halí, and Galen,
Serápyon, Rhazís of Baghdad, Ávicénna,
Áverros, Damáscién, and Constantine,
Bernárd, and Gáeddesdén, and Gilbertyn.
He also fed himself most carefully,   435
Permitting no excess to enter his belly,
Just nourishment both strong and well digested.
His studies rarely bothered with anything biblical.
His clothes were always red and blue, and lined
With taffeta and other silk of high   440
Degree. But spending money wasn't his plan:
Whatever he earned from sickness stayed in his hand.
Since gold's a restorative, in medical terms,
He cherished most the golden coins he earned.
    A goodwife came too, who lived not far from Bath;   445
Her ears no longer functioned well, alas.
She spun and weaved her cloth with such a touch
She easily surpassed all Belgians and the Dutch.
No woman in all the parish brought gifts to the altar
Ahead of her, and if that practice was altered   450
Her anger rose so quick and soared so high
That Christian charity just passed her by.
The kerchiefs covering her hair were heavily wound;
They surely weighed at least a good ten pounds
On Sundays, wearing them to church. Her stockings   455
Were red, full scarlet red and somewhat shocking,

Tightly laced. Her shoes were supple and new.
Her face was bold, and pretty, of reddish hue.
She'd been a worthy woman all her life;
The number of husbands she'd had amounted to five,   460
Excluding other men she'd known in youth.
But that is not my subject here, in truth.
She'd been three times a pilgrim in Jerusalem;
She'd seen a lot of foreign places, and men.
She'd been to Rome, and also to Bologne;   465
She'd seen Saint-James, in Galicia, and Cologne.
She'd done a lot of wandering down the road.
Her teeth were not the straightest you'll behold.
Her horse kept up an easy pace, she sat
Him well, wearing a wimple, and wearing a hat   470
As broad across as a shield, but not that fat.
An outer skirt was wrapped around her hips
(Quite large), a pair of spurs on her feet. She fitted
Well in the ways of the road, chatting, laughing.
She'd learned love's remedies along her path: 475
No one could lead her a dance on that old grass.
       A man of religion was also with us, a town
Parson—poor but abounding in goodness, crowned
With riches of holy thought and holy work,
And also a learnèd man who'd been a cleric,   480
And now was truly preaching Christ's own gospel;
With great devotion he taught as much as possible
To those in his parish. Humble, gracious, he never
Abandoned sinking souls, or flinched whenever
The way was hard. He proved himself again   485
And again. He hated to call down curses on men
Whose tithes had not been paid, but much preferred
To give away the bread from his table, fair
Bright gold from his purse, barley and oats from his stable.
He did not need what he had, for he was able   490
To live on little. His parish was large, its houses
Far apart, but neither rain nor growling
Thunder kept him from doors where men were sick
Or troubled, no matter high or low, and stick
In hand he made his way to their beds and hearts.   495

He showed his sheep a noble example, marking
Well how first he helped and then he taught.
Straight from holy gospel these words he caught—
Adding a homely metaphor: if gold
Is subject to rust, what hope can iron hold? 500
If priests, in whom we trust, turn out all gross,
Why be surprised if unlearned men are lost?
The devil sows, and then the devil reaps:
A shit-smeared shepherd and an honest sheep.
A priest is meant to lead, to illustrate 505
In flesh how life should best be lived each day
We're here. Priestly teaching should not begin
With renting a parish, leaving a flock in sin
And filth, while he runs off to London, seeking
Himself a churchly sinecure, or weekend 510
Posts with a prosperous tradesmen's guild. Stay
At home, feed your fold and keep away
The wolf, who's always waiting to snatch up prey,
A priest is a shepherd, not a merchant banker.
This priest was a holy man, but showed no anger 515
For men who sinned, was never severe or haughty,
But civil to all, and kindly as he taught
Others to be, showing sin could be caught
By virtue, and drawn to heaven by simple goodness
And example. This was his proper and all his business. 520
But any stubborn and snapping sinner, high
Or low, rich or mired in mud, he'd chide
And scold, sharp and straight and from the heart.
I know no better priest in any part
Of England. No one was asked to bow and scrape 525
For him, nothing was fuss and complicated:
All he taught was the law of Christ and twelve
Apostles, but first he followed that law himself.

     A Farmer came with him, a ploughman, who was his brother,
Who dug and carried dung like any other 530
Hard-hand honest man, as good as can be,
Living peaceful in perfect charity.
God he loved completely, with all his heart,
No matter how his own life ran. And part

Of his love he gave his neighbor, digging and pouring 535
For any poor man, in the name of Christ, and for
No pay at all, whenever he could afford to.
He paid his tithes to the church, he knew he should,
Some by labor of his hands, some by goods.
He wore a sleeveless coat and rode on a mare. 540
      A Steward was also there, and a Summoner,
A Miller, a Provisioner, and
A Pardon Peddler, and me—no other man.
      The Miller was a hefty rascal, stout
In flesh, and bone, and muscle, without a doubt 545
Prepared to fight in a flash. In wrestling bouts
With brawlers coming from everywhere, he routed
Them all, always winning. Thick-set and cringing
At nothing, he'd smash a door right off its hinges
Or run right at it, his head a battering ram. 550
His beard was red as a fox, so broad a span
It almost seemed the digging edge of a spade.
A wart his nose had sprouted out displayed
A tuft of hair, red as bristles wagging
Out a sow's sharp ears. His nostrils were black 555
As pitch, as wide as tunnels. By his side
He carried a sword, a shield hanging close by.
His mouth, when open, resembled a great brick furnace.
He was a coarse buffoon, who chattered like a bird,
Mostly prattling dirty jokes and tales. 560
He was good at stealing grain he milled, and played
With the prices he charged, but could not be called, in truth,
A thief. His coat was white, his hood was blue.
He carried a bagpipe, was able to blow it loud,
And that was how he led us out of town. 565
      A Provisioner, well-born, was also there,
From whom all purchasers of food might care
To learn a lesson or two. For whether he paid
In cash, or bought on credit, he always made
Himself a quiet but satisfying sum. 570
Now that must verify God's grace to men,
That someone never trained in anything
Could day after day be running casual rings

Around a flock of deeply learnèd folk!
His masters amounted to more than thirty dolts   575
Over-educated in matters of law,
At least a dozen of whom, or even more,
Could easily take posts as steward of income
And land for any lord in England, someone
For whom they'd steer a noble, debtless path   580
(Unless said lord was absolutely mad),
Or fix his life for him, as tight as a miser,
A lord with such resources that he could rise
To holding up and even sustaining a shire,
No matter what way the world might suddenly turn.   585
And yet these lawyers had all the wit of a worm.
        The Steward was a slender, choleric man.
He shaved his beard as close as any man can;
His hair was cut around his ears, like the least
Of the low, short at the top, in front, like a priest.   590
His legs were very long and very lean,
And like a stick or a staff, no calf could be seen.
No bill inspector knew how to get around him.
He measured days of drought and rain, and counted
Ahead to how much crop and grain he would grow.   595
This Steward held the reins for every horse
And cow his lord might own, and all that was stored
Away, and all the poultry, the sheep and swine,
And everything else, and governed this way from the time
His lord was twenty years old. No one could find   600
A flaw in his books, no grain of wheat was out
Of place. No bailiff, no shepherd, no servant doubted
His cunning, all were deeply aware of his theft.
But all were more afraid of him than of death
Itself. He lived in a cheerful house on waste land   605
Near the woods; tall trees shadowed the place.
He could have bought what he liked, better than his lord.
He'd gotten rich, but kept it secretly stored
Away. Pleasing his master was a trick he'd long ago
Learned, giving and lending his lord what belonged   610
To his lord, rewarded with coats and hoods in exchange.
As a youngster, he'd been taught a useful trade,

Remaining a very good carpenter and laborer.
And now he rode on a fine, strong stallion, gray
And dappled all over, a horse who earned his hay.   615
The steward's overcoat was long and blue,
And by his side hung a sword of rusty hue.
He hailed from Norfolk, this steward of ours, from a town
Called Baldeswell, no place of any renown.
He wore his clothes tucked close, just like a friar,   620
And always rode in the rear. That was his style.
      A Summoner was with us, there in that place,
Who had a fire-red cherubinish face,
Pimpled from top to bottom, and his eyes were narrow.
Hot he was, and lecherous like a sparrow,   625
His eyebrows black and scabby, and a balding beard.
Children looked at him and ran in fear.
No protoxide of lead, quick-silver, or brimstone,
Borax, white-leaded hydrate and carbon—none
Of the ointments, not even oil of tartar, could wipe   630
And clean his forest of white-headed pimples or slice
Away the knobs and bumps sitting on his cheeks.
He loved strong garlic, onions, and also leeks,
And swizzled the strongest wine, as red as blood,
And then he shouted and screamed as if he'd been drugged.   635
And when he'd drunk much wine, the only words
He'd utter were Latin, a language he constantly heard
As he did his work, and read in many decrees,
And papers he served as a summoner, but couldn't speak
With any understanding: a sprinkle of terms   640
Was his limit. And every man with ears has heard
A jay cry "water," as clear and correct as a pope.
Anyone able to test him, probe and grope,
Would find him empty of true philosophy.
"Questio quid juris?" Which law applies? he'd shriek,   645
And nothing more. But a gentle rascal, and kind;
A better companion would be hard to find.
Hand him a brimming quart of decent wine
And he would lend a good friend his concubine
For a month, or maybe a year, and say it didn't matter;   650
But knew how to cheat, and make himself feel better.

Shoulder to shoulder, drinking with someone new,
He'd show how little an official curse could do,
Unless you kept your soul deep in your purse,
For that was where church punishment was worked.   655
"Truly," he'd say, "the only real hell is that curse."
But as far as I'm concerned he lied in his teeth,
And ecclesiastical curses have endless reach.
For just as absolution will save your soul,
A priest's sharp curse will kill it, forever and all—   660
And don't forget: the earthly church has jails.
This summoner had at his mercy the girls
And boys of the diocese, and knew what they
Were up to, and how to help them on their way.
This cheerful pilgrim wore a garland high   665
On his head, almost as large and bold as a signpost.
A handsome loaf of bread was the shield on his chest.

    A worthy Pardon Peddler, one of the best
Of our summoner's companions, was with us. He'd been born
In Rouncival, and was just returned from Rome.   670
Loudly singing his salesman's pitch, "O hither,
Hither, love, to me!" And the summoner
Sang brassily along. No trumpet was ever
Half so loud. This peddler had hair like wax,
Yellow but hanging smooth as a hank of flax.   675
His locks were hung in careful little bunches,
Spreading down across his shoulders, clumped
In slender strips, and each one straight and good.
For the pleasure of looking different he wore no hood,
Packed it away in his bag, for the latest fashion   680
Was always on his mind; he dressed with passion,
And except for his cap, rode with his head all bare.
His eyes would glisten exactly like a hare's.
He'd sewn a Saint Veronica's kerchief to his cap.
He carried his bag in front of him, on his lap,   685
Stuffed to the brim with indulgences, hot
From Rome. His voice was thin and small like a goat.
He had no beard, nor would he ever grow one,
His face as smooth as freshly shaved. No one
Could say if he was truly gelding or mare.   690

But when it came to selling his holy wares
He stood at the head of his pack, for he declared
The silken pillowcase he stored in his bag
Was truly our Holy Lady's veil, and the fragment
Of a sail he showed was from Saint Peter's ship, 695
On which he plied the sea till Jesus' grip
Ended his fishing days. He carried a cross
Of brass, embroidered with stones, and in a glass
He'd filled, for display, with rattling old pig bones.
Employing these as holy relics, he won 700
More money from poor farmers than the parson
Would ever receive in a pair of months. He worked
With lying flattery, and knew what tricks
Would best deceive our simple folk, making
Both parson and parishioners his apes. 705
And so I'll end by telling you, at last,
In church he was a noble ecclesiast.
He read from scripture, or conjured up the magic
Worked by a saint, but best of all was the mass
In which he sang the offertory chant, 710
Knowing he'd have to preach with a silver tongue
To win pure silver, as he could do, and he sung
Both loud and merrily, right to the end.
        And now I've told you the truth about my friends,
Their status, how they dressed, and why they went 715
To Southwark as pilgrims, came to the inn that men
Still call the Tabard, not very far from the Belle,
And a gracious place to be. It's time to tell
How all our company behaved, that very
Same night when we first came together (and merry 720
We were); later I'll tell about our voyage
And everything else about our pilgrimage.
But first I need to ask you, for courtesy's sake,
That nothing written here shall ever be taken
As careless coarseness, or rudeness, although I speak 725
Directly and honestly the words that we
Then spoke, to show us talking when assembled.
Don't blame me, please, for words I've tried to remember,
For surely you know as I do, and will not dissemble,

That anyone who tries to describe other 730
People's speech and actions, even your brother's,
Must try to reproduce as close as he possibly
Can whatever was said and what it seemed
To mean, no matter how bad or rough it may be,
Or else he'll truly falsify his story, 735
Invent what never happened, and never worry.
He cannot hold back and hope to tell the truth.
In the Holy Bible, Christ himself speaks rudely
At times, and you know that rudeness has nothing to do
With *him*. As Plato says, to those who can read him, 740
Words must necessarily follow deeds.
And please, if you can, try not to be angry at me
For failing to properly show nobility,
Here in this tale, as nobility should be.
I'm neither noble nor smart, as you can see. 745
      The Host of the Inn was cordial to everyone,
And promptly to our supper set us down.
He served us only food of the very best;
The wine was strong, we drank it up with zest.
The host was a gracious man, pleasant to all, 750
A master of ceremony, ruler in his hall.
He carried a good deal of weight; his eyes were large;
Clearly, there in that hall, he was in charge.
He had good sense and manners, his speech direct:
A man among men, he only said what he meant. 755
Strong as he was, he was also a jolly fellow,
And just as our supper ended, he began a mellow,
Rambling speech designed to keep us merry
While our bills were paid, which wasn't very
Long. "Now gentlemen, I set apart 760
The welcome I want to give you. This is from the heart.
And let me tell you the truth—I swear by my soul—
It's been at least a year since I saw in this hall
As jolly a company as I see here today.
So I'd choose to keep you happy, if I knew the way. 765
And I've been struck by a mighty pleasant idea,
Truly delightful, which will not cost you a penny.
      "You're going to Canterbury.—God lighten the way,

And holy Saint Thomas grant you whatever you pray for!
I'm sure that, as you travel along the road,   770
You plan to talk, tell stories and, I suppose,
Amuse yourselves. Indeed, it isn't much fun
To ride in utter silence, dumb as a stone.
So let me offer a special diversion, a game
—As I said before—to help you entertain   775
Yourselves. So if you're willing to let me guide you,
Grant me authority, and I will provide,
By my soul, a wonderful way of passing time,
Beginning next-day morning, as you go riding
Off. I swear by the heavenly soul of my dead   780
Father, unless you're delighted I'll give you my head!
Raise your hands, without another word."
        We needed no talk, no negative voice was heard;
There wasn't much point, we saw, to further discussion.
Unanimously, we quickly gave permission   785
For him to be the leader and do as he wished.
"Gentlemen," he said, "please pay attention—
But mind, I'm not your leader, you're all free men.
This is the point, to tell it short and plain:
Each of you, to make our journey easier,   790
Will tell two tales—two, that is, in each
Direction, two as we go to Canterbury,
And another two as we travel home. And he
That tells a tale must tell it as it happened.
And whoever tells the best one—meaning that   795
Which offers us the ripest wisdom and the most
Of pleasure, earns the teller—if I may so boast—
The best of dinners at absolutely no cost
To him, when we return from Canterbury.
I hope that pleases, and makes you even merrier,   800
That I will join the journey, and be your guide,
Pay for myself and ride along at your side.
Let him who refuses to do just as I say
Pay everything we spend, along the way!
If that seems right, and you wish to make it so,   805
Tell me right now, so be it yes or no,
And I will puzzle my brain and make our plans."

　　　　We quickly answered yes, and every man
Of us was glad. We asked him most sincerely
To do exactly as he'd said, and really　　　　　　　　　　　　810
Be in charge, a leader indeed, not merely
In name, and be the judge and arbitrator
Of tales, arranging a dinner as he favored it,
For we were wholly governed as he chose,
In matters high and low. And so we closed　　　　　　　　815
Our agreement, once again by unanimous vote.
And then, to be sure, more wine was brought for our pleasure;
We drank, and later we went to sleep at our leisure,
Each and all well stuffed with food and wine.
　　　　The next day, soon as the sun began to shine,　　820
Up rose our host and, like a feathered cock,
Gathered us all together in a cheerful flock,
And off we rode, as far as a brook at the second
Milestone leading to Kent. Our host beckoned
Us all to stop. "Gentlemen," he said,　　　　　　　　　825
"Please listen. We've made an agreement, you know what we meant
To do, but let me remind you. If what we decided
To do, last night, is what we do in the rising
Sun, let's see who's chosen to tell the first tale.
I swear by the wine I drink, and also the ale,　　　　　830
That anyone who rebels against my judgment
Must pay, as we agreed, our travel expenses.
So before we travel, come hither, draw your straws:
Whoever pulls the shortest will speak before
All others. Sir Knight, my master and my lord,　　　　835
Draw first." The knight duly obeyed his word.
"Come near," said our host, "my Lady Prioress.
And you, Sir Cleric, shed your bashfulness,
Don't study these straws! Everyone, use your hands!"
They came quite quickly, each and every man,　　　　840
And not to waste more words, but tell my tale
Just as it happened, bad or good, the scale
Tipped toward the knight, and he was to be the first,
A choice that no one thought would be the worst
We'd have. The promise once made, reason demanded　　845
That promises be binding on every man.

The logic was simple and straight, no one was hasty.
You know what they pledged. Why bother with explanations?
It had to be one or the other, and he was the one.
The good knight saw, as wise men must, it was done,   850
He had to accept the task they'd all agreed on.
"I have to begin?" he said. "God save the straw!
Let's ride, and you shall hear what I once saw."
And with that word we rode off on our way.
The knight was hardly a man at ease, saying   855
Many words in public, but he smiled, that day.

THE KNIGHT'S TALE

And now, Theseus drawing near his native land in a
chariot covered with laurel wreaths, after fierce fighting,
is greeted with happy applause.
　　　　　　　　　　　　—STATIUS, *Thebaid*

Once, as many ancient stories tell us,
There was a duke who bore the name of Theseus;
He was the lord of Athens, its governor,
And in his time was such a conqueror
That none was greater, nowhere under the sun. 5
Many a wealthy country had he won.
Blessed with wisdom, and mighty chivalry,
He conquered the Amazon land called Feminee
(Previously known by the name of Scythia),
And married its powerful queen, Hippolita, 10
Then in great splendor and polished ceremony,
He took her home with him, to his own country,
She and her younger sister, Emily.
And now I'll leave this duke, as he rides to Athens,
He and his mighty army proceeding together. 15
　　　But surely, except it's much too long to hear,
I would have told you, in great detail, the fearsome
War he fought, in winning Feminee
(Lord Theseus, of mighty chivalry),
And especially the ferocious battle he won, 20
Pitting Athens against the Amazons,
And how Hippolita suffered, as he besieged her,
Barbaric, beautiful queen, with fierce Greek legions.
And I'd have told you, too, of their wedding feast,
And the tempest Athens made, to give them greetings. 25
But nothing like that can be included here,
For I have, by God, tremendous fields to clear,

And the oxen pulling my plow aren't strong.
The rest of my tale is more than sufficiently long.
I've no intention of keeping any one   30
From telling his tale, each in turn, when I'm done.
All right, we'll wait and see whose tale is best.
And now I resume at just the place I left.
  This duke, the one I'm telling you about,
Had almost reached his home, happy and proud,   35
Amid the noise, the waving banners, and crowds,
When suddenly he saw, right at the edge
Of the highway, a group of weeping ladies begging
For his attention, kneeling, all of them clad
In black, two by two in rows, and madly   40
Calling for him to stop and hear them, creating
Noises so wild, unending, clearly half crazed
With woe far worse than anyone alive
Had ever heard, never stopping their cries
Until, by reaching up, they grasped his bridle.   45
  "Who are you," said the duke, "at my home-coming,
To thus disturb my welcome? I find myself stunned
To hear you. Are all you ladies so proud of your lord,
The honor he's getting, pushing yourselves thus forward
And crying? Or have you been insulted, offended,   50
Hurt? Tell me if this can be brought to an end,
And why you're all now clothed in deadly black."
  The oldest lady among them answered him back—
First fainting away, with a face so deathly white
It was sorrowful to see, a pitiful sight: 55
"My lord, Fortune has made you all-victorious,
Enabled you to live a conqueror's glory,
And neither your glory nor your honor displeases
Us, for all we wish is simply freedom
From woe. Great lord, we stand here, now, to appeal   60
For noble mercy. O let a drop of pity fall
Upon the wretched women we are, for all
Of us, in sober truth, have never been
Less than a highborn duchess or glorious queen,
And now we're worthless, nothing, as you have seen,   65
Because of Fortune's cheating wheel that forever

Turns and throws us off our perch, never
Safe. I tell you, lord, awaiting your presence
We have been standing here, at Clemency's shrine,
For two long-suffering weeks, or more. Right   70
And justice are with us. Help us, lord, with your might.
     "Wretch that I am, weeping and wailing thus,
I once was the wife of King Capaneus,
Who died at Thebes—I curse that unlucky day!
And all of us, wearing this black array,   75
Weeping and wailing, as you have seen and heard,
We each and all of us lost husbands there,
While Thebes' great walls were pressed, the city besieged.
And now old Creon, alas, is that city's liege
And lord. Filled with rage and dreadful vice,   80
Impelled by tyranny and unnatural spite,
He's now committed acts of disgraceful shame.
The villain has taken the bodies of our naked
Dead, awaiting decent and necessary
Burial, and piled them in heaps and will not agree   85
Either that they be buried or even burned,
But sends out hounds to eat the bodies, turning
Law and decency all upside down."
     Hearing these words, the women fell to the ground
At once, groveling, crying in desperation: 90
"Have mercy on these wretched women. O patient
Lord, allow our sorrow to sink in your heart!"
     The noble duke dismounted, feeling a sharp
Pain in his breast, hearing the words they'd spoken.
It seemed to him his heart was almost broken,   95
Seeing these noble women so torn and dejected,
Thrown down from their high estates, alone, rejected.
With his own arms he drew them up, one
By one, and tried to console them, said what would be done
—As he was a knight, and true. It would be so thorough,   100
So final, that everyone in Greece would know,
And all would say, that tyrant Creon had met
The end he deserved, a short and bloody death
At the hands of Theseus, whose will and might
Would turn a wrongful disaster to decent right.   105

Without delay, he raised his banner high
And he and all his men began to ride
Toward Thebes, ignoring Athens, now so close by,
Not stopping even to rest for half a long day,
Riding hard into the night, on his way   110
To justice. Before he finally slept, he had
Hippolita, his queen, return to his land,
With Emily, her lovely young sister, remaining
While he would finish the task he'd undertaken,
And promptly in the morning, again rode hard   115
Toward Thebes. What else can I say? He was doing his job.
    And on the great white banner he rode beneath
Was Mars, all painted red, with spear and shield,
Bobbing up and down as they rode on fields
And hills. And his golden pennant they also bore,   120
Embroidered with an image of the Minotaur,
The monster Theseus had killed in Crete.
The duke rode on, rode on and on, I repeat,
And in his army the flower of chivalry,
Until he came to Thebes and stopped in the middle   125
Of a field, which seemed to him just right for battle.
And then he killed old Creon, fighting hand
To hand, as knights should fight, man against man,
Then drove the dead man's followers off the field,
Assaulting Thebes itself. He forced it to yield,   130
Then tore down its walls, its wooden beams and rafters,
And gave the sorrowing ladies their husbands' bones,
Rescued half-torn corpses from piles they'd been on,
For consecration in fire, as then it was done.
I can't be bothered recounting how these women   135
Sobbed and wept and cried as the burning went on,
And the noble display of honor Theseus showed them,
The mighty conqueror, when they went home,
When Theseus was finished with what should be done.
All that would take too long. I'll abbreviate   140
This story, for wordiness is not my way.
    And then this Theseus, this worthy knight,
Having killed old Creon, slept that night
Right in the open field where they'd fought their fight,

And after that he dealt with Thebes as he liked. 145
  The pillagers went up and down the field,
Stripping bodies of their clothes, their shields,
Their weapons, working hard at a dreary task,
Which always follow the hardships of war, the clashing
Of swords and spears. And there among the piled-up 150
Corpses, they found two knights, both young, lying
Side by side, wounded but neither dead
Nor alive. The Thebans identified these men
As Palamon and Arcite, cousins and friends,
Knights of the royal family, born to a pair 155
Of sisters. Quickly pulled from the pile, they were carefully
Carried to the duke's own tent. Then Theseus sent them
To Athens, to be locked in prison and kept there forever.
There'd be no ransom; he chose security.
And having finished his work, Theseus knew he 160
Could leave, and so he did; he and his army
Went home to Athens; he was welcomed with laurel wreaths,
And passed his life in joy and honor, not grief:
What more can I say? But high in a tower of stone
And iron, Palamon and Arcite knew woe 165
Unending. Gold would never buy their freedom,
Nor anything rich and rare from the Theban kingdom.
  So year by year went by, and day by day,
Until one sunny morning in the month of May
When Emily, far lovelier to see 170
Than lilies growing on slender stalks of green,
And fresher even than May, bursting with new
Flowers, competing with her rosy hue—
And who can pick the finer of these two?—
Rose up from bed before the break of day 175
And dressed and readied herself, as she preferred,
For May won't tolerate a lazy sluggard.
This is a season that stirs all noble hearts,
Tugging them out of sleep with a gentle start,
Saying "Arise, and practice what I preach." 180
So Emily remembered what springtime teaches,
And rose to observe her obligation to May.
Let me describe how bright she looked, how gay:

Her yellow hair was woven into a tress
Hanging down her back, and not much less   185
Than a yard. She was out in the garden when the dawn
Broke through, slowly walking up and down
And gathering flowers that caught her eye, some red,
Some white, to fashion a garland for her head,
Singing as she went, like an angel in heaven.   190
The massive tower which served the castle as a dungeon
(In which the pair of Theban knights were held,
The two I've told you about, and surely will tell
You more) was next to, and rose above, the walls
Of the garden where lovely Emily, all   195
Alone, was strolling from place to place, half
Amusing herself, half celebrating with laughter
And song. The sun was wonderfully bright and clear,
And that woeful captive, Palamon, was near
The top of the tower (where he was allowed to go,   200
By his jailer's permission), looking to and fro
At Athens, great city stretching far and wide,
And also the garden, full of flowers and bright
Green leaves, and graced by beautiful Emily,
Roaming below him, bright as the garden that she   205
Was walking through. And sad-faced Palamon
Was walking in his prison, up and down,
From wall to wall, complaining to himself
About his sorrows. He often said "Alas
That I was ever born!" And as he passed   210
A window, filled with iron bars as thick
As yards, and even masts, of a sailing ship,
His glance somehow or other fell on the shining
Girl and he staggered back, loudly crying
"Ah!" as if some dart had stung him, deep   215
In his heart. Arcite was startled out of sleep
And exclaimed, "My cousin! What on earth has happened
To you, so suddenly gone as pale as ashes?
What made you cry out? Has someone hurt you? But how?
For the love of God, oh bend your head and bow   220
To pain and suffering, for this is how it will be,
Here in our prison. Our fate is adversity.

Some evil astrological constellation,
Some angular turn spun by Saturn, has taken
Away our lives, no matter what we thought. 225
The heavens aligned against us when we were born.
We must endure it. The truth is brief and plain."
    Palamon replied and said, again:
"Cousin, this is a set and stubborn opinion,
Born of a worthless, futile imagination. 230
I didn't start and cry out because of this prison,
But because my eyes had seen an incredible vision
And driven it straight to my heart. I will never recover.
The beauty of the lady I saw, in that garden below—
Walking, so noble and lovely, to and fro— 235
Was the sole and entire cause of my startled cry.
Is she a woman? or goddess? From just what I
Have seen, in that narrow window, I believe it is Venus."
And then he dropped to his knees and declared: "Venus,
If you, O heavenly goddess, have chosen to burn 240
My eyes with the sight of you, walking on earth—
I, so wretched, a sorrowing, miserable creature—
I pray you, goddess, help us, give us freedom.
But if our destiny has been determined
By eternal decree, and I will die in this prison, 245
Have mercy on our family, struck to the core
By tyranny, and a tyrant's vicious law."
But even as he spoke, his cousin saw
The lady roaming up and down the garden,
And at that sight her beauty struck him hard. 250
However sorely she'd struck his cousin's heart,
Arcite was wounded as much as him, or more.
And sighing deeply, he said these pitiful words:
"The shining beauty of her, walking this earth,
So overwhelms my heart and being, that unless 255
She graces me with her lovely glance, and blesses
Me with her heart, so I may walk beside her,
I am as good as dead. It has been decided."
    But Palamon, hearing his cousin's speech,
Replied, frowning and scornful: "Tell me, Arcite, 260
Whether you say this in earnest, or only in play?"

"No!" said Arcite. "In earnest, by my faith!
God help me, cousin, I've nothing playful to say."
    Palamon's frown grew deeper and, eyebrows raised,
He said: "Arcite, it cannot bring you much honor   265
To tell me lies, or turn yourself a traitor
To me—I, your cousin and your brother,
Sworn to the root, by each of us to the other,
That we would never, no matter the pain, stand
In each other's way, when love is the matter at hand—   270
No, not till death will separate one
From the other—indeed we're each of us truly sworn,
Not only in matters of love, to assist the other
In any and every way, as brother to brother.
You swore to this, and surely so did I.   275
You cannot take this back. I was not lying.
You heard me declare my love, seeing this girl,
And now, like a hypocrite, you say you're burning
With love for my love, the lady I serve and adore,
And always will until I am no more.   280
No, Arcite, you liar, you cannot love her.
I loved her first, my primacy is proven,
I told you only because of who you are,
My trusted friend, and cousin, and counselor,
Sworn to aid and assist me, as I said before,   285
In any and every way you possibly could,
Or else renounce your honor, as a true man would."
    Arcite then answered, proud and swift and sharp:
"You're the liar, not me. Yours is the heart
That's faithless and false, I throw that right in your face. 290
As far as loving goes, I stand in the place
You want. You're talking nonsense, cousin; you plainly
Said you did not know if this was goddess
Or woman. Your tongue confuses a man confessing
Holy feelings or a man in love with a living   295
Human. My love is real, and you were given
That knowledge because of oaths we certainly swore.
For argument's sake, suppose you loved her before
I did. What would the ancient men of law
Tell you? 'Who shall bind a lover by law?'   300

I say that love is truly the greatest law
That any living man can know and adore,
And every day of the year whatever law
You like is always broken because of love.
A man is obliged to love, if he approves   305
Or not. He may be sluggish, but still needs love,
Whether she's virgin, widow, or someone's wife.
Nor is it likely she'll love you all your life,
And this applies to us both, to me and to you,
For you're aware, as I am, cousin, my brother,   310
That you and I will never live in another
Home, but only here. We cannot be ransomed.
We fight like snarling dogs for a meatless bone.
Remember? They fought all day and what they won
Was nothing. A hawk came down, as they snarled and growled,   315
And carried away the bone while they were howling.
At this king's court, my brother, it's each for ourselves.
We're helpless to help each other or our self.
Love, if it pleases you, and I'll love too,
And this, my cousin and brother, is all we can do.   320
We're locked in prison, and here is where we'll stay,
And each of us can love, each in his way."
        They snarled and quarreled, were hardly ever silent,
And I'd tell you all, if I could—but fate finally
Interrupted our story. It happened, one day   325
(To tell this tale as briefly as I may),
That another noble duke, Perótheus
By name, a very old friend of Theseus—
Indeed, a childhood friend, with whom he'd played
As a boy, and loved to play with, still—came   330
To pay his friend a visit, as he often did,
Loving no one else as he still loved him,
Renewing his love each time they met again.
Indeed, our ancient books have always claimed
That after one of them died, or so the books tell,   335
The other went to visit him in hell.
—But that's another story and not the tale
I'm trying to tell, at least not today.
Over the years, Perótheus had come

To know Arcite, and love him, so he offered to ransom   340
This other friend, and then, when that could not
Prevail, he sought to rely on friendship, and would
Not relent, until at last Theseus freed
Arcite, but not entirely, for he
Required a limitation on this freedom.   345
      In a word: Arcite was free, by solemn agreement,
And all the world was open to him—but not
A country ruled by Theseus. Caught
In any such place, for even a single hour,
Arcite agreed—what choice did he have? what power?   350
—A very sharp sword would quickly cut off his head.
This was his only chance for freedom; he said
He'd live by these terms. And then homeward he sped,
Having swiftly made his farewells. But death
Hung over his head; he'd made a fateful pledge.   355
      And how Arcite was suffering! A plague gnawed
At his heart, a pestilence far worse than before.
He wept, he wailed, he cried most pitifully.
He longed for death, and waited, secretly,
For a suitable moment to kill himself. "Alas,"   360
He cried, "The day that I was born! This vast
Prison of the world is worse than my dungeon cell!
I'm fated to live eternally in hell,
Not merely purgatory. Alas that I ever
Knew Perótheus! Locked forever   365
In Theseus' prison, I would have lived
In bliss, freed from woe and given the gift
Of seeing the lady I must and always will serve,
Though more than sight may not be what I deserve.
The sight of her would be enough for me.   370
Belovèd cousin Palamon," said he,
"You are the winner in this knightly bout,
Permitted to stay in prison, her sight surrounding
You. In prison? O no, in paradise!
Fortune has perfectly managed your throw of the dice.   375
You have the sight of her, I have her absence.
By now, you might have more, having her presence,
Since you are a knight, a worthy knight, and able,

For Fortune is fickle and always capable
Of change, and you may win what you desire. 380
But I, I live in exile, with empty hands
And no chance for grace, I live in total despair,
For neither earth nor water, fire nor air,
Nor any creature composed of these elements
Can help me, give me any comfort. I'm meant 385
To starve and die in sad despair and distress.
Farewell my life, my love, and all my gladness!
    "And why, so often, do people loudly complain
Of what they've gotten from God, or from Fortune gained,
When what they're given is cleverly disguised 390
And worth far more than they themselves could provide?
People who hunger for gold will sometimes find
That wealth can sicken them, or cause them to die,
And those too eager to leave their prisons, and welcome
Release, may find themselves soon murdered at home. 395
Danger is not dependent on human choice:
Our prayers may be granted, but by the Devil's voice.
We stagger through life as drunk as any mouse.
A drunk man knows for sure he has a house,
But how to get there proves to be the problem, 400
For all roads slide away from drunken men.
And that is certainly the way we live.
We hurry after happiness, and often
See, too late, that everything's gone wrong.
So everyone can say, and especially me, 405
Who fancied happiness would follow freedom,
Believing that if, somehow, I made my escape,
I'd live in joy and perfect peace. But Fate
In fact has exiled me from all my bliss.
And now I cannot see the face I miss 410
More than freedom, and nothing can help me in this."
    The other side of the coin shows Palamon,
Who when he learned that Arcite was free, and gone
Away, shed such tears, and howled such sorrow
That echoes went up and down the great stone tower. 415
The very chains that dangled on his legs
Were flooded over, hanging dank and wet.

"Alas," he said, "my cousin, dear Arcite,
Your victory ends our quarrel, I know I'm beaten.
Now, you walk through Thebes whenever you please,   420
You're free of any responsibility
For me. Being the excellent knight you are,
You'll gather together our family and friends, make war
On Athens, and fight so fiercely and well that either
By force, or chance, or even duplicity,   425
You'll end with Emily, she'll be your wife.
She holds my heart in her hands, and thus my life.
But in terms of every possibility
You've gained the advantage, now, by being free,
And being also a lord, while I starve in a cage.   430
You've won decisively, for I must rage
And weep and wail as long as I live,
Burdened with all the woe that prison gives,
As well as pains that love must plant in my heart,
Doubling torment and woe, like poisoned darts."   435
And then the fire of jealousy would start up
In his breast, and burn so fiercely in his heart
His face took on the yellow pale of hardwood
Trees, or ashes of fire long dead, gone cold.
    And then he said: "You cruel gods, who govern   440
The world with ropes woven of your eternal
Words, inscribed on stone, hard ádamánt,
Your permanent decrees, your potent grants,
What do you care about men, how can we hold
Your eyes much more than frightened sheep in the fold?   445
For men are slain just like the other beasts,
Locked in prison cages, whipped and beaten
And given sickness and sore adversity,
And often for no good reason, no guilt, no evil.
    "You govern by making the future happen. What sense   450
Can there be, when you can punish the innocent
And never suffer? I should not complain, but offer
Homage: God's law requires us to proffer
Renunciation of all our wills and desires,
While beasts may enjoy whatever they please and like.   455
And after a beast is dead, he suffers no pain,

Having no soul. But we must weep and strain,
No matter how, in this world, we suffered woe.
This is how it is, and how it will go on
Being. Let theologians resolve this conflict;   460
I understand that life is painful and sickly.
Alas, I see a poisonous snake, or a thief,
Doing infinite harm, causing much grief
To innocent men, never punished or imprisoned.
But only since old Saturn wants me in prison,   465
And crazy, jealous Juno works her will,
Half the nobles of Thebes, at least, were killed,
And its great walls destroyed and scattered wide.
And Venus is murdering me, on the other side,
For ancient jealousies and fear of Arcite."   470
    Leave Palamon, now, exactly where he is,
Miserably locked in prison, where he dwells,
And turn to Arcite. I'll tell what I need to tell.
    Summer comes, and long, long nights go on
And on forever, doubling pain for the wan   475
Lovers, one in prison, the other locked
Outside. Who can say which was wracked
The worst? There is Palamon, on one side,
Chained in prison until his life is done.
Arcite remains in exile forever, and will lose   480
His head if torments of love force him to choose
Some secret visit, if only to see his lady
Once, disregarding the awful danger.
    You lovers, now I need to ask this question:
Which existence is worse, Palamon's   485
Or Arcite's? One can see his lady, day
By day, but never lose his prisoner's chains;
The other may ride wherever he wants to go,
But will not see his lady any more.
Judge it as you please, you who can,   490
For I will go on telling as I began.

PART TWO

Once poor Arcite was home, gone back to Thebes,
All he could do was say "Alas!" and weep,
Knowing he'd never see his lady again.
Let me sum up the sorrows of this woeful man   495
By saying, simply, that as long as the world may last
No creature, now or then, will ever have had
Such miserable days. He was robbed of sleep, of meat,
Of drink, and grew as lean and dry as a bean.
His eyes were hollow, and terrible to see,   500
His skin was pale, and yellow; he was solitary,
Always completely alone, and spent his nights
Wailing and weeping, moaning and groaning in frightful
Tones, and if he heard a song being sung
Or music being made, his heart was wrung   505
With endless tears. So feeble his spirits, so low,
And he so changed, that no one, listening, could know
His voice or understand his words, when they heard them,
And the way he behaved to everyone in the world
Not only resembled the god of love, Eros   510
Himself, but insanity, brought on by wearisome
Sadness, and a spreading melancholic, futile
Sense, born in imprisoned love for his beautiful
Lady. In a word, all his earthly being,
His character and habits, were easily seen   515
To be upside down, and this was now Arcite.
    Who could write it all? And who would read it?
After enduring this pain for a year or two,
Living at home in Thebes, as I've said to you,
While sleeping one night, he thought that Mercury,   520
The wingèd god, had come to his room, his sleep-
Inducing rod in his hand, and also that
Covering his gleaming hair was a kind of hat.
And Mercury was telling Arcite to be merry.
The god appeared to the sleeping man to be very   525
Like how he'd looked, when putting Argus to sleep,
Then killing him, for stealing Zeus' sheep.
"Leave for Athens," he said. "Your sorrows will end."

And then Arcite awoke. "However this ends,"
He swore, "I'll leave for Athens immediately: 530
No fear of death will keep me, now, from seeing
Emily, the lady I love and serve.
If I die in her presence, death will be deserved."
    Saying these words, he took up a great, clear mirror
And saw that his face and hands were truly colored 535
Highly unlike the hue they had known before,
And suddenly realized that all this changed
Appearance might well protect him from the fearful dangers
There in Athens. These years he'd spent in sorrow
Might make it possible, today and tomorrow, 540
To actually live in Athens, remain unknown.
And then, if he was careful and kept himself low,
He might see his lady almost every day.
Quickly, he changed his clothing, so people would say
And think him a workman. He would go alone, 545
Except for a squire, also disguised, who would know
His deepest secrets and who and what he really
Was. By the shortest route, quite naturally,
The very next day he went to Athens, and there
He took himself to the court and offered to bear 550
And carry, as working men must, whatever needed
Doing. And, in a word, the trick succeeded:
Arcite was now in service to a man whose daily
Duties were rooms in the house where Emily stayed.
Arcite was no fool; he quickly learned just who 555
Was working where, and when, and what they would do.
Arcite could carry water, and chop up wood,
For he was young and could do what he needed to:
He was taller than most, his frame was solid and heavy,
Strong enough to manage the work they gave him. 560
And so for a year or two he served as a page
In the house of Emily, his lady fair.
And Philostratus was the name he was known by, there.
But half so well-beloved a man as he
Had never been seen in court, for Arcite could be 565
Wonderfully charming and kind, gentle and worthy
Of real affection; he earned the highest degree

Of commendation. Everyone said, indeed,
That Theseus should raise him to noble standing
And give him noble duties, allowing the man 570
To truly make use of his natural powers and grace.
His fine behavior grew his fame so fast,
Helped by his worthy tongue and his excellent taste,
That Theseus had placed him close to his side,
And raised his stature to that of a courtly knight, 575
Giving him gold to maintain his reputation—
Though year by year, men of the Theban nation
Brought him, in secret, the income his property earned.
Arcite was careful, money never burned
In his pocket, and no one wondered where it came from. 580
For three whole years he went on living this laboring
Life, carrying himself, in peace and war,
So well that Theseus held no one so dear.
Now let me leave Arcite in this state of bliss,
And turn to Palamon for just a bit. 585
  Tormented, wasted by suffering, locked in prison,
Palamon had been sitting, helpless, season
After season, afflicted with woe and distress.
Who could feel the sorrow and heaviness
That Palamon knew, beaten down with grief, 590
Half driven out of his mind, beyond all belief?
And you must remember that Palamon is in prison
Forever, not for just a year or a season.
  Who has so well mastered English rhyme
That he can describe Palamon's state? Not I. 595
So let me move on, as lightly as I may.
  And then it happened, in the month of May,
The third of that month (as ancient books explain,
That tell this story much more clear and plain),
Occurring by accident or destiny— 600
For just as things are intended, things shall be—
Shortly after midnight Palamon,
With a helping hand from a friend, broke out of prison
And fled the city as fast as he could go.
He'd offered his jailer claret wine, and thrown 605
In the glass a dose of opium and other

Narcotics, grown in the soil of Thebes, that wonder
Of wonders, no one could shake the fellow awake;
No matter how hard they shook him, he stayed in that state
All night. And Palamon hurried as fast as he might.   610
He'd started late, and little was left of the night,
And dawn was near, he knew he needed to hide.
A grove of trees, growing close beside
The road, was the best—the only—place he could find,
And, fearfully, right in he went, expecting   615
There to spend the rest of the day, protected
By trees. When daylight was done, he meant to take
His way toward Thebes, hoping he could persuade
His friends to aid him. He'd shaped his plans, he'd make
War on Theseus, and lose his life   620
Or win his Emily and make her his wife.
That was his plan, and all I need to explain.
     Now let me turn to Arcite, yet once again,
Who had no idea how close he was to trouble,
Till Fortune fell and broke his blissful bubble.   625
     The busy skylark, messenger of day,
Sang his song, greeting the morning, still gray
And dim, till fiery Phoebus rose so bright
That everything eastward laughed at the streaming light,
Beams of which went gleaming among the trees,   630
Drying the silver drops of dew on the leaves.
And happy Arcite, now first of knights at the court
Of Theseus, rose and smiled at the day,
Which was merry. In order to do his duty to May,
And keeping his mind well-fixed on what he most   635
Desired, the highest goal he could ever hope for,
He mounted a horse, skittish as leaping fire,
And rode in the fields, went out as far as required,
A mile or two at most from the ducal court.
An impulse took him into a green-leaved grove,   640
Intending to fashion a garland from branches and boughs,
Or else perhaps from woodbine or hawthorn leaves,
And riding along in the warming sun, he greeted
The glowing light from the sky, singing this song:
"May, with all the flowers I ride among,   645

And all your green, welcome, fair fresh May."
His horse went cantering quickly, with a lusty heart,
And Arcite rode him even faster, starting
To gallop up and down the leafy path,
Where Palomon, by the merest twist of chance,   650
Was crouching down in a bush so no one could see him,
As deeply afraid of death as a man can be.
Not knowing who was on the horse, or might be,
Not thinking it could be Arcite—he wouldn't have believed it—
But the proverb says, and has said it for many years: 655
"Fields have eyes to see with, and trees have ears."
A man must keep himself forever steady,
For things will always happen, you must be ready.
Arcite had no suspicion his cousin was there,
Listening to every word with attentive ears,   660
Now sitting very still in his green-leaved bush.
     When Arcite had finished his gallop on the rush,
And singing all the ballad songs he knew,
He sudden fell in a brownish study, musing
As lovers always do, sometimes up   665
And sometimes down, back and forth, dropping
Water like a bucket. Workers know
That days they needn't labor are perfect for snow
Or rain, and then sunshine. So Venus toys
With lovers' hearts: a day they think they'll enjoy   670
Suddenly brings them tears and woeful pain,
Just as Venus, high in the sky, changes
Her aspect. Nothing about her stays the same.
Days are never free, for workers or lovers.
     Arcite had just been singing; now he smothered   675
His songs, and abruptly dropped to the ground, like a stone.
"Alas the day," he said, "when I was born!
O Juno, how long will godly cruelty
Strangle Thebes, once so great a city?
     "Alas, the blood of Cadmus and Amphion,   680
Great kings—for it was Cadmus who founded the town,
And first to wear the noble city's crown.
And I, now lowly knight in service, descend
By proven, perfect line of blood from men

Of royal stock, a miserable wretch, forced 685
To bow and scrape to the very man who brought me
The pain of prison—Theseus, my enemy.
And I have become his knight in captivity!
Day by day I live a virtual slave.
And still great Juno showers me with shame, 690
And always more: no one must know my name.
Once I was called Arcite, and lived in fame;
Now I am Philostratus, not worth a penny.
O cruel Mars! Alas, O savage Juno!
Destroyers of my family, bringers of woe. 695
I and wretched Palamon remain,
And he lies martyred, bound with iron chains.
And yet, in addition to this, in order to slay me
Completely, Cupid with his deadly aim
Shot his burning arrow so deep in my faithful, 700
Sorrowing heart that my death was guaranteed
Even before I could walk. O Emily,
I'm slain by your eyes, and death will come to me
Through you. I care so little for the rest of the earth
That no one and nothing, now, would have any worth 705
If only anything I did could please you."
Then down he fell in a trance, a motionless fit,
And lay there long, before he came out of it.
  Then Palamon, who felt as if an icy
Sword had suddenly pierced his heart, was so wild 710
With anger he could no longer stay in hiding.
Hearing Arcite's bemoaning, woeful tale,
Bursting out of the bushes he came, as pale
As death, with all the appearance of a man insane,
Crying "Arcite, you traitor, you liar, you slave 715
Of evil, now I've caught you—you so on fire
With love for my lady, you who have brought me dire
And dreadful pain, my cousin, my brother, sworn
To support and help me, as I have told you before—
Here you are, ensnaring Theseus too, 720
Wickedly even changing your name! O you
Will either die or bring me death at your hands,
For you are forbidden to love her, the only man

Who ever will love my Emily is me,
For I am Palamon, your enemy! 725
And though I have no weapons, here in this place,
I've broken out of prison, by God's great grace,
And either you or I will have to die
To keep you from loving my Emily. Don't try
To escape, take whatever choice you like!" 730
  Then angry Arcite, with hatred deep in his heart,
Recognizing his cousin, hearing his sharp,
His fervent words, drew his sword like a charging
Lion, saying, "By God who sits above,
If you weren't sick, and wild as you are with love, 735
And here in this place carry no sword in your hand,
You'd never leave this grove of trees, or stand
Anywhere else on earth. I'd kill you right now.
For I dissolve all promises and vows,
All grants you think I've made, all guarantees. 740
You fool, don't you know that love is free,
And I would love her whether you weren't or were?
But you're a knight, worthy as any on earth,
And ready to choose who'll have her, by mortal combat,
So here is my answer: tomorrow I'll come back 745
Without the knowledge of anyone in Greece,
And come as a knight, with all the equipment you'll need,
And you may take the best, leave me the worst.
And later tonight, when all who live on earth
Are in bed, I'll bring you food and drink, and blankets 750
Sufficient to give you a sound, soft sleep. No thanks
Are due me: either you or I will win
My lady, and if it's you, rejoicing in
Her love when I am dead, why then you'll have her."
  Palamon replied: "I accept your offer." 755
And so they left each other, until next morning,
Each expecting faith would bring them glory
  O Cupid, never known for charity!
O deadly ruler of love who's always been
Alone: as men have truly long declared, 760
Love is sovereign, it won't permit sharing
Its rule with anyone, no one its peer,

As both Arcite and Palamon are learning.
Next morning, when dawn had not yet opened the sky,
Arcite left Athens, bringing, all secretly,   765
The battle equipment each of them would need,
Carefully chosen to make the battle fair
As well as fatal. Each of them would wear it.
Arcite came riding, he alone, deadly
Weapons, heavy armor and shields spread   770
On his horse's back. And at the time they'd set,
Arcite arrived. Two cousins and brothers met
And both changed color, turning pale in the face,
Exactly like hunters of bears and lions, in Thrace,
Knowing a beast is rushing under the trees,   775
Smashing branches and boughs, pulling down leaves,
And thinking, spear upraised, ready for throwing,
"Here comes my mortal enemy, knowing
I am determined to kill him, as he'd kill me.
Either he dies, here where the woods grow thinner,   780
Or I have failed, and he becomes the winner."
Each one knew what the other thought. Their faces
Went white and red, lost for the moment, dazed.
  And then, with no formalities of greeting,
Without a word from either man, no speaking,   785
They set to work, each of them helping the other,
Fastening, tying, like a pair of friendly brothers.
And then, immediately, their sharp spears strong,
They fought each other, fought the whole day long.
You'd surely expect that noble Palamon   790
Would fight like a lion fresh from the woods, and someone
Like Arcite would slash and cut like a tiger.
They fought like a pair of fierce wild boars, white
At the mouth with frothy foam of anger. They fought
Up to the ankle in blood they freely poured.   795
And there I leave them, while they continue fighting,
And turn to Theseus, another brave knight.
  The only mover and shaker of all this world
Is Destiny, who executes on earth
The providence long since decreed by God,   800
The power of which prevails, so firm and hard

That whatever our world may think, one way or another,
God's will will always be done, no matter whether
It takes a thousand years to fall on our heads.
And this is certain: whatever we want, for better   805
Or worse, for war, or peace, for hate, or love,
Is always entirely ruled by foresight above.
      I mean to prove this point by Theseus,
That mighty man, who hungered hard, in truth,
To celebrate this May by hunting down   810
Some huge old stag, and every day, with hounds
And horns and huntsmen by his side, he rode
As soon as morning came, right after dawn,
Finding in his hunting such delight
That it became his joy and appetite   815
To slay some noble deer, its branching horns
Showing how he was to Diana sworn.
      The day was clear—I think I've told you this—
And Theseus, blissful, reveling in happiness,
Had taken with him Hippolita his queen,   820
And also Emily, who was dressed in green.
So royally they rode until they came to
A nearby grove, where—it was said—a famous
Stag could be found. Theseus went riding straight
To the clearing amidst the trees, knowing deer   825
Would run that way, as soon as they could hear
The hunters. They'd jump a brook and be on their way.
And the duke would have a chance with his hounds, that day,
To run the animal down, for his hounds were swift
And Theseus himself had a hunter's gifts.   830
      But when he reached the clearing, and looking under
The sun, why, all at once—like lightning and thunder!—
He saw this Palamon and this Arcite,
Fighting hard, like two wild boars in a field.
Their shining swords were slashing to and fro   835
So terribly that even their lightest strokes
Seemed as though they'd surely fell an oak.
But who and what they were he could not say.
He spurred his horse directly in their way,
And stood between them, quickly as his horse could go,   840

And drew his sword and loudly shouted, "Ho!
Stop, no more, on pain of losing your head!
By mighty Mars, he shall be put to death
At once, he who swings another stroke.
But tell me who on earth you are, both   845
Of you, and bold enough to be fighting here,
Absent any sanction or officer,
To judge and assess your actions properly."
  Palamon's reply to the duke was hurried:
"Sire," he said, "why bother with words any more?   850
Death is what we both deserve. Two woeful
Wretches are we, miserable, captive men,
Our lives too heavily burdened again and again,
And you as righteous lord and honest judge
Should not award either of us your refuge.   855
But kill me first, for God's own charity!
Then kill him after, being done with me.
Or kill him first, for you are not aware
That he is Arcite—the name he rightly bears—
Whom you have long since banished, on pain of death,   860
And having returned, he now deserves to be dead.
For he is indeed the man who came to your gate
And said he was Philostratus, a workman, in faith,
And worked at deceiving you, both night and day
For a year, until you made him your knight in chief.   865
And he has long been in love with Emily.
And now that I know my death is here at hand
Let me confess myself, for I am the man
Named Palamon who wrongfully broke your prison,
Thus making myself your eternal foe and a sinner   870
Only worthy of death. I'm also he
Who burns with love for Emily the fair,
Who soon will witness my death, right where we are.
These are your reasons, lord, to put us to death,
The two of us together, slain in one breath.   875
And death is what we deserve, simply said."
  Theseus replied, not waiting, declaring
With equal haste: "Your sentence has been prepared
By the words out of your mouth, a complete confession

Of guilt. You both must die, there are no questions   880
To ask, no need for torture to pry out the truth.
And by mighty Mars, this I will swiftly see to!"
    But then his queen, in womanly sympathy,
Began to weep, and so did Emily
And all the ladies among their company.   885
How dreadful a shame, every lady thought,
For such a disaster to happen, such pain to fall
On two such gentlemen so noble, so tall,
And just because of nothing more than love.
The women could see the wounds they bore, covered   890
With blood, and each and all bewept their fate,
Crying with just one voice, servants and ladies,
"Have mercy, lord, for the sake of womanhood!"
They knelt and would have kissed his feet if they could,
Until at last his anger passed and departed,   895
For pity quickly stirs in noble hearts.
And though at first he fairly shook with passion,
Having swiftly seen their guilt, and fashioned
A perfect sentence for crimes they both admitted,
He saw that though his judgment was fully permitted   900
It was angry, and reason just as fully excused
Them both, for who, he thought, could be refused
The right to follow love as best he was able,
Even climbing out of prison's chains?
The duke was moved, too, by the intensity   905
Of womanly weeping, shed in a flood of pity,
And in his noble heart he said to himself,
Softly, "Fie upon a lord who is deaf
To mercy, always a lion both in word
And deed, not simply spiteful to some, a hard,   910
A cruel man, but also to the fearful,
Confessing guilt as proud men never will!
A lord has little wisdom who cannot tell
The differences in different cases, striking
Down the proud and humble, both alike."   915
And in a word, when time and reason, helped
By women's tears, had washed away his hot-felt
Anger, his face grew lighter, and lifting his head,

Eyes bright, he raised his voice and happily said:
    "The god of love, ah may he blessèd be!   920
How mighty, how truly great a lord is he!
Nothing can stand in his way, no obstacle
Resists him. Call him a god, for his miracles,
For he can fashion paths for the human heart
And lead us down a road, no matter how hard.   925
Just consider Arcite, and Palamon,
Escaping out of chains and from my prison,
Able to live in Thebes as royally
As ever. Knowing me their mortal enemy,
Aware I would not hesitate to kill them,   930
And with their eyes wide open, completely willing
To come to Athens, where death awaited them both.
What could be more foolish, by my oath!
Who can be an utter fool, but a lover?
Just look at them! For the sake of God above,   935
See how they bleed! How well they're sprayed in red.
Thus the god of love, their lord, has paid
Their wages for all the high devotion they gave him!
And still these lovers worship love, whatever
Happens, think it beautiful forever.   940
And here is the height of every irony:
The woman for whom they played this fantasy
Could not be grateful to them, not even to me,
Knowing as much about this whole affair,
By God, as cuckoos up in a tree, or hares!   945
But life requires testing, hot or cold:
A man must be a fool, if young or old—
As I can testify from my young years,
When I was a lover, hot behind the ears.
And thereby knowing something of love's fierce pains,   950
And how they seize you sharply, again and again,
And having myself been caught in mortal snares,
Your guilt, for all your crimes, I hereby declare
Forgiven, to honor my queen, now kneeling here,
And also of Emily, my sister dear.   955
Arcite and Palamon must therefore swear
They'll never injure Athens in any way,

Never make war on me, by night or day,
And be my friends in all they do or say.
You both are fully forgiven in every respect." 960
And they replied by swearing, without objection,
Begging him for mercy and lordly grace,
All of which was granted. And then he said:
    "Let me now speak of riches and royal blood.
Even were Emily a princess or queen, 965
Either of you are worthy, and would so be,
To ask for her hand. I speak on her behalf,
She for whom you fight, wound and batter
Yourselves. You know she cannot marry you both
At once, no matter how jealous you are, by my oath— 970
Not even should you fight tomorrow and after!
One of you two, either in tears or laughter,
Can go and blow his whistle in an ivy leaf.
However angry you are, or jealous, believe me,
She must say 'yes' to only one of you. 975
So let me place you, gentlemen, where one
Can win, one lose, and no one needs to die.
The fate of each of you will be decided
By you yourselves. So listen carefully.
    "Bluntly, here is what you'll now agree to— 980
Without discussion or any argument,
Like what I say or not. And my intention
Is this: without a ransom, without any threats,
You'll each go freely wherever you think it best,
And fifty weeks from now, here you'll appear, 985
Each of you with a hundred worthy knights,
Armed in all respects for tournament fighting.
Then you can joust and battle for her hand.
I promise this, to both of you young men,
Upon my truth and honor as a knight, 990
That which of you is winner in the fight—
Either by driving the other out of the lists,
With all his hundred, or striking him dead as a fish—
He who wins this tournament, I swear,
Will win my sister Emily. And here, 995
Right here, this grove of trees, this very same place,

The grounds will be prepared. When Fortune's grace
Is granted, whoever it is, will have her. God
Have mercy on my soul, but on this same sod
I will be the judge of who has won. 1000
And that is all, no other way will be done.
Tell me if you approve my plan; be pleased
That neither of you lies dead or about to be seized
And imprisoned. Thus we'll reach the end of this road."
  And who but Palamon is light as a foal? 1005
Who but Arcite is truly jumping for joy?
Who could describe the universal enjoyment
Felt by all who stood in that fairest place
When Theseus granted them all so fair a grace?
Everyone there fell to their knees, thanking 1010
Theseus with all their heart and their might,
And loudest of all were the pair of Theban knights.
And so with good hopes, filled with pleasure and high
Good humor, Arcite and Palamon go riding
Home to Thebes, with its walls so great, so wide. 1015

PART THREE

  I think most people would think me negligent
If I didn't go on to tell you the enormous expense
Duke Theseus incurred, working so busily
To fix the tournament lists, construction royally
Done—truly, an ampitheater, designed 1020
For thousands, larger than anything like it.
The inner ring, where men would fight, was a mile
Around, walled in stone, with a ditch outside.
And overall, to speak like geometry,
Its shape was a great round circle, with steps in degrees, 1025
Running almost sixty yards high, carefully
Set so men, wherever they chose to stand,
Would never block the sight of another man.
  To the east there stood a gate, built of white marble,
And to the west another. Men might marvel 1030
That in so short a space of time such
A place was erected, but only in this duchy

Were there so many men so zealously skilled
In arithmetic and geometry, willing
Workers in paint on canvas, or carving in stone, 1035
For Theseus paid them sumptuous wages, and sought
Them out, to build this ampitheater quickly
And well. In reverence and devotion he picked
The top of the eastern gate for a chapel and altar
Dedicated to worship of Venus, and for Mars, 1040
On top of the western gate, he erected a second,
In size the same but built at a cost that reckoned
More than a carriage-load of purest gold.
Then to the north, in a turret on the wall,
Built of snow-white alabaster and coral 1045
Red as blood, he set a third great chapel,
Wonderfully rich, as any man could tell you,
In worship of chaste Diana, goddess of hunts,
Making sure that it was beautifully done.
      But there! I've half forgotten to let you see 1050
The noble carvings, the bright and gracious paintings,
Carefully shaped in bodies, as in faces,
Wherever you looked in each of these three buildings.
      High in Venus' chapel, created right
On the wall, and every bit as sad a sight 1055
As ever seen, are lovers trying in vain
To sleep, their desperate sighs, their tears, their wailing—
All the burning strokes of helpless desires
The servants of love endure in love's hot fires,
Not to mention the oaths these people are sworn to, 1060
And portraits of Recklessness, Pleasure and Hope,
Youth and Beauty, Riches, even Pimping,
Magic Potions, and Force, Delicate Primping,
Lies and Expenses, Jealousy and Exertion,
All wearing golden garlands, and in addition 1065
A cuckoo sitting directly on their hands—
And feasts and violins, carols and dances,
Clothing and lust, all the circumstances
Inherent in love: I saw and studied them all,
And will study again, painted there on the wall, 1070
As well as others I cannot pause to mention.

Even great Mount Cithaeron was present,
There, where Venus finds herself at home,
Portrayed with all the alleys lovers roam,
The gardens, and most of all their lustiness.   1075
Her doorman, too, was painted, old Idleness,
And her handsome ancient hero, Narcissus,
And even Solomon's gross and ugly folly,
The power and strength of Hercules, the jolly
Enchanting of lovely Medea, and also Circe—   1080
Not forgetting Turnus, whose courage burned fiercely,
Or gold-ridden Croesus, enslaved by what he owned.
And so, if you look you see how Venus is stone
And steel, compared to riches or earthly wisdom,
Cleverness or beauty, strength or kingdoms   1085
Conquered, nothing can equal Venus' power,
For she can spin the world, hour by hour,
As she likes. See all these people caught in her trap,
So often sighing, "Well-a-day" and "Alas."
You'll see enough, I think, with even these few   1090
Examples; finding more would be easy to do.
        The glorious statue of Venus herself was naked,
Showing her taking her bath in the open sea,
Green waves, like blankets, covered her body from
The navel down, waves as bright as the sun.   1095
Her right hand held a zither, and on her head,
Lovely to see, was a garland of roses, fresh
And sweet to smell. Her doves were fluttering
Above her hair; Cupid, her son, stood near her,
Wings sprouting from each of his bare shoulders;   1100
And he was blind, right as old pictures show.
His arrows were bright and keen, he carried a bow.
        But why should I stop before I've told you all
The paintings also found upon the wall
Of the temple made for Mighty Mars the red?   1105
This wall was fully painted, in length and breadth,
Just like the inside of that grisly place
Known as the temple of Mars in far-off Thrace,
That frosty, distant, cold and dismal region
Where Mars long since had built his lordly mansion.   1110

The first scene painted on the wall was a forest,
Completely empty of either man or beast,
Its trees all knotty, gnarled, and barren, and old,
With stumps so sharp they're awful to behold,
Through which the forest rumbled a sighing sound,   1115
As if a storm were coming to break the boughs.
And downward from a hillside, under a cliff,
You saw the temple of Mars the omnipotent,
Wrought of burnished steel, and the entryway
Was long and narrow—ghastly, by my faith!   1120
And from this passage, rushing with frenzied roars,
Came blasts that shook and rattled the massive door.
There were no windows; the only light was across
The entryway, shining down from the north.
There was no other way to see. The door   1125
Was made of eternal ádamánt, attached
From side to side, its entire length, with clamps
Of tough and hammered iron. To make the structure
Sure and strong, every single pillar,
Thick as barrels, was shining iron, well-milled.   1130
   Inside this temple, the first of the pictures I saw
Was Felony, with all his disorder, dark
And secret; and then it was Anger, red as fire;
There were thieves to see, and justly terrible Fear;
And smiling men, with knives under their cloaks;   1135
And a farmer's dairy, covered with thick black smoke;
Treachery and nighttime murder in bed;
War itself, with swords all smeared with the red
Of blood; and fighting, with knives, and wounds, and menace.
The whole depressing temple was filled with threatening   1140
Sounds. I also saw a suicide,
His hair well-smeared with blood, his eyes gone wide,
A nail he'd hammered into his head at night,
Death all cold, his mouth that gaped upright.
And there, right in the middle, sat Bad Luck,   1145
His head hung down, his face all sorrow-struck.
And then it was Madness I saw, laughing, raging,
Quarreling, knives in hand, and screams of outrage;
A corpse lay in the bushes, his throat well carved;

Thousands dead, but not by the plague, not starved!   1150
A tyrant with all the plunder he's carried off,
A town destroyed, no single thing was left!
I saw ships burning, tossing in the waves,
And hunters crushed to death by bears in caves,
And sows devouring babies, right in their cradles,   1155
And a cook well-scalded, despite the length of his ladle.
The evil influence of Mars was imparted
By showing a carter crushed to death by his cart:
He lay there, stretched at full length, under the wheels.
And, unforgotten, in Mars' wide astral fields,   1160
Were barbers, butchers, and blacksmiths hammering hard
On forges, turning out swords too keen, too sharp.
And above the rest, painted high in a tower,
Was Conquest, seated, surrounded by royal honor,
And yet with a sword hanging over his head,   1165
Dangling down from a thin and fine-spun thread.
I saw the slaughtering of Julius Caesar,
And Nero the great, and Antony in his weakness—
All this despite historical fact, for these men
Were not yet born, at that time, but Mars had bent   1170
Chronology by wicked threats, and there
They were, painted truly (though out of fear),
For everything is seen by movements of stars,
Who must die of love, and who be carved
By swords. We know all this from stories of old.   1175
I cannot tell them all, though I wish I could.

     Mars stood in a chariot, a statue showed,
Armed and looking grim, scowling, but cold.
Two figures known to all who study the future,
And how it can be told, hung in their usual   1180
Style above his head. They were not beautiful.
But there below them, all the same, stood the god
Of war, a wolf at his feet, staring hard
At what was left of a man he had finished eating.
A deft and delicate hand had drawn this scene,   1185
In adoration of Mars, and what he has been.

     And now, at last, to the temple of chaste Diana,
As quickly as ever I can possibly manage,

I'll give you descriptions, brief and clear as I'm able.
The walls were painted from top to bottom: it may be 1190
Good to start with the picture of woeful Callisto,
When great Diana was angry with her and showed
Her powers by turning the girl into a bear,
But Jove allowed her to be the shining North Star,
And that was how it was painted, as I've just said. 1195
Later, Callisto's son, Arcas, went
The same way; he too is now a star in the sky.
Then I saw Dane—or was it Daphne?—I'll try
To tell you truly, but whatever her ancient name
(It wasn't Diana) eventually she became 1200
A tree. I saw how Acteon became a stag
Because he'd seen Diana naked in her bath.
The painting showed the poor man's hounds catching
And eating him, not knowing the stag was their master.
Nearby was painted the huntress Atalanta, 1205
Trapped into marriage by famous golden apples,
And warrior Meléagra, and many more,
For whom Diana had cares and sorrows in store.
I saw a host of marvelous tales, well drawn.
But alas! my memories have faded and gone. 1210
    Diana, high on a stag's great back, could be seen
With little hounds around her toes, and beneath
Her feet the painter placed a moon, waxing
Almost full, but waning soon. Her statuesque
Picture showed her dressed in gaudy green, 1215
A bow in her hand, and a quiver of arrows, teeming
Full. Her eyes were directed rigidly down,
Looking at Pluto's dark, unwholesome ground,
Where a woman was hard in labor, mired in a birth
Unfinished, calling Diana for heaven's assistance: 1220
"Come help, come help!" the suffering woman called,
"For yours are remedies the best of all!"
The man who gave us this was a master, well-taught,
And must have steeply paid for the paints he bought.
    And so the lists were constructed, and Theseus, 1225
Obliged at great expense to pay for this—
Temples and amphitheater, and all the rest—

Was pleased at what he'd done to provide the test.
But Theseus having had his turn at the fore,
Let me go back to our Theban knights once more.   1230
    Palamon and Arcite were due in Athens,
Each man bringing with him a hundred men
At arms, to stage the battle, as you've been told,
Exactly as promised. A hundred well-armed, bold,
Experienced knights now came with each of them,   1235
More than ready for battle once again.
And those who saw these stalwart warriors arriving
Believed, and rightly, that never in their lives,
Or before them, over every sea or land
God made, had better knights assembled, each man   1240
A certified hero, in small but noble bands.
For every knight who worshipped chivalry,
And longed for eternal fame, was desperate to be
Elected one of this number, and surely he
Who'd been selected was more than satisfied.   1245
And were there, tomorrow, another such chance, whose pride
And fixed, intense desire for fame and the love
Of beautiful women could resist it? Here they could prove
Their greatness: whether it was in England or elsewhere,
All yearning knights, if they could, would surely be there,   1250
Fighting for a lady's favor—O blessèd be he!
And what a joyous sight for us to see.
    By God, thus thought those riding with Palamon!
He'd brought a hundred heroes along with him,
Some well-armed in shining coats of mail,   1255
Some with glistening tunics, and strong breastplates,
Some with double armor, thick and straight,
Some with a wooden shield, or one that was made
In Prussia, some with rugged legs in shin-plates,
Wielding an axe, or a vicious club of steel—   1260
No fashion is new that's never been old, on these fields.
Knights have always chosen weapons they like
The best. They choose what they think is good, then strike!
    You could have seen, coming with Palamon,
Lycurgus himself, king of Thracian men.   1265
His beard was black. A noble, manly man,

The pupils of his eyes were red, or tan,
Or yellow, making him look like a savage griffin;
His brows, with hair like briars, jutted like grim
Great lions. His muscles were hard and strong, on arms   1270
And legs, his shoulders were broad, heavy and brawny.
As Thracian knights preferred, he rode in a golden
Chariot, pulled by pairs of pale white bulls.
He wore no armor over his battle dress,
No nailed-in steel, gleaming across his chest,   1275
But only an old bear skin, black with age.
He wore a golden wreath, huge and flaming
With bright-cut gems, rubies and diamond stones;
Wolfhounds, white as snow, leapt and roamed
Around his chariot, dogs as large as steers,   1280
Fit for hunting lions or quick-hooved deer,
Now muzzled, collars colored as if of gold,
Tied on with thongs. Twenty hounds, all told.
A hundred lords would follow wherever he went,
Stern and stubborn, proud and well-armed men.   1285
     Riding with Arcite was Emítreús,
Indian king. His horse's armor was trussed-on
Steel, covered with golden cloth, of cross-patched
Wool, looking for all the world exactly
Like Mars himself. His coat was Persian silk,   1290
Embroidered with pearls, great, and white as milk.
His saddle was hammered out of bright new gold,
And the mantle hanging high across his shoulders
Was heavy with fire-red rubies, sparkling in sunlight.
His curly hair was wound in rings, and was bright   1295
And yellow, gleaming like gold lying in the sun.
His nose was high, his eyes were bright, of citron
Hue, his lips were round, his color full;
Freckles sprinkled his face, which seemed a dullish
Blend of black and yellow. He peered around   1300
Like a lion ready to take a buffalo down.
His beard had begun to grow, his voice rose
As loud and clear as if a trumpet were blowing.
His head was crowned with a garland of green, laurel
Fresh and a joy to see. On his hand he wore,   1305

As if well-tamed by him, for his delight,
An eagle whose feathers were pure and virginal white.
He too was followed by a hundred loyal knights,
Lords in heavy armor, with swords and spears.
But nothing at all on their heads. Their other gear, 1310
In every possible way, was richly assembled,
For trust me, when I tell you, that in this assembly
Dukes and earls and kings had come, to be
Enrolled in this high noble company,
For love and for the sake of chivalry. 1315
On every side, there ran around this Indian
King, lions and leopards, tamed and friendly.
So one and all, lords from everywhere,
Came to Athens, that Sunday, waiting to appear
Where fighting would start in middle-morning light. 1320
    Now Theseus, this duke, this worthy knight,
Not only brought these lords to Athens, his shining
City, ensured that every one of them
Was housed like lords, which they were, and gave them festive
Nights, made them feel at home, and honored 1325
Them in every way he could. His labor
Was immense. No one could ever do it better.
    The music and entertainment, the waiting-on-tables,
The costly gifts to lords and men of the stables,
The gorgeous displays at Theseus' palace, 1330
And who sat first or last upon the dais,
What ladies were most lovely or danced the longest,
Or which of them were best at dance and song,
Or who was able to speak most fervently
Of love, or just which hunting hawks were perched 1335
Way high above them, which hounds were sprawled on the floor
Below, I will say nothing, and tell no more,
For just what happened should, I think, be enough.
And now to unwind the tale, with a gentle touch.
    That Sunday night, before the sunlight shone, 1340
When Palamon could hear the lark's gay song
(Although the day was still two hours off,
The lark was singing), he rose and climbed the stairs
To the shrine of Venus, holy, divine, bearing

A heart well sanctified and full of courage,   1345
Making his earnest, hopeful pilgrimage
To a goddess he had always known as kind.
At exactly the hour for a proper visit to Venus,
He climbed to where her temple stood, and kneeled,
Neither proud nor arrogant, with feelings   1350
Of due humility, his heart in pain,
He said: "Fairest of fair, O lady mine,
Great Venus, daughter of Jove, Vulcan's wife,
She who brings Mount Cithaeron to life,
On account of the love you felt for human Adonis,   1355
Have pity on my heart, my sorrow, my tears,
And let my prayers reach into your heart.
Alas! I do not know the words to tell
The causes or the torments of my hell,
Mine is not a heart to spin out its tale,   1360
I kneel here so confused I've nothing to say
Except, 'O mercy, O lady bright, who knows
My thoughts, and sees the wounds from which I groan!'
Consider all this, take pity on my sorrow,
As I, for now and always, forever more,   1365
Am and will be your faithful servant. I know
You endlessly make war on chastity,
And so I pray you wrap your mantle on me,
You to whom I pray, come and help me!
Winning this tournament means nothing to me,   1370
Nor any kind of fame, or knightly glory,
Reputation in worldly stories or songs,
But only Emily, for whom I long,
Who belongs to me. I can die if I have her. Who
Can tell you how or what you ought to do?   1375
It makes no difference whether I or Arcite
Is victor, so when I lay me down to sleep
I have my love in my arms. Mars is the chief
Of warfare, but Lady, it's ever been my belief
That yours, in heaven, is power stronger than his: 1380
If you wish it, Emily's my wife.
I'll worship you and your temple the rest of my life,
And on your altar, Lady, I'll sacrifice

And light your holy fire in sacred urns.
And if you think I do not, here on earth, 1385
Deserve my lady Emily—O dearest
Venus, let Arcite's spear swiftly pierce
My heart and let him have the glorious triumph
As well as the lady. That is the end of my cry,
I've nothing else to ask or say. O high 1390
Venus, my Lady dear, give me my love!"
  After Palamon's prayer had been said and done,
He performed his sacrifice, and did it at once,
Most pitifully, observing procedure in full
Detail, though details here are unnecessary. 1395
But, finally, the statue of Venus shook,
And made a sign, and this the lover took
As meaning his prayer had been accepted, that day.
Despite the sign's nature, showing delay,
He left the temple sure he'd been successful, 1400
Cheered to win support from the mighty goddess.
  Shortly after Palamon had gone
To Venus' temple, the sun shone in the sky
And Emily rose from her bed, to pray and sigh
To Diana, goddess of the moon and protector of women. 1405
Her servants followed behind, bearing incense,
Hot coals for the fire, white clothing, and everything else
Essential for the sacrifice: flagons full
Of mead, as custom required—O they brought it all.
Nothing was missing that ought to belong, when calling 1410
Diana, huntress of the moon, opponent of men.
They circled the temple, crowded with praying women,
Burning incense in hand, and Emily,
Her heart well-humbled, washed her beautiful body
With water out of the temple's brimming well. 1415
But how she performed her rites I dare not tell,
Except, as I have, entirely in general
Terms. What fun it would be to tell it all!
(No one knowing I mean that well is offended.)
The girl's bright hair was combed, and all untressed 1420
She wore upon her head a crown of fresh
Oak leaves, forever green. She set two fires

On the altar, doing as the goddess required,
As men can find described in ancient books
Like those of Statius of Thebes. You may go look! 1425
And as the flames rose up, her face unhappy,
This is what she said, just as it happened:
　　"O goddess, chaste, of green and fruitful forests,
Who sees both heaven and earth, including restless
Ocean, queen of Pluto's deep, dark realm, 1430
Goddess of virgin girls: my overwhelmed
Poor heart is known to you, you know what I long for,
But let me be immune to your anger, stronger
Than any lion's, as Acteon had to learn.
Chaste goddess, you of all in heaven have heard 1435
Me ask that I may stay a virgin forever.
O keep me free from love, let me never
Be married! You know I am a huntress, like you,
Pursuing game in the forest, or silent woods,
Where I walk, alone, and only wish I could 1440
Remain so, never married, never a mother.
I've never known much of men. Now for those other
Womanly forms I bear, and share with you—
Proserpina and Luna—help me, do
As only you can! This Palamon, so madly 1445
In love with me, and Arcite, who wants me so badly
(Facts which I mention, but mean no more than that),
Let there be love and peace between those two,
And turn their hearts away from me, do
Not let them fan the flames of hot desire, 1450
Let them love elsewhere, or else extinguish their fires.
End their torments, dear goddess, and also mine.
But if it be my destiny to be taken
By either of them, O goddess, let me make
My life at the side of whichever victorious knight 1455
Truly wants me the most. I admit my fright:
See, O goddess of chastity, pure
And clean, see the bitter tears I endure.
And you, the guardian of unmarried women,
I pray you preserve my virgin state, in which men 1460
Have no part. I will serve at your altar as long as I can."

        While she spoke, the fires continued clear,
Unchanging. But as she finished her tearful prayer,
She saw a strange and unfamiliar sight,
For one of the fires went out, and then burned bright   1465
Again, and immediately the other flickered
And whoosh! was suddenly dead and gone. But quickly,
As it died, the fire whistled (as wet wood will,
At times), and just as swiftly, out the end
Of the glowing, but now extinguished branch, were sent   1470
What seemed to be drops of blood, which kept on flowing.
Emily was so deeply shocked, not knowing
What these signs were supposed to signify,
She thought she might go mad, and began to cry;
She wept so pitifully that simply hearing   1475
Those tears, you would cry, but all it was was fear.
Immediately the image of Diana appeared,
Bow in hand, a huntress as all might witness,
And said: "Daughter, end this heaviness.
Here among the gods, we have affirmed,   1480
Written by eternal word and confirmed
That you must marry one of these two men
Who've suffered so long for your love, in endless torment.
But which of them I'm not permitted to tell.
I cannot stay here longer. Daughter, farewell.   1485
The fires you've seen, burning on my altar,
Already should have told you, before you depart
From here, the true and final course of your loves."
And after those words the arrows she carried, in proof
Of who and what she was, clattered and clanged,   1490
And Diana was gone. Emily felt no anger,
Astonished by the goddess, so quickly vanished.
"What does this mean?" she said. "O and alas!
I put myself, Diana, in your protection,
And in your hands. I promise no objection,   1495
Whatever your choice may be." She went on her way.
This is what happened. There's nothing more to say.
        An hour later, the hour of Mars arrived,
And Arcite entered the temple, grim and dire,
Fully prepared to make his sacrifice,   1500

With all the rites his pagan religion required.
With high devotion and a heart half sick with sadness,
He prayed, hoping tomorrow would bring him gladness:
     "O powerful god, honored in icy Thrace,
And lord of all that realm, who has his place   1505
In every land and kingdom where swords and spears
Are known, holding armies at your fierce
Command, and giving victories as you choose,
Accept my sacrifice, the honor my duty
Offers. Young as I am, if I deserve   1510
Your help, and I am worthy enough to serve
Your godhead and be a man of your very own,
I pray you, mighty Mars, O only look down
And see what pain, what sorrow, I have known.
For you, when younger, were burned by this same fire,   1515
And relished its flames, enjoying the heat of desire
With Venus, beautiful, noble, fresh, and young,
Whom you could hold in your arms whenever you longed to—
Though once upon a time you were caught in a snare,
Vulcan coming home and finding you there,   1520
Lying with his lovely wife, alas!
And for that sorrow, deep in your heart, as
It is deep in mine, have pity on my woe.
I'm young, untried at war, as you well know,
But love, it seems to my heart, has injured me   1525
More than any other living creature,
Since she for whom I constantly burn pays no
Attention to whether I sink or float on the waves,
And O! I understand she'll make no promise
Until I win her in this tournament's lists—   1530
A combat, I also know, I'll never win
Without your help: no matter my strength, I cannot
Win, alone. Then help me, lord, manage
My battle, tomorrow, in honor of the fire which burned,
Once, in you, as well as the fire and yearning   1535
In me, and arrange that, tomorrow, victory is mine.
Let mine be the work, and yours the glory divine!
And I will honor your sovereign temple far past
All places on earth, and work with my heart and hands

To beautify your shrine, until your temple surpasses 1540
All others, my banner hanging high on your walls,
And my men's flags and banners, each one and all,
And forever more, until the day I die,
I guarantee that on your altar fire
Will be burning. You may be sure this vow will bind me: 1545
My beard, my hair, flowing full behind me,
Neither of which has ever felt the edge
Of a razor, or snapping shears, I hereby pledge
To your altar, and swear to be your servant in this life.
So, lord, show pity for my sorrow and grief, 1550
And make me win. There's nothing else I ask for."
    Strong Arcite had finished his prayer, his task
Was done—but suddenly the tight-wound rings
On the door began to clamor, the doors were swinging
Fast, and Arcite could feel a tremor of fright. 1555
The altar fires began to flame, and brightly
Lit the enormous temple, always so gloomy.
The very floor began to tremble, and a perfume
Rose. So Arcite sprinkled a bit more incense
Onto the leaping flames, and quickly commenced 1560
A number of other pagan rites, and prevailed
On the statue of Mars to shake his coat of mail,
And at that sound Arcite heard gentle murmurs,
Low and dim, and a voice which uttered one word:
"Victory!" Honor and glory to Mars, 1565
Arcite pronounced in his heart, and left the once-dark
Temple with hope and joy swelling in his soul,
Walking back to his lodgings, there in the old
City of Athens, happy as a bird in the sun.
    But quickly, high in the heavens, fierce strife had begun 1570
About what Mars had granted, with Venus, goddess
Of love, attacking Mars, omnipotent
In war, and Jove required all his strength
To contain it, until pale Saturn rose, old
And rich in experience, so deft and artful 1575
That soon the quarrel was settled in all its parts.
For truly it is often said that age
Has many advantages, for time has conveyed it

Both great wisdom and practice at making that useful.
Young men run faster than old, but though not youthful 1580
The old are quicker of mind. Saturn is hardly
A mediator born—indeed, his heart
Lies elsewhere—but he meant to stop this quarrel.
    "My dear and beautiful Venus," Saturn explained,
"Because my orbit stretches so far in space, 1585
It sweeps up power more than any man knows.
Pale drowning is mine, when men must sink in the ocean;
Living interment is mine, locked from notice;
Strangling is mine, when men are hung by the throat;
Grumbling, before the dullish peasants revolt, 1590
And loud complaints, followed by poison in soup;
I am in charge of vengeance, and beatings, in truth,
When I go swinging into Leo, sign
Of the lion, old halls that topple down are mine,
And towers, and also walls, that roll, inclining, 1595
Onto the heads of carpenters, or miners.
I killed strong Samson, fiercely shaking the pillar;
And sneaking diseases, even malignant killers,
Are mine, like treason's darkness, age-old plots.
One glance of mine, and plagues spring out of plots 1600
Of ground. So weep no more, Venus, I'll take
Good care of Palamon, he'll have his lady
Exactly as you said he would. Mars
Must be allowed to help his knight, but quarrels
Between you two must somehow be at end, 1605
Although you cannot be the best of friends,
You two who've always fractured heaven's peace.
I, your father's father, will do as you will,
So weep no more, I'll do what you said you will."
    Now let me leave the gods, so high above us, 1610
Mars and beautiful Venus, goddess of love.
And what I'll tell you, as plain as anyone can,
Is the great result for which this tale began.

PART FOUR

Athens was celebrating, all that day,
Helped by gaiety inherent in May,   1615
Which made the people so completely happy
They played war games, and danced, all through that Monday,
Spending energy in the holy service
Of love. But knowing they had to rise so early
Next morning, to see the great, magnificent fighting,   1620
They all dutifully went to bed that night.
And when it was dawn, and they saw the emerging light,
The sound of horses, of equipment clattering, they rose
From every house and inn in the town, rows
Of lords on riding horses and gentle palfreys,   1625
Making their way to the duke's great noble palace.
You would have noticed equipment the like of which
You'd never seen, fashioned by jewelers, and richly,
Beautifully embroidered metals, and steel,
Armor on their heads and their horses, as bright   1630
As their shields, their pure gold helmets, their axes and lightweight
Armor; some lords in robes of state, and knights
In Athens' service. And squires were busy tightening
On the spear-heads, and buckling up the helmets,
Fastening straps on shields, then lacing them well—   1635
Whatever needed doing, someone was doing
Those things. Horses gnawed at bridles, frothing
As they chewed on gold, and armorers were hurrying
Back and forth, carrying files and hammers;
Yeomen walked, as did the common rabble   1640
Of soldiers, lugging short staffs, thick as barrels;
Flutes and trumpets, kettledrums, and clarion
Were brought, instruments of battle sounds;
And the palace was full of people, both up and down,
Three here, there ten, holding their discussions   1645
Of these two Theban knights. These were questions
No one could answer. Some said this, and some
Said that. Some favored the knight with a long black beard,
Some the knight half bald, or else the thick-haired
One. Some said he would fight, and thought he looked grim.   1650

"His battle-axe weighs twenty pounds. Watch *him*!"
And thus the hall was full of wondering and guesses,
Long after the sun was shining, bright and pleasant.
　　Great Theseus had lost his sleep, so loud
Were noises of music and a huge and lively crowd, 1655
But carefully remained in his palace rooms,
Until the Theban knights were brought to his home,
Each of them equally honored. The duke had gone
To an open window, sitting like a god enthroned.
Quickly, the crowds came pushing in his direction, 1660
Anxious to see him and show their appreciation,
And also to hear his commands. His thoughts were law.
High on a scaffold, a herald called out "OOOO!"
And kept it up till all the people were quiet.
Seeing noise had been stilled, he was satisfied, 1665
And told them rules on which the duke had decided:
　　"The great lord's judgment, on careful consideration,
Concludes that spilling noble blood would be wasted,
If he allowed the knights appearing here
To fight as if mortal battle were called for. Wherefore, 1670
To keep these knights from futile, wasted dying,
His basic purpose has now been modified.
No man in these lists, on pain of death,
Shall knowingly carry into this tournament
A missile of any sort, no pole-axe or dagger, 1675
Not even his squire or other man may so carry;
No man may bring, and is strictly forbidden to draw
A short-sword, with its piercing point; nor
May any man attack his opponent more
Than once, riding with a sharp-ground spear; 1680
But men may parry on foot, to defend themselves.
A wounded man in obvious trouble shall be held
Away from battle, off to the side, and compelled
To come there; he'll have no choice. There he stays!
And if the leaders, Palamon or Arcite, 1685
Shall be conclusively captured, or in fair fight
Either leader shall kill the other, no further
Fighting will be allowed; the tourney must end.
God speed you all! Go forth and lay on hard!

Fight with maces, at will, and with long swords.   1690
Go forth now. These are the words of the duke your lord."
     The people's shouts rose up almost to heaven,
So loud their voices, so lively and great their pleasure:
"God save a lord that was, and is, so good,
Wanting no useless spilling of human blood!"   1695
Trumpets began to sound, and songs could be heard,
And all the knights in the tournament were ordered
To ride together, through the streets of the town,
Where golden banners were hung, to the fighting ground.
     Exactly like a monarch, the duke came riding,   1700
Each of the Theban knights on either side,
Then came Hippolyta, then Emily,
And after them came groups of people, he
And she, of this and that, by height of standing.
And so they passed across the city, grandly,   1705
Reaching the tournament grounds exactly on time.
They'd started not long after dawn; now it was nine,
Theseus was seated, rich and high,
Hippolita, his queen, and Emily,
And other ladies, according to their station.   1710
The mob came rushing, taking places they could
Get. Westward, through the gates of Mars,
Came Arcite, and then the hundred of his party,
Riding swiftly, bearing a bright red banner,
And at that moment Palamon appeared   1715
At the eastern gate, which belonged to Venus, their banner
White, their faces brave and strong. No manner
Of paired-off groups of knights, hunted around
The world, both up and down, would seem so proudly
Matched, so evenly chosen, so much alike.   1720
No one alive could choose between them, wise
Enough to say that one was perhaps too old,
Or this one might have been better, if just a bit nobler:
Split two hundred knights up the middle, and change
Nothing. Their ranks were neat, well-ordered arrangements.   1725
In order to show that all of them were the men
Elected, and tricks were not being played, again
Their names were read aloud. Then the gates shut tight,

And they heard: "Now do your duty, you proud young knights!"
    The heralds left their jogging up and down,   1730
Now clarions sounded, and trumpets blared out loud.
There's nothing more to say. East and west
Spears were put in position, firmly set,
Sharp spurs were dug in two hundred horses' sides.
Now we'll see which men can fight and ride,   1735
Spear shafts will shiver and split on shields well-thickened,
Knights will receive their breastbone bruises and pricks,
Spears will go springing twenty feet in the air,
Out come the swords, bright as shining silver.
They'll hew helmets, shred the leather to pieces,   1740
And mighty maces will smash up bones. This one
Through even the thickest throng will thrust and stun,
Steeds will stumble, though strong, and down comes all,
And that one rolls under foot, just like a ball,
Using his spear shaft, though standing, he parries thrust,   1745
And forces rider, and horse as well, to the dust;
That other one is pierced through the body, and captive,
And though he doesn't want to surrender, he has to,
Because the rules were agreed, and the rules were obeyed.
Another young knight, from the other side, does the same.   1750
Then Theseus orders that everyone take a rest,
And eat, or drink, or wash, as suits them best.
The Theban knights had often crossed their paths,
And done hard damage with a stroke or a smash.
Each had knocked the other to the ground, just once.   1755
Arcite was every bit as cruel a hunter,
Stalking Palamon like an angry female
Tiger in a valley, when her cub is stolen, chasing
The guilty party, sniffing after his trail.
But Palamon, in search of his cousin Arcite,   1760
Was like an African lion, hoping to leap
And claw and bite and drink the other man's blood,
Praying for the chance, wishing his time would come.
Each time they met, jealousy rang in their strokes,
They beat their blades, hoping helmets were broken.   1765
Each was bloodied, red ran down their sides.
    But all things come to an end, and have their time.

Just before the sun went off to rest,
Mighty king Emétreus had set
Himself at Palamon, who was busy seeking   1770
To kill Arcite, and his sword cut terribly deep,
After which a force of twenty knights
Pushed Palamon off the field. Lycurgus tried
To rescue him, and strong as he was he failed.
And king Emétreus, already famous   1775
For strength, was sent from his saddle, fiercely knocked down
A full sword's length away from his horse by angry
Palamon, before he was forced away.
It could not help him, it did not save the day.
Boldness of heart was no match for twenty who came,   1780
And having been caught, there he had to stay,
For these were the rules he had agreed to play by.
    Who was lost in sorrow, now, and pain,
Than woeful Palamon, who'd lost the game?
And as soon as Theseus saw this decisive stroke   1785
He stood and loudly called to the fighting folk
To stop: "Ha, no more, it's over and done.
I am an honest judge, and the battle's been won.
Arcite of Thebes shall have his Emily,
This fortunate man, who's won her fair and free."   1790
Those who were watching raised a noisy cry
Of joy, so loud, so heavy, so piercing high
It seemed the lists themselves would crumble awry.
    And now, what can Venus, poor goddess, do?
What can she say? What the queen of love could do,   1795
And did, was weep and cry, for sheer frustration,
Shedding tears that fell, a strange libation,
On the lists. "I'm shamed," she said. "And that is the truth."
    Saturn answered: "Be quiet. He has his fruit,
But he won't eat it. Mars has won, but his joy   1800
Won't last. Watch, you won't be disappointed."
    The sounds of music, rising from below,
Were loud and unrestrained, trumpets blowing
And heralds crying in praise of "Don Arcite."
But listen to me, keep yourselves in your seats,   1805
And see what miracle will come from the ground.

    Arcite had quickly undone his helmet, and round
And round he was riding, showing the crowd his face,
Galloping back and forth across the whole place,
Looking up for the sight of Emily,   1810
Who was looking down at him with a very friendly
Glance (for women, as is commonly known,
Tend to follow the path shaped on the ground
By Fortune, fully as fickle as them), and the sight
Meant everything to him, and was his delight.   1815
    Then out of the earth an infernal fury burst,
Delivered there by Pluto, at Saturn's request,
And Arcite's horse too quickly tried to get
Away, leaping aside, and as he leapt
He stumbled, and Arcite could not take command.   1820
The horse pitched him straight at the ground, his head
Hit first; he lay there, looking as good as dead,
His chest smashed in by his jutting saddle-bow.
He looked as black as coal, or a buzzard crow,
So swiftly had blood gone draining from his face.   1825
As fast as they could, they carried him out of that place,
Everyone looking grim, to the duke's great palace.
And there they cut him out of his battle-harness,
And quickly laid him down in a handsome bed,
For he was conscious, still alive, not dead,   1830
And never stopped his calls for Emily.
    Now Theseus, with all his company,
Was riding back to Athens most happily,
Celebrating, in proper dignity,
An event that surely misfired, but after all   1835
Had been a success, despite Arcite's sad fall.
He did not wish his people disappointed,
For men were saying Arcite could be anointed
With life-saving balms and did not have to die.
And they were happy, too, that those who'd been fighting   1840
Were all alive, though many were wounded and sore,
Especially one whose chest had been pierced by a spear.
For other wounds, and even for broken arms,
There were herbs and salves, and also there were charms,
Boiled-up froth of special leaves, for drinking   1845

And saving damaged lives. And they were thinking,
Like Theseus, who tried to keep them pleased,
All celebrating together, which was what they needed
To do, as custom was, drinking all night
To honor every noble lord, knights   1850
From everywhere—all this was perfectly right.
No one spoke of defeat, but of celebration,
For truly no one had lost, or damaged their station.
Falling, they said, is strictly an accident,
And what had happened to Palamon just meant   1855
He'd been held down by superior numbers, forced
To yield, compelled by twenty knights on horses—
One man and twenty, with no one else to save him,
Dragged along and his horse well-beaten by staves,
Pushed by footmen, yeomen, and even slaves—   1860
Why that, they said, can hardly be thought disgraceful.
No sensible man could think it cowardly.
And Theseus had all of this proclaimed,
To stop all quarreling and silly calling of names,
Affirming the equal rank of knights on both sides, 1865
For though opposed, they seemed two groups of brothers.
He gave them gifts, each one receiving what other
Men would think proper, and feasted them three days,
Treating them worthily, as was his way,
And then conducted his royal guests on their way, 1870
Riding beside them a full day's journey. All
They said, on departure, was a quick "Goodbye, we'll call
Again some day." And now I'm done with this fighting.
Let me mention some of our Theban knights.
  Arcite's whole chest was swollen, and the swelling pressed 1875
More and more against his heart. The best
That anyone could do for him was worthless,
For all the clotted blood stayed in his veins,
And neither leaching nor drawing blood could drain it
Away. He drank the herbs they gave him, but in vain. 1880
The body's power to eliminate whatever
Needs to be forced from flesh, a power that everyone
Thinks belongs to our nature, here was blocked.
The tubes deep in his lungs were swollen, half stopped

Already, and every muscle from his chest on down   1885
Was infected, incapable of carrying on.
In order to save his life, he needed to vomit
Upward, or expel from the rear, but all the dominate
Forces throughout his body were broken and stilled.
Nature no longer controlled what his body could do.   1890
And one thing is sure: when Nature no longer works,
Goodbye doctors! Go bring the man to church!
Thus is the story told: Arcite must die.
And so he asked for a visit from Emily,
And also from Palamon, who loved him dearly,   1895
And this is what he told them, so listen well:
"My heart's hard sadness is greater than I can tell
To anyone, but most especially
To you, my lady, for whom my love will be
Eternal. Even after I die, my spirit   1900
Is pledged to your service, more—far more—than it
Will give to any other living creature;
I know my life on earth cannot endure.
Alas, for the sorrows! Alas, for the terrible pains
I suffered for you, again, and again, and again!   1905
Alas, for death! Alas, my Emily!
Alas, for the binding together of you and me!
Alas, queen of my heart! Alas, my wife!
Only lady of my heart, for whom my life
Ends! What is this world? What can man have   1910
And hold? Now with his love, now in his grave,
Alone, forever deprived of her company.
Farewell, my foe, my sweetest Emily!
Take me gently in your arms, I pray,
For love of God, and listen to what I say.   1915
        "My cousin Palamon and I have fought
Bitterly and long, all for the thought
And love of you, and for my jealousy.
May all-wise Jove incline my soul to be
What honest, truthful lovers ought to be,   1920
To serve in all we do most properly—
That is to say, in knighthood, integrity,
And honor, in wisdom, nature, and humility,

Generous to friends and family—
So Jove may own and relish a share of my heart,   1925
Which knows no man so worthy to share your heart
Than Palamon, my belovèd cousin, part
Of my being, and in your service as long as his life
May last, so if you ever become a wife
Remember him." As he spoke those words, death   1930
Came near him, its coldness stealing away his breath,
And now, because his body lost its strength,
His arms could no longer move. He still had left
His mind, and nothing else but his failing heart,
Still sick, still sore, and even that heart started   1935
To falter, feeling death's swift frigid approach.
His eyes went dark, but before the final stroke
Took his breath away, once more he spoke:
"Mercy, Emily!" Then he spoke no more,
His spirit left his body and went off there,   1940
Which I have known, but cannot say just where.
I'm not a theologian, so I desist,
And even the ancient books contain no list
Of souls, and their opinions being no better
Than mine, I'll hold my tongue, and stick to the letter   1945
Of my tale. Arcite is dead, may Mars be easy
On his soul! And so I return to Emily.

    Emily screamed, and Palamon wept out loud,
And Theseus quickly carried his sister out
Of the room, to keep her away from the corpse. What good   1950
Would it do, except to waste our time, should I
Describe how Emily wept that night and the day
That followed? When death's in a house, this is the way
That women are, shedding their tears for a husband
Long dead, which only makes them cry more sadly: 1955
Sometimes they make themselves sick, and finally die.

    But others in Athens mourned and wept for this Theban's
Death, old folks' sorrows, tears for the man
Falling hardest, yet young folks too. Men,
And women, and children wept for dead Arcite.   1960
This was greater weeping than you might have seen
In Troy, when Hector's body was carried in.

This sorrow was so intense, so hard to bear,
That people tore at their cheeks and pulled out their hair.
    "Why should he be dead," these women were weeping,   1965
"He who had gold enough, and Emily?"
    No one could comfort Theseus, except
His father, Égeús, old man who'd met
Over and over again the world both going
Up and going down, and knew the flow   1970
Of joy and woe, and woe and joy, and told
His son what he had seen and had concluded:
    "No man has ever died before he was due,
Here on this earth, some share of what we call life.
Nor has there ever," he said, "been a man alive,   1975
That some time or other has not finally died.
This world is only a thoroughfare of woe,
And we are pilgrims, passing to and fro.
No matter the pain, it's gone when we are dead."
And on this subject there was more he said,   1980
Wisely exhorting his son and all his people
To search for comfort and try to end their weeping.
    Duke Theseus, trying to stem his grief,
Now planned how he and Athens would take their leave
Of good Arcite, the funeral this knight   1985
Deserved, for both his birth and deeds. The right
Decision he finally came to was this: Arcite
And Palamon, not expecting to meet,
Were forced to fight, driven by passionate love,
In a sweet and green, well-isolated grove   1990
Where pale Arcite had sung and sworn his desire,
And suffered much, burning in love's hot fires.
That grove should be the setting for a funeral pyre,
Where proper rites would join a blazing fire.
And so he commanded that ancient oaks be turned   1995
To brands, arranged in rows best suited for burning.
And then he sent his servants to make arrangements
As fast as they could; without the slightest complaint
They ran and rode to do as he had directed.
And then, when that was done, the duke selected   2000
A burial stand, a bier covered by golden

Cloth, the richest this royal dukedom owned,
And dressed Arcite in clothes of the same material,
And a pair of white gloves on his hands, and a green funereal
Crown of the greenest laurel; and then he placed   2005
A sword in his hand, a shining weapon, and keen.
He laid him on the bier, so people could see him,
Exposed his face. Then Theseus started to weep.
And so his people could see the corpse by light
Of day, he brought the bier to his hall, and the sight   2010
Brought forth a reverberating roar and din.
      Then sorrowing, weeping Palamon appeared,
His hair all wild and sprinkled with ashes, his beard
Fluttery, his clothes all black and wet with tears.
Far surpassing anyone's weeping and woe   2015
Was Emily, most sorrowful of all.
Theseus, wanting the funeral to be
Even more noble and rich, came leading three
Great horses, armored over with glittering steel,
And wearing heraldic arms of noble Arcite.   2020
These steeds (each of the three was gray and white)
Were being ridden by solemn Athenian knights,
One of them carrying, high in front of his saddle,
The dead man's shield, another holding his battle
Spear, and the third bearing his Turkish bow   2025
(The quiver was burnished gold, and the straps were, too).
Their faces drawn and somber, all of them rode
From the palace, heading toward the sweet green grove.
The duke had chosen the noblest Greeks in his city
To carry the bier on their shoulders. They rode through the streets,   2030
Slowly, their red eyes wet with recent weeping,
And down the broadest road in the quiet city
They came, the pavement blackened. Beyond the street
The houses, too, hung high with blackened sheets.
Riding to the right of the slow-moving bier was Égeus,   2035
And riding to the left was his son, Duke Theseus,
Each of them bearing in hand a golden flask,
Filled with milk, and honey, and wine, with a splash
Of blood; and Palamon was there, with many

Men; and then came woeful Emily,   2040
Carrying fire in her hand (which was then the custom),
To burn the corpse, as a proper funeral must.
  Much hard labor was done; great preparation
Was needed both for the service and fire-making,
So that the pyre's top reached for the heavens.   2045
And the pyre's width was a full hundred and seven
Feet—that is, the laid-out boughs were that broad.
Incredible loads of straw filled the holes.
But exactly how they built the fire that high,
And the names of all the different trees, like pine,   2050
And oak, and evergreen-oak, fir, birch, holm, aspen,
Poplar, willow, chestnut, linden, and ash,
Laurel, maple, hazel, plane, and box,
Alder, thorn and yew, whipple and box,
I'll make no listing, nor how old deities   2055
Were running up and down, losing their trees,
In which they'd so long rested and been at peace,
Nymphs, and fawns, and hamadryads, nor how
The birds, the beasts both large and small, fled
In fear, when wood came toppling down on their heads,   2060
Nor how the ground was frightened by sudden light,
No longer accustomed to seeing the sun so bright,
Nor how they laid the fire, at first, with straw,
And then with three dry sticks, carefully cloven
In two, and then with wood that was green, and spices,   2065
And then with golden cloth and splendid trifles
Of goldsmith's making, and garlands hung with flowers,
And myrrh, and incense, with their perfumed odors,
Nor how Arcite was lying, in the midst of this,
Nor what the richness around his body was,   2070
Nor how pale Emily, as was the custom,
Brought them the fire for funeral combustion,
Nor how she fainted when the flames were leaping,
Nor what she spoke or if she meant to speak,
Nor precious jewels that men threw in the fire,   2075
When flames grew huge, and smoke went floating higher,
And some threw shields, and some threw in their spears,

And some their clothing, or how each garment appeared,
And many cups of wine, and milk, and blood
(The fire was hot enough to drink it at once),   2080
And how the Greeks, in enormous cavalry groups,
Rode three times round the fire, in galloping loops,
Shouting loud as they rode, not simply waving
Their spears but fiercely clattering one against
The other—and how the ladies went on crying,   2085
Nor Emily, who had to be led right
To the palace gates, when Arcite's ashes lay still,
Nor how they held a wake, which lasted until
The morning, nor how and what funereal games
Were played—none of all this do I care to say,   2090
Not even who was the best of the wrestlers, anointed
With oil, nor which of them won the prize, appointed
The best. I won't describe how homeward to Athens
They went, when all the funeral games had ended,
But briefly to the point I'm carefully heading,   2095
To bring this long and winding tale to an end.
      The passage of time, and also a number of years,
Finally ended the mourning in Athens, and the tears
Of the Greeks, by universal common assent.
I have the impression there was a parliament   2100
At Athens, to deal with diplomatic issues,
And one of the matters raised was carefully pointed
At finding allies in quite a number of countries,
Including Thebes, with which they were now at peace.
Palamon was summoned to Athens, but not   2105
Told why. He came, still dressed completely in black,
Visibly still in mourning, hurrying back
To Athens, to which the city of Thebes was subjected.
And Emily was there. But Theseus said
Nothing, letting the silence remain unbroken,   2110
His attention fixed on all the strong emotions
He'd been preparing to deal with, when in his wisdom
He thought it best to speak. And after giving
Them time, he quietly sighed and with a somber
Face, said what he'd long been pondering, as follows: 2115

"The First great Mover, high in heaven above,
Created the very first shining chain of love;
The consequences were large, for he'd aimed high.
He knew exactly what he'd intended, and why,
For with that beautiful chain of love he bound 2120
The fire, the air, the water, and also the land
In well-fixed limits, so none of them could flee.
That same heavenly Prince and Mover," said he,
"Established in this wretched world below
The length of days, fixed spans of life and woe 2125
For every living thing this globe engenders,
Limits beyond which lives will never go,
And yet, those spans can always compress and shorten.
No written texts are needed, these important
Facts are perfectly proved by worldly experience. 2130
But let me tell you, now, my sentiments.
These fixed arrangements make all men aware
That this same Mover is stable, and always there.
Men can plainly see, unless they're fools,
That everything derives from larger wholes, 2135
For Nature was not made, in the very beginning,
As only a fragment, a separate, small existence,
But born of a greater thing, perfect and stable,
And staying so until it turns corruptible.
And so our God, from wisdom and foresight divine, 2140
Has carefully established every line,
Allowing different species living on earth
To endure by succession only; first comes birth,
Then death. Life on earth is never eternal.
These are things you can see and know for yourself. 2145
    "Look at the oak, which slowly grows itself
Tall, from seed to stout and thickened tree,
And lives exceedingly long, as we may see,
Yet in the end, like everything else, it's gone.
    "Consider, too, that even the hardest stone 2150
Under our feet, on which we walk and run,
Slowly wears away, and then it's done.
The broadest river can go completely dry,

The greatest towns and cities can fade and die.
We learn from every side that all things end.   2155
    "And man and woman show these truths extended
(Whoever needs it), in either one of two ways,
That is, either in youth or else in old age.
A king can die, exactly like a page;
Some in their beds, some in the depths of the sea;   2160
Some right out in the fields, as all men can see.
There's nothing to do, this is the way it is.
For each and all of us, death does his business.
    "Who makes and drives our living and dying but the king
Of this world, great Jove, the cause of everything,   2165
Turning whatever grows back to the source
From which it derived, and where it belongs? And of course
No living creature, no matter its stature, has force
Enough to resist any of great Jove's laws.
    "And so it is wisdom itself, it seems to me,   2170
To make a virtue of simple necessity,
And understand that there is no escape,
Thinking we are better than monkeys or apes.
Those who grumble at Jove are utter fools,
Rebelling against our lord, who guides and rules.   2175
And surely a man achieves the highest honor,
Dying at the height of his worth, when life has flowered
And he's secured the reputation of his name,
And thus he does himself, and his friend, no shame.
And his friend should always be happy, reaching his death,   2180
To see the worth of his life in the public breath,
Instead of fading away as time goes by
And his fame has shrunken away until it dies.
Worldly reputation will last much longer
When men are dead with names both high and strong.   2185
    "The opposite of this is wilfulness.
Why do we grumble, oppressed with heaviness,
Because Arcite, flower of chivalry,
Has died with honor, always doing his duty,
Departing this foul prison of our life?   2190
Why are they complaining, his cousin, his wife,
About his welfare, he that loved so well?

And would he thank them? No, by God, not at all,
Because they injure both his soul and himself,
And cannot find the way to their lives' fulfillment. 2195
    "What conclusion is reached, after this series
Of statements? After woe, we need to be merry,
Thanking Jove for his unending grace.
And then, before we rise and leave this place,
I think we ought to turn a double sorrow 2200
Into a single perfect joy for tomorrows
Evermore. The misery you're in,
You two, is just the place where joy should begin.
    "My sister," he said, "this is what I want,
Fully endorsed, right here, by my parliament, 2205
Which is that Palamon, your own brave knight,
Who serves you with ready heart, and all his might,
As he has done from the very time you met him,
And you must, by your grace, take pity on him,
And have him as your husband and your lord. 2210
Give me your hand, for these are my royal words.
Show me, now, your sense of womanly pity.
His father was brother to a king, in his city,
And were he nothing more than a poor young student,
He's served you long and well, and has every intent 2215
Of continuing. He's suffered greatly for you,
Things must be seen as they are, and your favor is due him.
Noble mercy should always prevail over right."
    And then he said to Palamon, the knight:
"I take it you don't need much sermoning 2220
To give your happy, total assent to this thing.
Come closer, take your lady by the hand."
    It did not take much time before they were man
And wife, now knotted each to each by that bond
Well known as matrimony (or simply "marriage"), 2225
Approved by council and lords of the baronage.
And so in happiness, and with much singing,
Palamon and Emily were linked
In marriage. And God, who made this entire world,
Brought him the love he had worked so hard to deserve, 2230
And now our Palamon is filled with bliss,

Living in riches, health, and happiness,
Loving Emily so tenderly,
And always treating her with gentility,
So neither would speak a word, harsh or senseless,   2235
Or were jealous, or said what either would find offensive.
    Now Palamon and Emily are finished.
May God have mercy on those who were here to listen!

THE MILLER'S PROLOGUE

When the Knight had finished, all his tale was told,
No one who'd heard his tale, young or old,
Could have denied that this was a noble story,
Well worth keeping fresh in memory—
And especially the pilgrims of loftier breeding.   5
Our Host was laughing, then he swore: "This thing
Is going right, by God! We've gotten the bag
Open. Who'll pull the second tale from the sack?
Truly, our game has well and swiftly begun.
Now tell us, sir Monk, if as it happens you know one,   10
A tale to match the one which the Knight spun out."
The Miller, drunk from all the ale he'd downed,
Was pale and not completely stable-mounted.
Not a man to doff his cap to the worthy,
Sitting and waiting, nor skilled in courtesy,   15
He raised his voice to the level of actors playing
King Pilate, and swore, "By the very bones of God
I know a noble tale that cries to be told,
So now I'll tell it better than the Knight told his."
The Host could see that ale had gone to his head: 20
"My brother," he said, "just let a better man
Tell us another. Wait, we'll work as we can."
    "By God's own soul," said the Miller, "damned if I wait!
Either I tell it, or else I ride on my way."
Our Host replied: "Tell on, we'll hear your story!   25
You're a fool, and drunk as a pig. Your brain's been boiling."
    "You listen to me," said the Miller, "both all and some!

But first I have to affirm just what I am.
I'm drunk, I hear that when I talk. My words
May not be good ones. All right! If I slop and slur,   30
Blame it all on Southwark ale, I pray you.
I want to tell a story that's also a life,
About a carpenter, and also his wife,
And a cleric, who put a cuckoo cap on the fool."
        Up spoke the Steward: "Stop this ranting drool!   35
Spare us all your stupid, drunken cursing.
Slandering men is sinful, defaming is worse,
And so is hurting the reputation of wives."
        This drunken Miller's answer was quick and lively:
        "You ought to think, and remember, dear brother Oswald,   40
A wifeless man can never be a cuckold.
Which isn't to say that you yourself are one.
For who could count the number of decent women?
And a thousand good ones, by God, for one that's bad.
A man who doesn't know that is downright sad.   45
Why be so angry at a story I haven't told?
I'm married, too, if a miller can be so bold.
But one is enough, I swear by the ox in my plow,
Who needs another? Let some fool take a vow
That I'm a cuckold, as long as I know it's a lie.   50
A husband should not go sniffing, inquiring
In God's affairs, or what his wife has done,
So long as God's own plenty is there at home.
Whatever's left over, I leave it strictly alone."
        What else can I tell you, now, except that no one   55
And nothing could stop the flow of this Miller's words:
He told his vulgar tale in vulgar terms.
Alas, I need to repeat his language, here,
Imploring enlightened people to understand,
For the love of God, that telling this tale was a man   60
With a vulgar, drunken mouth, but what he said
Was what I have to write, if I hope to be true
To my tale, and not tell lies, as I never do.
But anyone who doesn't like what's here
Can turn the page, and cleaner tales will appear: 65
Historical writing that touches on noble matters,

And also morality and holiness,
All easy to find, in a large collection like this.
But don't blame me, if you happen to choose amiss.
The Miller's a vulgar man, you know this well,   70
And so is the Steward, and others here, I tell you,
And vulgar words and deeds abound in their tales.
So be on notice, and don't give me the blame.
No one should be too serious, playing a game.

THE MILLER'S TALE

Once upon a time there lived, in Oxford,
A boor, and rich, who took in paying boarders;
He was himself a carpenter by trade.
His boarder, a scholar, was poor at the time of this tale,
He had studied some, but took a passionate fancy   5
For learning the cosmic art of astrology,
Progressing to the point of solving problems—
As if, let's say, people brought with them
Questions about the weather, good or bad
On certain days, if drought or rain, for planting   10
Crops, or what would happen because of this
Or that. I cannot give you a detailed list.
       This cleric was known by the name of Handy Nicolas.
He had studied illicit love, its pleasurable practice,
But was sly, and kept completely hidden and private,   15
Appearing, like a virgin girl, quiet
And meek, living alone, in a room in the carpenter's
House, and keeping to himself—a room well-scented
With herbal perfumes, prepared by his good fingers;
He too was scented, sweet as spicy ginger   20
Or the delicate root of licorice. Lying
Near his bedside was the Ptólemáic bible,
The *Almageste,* and many other precious
Books, and his stones, marked for his abacus.
His storage chest was covered with a cloth, coarse wool,   25
And red, and his dulcimer was ready for use,
On which he'd play his nighttime songs, tunes

So sweet the whole room rang with sensuous music.
And then he ended with "The Good King's Tune."
He used his merry throat sweetly and often.   30
And thus this gentle cleric spent his time,
Spending his good friends' gifts, and what else he could find.

    The carpenter had newly wedded a wife,
A pretty girl he loved far more than his life:
She was exactly eighteen years of age.   35
Jealous he was, and kept her tight in a cage,
For she was rebellious and young, and he was old,
And thought himself quite likely to be a cuckold.
His education was small, like his mind. He'd never
Read Cato's book of maxims, which says that every   40
Man should choose a wife like himself: age
And youth will often fight like rats in a cage.
But now he'd caught himself in exactly that snare;
Like all the world, he had to be prepared.

    His youthful wife was lovely, with a body as slender   45
And delicate as a well-fed weasel, wearing
Around her waist a belt, with bars of silk,
And an apron white as the freshest morning milk
Wrapped around her loins like a narrow skirt.
Her under-vest was white, the front as well as   50
The back embroidered, as was her collar all
Around. Her cap was white, but covered with small
Bright ribbons. Her headband was silk, she wore it high,
And surely she pranced about with a lecherous eye.
Both her brows were plucked, neatly done,   55
Arched and black as berries dark in the sun.
Looking at her was a far more blissful sight
Than even early pears on the tree, and she might
Be softer, all told, than even the fluffed-out wool
Of a ram. A leather purse hung from her belt,   60
Tasseled with silk, spangled with burnished metal.
In all this world, if you search it front and behind,
No man can fashion images in his mind
So dainty, delightful, and easier on the eyes.
She shone more brightly than golden coins you'll find,   65
Newly forged and burnished on either side.

And when she sang, it sounded loud and charming
Like any swallow sitting high on a barn.
And she could skip and play at dancing games
Like any kid or calf, behind his dame.   70
Her mouth was as sweet as honeyed ale or mead,
Or well-stored apples, laid in hay or heath.
She was as skittish as any bouncing colt,
Tall as a mast, and straight as an arrow bolt.
She wore a brooch on her under-collar, broad   75
And round, like a shield's projecting, shiny center.
The laces tied around her shoes went
Almost to her waist. She was a cowslip, a fairy
Flower, fit for any lord's high bed,
Or even any good farmer to take and wed.   80
　　　Now, my lords, and then it came to pass
That once upon a day, this Handy Nicolas
Happened to flirt and fool about with this pretty
Wife, when her husband was working in another city.
Clerics are smooth, and sly, carefully taught,   85
And suddenly he caught her by the crotch
And said: "By God, unless I take you to bed,
Sweetheart, I want you so badly I'll end up dead."
He gripped her thigh-bones hard, and pressed against her,
And said: "Sweetheart, let me love you this minute,   90
Or I will really die, may God preserve me!"
She jumped like a restless colt, bound to a fence,
Twisting and quickly pulling her head away,
And said, "You'll get no kisses from me, by my faith!
Let go, let go," she said, "let go, Nicolas,   95
Or I will scream for help, 'O save me, please!'
Take off your hands and stop this silly rudeness!"
　　　Nicolas talked so gently, giving up crudeness,
And spoke so well, advancing himself so fast
She truly began to really love him, at last,   100
And swore an oath, by sainted Thomas à Beckett,
That she'd be willing to take him to bed in a minute,
The moment she knew for sure it was safe to do it.
"My husband's always hot with jealousy.
You must be patient, make sure he doesn't see   105

A thing, or I'm as good as dead," said she.
"You have to work in the dark, be secret as night."
  "Ah, don't you worry yourself," said Nicolas nicely.
"A cleric would surely have wasted his studying time,
If he couldn't put a blindfold on a carpenter's eyes."   110
So they reached a quiet agreement, and swore to be true,
And wait for a while, just as I've told it to you.
  Having accomplished this much, Nicolas went back
To stroking her thighs, and did it so well that she asked
To be kissed. He did it sweetly, then turned to music   115
And played his dulcimer hard, eagerly tuneful.
  And on a holy day, it happened, as usual,
This good wife finished her tasks and went to church,
To pray and do our good Lord's holy work.
Her forehead glistened like the sun at noon,   120
Because she'd washed it, before she left her home.
Now at that church there was a parish clerk,
Named Absalom. His hair was curly, worked
To sprout around his shoulders, shaped like a winnowing
Basket, but gleaming like gold, the part showing   125
Straight and even, right down the center of his head.
His face was red, his eyes gray as a goose.
Complex designs were carved on both his shoes;
In long red stockings, he walked most graciously.
The tunic he wore was fine and handsomely made,   130
Blue of a light and carefully handled shade,
Freely punctuated with leather laces.
And over the rest he wore a clerical gown
White as blossoms sprouting on the bough.
He was a happy child, so help me God,   135
Good at clipping and shaving, and drawing blood,
And he could draft all sorts of documents.
He knew how to dance in twenty different modes,
But all according to Oxford styles, old,
Outdated. He kicked out his legs, went to and fro   140
While playing songs on a small-sized, squeaking fiddle.
And sometimes he sang much higher than most men did.
He played the guitar as well as he played the fiddle.
There wasn't an ale- or brew-house he didn't visit,

Entertaining those who were drinking their beer. 145
His eyes saw only the pretty barmaids there.
But I must admit, he was terribly shy about farting,
Over-careful of speech, when coming or departing.
    This Absalom, who was pretty rather than handsome,
Was out in front of the church, eager and passionate, 150
Shaking incense on parish wives, on arrival,
And pretty faces he made at them, all the time,
Especially the lovely carpenter's wife.
Looking at her, he thought, was a perfect life,
She was so neat, so sweet, so lecherous 155
It seems to me that had she been a mouse
He would have swallowed her down, right on the spot.
This parish clerk, this amorous Absalom,
Lived with a heart so flooded, longing for love,
He would not accept a cent from anyone's wife; 160
It seemed to him proper, he said; they looked so fine.
    When darkness fell, the moon was shining bright,
And Absalom's guitar could be used, that night,
To wake up sleeping lovers, simply for fun,
And off he went, happy and amorous, 165
Until he'd gone as far as the carpenter's house.
A moment or two before, the cocks had been crowing.
He posted himself beneath a small hinged window
(The carpenter hung it himself, low on the wall),
And then he sang, in his sweet and dainty tone, 170
"Now, dear my lady, if it your will may be,
I pray you shed your mercy down on me."
Absalom meant to break his listeners' sleep:
The husband woke as the clerk's guitar was ringing,
And turned and said to his wife, quickly and sharp: 175
"What! Alison! Do you hear that idiot Absalom
Singing like this under our bedroom wall?"
"John, God knows I hear it, and every bit."
    And Absalom did it again. And again. This
Went on, day after day. He wooed her like this 180
Until he convinced himself that love was his fate.
He did not sleep at night, nor during the day;
He combed his spreading curls, and dressed himself up;

He got other people to tell her how good he was,
And swore he'd be her everlasting page;   185
And he sang, he sang like a trilling nightingale;
He sent her spiced wine, and mead, and flavored ale,
And pastries, fresh and hot from the baker's fire;
She was a city girl, so he offered her bribes:
Persuasion is sometimes done by silver and gold,   190
Sometimes by a blow in the face, or by nobility.
    At times, to show his depth and facility,
He acted the role of Herod, on a platform stage.
But what was the point? She was already crazy
In love with Nicolas, and Absalom   195
Could strut and fuss and keep on carrying on,
And he got nothing from her but laughter and scorn.
She turned him into her ape, her little monkey,
Whatever he tried kept making him look like a donkey.
The proverb tells it all, and this is no jest: 200
"A subtle hand that has her right where she rests,
Makes an absent lover look like a toad."
Absalom could be happy or sad, but both
Or either meant nothing; he would never shine bright,
For Nicolas forever stood in his light.   205
    Now watch yourself, you Handy Nicolas,
So Absalom may sing and wail "alas."
And then it happened, one easy Saturday,
The carpenter had business, and went away,
And Handy Nicolas and Alison   210
Agreed that something simply must be done:
Nicolas should now invent some trick
To keep her husband safely out of it.
And if the trick succeeded, she could sleep
All night in his arms, and how she wished it could be,   215
Exactly as he desired, and so did she.
So without another word, and moving quickly,
Nicolas began to prepare his trick,
Quietly taking up to his room meat
And drink enough to last two days—or a week!   220
—And telling her to say, if her husband inquired,
She hadn't the faintest notion, and no idea

Just where the fellow was, for she hadn't seen him
All day long, and perhaps he might be ill,
For when she called him, he never answered, stayed still, 225
And whatever might happen, this was what he would do.
   And what indeed he did, no matter who
Approached his room. He remained just as he was,
Doing whatever a scheming cleric does.
Another day, and the foolish carpenter, 230
By nightfall, became enormously concerned
About poor Nicolas and what had happened
To him. "In the name of Saint Thomas," the carpenter said,
"I'm afraid that something's wrong with Nicolas.
God forbid that our friend just might have passed 235
Away. The world can change wonderfully fast.
This morning I saw a corpse carried to church,
But Monday last I saw the man at work."
   "Go on upstairs," he suddenly said to his servant,
"Call him, or use a stone to knock at your service. 240
See what's what, and tell me right away."
   The fellow went stomping up, as quick as he may,
And standing directly in front of the door, he shouted
And knocked, loud as a madman, without a doubt:
"What! And how! What are you doing, my master? 245
You can't be sleeping all day. What! Are you fasting?"
   He was wasting his breath, Nicolas said not a word.
He found a hole, down at the bottom of a board,
Through which the cat entered and left the room,
And he looked and looked, and finally saw the man. 250
And there he sat, all bolt upright and staring,
As if he were watching the moon's nightly appearance.
So down the stairs he went, and told his master
What he had seen, and what might be the matter.
   The carpenter quickly crossed himself, and said 255
To the patron saint of Oxford: "O Fridesweed,
Help us! A man can't know what's waiting for him.
This cleric's astronomy has suddenly driven him
Mad. Or maybe he's sick, maybe he'll die.
I thought as much. This is the price for prying 260
On things that God didn't want us ever to see.

Ah, ignorant men are truly blessed, believing
Only what they believe, and knowing what they know.
It happened to another cleric, this astronomy.
He always walked in the fields, trying to see   265
In stars whatever the future might hold for our kind,
Until he fell in a clay-pit, and then he died,
Not having seen it there. But by Saint Thomas,
I really feel bad about this Nicolas.
He'll have to be scolded for studying all this hard—   270
If I can, by Jesus, heaven's king and my God!
Get me a staff, Robin, so I can pry up
The door from underneath, and you push it out.
I'll pry him out of his books, I'll go and shout him
Down." With staff in hand, he went to the door.   275
His servant was strong, and drove it flat on the floor,
Pushing one way, gripping it by the hasp,
While his master pried from beneath. It went down with a crash.
But Nicolas stayed as he was, still as a stone;
Continually looking skyward, he never moved.   280
The carpenter grew frantic, and took his tenant
By the shoulders, shook him very hard and said,
Loudly, "What! What how! Now, now! Look down!
Wake up and think of Christ and his thorny crown!
Here, with this sign of the cross, I free you from evil   285
Creatures." And quickly he said a prayer for the devil
To leave not only the room where Nicolas dwelt,
But every corner of the house, inside and out:
"Jesus Christ, and holy Saint Benedict,
Keep us and this house from all the devil's tricks,   290
And from all the spirits out in the dark, our Father
And Lord, save us like Saint Peter's sister!"
        And finally Handy Nicolas sighed, as if
In pain, and said, both low and deep, "Alas!
Must this whole world be drowned all over again?"   295
        The carpenter exclaimed: "What in God's name
Are you saying? Rely on God, as we working men do."
        And Nicolas answered: "Fetch me a drink. Go.
Then you and I shall sit here, but all alone,
And I will tell you what you need to know.   300

This isn't for anyone else in the world to hear."
    The carpenter went down and came back, bearing
A brimming pitcher of the strongest ale he knew,
And after each of them had drunk his due
Nicolas picked up the door and locked it tight,   305
And then he came back and sat by the carpenter's side.
    "John," he said, "my host, belovèd and dear,
Before I tell you, you must solemnly swear
Not to tell this secret to a man in this world,
For these are Christ's own words that you shall hear.   310
If you repeat them, your soul will be damned forever,
And all the rest of your days you will never, never
Be sane again, but roam the woods like a dog."
"No, Christ forbid it, by his holy blood!"
Answered this foolish fellow. "I'm no blabbermouth.   315
If I say so myself, I don't run off at the mouth.
Tell me whatever you like, I'll never tell it
To child or woman, by him who battered hell!"
    "Now John," said Nicolas, "I'll tell you no lies.
I have now found, by searching in the skies,   320
Looking deep in the moon's bright eye, all bright,
That Monday next, just before the light
Returns, rain will fall so crazed and wild
That even Noah's flood didn't see the like.
In less than an hour," he said, "the entire world   325
Will be drowned, so fast and hard will the waters swirl.
The entire world. And every man will be dead."
    The carpenter cried out: "Alas, for my wife!
Must she be drowned? Alas, my love, my life!"
The pain he felt came close to knocking him down.   330
"Can anything be done? Can a way be found?"
    "Well yes, by God," said Nicolas. And then:
"If you will take advice from learnèd men.
There isn't knowledge enough in your silly head.
It's totally true, what wise old Solomon said: 335
'Listen to counsel, and you will never be sorry.'
And if you do as I tell you, never worry,
I guarantee, although we have no boat
To save us, she, and you, and I will float.

Haven't you ever heard, before, that Noah   340
Himself was saved before the rains came down?
Because our God had warned him, he didn't drown."
    "I heard it, yes," said John, "but years ago."
    "And did you also hear that his people said, no,
Your wife will not be allowed to come on board?   345
I'm sure he thought, right then and there, that rather
Than filling a ship with sheep, he'd like to give her
A ship of her own, just she herself, alone.
Can you imagine, now, what needs to be done?
Haste is required, and something this urgently needed   350
Must not be left to words. So listen, and heed me.
    "Hurry and fetch us kneading troughs, one
For each of us, or else three brewing tubs;
Make sure that every single one is large,
So we can comfortably float, as in a barge,   355
With food and water for just a single day.
And who needs more? The water will drain away
Early next morning, more or less by eight.
But Robin, your servant, will have to accept his fate,
And Gilly, your maid: these I cannot save.   360
Don't ask why not, I'm not allowed to answer;
God's secrets are not for merely human ears.
You ought to be happy enough, unless you're mad,
To receive the kind of grace that Noah was granted.
I'll save your wife, to be sure, no doubt about that.   365
Now go, and hurry, fetch us our life-saving vats.
    "And when you have them, one for each of us three,
Here is the rest of your work: these tubs must be
Hanging extremely high, close to the roof,
So no one else can find the living proof   370
Of our plans. That done, and when the drink and food
Are set inside, and an axe as well, so the roof
Can't trap us when the water rises: we'll smash
Three holes, each one up high and in the gable,
Facing toward the garden, over the stable,   375
So we can freely float along our way,
Once the terrible rain has passed away.
I think I see you swimming, John, like a duck

Chasing after her drake! We'll bless our good luck,
And I will call, 'How Alison! How John!   380
Enjoy yourselves, the flood will soon be gone.'
And you will answer, 'Master Nicolas,
Now hail! I see you clearly, this water's like glass
In the sun.' And spend the rest of our happy lives
As lords of all the world, like Noah and his wife.   385
    "But one thing more. Listen with all your might.
Remember, set it hard in your head: that night,
When we have gone aboard our separate ships,
None of us may utter a word or whisper,
No calls, no cries, nothing but silent prayer.   390
This is our God's decree, so listen and hear.
    "You and your wife must stay completely apart,
So sin will not take place between you, in heart
Or look, in any form of amorous deed.
My words are done. Go, and now God speed!   395
Tomorrow night, when other men are asleep,
We three will go to our kneading tubs, creeping,
And sit there, silent, awaiting the grace of God.
So go now, go along, and do your part.
We haven't time for me to give you more   400
Instruction and holy explanation. The saying
Is, among men, 'Just send a wise man and say
Nothing.' You are so wise, you need no teaching.
Go, and save our lives. This I beseech you."
    This carpenter fool hurried off on his way.   405
Often he said, "alas," and "wellaway,"
And, of course, he told his wife his sacred secret,
Which she had been told, and knew far better than he did,
Just what this strange adventure was all about.
But she made a great pretense of fear and doubt,   410
And said, "Alas! Hurry, that it may be done.
Help us escape, or we will be dead, one
And all! I am your true and wedded wife.
Go, dear spouse, and help us save our lives."
    What incredible things flow in our emotions!   415
Men can kill themselves with imagination,
So hard and deep and dangerously we feel.

This fool of a carpenter began to reel
And quake, believing that in truth he'd see
Noah's flood come rolling like the sea   420
To drown poor Alison, his honey dear.
He wept, he wailed, he felt his stomach quiver;
He sighed with sorrowing, wrenching, heavy breaths.
And then he went and got a kneading trough,
And then a pair of brewing tubs, enough   425
For them all, and had them brought, in secret, to his home.
And then he made three ladders, working alone,
So they could climb from the floor, rung by rung,
Up to tubs in the rafters, where he had hung them.
He stocked three tubs with food and drink, good jugs   430
Of ale, and bread and cheese, more than enough
To last them through a long and worrisome day.
But before these things were ready and all arranged,
He sent his servant, and also his serving maid,
To London, on matters of pressing business need.   435
And when the evening came, and night was near,
He shut his door in the dark, lighting no candle,
Completed all his work, most handily.
And soon all three of them went up their ladders.
And then they sat in silence, as if in sadness.   440
        "Now in our Father's name, we all stay mum!"
Said Nicolas. "Mum," said Alison,
And "Mum," said John. The carpenter sat there praying,
Sitting very still, and fervently praying,
Awaiting the mighty rain coming his way.   445
        Anxiety, and hurried, desperate labor
Soon put this foolish carpenter to sleep:
By curfew time, at eight, he could not keep
His tired eyes open, but still he sighed and groaned,
Lying uncomfortably, and constantly snoring.   450
Then Nicolas came cautiously down his ladder,
And Alison went softly, quickly after,
And without a word they crept to the bedroom, and into
John's bed. And what a party they had, long into
The night, lying together in pleasing pleasure,   455
Taking their time and making love at leisure,

Until the bells of morning prayer were ringing,
And friars in church and chancel had started singing.
    The parish clerk, our amorous Absalom,
Drowning in love and always woebegone, 460
Had gone on a picnic, earlier that day,
For sport with some of his friends, running and playing.
On coming back, he quietly asked a cleric,
As if by chance, but pulling him out of the church,
What news he had of John the carpenter, 465
And the monk replied: "No news. He wasn't working
In town, the other day, so maybe he's searching
For timber, and maybe our abbot sent him out,
As often he does, and John will be looking around
For a day or more, and sometimes he'll stay at our farm. 470
He may be sleeping out there, alone in the barn,
Or maybe he's home. I really do not know."
    Absalom was happy, and ready to go
On an all-night spree, staying awake till dawn.
"I haven't seen him anywhere," he thought, 475
"Nowhere, since the sun came up, all bright.
By God, at cock's crow, just before the night
Is done, I'll go and quietly knock at his window,
The one in his bedroom, hung conveniently low
On the wall, and tell her everything I long for, 480
And at the very least I'll get her to kiss me—
I need some sort of comfort, some solace, some bliss.
My mouth's been itching, almost all this day.
Which is surely a sign, at least, of heavy kissing.
And last night I dreamed of attending a jolly feast. 485
So let me take myself an hour of sleep,
And when I wake, I'm well prepared to play."
    And when the very first cock was crowing, awake
He was, this playful lover, Absalom,
Who dressed himself to absolute perfection. 490
But first he chewed some spice and licorice,
Perfuming himself, before he combed his locks.
He put a true-love flower under his tongue,
To make himself as welcome as he could long for.
And then he strolled away, to the carpenter's house, 495

Standing under the window, still as a mouse—
The window was low enough to press on his chest—
And coughing most softly, in a tiny voice, he said:
"How are you, Alison sweet, my honeycomb,
My beautiful bird, my sweetest cinnamon?   500
Wake up, my sweetheart, come and speak to me!
You should pay more attention to the sorrows I feel,
So woefully I walk, thinking of you,
I actually sweat—and no wonder I melt for you,
I mourn like a lamb wanting its mother's milk.   505
O yes, sweetheart, my beauty soft as silk,
My love is like a turtle-dove, all true.
The only appetite I have is for you."
        "Just go away from the window, Jack fool," she said.
"So help me God, you'll get no kisses from me,   510
My love is for someone else, so you can leave!
He's worth far more than you, you Absalom!
Take yourself off, or I'll say goodbye with a stone!
Now let me sleep, just leave, just go away!"
        "Alas," said Absalom, "and wellaway!   515
True love should not be spurned, this ugly way.
At least give me a kiss, if nothing better,
For love of Jesus, our lord and loving savior."
        "And if I do," she said, "will you go away?"
        "O yes, my sweetheart," he was quick to say.   520
        "Make yourself ready," she said, "for here I come."
        She whispered to Nicolas, who was playing dumb,
"Keep quiet, and then you can laugh as much as you please."
        Absalom carefully set himself down on his knees,
Saying, "I am noble, in every way,   525
So after this, let there be more, I pray.
O sweetheart, your grace! O lovebird, your mercy, this day!"
        She undid the window, and opened it very swiftly.
        "All right," she said, "come on, and do it quickly,
Or else our neighbors, alas, might see you there."   530
        Absalom hurriedly wiped his lips all clear.
The night was dark as pitch, as dark as coal,
And out of the window she stuck her bare asshole,
And Absalom, who could have done much worse,

Put forth his mouth and lovingly kissed her ass,   535
Licking his lips, as it were, before he'd grasped it.
He jumped right back, knowing something was wrong,
He knew no woman was bearded—and this was a long one!
The skin was coarse, and rough, the smell was strong.
    "O God, alas," he said. "What have I done?"   540
    "Tee hee," she said, and slammed the window down,
As Absalom went walking slowly off.
    "A beard! a beard!" said Handy Nicolas.
"By God's own corpse, this is worthy of laughter."
    Our foolish Absalom heard him, every word,   545
And bit at his lip, angry, anxious to return
The favor as soon as he could. "I'll do it, by God!"
    Who was rubbing, now, wiping his lips
With dust, with sand, with straw, with cloth, with chips,
But Absalom? And who kept saying "Alas!   550
I'd give my soul to Satan—but better he has
Everyone in this town, than I should fail
To avenge an insult against my soul and name.
Alas!" he said, "that I never turned away!"
His burning love was cold, snuffed out: from the moment   555
He knew he'd kissed her ass, Absalom went
From adoring love to thinking it less than nothing.
That sickness had now been cured, and turned to something
Closer to hate. He started denouncing it,
Then weeping like a child who's just been whipped.   560
    And then he walked slowly across to the place
Where a blacksmith worked, a man called *Don* Gerveys,
Hammering plows, many of which he made.
He sharpened plowshares, and colters, turf-cutting blades.
Absalom softly knocked at the blacksmith's door,   565
And said, "Come open up, Gerveys, at my call."
    "And who are you?" "It's me, it's Absalom."
"What, Absalom! For the sake of Christ's sweet tree,
Why are you up so early? Blessed may you be,
What's the matter? Which pretty girl, God's brows,   570
Has got you out on the street, and prowling around?
By all the saints, you understand what I mean."
    Absalom did not give a damn or a bean

For the blacksmith's jokes; he could not play the game;
He had more important things on his mind than play, 575
Which Gerveys could not know. "My friend so dear,"
He said, "That colter, hot in the fire, there,
Lend it to me, please. I need it to do
Something. You will have it back, and soon."
  Said Gerveys: "Of course. Were it made of gold, 580
Or a nobleman's purse all filled with wealth untold,
I'd lend it to you, as I am an honest smith.
By Christ's own toe, what will you do with it?"
  "All in good time," said Absalom. "I'll say
Nothing now, but tell you tomorrow-day." 585
He took it by the steel handle, which was cold,
And quietly walked away from the blacksmith's door,
Heading straight for the carpenter's windowed wall.
First he coughed, just as he'd done before,
And then he knocked, as if he were paying a call. 590
  Again, Alison answered, "Who can it be,
Knocking like that? It's bound to be a thief."
  "O no," said he, "By God, my sweetest love,
I'm Absalom, my darling. And here, to prove it,
I've brought you a golden ring. My mother gave it 595
To me. It's very fine, may God save me,
And very well shaped. I'll give it you, for a kiss."
  Nicolas had risen, intending to piss,
And thought he might improve the game, by this:
The clerk could kiss another ass, if he liked. 600
He went to the little window and in hasty excitement
Threw it open, and stuck his ass in the air.
"Sweet bird," said Absalom, "I don't know where
You are." Then Nicolas let loose a fart
As fierce and hot and heavy as a thunder-dart, 605
So Absalom was almost blind in the darkness,
But he was ready with his red hot colter,
And shoved it in, almost up to his shoulder.
  The skin burned off, a hand's breath all around,
And Nicolas felt his ass on fire, molten, 610
And thought this wound would surely make him die.
And like a maniac he screamed and cried,

"Help! Water, water! Help! By God's great heart!"
    The carpenter woke, and with a frightened start,
Hearing someone wildly shouting "water,"   615
He thought: "Alas, now it's Noah's flood!"
He straightened up, not saying a single word,
And wielding his axe, he cut the rope like a swordsman,
And fell to the ground, not stopping to barter his ale
Or bread, until he hit the floor, with a smashing   620
Blow, and fainted dead away, from the crash.
    Alison and Nicolas went dashing
Down the street, screaming, "Help! Out!"
All their neighbors came rushing from their houses,
Then stopped, in amazement, gaping down at John,   625
Still unconscious, and very pale and wan,
Because his crashing fall had broken his arm.
But when he awoke, and spoke, he did himself harm,
For Alison and Nicolas declared him mad,
Telling everyone there that Noah's flood   630
Had frightened him out of his wits, and his fantasy
Had met its match in his broken-headed folly,
Buying three enormous, heavy tubs,
And hanging them all up high, from the roof above,
Pleading with the others, for God's great love,   635
They ought to join him there, for company,
    Everyone laughed and jeered at this fantasy,
Gaping, staring at his house, and what he'd done,
Turning the whole adventure to public fun.
Whenever John attempted to frame an answer,   640
No one listened, hearing only his fancy.
They joked and swore, so utterly bearing him down,
That public judgment declared him mad, in the town.
And, of course, all clerks and clerics stick together,
Saying, "This fellow's insane, my dearest brother."   645
And everyone laughed at this silly, fussing strife.
Thus well and properly had, was the carpenter's wife,
Despite the cautions of his jealous life.
And Absalom had kissed her, right on the ass,
Where Nicolas was badly scalded, alas.   650
Which ends my tale. God send us all his grace!

THE STEWARD'S PROLOGUE

Everyone laughed at this silly, foolish, and funny
Story. But some among them saw it one way,
And others insisted on seeing it differently.
Yet most were laughing, which showed their common sense.
Of all who were there, I saw one single face   5
Show true distress, and that was Oswald, whose place
In the world was high, as a Steward, but who had first
Been a carpenter, and resented jokes at his craft.
He began to grumble, and said the story was bad.
    "And if I cared to," he said, "I'd pay it back,   10
And humble a cocksure miller's bleary eyes,
If I had a taste for obscenities and lies.
But I'm too old, such things are not for me.
Grass time is done, dry winter food must be
My diet. This snowy hair proclaims my years;   15
My heart's decayed, and so, alas, have my ears.
And here I am, molding on with age,
Rotting away, and worse each livelong day,
Headed, like garbage, for wasting in a pail,
And knowing this is what we old men fear: 20
Our only way to ripen, now, is weary
Decay. And still we keep on dancing, for as long
As the world is willing to play a tune or song.
We live our dreary lives pierced by a nail,
Combining a hoary head and a greenish tail,   25
Just like a leek. Our strength is driven down,
But we wish and will as if we still had power.

Whatever we cannot do is what we talk
About. But the fire's done, we're ashes and chalk.
  "Four glowing coals are all old age possesses: 30
Boasting, lying, anger, and greed. The rest
Is gone, but these dull sparks belong to us.
We cannot kick our heels, or make much fuss,
But emotions never fade, and that's the truth.
And still I feel in myself a brash colt's tooth,   35
No matter how long the water of life's been running,
Well aware that my life is almost done.
Surely, the moment I was born, it was death
That opened the faucet, and let my very breath
Flow on and out and away. The barrel is empty,   40
Life's current hangs like drops on the barrel's rim,
And no matter how hard the foolish tongue can chime,
And complain, we've used our lives, we've had our time.
Dotage is all that's left us, nothing more!"
  Our Host had found this sermon-talk too boring   45
For words, and quickly protested, like an angry king:
"What good is all this chewed-up learning and wit?
Why should we talk all day about Holy Writ?
Only the devil's hand can make a preacher
Of a steward, or a cobbler a sailor, or you our teacher.   50
Just tell your story, man, and save us time.
We've come as far as Deptford, and in a while
We'll be in Greenwich, where wretches and rascals thrive.
Begin your story, while we're still alive."
  "Gentlemen," said Oswald the Steward, "your pardon.   55
I did not intend to bore you. Here is my problem:
I need to answer our drunken Miller, use force
Against his lies, not my usual course.
  "This Miller has told us a tale, my friends, right here
And now, about deceiving a carpenter,   60
Probably aimed at me, that being my trade.
With your permission, this fellow will be repaid,
And I will use the vulgar words he has chosen.
I pray to God his neck might soon be broken!
Seeing a bit of stick caught in my eye,   65
He's blind to the beam in his own. But it's easy to spy."

The Steward's Tale

At Trumpington, a town not far from Cambridge,
There is a brook, and over that a bridge,
And standing beside that brook there is a mill,
And these are simple truths, these things I tell you.
A miller had been in that mill for many a day.   5
And he was proud as a peacock, and loved to play.
He played on a bagpipe, he fished, he knitted torn nets;
He carved wood cups; he could shoot a gun, he wrestled;
He strutted around with a cutlass stuck in his belt,
And the blade was sharp as any sword, well whetted,   10
And in his pouch he carried a fine little dagger.
No one bothered him, for fear of danger.
His stockings were long, and held a Sheffield knife.
His face was round, his nose was stubby and wide.
His skull was bald, as naked as any ape.   15
He was a noisy braggart, a loafer, a chaffer.
No one got close enough to touch his skin
Without a warning: this miller's patience was thin.
And of course he was a thief of wheat and meal,
A sneaky scoundrel, well accustomed to stealing.   20
This hot and haughty fellow was named Simkin.
His wife had come from a family of noble kin,
And the local priest himself had been her father.
Simkin was very well paid for making that marriage:
The priest welcomed that kind of blood in his family.   25
Simkin's wife had come from a nunnery,
For he would not have agreed to anyone

Without a warrant of virtue and education,
Proud as he was of his sterling yeoman station.
And she was proud, standoffish as any magpie.   30
The two of them were truly a splendid sight,
On holy days, when he would walk ahead,
A brilliant scarf tight wound around his head,
And she came after, wearing a gown of red,
And Simkin's stockings displayed the same bright shade.   35
No one dared to address her, except as "my lady."
No one was brave enough to flirt as she walked
(Though clothes and manners attracted attention, of course),
Unless he chose to be pierced by Simkin's cutlass,
Or with his knife, or his dagger. And that was the truth.   40
Jealous folk have always been dangerous people—
Or at least that's what they want their wives believing.
And since her birth was stained, she being illegal,
She was so dignified she seemed quite regal,
Full of legitimate scorn and infinite mockery.   45
Simkin held that the lady was rightly haughty,
Considering her education and family,
And everything else she'd learned in that nunnery.
    This well-matched pair had first brought forth a daughter,
Now twenty years of age, and then a brother,   50
Still in his cradle, and a fine and handsome boy.
The girl was rather stout, with a well-grown body,
And a stubby nose, and eyes as green as glass,
Her buttocks broad, her breasts round as her ass.
But her hair was long and fair, a worthy asset,   55
Because the local priest, seeing her hair,
Intended to make her wealthy: she'd be the heir
Of all his herds and his many acres of land,
And he'd made a fuss of her marriage, carefully planned
To link his family tree to one so high   60
That noble blood would give her an ancestry
Worth having. Holy church's wealth should be
Allotted to people born from holy church-hood,
And so he honored in her his holy blood,
No matter that holy church was consumed by his brood.   65
    The mill had made the miller rich, no doubt,

Grinding wheat and malt from lands around him,
And especially from the fields of a noble college
Called Hall of the King, set in ancient Cambridge.
The miller ground up every sheaf of their wheat   70
And malt. Now one fine day, as it happened to be,
The college provisioner was too sick to drive,
So sick, in fact, he was expected to die.
Freed from his supervision, the miller stole
With two hands, infinitely more than ever before,   75
For with supervision he stole quite courteously,
But now he was a thief outrageously.
The college warden scolded, and made a fuss,
But the miller knew his business and would not budge,
Boasting and swearing these accusations were false.   80
    A pair of poor young scholars dwelt in this hall,
Headstrong youngsters, clever, and fond of play,
Not truly concerned with college affairs, but able
To see all possibilities for amusement,
And so they approached the warden, offering to use   85
Their well-trained minds against the miller's will,
Declaring they'd escort college grain to the mill
And back, and like all youngsters willing to bet
The miller would never steal a half of a peck
Of wheat, neither by tricks or force, with them   90
In charge. Reluctantly, the warden consented.
John was the name of the first, and Allan the second.
Both had been born, far to the north, in a place
Called Strother, of which I know nothing, and have seen no trace.
    This Allan prepared his gear, then hefted their sack   95
Of grain and threw it up on the horse's back.
And off they trotted, riding in front of the wheat;
Each one had at his side a sword and a shield.
John knew the way, he needed no one to guide him.
And when he saw Simkin, he dropped their sack beside him.   100
Allan spoke first: "All hail, Simkin, in faith!
How is your pretty daughter, and how is your wife?"
    "Welcome, Allan," said Simkin, "I swear by my life!
And John, too. How now, what do you say?"
    "Simkin," said John, "Need will have its way.   105

A man who has no helpers must help himself,
Or else he's a fool, as clerics like to tell us.
Our provisioner, I fear, is as good as dead,
So painful, now, are the molars back in his head.
So I have brought our grain, and Allan with me, 110
And we hope you'll grind it up, and do that swiftly,
So we can turn around, and ride home quickly."
    "That I will do," said Simkin, "by my life!
And what will you do while your wheat is busy grinding?"
    "So help me God," said John, "I'll stand by the hopper, 115
Watching how grain is ground, and done right proper.
Never in all my life have I seen the process
Of grain to flour—and that's plain truth, not nonsense."
    And Allan added, "Is that what you'll do, friend John?
Then I'll go underneath, and see how the flour 120
Goes sifting down. That I could watch for hours,
It's my idea of truly excellent sport.
Like you, friend John, I know almost nothing of milling,
But I'm ready to learn: knowledge will come to the willing."
    The miller smiled at these school men's silly tricks, 125
Thinking, "This is a stupid game. I'll fix them!
They think they're high and mighty, no one can cheat them.
But I know my business, I can easily beat them,
No matter what clever philosophers they've read.
The more cute tricks they try, the more bread 130
I'll bake for myself, with the grain I'm going to steal.
I'll fill their bag with husks, and say it's meal.
'The greatest clerical minds are the stupidest men,'
As the wolf said to the mare, in the Reynard yarn.
These are just children's games, they'll do me no harm." 135
    They were far too busily watching to see him sneaking
Out at the door, careful that nothing creaked
And gave him away. Looking up and down
He found their horse, standing where they'd bound it,
Behind the mill, in the shade of a clump of trees, 140
And straight to the horse he went, and quickly freed him,
Stripping off the bridle by which he was tied.
The minute the horse was loose, he was last seen bounding
To nearby marshlands, where wild mares could be found,

Snorting "Weehee" and trampling bushes down. 145
    The miller went back to his mill, not saying a word,
Doing his business while joking with both the students,
Till all the grain had been ground, the job well done.
And when the flour was sacked, and the sack was tied,
John went out the door and, walking outside, 150
Saw his horse was gone. "Wellaway!" he cried,
And "Help! Allan, our horse is gone! By God's
Own bones, come here and quickly, our horse is gone!
O God, our warden's lost his horse! O God!"
    Everything else fell out of Allan's head, 155
His supervising flew off, and his thoughts of their bread.
"What!" he cried. "Which way did the creature run?"
    The miller's wife came leaping toward the young men.
"Alas! Your horse is headed for marshlands, where wild
Mares are running. He's galloping fast, and excited. 160
No thanks are due the hand that tied him so loosely:
Whoever can do it better had better do it!"
    "Alas," said John, "for the sake of Christ's great pain,
Lay down your sword, and I will lay down mine.
God knows, I'm able to run as fast as a doe, 165
By God's sore heart, he won't escape us both!
Why didn't you shut the horse in Simkin's barn?
Bad luck! By God, Allan, you're a dumb one!"
    They ran as fast as two men have ever run,
Heading for marshlands together, Allan and John. 170
    And when the miller saw them running off,
Half a bushel of flour came out of their sack.
He told his wife to knead and then to bake it.
He said, "Those scholars had notions in their heads.
But no one pulls the hair in a miller's beard, 175
Whatever their learning. See them running away!
Lord, how they run! Well, let the children play!
Catching that horse won't be an easy game."
    These scholars ran up and down, and everywhere.
"Keep! Keep! Stand! Stand! Down here! Look out back there! 180
Go whistle over there, I'll keep him here!"
But try as they could, until it was night, and dark
They couldn't catch the creature, no matter how hard

They tried. The horse kept running away, so fast
Until in darkness he was trapped in a ditch, at last.   185
    Weary and wet, like horses in the rain,
Foolish John returned, and Allan, again.
"Alas," said John, "the very day I was born!
Now we've shamed ourselves—and how we'll be scorned!
Our grain has surely been stolen, they'll call us dullards,   190
Both the warden and our laughing fellow scholars,
But especially the miller! Wellaway!"
    So John complained, trodding to the mill, that day,
Holding tight to Bayard, the horse, on the way.
They found the miller sitting near his fire,   195
And knowing that in the dark they could not ride
Safely, they asked him to shelter them that night,
Both food and a bed, for God's sake, and for a price.
    The miller replied, "Whatever bed we may have,
Such as it is, you're welcome to at least a half.   200
My house is small, but with your education
You know enough to create extra space
A good mile broad, given a ten-foot place,
Or turn it round with your learnèd arguments."
    "Simkin," said John, "now by Saint Cuthbert, that pleasant   205
Host, you've a merry tongue, you've wagged it for your pleasure.
I've heard it said that 'A man takes one of two,
Whatever he finds, or whatever he brings.' But you,
Dear host, I most especially pray for your food
And drink. Now John and Allan are in no mood   210
To quibble, we'll pay you properly, and in full.
Men with empty hands can't catch a hawk.
Look, here's our silver. Let it do the talking."
    Into town the miller's daughter went walking,
For bread and ale, while he roasted them a goose,   215
And tied their horse so well it couldn't get loose,
And in his own bedroom made them a bed,
With sheets and blankets folded and neatly spread
No more than ten or twelve feet from his bed.
His daughter had a bed all to herself,   220
Right in the room with the others, side by side.
There was no choice. Do you know the reason why?

There never had been a spare room in the house.
They ate and talked, the scholars found some solace,
Drinking good strong ale, some of the best.   225
At midnight, more or less, they went to rest.
The miller had thoroughly varnished his sweating head;
He was pale from drinking, rather than rosy red.
He hiccoughed, and spoke entirely through his nose
As if he were growing hoarse, or had a cold.   230
To bed he went, and with him went his wife.
And she was happy as a blue jay, bright and nice,
Her jolly whistle, too, was thoroughly wet.
The baby's cradle was at the foot of their bed,
For rocking, and also in case it had to be fed.   235
The pitcher of ale was empty, they were ready to sleep.
Their daughter lay down first, feeling the need,
And then came Allan, and after him came John.
And that was all. None of these five wanted
Herbal help in sleeping. The miller had drunk   240
So much that, for the first hour, he constantly snorted,
And didn't worry how often or loud he farted.
His wife supplied a counterpoint: their snoring
Could have been heard from at least a couple of furlongs.
The daughter too was snoring, the family was one.   245
     Allan lay there, hearing these jolly songs,
Then poked at John and said, "Are you actually sleeping?
Have you ever in all your life heard music to compete?
What an evening song this family is roaring.
May wildfire drop from the sky and extinguish their noise!   250
Who in this world has heard such counterpoint?
They'll surely have the kind of death they deserve:
This whole long night I'll never get to rest.
And still, no matter. Everything's for the best.
For, John," he said, "I swear by my own true head,   255
I think I'll try to have the girl in that bed.
Some higher recompense has been granted us,
For, John, there is a law providing thus:
A man who suffers, here, on this one side,
Must then at some other point be satisfied.   260
Our grain has been stolen, there's no denying that.

And we have had a terrible day: that's flat!
And since what's lost is gone for now and ever,
I have to find repayment, and find it wherever
I'm able. By God, and that's the way it will be!"   265
    Then John answered: "Allan, take care. He
Is a very dangerous man, and suddenly
He might wake up, and we'd be facing an angry
Man armed with a sword and a knife and a dagger."
    Said Allan: "He worries me as much as a worm."   270
He rose and crept carefully toward the girl,
Who was lying flat on her back and fast asleep,
And then he got so close that, should she see him,
It would have been too late—and then there he was,
And doing what each in his place have always done.   275
Play on, Allan! Now I'll talk about John.
    John lay still, not far from where Allan had gone,
Sickening himself with worry and woe.
"Alas!" he thought. "This isn't a proper joke.
After this day, I'll know myself an oaf.   280
But here's my friend, repaying himself for our loss,
Lying in her bed, the miller's daughter in his arms.
He tried, and he succeeded. And I'm as harmless
As a fly, lying as unrequited as a sack.
This tale will be told again, and I'll still be lacking   285
Courage, you helpless fool, you cringing sissy!
By God, so what can happen? I'll try, I'll miss it.
And then? Who cares? 'Frightened men are unlucky.'"
So quietly he rose, and then he went
To the cradle, picked it up, then back to his bed   290
Again, and kept the cradle at his feet.
    Soon the snoring wife broke off her sleep
And her snoring, woke up and went outside to piss,
And then came back, but found the cradle missing,
And groping all around, in the dark, found nothing.   295
"Alas!" she thought. "I almost committed a foolish
Mistake, returning not to my own but the scholar's
Bed. Bless me! That would have been a horrible
Thing." She groped her way, and found the cradle,
Then groped a little farther and then was able   300

To find the bed, and was pleased she hadn't made
A serious mistake: the cradle vouched,
In darkness, for her decision: her judgment was sound,
So in she crept, and lay down next to John,
Staying very still, and almost asleep.   305
But suddenly the scholar fairly leaped
Upon her, and laid it on this wife so hot
She had a merry time, a pleasure not
Her usual fare. John worked hard and stopped
For nothing. This was the scholars' jolly time,   310
Until the third cock crowed the daylight sign.
     When dawning came, our Allan was good and tired,
For he had been at work the whole night through.
"Farewell, Maylin," he said, "You are a true
Sweetness. Though daylight's come, and I must be gone,   315
Wherever I walk or ride, from this day on,
My heart belongs to you, God save my soul!"
     "Sweetheart dear," she said, "goodbye and farewell!
Before you leave, there's something I must tell you.
Riding homeward, beside my father's mill,   320
Right behind the door, when it's open, there is
A half-bushel loaf that's baked from what is yours.
I know, because I helped my father rob you.
But it is yours, so take it with you. Now go.
Yet sweetheart dear, the Lord God save and keep you."   325
And with those words she almost began to weep.
     Allan stood up, and thought, "Before it's dawn,
I need to creep to the bed I ought to be in."
But his groping hand immediately found the cradle.
"My God," he thought, "what a desperate mistake.   330
My head must be swimming, after this long night's work,
Leading me where I must not be. Alertness!
There's the cradle, so that's where I shouldn't be,
Here's where the miller is lying, his wife and he."
And so he proceeded, twenty devils away,   335
To the bed where, in fact, the sleeping miller lay,
Expecting the bed would hold his comrade John.
And creeping in, he tapped the miller's arm,
Put his hand on his neck, and whispered these words:

"John, you pig's head, wake up! you sleeping worm,   340
And hear, by Christ's own soul, a noble game.
For by that holy spirit we call Saint James,
I've three times screwed, in only this short night,
The miller's daughter, I tell you I've done it right,
While you, you coward, are too afraid to try it."   345
    "Ho, you cheating beggar," the miller cried,
"Have you now? You lying scholar," he roared,
"I'm going to kill you, in the name of God above!
You, so boldly disgracing my daughter's blood,
And you a dustball, a book-bug, and she so noble!"   350
He grabbed Allan by the throat, and whacked him hard,
And then he shook him, and hit him again and again,
Smashing his fist at Allan's nose. A stream of blood
Came rushing down Allan's breast. He fell to the floor,
Blood pouring out of his mouth and also his nose.   355
They rolled about like a pair of pigs in a poke,
First up they went, then soon were down once more,
Until the miller tripped on an empty pot
And fell straight backward, right upon his wife,
Who had no knowledge of this foolish fight,   360
For she had fallen asleep, right next to John.
Bewildered, she woke and started calling for aid:
"Help! O Holy cross of Bromholm," she said,
In manas tuas! Lord, we're in your hands!
Awake, Simkin! The fiend himself has fallen   365
On me, my heart is broken, my life is all
But ended! There's one lying on my womb and my stomach!
Help! The traitorous clerks are fighting each other!"
    John woke up as fast as ever he could,
And groped at the walls, hoping to find some wood   370
To hit with. The wife, too, jumped out of bed,
And having better knowledge of where it might be
She quickly found a heavy staff, and could see
Through a hole, a slender, shimmering shaft of light
Where the moon shone through, and saw the two men fighting,   375
But was not able to clearly recognize them.
A bit of white on one man's head then caught her eye.
Remembering that one of the scholars had worn

A white nightcap, she drew up closer, warning
Herself she had to hit him square on the head, 380
And standing on tiptoes she swung as hard as she could,
And hit the miller right on his shining bald skull.
And down he went, crying, "Help! I'm dying!"
Both scholars beat him hard, then let him lie.
Swiftly, they dressed themselves, and fetched their horse, 385
And also their flour, and easily altered their course,
Collecting, as they passed the mill, their loaf
Of bread, half a bushel worth, and well baked.
     So the arrogant miller didn't get his cake
Or eat it, and lost his flour, and got well-beaten, 390
And out of his purse purchased what scholars had eaten—
Allan and John, who'd administered his beating.
His wife had been screwed, and so too had his daughter.
Ah, cheating millers are served with what they've ordered!
And that's what this little proverb is all about: 395
"Evildoers are not rewarded, by God!"
Cheaters will end by being cheated themselves.
May God, who's sitting in heaven high above us,
Save every pilgrim here, both noble and common!
And so I've repaid the miller, that drunken man. 400

THE COOK'S PROLOGUE

The London Cook, hearing the Steward speak,
Rejoiced as if the man were scratching his back.
"Ha!" he said, "I swear, by the passion of Christ
This miller made a mistake, by God's own eyes,
Expecting to crucify the Steward and his friends.   5
You've got to be careful, Solomon once said:
'Don't open your door to every man who asks.'
Taking nighttime lodgers is a dangerous craft.
People have to watch who enters their doors:
Keeping private is a noble cause.   10
By God's name, and my own (I'm Roger of Ware),
Let me live in endless sorrow and care
If ever I heard a miller better paid off.
He learned how darkness can make things risky and rough.
But God forbid we stop, coming this far.   15
So if you're willing to bend a friendly ear
To a tale from me, a poor and simple man,
I'll tell you all a story as well as this man can,
A small adventure that happened, once, in my city."
        The Host replied, saying, "Please feel free.   20
Tell on, Roger, be careful to tell it right—
Because we know that cooks can cheat on their pies,
And sometimes sell as fresh what's really old,
Reheated twice, and twice been lying cold.
Many pilgrims have hoped that Christ would curse you,   25
Their stomachs suffering cramps, and sometimes worse,
Swallowing too much of your fatted goose,

Because your shop has flies, and they're on the loose.
Tell us your tale, Roger of Ware by name.
Yet never mind our teasing and playing games. 30
A man can say what he likes, when fooling around."
    "You speak the truth," said Roger, "by God's own wound!
Yet 'true jokes always bad jokes,' as the Flemish say.
So, Harry Bailey, listen with a friendly ear,
And don't get angry, before we leave from here, 35
In case my tale concerns another host.
Not now: I'll save that tale for later. By the ghost
Of heaven, I'll catch your tail, and you will know it!"
And then he laughed, and made a merry face,
And told a tale—which follows after a space. 40

The Cook's Tale

Some time ago, an apprentice lived in our city,
Who worked in the guild of provisioners. And he
Was a jolly fellow, as merry as a goldfinch in a tree,
Brown as a berry, short but very proper,
His black hair always combed and kept in order. 5
And he could dance so well, so gaily sing,
That he was known as Perkin, the Happiness Bringer.
He was as full of love and burning passion
As a hive is full of honey, sweet for the asking.
A girl who got her hands on him did well. 10
At every wedding feast he'd sing and hop;
He loved the tavern better than the shop.
Whenever deliveries were loudly called for
He fairly went leaping out the shop's front door.
And till he'd seen whatever was there to see, 15
And danced up a storm, the shop was not where he'd be.
He gathered around him people like himself,
Hopping and singing, merry as a band of elves,
And sometimes they'd make appointments for the group to meet
And gamble at dice, in such-and-such a street. 20
Nowhere in all the town was there an apprentice
Who handles a pair of dice with such a sensitive
Hand, so Perkin managed to afford
Expenses high as any noble lord's.
The shop's good owner found Perkin's traces in his cash 25
Container, often open and distinctly bare.
Clerks who work too hard as happiness bringers,

Busy at dice, extravagance, and singing,
And love, will lower profits at any shop,
Although the owner himself won't sing or hop.   30
Debauchery and thieving go hand in hand,
Two tunes but played alike by a single band.
Dancing and decency, in a common man,
Are always at war, as you can understand.
    This jolly apprentice stayed in his master's shop   35
Almost until he'd served his apprenticeship out,
Scolded and sometimes roared at, early and late;
Sometimes, playing too hard, he ended in jail.
But when he finally asked to be freed from service,
His master scratched his head and remembered words   40
From a proverb: "You'd better get rid of a rotten apple
Before it rots what else you've got." It happened
That way: a bubbling, boiling, riotous man
Should be disposed of, before (like a dog with fleas)
He scratches too many around the shop. So please   45
Our lord, the apprentice got his deed of release,
Asked to leave, with sorrow but great relief.
And thus this jolly apprentice obtained his freedom,
Let him dance all night, or not, as he pleased.
And since no thief is ever without an accomplice,   50
Assisting him in all his confidential
Endeavors, which means, in truth, robbing and stealing,
The things he had in his master's house went wheeling
Off to a friend, as good a thief as he was,
Another fellow who stole, and danced, and diced,   55
Married to a girl who ran a shop, for convenience,
But for her living sold her body to men.

[unfinished]

Introductory Words to the Man of Law's Tale

Our host could readily see the shining sun,
Tracing the day's slow arc, had certainly run
One end, and half another hour past it.
No astronomer he, but he knew without asking
That we had reached, by now, the eighteenth day   5
Of April, the messenger which announces May,
And without any trouble could very easily see
The shadow cast on the ground by every tree
Was absolutely equal in quantity
To exactly the height that caused the shadow to be.   10
Bright Phoebus had climbed to forty-five degrees,
And for that day, and in that latitude,
It was ten o'clock, and that was his conclusion.
Then suddenly he turned his horse around.
        "Now gentlemen," he said, "Let me sound   15
A warning. A quarter of this day is gone.
Now for the love of God, and of Saint John,
Waste no time, as carefully as you may.
Time goes trickling off, both night and day,
And robs us, what with sleeping long in our beds   20
And carelessness, indifference running our heads.
Time's like some stream that never turns again,
Descending down from mountain into plains.
Seneca and other philosophers
Worry more about time than gold in their coffers,   25
For 'property lost can be recovered, but time
Once gone will surely ruin us,' Seneca claimed.

Without a doubt, it never comes again,
Just like a wayward woman's virginity,
Once it's been lost to capricious, self-willed glee.　　　　　30
We must not throw away time, in this company.
　　　"My noble lord of the law, now tell us a story,
As we have agreed. Your free assent has decreed
That, in these matters, my judgment will be your law.
Absolve yourself, fulfill your contract, without　　　　　35
Delay. Do your duty: the court so orders."
　　　"Host, in God's name, I fully and freely assent.
Breaking my contract was never my intention.
Duty is debt, so I will pay mine off,
And gladly submit to your honor's order at once.　　　　　40
Whatever law a man imposes on other
Men, he must apply to himself as well.
That can stand as my scripture. But how can I tell
A story when Chaucer, although his meter and rhyme
Are crude, is busily spending all his time　　　　　45
With telling stories in English, as he's able,
Borrowing from our ancient language and fables?
If Chaucer hasn't told them, believe me, brother,
In one book, he's certainly told them in another.
He's written lovers' tales, now down, now up,　　　　　50
And more than even Ovid, and Ovid gave up
His writing, along with his life, years gone by.
Why should I tell such tales, when Chaucer's told them?
　　　"When he was younger, he wrote of Álcyóne
And Céyx, her husband; since then he's written, one　　　　　55
By one, of everyone, of lovers and their wives.
Whoever picks up his enormous book on fiery
Cupid, *The Legend of Good Women,* will find
He's told, and described, Lucretia's fatal wounds,
And the story of Babylonian Thisbee, and the sword　　　　　60
That Dido wielded, killing herself for false
Aenéas, and Dèmophon, who deserted Phyllis,
Who hanged herself, and Díaníra, who killed
Her husband, Hercules, but did not mean to,
And Hermíoné, and Áriádné on Naxos,　　　　　65
Barren island in the sea, deserted by Theseus,

And the nun for whom Leander drowned himself,
Helen of Troy's hot tears, and those of Briséis,
Achílles' lost slave, the cruelty of Medea,
The little children hanging by their necks 70
Because of Jason, whose love was false and reckless.
O my Penèlopé, and O Alceste,
Your wifehood Chaucer praised among the best!
    "He never wrote a word, of course, of wicked
Cánacé, whose love was incestuous, committed 75
Together with her brother: to all such cursèd
Stories I say 'for shame, for shame,' and ignore them.
Nor did he write of Ápollóniús
Of Tyre, or how that cursèd Antíochús
Threw his very own daughter to the ground and forced 80
Himself upon her, taking her maidenhead—
A tale I find it horrible to read!
But Chaucer, now, no matter how he harangued
His readers, would never play the goose to that gander
And trouble weary ears with abominations. 85
Nor will I repeat them, if you have no objections.
    "But what am I supposed to tell you, today?
I doubt that I am thought of, in any way,
As under the influence and guidance of the Muses,
Like Ovid, who wrote so well that I refuse 90
To imitate him. But on the other hand,
It hardly matters, these days, that Chaucer stands
At the head of the field, for I speak prose, and rhymes
Are his professional business, not at all mine."
And saying so, not smiling even a bit, 95
He began his tale, exactly as you'll now hear it.

Prologue to the
Man of Law's Tale

O horrible state, to be living in poverty!
By thirst, by cold, by hunger torn apart!
Asking for help shames you, wounds your heart,
But asking no one doubles tears and grief:
Need discloses what was hidden so deep!   5
Your feelings don't matter. All that counts, by now,
Is what you steal, or beg, or borrow, but not how.

You lay the blame on Christ, and bitterly,
Declaring how wrong he was to scorn the rich.
You gripe at your neighbor, angry and sinfully,   10
Declare you have too little, he has too much.
"By God," you say, "some day he'll burn in the filth
And fire of hell, his tail will roast like his head,
He'll pay for never helping the poor and needy."

Now hear what wise men say of this horrible state: 15
"You're better off dead than alive, a helpless beggar."
"Your neighbor sees you each day, and comes to hate you."
No one respects the poor, but disregards them.
And wise men also say, "No one can pardon
The poor, for all their lives and days are evil."   20
Think hard, before you drop in the hands of the devil!

Your brother despises the poor, despises you,
And whatever friends you had will run at your sight!
O rich and noble and careful folk, be advised,

O wealthy merchants, living in golden delight, 25
You're never haunted by dark and dreamless nights,
Remembering chances fumbled, business lost,
At Christmas time you're merry, whatever the cost!

You rake in profits from every land and sea,
You're sage and knowing, aware of princes and kings, 30
You always know the news of everything
That happens, whether of peace or war and defeat.
And I'm as empty of stories as a man can be.
Here's a tale a merchant, now dead, once told me,
So if you dislike his tale, you can't scold me. 35

The Man of Law's Tale

In Syria, not long ago, were a group
Of wealthy merchants, honest, really truthful,
Who sold their spices all over the face of the earth,
And their golden cloth, their satins, rich of hue.
They bargained so well, trading so fresh and new,   5
That everyone sought their business, to buy or sell,
Their strengths were clear, their fortunes too great to tell of.

It happened that those in charge of this mercantile business
Were planning a trip to Rome, but whether for trading
Or pleasure they would not say. Whatever their reasons   10
They surely were more than enough, for they were sailing
Soon, and that was the end of that. Making
This trip (as they had done before) was quick.
Before too long they were there, and in their lodgings.

And there they stayed for a while, doing whatever   15
It was they had come to do. And then they happened
To learn the golden reputation of the Emperor's
Daughter, Constance, information they gathered
In great detail, from sources and circumstances,
Day after day, as at the proper time   20
I'll fully disclose and explain, as you will find.

Every voice in the city of Rome agreed:
"Our Roman Emperor is blessed with a daughter unlike
All others, as we (and God in heaven) can see.

A girl so good and beautiful will strike   25
All hearts and eyes: may heaven recognize
And preserve her! This is a girl who deserves to reign
As Queen of France and Germany and Spain!

"Her great and flowering beauty has never made her
Proud; she's young, but neither green nor foolish;   30
Whatever she does is regulated by Nature,
With virtue and humility as rules,
Kindness and courtesy like a workman's tools;
Holiness fills her heart, like a blessèd chamber;
Her hand's an agent for generous help to the poor."   35

This common voice was correct, as God is true.
But now I'll turn to my story once again.
These merchants filled their ship with the best and newest
Goods, and once they'd actually seen this maiden,
Off they went to home, flying full sails,   40
Doing exactly what they always did,
Most prosperously. There's nothing more to be said.

These merchants happened to be in excellent standing
With Syria's Sultan, held by him in such high
Regard that when they came home he always commanded   45
For them a noble reception, fine food, fine wine,
And intimate conversation, frankly inquiring
What was truly occuring in faraway lands,
Anything wondrous they'd seen, or heard, or handled.

And among the many matters they chose to tell him,   50
Most of all they talked, and in great detail,
Of Constance, this Roman lady so beautiful,
So virtuous and noble, until he'd taken
So great a fancy he felt he had to make her
His own: his only love and sole concern   55
Would be her, for all the rest of his days on earth.

Perhaps in that great book which men have called
The heavens, where everything's inscribed in the language

Of stars, it might have been written, when he was born,
That he should die, alas! in the fiercest anguish   60
Of love. We live and die on earth, languish
For lack of certain knowledge, clearer than glass
If we could read it and know what's coming to pass.

     The Sultan called his private council in session,
And quickly told them what was on his mind,   65
Making an open secret, a true confession
Of how he wanted, and needed, her for his wife:
Without her, he would die. To save his life
They had to be swift, and do whatever needed
Doing so he could have her. They had to succeed!   70

     The counselors discussed his situation,
Wrangling this way and that, some taking one view,
Some taking another, with complex explanations,
Considering what magic and witchcraft might do.
But in the end, no matter how much they knew,   75
They all agreed that nothing had the advantage,
And practicality, of a lawful marriage.

But therein lay some large inherent problems,
Especially, to put the matter plainly,
Because they were dealing, here, with two religions,   80
Two sets of laws and beliefs, and they feared they would fail.
"Let us remind you," they said, "that what we face
Is this: No Christian prince will allow his daughter
To walk, beside a Mohammadan king, to the altar."

And he replied: "Rather than give up Constance,   85
My certain choice will be to become a Christian.
I love no other, she is the only one.
So hold your peace and put me in position
To have her. The only matters left for decision
Are details, and you will arrange them as fast as you can,   90
For I am in need, and not a patient man."

Why fuss and prolong this business any farther?
Ambassadors went this way and that, treaties
Were written and signed, and then our Holy Father
In Rome, and the Church, and all knights of chivalry   95
Decided that any destruction of Moslem beliefs,
And further spread of Christianity,
Was an excellent idea, as you will now see:

The Sultan and all the barons attached to his court,
And everyone under his rule, would quickly be christened,   100
And Constance would be his wife, and it was ordered
That a certain amount of gold be given in pledge,
I cannot say how much, but whatever was said
Was done. And oaths were sworn in Syria
And Rome. For Constance this was fact, not theory.   105

Some of my readers, perhaps, are patiently waiting
To hear exactly what the Emperor
Of Rome would give his daughter as dowry. Your patience
Cannot be rewarded. A dispensation
Of such complexity can't be explained   110
In a stanza or two of idle poetry:
Such great events are not for us to see.

Bishops were chosen to go along with the lady,
And lords and ladies, knights of high renown,
And many, many more than many, I cannot   115
Name. In every city, in every town,
All men and women were solemnly urged to kneel down
And pray that Christ would welcome word of this marriage
And guard our Constance, sailing forth on her voyage.

The day of her departure finally arrived.   120
I say once more, the woeful, fatal day
Has come: waiting is done, she'll be a wife.
Preparations had been completed, the way
Was open. Constance herself was sad, not gay:
She woke up pale, and dressed herself for leaving.   125
She had no hope, oppressed with heavy grieving.

Alas! Who could wonder at her tears,
Forced to go to a nation totally strange,
Away from friends who carefully soothed her fears,
Bound to an unknown man. What a great change! 130
Who could know in advance how his feelings ranged?
Husbands, of course, can be good, have been so before.
Wives know that. But I'd better say no more!

"Father," she said, "Constance, your wretched child,
The little girl you raised so gently and well— 135
And you, my mother, taken to heaven by Christ,
Your love and tender care are with me still:
I constantly pray for your angelic help,
And your heavenly grace—for to Syria I must go,
Never to live in Rome with you, any more. 140

"Since you have made the choice for me, I obey,
And for that Barbarian nation I leave this day.
I pray to Christ, who died to redeem all human-
Kind, to grant me grace to fulfill His commands!
A wretched woman, whose tears mean nothing to a man, 145
We women are born to servitude and penance,
Always ruled by some man's governance."

Even at Troy, when Pyrrhus broke the wall
And Troy was burning, or at the city of Thebes,
Or Rome, for the wreckage wreaked by Hannibal, 150
After Rome had three times vanquished his city,
Such tender piteous weeping had never been seen
As in these rooms, as she readied herself to leave.
But leave she must, whether weeping or singing.

O, primeval, cruel heavenly stars, 155
Bustling day by day from east to west,
And hurling out of your path whatever portions
Of sky would rather proceed in different directions,
Your pushing and shoving made the misdirections
Which, as this voyage began, allowed fierce Mars 160
To attack and destroy this marriage from the start.

The unlucky, oblique angle by which the ascendant
Star soared up had left the Sultan helpless,
Unprotected, alas, falling down
From his proper place to the darkest and least transcendent!   165
O cruel Mars, O feeble moon, dependent,
Swung away from where you belong, to an alien
Orbit, unable to work, weakened, strained.

O careless Emperor of Rome, alas!
Were there no astronomers in your city?   170
An event of such importance should not take place
Without precautions. Either good sense or pity
Should have moved you. What could you have been thinking?
The necessary calculations are known,
But humankind is too dull, or else too slow.   175

Woefully, this beautiful girl was brought
To her ship, solemnly, magnificently
Attended. "Now Jesus Christ be with you all!"
She said. They said, "Farewell, O lovely Constance!"
She managed to keep a cheerful countenance.   180
And now I'll let her sail along that day,
And turn my story forward in a different way.

The Sultan's mother, who was a well of vices,
Had certainly taken note of her son's intentions,
And knew he'd give up making sacrifices.   185
She quickly called together her own wise men,
Her council, all of them anxious to hear what she meant
To do. And when she had their full attendance,
She seated herself—and here is what she said:

"My lords: now each and all of you surely know   190
My son is on the verge of abandoning
The holy laws of the Koran, given and known
To us by Mohammad, messenger of God.
But I have sworn to God, the highest one,
Life will leave my body before my heart   195
Can or ever will abandon Mohammad.

"What will these new, these dreadful Christian laws,
Do to us? They'll bring us sad abuse
And slavery, knowing well we'll be drawn
To hell for recanting our faith in Mohammad's beautiful   200
Rules. Now lords, who will to swear to the truths
I tell you, and follow me, and obey my commands,
So I can keep us safe, in this our land?"

Every one of them swore, and fully agreed
To live and die with her, and stand at her side,   205
And each and every man would struggle to bring
To her cause, as best he was able, all his friends.
And so she launched her attack, as she had intended
To do, and you will hear her malicious plan,
In her own words, spoken to all her men: 210

"We must begin by acting as if we accept
This Christian faith: cold water won't be painful!
And I will stage a feast and festival
That's certain to overwhelm my son, our unfaithful
Sultan. However his wife has been christened, white   215
As snow, how can she wash away the red,
No matter what barrels of Christian water she has?"

O Sultaness, O root of iniquity!
O wicked shrew, O Semiramis the second!
O serpent hidden in femininity!   220
The serpent bound in hell, who forever beckons!
Deceitful woman: whatever wounds and threatens
Virtue and goodness, because of your poisoned womb,
Was nourished in you, O nest of evil, O tomb!

O Satan, jealous ever since the day   225
That you were forced to flee away from God,
How knowing you were with women, in olden days!
Seducing Eve left humankind trodden
By sin. For spoiling a Christian marriage, your rod
And tool will once again be a sinful woman!   230
Lying and deceit by women fulfill your plan.

This Sultaness, against whom I warn you, and accuse,
Sent her personal counselors away.
Why should I waste more time on what she does?
She rode to see the Sultan, one fine day,   235
Saying she'd surely recant her Moslem ways,
And let herself be christened by priestly hands,
Repentant of her long adherence to Islam—

Indeed, she begged that she might have the honor
Of giving their Christian visitors a feast.   240
"This I will do," she said, "as a personal labor."
The Sultan said: "It will be as you request,"
And kneeling, thanked her for her generous gesture,
Rejoicing so keenly, he had no words to say.
She kissed her son and homeward made her way.   245

PART TWO

The Christian visitors arrived on Syrian
Soil, a large and impressive group of men,
And swiftly, the Sultan then informed his imperial
Mother, and all his people, that now the woman
He'd marry had made her happy way to their kingdom.   250
He urged his mother to ride and welcome the queen,
As a matter of royal honor, and princely esteem.

The crowds were huge; how gorgeous were the clothes
Of Syrians and Romans, meeting together.
The Sultan's mother, most cheerful, let it be known   255
How pleased she was, greeting the Roman girl,
Embracing her, as a mother might, as her dearest
Very own daughter, kissing her son's new wife.
Then slowly and solemnly they rode to the nearest
City, to complete their ceremonious arrival.   260

I do not believe the royal welcome of Julius
Caesar, so proudly celebrated by Lucan,
Was any more elaborate or intense

Than welcoming this band of innocent Christians.
And yet this scorpion, malicious spirit,   265
For all her blissful words, she too had a hidden
Weapon of destruction, and meant to use it.

Soon the Sultan himself rode up to join them,
Gave his Christian visitors his welcome,
And warmly saluted his mother, glad she'd come.   270
And so, in mirth and joy, I'll let them dwell:
The end result is what I'm going to tell you.
When, at a certain time, they thought it best
To pause in their celebration, they took their rest.

And then, at a later time, this Sultaness   275
Presented them with the feast I've already mentioned,
And the Christians came, in peace and happiness,
Joined by many others, a great convention
Of rank and royalty, who gave their attention
To delicious food I will not here describe.   280
They paid for it in blood, before they could rise.

O sudden disaster, which always follows after
Worldly bliss, sprouted by bitterness!
Such is the end of all our worldly efforts!
Woe is where we come to, for all our gladness.   285
Keep these cautions in mind, for your own protection:
Whenever you're bright and gay, always remember
The unknown sorrow, waiting to make you surrender.

To tell it briefly, all the Christians as well as
The Sultan were suddenly cut down, hacked   290
And stabbed where they sat, every one of them killed,
Except the Sultan's new widow, Lady Constance.
The ancient Sultaness had concocted this plan,
She and her many friends, in order to place
The Syrian kingdom completely in her hands.   295

Nor were there any Syrians converted,
As far as the royal council ever heard:
The Sultan was cut to pieces before that started.
And Constance was taken, almost as quick as a bird
Can fly, down to a ship without a rudder,   300
And they sent her out to sea, advising that she
Should teach herself the way to Italy.

They gave her a certain amount of gold, and truth
To say, they fairly filled the boat with food,
And allowed her most of the clothing she'd brought from Rome—   305
And out on the open sea, the salty foam,
She went! O Constance, model of human kindness,
The Emperor's dear young daughter, far from home,
May He, the Lord of Fortune, steer your boat!

She crossed herself, and pitifully she called   310
To the cross of Christ, saying, "O shining altar,
Bountiful source of blessings, O holy cross,
Red with the blood of the lamb, O pitiful loss
That washed the world completely free of sin,
O save me from the devil's terrible claws,   315
Whenever I drown and sink beneath these waves.

"O tree of heavenly triumph, final protector
Of truth, the only wood full worthy of bearing
The King of Heaven, with fresh and bloody wounds,
He, the white lamb, his side stabbed through by a spear.   320
As over him, devils' destruction, you once
Extended your arms in shelter, O cross, give me
That same protection, lend me the strength to go on."

For years and days the woman fled, sailing
Back and forth across the Grecian Sea,   325
As far as the strait of Morocco: thus it would be.
She ate full many a sorry, soggy meal.
By the time she died, or so it often seemed,
High and breaking waves would still not drive
Her ship to where she prayed it might arrive.   330

Why, you may wonder, was she not slain with the others,
At the savage feast? Who was there to save her?
Again I answer: There once was a man, Daniel
By name, thrown in a pit with many others,
Every one of whom was swallowed by   335
The lion, except for Daniel, until he escaped.
Who saved him? God, and God alone, saved Daniel.

God chose to show his high miraculous power
In her, so we might see what might he wields.
Christ, who knows the remedies for whatever   340
Happens, by secret means, just as certain
Clerics are capable of achieving things
That most of us, as ignorant as we are,
Can understand as much as a man in the dark.

Clearly, she was not killed at the Syrian feast.   345
Who kept her from drowning in deepest ocean waves?
How did Jonas live, caught in the fish's
Great mouth, till spouted up at Nineveh?
Men must remember this too was worked by God,
Who also saved the Hebrew people from drowning,   350
Crossing the great Red Sea, their feet still dry.

Who ordered the four great spirits commanding the winds,
Capable of harming land and sea,
The north wind and the south, the west and the east:
"Do not annoy a sea, a land, a tree"?   355
Clearly, the same commander of us all
Who kept the stormy winds away from this woman
As quietly when she slept as when she woke.

Where could this woman ever have obtained
Meat and drink for three long years or more?   360
Who fed Saint Mary the Egyptian, both in the cave
And in the desert? No one but Christ could save her.
The miracle was no greater, when he fed five thousand
People with only two fish and five loaves of bread.
God gave his plenty, seeing what Constance needed.   365

Her ship went dashing out into our ocean,
Back and forth on the sea, until at last
The waves threw her to shore, right near a castle
—I do not know its name—in Northumberland,
The keel of her boat striking deep in the sand 370
And sticking so fast no tide would ever be strong
Enough to lift it. Here, said Christ, you belong.

The castle warden trekked across the sand,
To inspect this wreck, and searched the entire ship
Until he found this woeful castaway woman, 375
And also all the gold and valuables
She'd brought. Then speaking in her language, she begged
The warden to kill her, right where she stood, she was in
Such sorry straits, and such sorrow, she could not continue.

Her speech was like a kind of corrupted Latin, 380
But any half-trained man could understand her.
Once the warden completed his inspection,
He took her off the ship and onto dry land.
She knelt and thanked the Lord for his intervention,
But would not tell her name or where she was from 385
To no man whatever, even if they killed her.

In truth, she said, she'd been so dazed, so lost
And battered at sea, she'd truly lost her mind.
The castle warden, along with his wife, sorrowed
With her, both of them freely shedding tears. 390
She worked so hard to help them, never lazy,
Always trying to please them all, in that place,
So everyone loved her, the moment they looked at her face.

The castle warden, and Hermengild, his wife,
Were pagans, as everyone was in that land, at the time, 395
But Hermengild loved Constance as she loved her own life.
And Constance remained, staying so long that her constant
Prayers to Jesus, recited through bitter tears,
Brought down his grace: the Lord converted her,
Made Hermengild, the warden's wife, a Christian. 400

Christians did not come to that land; whatever
Christians had lived there, once, had fled away,
Because the whole of these far northern regions
Had now been conquered by pagans, by land and sea.
The Christian Bretons who'd lived there went to Wales,   405
Finding safety and security there
In that far-off place, at least for a space of time.

Yet not the whole of these Christian Bretons had fled,
Though the few who remained were careful to keep their religion
Secret, honoring Christ and deceiving the heathens,   410
And near the castle three of them were living.
One of them was blind, unable to see
With his eyes, but even so he could see with his mind,
As some men can, when their sight is gone, and they're blind.

This summer day, the sun was shining bright,   415
So Constance, with the castle warden and his wife,
Came walking down the path that led to the sea,
Intending to find whatever there was to see,
On land and strolling down along the beach.
And as they walked, they came upon this blind man,   420
Old and crooked, walking, eyes shut tight.

"In the name of Christ," the blind old Breton cried,
"Dame Hermengild, give me back my sight!"
His words were terribly frightening to Hermengild,
Whose husband did not know she was now a Christian,   425
And might, for her love of Jesus, have her killed.
But Constance stiffened her spine: whatever work
Christ wished of her, she was bound to, by his church.

The warden was stunned, surprised and not at all happy,
And said: "What's going on, what does this mean?"   430
Constance answered: "Good sir, you see Christ's might,
He saves poor people, saves them from devils' claws."
Before the darkness fell, that night, she
Had talked him around, and he was also converted,
Made a Christian, firm in Christ's belief.   435

The warden was not, of course, the lord of this place,
There where Constance had landed, and he had found her,
But only custodian in winter times
For royal Alla, King of Northumberland,
A wise, experienced ruler, whose glory was gained   440
Fighting the pagan Scots, a story familiar
To most. But in this matter I must restrain
Myself, forget all history, and tell my tale.

Satan, forever attempting to cheat and deceive us,
Saw the saintly perfection of Lady Constance,   445
And wondered how he might assault her belief.
He used a young knight, living there in that town,
Heated him up with love of a nature quite foul
And turned him absolutely so upside down
The knight was convinced he'd either have her or die.   450

He tried to woo her, but totally in vain;
There was no way she would commit such sin.
And then, most spitefully, he made up his mind
To force upon her a shameful death. He contrived,
By careful watching, to seize a night when the warden   455
Was out, and quietly crept into the room
Where Hermengild was lying in her bed.

Weary, exhausted from all the prayers she'd said,
Constance was fast asleep, and Hermengild too.
At Satan's evil urging, this knight approached   460
The good wife's bed and cut her throat in two,
And then he laid the bloody knife next to
Constance's bed, and left as secretly
As he had come—may God now strike him down!

Later that night, after the warden came home,   465
And saw his wife slaughtered so brutally,
So pitifully, he wept and wrung his hands,
Not once but over and over. And then he found
The bloody knife lying in Constance's bed.

And what, alas! could Constance say? Her head 470
Spinning, she could not comprehend a thing.

King Alla was quickly informed of this unfortunate
Deed, and when it took place, and where, and also
Informed how Constance had come, alone in a ship,
All of which I believe you already know. 475
Pity wrenched at good King Alla's heart,
When he saw so clearly good and kind a creature
Somehow fallen in dark and fatal adventures.

Just as an innocent lamb is carried to death,
So Constance, pure of heart, awaited his judgment. 480
The wicked knight who'd done this evil thing
Swore she was indeed the murderer.
But most of the people did not believe him, refusing
To think of her as a killer, savage, malicious.

For they had seen for themselves her virtuous nature, 485
Loving Hermengild as she loved her life.
Every castle resident felt this way,
With one exception: the man who'd killed with his knife.
The noble king was much impressed by all
The witnesses, and thought he needed more 490
Investigation, before the truth was uncovered.

Alas, O Constance! Alone, without a champion!
You cannot fight for yourself, your life is in danger!
But he that died to save our human souls,
And swept to hell, destroyed it, and tied up Satan, 495
Let him become your champion, and save you this day!
For unless the Lord produces a miracle,
Despite your innocence, you'll be dead today.

Constance went on her knees, and spoke these words:
"Immortal God, O once you saved Susannah, 500
Accused, but innocent! O Mary, Christ's mother,
And virgin daughter of Saint Anne, before

The two of you all angels sing Hosannah:
If I am innocent of this terrible crime,
Help me, or otherwise I'll surely die!"   505

You must have seen, and more than once, one face
In a crowd, so white, so pale, you knew at the sight
This man was walking to death, and could not escape:
Just seeing the absence of color, the utter paleness,
You knew he'd been convicted, would find no grace,   510
He, that single one, of all the crowd.
So Constance looked, her eyes searching about.

O queens, who live in high prosperity,
Duchesses, and all you noble ladies,
Take pity on this woman's adversity!   515
An emperor's daughter, standing alone and afraid,
No one she could call on, to comfort her fears.
O emperor's daughter, exposed to such foul danger,
Your friends so far away, so helpless your neighbors!

King Alla watched her, and felt so much compassion,   520
His noble heart was filled with so much pity,
His tears were pouring down, this sad occasion.
"Fetch me a book," he ordered, "and hastily,
And let us see if this knight will swear that she
He accuses truly did this deed, and if   525
A judge must be appointed to hear this case."

A Breton book, translated out of the Bible,
Was brought, and on this holy book the knight
Immediately swore to her guilt, and just at that time
A hand appeared, and struck so swift and righteously   530
Hard, he staggered, and fell to the ground like a stone.
Both his eyes went bursting out of his head,
Which everyone saw, and knew that he was dead.

And then a voice was heard, speaking out loud,
Saying: "This man slandered the daughter of holy   535

Church, a guiltless woman of whom I am proud!
You were guilty. I now say nothing more."
Everyone was astonished, the entire crowd
Standing as if in a charm, rooted to the floor,
Afraid of punishment—except for Constance.   540

Those who'd thought she was truly guilty shook
With fear, filled with repentance, for she had been close
To death, falsely accused, but innocent.
This miracle converted both the king
And many of his subjects, there in that place,   545
To Christian belief: give thanks to Christ for his grace!

King Alla hurriedly passed post mortem judgment
Upon the dead knight, closing the case on the spot,
Though Constance pitied his death. And then, God
Be praised for his mercy, Alla immediately   550
Took Constance to be his wife, and his people could see
This holy maiden, shining so bright, as their queen,
Transformed from wretch to ruler by Christ, our God.

The only living person in all that land
Regretting this marriage—and she alone—was the king's   555
Old mother, Donagild. A wretched thing
Like Constance, plucked from the gutter at his command
And made his mate? She shuddered at thought and deed.
Her royal heart almost breaking in two,
Her merciless mind turned to what she might do.   560

Myself, I do not care for stories that mix
Too much of chaff and straw along with their wheat.
As if you cared (I don't) what nobles were seen
At the marriage, or what was eaten first, what next,
Or who was blowing a trumpet and who a horn?   565
The only way to describe a wedding is to say
They ate, they drank, they danced, they sang, they played.

They went to bed, as it was reasonable
And right, for even the holiest of wives
Must marry patiently, and know that at night   570
Such things must happen as mankind always delights in,
After they've taken themselves a wife, and given her
Rings, putting holiness aside
For a while, for that is marriage's plan and design.

It didn't take long for his wife to be with child.   575
King Alla was called to Scotland, where war was declared.
Consigning his pregnant wife to the care of a bishop
And his castle warden, Alla rode off to fight.
Beautiful Constance, humble as she was meek,
Was now so very pregnant she had to keep   580
Herself in her rooms, waiting for God to relieve her.

The time arrived, and she produced a son,
Who was named Maurice, when baptized at the font.
The warden wrote a letter, addressed to the king,
Announcing this happy news. A messenger   585
Was summoned and given this and other things
To deliver as fast as he could. I wish I could say
He got on his horse and galloped forth on his way.

Seeking to curry favor with the king's old mother,
He rode, instead, to her house, then bowed, and spoke   590
To her in the courtliest words he knew. "Madame,"
He said, "I know you will be thankful to God,
Properly grateful and happy as happy can be,
For my lady queen has given birth to a son,
And joy resounds across this kingdom and people!   595

"Here are the close-sealed letters, fully explaining
These matters, to be delivered swiftly to our king.
If you desire to send your son some word,
I am your servant, as you may wish, both day
And night." She answered, "Not now, not yet, nay.   600
I wish you to take the night and rest well here;
Tomorrow morning there'll be a message to bear."

This messenger drank deep and long, both wine
And ale, then as he slept like a sodden swine
Donagild took the letters out of his box   605
And craftily she counterfeited another
Message, making it look like his warden's hand,
But telling the king some truly horrible lies,
As I will tell you in the following lines.

She told her son the queen had given birth   610
To a devilish-looking creature, awful to see,
And so repulsive to everyone in his castle
That no one could spend much time around this being.
The queen, she said, was probably an elf,
Maliciously transformed, by magic, to seem   615
Like a human; no one wanted to be around her.

The king was full of grief, reading these words,
But never spoke of his woe and sorrow. In his own
Hand, he wrote this reply: "Whatever Christ sends me,
Now that I have learned the truth of his message,   620
Is welcome! Lord, your hands now hold my pleasure,
Your words will ring in my heart for ever more,
And every desire I know is for you to award.

"Preserve and care for this child, whatever it
May be, and also my wife, until I return.   625
If Christ so pleases, he'll send me another heir,
More to my liking, better made for my throne."
He sealed this letter, quietly weeping, alone,
And soon the messenger was back on his horse,
Hurrying this pitiful letter home.   630

O messenger, drunk to the top of your head,
Your breath is stronger by far than your arms or legs,
And secrets stay as safe with you as eggs
In a cuckoo's nest. Your brains are scrambled, a jay
Makes better sense of its chatter, and your silly face   635
Changes its appearance, from day to day.
Nothing's secret, when drunkards take their place.

O Donagild, my English words cannot
Do justice to your malice and cruelty!
I leave you to Satan, whose care you richly deserve: 640
Let him write verses about your wretched betrayal!
For shame, you ghastly woman—but no, by God!
You once were a woman, but now you're simply a devil.
You walk on this earth, but your spirit lives in hell!

The messenger arrived, and just as before   645
He rode straight to the king's mother's court,
And she was delighted with him, and what he brought,
And tried to please him in every deed and thought.
He drank so much that his belly sprouted forth.
He slept, and in his usual style, snorted   650
And snored through the night, until the sun came out.

Then Donagild, once again, opened his box,
Destroyed the king's true letter, put this in its place:
"Hereby the king commands his castle warden,
On pain of being hanged, in the name of the law   655
Not to allow the lady Constance to stay
In his kingdom, no matter what the reason, for more
Than three whole days, and not a minute longer,

"And he must put her back in the very same ship
On which she came, she and her son, and every   660
Thing she owns, then shove her out to sea,
Away from our land, never ever to return."
O Constance, well might your spirit sink in fear,
And when you sleep, well might you dream of penance,
When Donagild unleashed on you this menace.   665

And in the morning the messenger awoke,
And plodded slowly up the castle road,
And carried his letter straight to the castle warden,
Who read it with utter horror, constantly saying
"Alas! and wellaway! O wellaway!   670
Lord Christ," he said, "how can this world endure
When sin controls so many worldly creatures?

"O mighty God, how can it be your will,
Since you are a fair and righteous judge, to spill
So many innocent lives like water on the ground,   675
While wicked people rule the world, and are rich?
O Constance, so good, alas! that I am found
Tormenting you, on pain of being killed.
In this quite awful matter, I have no will."

Both young and old were weeping, there in that place,   680
Hearing the cursèd words of the king's letter.
And Constance, slowly walking, dead pale of face,
Went as ordered, at the end of three more days,
Back to her ship. Sad, but not complaining,
She knelt in the sand, and lifting her hands to the Lord,   685
Said, "Christ, welcome forever are all your words.

"He who protected me when I was falsely
Accused, here in good king Alla's land,
He can protect me forever from any shame
And any harm, when I am on the salt sea.   690
He has the sacred powers he always had,
And I trust in him, and in his mother dear:
These are my sails, these are who will steer me."

Her little child lay weeping in her arms,
And she knelt down beside him. "O peace, my son,"   695
She said, "For I will never do you harm."
She took the kerchief wrapped around her hair
And covered over his little face and eyes,
And began to rock him slowly back and forth,
Her eyes now peering high into the heavens.   700

"Mother Mary," she said, "O Virgin so bright,
I know how true it is that mankind fell
Because of a woman's fault, and was damned to die,
Because of which your son was nailed to the cross.
Your blessèd eyes could see the pain he felt.   705
No pain could ever be worse than yours, no man
Or woman can ever feel such woe and sorrow.

"You saw your son being killed in front of your eyes,
And yet, by God, my little child is alive!
O shining lady, all woeful people cry   710
To you, the glory of all women, lovely
Virgin, haven of refuge, bright star of day,
Take pity on my child: your noble breeding
Has always made you pity the woeful and needy!

"My little child, O how could you be guilty,   715
And of what, too young ever to have sinned?
Why should your rock-hard father want you to die?
Have mercy, dear warden!" Constance pitifully cried,
"Let this little child stay here, with you,
And if you dare not, if you are too afraid,   720
At least come kiss him once, in his father's name!"

And then she stood, looking back at the land,
And said, "Farewell, my ruthless, merciless husband!"
And then she rose, went slowly walking toward
The ship, along the sandy shore, a crowd   725
Behind her, doing her best to keep the child
From crying. And then she reached the vessel, said
Farewell, crossed herself, and entered the ship.

Provisions had been brought aboard; food
Would not be a problem, nor would other supplies: 730
From bow to stern the ship had been filled with enough
To last, thank God, for who could say how long!
May God Almighty supply both wind and weather
And bring her home! That prayer is all I can say.
Out on the waves, now, her ship is under way.   735

PART THREE

Soon after this, King Alla returned to his castle
(About which you have, by now, been abundantly told),
And asked to see his wife and child. He asked,
But the warden could barely speak, his heart went cold.

He managed to speak, and informed the king, as plainly   740
As he could, exactly what had happened, no better,
Showing the king his seal and also his letter.

He said, "Lord, as you commanded me,
On pain of death, I have done, and nothing more."
The messenger was tortured, and finally he   745
Was obliged to tell, in plainest terms, detailed,
Where he had gone, each night, and where he had lain
And slept, and thus, by subtle investigation,
It was perfectly clear just who was the instigator.

The letter's handwriting, too, was identified,   750
And all the venom behind this cursèd deed,
Although the entire procedure is not known by me.
The net result, in a word, was that the king
Ordered his mother killed (as you might have expected)
As a vile traitor to both the king and kingdom.   755
And so farewell, old Donagild, God damn you!

No tongue can possibly tell the sorrow that Alla
Felt, both for his wife and for his son:
He mourned them, weeping, by day and also by night.
But now I must turn and tell you the pain and woe   760
Constance endured, sailing over oceans
Five years or more, as God willed that she do,
Until at last her ship returned to the land.

The shore lay down beneath a heathen castle,
The name of which does not appear in my text,   765
And there the ocean cast them up, Constance
And her son. You need to be aware of them,
Almighty God, they'll be in heathen hands,
And very soon, poised for a brutal death,
As I will explain in just a moment or two.   770

Many people came down from the castle, gawking
At this crewless ship, clearly without a captain,

But only a solitary lady. That night,
The castle's steward—may God bring him bad luck!—
A thief who had turned his back on everything Christian,   775
Boarded the ship in the dark, and told Constance
She'd sleep with him, whether she liked it or not.

The wretched woman began to wail, her child
Cried, and she wept bitter tears beside him.
But our blessèd mother in heaven came to her aid,   780
For Constance fought with him, as well as she could,
Until the thief slipped on a bit of loose wood
And fell into the sea. He could not swim,
And drowned. Thus Christ had kept Constance from harm.

O, licentious lust, foul and often   785
Fatal! You weaken the minds of men, but soften
Their muscles, too, the easier to destroy them.
Blinded lust produces good cause for mourning
And nothing more. How many men, simply
For even thinking of this, not doing a thing,   790
Have lost their reputations, or else been killed!

How could a well-born woman, gracious and weak,
Defend herself against this renegade?
O Goliath, tall and strong as a tree,
How could little David grind you down,   795
So young, possessing no armor or weaponry?
How dared he even look at your fearful face?
It's plain he only won because of God's grace.

And who gave Judith the boldness, the courage to kill
Hóloférnes in his battlefield tent,   800
Thus to deliver out of wretchedness
The people of God? My purpose in saying this
Is simple, for just as God Almighty sent
The spirit of strength to them, saving them both
From misfortune, he now sent courage and vigor to Constance.   805

Her ship went sailing past the Moroccan bays,
Then through the narrow mouth of Gibraltar, pounding
Forever on, to the west, then north and south,
And sometimes east, for many a weary day,
Until Christ's mother—O blessèd is she always!— 810
Plotted out, through her eternal goodness,
A path for ending all this heaviness.

Now let us leave our Constance, for just a moment,
And turn these pages back to the Emperor of Rome,
Who had been informed, by letters sent from Syria, 815
Of the slaughter of all the Christian folk he'd sent there,
And also of the dishonor inflicted on
His daughter by the wicked Sultaness,
A cursèd traitor killing men who were helpless.

And because of this the emperor immediately sent 820
His councillor and many other lords
To Syria, armed, and given royal orders
To take high vengeance. This they did, burning
And slaying across the land with power and zest—
That's all you need to know. The invasion ended, 825
They boarded their fleet of ships and headed for Rome.

This councillor was sailing royally,
Flushed with the satisfaction of victory,
And met the unmanned ship, and the woman and boy
Sitting alone on its deck, most piteously. 830
He neither recognized the lady nor knew
Who and what she was, or why she was there,
And she, as ever, refused to disclose the truth.

He put her on his ship and took her to Rome,
Handing over Constance, and also her son, 835
To his wife. And there she stayed, living on.
Our Lady had brought her out of sorrow and woe,
As she had done so many times before.

She lived in the councillor's house a very long time,
Performing holy works, as her heart inclined her. 840

Indeed, the councillor's wife was in fact her aunt,
But never recognized or knew her niece.
And that is enough of that: let them live in peace,
While I return to Alla, a sad-faced king,
Who still was sighing and weeping for a long-lost wife. 845
That is, I'll leave Queen Constance right where her life
Has brought her, as Alla, her husband, thinks life is behind him.

Alla had killed his mother, as I have told you,
And sorrowed because of her life and also her death,
Repenting what she had done and forced him to do, 850
He came to Rome, seeking papal penance,
And putting himself completely in holy governance,
Praying continually, in sorrow and woe,
That Jesus Christ would forgive his wicked works.

Word that Alla was coming to Rome—important 855
News—was carried across the sea before
He arrived. This was a pilgrimage of note.
That day, the councillor's horse, and others, took a road
To the harbor, welcoming the king, he
And many family members, proudly showing 860
Off his splendor while playing the role of host.

He played his part with great magnificence,
And Alla responded just as splendidly:
They offered each other cordiality
With open hands. It happened, quite naturally, 865
That Alla invited the councillor to dine,
And though I cannot tell you how or why,
He brought Queen Constance's son with his company.

I know some people might say that Constance, in fact,
Begged the councillor to bring the boy 870
Along. These matters involve some circumstances
I am not free to reveal. Don't think me coy:

This is plain truth. But I am allowed to say
She told her son, during this dinner, to stay
Where Alla could see him, and stare at his father's face.   875

King Alla stared back, astonished, surprised, half stunned,
And finally asked the councillor directly,
"Who is that handsome boy, standing to your left?"
"I have no idea," was the answer, "By God and Saint John!
He has a mother, I know. But a father? He has none."   880
And truth to tell, in another half a moment
He told King Alla how the child was found.

"God knows," the councillor went slowly on,
"No one I've ever known, in all my life,
Lives so holy an existence. There's not another   885
Woman like her, whether virgin or wife.
She seems to me a lady who'd rather a knife
Were stabbed through her breast than do a wicked deed.
No one, I swear, could force her into evil."

No creature walking the earth could possibly be   890
As like the lady Constance as this unknown child.
King Alla remembered her face most perfectly,
And began to wonder in silence, to himself, if she
Might prove, indeed, to be Constance in the flesh,
Long lost, now found. He sighed, though secretly,   895
And left the table as soon as he decently could.

"By God," he thought, "I'm living in fantasy!
If I had control of my senses, I'd surely know
She's dead and drowned, lying on the floor of the sea."
And then he changed his tack. "Yet, although   900
That's reason itself, what if Christ might be
The force that brings me to her, just as he
Might well have ordered her journey out of Syria?"

That afternoon, Alla paid a visit
To the councillor's home, wanting to make the best of   905
This miraculous chance. The king was received

With the greatest honor, and Constance was hastily sent for.
Believe me, seeing just who the visitor was,
She did not feel like dancing. Indeed, I suspect
It was hard enough to simply stand on her feet.   910

Seeing his wife, he greeted her courteously,
And wept so freely the sight was hard to see,
For he had recognized her immediately,
For him there was not the slightest shade of doubt.
And she, in her sorrow, stood frozen in place like a tree.   915
Remembering the harsh decisions she thought
He'd made, her heart was shut against him, and hard.

And yet, she fainted twice, quite dead away;
He wept, and tried to explain what had happened that day.
"May God," he said, "and all his shining saints   920
Who know his mercy, in truth take pity on me,
For I'm as innocent of harms that were done you
As my son Maurice, who looks so much like you,
Or let the devil take me to hell today!"

Both of them sobbed for a very long time; their pain   925
Was bitter, and woeful hearts were terribly tested.
Standing and hearing their sorrow was a dreadful strain.
Releasing her sorrow made things hurt more, not less.
Allow me, please, to let my struggles stop
And describe her sorrow another day, if I can,   930
For I am very weary of telling these woes.

At last, and finally seeing he'd told the truth,
And never given orders for the terrible crimes
Against her, I swear they kissed a hundred times,
And such a happiness had swept them both   935
That, except for heaven's joys, no one alive
Or dead had ever seen, or will see, the like,
Not while this world of ours has still endured.

And then she asked her husband, most quietly,
In relief of all her long and piteous pain, 940
To ask her father, the mighty Emperor of Rome,
If he would invite Alla to dine at his home,
Whenever his majesty might so incline,
But saying nothing of Constance, daughter and wife,
No word to her father, who thought she'd left this life. 945

It has been said that their little son, Maurice,
Brought this message to the emperor's palace,
But I do not think that Alla, a king, and wise,
Was ignorant enough to use a mere child
When dealing with the Emperor of Rome, 950
Flower of Christian folk, but would have gone
Himself: that seems to me the way it happened.

The day arrived, and Alla wore his finery,
As did his wife, wanting to make a graceful
Impression, and off they rode, both of them gleeful. 955
But when they arrived and she saw her father waiting,
She dismounted, dropped, and fell full prone at his feet.
"Father," she said, "you do not remember your child,
Constance, the daughter you loved so very well.

"But I am that daughter, I am Constance," she said, 960
"Who once you sent to be married in Syria.
It was me, father, who soon was put in a ship,
Completely alone, and left to die in the sea.
O my good father, let me beg for mercy!
No longer send me off to distant heathens, 965
But welcome and thank my husband, for his kindness."

Who could possibly describe the joy
Of the three, meeting this unexpected way?
But I will have to end this tale today,
And not tomorrow; darkness will soon be upon us. 970
These happy people sat down to dine together,

And there I will let them stay, enjoying their bliss
Better a thousand times, just left alone.

At a later time, this child, Maurice, assumed
His grandfather's throne, by papal command, and lived   975
Like a Christian. He honored the Church and his royal gift.
But that is a tale for which I have no room;
Constance remains the center of the story I'm telling.
Ancient Roman tales will certainly help you
Follow Maurice to his end, which I've forgotten.   980

King Alla remained in Rome as long as seemed
Quite proper, then took his sweet and holy wife
And sailed directly to England, where they lived good lives
Of joy and peace. No one, I warn you, can dream
Of keeping worldly happiness for more   985
Than a very short time, for joy in this world can't last,
Changing back and forth as days go past.

Who has ever lived in such delight
For a single day, unaffected by anger,
Pity, desire, or perhaps some relative's fright,   990
Or envy, passion, pride, or the poisoned fangs
Of insults? Yet all I'm doing is telling this right
As it happened, for the joys and pleasures of Alla and Constance
Were short—and here, in brief, are the circumstances.

Death takes his due, no matter low or high,   995
And though the dates are not clear, it seems to have been
Little more than a year when Alla died,
And Constance was left in very great sadness and pain.
We all should pray that his soul was received as sinless!
And Constance, thereafter, made her way again   1000
To Rome, as I will somewhat fully explain.

When she arrived in that city, this holy creature,
She found her family and friends in great good health.
All her grim adventures were done, she'd reached
Her destination. She went to her father and fell   1005

On her knees, weeping for tenderness, not sorrow.
Her heart brim full with happiness, for which
She thanked our God, a thousand times and over.

Living in holiness, and the giving of alms,
She and her father shared his house, never   1010
Separated again, except by death.
And now farewell, my story! Your time has ended.
And now I pray to Jesus Christ to send us
Joy after woe, and govern us all in his grace,
And grant us all salvation, here in this place.   1015
Amen.

EPILOGUE TO THE MAN OF LAW'S TALE
[OF DISPUTED AUTHENTICITY]

Our Host at once stood straight, right up in his stirrups,
And said, "Good men, all of you listen and hear us!
This was a proper tale to be told to us!
Sir Parish Priest," he said, "by God's great bones,
Tell us a tale, as you agreed before.   5
I see quite well how you learnèd men perform,
Knowing so much, by the dignity of our Lord!"
    The Priest replied, "Blessings on you, my son.
But why do you swear so much, so terribly often?"
Our Host replied: "Ho ho, so that's where you are!   10
I smell the scent of Reforming blown in the air!
Good men, come now!" said our Host. "Listen to me.
By the passion of God, a sermon is now what he
Will give us, reformed to the tune he likes to sing.
Attend most carefully to what he'll bring us."   15
    "By my father's soul, that won't be happening!"
The Shipman swore. "I see no happiness
In preaching. Shove no gospel down my throat.
We're living under God," he said. "You can quote me.
The Parson plans to sow some prickly oats,   20
Or spread sharp thorns in our good, edible wheat.
And so, by God, Sir Host, I'll do what I need to,
To stop him. I'll tell a better tale myself.
I'll clink and clang a good one, right off the shelf,
And wake up all the folk in this company.   25
But it won't, by God, be a tale of philosophy,
No frissy-fussy, haughty words of law.
This sailor never knew Latin, and doesn't want more!"

The Wife of Bath's Prologue

"Experience, no other authority,
Is good enough ground to stand on, and enough for me
To speak of marriage, its sorrows and its woes.
For, gentlemen, since I was twelve years old
I've walked away from church with five good husbands—   5
If five times married is legal, by the law of this land—
And each were worthy men, all things considered.
But I've been told that Jesus only attended
A single wedding, up in Galilee,
And this example, it's said, should truly teach me   10
That I should not be married more than once.
And here are biting words that Christ pronounced
Beside a well—Jesus, both God and man,
Speaking to a woman, a Samaritan:
'You've had five husbands,' he said, scolding the lady,   15
'So the man who has you today, I tell you, is surely
Not your husband.' And that's what he said, truly.
Yet exactly what he meant, I cannot say,
Except to ask just why the fifth of her men
Was not, in fact and law, an honest husband   20
For this Samaritan? For just how many
Men was she entitled to take in marriage?
Numbers have never been counted: people have managed
To marry without arithmetic. I've never
Heard of such a definition. Whatever   25
Learnèd men may guess, and interpret, down
And up and all around, here's what counts

For me: God has ordered us to wax
And multiply. That is a noble text
I perfectly understand. And he also said   30
My husband should leave his mother and father for me.
He didn't talk about numbers, that I can see,
Or bigamy—or even octógamy!
Why should men speak of this as villainy?
     "Hear the wise old king named Solomon.   35
I guess he married a lot more times than once!
I wish our God would make it legal for me
To have my fun half as often as he!
O, the gifts of God he had for his wives!
No living man could try it and hope to survive.   40
God knows, and the Bible says, the very first night
He slept with every single one of his wives.
God be blessed that I have married five!
I welcome the sixth, whenever he arrives.
Frankly, I have no use for chastity.   45
Whenever my husband leaves this world behind,
Some other Christian man will make me his wife,
Without any need for delay or silly waiting.
The apostle says so himself: a wife with no mate
Is free to marry wherever she thinks it's best,   50
Marriage, he said quite clearly, is not sinning,
For marrying, he stressed, is better than burning.
Why should it matter to me if people curse
Old Lamech, who had two wives? Is that bigamy?
Now Abraham seems holy enough to me,   55
And also Jacob, as far as I can see,
Yet both of them had many more wives than two,
And other holy men, they did it too.
Look in the Bible. Where do you see the word
Of God, in clear and unmistakable terms,   60
Forbidding marriage at any age? Where?
And where does God command virginity?
I know as well as you, without a doubt,
That when the apostle talked of maidenhood
He said that God did not command it. Men do,   65
And they can advise it, but then it's up to you:

Advice about something is not what you have to do,
But what you choose for yourself, using your judgment.
If God had commanded virginity for women,
He would have denied all marriage—and you know he didn't.   70
Remember, too: if seed is never sown,
Where could virginity be ever grown?
Paul knew very well he could not command
Something his master had clearly never demanded.
Announce a contest, and a prize, for virginity: 75
All women can run, but who runs the best? We'll see.
    "But Paul is not addressing the entire world:
Those inspired by God will hear his words.
And of course the apostle himself was surely a virgin.
But yet, although he said in the clearest words   80
He wished all men would share his virginity,
His preference is not a command, nor should it be.
And those who prefer to be married can never be
Condemned as sinners, which is good enough for me.
If my husband dies, I marry again, free   85
Of sin, exempt from charges of bigamy.
Paul's wish that good men's hands would keep from touching
Apply to women in bed or lying on couches,
Since fire's not dangerous unless there's tinder.
This is a scene that most of you remember.   90
In short, Paul says that good virginity
Surpasses a thing of impossibilities—
Impossible, that is, unless the he
And she agree to live in chastity.
    "That's fine with me, I've no desire for a life   95
Like that—though abstinence is better than outright
Bigamy: body and spirit unstained.
I make no boast, my life has been open and plain.
You're all aware that a lord's expensive household
Contains some cups and spoons not made of gold.   100
Some are plain wood, and the lord is satisfied.
God calls our spirits to him in different styles,
But all these differences are put inside us
By God, a little of this and of that, as he likes
    "For sure, virginity is a great perfection,   105

As continence can come from great devotion.
But we know the source of all perfection is Christ,
Who told the people who heard him to change their lives,
Sell everything they owned and give it to the poor,
And then they could follow him, be perfect and pure.   110
But gentlemen, excuse me, I couldn't endure it.
At whatever age I am, I want to bestow
The flower of my body in the acts and fruits of love.
        "Tell me, indeed, why are our bodies shaped
With parts and places made for procreation,   115
And made so by God, the perfect body maker?
Believe me, they're not made *not* to be used.
Interpret things as you like, and say what you choose,
Declare one part was made for urine excretion,
And that, and our female parts, are an explanation   120
And guide for telling one sex from the other,
And say it, both up and down, as a source for that knowledge,
And nothing more. Do you think that stands for the truth?
Experience tells you it's certainly not true.
To keep religious folk well satisfied,   125
I say all uses are good, and all have been tried—
That is, our natural parts are good, and they work,
And whatever they do, God's pleased (if not his church).
Why else should wise men write in their holy texts
That a man is bound to pay his marriage debt   130
To his wife? How could he possibly make that payment
If he never used his God-given implement?
God gave his creatures these tools for urine excretion,
And also for making new lives in God's creation.
        "But no one, I say, should think themselves compelled   135
To use this equipment, given by God himself:
No one must be obliged to populate
The earth. Chastity is too little too late.
Christ was a virgin, but shaped like any man,
And so were many saints, since the world began.   140
They chose the road of chastity for themselves.
But I will not, I tell you that myself.
Let them be seen as bread whiter than snow,
And call we women loaves of the darkest brown.

And yet, with good brown bread, as Mark has written,   145
Our good Lord, Jesus, fed a host of men.
However God himself has made us, there
I'll stay; brown bread or black, I do not care.
When I'm a wife, I'll use his gifts to me
As he has given them, all generously.   150
If I am ever reluctant, God send me sorrow!
My husband will have it at night, and in the morning,
Whenever he wishes to come and pay his debt.
And I want a husband, the youngest one I can get,
And he will owe me my debt, and serve me, too,   155
For I will make my pound of his flesh a duty
He must fulfill, as long as I'm his wife.
His body owes me this, for the rest of my life,
And nothing can interfere or ever deprive me.
This is what the apostle has guaranteed me,   160
Commanding our husbands to love us well, and be
Our mates in every sense of that blessèd word—"
    At this, the Pardon Peddler interfered:
"Now, lady," he said, "by God and by Saint John!
You make a noble preacher, by God's own bones!   165
I was just about to marry a wife: O Lord!
Why should I give her my flesh, so she can gorge
Herself? I'll reconsider, and think this over!"
    "Wait!" she said. "I haven't begun my tale.
You'll have another refreshment to put in your pail,   170
And it won't taste as fresh and winning as ale.
After you've heard my story through to its end,
And learned the pains and perils of marriage first-hand,
From someone who's been an expert for as many years
As I've lived, for I have shed tears, and I have been fierce—   175
By then, you can choose for yourself which barrel to open,
Which drink to taste, and perhaps be able to cope.
You'll need to be careful, before you get too close.
I'll cite you examples, ten or even more.
If other men's experience has not taught you,   180
You'll be an example to others, by being caught.
Great Ptolemy has spoken these same words:
Look in his book, and you will find it there."

"Lady, I beg you, should it be your pleasure,"
The Pardon Peddler said, "teach us your treasure 185
Of a story, continue just as you began,
And let your practice inform us younger men."
    "More gladly," she said, "because it's likely to please you.
Yet let me inform you all I'm not a preacher,
But only indulging myself with what delights me. 190
Take nothing to heart. If it happens that you dislike
What I say, remember: I speak only in play.
    "Now then, sir, I'll continue on with my tale—
I swear on whatever wine I drink, or ale,
I'll tell you the truth about every husband I had, 195
Since three of them were good, and two were bad.
The three were good men, they were rich, and old,
And never found it easy to uphold
The law establishing their debt to me.
I'm sure you understand me well indeed! 200
So help me God, I laugh when I remember
How hard, at night, I made them use their members!
And I recall how little their labor meant.
They'd handed over all their land and treasure,
I had no need to worry about their pleasure, 205
Or play at being in service: I'd won their love.
Their love for me was such, by God above,
I took it for granted, and set no value on it!
Smart women sweat for love, when they really want it,
And being without it is really when they want it. 210
But since I held them entirely in my hands,
And since they'd long since given me their lands,
Why should I worry myself with what might please them,
Unless I stood to gain, and make life easier?
I had them all so busy, by my faith, 215
That many a night they sang 'O weylaway!'
The prize for never quarreling, given they say
In Essex, would never be awarded to them.
I ruled so hard, and kept them under my thumb,
That they were truly happy, bringing me prizes 220
They'd won at the fair, glad to so surprise me.
And they were pleased when I chose to treat them nicely,

Because, God knows, my tongue was tart and spicy.
    "Now listen to how I handled them so well,
You knowing wives, who comprehend what I tell.   225
Always assume, and speak that way, that they
Are in the wrong, for there isn't a man who can play
At lying and swearing as any woman can.
Not that they always do, but that they're able,
If something goes wrong, to be bold and fiercely capable.   230
A wife who cares for herself protects her status
By stamping her foot and swearing the man has inflated
A mouse-tail into a tiger, and call on her maid
To tell whatever story the wife has created—
Like this: 'Sir, you old sluggard, look at my dress!   235
Our neighbor makes sure that *his* wife's clothes are the best!
They honor her, at sight, all over town,
While I sit home, having no decent gown.
And you are always seen at our neighbor's house:
Is she so pretty? Are you so amorous?   240
What do you whisper in our maid's ear? Bless me!
You old lecher, you're up to old tricks, I guess!
But I, if I have a lady friend, or any
Friend at all, without good reason, you ninny,
You scold like a wild-eyed devil, if I just dare   245
Approach his house, or go in anywhere!
But you come home as tipsy and drunk as a mouse,
And mount your high horse, and preach like mad, with no ounce
Of reason or proof! You say that it's an awful
Mistake, to marry a dirt-poor woman: she costs   250
Too much! But then a rich one, you say, of high
Descent, torments you with her moods and her pride.
And when she's pretty, you rascal, you say that lechers
Follow her like flies, go everywhere
She goes. How can a woman ever be chaste,   255
Harassed first here, then there, in every way?
    "You say that some folk want us for our money,
Some for our body, others for beauty, our honeyed
Singing, our dancing, our fabulous sweetness, our noble
Manners; some like us because we flirt, and are bold;   260
Some like our tiny hands, our delicate arms—

And the devil will catch us all, despite our charms.
How can men, you say, defend the wall
Of a castle so assailed; it is bound to fall.
    "Oh, but if she's ugly you say she yearns   265
For every man she sees, her lust so burning
Hot she jumps at men like a spaniel puppy,
Until she finds a fellow who'll take her up
On her offer. There's no gray goose that swims in the lake,
According to you, that doesn't long for a drake.   270
O, you moan, how hard it is to control
Something no man will willingly take hold of.
You say these things, you loafer, as you climb into bed,
Exclaiming that no wise man is better off wed—
At least if he expects to go to heaven.   275
May blasts of thunder and lightning bolts as deadly
As clubs fall on your neck, and may it be broken!
    "You say that collapsing houses, and clouds of smoke,
And scolding wives are reasons for men to flee
Away from their houses: Ah! May Jesus bless me!   280
What's wrong with such an old man, that he scolds and yelps?
    "You say we women hide our vices until
We're married, and then we roll them down the hill—
A fitting proverb for a man so ancient and shrill!
    "You say that every living ox and horse,   285
And asses and hounds, are tested as a matter of course;
Basins and wash-bowls, before men buy them, and spoons
And stools, and all the things a household owns,
As well as pots and all the clothes we wear.
But women are not tested, no one would dare,   290
Until they're married. You feeble-minded rascal!
    "You also say—and you lie in your throat!—I'm after
You, O all day long, to praise my beauty,
Insisting that staring at me is your bounden duty,
And wherever we go you have to call me 'fair lady.'   295
And I require of you a birthday feast,
And a celebration, with plenty to drink and eat,
And you've had to honor the chambermaid who tends
My room, as well as the nurse we pay to attend to
The children, as well as my father's people and his friends—   300

Old barrelful of lies, that's what you pretend!
　"You've fabricated a crazed and false suspicion
That I am in love with Jannkin, our apprentice,
Who's constantly with me and squires me everywhere,
And only because of his curly golden hair.　　　　　　　305
I wouldn't have him, if you were dead tomorrow!
　"Just tell me this: why do you hide—O sorrow!—
The keys to your money box? I cannot find them.
All our goods are shared, they're yours, they're mine:
This house has only one lady. Why do you shame me?　　310
I say, by God and by the good Saint James,
No matter what you think, you will not be
Master of my body and my property,
Not even if you roar most angrily.
Give that one up, old man—god damn your eyes!　　　315
What can you accomplish by peeping and spying?
Perhaps you'd like to lock me in that box?
You ought to say: 'Now wife, go where you like,
And have your fun, I won't believe these tales.
I know you're good and true, my wife and lady.'　　　320
Women don't love a man who watches so closely;
We need be free, we need to make our own choices.
　"Blessings on that man, most blessèd ever,
Great Ptolemy, wise and almost never
Wrong: hear a proverb from his *Almageste:*　　　　　325
'He who ranks the highest among the blessed
Is he that does not care who rules the world.'
Let me explain the meaning of these words:
If you have enough, why does it make any difference
How happy your neighbors are, just over the fence?　　330
And you, old goat, are certain sure to get
As much as you can handle of very good sex.
How niggardly a man must be if someone
Asks a light from his match and he gives him none?
A loan of light, by God, deprives him of nothing!　　335
If you have enough, why bother with silly moaning?
　"And yet you say of us, all dressed to the nines,
Our clothing bright, our jewels shining fine,
That this endangers our precious chastity.

And then you think you've reinforced your plea 340
By quoting, to your shame! the apostle's words:
'The clothes you women wear should always be worked
In full acknowledgment of chastity
And shame. No overdone hair or shining jewelry,
No pearls, no gold, no gowns to show your position.' 345
To his old words, and your offensive petition,
I give as much attention as I would to a gnat.
    "And you insist that, truly, I'm like a cat.
But whoever fusses over a cat's fine skin
Would like the cat in his house, to live with him. 350
And if that skin, as it happens, is sleek and bright,
That cat won't stay indoors all day and night,
But out she'll go, before the day has dawned,
To show her skin and join the caterwauling.
Which means, you ancient villain, if I look bright 355
I'll run right out and show the world my light.
    "My lord, old fool, I'll ask you again: why spy?
Even if Argus, blessed with a hundred eyes,
Agreed to watch over me, as he knows how to do,
Unless I wished it, he'd do no better than you. 360
I know how to make a fool out of Argus, too!
    "You also say that, universally,
The things that trouble all the earth are three
In number, and a fourth that sweeps away
All living men. You ancient rascal, now may 365
Jesus shorten your life! You love to claim
A hateful wife is one of these pestilences.
You say so, but is there, in truth, no greater resemblance
To other things, more fitting to your beliefs,
Than an innocent wife, dutiful, helpless, weak? 370
    "Women's love, you say, can only be
Compared to hell, to land so barren that water
Dries away. You paint an even broader
Picture: women's love is fire, forever
Consuming all in its path, and endless, never 375
Sated. As worms can eat up trees, so wives
Will always destroy their miserable husbands' lives.
Once tied to a wife, all men will understand."

"Gentlemen, this was my marital stance:
My doddering husbands were tightly held in hand,   380
And when they were drunk they'd always claim what you've heard.
I lied, of course, but even the most absurd
Were confirmed by Jannkin, and also by my niece.
O lord! The sorrow I brought them, the awful pain,
But they were innocent, in God's own name!   385
But I could bite like a horse, and I would whine,
Complaining hard, although the guilt was mine,
Because I would have been ruined if I'd told the truth.
Whoever's first at the mill, is the first to have flour.
And I was always first, which ended our wars.   390
They were glad to surrender, and go and lick their scars
For sins that none of them had ever committed.
O how I ranted and raved about their wenching,
When they were too sick in bed to answer a question.
     "And yet, I tickled his heart, because he knew   395
I had so much affection for him! It was true,
Although I swore that every time I walked forth
At night, I was spying on wenches that he'd had intercourse
With—my standard excuse for making merry!
That quickness of mind is given, at birth, to every   400
Woman: lying and weeping are birthright gifts
From God, natural weapons to help us live.
My one particular boast is exactly this,
That in the end I always won, whether
By tricks or force, or anything whatever.   405
For example, complaining that never stopped. Being
In bed was my special opportunity:
I'd scold and scold, and give them no pleasure; I'd lie
Beside them, but not too close, and I'd run and hide
If they touched me, I'd leave the bed and stay away   410
Until, whatever it was I wanted, they gave me.
And then I'd let them do what all men savor.
Whenever I talk to men, I tell this tale:
Earn what you can, since everything's for sale.
No one catches hawks with an empty hand;   415
To win what I wanted, I'd gratify the man,
Pretending that he had what my heart desired,

Though weary old meat could never set me on fire,
And I paid them back by scolding, night and day.
Even if the pope had sat at our table, 420
I couldn't let up on my husband. This is no fable:
I'd hammer the man as hard as I was able.
I swear by God in heaven, omnipotent,
That were I, right now, making my testament,
I've long since paid him back for whatever he said. 425
I ran them around in circles, and my tongue had a bite
That made them surrender, or the house would never be quiet.
He could growl like a lion, it made no difference,
He never got to eat till he showed me deference.
    "And then I'd say: 'My dear, have you ever noted 430
What a gentle face our sheep, Willkin, shows us?
Come here, my husband, allow me to kiss your cheek.
Always be patient, my dear, always be meek,
Act and speak most sweetly, with gentle feeling—
Exactly what you find in Job, when you teach. 435
Suffer in silence, practice the words you preach.
And if you do that, then you will certainly see
How pleasant it is to have a wife who's peaceful.
For when we argue, someone is bound to win,
And since you men are reason-born, begin, 440
In good reason, not to be impatient with us.
What need do you have to grumble, and groan, and fuss?
Are you worried that someone else might share my crotch?
Why, have it all, take it, if you need so much!
O by Saint Peter! I scold you, but you know you like it. 445
For if I wanted to sell myself, I'd be rich,
I could have whatever I wanted—this!—and then this!
But I'll keep it fresh for you, since you like my taste.
But I'll go on scolding: I see my words aren't wasted.'
    "That was how we argued, back and forth. 450
And now I'll talk of my husband number four.
    "This fourth husband of mine was a partygoer,
A dancer and drinker, and he had a paramour,
And he kept her even after we were married.
And I was young, and very hard to manage, 455
Stubborn and strong, as active as any magpie.

I danced most beautifully to a gracious guitar,
And I could sing, by God, like a bird in the air,
After I'd drunk a single glass of sweet wine!
Mettéliús, a disgusting slob, a swine,   460
Beat his wife to death for drinking wine,
Beat her over and over with a heavy staff,
But he couldn't have stopped my drinking, were he my husband.
And after wine, my mind, and body, began
To think of Venus, for just as cold makes hail   465
A lecherous mouth produces a lecherous tail.
Drunken women have no desire to say "no."
This is something lechers have always known.
        "But good Lord Christ! When I remember my youth,
That sparkling brightness, that constant joy, the roots   470
Of my heart reverberate, and sparkle again.
My heart is forever pleased with what I did then,
For I have had my world as in my time.
But age, alas! poisons us on the vine,
It's stolen away my beauty, and also my strength.   475
So let it go, farewell! The devil go with it!
The smooth, cool flour is gone, that's all I can tell you.
Husks and bran, when I'm able, is all I can sell you.
And yet, to try to be merry is a better plan,
So let me tell you more of my fourth husband.   480
        "My heart, I admit, was churning with bitter rage
Whenever he took his pleasure from a different page.
But I got even, by God and Saint Joducus!
I took that wood and made him his own sharp cross—
Not with my body, I would not let that happen,   485
But working hard at making other men happy
I let his anger, the bitter grease inside,
Flame like a fire and fry his jealous mind.
By God! In this world I was his purgatory,
For which I hope his soul is now in glory.   490
God knows it's true, he often sat and sung
His sorrows, pinched by his woe, his heart hard strung.
No one in all the world, save God and he,
Knew all the many torments I made him feel.
After I came home from Jerusalem,   495

He died, and is buried under the high crossbeam,
Although his tomb is not a work of art
Like the sepulcher of Dáriús, carved
By the famous painter, Ápellés. For me,
It's waste to bury so expensively. 500
I bid him farewell, God grant his soul may rest!
He lies in his grave, a treasure set in its chest.
　　"And now my fifth husband's story is what I'll tell.
God keep his soul forever out of hell!
And yet he treated me by far the worst: 505
I feel it, rib by rib, all down my chest,
And always will, until my dying day.
But in our bed he was so fresh and gay,
And knew exactly how to lead me on
Till what he wanted was what we had done, 510
And though he'd beaten me from bone to bone
He was so good at winning me again.
I think I loved him best, because in fact
His love was such a trembling high-wire act.
We women have, and here I'll tell no lies, 515
A strange approach, a secret fantasy:
Whenever what we want is hard to get,
That's what we crave, and cry for, and deeply regret.
Forbid us something, that's just the thing we cherish;
Pursue us hard, we run away like deer. 520
How carefully we spread our merchandise;
Pushing and shoving at market raises the price.
When women know this, we can call them wise.
　　"This fifth of my husbands, O God please bless his soul!
I took him for love, and for riches not at all, 525
For he had been a cleric, schooled at Oxford,
But left there, then came home and went to board
At Alison's house, she my very best friend
In town. May God preserve her soul, in the end!
She knew my heart, and all my private affairs, 530
Far better than our parish priest, whose ears
Had heard my confession: by my faith that's the truth!
My confessions to her were complete, and completely true.
For if my drunken husband had pissed on a wall,

Or committed a sin that could have cost him his all, 535
She was the one I told, and one other woman,
And also my niece, for whom I had great affection.
I would have told his doings to all of them,
And many times I did, truly, I hid
Nothing, and hearing them say it he turned red 540
In the face, hot with shame, blaming himself
For telling me such a secret, God so help me.
　　"And as it happened, once on a day in Lent—
Of course, my good friend's house was where I went,
For what I loved of all things best was pleasure, 545
Walking in March, and April, and May, at my leisure,
From house to house, hearing all the gossip—
My cleric, Jannkin, and also my friend, good Alice,
And I, out in the fields together we went.
My husband was in London all that Lent, 550
And I had perfect leisure to let myself play,
And see what I liked, and show myself both day
And night to merry folk. How could I say
What luck I'd have, or in exactly what place?
Accordingly, I made my visitations 555
To evening vigils and also church processions,
And sermons, too, and pilgrimages like these,
Holy drama performed, and marriage rites,
And wore my best and brightest gowns, the red ones.
Moths, and worms, and all cloth-eating bugs 560
Left them alone, ate not a single bite—
And do you know why? I wore them day and night.
　　"And now I'll proceed with telling what happened to me.
I told you we walked in the fields, most regularly,
And more and more we played, and flirted, and toyed, 565
This cleric and I, and at last I told him my choices
Were all my own, I needed no additions,
And if I were widowed he could take the position.
For surely, it was no boast, this proposition:
I always made sure my larder was fully stocked, 570
To provide for marriage, or anything else I wanted.
A mouse would certainly have the heart of a fool,
If all it possessed in this life was a single hole,

For if that failed, down comes the world as a whole.

    "I pretended to Jannkin that he had enchanted me— *575*
That was a trick I learned at my mother's knee.
I also said I dreamed of him all night,
Dreamt that he had slain me, as I lay upright,
And then my bed was all awash with blood;
I hoped, I added, that he would do me good, *580*
For blood, as I was taught, was a symbol of gold;
And all of this was a lie, these things I told him.
I always followed the path my mother had shown me,
In this, but also in many other ways.

    "But now, sir Host, let's see, what should I say? *585*
A ha! By God, I have my tale again.

    "Seeing the fourth of my husbands about to be buried,
I sobbed and wept, and fussed, and acted flurried,
That being clearly expected how wives should behave;
And I wound my kerchief all around my face; *590*
But since I already knew I would have a mate,
My weeping was modest, I guarantee the case.

    "My just-dead husband was carried to church, on the morrow,
And neighbors went along, and showed their sorrow,
And Jannkin, my cleric, was there among the others. *595*
So help me God! As I watched him walking behind
The bier, the thoughts that circled around in my mind
Were focused on his straight legs, and on his feet,
And I put my heart completely in his keeping.
He was, I think, no more than twenty years old, *600*
And I was forty, to tell the truth, but a colt's
Young appetite had always been my style,
My teeth were wide apart, which is a sign
Of Venus, and I bore her birthmark on my body.
So help me God! But surely I was lusty, *605*
Pretty, rich, and very well situated.
And truly, as my new husband often stated,
My crotch was just as perfect as that part can be.
I'm truly born of Venus, most certainly,
In all my feelings, but my heart belongs to Mars. *610*
Venus gave me desire, and all the parts
I needed, but it was Mars that made me daring.

My astral ascendant was Taurus, with Mars sharing
The sky. Alas, alas! that love should be sinful.
I followed the path my stars had placed me in,   615
I had no choice but to be what I have been.
I never was good at holding back: my chamber
Of Venus was open to any man who was able.
And yet, remember, I wear Mars on my face
And also in another private place.   620
May God be guarantor of my salvation,
In making love I never used discretion,
But always followed after my appetite,
Whether a short man, or tall, or black, or white.
It made no difference, if I felt he wanted me,   625
How poor he was, or how high in the world he might be.
      "So what must I say? Before the month was over,
This jolly cleric, Jannkin, who had been my lover,
Became my husband, with great solemnity,
And I gave him all the lands, and all the deeds,   630
That others had given me, in years before,
Which later, how I regretted, my heart so sore,
For nothing I wanted mattered to him any more.
By God! Once he hit me right on the ear,
Because I tore a page from a book he held dear,   635
And that ear went deaf, slowly across the years.
But I was just as stubborn as a lioness,
And my chattering tongue stayed every bit as excessive,
And I'd walk out when I wanted, as I'd always done,
From house to house, no matter what he had ordered,   640
So he would often preach about my errors,
Quoting Roman tales of woes and terrors,
Like Símplicus Gállus, who walked away from his wife
And never returned, the entire rest of his life,
For nothing more than looking out the door   645
And seeing her with her head uncovered, and bare.
      "And another Roman—he told me, but I forget
His name—when his wife attended a sporting event
Without his knowledge, he too forswore her forever.
And then he'd rattle through his Bible pages,   650
Hunting the proverb where Ecclesiastes

Commands, in language strong and terms as harsh,
Husbands must keep their wives from walking at large.
And then he'd say, like this, in angry voice:
    "'Whoever builds his house of willow sticks,   655
And rides a dead-blind horse through well-ploughed strips
Of land, and lets his wife go seeking shrines,
Ought to be hanged for all his stupid crimes!'
But he was wasting his time, his classic quotations
Affected me no more than bugs on a basin,   660
Nor, sir, was I about to let him rule me.
A man reciting my vices can go climb a tree!
God knows, most women would cheerfully agree.
This drove him wild, he'd lose his temper completely,
Which made no difference, no one ever owned me.   665
    "But let me tell you, in truth, in Saint Thomas's name,
Why I ripped from his book that silly page,
For which he hit me, and made my ear go bad.
    "He had a book that he would read, and gladly,
Night and day, he loved that book so madly   670
He called it Valériús and Théophrástus—
And how those pages always made him laugh!
And there had been a cleric, once, in Rome,
A cardinal, now known as Saint Jerome,
Who wrote an angry book on Jovínián   675
Which also had to do with Tértulán,
Crisíppus, Trótulá, and Héloíse,
Who was an abbess somewhere close to Paris.
And there were Parables by Solomon,
And Ovid's *Art of Love,* and many more,   680
Bound together in one immense big book.
And every night and day you'd find him looking
There, when he had time, and some vacation,
And leisure from his worldly occupation,
Reading this book on the wickedness of wives.   685
He knew more legends of them, and of their lives,
Than tales of good wives written in the Bible.
There is no greater impossibility,
In truth, than clerics praising wives would be,
Unless the woman is a holy saint: 690

No other women deserve a word of praise.
Pictures of lion-killing show a living
Man. But what if a lion had painted the picture?
By God! If women had written as much as clerics,
They'd surely inscribe more wickedness of men   695
Than all the males from Adam on could defend.
The signs of Mercury and Venus produce
Two very different kinds of human youths,
For Mercury favors wisdom, and loves all science,
While Venus loves good parties, and huge expenses.   700
And simply because their marks are wholly opposed,
One being down will drive the other up.
Thus Venus rules when Pisces is climbing high,
And Mercury lies flat, helpless, deprived.
And Venus falls when Mercury is rising.   705
Clerics can never praise a creature of Venus,
And when these clerics grow old, and cannot do
Much more of Venus' work than their old shoes,
They sit themselves down, and write in their helpless dotage
Books about women unable to preserve a marriage!   710
     "But back to my purpose, and why I told you about
A book that caused my beating, with a rare good clout.
My husband, Jannkin, was reading a book one night,
Beside the fire (as much for heat as light),
The subject of which was Eve, whose wickedness   715
Brought all mankind to endless wretchedness,
Which then required that Jesus Christ be slain,
Everyone redeemed by his blood again.
You see? he was saying, here's the proof you can find
That women were the ruin of all mankind.   720
     "He read me, then, how Samson was shorn of his hair,
For while he slept, his sweetheart cut it with shears,
And that betrayal cost him both his eyes.
     "Then he read me (this is truth, not lies),
Of Hercules and lovely Dianeira,   725
Who accidentally set her man on fire.
     "He left out not a jot of the care and woe
Old Socrates had suffered because of both
His wives: Xantíppa threw hot piss on his head,

But the stupid man just sat there, as if quite dead,   730
Wiping his face and hair, afraid to say
Much more than, 'After thunder, here comes rain!'
    "He thought, maliciously, Phasípha's tale
Was sweet, because her lover was a bull.
Fy! No more, the story's far too grisly,   735
Horrible, disgusting, rather than silly.
    Clytemnestra's story he read with devotion:
Her husband had been at Troy, and sailed the ocean
To return; she welcomed him with a bath and a knife.
    He talked about Amphíoráx's wife,   740
He who died at Thebes because the Greeks
Were told his hiding place, as soon as she
Was given a golden necklace to tell his secret
(She tried to make sure that no one knew, but he
Was one of the Seven who fought against Thebes). The Greeks   745
Then nosed him out and killed him where he lay.
    He told me of Lívia and Lucíla, that day,
Both of whom caused their husbands' death by poison,
One for hate, the other for love. The first one,
Lívia, killed a husband who was in the way: 750
She loved her lover, her husband had to be hated.
Lucíla literally loved her husband to death:
She gave him a love-drink, to make him love her better;
He took it, went to bed, and never woke up
Again. Jannkin assured me this was no joke,   755
But just what husbands have always had to suffer.
    "And then he told me how Latúmyús,
One day, complained to his neighbor, Árriús,
That he had growing in his garden such
A tree that each of his wives, and he'd had three,   760
Had hanged themselves on its branches, for hate and malice.
'My dearest friend,' this Arrius fellow answered,
'Give me a shoot of this blessèd tree. I'll plant
The little stick in my garden, and make it grow.'
    "In a book more recent, my husband told me he'd read   765
Of wives who'd murdered husbands right in their bed,
And while the corpse was lying stiff on the floor
Had spent the night with their lovers, and loved them much more.

Some wives, he read, had killed with poisoned drinks.
He rattled off more murders than a man can think of,   770
And quoted them, with many more sayings and proverbs
Than grass can grow the whole world over, and herbs.
    " 'You're better off,' said he, 'to share your dwelling
With a savage lion or the foulest dragon than a helpmate
Wife who's always chattering and scolding.   775
It's better,' he said, 'to lie on the roof, in the cold,
Than down inside the house with an angry wife.
These women are so wicked, so fond of quarreling,
They hate what their husbands love, as they hate the devil.
A woman,' he'd say, 'throws her shame away   780
As soon as she undresses,' and then he'd say,
'A beautiful woman, who's also chaste and knows
Her place, is a golden ring in a sow's fat nose.'
Who could imagine, who could ever suppose,
The sorrow I felt in my heart, the woe and the pain?   785
    "And when I saw, at last, he'd never refrain
From reading that cursèd book, not all night through,
I suddenly yanked three pages out of the book
And threw them onto the floor, and also hit him
Right on the cheek, hard, with my balled-up fist,   790
So hard he fell down backward, landing right
In our fire. He came up roaring, and swift as lightning,
Fierce as any lion in the wood, he struck me
Flat on the head, a tremendous blow that knocked me
Straight to the floor, flat as if I were dead.   795
Then seeing how I did not move, stretched out,
Perfectly still, he was truly frightened, aghast,
And might have fled away, except at last
My eyes opened and I was able to breathe.
'O!' I said. 'And have you killed me, you sneaking   800
Thief? And for my land you've murdered me?
Before I die, bend down and kiss me, please.'
    "He came to me, and knelt himself at my side,
Saying, 'O dearest Alison, my bride,
So help me God! I'll never hit you again.   805
You forced me to it, you drove me to violence.
Forgive me, please, I beg you. Forgive me, dear wife.'

And then I hit him on the cheek, and smiled:
'Thief,' I said, 'thus I take my revenge.
Now I can die. My life is about to end.'   810
Somehow, at last, after much trouble and woe,
We managed to fold ourselves together and go
On living as one. He passed the bridle to my hand,
So I could govern both the house and land,
As well as his tongue, and also his hammering fist.   815
But I made him burn that book, and he went and did it.
And when my strength and skill had gotten me
Control of everything, and mastery,
And he had declared, 'My own true, dearest wife,
Do as you wish the entire rest of your life.   820
Keep your honor, and observe my rank and station,'
Why then, thereafter, we never again debated.
God help me so, I was as kind to him
As any wife from Denmark to India,
And also faithful, and so was he to me.   825
I pray to God, who sits in majesty,
To bless his soul, as he is given to mercy.
And now I'll tell my tale, if you want to hear it.'

Behold the exchange between the Friar and the Summoner

    The Friar laughed, when all of this had been heard:
"Now lady," he said, "as I have joy or bliss,   830
Your tale has a long preamble, I tell you this!"
And when the Summoner heard this jolly oath,
"Lo," he said, "by God's two arms, and by both!
A friar always sticks his nose in the broth.
Lo, good men, how flies and also friars   835
Will fall in every dish, always inquiring!
Why are you dragging in preambulation?
What! Amble, or trot, or hush or go sit down!
You're in the way of our pleasure, as befits a friar."
    "O really, Mister Summoner?" answered the Friar.   840
"Now by my faith, before we're done and we're leaving,
I'll tell you a couple of summoner tales, believe me,
You'll all be shaking with laughter, here in this place."

"Hear this, you Friar, I curse your ugly face,"
The Summoner said, "and I would say 'curse me'   845
If I kept myself from telling two or three
Of friars, before we come to Sittingbourne,
Tales to wrench your heart, and make you mourn;
I see that all your tolerance is gone."
    Our Host cried out, "Peace! And right away!   850
Now let the woman speak her tale this day.
You act as if you're drinking too much ale.
Now, lady, tell your tale, just as you wish."
    "I'm ready, sir," she said, "since you want to listen—
Assuming I have my leave from our worthy Friar."   855
    "O yes," he said, "proceed, and I will hear you."

THE WIFE OF BATH'S TALE

In ancient times, in the days of good King Arthur,
Of whom the British speak with grateful honor,
All this land of ours was filled with fairies.
The elf queen, with her jolly company,
Was often seen, dancing in soft green meadows.   5
That, at least, was the old account I've read,
And I speak, of course, of hundreds of years ago.
But now these elves are not to be found any more,
Since, these days, higher charity and prayers
By friar-beggars, and other holy friars   10
(Searching every land and every stream),
Are thick as dust motes speckled in the beams
Of sunshine, blessing halls, and kitchens, and bowers,
Cities, townships, castles, even high towers,
Villages and barns, ships, and dairies—   15
And this explains the absence of our fairies.
For where we used to see a strolling elf,
A friar-beggar, now, will walk himself,
Equally in afternoons and mornings,
Selling ritual prayers and holy things   20
As he goes walking through the lands allowed him.
Now women may go safely up and down.
In every bush, or under every tree,
There is no other demon, now, but he,
And he's no rapist: all he does is dishonor.   25
      And as it happened, this great king called Arthur,
Had in his house a lively bachelor,

Who once upon a time rode by a river,
And as his horse came slowly jogging along
He chanced to see a girl walking before him. 30
And strong as he was, no matter how hard she fought him,
Against her will he took her maidenhead.
Word of this crude and vicious violence spread,
And many people petitioned Arthur for his death.
And since that seems to have been the law in effect, 35
It was decreed that he should lose his head.
But Arthur's queen, and other ladies of grace,
Bombarded Arthur with such complaints that, in place
Of beheading, the king declared that the young man's fate
Would have to be decided by his queen: 40
He would live or die, exactly as she deemed.
     The queen then thanked the king with all her might,
And later, when she saw the time was right,
She spoke quite plainly to the waiting knight:
"Just now," she said, "you have no guarantee 45
Of either life or death. Which will it be?
I grant you your life, if you are able to give me
A statement of what we women most desire.
Be careful, keep the axe's blade from your neck!
But if you cannot give me an answer, as yet, 50
I grant you a year and one day to ride where you choose,
Seeking an adequate answer which you can use
On your return. But before you leave us here
I need your pledge that you will surely appear
On or before the time, on your knightly honor." 55
     These were not cheerful words; he sighed in sorrow,
Yet could no longer act as he was used to.
At last, with heavy heart, he was forced to choose
This strange new form of hunting. He could not refuse,
For whatever God might provide was his only hope. 60
He said his farewells, and started down the road.
     He asked at every house, and every place,
Anywhere he might be blessed with grace,
And learn whatever it was that women wanted.
But everywhere he went, confusion was boundless, 65
No two of those he questioned answered the same.

Some said what women wanted most was fame
And riches. Some said that honor was what they sought,
Some said that amorous play was their favorite course,
Some would say rich clothing, some pleasure in bed,   70
And often a wealthy widow, and often re-wed.
Some said that women's hearts were mostly eased
When we have been well flattered and well pleased.
And that comes close to the truth, I have to agree.
A man can win us best with flattery   75
And constant service, always at our elbow:
Those are snares that catch us, one and all.
　　　　Others said that what we love the best
Is freedom, doing what we choose, and blessed
With no one able to scold us afterward,   80
But only say we're wise and follow our hearts.
And truly indeed, no woman alive will accept
Blunt criticism, hitting our faults directly:
We'll kick a man like that, until it hurts.
This is the truth, and you will find it works,   85
For any woman deeply mired in sin
Wants to be told how pure she is, within.
　　　　Some others say our perfect joy and delight
Is a reputation for steadiness, and tight-mouthed
Secrecy, and sticking to the path we're on,   90
Never revealing whispered information.
But that's hot air, not worth a bony eel.
Pardon me, please: we women cannot conceal
A thing. Consider Midas—shall I tell the tale?
　　　　In one of his shorter stories, Ovid reveals   95
That Midas, under his long and flowing hair,
Had growing on his head two donkey ears,
A blemish he did his very best to hide,
Thus carefully, from public and private eyes,
For only his wife was allowed to know this fault.   100
He loved her dearly, and trusted her in thought
And deed. He begged her never to reveal
To any man the deformity he concealed.
　　　　She swore it, up and down, to the end of the world:
She'd never commit so villainous a sin,   105

Bringing down on her husband so awful a name,
For in the telling she would herself be shamed.
But nevertheless the secret drove her wild,
It almost killed her, always having to hide it,
She felt it swelling so sorely in her breast   110
That, surely, some day, words would break through her chest.
She did not dare say it to a living man,
And so, one day, into a marsh she ran,
Her heart burning as over the grass she came,
And like a heron, whose booming call is famous,   115
She set her lips down in the flowing stream:
"O never betray me, water, with what I reveal:
No one but you will ever hear my sigh.
My husband's head has a donkey's ear on each side.
O ah! My heart is whole again, it's out   120
At last! I couldn't have held it, without a doubt."
Thus you can see, though a woman holds it a while,
It has to be spoken, no secret stays inside us.
If you want the rest of this story, go to the poet,
And Ovid will tell you. If not, you'll never know it.   125
       My tale's about this knight, who when he saw
He could not find the answer he desperately sought
To this awesome question, what women want the most,
His spirits sank, his heart was sore: he was almost
Dead. So homeward he went, he could not delay,   130
The time for his return was only a day
Or two away. His head bent down, he rode
Along the edge of a forest, and saw a crowd
Of ladies dancing, two dozen or even more.
He quickly drew as near as he could get,   135
Hoping these fairy women would save him yet,
But before he actually reached them, all the dancers
Suddenly vanished, and the only sight his glancing
Eyes could see, sitting on the grass,
Was an ancient hag, as ugly as death, alas!   140
This awful creature rose, and went to meet him,
And said: "Sir knight, from here no roadway leads
To anywhere. So tell me what you are seeking.
Perhaps, who knows? I might be able to help you.

Older folks have wisdom stored on their shelves."   145
    "My dear old mother," replied the knight, "I'm sure
To die unless I am somehow able to procure
This knowledge: What do women want the most?"
    "Pledge me good faith," she said, "and give me your hand,
Swear that whatever favor I ask you'll grant me,   150
As long as it is something in your might,
And you'll have your answer before this day turns night."
    "You have my promise," said the knight. "I hereby grant it."
    "Now then," she said, "I'm able to safely boast
Your life is saved. You and I will go   155
Before the queen together, I at your side,
And the queen will agree with me, upon my life.
Let's see if even the proudest woman, tall
And wearing a jeweled headdresss over all,
Will dare deny what you've been taught to say.   160
Now we can go, I see no point to delay."
A secret message she whispered in his ear,
And told him he should be glad, and have no fear.
    And when they reached King Arthur's court, this knight
Announced his promise was kept, he'd come on time,   165
Well prepared to reply to the queen's hard question.
Many noble wives, and unmarried ladies,
Were gathered there, and widows, too, all waiting,
Many wise with long experience
Of marriage, anxious to hear whatever was said.   170
The queen herself was in front, sitting in justice.
The women were whispering low, their dresses rustling.
    The knight appeared, and the queen commanded silence,
Then ordered the knight to tell, in open audience,
What was the thing that women wanted most.   175
Speaking straight and clear, the knight answered,
In a manly voice, and all assembled could hear him.
    "My royal lady," he said, "what women want,
Most usually, is sovereign power in their hands,
Not only over husbands but whatever lovers   180
They take. They wish to be masters, high above them.
This is your strongest desire, though you may kill me
For telling this truth. You are the judge, your will

Is my rule." No wife, no girl, no widow denied
His answer. All agreed that he'd saved his life 185
And ought to be freed. And at those words, the old wife,
Who'd waited patiently with the other women,
Quickly rose to her feet and approached the queen:
"Mercy," she said, "my sovereign lady supreme!
Before your court adjourns, affirm my rights. 190
It was I who taught his answer to this knight,
For which he gave me his vow, both then and there,
The very first thing I asked of him, he'd swear
To do it, if it was something he could do.
Accordingly, in front of this court, my true 195
And faithful knight, I ask you to make me your wife.
You're well aware that I have saved your life.
If I am lying, deny this wish, by your faith!"
     This knight replied: "Alas! and wellaway!
I can't deny it, it's what I promised to do. 200
For the love of God, ask anything else you choose!
My wealth is yours, if you let my body go."
     "No," she declared. "I'd have to curse us both!
For though I am ugly, poor, and very old,
I spurn the gold, the silver, the jewels, and the ore 205
Beneath the ground, and even high above it.
I wish to be your wife, and have your love."
     "My love?" said he. "O no, but my damnation!
Alas! That someone of my birth and station
Should ever be thus fouled in high disgrace!" 210
But all for naught. The trap could not be escaped,
He had no choice. And so these two were wed,
And he took his ancient wife, and went to bed.
     Now here, some people might say that I neglect
My audience, who rightfully expect 215
A full description of their wedding day,
Its joys—the food, the clothes. It wasn't that way.
For better or worse, there was no party, no play,
No feast, there was no joy at all, that day,
Just somber heaviness, and endless sorrow. 220
The marriage was made next morning, all in good order,
But privately, and no one else was there.

And then the rest of the day he hid like an owl,
It brought him such woe, seeing his wife so foul.

His mind was woefully afflicted, his thoughts 225
All dismal when, inevitably, he was brought
To bed with her; he tossed from side to side.
His wife lay still and, all at peace, said smiling,
"O my dear husband, heaven bless us both!
Is every knight, indeed, so terribly loath 230
With his wife? Is this the law of Arthur's house?
Are all his knights so fearful, bold as a mouse?
I am your righteous love and also your wife,
And I am also she who saved your life,
And certainly I've never done you a wrong. 235
Just why are you so weak, when you should be strong?
You're acting like a man who's lost his mind.
What have I done? Tell me, please, I pray you,
And whatever it is, I'll cure it, if I may."

"Cure it?" said this knight. "Alas, O no! 240
Nothing can be done for ever more.
You are so ugly, and also very old,
And even worse, you surely must be born
To peasant parents. How can you even wonder
At my sorrow? O God, just break my heart asunder!" 245

"Is this," she said, "the cause of your unrest?"
"O yes," said he, "this is surely it."
"Now sir," she said, "these are things I can fix,
If I wish to—three days at most. I can do this quickly,
If you can treat me as well as I prefer. 250

"But since you mention the noble line you're heir to,
Descended out of riches, down the years,
Your words should come from the hearts of gentlemen:
Such arrogance is really not worth a hen!
Whoever is truly a man of virtue, whether 255
In public or private, should always strive to be better
And do whatever noble deeds he can.
No one but he should be thought a gentleman.
Nobility, says the Lord, should be based on our souls,
Not claimed because of what our fathers owned. 260
They certainly can leave us all their gold,

And we can say we came of noble folk,
But ancestors cannot bequeath their virtue,
Which made them gentlemen. That is the truth:
A virtuous life must come from a virtuous soul,   265
Which no one on earth can inherit, no one at all.
    "And on this topic, the wisest poet of Florence,
Whose name is Dante, can speak with noble purpose:
Lo, here are Dante's words in my translation:
"Personal efforts alone can seldom raise   270
A man, for God, in heavenly goodness, wishes
Us to claim nobility from him."
What we can claim to inherit, in truth, is no more
Than merely worldly things, which men can destroy.
    "And every man knows this as well as I do: 275
If nobility were implanted in a certain line
Of descent, separate and apart, Nature
Would make sure that all such men were virtuous,
Unable to practice vice or villainy.
    "Carry fire to the very darkest house   280
From here to the far-off mountains of Caucasus,
Then shut the doors and leave. The fire will go on
Blazing and burning just as high and hot
As if some thousands of men were there to watch it.
What nature gives it to do, the fire will go on   285
Doing, I swear by my life, until it's gone.
    "Thus you may see, with crystal clarity,
That nobleness is not attached to money,
For people, plainly, do not always act
The same, as fire does. And these are facts.   290
God knows, we sometimes see a nobleman's son
Steeped in shame, behavior infamous.
He who celebrates nobility
That he was born to, in a noble line,
Where every man was noble, true, refined,   295
But won't behave as noble men must be,
And as his fathers lived, in nobility,
He is not noble, although he bears a title:
Ignoble deeds turn noblemen to triflers.
Nobility you claim because your fathers   300

Had it, earned by constant goodness and other
Virtues, isn't yours if you have not lived it.
This is a blessing that only God can give.
He is the source of nobility, by grace;
There's no connection to titles, place, or station.   305
    "Remember, as old Valerius tells us, how gracious
Cicero made himself, born to no station,
Rising from poverty to noble high place.
Read Seneca, and also Boethius,
And find, expressly framed, this simple truth: 310
A man is noble who behaves with virtue.
    "And so, dear husband, the lesson must be learned:
Although my fathers were nothing, poor, unlearned,
High God may grant me, I hope, a noble state,
Because my life is virtuous, by his grace.   315
A man becomes a noble when he begins
To live his life in virtue, and gives up sin.
    "And as for your assertion that, being poor,
I must be nothing, God himself, for sure,
Chose to live his life in poverty.   320
And every man and girl, wife and widow,
Can comprehend that Jesus would not live
A vicious life, for he is heaven's king.
Happy poverty is an honorable thing,
As Seneca and many clerics have said.   325
A poor man satisfied, his days not sad,
To me is rich, although he does not own
The shirt on his back. A greedy man has a soul
Of poverty, wanting what isn't his.
But a man with nothing, who wants no more than he has,   330
Is rich, although you call him a dirty slave.
Poverty that's honest sings its own song,
As Juvenal cheerfully says, and he's not wrong:
"The poor man, merrily going on his way,
Surrounded by thieves, can sing and dance and play."   335
Not that poverty is good: it's hateful,
Piling care and woe on a poor man's back.
But poverty can also cure a lack
Of wisdom, for one who lives it in calm and peace.

Wretched as it is, no one will steal it,   340
No one will fight to have it, no law will repeal it.
And poverty, although it knocks you over,
Can help you know yourself, and God's great love.
It works like a pair of glasses, and lets you see
How many friends are true, how many will grieve you.   345
And so, sir, since I haven't brought you grief,
I ask you, on this subject, to hold your peace.
    "Now, sir, you've also reprimanded me
For being old. I cannot cite you written
Words, but surely noble men are bidden,   350
Generally, to honor agèd folk,
And call them 'father,' a mark of honor you know
They like. If you wish, I'll find some authors to show you.
    "You say that I am ugly and old; I admit it;
But you can be sure I'll never be anyone's mistress.   355
And filth and age are preventatives, you see,
Helpful guardians of chastity.
But knowing, now, more clearly what you desire,
I will proceed with my plan to satisfy you.
    "Now choose," she said, "according to your will: 360
Either you have me ugly and old, until
I die, remaining a true and humble wife,
And never displease you, across the length of my life,
Or else, if you wish me young and captivating,
You'll take your chances with all the men just waiting   365
For me to fall, here in your house, or elsewhere.
    "Take your choice, sir. Tell me, let me hear it."
    The knight sat contemplating, with heavy sighs.
Then finally he said (will you be surprised?):
"My lady and my love, my wife so dear,   370
I'll let you answer these questions, you see more clearly,
And so I ask you to make the choice yourself,
Whatever may bring both pleasure and honor to our selves.
It does not matter to me, your choice will be right,
I'll leave it to you, and be more than satisfied."   375
    "Then I will be in power, not you?" she said.
I will choose and govern as I think best?"
    "Yes, certainly," he said. "That's what I wish."

"Kiss me," she said. "There's no more anger left.
For by my faith, you'll have both choices and more: 380
I will be beautiful, and good as gold.
Let God on high drive me insane, and dead,
If I'm not good and true as any wife wed
Since ever this world was fashioned, bright and new.
When I walk out, tomorrow, people will view   385
A woman lovely as any empress or queen
Between the east and west of the world, seen
As a lady, or you can treat me however you wish.
Now lift the curtain, see just how it is."

  And then the knight could tell it really was true,   390
She had become a beauty, and his two arms
Reached out and wrapped around her. He kissed her, too,
Perhaps a thousand times in a row, or more.
And when they fell to making love, he led
The way, and she obeyed, and they rocked the bed.   395

  And this is how they lived, till life was ended,
In perfect joy. And Jesus, may he send us
Obedient husbands, young, and fresh in bed,
And give us grace to live on, when they are dead.
And I also pray that Jesus shorten their lives   400
Who do not allow themselves to be ruled by their wives.
And foul old misers, angry at a wife's expense,
May God—this moment!—send them a pestilence!

THE FRIAR'S PROLOGUE

This worthy beggar-friar, this noble Friar,
Constantly wore a frown whenever he stared
At the Summoner, but preserving dignity
He'd spoken no vulgar words. But finally
He said, addressing himself to the Wife of Bath: 5
    "Lady, God give you good life, and never his wrath!
You've touched, by God, and spoken most interestingly
On scholarly topics of serious difficulty.
You've made some very useful remarks, I say.
But lady, while we're riding along the way   10
We're better off, when we speak, to amuse ourselves,
And leave the scholarship, by God's own self,
To those who preach and those who study scripture.
If it's of interest, my friends, I'll paint a picture
Of a summoner. Of course, you know that name   15
Is linked with wicked things, and always with shame:
I hope you won't be displeased, hearing this tale.
A summoner goes running up and down,
Serving criminal summons for fornication,
And takes a beating at every end of town."   20
    Our Host then said: "Ah, sir, you must be polite,
Courteous, as a man with a worthy title.
Here in this company, we'll have no fighting.
Tell your tale and let the Summoner be."
    "No," the Summoner said, "let him say to me   25
Whatever he likes. Then, when I take my turn,
By God! I'll say such things his ears will burn!

I'll make it clear exactly how much honor
Goes with being a flattering beggar-friar,
And I'll describe a number of different crimes   30
Which do not require description, not at this time.
And I'll tell you what his duties involve, by God."
    Our Host replied: "Peace, this will have to stop."
And after this he turned to the Friar, and said:
"Please tell us your tale, my master, as we move on ahead."   35

THE FRIAR'S TALE

Some time ago, in my own town, there dwelled
A bishop's enforcer, titled archdeacon, hellishly
Fierce at punishing all sorts of crimes,
Like fornication, witchcraft (black and white),
Pimps, procurers, panders, and go-betweens,   5
Slander and defamation, and adultery,
Stealing from churches, but also probation of wills,
All manner of contracts, people found unwilling
To keep their vows, obtaining church office by selling
And buying, and usury. He was hardest on lechers   10
And other sex offenders (he enforced to the letter),
And those whose tithes were less than they should be
(Turned in by neighbors and ancient enemies).
When it came to fines, no possibility
Escaped him: cheating on tithes and offerings   15
In church were punished hard, he made them sing!
Before they reached the bishop's episcopal hook,
Offenders were enrolled in the archdeacon's book,
For he possessed, by virtue of jurisdiction,
Power to make them suffer his brand of correction.   20
He had a ready summoner at hand,
No rascal craftier in this British land,
For he'd created a skilful net of spies,
Who watched for him as they roamed (procurement eyes).
A turncoat pair of lechers he could spare,   25
Since they could help him catch two dozen more.
And though our Summoner here may foam at the mouth,

I'll tell his wickedness from north to south.
We friars can't be touched by his correction,
We're not included in their jurisdiction, 30
Nor will we ever come between their claws.
    "Saint Peter! So are panderers and whores,"
The Summoner said, "exempt from all our laws!"
"Peace!" Thus said our Host. "This is bad luck,
And bad fortune, too! Let him go on. No talking! 35
Friar, proceed, ignore this Summoner's wailing,
And don't hold back, my master, dear and able."
    This lying thief, this summoner, said
The Friar, had plenty of pimps and panders ready
At hand; like hawks that swoop from out of view 40
They hunted secrets, and told him all they knew
(For their acquaintance wasn't anything new).
They were his unknown agents, secret spies,
And money flowed to his hands, as if from their eyes;
The summoner's master knew just part of his gain. 45
He needed no summons, with ignorant man or maiden:
They feared him, knowing they should be afraid.
Indeed, they were glad enough to fill his purse,
And cheerfully paid for drinks and snacks at the alehouse.
Just as Judas had a purse that was always 50
Empty, and also was a thief, theft was his trade.
His master got one half of the money paid him.
This summoner, to give him praise he's owed,
Was summoner and thief, and also a bawd.
And the girls he had in his hand would always report— 55
Whether they lay with Sir Robert, Sir Hugh, or Jack
Or Ralph, whoever they were—who'd been in the sack
With them. Thus he and the girl were on the same track.
Whatever they told him, he'd use to issue a note
For fornication, haul them both to court, 60
Release the girl, and rob the fellow blind.
And then he'd tell him, "Friend, with your welfare in mind,
I'll strike your name out of my archdeacon's book,
And you'll be spared all further trouble. But look,
I am your friend. Call me whenever you need to." 65
He had an expert's touch, in bribery,

More craft, than I can tell in a year of talking.
In spotting which deer to chase, no hunting dog
Could better rely on his nose than this man, knowing
Who were sinners and who he should ignore. 70
And since those scents were sources for his living,
To them his hours, both day and night, were given.
        And so it happened, once upon a day,
This summoner, who always watched for prey,
Went riding after an ancient widow, not 75
For actual sin, but something he would concoct.
And as he rode along, by chance he saw,
Ahead on the road, when passing through a forest,
A groom, who bore a bow and shining arrows,
Sharpened and keen. His shortcoat was green, the hat 80
He wore upon his head had fringes of black.
        "Sir," said this summoner, "hail and very well met!"
        "Welcome," the groom replied, "to all good fellows!
Where are you headed, under these green-wood shadows?
Have you some far-off place in mind today?" 85
        This summoner answered him, and said, "Nay,
Really not much farther from here. I intend
To ride there, because I need to collect a rent
Owed to my master, and longish over-due."
        "Are you, then, a bailiff?" "Yes," said he, 90
Not daring, for its very filth and shame,
To say his post was summoner, by name.
        "In the name of God," declared this groom, "dear brother,
You are a bailiff, and I, dear friend, am another.
I don't know much about this county of yours, 95
So if you'd like an acquaintance, I'd be glad for that,
And brotherhood, too, if that would suit you better.
I've gold and silver stored away in my chest,
So if, by chance, you ride across to our shire,
I'll give you whatever you need, as you desire." 100
        "Many thanks!" this summoner said, "by my faith!"
And then they solemnly shook hands, and said
They'd be sworn brothers all the rest of their lives.
They fell to chatting, enjoying themselves while riding.
        This summoner was a man as full of babble 105

As butcher-birds are ripe with malice and venom;
He could not keep himself from asking questions.
     "Brother," he said, "where would I find your house,
Some other day, if I came and sought you out?"
     The groom's deep voice, as he answered, turned mild and soft: 110
     "Brother," he said, "it's very far in the north,
But I hope to see you there, if you do ride forth.
Before we leave, I'll tell you all of this,
So when you ride up there, you'll never miss it."
     "Now, brother," this summoner said, "Let me pray you,   115
Teach me—as we're riding along the way,
Since you are truly a bailiff, as am I—
Some trick of the trade, with all the nice details,
So I can use it in this post I'm in.
And please don't hesitate, for conscience or sin,   120
But tell me, as my brother, how you work it."
     "Now truly, brother dear," the groom replied,
"Since I, as a matter of course, can't tell you a lie,
My wages are very low; they've stayed so for years.
My lord is hard to deal with, as befits a peer,   125
And what I do requires such great exertion
That my livelihood, in fact, is earned by extortion.
Indeed, I take whatever men will give me.
Somehow, by sheer deceit, or violent means,
From year to year I manage to earn what I need.   130
Truly, in faith, I cannot put it better."
     "The same," this summoner said, "for me, too,
That's how it is. I take what I can, I do,
Unless it's maybe too heavy or even too hot.
Whatever I can squeeze, in daylight or darkness,   135
I worry no more for conscience than a fox or a shark.
Without extortion, indeed, I'd surely be dead,
And I never confess these sins," he proudly said.
"I can't be bothered with conscience or compassion:
The devil with these priestly father confessors!   140
We're well met, I say, by God and Saint James!
And now, dear brother, I wish you'd tell me your name,"
This summoner said. And then the groom began
To smile, a slow and sober, dangerous grin.

"Brother," he said, "do you really want me to tell?   145
I am a devil, and the place I live in is hell.
On earth I ride about, looking for business,
Searching for men who'll give me what's in their interest.
All my profit depends upon this income.
And you are riding about for this same reason,   150
To get what you can, no matter person or season.
I do exactly the same, for I would go
To the end of the earth to catch myself a soul."
    "Ah!" this summoner said. "God bless me! Really?
To me you seemed a groom, really and truly.   155
You looked exactly like a man like me.
Have you some regular shape, a body you use
In hell, when you are doing whatever you do?"
    "Certainly not," he said. "Why would we ever
Need a body? But we take on whatever   160
Shape we like, or make you believe we're human,
Or like an ape, and we can even assume
An angel's shape, and use it here in this world.
It's neither marvelous nor even absurd:
A lousy juggler can make your head go spinning,   165
And really, if he and I competed, I'd win."
    "But why not pick yourself a regular shape,
So whether you ride or walk, you'll look the same?"
    "We have a purpose," he said. "We change our shape
To whatever helps us most in catching prey."   170
    "But why take on this very strenuous labor?"
    "Many reasons, my dear sir summoner,"
The devil answered, "but all things have their time,
The day is short, the sun is already shining
Bright, and I've earned nothing at all, as yet.   175
Let me stick to business and see what I get,
And not just ride, while trading information.
Because, dear brother, I see your mind's not able
To fully understand whatever I told you.
But since you ask just why we work so hard: 180
Sometimes we're servants of God, his instruments
And means for enforcing high and heavy commandments,
At his great pleasure, upon his human creatures,

Employing different devices and different figures.
We have no way of defiance, dealing with him,   185
We cannot reject whatever command he sends us.
But sometimes, when we ask it, we have his leave
To torment a body, leaving the soul quite free,
As witness the case of Job, to whom we brought pain.
Sometimes we're given even fuller reign,   190
Comprising body and soul together. And then,
Sometimes, our powers are strictly limited
To a soul; the body we may not touch. The list
Is endless, you see, and always for the best.
A man who stands and fights our sweet temptation   195
Will find, in time, the strength for his salvation,
That being not our purpose, not at all,
For what we're after is his filthy soul.
Sometimes, alas, we're forced to serve you men,
As once we were to Bishop Saint Dunstan,   200
And I was servant to Saint Paul, by God."
        "Tell me," said this summoner, "straight and hard,
Do you always make new bodies, like yours, of basic
Elements?" The devil said: "We change it.
Sometimes it's all deceit, sometimes we rise   205
From the ground, in very dead bodies, in various styles,
Speaking as fluently, and fair, and well,
As the Witch of Endor was once addressed by Samuel
(Though some of your doctors of theology
Say different—the devil with your divinity!).   210
But let me warn you, this is not a trick:
You'll have the chance to see the heart of this.
Give yourself time, dear brother, for you will later
Reside where all this information is plain.
Your own experience, by then, will teach you   215
Professorial knowledge so full, so deep,
That even a living Virgil could not reach,
Nor Dante, either. Now let us ride on quickly,
For I would like to stay in your company
Until, however it happens, you leave me."   220
        "O no," this summoner said, "that won't be the case.
I am a person known all over this place,

And I will stick to my vow. Though you were the devil
Satan, I promised you, and I'll hold myself
To my vow, to be your brother, as you have to me,   225
And we are sworn to all eternity,
True brothers both, riding along this ground,
Ready to take whatever's ready and is found.
You take your share, whatever they wish to give,
And I'll take mine, and so we both may live.   230
And if it happens that either has more than the other,
Let him be faithful, and share it with his brother."

     "Agreed," the devil said, "and by my faith."
And with those words they rode along their way.
And just before they reached the village limits   235
(The neighborhood this summoner planned to visit),
They saw a cart well loaded up with hay,
And which the carter meant to carry that day.
The road was deeply rutted, the wheels stuck fast,
The horses couldn't move them, so the carter lashed out: 240
"Giddee up, Badger! Hey, Scot! Don't stop for these stones!
The devil," he said, "may take you, body and bones,
From top to bottom, nose to hooves! Have you ever
Been worth as much as you eat? Likely you never
Will! Take all, horses, cart, and hay!"   245

     This summoner thought: "Here's a game we can play."
He rode right up to the devil, feeling no fear,
Bent over and whispered right in the devil's ear:
"Listen, brother, listen, by your faith!
Don't you hear the things this carter's saying?   250
Go take it all, he's given you everything,
The hay and the cart, and three good horses to boot."

     "No," the devil answered, "God knows it's not true.
The carter doesn't mean those words. Trust me.
Ask him. Do you find it hard to credit me?   255
Or else just wait a while, and then you'll see."

     The carter whacked his horses across their backs,
And they began to draw, the cart advanced.
"Hey now!" he said. "May Jesus Christ come bless you,
As he blesses every man, greater and lesser!   260
Badger, my boy, my own, you pulled like a beauty.

May God save you and bless you, for doing your duty!
By God, my cart is out of the ditch, all's well!"
    "Lo, brother," the devil said, "what did I tell you?
Here you can see, my very own dear brother,   265
The peasant said one thing, but he meant another.
Now let us ride along, the rest of our voyage;
There's nothing here for me, no horse, no carriage."
    When they had ridden out of town a bit,
This summoner turned to the devil and carefully whispered: 270
"Brother," he said, "a cranky old widow lives here,
Who'd almost rather break her neck than spare
A single penny out of her slender purse.
I want twelve pence, no matter how she curses,
Or else I'll summon her to the archdeacon's court,   275
Although as far as I know she's done no wrong.
Now watch: no stranger here can earn his keep,
So notice well my method for getting my fee."
    This summoner rang the bell on the widow's gate:
"Come out," he said, "and show your wicked old face!   280
I know you're sharing your bed with some priest or friar."
    "Who's ringing?" asked the old woman. "God bless my soul!
God save you, sir, what are you looking for?"
    "Here," he said, "I hold in my hand a summons.
You've been accused of cursing, so you, old woman,   285
Are called to come to court tomorrow, and bend
Your knees and answer well for your many sins."
    "Now Lord," she said, "O Jesus, king of kings,
I'm weak, I need your help with wicked things.
I've been so sick, I've lain in bed for days.   290
I'm barely able to walk. How could I ride?
A horse's bobbing would stab me in the side.
I ask you, please, for a copy of your bill,
And though I cannot appear, my lawyer will,
And deal with everything I've been accused of."   295
    "Yes," this summoner said, "let's see, I've reviewed
The charges. Pay me twelve pence, that will do it.
There's not a lot for me, my master's eye
Is sharp, he takes the biggest share, not I.
So come and pay me, let me ride away.   300

Give me twelve pence, I haven't got all day."

"Twelve pence!" she said. "Now Mary, mother of God,
Surely you will help me out of this bog
Of sin. The wide world's gold may fall on this floor,
And I would still have nothing, just as before.   305
And you know well that I am poor and old.
Have mercy on this woeful, poor old wretch."

"Now then!" he said. "The devil himself come fetch me
If I release you. Sin must pay its bills."

"Alas!" she said. "God knows I am not guilty."   310

"Pay me," he said, "pay me right on the spot,
Or I will carry off your brand-new pot,
Since your account with me is already in debt.
When you were sleeping with every other fellow
In town, I paid your fine. What's under your pillow?"   315

"You're lying!" she said. "By my every hope of salvation,
Until this moment, neither as widow nor wife,
Have I been brought to court in all my life.
And never have I been anything but true
With my body. The devil, black and rough, take you!   320
I give him your body, and give him my pot—that too!"

Hearing these curses, uttered on bended knees,
The devil suddenly spoke. "Now tell me, please,
Mabel my dear, my own dear mother, pray,
Do you mean, in truth, these words I heard you saying?   325

"The devil," she said, "can come and fetch him right here
—Him and my pot—unless he repents sincerely!"

"No, you old cow, repentance is not on my mind,
I don't regret a thing. What's yours is mine,
I want your clothes as well as your pots and pans!"   330

"Now brother," the devil said, "please don't be mad,
Your body, and this pot, are now mine by right.
And you will be in hell with me, tonight,
And learn much more about our devilish ways
Than doctors of the church, may God be praised."   335

And, saying this, the foul devil took him.
Body and soul, he went where devilish hooks
Are waiting for summoners, their heritage.
May God, who made mankind in his own image,

Save and wisely guide us, all and some,   340
And let these summoners righteous men become!
    Gentlemen, this Friar said, I could
Have told you, had I leisure, things that would
Have filled your hearts with terror—taking it all
From texts by Jesus, Saint John, and by Saint Paul,   345
And many other masters of holy writ—
Detailing the pain of existence in hell. But that
Would take a thousand winters, all and entire.
To keep yourself from burning in those fires,
Wake, and pray to Jesus for his grace,   350
And may he keep us out of Satan's embrace.
Just listen to this! Take care, as it is said:
"The lion is lying in ambush, he is always
Prepared to kill an innocent, if he may."
You must prepare your hearts, so they can withstand   355
The devil, forever ready to find and grab you.
Though he is stronger than any single man,
Christ can save you, we all know he can.
And pray that all these summoners repent
Before they're gone, for we know where they went!   360

THE SUMMONER'S PROLOGUE

This Summoner stood up high upon his stirrups,
So angry at the Friar, his heart stirred up,
That like an aspen leaf he shook with ire.
    "Gentlemen," he said, "all I desire,
And I beseech, is now your calm attention—   5
Having heard this Friar's false inventions—
To what, with your permission, I now will tell you.
This Friar boasts how much he knows of hell,
By God, that's no surprise, no one will wonder,
For friars and fiends are hard to tear asunder.   10
Please pardon me, I'm sure you've heard men tell
How, once, a friar's spirit was swept to hell
In a nighttime vision, where he was led about
By an angel, carefully taking him up and down,
Showing torment, and souls both burning and bound.   15
Wherever the friar looked, no friars were found,
Though plenty of people met suffering and woe.
And so he asked the angel to tell him more:
    "Sir," he said, "do friars have such grace
That none of them are ever seen in this place?"   20
    "O yes," said the angel, "friars are here by the million!"
And then he led him to where huge Satan was lying.
"You see," he said, "that Satan has a tail
Broader across than a tall ship's flapping sail.
Lift up your tail, you Satan, there!" said he.   25
"Open up your ass so this friar can see
The friar's nest, and where it's kept in this place!"

In less than a minute, so quickly they came passing,
Like buzzing bees swarming from a hive,
Twenty thousand friars came tumbling, driving   30
Out of the hole in Satan's enormous ass,
Running all over hell, then just as fast
As they'd been rushing out, came hurrying back,
And crept, the whole great lot, up into his ass.
Satan slapped down his tail and again lay still.   35
      This friar, after seeing more than his fill
Of horrible pain and torments in this sorry place,
Found his spirit restored, by God's great grace,
And inhabiting his body. He quickly awoke.
But all the same he lay there trembling, he shook   40
With fear of the devil's ass, for it burned in his mind
That this was the destination of all his kind.
God save you all—except this cursèd Friar!
This prologue to my tale will end right there.

THE SUMMONER'S TALE

Gentlemen, in Yorkshire, more or less,
You'll find a marshy place called Holderness,
And there a beggar-friar went about,
Preaching—but mostly begging, I have no doubt.
And so it happened, one fine day, this friar   5
Had been in a church, and preached—in his own manner—
And especially, above all other things,
He stirred the people, in what he called his preaching,
To open their purses and give, for God's own sake,
Funds with which the friar Orders could make   10
More houses, and friar service receive due honor,
Not wasted, as in churches, consumed, devoured.
He stressed there was no need for them to give
To priests or monks, for they are clerics who live,
May God be praised, in wealth and true abundance.   15
"Our masses for the dead," he told them, "lift penance
From dear ones' souls, old as well as young.
But when a mass is hurried, hastily sung,
It makes the priest important, he laughs, he's gay—
Remember, *he* sings only one a day.   20
We need to free those souls: deliver all souls!
Think of your loved ones speared on hooks, clawed
By iron spikes, burned and baked and raw.
Give us the money to help them, by God's own soul!"
And when the friar had said whatever he meant to,   25
He murmured part of a prayer, in Latin, and left:
When congregations had clearly given their all,

He took the money and headed down the road.
    Bearing his pointed staff, his robe tucked high,
From house to house he peeked and poked and pried,   30
Begging flour, or cheese, or unthreshed grain.
The partner he was required to beg with would make
A record, writing on marble tablets coated
With wax, his stylus fine and polished; he noted
Every name of every person who gave them   35
Anything worth while, as though he engraved
For helping remember names in his prayers for atonement.
This partner's staff had a point of ivory horn.
"Give us a bushel of wheat, or malt, or rye,
A little God cake, or else a chunk of cheese—   40
Whatever you like, we're not the least bit choosey:
Half a penny for God, a penny for a mass,
Or a piece of pork, if there's any in your house.
A piece of undyed wool you've spun, good wife,
My dearest sister—see, I've just inscribed   45
Your name! Bacon, or beef, whatever you find."
    They had a sturdy servant, who walked behind them,
Bearing a large and well-sewn brownish sack.
Whatever they got, he carried it on his back.
But as soon as the writer of names was out the door,   50
He planed away whatever he'd written before,
Each and every name of every donor:
Every word he said was a lie and a fraud.
    "That's a lie, you Summoner!" the Friar said.
    "Peace!" said our Host, "by the Virgin Mother's head!   55
Keep on with your tale, and whack away as you like."
    "O that's what I'll do," said the Summoner, "by God's own life!
    The Friar kept walking, house by house, till he
Had reached a home where he could expect to be
Refreshed far better than hundreds of other places.   60
The good man was sick, he for whom this place
Was home; he lay on a couch, and could not rise.
    "May God be here!" said the Friar. "O Thomas, my wise
Good friend!" He spoke in a courteous voice, and softly.
"Thomas," he said, "I pray that God restore you!   65
How often, here on this bench, I've been well treated,

How often, here, I've eaten merry meals."
And off the bench he pushed a sleeping cat,
And lay down both his staff and his well-worn hat,
As well as his holy texts, then sat himself down.   70
His partner had gone ahead, walking to town
Along with their servant, to an inn where they would try,
The three of them, that night, for a bed they could lie in.
    "My master dear," the sick man said, "how
Has it been with you, since March came blowing in?   75
I haven't seen you in a pair of weeks, or more."
"God knows," the Friar said, "I've labored hard and sore,
Especially for you, and your salvation.
I've uttered many a precious prayer and vocation
For other friends as well, God bless them all!   80
Today I attended mass at your church; I was called
To the pulpit, I spoke the kind of simple sermon
I'm known for, not according to gospel words.
Still, you may find it hard to understand,
So let me tell you the message I had planned—   85
An explanation is surely a glorious thing,
For as we clerics say, words can be killing.
What I have taught is the need for charity,
Give where goodness is simple and plain to see.
And then I saw our wife. Ah, where is she?"   90
    "Yonder in the yard, I guess she'd be,"
Her husband said, "and she'll be coming soon."
    "Hey, my master, you're welcome, by Saint John!"
The good wife said. "Truly, how are you doing?"
    Full curteously, the Friar rose and threw   95
His arms around her, and hugged her very tight,
And kissed her sweetly, like a sparrow lightly
Chirping. "Good wife," he said, "I'm very well,
Remaining your servant most heartily in all
I do. May God be thanked for your life and soul!   100
I looked around the church, today, and none,
My dear, were nearly as pretty as you, by my soul!"
    "May God remove my faults, sir," answered she.
"In any case, you're always welcome, in faith!"
"Thank you, good wife, I've always found it so.   105

But of your goodness, now, and by your leave
—I hope I won't annoy you, or cause you grief—
I wish to spend a little time with Thomas.
These priests are far too lazy, slow, and pompous,
They never set themselves, in confession, to grope   110
A tender soul. But preaching's where I work hardest,
Meditating Peter's words, and Paul's.
I walk, yes, but I fish for Christian souls,
Working for Jesus, and eager souls to send him.
To spread Christ's words is always my attempt."   115
     "Then by your leave, dear sir," she said, "scold him
Soundly, for by Saint Trinity, he's bold
And angry as a biting ant, although
He wants for nothing, whatever he desires
I give him, I always cover him warm, at night,   120
And I rest either my leg or arm at his side,
But he groans just like our boar, out in the sty.
No more than that; I get exactly nothing;
He takes no pleasure in me, or in anything."
     "O Thomas, I say to you, Thomas! Thomas!   125
You're helping the devil, this must be changed, I promise you!
Anger is something God in heaven forbids,
And so, for a little, I'll turn my attention to this."
     "Now, master," asked the wife, "before I go,
What would you like to eat? I'll have it done."   130
     "Now wife," he said, "It's good of you to mention,
But all I really need is some capon liver,
And your soft bread—but just the tiniest sliver,
And after that the roasted head of a pig—
Although I'd rather no beast were killed for me—   135
Such plain and homely food would make a fine meal.
I am really not a man who cares a good deal
For food. My spirit feeds upon the Bible.
Constant rising at night, for saying prayers,
Is sure to weaken appetites, it wears   140
Us down. I hope this friendly advice of mine,
Thus freely offered, causes you no pain.
By God! I speak like that to a very few."
     "Now sir," she said, "I have a few words for you,

Before you're alone with Thomas. Two weeks ago,   145
My little son died. It was after you had gone."
    "I saw his death," said the Friar, "in a revelation,
When I was at home, in our dormitory. It can't
Be more than an hour later, I saw God grant him
Bliss in heaven. Praise the Lord forever!   150
So too our sexton saw it, and the holy friar
Who tends our infirmary, both of them holy
Men, the sexton for fifty years—and wholly
On that account, he is allowed to walk
Alone, wherever it pleases him to talk   155
And rest, or happily sing songs for God.
My brothers and I climbed out of bed (my cheeks
Were wet with tears). Without any drums to beat
Or bells to ring, we sang a pure *Te Deum,*
And nothing else, only our words to praise Him,   160
Except that I sent a passionate prayer to Christ,
Thanking him for his visionary advice.
For trust me, good wife and husband, our prayers have effects,
And we are allowed to see, at Christ's direction,
Things unseen by non-religious folk,   165
Not even by kings. We bear the heavy yoke
Of poverty, we practice abstinence,
While ordinary men have huge expenses
For meat and drink, and other such excesses.
The world's desires take no hold in our hearts.   170
Lazar the beggar, and wealthy Dives, lived
Two different lives, rewarded with different gifts.
For proper prayers, a man must fast and be clean,
And fatten his soul as he keeps his body lean.
We follow Paul, the apostle: clothing and food   175
Are enough for us, whether they're bad or good.
The purity and fasting of holy friars
Persuades Lord Christ to always hear our prayers.
    "Lo! Moses fasted for forty days and nights
Before our God, high up in heaven, our mighty   180
Lord, would speak with him, there on Mount Sinai.
On an empty belly, fasting so many days,
He received those laws, written by God's own fingers,

And prophet Elijah, in a cave of Mount Oreb, lingered
Long, fasting as ordered, and only then 185
Did the Lord agree to give him an audience—
God, who as you know, can cure our souls.
    "Aaron, put in charge of the temple by God's
Command, was ordered neither to eat nor drink—
He and every one of the other priests— 190
Before they entered the temple and prayed for the people,
Strictly commanded to shun all alcohol
And remain awake, however long they were there,
Or he would kill them. Pay heed to these my words!
Remember: those who pray for the people are sober 195
Or dead.—I do not need to say that again.
Our good Lord Jesus, we read in our Testament,
Gave us many examples of fasting and prayers.
And so we mendicants, we innocent friars,
Are married to poverty and self-restraint, 200
To humble charity and abstinence,
Sometimes to persecution, for righteousness.
To weeping, purity, and innocence.
And thus it may be said that our warm prayers—
I speak, of course, of all the Orders of friars— 205
Are far more certain to reach our high God's ears
Than yours, who feast and drink across the years.
Driven from Paradise, I dare not lie,
Man suffered, from the first, from gluttony.
And man was driven out, not asked to leave. 210
    "But Thomas, pay attention to what I say.
I have not drawn this message out of some text,
But only from my subtle explanation
That Jesus, when he spoke the words I'll say,
Was truly speaking of us friars: hear it: 215
    " 'Blessèd be they who live in poverty's spirit.' "
And by the holy gospel you plainly see
Which profession fits his words more closely,
Our Orders, or those that swim in property.
Fie on their pomp and on their gluttony! 220
Their ignorance and coarseness must be mistrusted.
    "To me they're like that heretic, Jovínian,

Fat as a whale, but trying to walk like a swan,
As full of wine as bottles in the cellar.
Great reverent words will steep these priestly prayers,   225
Reciting David's psalm for people's souls:
"Hrrumph, hrrumph, he makes me burp good prose."
But friars like me are humble, chaste, and poor,
Forever following Christ's path, and working
Every word of the Lord. We are not shirkers.   230
And so, like hunting hawks, springing up
To the air, friars' prayers will never stop
Until they've reached and entered God's own ears.
Thomas! Thomas! God is listening, he hears
Me praying as I ride or walk, and you,   235
Our brother dear, are always prayed for, too,
I and all the friars in my Order
Day and night beseeching Christ to hold you
Up and quickly make you well and fat."
    "God knows," said Thomas, "I'm feeling none of that!   240
So help me Christ, in these few recent years
I've spent, on every single kind of friars,
A horde of gold, but I grow worse and worse.
But one thing's certain: friars have emptied my purse.
Farewell, my gold, for you have flown away!"   245
    The Friar answered: "O Thomas, what are you saying?
Why do you need to seek out other friars?
Why does a man who has a perfect doctor
Go looking for other assistance in his locale?
You harm yourself, not help, by running about.   250
Do you think that I, or else my brothers, are doubtful
Godly support, our praying insufficient?
You have yourself to blame. You haven't sent us
Enough: you are the 'in' in 'insufficient'!
Hah! Just give that house a sack of oats!   255
Hah! Just give that house a purse of gold!
Hah, give that friar a penny, and let him go!
No, no, good Thomas, that never can be so!
How much is a quarter-penny divided in twelve?
Lo, any thing complete unto itself   260
Is stronger than when, like wind, it's swiftly scattered.

Thomas, the thing I'll never give you is flattery:
You wanted to have our labor all for free.
Our God on high, who all this world created,
Declared the workman worthy of his hire. 265
Thomas, there's nothing you own that I desire:
It's not for me, but only to help make sure
My brothers continue constant praying for you,
And also for the construction of God's own church.
And if you'd like to read of this high work, 270
Namely, the building of churches, you can read
The life of Saint Thomas, who saw how India needed
Churches, and built them. You lie here, full of ire,
With which the devil sets your heart on fire,
And here in your home you scold your simple, innocent 275
Wife, truly meek, profoundly patient.
So Thomas, trust me, please, and if you wish to,
Give up your quarrels with her. That would be best.
And keep these words in mind, now by your faith,
O hear what once the wise man rightly said: 280
'Be wary of being a lion under your roof,
Be careful not to oppress the weak and poor,
And never make your friends avoid your door.'
And Thomas, I warn you again, stay on the watch
For secret serpents your own weak heart may hatch, 285
For creatures like that can creep beneath the grass,
And they will sting you, without your knowledge, alas!
Be careful, my son, and listen with patient calm
To my words: twenty thousand men have gone
From this earth, killed for fighting with lovers and wives. 290
Take notice: having so holy and meek a wife,
O Thomas, why do you need to indulge in strife?
I tell you this: no serpent has ever existed,
Half so cruel, or fatal to man's existence
When he steps on its tail, as a woman roused to anger. 295
Vengeance becomes the only thing they long for.
Anger's a sin, one of the mighty seven,
Each of them hateful to God, above us in heaven.
And anger is pure destruction, once it owns you.
No one's too simple of mind, unable to know this, 300

And all will tell you anger leads to murder.
Truly, anger's the sheep, but pride is the herder.
O I could tell you more of the sorrows anger
Leads to, but the tale would last till tomorrow, or after.
And one of my prayers, I say it both day and night, 305
Asks God to grant no angry man much might.
It does great harm, and becomes an awesome pity,
When angry men are raised for all to see.
  "Once there was an angry potentate,
Says Seneca, who when he ruled the state, 310
Was asked to rule on a simple-seeming case:
Two knights went riding, one fine and sunny day,
And just as Fortune gaily wished it to be,
One came home, the other was nowhere seen.
And when the returning man was brought to trial 315
He was told, 'Surely, you killed your friend. You will die
For this, and not tomorrow afternoon
But now.' He ordered another knight to do it.
But as they rode to the place of execution,
They met the supposèd dead man, which seemed a solution: 320
Surely, once the mighty potentate
Had seen that both preserved their living state,
The case would be ended. 'Lord,' he said, 'no man
Was killed, the dead man's alive, and here he stands.'
'You all will die,' was the answer, 'may I be heard! 325
I mean all three, the first, the second, the third!'
And then, to the first of the knights he said: 'I sent you
For killing; as far as I'm concerned, you're dead
Already.' To the second he said: 'You lose your head,
As well, for you're the cause of this man's death.' 330
And then he turned to the third knight: 'You will be dead,
Because you disobeyed an order I gave you.'
He wiped the slate quite clean, no one was saved.
  "Angry Cambíses, of Persia, was also a drunkard,
And always took delight in being a scoundrel. 335
A lord of his, beside him one day, a man
Who believed in morals and virtue, alas! happened
To speak to the king of what he thought was virtuous:
  " 'A lord is lost, when his behavior is vicious,

And drunkenness, too, creates a foul report   340
On any man, but especially a lord.
Many open eyes, and many good ears,
Are always watching a lord, and how he appears.
For the love of God, try to drink much less!
Wine can rot your mind, and over the years   345
Can cause your limbs to fail you, one by one.'
      "Cambíses replied: 'I'll prove you totally wrong,
And you can test it, watch this experiment,
For wine is guilty of no such foul offense.
No wine exists that strips me of the might   350
Of hand or foot, or affects my sharp-eyed sight.'
Contemptuously, he began to drink much more,
A hundred times as much as ever before.
And soon this angry king, this cursed wretch,
Ordered this lord's young son immediately fetched,   355
Commanding that he stand across the room.
Then suddenly he took his bow, assumed
A hunter's stance, and pulled the string to his ear,
And with his arrow killed the child, right there.
'Now do you think my hands have lost their touch?   360
My strength's all gone? Has drinking cost me that much?
And has it ruined my once so fabulous sight?'
Why bother repeating whatever this grieving knight
Replied? His son was dead. What else can I say?
Watch your tongue, when a king is across the table.   365
Sing 'yes, O yes,' and 'I'll do what I can.'
But free your tongue, with a poor and simple man,
Who needs to be told how much he's sinned. So tell him.
But never a king, not even to keep him from hell.
      "Lo, angry Cyrus, who built the Persian empire,   370
Drained a Syrian river almost dry
Because it had drowned his horse, on his expedition
To conquer Babylon. He made that river
No more than a tiny creek, running so low
That women were able to wade from shore to shore.   375
And what did Solomon, the teacher, say?
'Never become the friend of an angry man,
Or even walk beside a man who's mad,

Or you'll be sorry.' What else could I add to that?

    "Now Thomas, dear brother, let anger fall by the way.   380
Think, and see precision in these words I say.
Don't go on pressing the devil's knife to your heart—
O anger hurts you, injures every part!—
But let me hear your true, complete confession."

    "No," said the sick man, "in the name of old Saint Simon!   385
I made confession, today, it was heard by my priest.
He knows what needs to be known, it's done and complete.
There's nothing, now," he said, "I need to repeat,
Unless I wish, devoutly feel a need to."

    "Then give me some of your gold, to build our cloister,"   390
Said he, "for many a mussel and many an oyster
Have been our food, as we have struggled to raise
Our building, while other men enjoyed their days.
And still, God knows, we haven't finished the base
And not a brick has been laid, not anywhere.   395
By God! we're forty pounds in debt right there.

    "Now help us, Thomas, for the sake of Jesus Christ!
Or else we'll be selling books for whatever price
We can get. And if the world won't have our preaching,
Death and destruction will follow. So says our teaching.   400
And any man who wants us out of the world,
May God preserve me, Thomas, by His word,
That man desires the death of the sun itself,
For who can preach like us, if I say so myself?
Nor are we new in this world," he said, "though some   405
May say so. But since Elijah, or Elisha, one
Or the other, friars are found in the written record,
Renowned for charity, I thank the Lord!
Now Thomas, help, for holy charity!"
And then the passionate Friar fell to his knees.   410

    The sick man felt his anger swell like a fire;
He wished the Friar burned to a crisp as a liar,
And all his cheating and false dissimulation.
"Some things I happen to have in my possession,"
He said, "I'm able to give you them, but no other.   415
Yet tell me, first, how I became your brother."

    "O yes, believe me," the Friar said, "trust me.

Your wife has a letter that says so, with our seal upon it.
    "All right," the sick man said, "I'll manage to give
A little to your holy house, as long as I'm living.   420
Indeed, you'll have it in your hand, and soon,
But on this condition, this single thing alone,
That you divide it so, my dearest brother,
That every friar receives as much as another.
You'll have to swear to this, with holy vows,   425
In total truth, and the name of your holy house."
    "I swear it," the Friar said, "and by my faith!"
The Friar's eager hand was solemnly placed
In the sick man's. "All my faith, with nothing lacking."
    "Now then, put your hand right down my back,"   430
The sick man said, "and feel around behind.
It's under my buttock, and there your fingers will find
A secret thing, something that's long been mine."
    "Ah ha," this Friar enthused, "I think that's fine!"
He shoved his hand right down to the buttocks' cleft,   435
Hoping that there he'd find some precious gift.
And when the sick man felt this eager Friar
Groping around his asshole, here and there,
Right in his hand he let go a monstrous fart,
So huge no nag, hitched ahead of a cart,   440
Could ever emit a fart that matched this sound.
    The Friar jumped like an angry lion up-bounding.
    "Ah! You lying peasant," he cried, "for the bones
Of our Lord! For this deliberate sin you'll atone!
You'll pay for this fart, if I have a thing to say!"   445
    The servants, having heard these angry statements,
Came running in and chased the Friar away.
As he stalked out, his face wore a furious scowl.
His partner had stayed behind, and he sought him out.
Looking, in truth, like a savage boar on the prowl,   450
Grinding his teeth, so bitter was his wrath.
They walked off quickly (it wasn't very far),
To the house of a man who made his regular
Confession to this Friar, and was the lord
Of the town, and someone, indeed, of very great honor.   455
He was seated, now, eating at his board.

The raging Friar could not say a word,
At first, but finally managed a greeting: "God save you."
  The lord looked up, and said, "Now blessings on you!
What! Brother John, what must be going on?   460
I see at once that something's gone all wrong:
You look as if the world were filled with thieves.
Sit down at once, and tell me what your grief is,
And I will make it right, if that I may."
  "I have," said the Friar, "been so insulted today,   465
God yield you his grace, right here in your little village,
That nowhere in all this world can there be a villainous
Boy who'd welcome the filthy kind of grief
That I have just experienced, here in your fief.
And yet, there's none of it afflicts me so sore   470
As that this ancient peasant, his head gone hoary,
Also blasphemed against our holy convent."
  "Now, master," said this lord, "please be content. . . ."
  "No master, sir, but only your servitor—
Although I've earned a degree which gives me that honor.   475
Though God prefers 'Rabbi,' it's not what we're called,
Neither out on the streets nor in your hall."
  "No matter," said the lord. "But tell me your grief."
  "Sir," said this Friar, "a piece of odious mischief
Has happened, this day, both to my Order and me,   480
And thus, inevitably, to the dignity
Of our holy church (may God amend it soon)!"
  "Sir," said the lord, "you know what needs to be done.
Do not be vexed. You are my holy confessor,
The salt of the earth, and you give the world its savor.   485
For the love of God, keep your patience firm,
And tell me your grief." So the Friar said what you've heard
Before, and you know the entire history of that.
  The lady of the house, meanwhile, quietly sat
Until she'd heard the tale the Friar told.   490
  "O mother of God," she said, "O lamb in the fold!
Really, can that be all? Do tell us more."
  "Madame," he said, "that's all. Please tell me your thoughts."
  "My thoughts?" she said. "They're not very hard to read.
I say, a peasant has done a peasant's deed.   495

What else can I say? May God deny him his peace!
He's sick, and his head is full of vanity.
Really, I think he lives in a kind of frenzy."
        "Madame," he said, "by God, I can't speak a lie,
But other avenues of revenge are open,   500
I'll cover him with disgrace, where my word is spoken,
This low, this lying sinner, offered me
A share of a stinking thing that cannot be
Divided in equal parts. May he be damned!"
        The lord, meanwhile, sat like a man entranced,   505
And in his heart kept rolling it up and down:
"How could this peasant have the imagination
To postulate so dense a problem to our Friar?
I've never known a puzzle quite so surprising.
It must have been the devil, at work in his heart: 510
Nothing in logic has ever dealt with a fart,
No one, till now, has ever raised this question.
Who could evoke so clever a manifestation—
Proving that every man must have his part,
Equally sharing the sound and savor of a fart?   515
A proud, rebellious peasant, I curse his face!
Now sirs" (he said aloud), "may he receive no grace!
Who ever heard of such a thing, till now?
Equally to every man? But how?
This is impossible, it cannot be.   520
O foolish peasant, away with your vanity!
The rumbling of a fart, its every sound,
Is nothing but echoing air spinning around
Until, in the end, it slowly dies away.
No man alive can judge, I swear by my faith,   525
That it was truly divided equally.
But hey, my peasant, hey, how cleverly
He spoke and dealt with my confessor, this day!
He's surely possessed by the devil, that's what I say!
Well, finish your food, and let the peasant go play,   530
Or let him hang himself, as the devil says!"
        The lord's young squire was standing near the board,
To carve his master's meat, and word by word
Listened to what you have already heard.

"My lord," he said, "your pardon for interfering,   535
But I would be able, for the cost of cloth for a gown,
To tell both you and the Friar exactly how
(With the Friar's leave, and yours) this fart can be shared
To one and all the same, if you wish this heard."
    "Tell us," said the lord, "and by Saint John   540
Cloth for a gown is yours! Now tell it on!"
    "My lord," he said, "on a day when the weather is fair,
Without any wind or perturbation of air,
Let be a cartwheel carried into this hall—
But note this caution: the spokes of this wheel must all   545
Be in place; usually, they're twelve in number.
Then let twelve friars appear. Why this sum?
Because a convent requires a full thirteen,
And your Friar, here, will thus supply what's needed.
The Friar's colleagues will then be asked to kneel,   550
Each at a spoke of his own, beside the wheel,
And each man's nose pressed at the end of his spoke.
Your noble confessor—may God reward his devotion!—
Shall hold his nose stiffly against the hub.
And then the peasant, his belly stiff and taut   555
As any drum, must here in your hall be brought,
And set him directly on the wheel of this cart,
Right at the hub, and let him release a fart.
And then you'll see—I swear it by my faith—
That, clear and plain, this truth will be demonstrated: 560
In equal measures, the sound of the fart will be sent,
As also its stink, straight to each spoke's end,
Except that this worthy man, your own confessor,
Because of his honor, and all his many blessings,
Will have the very first fruit, as reason requires.   565
This is, indeed, the noble custom of friars,
The worthiest man must be the first who's served,
As certainly this Friar has surely deserved.
He taught us, today, so much of holy goodness,
Preaching down from the pulpit where he stood,   570
That I can guarantee, though I speak for myself,
That he'd had three farts already, or at least their smell,
As each of his colleagues would, I can truly swear it,

All of them handsome men, of holy bearing."
    The lord, his lady, and all, except the Friar,   575
Affirmed that in this matter the lord's young squire
Had figured as well as Euclid or Ptólemy;
As for the peasant, they said, he'd spoken with skill
And understanding, framed by his wit and will,
Neither a fool nor simply a man possessed.   580
The squire got his gown, as you must have guessed.
My tale is told, and here we can stop and rest.

The Cleric's Prologue

"Sir Cleric of Oxenford," our Host then said,
"You ride as shy and quiet as any maiden
Newly married, seated at the marriage board.
The whole of this day, your tongue's not spoken a word!
I think you're contemplating some scholar's rhymes,   5
But Solomon says, 'all things must have their time.'
    "For God's sake, try to be a bit more cheerful!
We haven't come for studying—not here!
Tell us something merry, by your faith!
Any man who joins up in a game   10
Must truly enter into all the playing.
Don't preach at us, as friars do in Lent,
Making us weep for ancient sins long spent,
Or tell a story that draws us into tears.
    "Tell us some merry tale of high adventure.   15
Let rhetoric, and stale scholastic figures
Stay in storage, held for when you write
To kings and popes, and need the highest style.
Pray you, speak to us in plain and simple
Words, so nothing will be too difficult.   20
    This worthy cleric gave a gracious answer:
"Host," he said, "you're in charge, the master
Of all, as we've agreed, and we have meant
To show you by our easy obedience—
As much as reason requires, most certainly.   25
    "I'll tell you a tale I learned from a worthy cleric
In Padua, Petrarch was his noble name,

And all his writings show his eternal fame.
He's long since dead, and nailed up in his coffin.
I pray he's gone to God: may his soul rest softly.　　30
　　　　"A word or two more: Francis Petrarch, laureate
Poet, whose gift of the sweetest rhetoric
Shone in Italy like the brightest star,
As once, in philosophy, but ranging far
To law and many other noble arts.　　35
Lynyáno did, as well. Death's rule is hard
And inflexible, and fast as a twinkling eye
He slew them both, as all of us must die.
　　　　"But Petrarch, in particular, was the man
Who taught me this tale, as a moment ago I began　　40
To say. His style, at the start, was noble and high:
Before he reached his story, he swept in widening
Circles, creating a prelude which described,
In gorgeous, perfectly chosen words, the setting
In which his story would soon roll forth, in Piedmont　　45
And also Salúzzo, the hills of the Ápennines,
Which form the boundary of western Lombardy,
And especially Mount Viso, where the River Po
Springs up and remains that river's eternal source
As eastward it takes its ever-increasing course　　50
That runs along to Ferrara, and ends in Venice—
All this, it seems to me, is irrelevant,
And far too long to force on your tired ears.
Petrarch penned this description for Italians to hear,
Reminding them of scenes they'd all of them seen.　　55
So here's his tale, which still sounds fresh and green."

THE CLERIC'S TALE

Right at the western side of Italy,
Down at the foot of cold and frozen Viso,
There is a plain of lush fertility,
Filled with many castles, and ancient cities
Founded and built by the fathers of this country,   5
And there you can see all manner of pleasant sights,
And the region all around is known as Salúzzo.

Once, a marquis ruled across that land,
As had his worthy ancestors, before.
Obedient, always ready at his hand,   10
Were many vassals, both the less and more.
Thus he lived in pleasure, as he had of yore,
Beloved and respected, because of the favor of Fortune,
Both by his lords and the folk we like to call common.

In addition to that, he was by líneáge   15
The noblest man in all of Lombardy,
Handsome and strong, blessed by his youthful age,
And full of honor and of courtesy,
Wise enough to be his country's leader—
Except in certain ways that should have shamed him.   20
And Walter was this youthful leader's name.

I censure him because he gave no heed
To what, in time to come, might happen, thinking

Only of his present desire, meaning
Hunting and hawking, the play he was always seeking, 25
While other duties could slide from week to week;
Nor would he—and this, I say, was the worst of all—
Choose a wife, no matter what might befall.

His people's anxiety, on just this matter,
Finally drove a flock of citizens 30
To visit him, and one, wisest and saddest,
He to whom their lord would listen best,
Declared just what this worried visit meant.
Capable of the clearest explanations,
He explained to the noble marquis their perturbation: 35

"My gentle lord, your splendid humanity
Has always given us assurance and also
Confidence, whenever necessary,
Which lets us, now, express our grief and woe,
Believing that you, the noblest lord of all, 40
Will listen when we tell you of our pain,
Will hear and understand what might be disdained.

"Although I have, in this matter, no special place,
Nor have I done more about it than other men,
You, my lord, have always shown me favor 45
And grace, and so I come to you again
And ask, dear lord, that we, your citizens,
Be allowed to justify this crowding visit
And explain, though you, our ruler, have no need to listen.

"Certainly, lord, your people have such affection 50
For you, and all you've done, that there's no question,
For us, of greater joy and satisfaction
Than what we now enjoy—with one exception,
Which is, my lord, if it may be your election,
That you might marry a woman who'll give you joy, 55
At which your people, and I among them, will rejoice.

"We ask, in short, that you bow your neck to that yoke
Of blissful happiness, surrendering nothing,
But granting yourself what men call marriage, or wedlock.
Advise yourself, dear lord, and wisely think   60
How variously our lives are lived, but one thing
Never changes, and that is time itself,
Which always runs, and nothing we do can help that.

"And your green youth, as yet in perfect flower,
Will sooner or later find itself invaded   65
By age, and death can come at any hour,
For peasant or marquis, for no one ever escapes,
And though we never anticipate that date
We know it's coming, but no one knows just when,
Except that death is there and will strike when it's meant to.   70

"Let us take on this business, in your behalf,
We who have never refused a single command—
And we will find you a wife, if you trust our craft
And wisdom: we'll have this done as quick as we can,
And she will be from a noble, mighty clan   75
Of our Italy, and your marriage will be an honor
To God and you, and so it will seem to foreigners.

"Free us from our ever-haunting fear.
And take a wife, in the name of God in heaven!
For if it happened—and God forbid it, clearly!—   80
That you were dead, and left yourself no heir,
A man from some other place would be ruler here,
O woe to us, still living in this land!
This is our reason for taking the matter in hand."

This modest request, and the sorrowful look on their faces,   85
Brought a rush of pity to the marquis' heart.
"My own dear people," he said, "you wish to constrain me,
Oblige me to do what never seemed my part.
I've truly always rejoiced in my liberty,
And marriage has come to seem extremely hard.   90
There I was free; freedom now will be guarded.

"And yet I see your purpose is just, and fair,
And I trust your intelligence, as I've always done,
And so, of my free will, I do declare
I'll marry, as soon as a suitable bride is won. 95
But not the way you've offered to do it here.
Let me release you from any such attempt:
I'll choose my own wife, though your offer was clearly well meant.

"God knows that children are often quite unlike
Their worthy ancestors, and their parents, too. 100
Virtue is the grace of God, neither one side
Or the other of any great line is guaranteed virtue.
Because I trust God's bounty, I tell you truly,
His guidance will be mine, and all my lands,
And my high position, I hereby place in his hands. 105

"Please leave the choice of a bride to me alone:
This is a weight my back can surely endure.
What you must swear, on your lives, is to do her no wrong,
To worship her for her rank and her purity,
For however long she may remain among us: 110
Always praise her words and her good deeds;
Treat her like an emperor's daughter, indeed!

"And this, too, you must swear; no one in the land
Will ever complain about my choice, or oppose it:
Since I have agreed to lose my freedom, in answer 115
To your request, this matter must be closed:
Wherever I set my heart is my choice alone.
If you agree to these explicit provisions,
This issue is dead, and you go about your business."

With high sincerity they swore and assented, 120
No one opposing: no single man said nay.
They asked him, for his grace, before they went,
To tell them when he had set a wedding day,
As soon as he could do it—his people always
Worried that nothing was sure until it happened; 125
Ignoring things, they knew, was their ruler's habit.

In time, he set a day, as they'd requested,
On which without a doubt he would be wed,
Reminding them that this was their suggestion.
And they, most humbly, showed their obedience 130
By dropping on their knees and thanking him
With reverent pleasure. The issue thus foreclosed,
One and all went back to their work and their homes.

And then the marquis gave official orders,
Commanding his men to plan the wedding feast, 135
And all his personal knights and squires, closely
Attendant, were set their tasks, however he pleased,
And everyone obeyed, his wishes were heeded,
Dozens of servants working at their best,
So he could be wed with reverent festivity. 140

PART TWO

Not far from the marquis' palace, honorable
And ancient, where wedding rites would be celebrated,
A village stood, small but amiable,
Whose lowly inhabitants, though poor, were able
To keep their animals in well-built stables, 145
And working hard, they fed themselves from the earth,
Season by season, and passing year by year.

Among these people of little means, one
Was generally accounted the poorest of all,
But God in heaven will often send some 150
Of his holy grace to a tiny oxen's stall.
Janículá, the men of the village called him.
He had a daughter, sufficiently lovely to see;
Her name was Grisélda, good as a girl can be.

And if we're speaking only of virtuous beauty, 155
Then she was surely the fairest under the sun.
Having been born and raised in poverty,
No wild desires had even started to run
Through her heart. She drank her water as it might come

From their well, for virtue was for her a pleasure,   160
She knew hard labor, but never had knowledge of leisure.

And though this girl was barely grown, and was young,
Yet in the breast of her virginity
A ripe and stable heart had long since begun
Its beat, and with great honor and charity   165
She fostered her father, old and poor as can be.
While spinning their wool, she guarded their handful of sheep,
And never was still or idle, until asleep.

And when she walked back home, she plucked up cabbage-
Worts and other edible greens and herbs,   170
Then sliced them, and boiled them, and that would be their supper.
Her bed was hard, she felt no softness there.
Her constant goal was keeping her father alive,
Laboring hard and obediently, and he thrived:
She circled around him like a bee in a hive.   175

The marquis had always had his eye on this creature
Of poverty and, plainly, holiness.
Riding off to hunt, he would scan her features,
But not with lust or other foolishness,
But serious, somber, heavy thoughtfulness: 180
He'd watch her face and inwardly would think
She walked and held herself much like a saint,

And praised her, in his heart, for her womanhood
And extraordinary goodness, unlike the girls
So young an age, in looks and attitude.   185
For though poor peasants have no use for virtue,
He saw her goodness flower, and how it worked,
And came to the firm decision that if he wed,
This was the only woman he'd take to his bed.

The wedding day dawned, and still nobody knew   190
Who'd been chosen to be the marquis' bride,
And many men pondered, amazed at what was brewing,
Wondering (safely indoors) if their lord's great pride

Would stop him taking any woman to wife.
"Will he truly come to this wedding? Alas, the while!   195
Why should he cheat himself, and his people beguile?"

    Yet all this time, keeping everything secret,
The marquis had jewellers making gems of lapis
And gold, fashioned not for her to see
But wear, and a serving maid, young, with a shape   200
As like Griselda as Griselda herself, had served
As a model for dresses, all manner of other clothes,
And everything that a proper wedding bestows.

    At nine in the morning, the promised wedding day,
The place was fully prepared, swept and brightened   205
And richly adorned in every room and place,
According to rules of royal enlightenment.
Storage houses bursting with food and dainties
Were everywhere, all manner of food and drink,
Unmatched from Italy's alps down to the brink.   210

    Royally arrayed, and taking with him
Lords and ladies of his company,
All invited to celebrate with him,
And also younger knights-in-waiting, the marquis
Went, with music sounding melodies,   215
Across to the village I have already described,
Going, though no one knew it, to fetch his bride.

    God knows, Griselda was deeply unaware
That all this splendor, these sights, were for her to see.
She fetched her water from the well, as ever,   220
And hurried home with quick and happy feet,
Wanting to watch the happy wedding party,
If she could, and see whatever might be seen
By a peering peasant (about to be a queen!).

    She thought she'd make the time to stand at her door,   225
With other girls she knew, and perhaps have a glimpse
Of their ruler's unknown bride, while scrubbing a floor

And working at other things she might fit in,
Tasks she could work at, even lightly flitting
Out and back. "At least, I'll have a chance   230
To see the procession, if this is the way it passes."

But just as she came hurrying out the door,
The marquis arrived, and started calling for her.
Quickly, she set her pot down on the floor
Right at the threshold, in front of an ox's stall,   235
And then, obedient, on her knees she fell,
And silent, sober, knelt there perfectly still,
Waiting to hear whatever her lord might will.

The marquis' face was thoughtful, his familiar voice
Was grave, and this was how he then addressed her: 240
"O Griselda, where is your father?" Adroit
And simple, she quickly said, with reverence:
"Lord, he's here, I'll bring him to your presence."
Straight in she went, with no delay, and swiftly
Returned, presenting her father as her lord had wished.   245

The marquis took her father by the hand,
And said as follows, leading him off to the side:
"Janículá, I neither may nor can I
Keep my heart to myself, or my longing hide.
May I have your daughter for my bride?   250
This is who I've longed for, to be my wife,
To love forever, as long as we're alive.

"I know you love me, old man, I know it for sure,
And you have always been most faithful to me.
I think I safely can say that what I approve   255
You do, too—and I mean, especially,
One thing I've already told you, just before:
I want your daughter, I'll be your son-in-law,
She'll be my wife, if we agree, all three."

This blunt and sudden statement so astonished   260
The good old man that his face turned red, and his body

Trembled. He found it hard to make a longer
Answer than this: "Lord," he said, "what you want,
I want. I'll never oppose you, no matter what.
Whatever my dear lord wishes, I join his cause.   265
Do whatever you want, it will always be just."

     "Now what I wish," the marquis said more softly,
"That in your chamber I and you and she
Consult together, and let me tell you why.
I want to ask her whether she will agree   270
To be my wife, and live as I decree.
And this must all be done with you in the room;
I want to say nothing you do not hear and approve."

     Meanwhile, outside the room where this discussion
Took place—and you will shortly hear the rest—   275
Many people came pouring into their house,
Expressing great astonishment that she kept
Such wonderful order, as perfect as she could get it.
Griselda watched and wondered, silent and dazed;
She'd never seen a sight so truly amazing.   280

     But her amazement should not be a surprise:
No other marquis had ever been inside
Her house, neither had any others who followed.
Surely that explains her silent pallor.
And then the marquis asked her to join her father   285
And himself. And here's what the marquis said to this gracious,
Faithful, honest, virtuous young maiden:

     "Griselda," he said, "I'd like you to understand
Your father and I are each most fully agreed
That I will take you to wife. This is our plan,   290
And I imagine you'll have no difficulty
Accepting. But first, I need to ask," said he,
"That since the marriage is to be today,
Do you accept, or would you rather wait?

"And let me add, you must be fully prepared   295
For whatever I want, whenever I want, in any
Matter at all. You're never to grumble or stare,
You're never to sulk, whether by night or day,
And any time I say 'yes,' you'll never say 'nay,'
Neither the word nor a negative look on your face.   300
If you'll take these on oath, I pledge you my faith."

  Marveling at his words, and quaking with fear,
She said, "My lord, I know myself not worthy
Of this honor you've offered me, but since you appear
To want this marriage, I cheerfully agree.   305
And here I swear that never willingly,
Neither in word nor thought, will I disobey you,
Even to the point of death, though I'd hate to die."

  "That is enough, my good Griselda," he said.
Then out the door he went, his expression sober,   310
Fixed, to where the people waited to hear him
And Griselda followed after. "Good citizens,"
He said, "This is my wife, who's standing here.
Honor her, and love her, this I pray,
Whoever loves me. There's nothing more to say."   315

  Not wanting her to bring a single possession
Of her former life from this house to his, he asked
That women take her back inside and undress her.
This did not make these ladies terribly glad,
Having to handle the clothes in which she was clad.   320
But they did it, took this maiden of shining hue
And clothed her, head to foot, completely anew.

  They brushed and combed her hair, that lay untressed
And flat, and with their nimble fingers set
A garland on the head they'd finished dressing,   325
Then decorated her with jewels great
And small. And that, as to clothing, is all I will say.
No one found it easy to recognize her,
Transformed and beautiful, too shocked and surprised.

The marquis formally married her, with a ring   330
Brought along for that reason, and then he sat her
On a snow-white palfrey, a horse well-trained at ambling,
And took her by the longest route to his palace,
Accompanied by joyful folk who met her,
Happily led her, and thus their day was spent   335
In reveling, until the sun descended.

And to spur this tale along at a useful pace,
I'll say, quite briefly, this country's new marquesse
Clearly had God's favor, for he of his grace
So burnished her she seemed no more nor less   340
Than noble, not like someone born in rudeness,
From cottages, and wells, and oxen stalls,
But nourished in an emperor's great hall.

The people quickly learned to find her dear
And worshipful, and those from where she was born   345
And raised, who'd known her all along, from year
To year, came to believe—but would not have sworn—
The old man they knew, of whom you've heard before,
Had had a daughter, yes, but *this,* they conjectured,
Appeared to be an entirely different creature.   350

Although she'd always been a virtuous child,
This woman who'd married their marquis swiftly soared
To such heights of manners, and goodness so well refined,
So eloquent in speech, wise in both words
And deeds, so gracious, so worthy of being adored,   355
So able to reach to people's hearts, and embrace them,
That all of them loved her, as soon as they looked in her face.

Not only in Salúzzo, the town I named
Before, were her virtues known and celebrated,
But also in many other regions her fame   360
Had spread, and her excellence was venerated:
If this one spoke well of her, that did the same.
Both men and women, young as well as old,
Came to Salúzzo, wanting just to behold her.

So Walter married lowly—yet royally—   365
Wedded with noble honor, and fortunately:
The peace of God was given him, at home,
And he had more than sufficient outward grace.
Because he'd known that virtue and lowly place
Can come together, his people thought the marquis   370
A man of prudence, and that is rarely seen.

Not only was Griselda a clever woman,
And capable of making a comfortable home,
But also, under proper circumstances,
She understood the public welfare, and was drawn   375
To assist it. There was no discord, rancor, or woe
Anywhere in that country she could not appease,
And wisely help them back to rest and ease.

Although her husband was often away from home,
If gentlemen or others in her country   380
Had quarreled, she'd help them think of themselves as one.
She was able to speak of peace with maturity
And wisdom, and even-handed equity,
So men would often remark that she'd been sent
From heaven to save them, see their wrongs amended.   385

No great time after her wedding, perhaps a year,
Griselda gave birth to a daughter. The marquis, for sure,
Would rather she had produced a son and heir,
But welcomed the child; his people showed their pleasure,
Aware that though a girl was the first to be born,   390
She might be blessed, the next time, and bear a boy.
At least, she was not barren, and that was a joy.

PART THREE

It happened as, alas, it often does,
Before this baby girl was long at the breast,
Profoundly deep in his heart the marquis was   395
Determined to test his wife for her faithfulness,
And this determination grew, and festered.

He was wholly unable to drive it away.
Quite uselessly, he planned to affright her one day.

In fact, he'd tested her enough, before,   400
And always found her good. Why did he need
To tempt her again and again, and always more,
Though some men say it's clever, a kind of teasing?
As for myself, I think it's downright evil
To go on testing a wife when there's no need to,   405
Afflicting, frightening her, all needlessly.

And here is what the marquis decided to do:
He came to her alone, one quiet night,
As she lay in bed, a frown on his face, and truly
Stern in his manner. "Griselda," he said, "quite rightly,   410
Before I took you out of your poverty,
And lifted you to high nobility—
Do you still remember what I asked you?" said he.

"I hope, Griselda, that this dignity
In which I've put you, as both of us well know,   415
Will not make you forget, too easily,
That you were taken from poverty, quite low,
Knowing full well you had no property.
Now listen carefully to every word
I say; no one is near, we're unobserved.   420

"You surely remember how, that day, you appeared
In this house; it hasn't been so long ago.
And though you've shown me your loveliest side, and your dearest,
That isn't the side my nobles have been shown.
They're saying that, to them, it is great woe   425
And shame to be subjected and in service
To a woman from such an insignificant village.

"And now, especially, after your daughter's
Birth, they've spoken these words, and plentifully.
I wish to live my life with them, as I ought to,   430
And as I have done before, in quiet and peace.

These are not casual matters, I cannot be
So careless with them. Your daughter's destiny
Lies in my people's hands, and not with me.

"God knows, I don't enjoy saying such things.   435
Without your knowledge, of course, I'll take no action.
But what I want," he said, "is this. Bring
More patience into your dealings with men, react
More slowly, be what you swore to be, the day
We were married. Now, will you agree that your ways   440
Of behavior need to fulfill the virtues you've claimed?"

Hearing all the complaints he'd abruptly lavished
Upon her, neither her face nor her words expressed
The slightest disapproval, annoyance, or anger.
She said, "Lord, everything lies in your pleasure.   445
My child and I, as I have always attested,
Are yours, we belong to you, and whether you kill
Or save us, truly depends on your pleasure and will.

"Nothing on earth, as God may save my soul,
Displeases me, if it is what you like.   450
There's nothing I want to have or desire to own,
Nothing I fear to lose, except you alone.
And this is deep in my heart; no worldly might
Can change it, no time, not even death can displace it,
Or shift my love and devotion to another place."   455

The marquis was pleased at how she answered his question,
But his expression stayed dreary, his face was gloomy,
He scowled and grimaced, pretending dissatisfaction,
And looking upset, he turned and left the room.
He walked a hundred yards or so, and soon   460
Approached a fellow, to whom he gave commands,
Ordering them enforced on his wife by this man.

This was a bailiff, silent and secretive,
Whose services the marquis often employed
For serious matters: whatever orders he'd give   465

Were accomplished, even if it meant destroying
A life or two. There was no question of enjoyment:
The lord was well aware the man would obey him,
For fear and for love. The bailiff went to his lady.

"Madame," he said, "you must forgive me for doing   470
That which I am compelled to do. You're more
Than wise enough to know our lord's commands
Can neither be refused nor safely ignored.
Some orders make men weep, and women, too,
But what he wants is more than words: it's law.   475
So I obey him, as I've done before.

"I've been commanded, now, to take this child"—
And speaking no other word, rough and swift,
He snatched the girl, his eyes wide open and wild,
As if he meant to kill her before he left.   480
Griselda had to permit it, she could not protest.
She sat like a lamb, silent, meek, and still,
And let this cruel bailiff do as he willed.

She knew this man had an evil reputation;
His look was dark, his words were black as the devil,   485
Everything he did had this connotation.
The daughter she loved so desperately might well
Be slaughtered then and there, ruthlessly killed.
But nevertheless she neither wept nor sighed,
Bent as she was to behavior her husband liked.   490

But then she did begin to speak, most softly,
Meekly begging the bailiff, as he was a man
Of honor, to give her the opportunity she sought,
And had to seek, as a mother, to kiss and clasp
Her child before it died. He laid it in her arms,   495
And solemnly she kissed it, and blessed it, and lulled it,
As mothers do, and kissed it over and over.

And then she said, in her gentle, gracious voice,
"Farewell, my child! I'll never see you again.

But since I've marked you with the sacred cross   500
Of Jesus Christ, most blessed, most holy of men,
He who died for us, pierced on that cross,
I place your soul in his hands, my little child,
Obliged by your mother's sins, so soon to die."

    Even a servant, a nurse, would weep at this sight,   505
So painful, so terrible a thing to see.
Who could have blamed a mother if she moaned and cried?
But still, so strongly, steadily calm was she
That nothing could shake her, no adversity.
She handed over the child, and meekly said,   510
"Here she is, again, your little maiden.

    "Go now," she said, "and do as my lord commanded.
One final thing I ask for, by your grace:
Unless my lord forbids it, try at least
To bury this little body in some place   515
Where neither beasts nor birds will tear at its face."
He gave her no answer, had nothing more to say,
Just took the child and went about his way.

    And then the bailiff went to his lord again,
Reporting Griselda's words, and how she appeared,   520
Telling him point by point, speech short and plain,
And gave him his daughter—a child, in fact, he dearly
Loved. Pity was plain, in the lord's cold manner.
But nothing could sway him, once he had made up his mind:
Princes and kings are like that, an honest man finds.   525

    Then he ordered the bailiff to secretly wind
And wrap the child, all tenderly, with napkins
And gentle cloths, the softest he could find,
And carry it off in an open box, on his lap,
But warning him a mistake would mean his death,   530
Should anyone learn the mission he'd been sent
To accomplish, where he was from, or where he went.

His destination would be Bologna and the countess
Of Pánicó, who happened to be the marquis'
Sister, to whom he should bring the tiny foundling,   535
Requesting her to raise the daughter he
Had sent her, teach her well and royally,
But never under any circumstances
Reveal the girl's true name, or that of her parents.

The bailiff left, and did what he was told to.   540
But we will stay at home, and speak of the lord,
Who now went visiting his queen, Griselda,
Wondering what mood she'd be in, what sort
Of change he'd see, if any. She was as before,
For never could he find his wife except   545
As always she was, stable, kind, and respectful,

As happy, as humble, as active in her service
And her love, as she was always accustomed to be—
In short, exactly the same, impervious.
Not even a word was said of her daughter, and he   550
Was aware of nothing changed, no adversity
Displayed in her face or manner, all the same.
No mention was ever made of her daughter's name.

PART FOUR

Nothing happened at all, for four full years,
Before Griselda was pregnant again, and this time   555
Walter's child was a boy, a suitable heir,
Gracious and healthy, pleasant to look at, and fine.
When Walter's servants brought him the news, he smiled
And then the entire country joined him, happy
For child and father, and themselves, and God was praised.   560

But when the boy was two years old, no longer
Drinking from his nurse's breast, one day
Walter felt the familiar urge, strong
And insistent, the need to test his wife, if he may.

O this was more than needless, I need not say! 565
But married men are apt to feel this urge,
When wed to a woman who makes herself their servant.

    "Wife," said the marquis, "surely you've heard, by now,
My people have come to dislike the fact of our marriage,
And especially since I have a son, somehow 570
It's gotten worse, and this is causing damage,
Striking my heart and making me lose courage—
Indeed, this grumbling, since it's reached my ears,
Has filled my aching heart with worry and fears.

    "This is what they're saying: when Walter's gone, 575
The blood of Janículá will assume the throne
And be our lord, for where would we find someone
Else? This is the voice of fear, no doubt,
But I must hear that voice, for I certainly know
That such opinions quickly become a menace, 580
Even if never spoken aloud in my presence.

    "I'd choose to live in peace, if I only could.
But since I managed to deal with his sister, by night,
I'm now determined to follow that secret road
Again. It's served me once; it will do so twice. 585
I warn you, thus, to save you from losing control
Of your feelings, presented with this so suddenly:
Be patient, that's all that I can say," said he.

    "I've said this before," she said, "and always shall:
I've nothing to wish for, nothing I hope to gain, 590
Except what you desire. I've nothing at all
To grieve for, no matter my son and daughter are slain—
So long as that is your wish; I can say this plainly.
There's been no joy, in either of these two labors,
But sickness, first, and afterward woe and pain. 595

    "You are our lord; do what you wish with your own,
However you please. You need no advice from me.
For just as I left my clothing, when I left my home

And came to you, exactly so," said she,
"I left my will and all my liberty   600
When I accepted your clothing. Please, I say,
Just do what you wish, and I will that wish obey.

    "For, surely, had I happened to know in advance
Exactly what you wished, before you told me,
I would have done it at once, without delay.   605
Hearing, now, your wishes, and also knowing
Your plan, I once again affirm my stance.
And if I knew my death would put you at ease,
I'd gladly die, simply in order to please you.

    "It is impossible for death to compare   610
With your love." And hearing these words, the lord could see
How constant she truly was, and stood there, staring
Into the ground, perceiving but not believing
How she endured the treatment she was receiving.
He left her room with a dreary, woeful expression,   615
But his heart was happy, relieved, distinctly pleasured.

    The frightening bailiff, following the same
Repellent plan he'd used to seize her daughter—
Or something worse, if any man could claim that—
Had suddenly appeared and taken her other   620
Child, her handsome son. She seemed no more
Upset, too patient to show her heaviness,
But kissed her son; then, carefully, she blessed him.

    But, as before, she begged that if he might
He'd put those little limbs in an earthly grave,   625
Preserving that body, so fragile and tender a sight,
From hawkish beaks, and his flesh from jaws that crave it.
And then, again, he remained silent, gave her
No answer. He left as quickly as he'd come,
But gently carried the boy, too, to Bologna.   630

    The marquis was deeply puzzled, more and more,
By the patience his wife maintained, and had he not known,

Long since, that she had profoundly loved her daughter
And just as perfectly had loved her son,
He would have believed some subtle trick had been done,   635
Something based in malice, or pitiless courage,
Enabling her to endure with so steady a visage.

    There was no shadow of doubt in his mind that, next
To himself, love for her children was strongest in every
Way. But now I ask, of women, if expecting   640
More than what his tests had taught him was wholly
Necessary? What could a man, a very
Harsh man, invent to see how good a wife
He had, while he himself was stirring up strife?

    There are, indeed, people so strangely framed   645
That, once they've made up their minds, nothing can change them;
They cannot shift a direction, to left or right,
As if they were helpless, bound to a stake, tied
To a mountain, unable to move their glacial minds.
Once the marquis had first decided his wife   650
Should be tested, he held that course the rest of his life.

    He waited, and watched, to see if her face or words
Displayed some sign of shifting, deep in her heart,
But never noted the slightest twist or turning.
She was always the same, true in every part.   655
And, indeed, the older she grew, the more he thought her
Fixed more firmly faithful (if that could be),
More loving, more careful, to an infinite high degree.

    It seemed to him, in truth, that between these two
Only a single will existed, for whatever   660
Walter wanted was what she wanted to do.
Now God be praised, this marriage jointure never
Faltered, and she was right: a wife is forever
Intended to subordinate her life and will
To that of her husband, for he has become her ruler.   665

But Walter's reputation slowly sank,
For people began to say, and more each year,
He had a wicked heart, and her lower rank
Provoked him to kill his children. Such murmuring
Is hardly uncommon, but not unnatural, 670
For who had ever whispered to the public ear
Anything else? All they knew was their fear.

And so, although his people had loved him well,
Before, rumors kept spreading, and he was defamed
To the point where hate began to smother love, 675
For "murderer" is not a pleasant name.
Yet Walter still pursued his odd and shameful
Pleasure, deeply cruel, but firmly intended.
Never doubt his purpose; he did what he meant to.

So when his daughter had reached the age of twelve, 680
He sent a messenger to the papal court
In Rome, directing (both in secret and evil)
His servants there to counterfeit a lawful
Papal permission for the marquis to further his awful
End—namely, to marry again, if he liked, 685
In order to calm his people and avoid all strife.

They doctored up a false and lying bull,
Giving the marquis allowance to leave his wife,
In order to stifle rancor and stop all quarrels
Between himself and his people. They made it look right 690
And legal, fashioned properly and tight,
And—without a word to the pope—had it published,
Spread it abroad, so Griselda could quickly be banished.

The common people—and who should be surprised?—
Accepted this document as if it were real, 695
Though not expected. But to Griselda's eyes
It surely must have been woeful. Whatever her feelings,
This humble creature wouldn't show them, concealing
Her pain and sorrow, always and ever bent
To Fortune's wishes and whims, and its intent. 700

She'd always given her heart, and everything else,
To her husband's wishes, whatever gave him pleasure:
To her this constituted happiness.
But the marquis had also written a very special
Letter, setting out in detail the rest of   705
His plan, and—not to further prolong this tale—
Had secretly sent it to Bologna, by messenger mail.

The person to whom he'd written was the noble Earl
Of Pánicó, his sister's husband, requesting
The honorable and open, public return   710
Of both his children, as soon as the earl could best
Arrange this. But most emphatically, he asked
That no one be told, no matter who inquired,
Who was these children's father. That must be quiet,

He said, but told the earl that sooner or later   715
The girl was meant to be married to Salúzzo's ruler.
Whatever the marquis asked, the earl obeyed him,
And speedily he started off on his way,
Riding with many lords, richly arrayed,
Accompanying this pretty, royal maiden,   720
Whose younger brother rode happily beside her.

Indeed, the girl was already dressed for her marriage,
This fresh young lady, decked with gleaming gems.
Her brother, only seven years of age,
Wore proper clothes, well suitable for him.   725
And thus this noble parade, rich and trim
And very happy, made their way to Salúzzo,
Riding day after day, which they were used to.

PART FIVE

In addition to all these things, and according to
His evil custom, so he could further tempt   730
His wife to the farthest limits, the very border
Of heart and spirit—imagining he meant
To study just how steadfast her heart was set—

One day, in his court, in open audience,
He blared his news, in boisterous sentences: 735

   "Certainly, Griselda, marriage to you
Has been pleasant enough. You truly are very good,
And very truthful, and very obedient, too,
And not at all for your father's name or his goods.
But I have learned, through much experience   740
And consequential thought, that nobleness
As well as poverty must suffer in service.

   "I'm not allowed to do what any plowman
Can. My people are forcing me to take
A different sort of wife, and crying loudly.   745
And the pope, as well, will now allow me to make
A better marriage—acting, I think, for the sake
Of public peace. So now I can proudly state
My second wife is even now on her way.

   "Be strong of heart, and clear away her place,   750
And take away the dowry that you brought me,
Bring it back to your father, I grant by my grace,
And you return there, too, bring it along
On your back. Prosperity is neither strong
Nor lasting. My heart is calm as I advise: 755
Accept what Fortune has done. That would be wise."

   Yet once again, she answered patiently:
"My lord," she said, "I know, as I always have,
That no one can compare nobility
Like yours to powerless, low poverty   760
Like mine. Who could utter such idiocy?
I never thought myself worthy to be
Your wife—not even one of the servants you need.

   "And in this palace, though turned into a lady—
God on high will be my perfect witness,   765
He who surely lifted my heart and made me
Rejoice—I never considered myself its mistress,

But only a humble servant to your worthiness,
As I shall remain until the end of my life,
Sworn as your servant, lord, but not as your wife. 770

  "Your generosity in keeping me
So long, in honor and splendid nobility,
None of which I was ever worthy to be,
Is a grace from God as well as from you: may he
Reward you for your goodness. What more can I say? 775
I'll gladly turn my steps to my father's home,
And live there, content, until my time shall come.

  "I was born and raised and cared for, there, as a child;
I'll lead my life in that house until I'm dead,
A widow chaste in body, heart, and all. 780
And having given you my maidenhead,
My heart belongs to you: no one should expect
A great lord's wife—may God prevent such mistakes!—
To take another man as husband or mate!

  "And as for your new wife, may God in his grace 785
Grant you happiness and prosperity!
Most cheerfully, I yield to her the place
In which I lived so long and happily.
So since it pleases you, my lord," said she,
"You who have been my heart's tranquility, 790
I'll live in my father's house, where you wish me to be.

  "But all the dowry I ever brought you, my lord,
I'm well aware, were the wretched clothes I was dressed in,
All the clothes my father could ever afford,
Worth terribly little, and now perhaps still less. 795
O praises to God! How noble, kind, and gracious
You seemed, not just in your words but in your face,
That day our sudden marriage was celebrated!

  "But it's often said—and I agree it's true,
For its accuracy has surely been proven on me— 800
Love when it's old is not as it was when new.

But let me assure you, my lord, that adversity
Will never make me regret—in word or deed,
Not even given the threat of immediate death—
I gave you my heart forever, come worst, come best.   805

    "Recall, my lord, that in my father's place
You had my humble clothing stripped away,
And dressed me richly, by your royal grace.
And certainly, there was nothing else that came
With me, but destitution and maidenhead.   810
Here are the clothes you gave me; they're yours again,
And also the wedding ring you put on my finger.

    "All the rest of the jewels, once mine, are yours
Again, safely stored in the room I slept in.
Out of my father's house," she said, "naked   815
I came, and naked must I return once more.
I wish to do exactly what pleases my lord,
But I hope you do not want me to leave your door
Without so much as a dress to cover bare skin.

    "You could not do a thing that so disdains   820
Honor, letting the womb in which your children
Lay, go walking forth for every one
To see, but bare as the day I was born. I pray you,
Let me not go crawling along the road
Like a worm. Remind yourself, my own dear lord,   825
That I was your wife, though surely I was not worthy.

    "In consequence, as payment for the only
Thing I brought you, my maidenhead, which I
Will never have again, a due and proper
Reward would be to give me the kind of smock   830
I used to wear. I will wear it, once more,
To cover the womb of she who once was married
To you. Farewell forever: I will not tarry."

    "The smock," he said, "you're wearing on your back,
Keep it there, take it away when you go."   835

Regret and pity left him—it was most unusual—
Uneasy, speaking these words. And then he left.
Standing right where she was, in front of the public,
She stripped right off her outer garments; the smock
Was all she wore; her head and feet were bare. 840

    People followed her down the road, weeping
And cursing at Fortune as they walked along behind her.
Griselda's eyes were dry, she would not weep,
But from there to her father's house she did not speak
A word. Her father had heard the news she was bringing; 845
He cursed the day and time Nature had made him
A living creature, and father of this poor maiden.

    It must be confessed that Janículá, this poor
Old man, had always been suspicious of his daughter's
Marriage. It seemed to him, from the very first, 850
That when the lord had had as much as he wanted,
He'd turn to thinking how much he'd lowered himself,
Tying his noble position to such a lowly
Girl, and throw her out as soon as he could.

    He hurried out to greet his daughter, warned 855
By the crowd and all the noise it made, and brought her
The tattered old coat she'd worn, and wrapped it around her,
The only covering he could offer. Then he wept.
The coat was so old, indeed, its cloth so worn,
That nothing could make it fit her, not ever again, 860
For many years had passed since she last wore it.

    And so, for a time, this flower of wifely patience
Lived alongside her old and sorrowing father,
Never showing, by words or countenance,
For anyone to see, or even wonder, 865
About whatever feelings she had, of offense
Or regret. No one could ever tell, from her face,
That she remembered her high and stately place.

It's hardly surprising, for even life in the palace
Could not affect her depth of humility.   870
Her mouth could not be pampered, her heart was as
It had been forever; she had no pomposity
Or royal pretensions, but a simple dignity
And kindness, always discreet, not proud. Respect
And honor she showed to the world, as her husband expected.   875

Men talk of Job, and especially his humble
Spirit, as clerics, when they wish to, write—
But mostly of other men. Clerics fumble
And fuss about women, rarely praise them. But in right
And truth, no humble man can shine so bright   880
As a woman, and men are never half as faithful
As women—unless some change has come about lately.

PART SIX

Now from Bologna the Earl of Pánico came,
And everywhere the people spoke his name.
And in the ears of people high and low   885
Was heard this earl was coming, a girl in tow,
Meant to marry the Marquis of Salúzzo.
The earl escorted her in more ceremony
And pomp than ever seen in West Lómbardy.

The marquis had been arranging everything,   890
And knew the earl was coming. He sent a message,
Calling poor and innocent Griselda to him,
And she, with humble heart and cheerful visage
And neither injured pride nor any resentment,
Came when he called, greeted him properly,   895
Quietly setting herself down on her knees.

"Griselda," he said, "I am truly determined:
This maiden is coming here to be married to me,
And must be greeted, tomorrow, as royally
As any visitor here has ever been.   900

As well, my every guest, of any rank
And state, must be given courtesy
And all the pleasure visitors here have seen.

    "Alas, I have no woman competent
To order properly these many rooms   905
In the manner I want, and that is why I sent
For you, and ask you, now, to quickly assume
This task. You've long since learned the way I want
This done. And even though your clothing is scant
And poor, please do the job as well as you can."   910

    "Not only am I glad, my lord," she said,
"To do as you wish, but also I desire
To serve and pleasure you to whatever extent
I can, without any weakness, as you require.
So will it always be, in happy times   915
Or sad: the spirit I hold in my heart will never
Cease to love you best. And that is forever."

    And with those words she began preparing the palace,
Having the tables set, and the beds made ready,
And worked as hard as she could to insure that all   920
Was correct, urging chambermaids, in the very
Name of God, to hurry, quickly sweep
And shake, till she, the hardest worker of all,
Had every room prepared, and also the hall.

    Before high noon, the very next day, the earl   925
Arrived, together with the two young children,
And people ran to see the clothes they wore,
Rich, luxurious, and utterly splendid,
Saying among themselves that their noble ruler
Was surely not a fool to change his wife,   930
For certainly this maiden would better his life.

    They all agreed the girl was infinitely
More pretty than Griselda, and a great deal younger,
And fairer fruit would fall, quite naturally,

Between these two, so much more pleasant to see.   935
Her little brother, too, was a handsome child,
His hair, his eyes, all drove the people wild
With excitement, saying the marquis was always right.

"O stormy people! Unfaithful, forever changing!
As fickle and fallible as a weather vane!   940
Always delighted by anything new and strange,
Just like the moon, forever waxing and waning!
Clapping, shouting, for a world that has no pains!
Your judgment is bad, your constancy is worse:
Whoever depends on you is bound to be cursed."   945

      Thus said the sober folk who lived in that city,
Watching people staring up and down,
Enormously happy, just for the novelty
Of having a brand new queen live in their town.
Now let me close that page and move right on: 950
This time, once more, Griselda has my attention,
Showing how she indeed was faithful to him.

      For she was constantly active in everything
The wedding celebration needed done.
She hurried about, never ashamed of her clothing,   955
Though it was clumsily made, and in places torn.
Happily she went, with other folk,
To the palace gate, to greet their ruler's new wife.
And afterward went back to work, untired.

      She welcomed his guests with ready cheer, received them   960
Skillfully, each according to rank
And position, and none of the visitors perceived
A flaw, except they wondered who she might be,
Dressed in the poorest clothing they'd ever seen,
And yet displayed such noble reverence.   965
A bit bewildered, they praised her constant prudence.

      And all the time she showed her high approval
Of the girl, and also of her little brother,

Speaking with her heart, and kind intentions,
So perfectly phrased that nothing needed amending. 970
But finally, when dinner was served, and guests
Sat down to eat, the marquis suddenly called
Griselda, working hard in his busy hall.

"Griselda," he said, as if he were only playing,
"How do you like my wife and her youthful beauty?" 975
"Very well, my lord," she said. "In good faith,
I've never seen a prettier girl than she.
I pray that God will give her prosperity,
And hope that he will always send such pleasure,
From now to the final end of your lives together. 980

"One request I must make; it's also a warning.
Never torment this girl, as you've done before
To others, for I can tell that she's been raised
And nourished most tenderly; I'd be afraid
She could not deal with, nor could she endure, 985
The kind of adversity that only a poor
And narrowly nourished creature could be ready for."

And when this Walter saw, and truly knew,
Her patience, her happiness, so free of temper,
Despite his frequent, horrendous, and futile attempts 990
To offend her, she so sober, steady as a wall,
Forever preserving her innocence, for all
Her sorrow, this marquis, though harsh, readied his heart
For pity, and recognized and regretted his part.

"This is enough, O my Griselda," said he. 995
"No more! Don't be afraid, I won't be frightening.
Surely, your faith and your unending kindness
Were tried and tested as any woman's could be—
A queen by marriage, but dressed as in poverty!
And now I know, dear wife, your steadfastness." 1000
He took her in his arms, and began to kiss her.

Amazement made her unable to take in his words;
She did not hear a single thing he said,
Behaving like someone startled out of bed.
At last she steadied her heart, stood straight, and sighed.   1005
"Griselda," he told her, "I swear by God who died
For us, that you're my wife, I have no other,
Nor never had, or will, for this is your daughter,

"Whom you have naturally assumed and supposed
Would be my wife. That other child I hold   1010
As my heir: I've always intended that noble role
For him. You bore him, too, in your body, by God.
They've been in Bologna, I've kept them there in secret.
He's yours once more, accept your lawful son
And never say your children are dead and gone.   1015

"People have thought and said dark things of me,
But here and now I let them know that nothing
I did was meant to be cruel, or a work of malice,
But only to test your womanly constancy—
Never to kill my children, may God forbid it!   1020
I meant to keep them in secrecy and silence,
Until I knew your strength and innocence."

On hearing this, she fainted and fell to the ground.
But once she opened her eyes, came out of her swoon,
She called for both her children and wrapped them around   1025
In her arms, embracing them and weeping hard,
Then kissing them with tenderness, her heart
Filled with a mother's love, and her eyes with salty
Tears, which bathed her hair as well as her face.

O what a pitiful thing it was to see   1030
Her faint, and then to hear her humble voice!
"My endless gratitude, O God be thanked,"
She said, "for saving these two children for me!
If I were stricken dead, right now, right here,
I would not care, having your love once more.   1035
Death means nothing, having you two before me!"

"O tender, young, O dearest children of mine!
Your sorrowing mother had long supposed you dead,
Eaten alive by cruel hounds, or lying
In graves, consumed by vermin. But merciful God,   1040
And your kind father, in his noble tenderness,
Have kept you alive,"—and then, without a sound,
She fell like a stone, stretched out on the ground.

But even as she fell, she held her children
So tightly in her arms, embracing them,   1045
That both her daughter and her son were obliged
To squirm and wriggle, until at last they escaped.
O tears went rolling down on many faces,
All of those who stood beside the fallen
Mother, uncertain if they could help at all.   1050

Walter gave her comfort, her sorrow began
To ease. Feeling ashamed, she rose from her trance,
Her honor was freely and fully celebrated,
Till finally calm had settled back in her face.
Walter was so attentive, so careful to please her,   1055
That guests and all were glad, deeply relieved
To see this pair together, and a couple indeed.

The ladies, when they saw the time was right,
Ushered her to the bedroom, once hers to use,
And changed what had been a dirty dress, and frightful,   1060
To clothes of golden cloth, and bright of hue.
Wearing a crown all decorated with gems,
She returned to the marquis' happy hall with them,
Honored, now, as she should always have been.

Thus, a terrible day had a blissful end,   1065
With every man and woman determined to spend
This time in mirth and revel, till heaven sent
Its shining stars to brighten up the night.
This was a singular occasion, a sight
—The guests declared this—of such intense delight   1070
That none of them had ever seen its like.

They lived, these two, in harmony and rest
For many years of high prosperity.
The marquis married his daughter to one of the best
And noblest young lords in all of Italy,   1075
And then he took Janículá to the peace
And comfort of the spacious palace, and there he was kept
Until his shining soul from his body crept.

And when the marquis himself was brought to his rest,
His son succeeded him, in Salúzzo land;   1080
All was calm and peaceful. His marriage, too, was blessed
And happy, although he never thought of testing
His wife. This world is surely not as strong
As once it was, in ancient days of yore—
So hear the author's observations on this score: 1085

This story has not been told so all wives should
Attempt to ape Griselda's humility,
For that would be ghastly, even if they would,
But so that every one of us should be
Equally constant in adversity.   1090
This was Petrarch's position, when he finished writing
This story, the style of which he embellished to its height.

A woman having been incredibly patient
To a mortal man, how very much more we ought
To take in good part whatever God has sent us,   1095
For rightfully he tests what he has wrought—
But never severely tempts a man who's redeemed,
As James observes, in the holy Testament,
And we should read, and ponder, and see what he meant,

And learn to endure, and our spirit exercise,   1100
Thus using the sharpest scourge of adversity—
For no man living anticipates its bite—
Not to depend on human will, for he
Who made us has always known our frailty.
Accepting his will is always the road to take,   1105
For we must live in patience, for virtue's sake.

But gentlemen, allow me one word more.
These days, it would be very hard to find,
In any town, two or three Griseldas,
And tests like those I've told will nowadays show   1110
That girlish gold is mixed with so much brass
That though it glitters, when it meets the eye,
It might well break before it compromises.

On account of which, for love of the Wife of Bath—
May God preserve her life, and those of her sex,   1115
In control of this world, so we may enjoy the next—
I'll sing you, now, a song, from a cheerful breast
And a heart both fresh and green: it will meet your needs,
And help us leave behind all serious matters.
So here is my song, shaped to a happy pattern: 1120

CHAUCER'S HAPPY SONG

Griselda is dead, and so too is her patience,
Both of them buried deep in Italy,
Because of which I sing the many reasons
Why married men, these days, are never free
To test and probe for Griselda's calm acceptance: 1125
They'd only be wasting their time, and deserve their penance.

O noble wives, filled to the brim with prudence,
Never silence your tongue with humility,
Nor give a cleric good reason to condemn your usage,
Transform you into a monster of futility,   1130
Exactly like Griselda, whose cup of tea
Would be torture to you, as to every other she.

Imitate Echo, who cannot ever stay silent,
But offers an immediate reply.
Allow no scoffing at your innocence,   1135
But quickly grasp control, become the guide.
Keep this lesson clearly in your mind.
It might be useful to you both, you'll find.

O super wives, stand ready at defense,
Being in truth as strong as any camel,   1140
Allow no man to offer you offense.
You slender wives, though much too feeble for battle,
Be fierce, like tigers roaming far-off India—
Work your mouths like mills that grind up wheat.

Never be afraid, allow them no reverence,   1145
For though your husband wears his suit of armor
The arrows of your crabbèd eloquence
Will pierce his breast and split his heavy helmet.
Tie him up with ropes of jealousy
And he will cower like a stingless bee.   1150

If you are pretty, whenever people gather
Show off your face and all your fancy clothes.
But if you're ugly, open up a golden
Purse. Find friends for yourself, to back you up;
Always flutter around like a linden leaf,   1155
Let him be worried and sad, and weep and wail.

Now when this worthy Cleric ended his tale,
Our Host declared, and swore, "By God's own bones,
Rather than any brimming barrel of ale,
I wish my wife could hear this story just once!   1160
A noble narrative to bring back home.
So, let us now continue. That is my will,
And anyone who's disinclined, be still!

The Merchant's Prologue

"With weeping and wailing, care and other sorrows,
I'm well acquainted, evenings, nights, and mornings,"
The Merchant said, "and so are many more
Old married men. That's how it is, I think,
And certainly that's how it's been for me.   5
I have a wife as bad as wives can be,
For even the Devil himself, if married to her,
Would be beaten down. That's simple truth, I swear.
How can I catalogue and classify
Her malice? However you count it, she'd be the highest.   10
O there's an immense, a deadly difference
Between Griselda's soft and ideal patience
And my wife's surpassing perfect cruelty.
Were I divorced, how happy I could be!
I'd never ever fall in the trap again.   15
Sorrow and care are the trials of married men.
Ask anybody, pick and choose as you like,
They'll all agree, they know I've got it right.
I will not give details, there's more to be said,
But God forbid this savagery should spread!   20
     "Ah, good sir Host, I married two months ago;
I'd never been married before, I swear to God.
And yet some fellow, single all his life,
Faced with death by dagger, sword, and knife
Could never, in a million million years,   25
Describe the infinite woe that I, right here,
Could tell you, created by her wickedness!"

"Now Merchant," said our Host, "may God then bless you.
But since you are so learnèd in that art,
I ask you, heartily, to tell us some part." 30
  "Gladly," he said, "but not of my personal sorrow.
My heart's so battered I cannot say any more."

The Merchant's Tale

Once upon a time, in Lombardy,
There lived a worthy knight, from Pavia,
Who lived his life in great prosperity.
For sixty years a wifeless man was he,
Chasing after women for his delight,   5
Forever feeling a natural appetite,
Like every fool who hasn't become a priest.
But when he reached the age of sixty, he believed—
Whether for holiness or simple dotage
I cannot say—he felt a terrible rush,   10
This wealthy knight, to become a married man,
And day and night was doing all a man can
To figure out how to realize this plan,
Praying that God would let him be married soon,
Rewarding him with a perfect, blissful boon   15
He'd never yet known in all the years of his life,
The bonding of each and every husband and wife,
Living together under that holy bond,
Man and woman, made as one by God.
    "No other life," he said, "is worth a bean,   20
For marriage is so pleasant, so righteous and clean,
That in this world of ours it's paradise."
Thus said this knight, so much respected and wise.
    And certainly, as truly God is king,
To take a wife is in fact a glorious thing,   25
And even more when the man is old and hoary:
Ah, then a wife is the choicest flower of glory.

He ought to take a wife who's pretty and young,
On whom he might engender himself a son,
Leading his life in joy and perfect delight,   30
While bachelors are singing "Alas!" all night,
When they encounter any adversity
In love, as it's called: it's really vanity.
And this explains why bachelors' lives are so
Egregiously filled with moaning, pain, and woe.   35
They build on imperfect ground, and impurity
Will down them, though they think it's security.
Their lives are much like those of birds and dogs,
Running wild, with all the restraint of hogs.
But a married man, in a house maintained by a wife,   40
Leads a regulated, orderly life,
Gripped and bound by the yoke of sacred marriage.
His heart deserves to be joyful—if he has managed
To find a wife who's obedient, humble, gracious.
For who can be so true, forever anxious   45
At guarding him, in sickness or health, as his mate?
In happiness or woe, she won't forsake him.
She's not afraid of love, or matters more trying,
Although he's sick in bed, and ready to die.
     And yet there are some clerics who say it's not   50
The truth, and Theophrastus is one of that sort.
But what does it matter if Theophrastus is a liar?
"Don't take a wife," he says, "to keep from hiring
A servant, for when it comes to household expense
A real servant is far more diligent,   55
And does you much more good, than any wife.
For she will claim one half of your whole life.
And if you've fallen sick, in the name of God
Call on your true real friends, or even a doctor,
For the lady you married is waiting, and has waited long,   60
To inherit what you have, which she wants to own.
Further, any wife you let in the door
Is likely to pleasure herself with two or more
Others." This, and a hundred things much worse,
Are all from Theophrastus, may his bones be cursed!   65
Don't pay attention to such a fool as he:

The devil with Theophrastus! Just listen to me.
  A wife is truly God's ineffable gift.
Other kinds of presents that you may get,
Like land and rents, pasture, or pasture rights,   70
Or any sort of handy, moveable items,
Are from Fortune, and pass like shadows upon a wall.
But don't you worry (I need to tell it all),
A wife will endure, and stay in your house far longer
Than perhaps, it just may be, you still want her.   75
  A wife! Ah, Mother Mary, your blessing, please!
How can a man have any adversity
Having had a wife? I cannot speak to that.
The heavenly peace existing in marriage relation
Is far beyond all speech or meditation.   80
If he is poor, she helps him, works at his side;
She cares for what he owns, lets nothing slide;
Whatever her husband favors, she too likes.
She never answers "no," if he says "yes."
"Do such-and-so," he says. "It's done," she says.   85
O blissful state of wedlock, how utterly precious
You are, how very happy, how perfect in virtue,
And also so commended and approved
That every man who thinks he's worth a prune
Ought, on bended knees, and all his life,   90
Give thanks to God for sending him a wife—
Or pray to God that he will finally send
A wife, to last until his days are ended.
For then his life is set in security,
He may not be deceived, it seems to me,   95
As long as he does whatever his wife advises.
Wives are so true and, wherewithal so wise,
That once he's married he can hold up his head.
And this is why, if you listen to what I've said,
You'll always follow where your wife has led you.   100
  Lo, look at Jacob, as these clerics tell us,
Taking good advice from his mother, Rebecca,
Tied the skin of a kid around his neck
And won the special blessing from Isaac.
  Lo, Judith also, the Bible story makes plain,   105

Preserved her people by following good advice,
And killing Hóloférnes, monster of vices.
      Lo, Abigail, with good advice, saved
Her husband, Nábal, when David would have slain him,
And Abigail's daughter, Esther, kept old Haman   110
From killing Jews, the captive people of God,
And persuaded Áhasúerus, her husband, to slay
This Haman, give Mordechai, a Jew, his place.
      Nothing stands higher, in degrees of superlative,
As Seneca says, than a good man's humble wife.   115
      Endure your wife's sharp tongue, as Cato suggests,
She must command, and you must do your best
To follow, though she'll obey you, for courtesy.
A wife is ruler of domestic economy.
A man who's sick in bed must wail and weep,   120
If he has no wife to hold his house in her keeping.
Let me warn you: if you want to follow wisdom,
Love your wife, as Jesus loved his kingdom.
If you truly love yourself, then love your wife.
No man hates his family, but all his life   125
Keeps nourishing it along, so love your wife
As part of you, in each and every day.
Husband and wife together, wise folk say,
Is the road to follow (clerical folk aside),
So closely joined that no disaster pries them   130
Apart, and especially the wife upholds them.
      And January, the knight of whom I told you,
Considered such things (as he watched himself grow older)
As the joyful life, the holy, virtuous peace
That comes with marriage, and wanted that honeyed sweetness.   135
And so, one day, he called in some of his friends
To let them know his mind and his intention.
      With a sober face, this is the tale he told them,
Saying: "Friends, my hair is gray, I am old.
And almost, God knows, right at the edge of my grave.   140
It's time I thought of my soul, and my behavior.
My foolishness has well rubbed down my senses;
By God's great favor, this must be amended!
For I intend to be a married man,

And, surely, just as fast as ever I can.   145
Please, good friends, arrange without delay
My marriage to some young and pretty maiden:
Make it tomorrow, I can't, I will not wait.
Meanwhile, I myself will try to locate
Someone I can marry right away.   150
But you are many, and I am only one,
Your chances are better, of course, for getting this done,
And knowing who would serve and who should be shunned.
      "But let me warn you, dear friends, right here, in advance:
Consider no older women, don't even glance.   155
Someone, certainly, not a day past twenty:
I like old fish, but flesh that's young and plentiful.
A wife," he said, "has outgrown being a baby,
But tender veal is better than beef that's aging.
A woman of thirty is far too old for me: 160
They're only dried-out stalks and withered berries.
Besides, a ripe old widow has learned to steer
And fight, God knows; she's had a long career
Of swinging her tongue and fists, and breaking heads,
And battlers like that don't make for restful beds.   165
A broad experience is fine for priests,
But worldly women are educated beasts.
A man can guide and mold a nymph who's young,
The way we roll and model wax with our thumbs.
So let me say it plainly, once again: 170
I have no interest at all in older women.
For if I took that chance, and it misfired,
And sagging, ancient flesh had stifled desire,
I'd look for someone else, commit adultery,
And straight to the devil I'd go, the minute I died.   175
Nor would I have children, yoked to a dried-out wife:
I'd rather be eaten by dogs, at the end of my life,
Than know the property I left would fall
To no one sharing my blood, not a drop at all.
I'm not in my dotage, I know exactly why   180
Men ought to be married, and in addition I
Know well that many men who talk about marriage
Know less about it than horses pulling a carriage:

Nothing is what they know about taking a wife.
A man who cannot stay chaste, the whole of his life,   185
Should make himself marry with great and holy devotion,
And then, by sanctioned, lawful procreation
Create his children, to the honor of God above,
And not by chance, or paramour, or mere love.
Once married, they must surely eschew all whoredom,   190
And satisfy their wives, when that must be done.
And each of the married pair should help the other,
If bad luck happens, as sisters help a brother;
Both their lives should be chaste, divine and holy.
But, gentlemen, a chaste life's not for me,   195
For God be thanked! Truthfully I boast
That all my limbs are strong, and stout, and whole
And able to do whatever any man ought to.
I'm very well aware of what I can do.
I may be gray, but I function like a tree   200
That blossoms before its fruit can properly
Be picked—and a tree that's blossoming is not dead.
I feel myself gone gray just on my head.
My heart, and all my limbs, remain as green
As laurel bushes, which never lose their sheen.   205
And now that you have heard what I intend,
Let me suggest you give me your assent."
     Different men had different ideas. Some told
Familiar stories, examples more than old.
Some criticized marriage; some, of course, then praised it;   210
But in the end, it all came down, in a phrase
(As the sun began to set), to an altercation
Between good friends engaged in disputation,
As two of January's friends dug in
For a desperate battle (they still remained good friends):   215
One was named Placébo ("I will please"),
The other Justínus ("I'll tell the truth or leave").
     Placébo said: "O January, brother,
Surely you had no need to ask for others'
Opinions, for none of us, consulted here,   220
Can possibly outweigh you, brother dear.
Clearly, you wish to act as prudently

As Solomon: he told us all, said he,
'To do all things in council' (these were his words),
'And you will never have to regret your works.' 225
But in spite of Solomon's sage and sensible words,
My dearest brother, and also my dearest lord,
May God in heaven bring my soul to rest,
But I believe the wisdom you spoke is wisest.
This, my brother, is my view, in words quite brief, 230
For I have been a courtier all my life,
And though, God knows, I don't deserve their place,
Lords of singular wealth and high estate
Have always considered mine a worthy face.
But I have never joined in their debates, 235
Nor have I, truly, ever disagreed
With any of them. It's certain, as I see it,
That you, and every lord, know more than I do.
Whatever a lord has spoken, I say 'Ay' to,
And I echo his every word as well as I can. 240
A counselor must be a fool of a man
Who, serving a lord of noble place and station,
Presumes (or thinks of presuming) his own statements
Surpass whatever the noble lord is saying.
Lords can never be treated like fools, by my faith! 245
And you yourself have shown right here, today,
Such high good sense, so reverent and wise,
That I can only confirm you take the prize
For every word and all your grand opinions.
By God, there's no one in these grand dominions 250
Or all of Italy, who might speak better!
God takes delight in your words, in every letter.
And truly, that requires noble courage,
When any man who's well advanced in age
Will take a girl for his wife. By my father's kin, 255
Your heart will surely hang on an amorous pin!
But do exactly as you please in this,
For in the end that seems to me the best."

　　Justínus, who quietly sat and listened to this,
Immediately spoke and gave Placébo his answer: 260
"And now, my brother, please be patient, I pray;

You've had your turn, now hear what I have to say.
Seneca is surely a man whose advice
Is sound. He says that no one's acting wisely
Unless he's careful to whom he entrusts his wealth.   265
And if I need to consider extremely well
Who gets my land or receives my property,
How much more careful a man should always be
To whom I consign my body for the rest of my life.
I tell you, January, taking a wife   270
Without deliberation is playing with fire.
Inquiries must be made, I have to warn you:
Is she steady? wise? Or is she a downright drunkard?
Modest or proud? Or given to being shrewish
And scolding? Will she waste away your goods?   275
Is she rich or poor? Has she a craving for sex?
No one in this world, or even the next,
Is perfect, every human being has flaws,
Not even beasts are perfection incarnate: of course!
But nevertheless, inspection will let you know   280
Enough of any woman you take as your wife:
Has she good characteristics, to balance her vices?
Learning these things takes time, and careful inquiring.
God knows that I myself have poured out sighs
And tears, in private, since I have had a wife.   285
No matter who extols the marital life,
What I have found in marriage is expense and grief,
And unrewarding responsibilities.
And yet, God knows, my neighbors all around—
Especially women, naturally quite fond   290
Of the institution—heap praises on my wife,
For steadiness and meekness beyond all price.
But I know where my shoes are pinching me.
I think you can marry or not, just as you please,
But watch how you enter—you're not an ignorant child—   295
This marital realm. Young wives are apt to be wild,
If pretty. By him who made water, earth, and air,
The youngest man we have in this group, right here,
Works hard enough, preserving himself a share
Of his wife. On matters like this, put trust in me: 300

How many years can you fully please her? Three,
Perhaps, for I refer to pleasing her fully,
And a wife requires many sorts of duties.
Go marry. I hope you won't be sorry, later."
    "Well," said January, "have you more to say? 305
The devil with Seneca, and all your proverbs!
I'd rather have a basketful of herbs
Than heaps and hordes of academic terms.
Other men agree with my intention.
Placébo, do you hold to your position?" 310
    "I say it is a wicked man," said he,
"Who blocks the joyous road to matrimony."
    And with those words, the council rose as one,
Agreeing that their work had now been done,
And he should take a wife when he wanted one. 315
    Thoughts and images of marriage began
To press on January's soul. The man
Kept shifting, day by day, from one to another
Fancy. Beautiful faces and bodies rose
And fell in his heart, one night after the other, 320
As if you took a mirror, polished bright,
And set it in a crowded market-place,
And watched the many figures in that glass,
Passing back and forth. And the same strange visions
Flitted through his imagination, positioned 325
Beside him, there where he lay. He could not decide.
One would show a lovely, smiling face,
But another was blessed with truly outstanding grace,
Widely admired for affability,
And winning marriage points from many voices. 330
Some were rich, but bad. He found the choices
Highly difficult, but then in time
He settled on one, and fixed her firm in his mind,
Letting all the others fade from his heart,
And allowing his affections to play their part— 335
For love is always blind, and will not see.
Settled down at night, intending to sleep,
He pictured in his heart, and in his thought,
Her purest beauty, her tenderness, untaught,

Her tiny waist, her arms so long and slender,   340
Her noble stance, her sensible behavior,
Her seriousness and charming female savor.
And after she had finally been selected,
He felt his choice could never be corrected.
Once he'd finished making his decision,   345
He thought that all the other men had pigeon
Brains, incapable of valid objection
To his choice: in short, he lived a fantasy.
But still, he urged them all to come and see
For themselves, most urgently, how extremely well   350
He'd shortened their collective labor. He'd tell
A quick, decisive tale of perfect judgment,
From which, he said, he'd never again be budged.
      Placébo arrived, and then came all the others.
Their host began by asking that no one bother   355
Themselves, or him, by arguing against
This final choice he had already mentioned—
Which, he explained, was fine in the eyes of God,
Framing foundations for everything he had.
      He described the chosen maiden, there in that town,   360
Whose beauty already gave her great renown.
Although she rated low on the social ladder,
Her youth and beauty satisfied him better.
This was the girl he meant to have as wife,
For pleasure and holiness, the rest of his life;   365
He was grateful to God for having her completely,
So bliss need not be shared with anybody.
All he wanted them to do was arrange it,
And quickly, so nothing could intervene and change it.
That done, he said, his heart would be at ease.   370
"Nothing, then," he said, "will ever displease me,
Except one thing, which truly troubles my conscience,
And which I wish to discuss, here in your presence.
      "I've heard it said, though many years ago,
That no man achieves a perfect bliss in two   375
Main spheres—that is, in earth and also in heaven.
For though he keeps himself from the deadly seven
Sins, and also from every branch of that tree,

Because there is such perfect felicity
In marriage, I fear I'll have such joyous ease   380
And delight, and lead so very merry a life,
So wholly content, no touch of woe or strife,
That I will have my heaven here on earth.
But since that heaven on high was bought so dear,
With tribulation, and whips of infinite penance,   385
How can I be allowed to live such pleasure
As married men, of course, lead with their wives?
Can I rise to eternal bliss, where Christ now lives?
This is my fear, and you, my brothers, I pray
Will resolve this question, and leave me happy today."   390
      Justínus, who hated the raging folly he'd heard,
Plunged right in; he answered in sharp-edged words,
But because he did not intend a scholar's oration,
He left out all the heavy documentation,
And said: "Good sir, if this is indeed your only   395
Problem, God on high may send you a stony
Answer, and in his mercy may do this work
Before you stand to be wed, in holy church;
You may regret the facts of married life,
In which, you say, there's neither woe nor strife.   400
Moreover, the grace of God will usually send
A married man a host of occasions to repent
His choice—more opportunities for that
Than a bachelor gets. And therefore, sir, I am
Not able to offer better advice than this: 405
Don't worry yourself about your state of bliss,
For she may be, in truth, your purgatory!
Perhaps God's agent, in this marriage story,
A holy tool wielding a sacred whip:
Your soul may like an arrow go flying, skipping   410
To heaven. I hope, in time, you'll come to perceive
The illusion you have trusted, and come to believe in,
Of marriage as high felicity. It isn't,
And never was. Pursue the road to salvation,
Living by reason and discrimination,   415
Indulging yourself with your wife in moderation,
And never too much, and avoid all other sin.

That ends this lesson: my wit is dry and thin.
Don't be shocked by my words, my very dear brother.
Now let us leave this subject and try another.   420
The Wife of Bath, if you can understand her,
Handled this marriage business, now held in our hands,
Extremely well, and in a very short space.
Farewell for now, may you be granted his grace."
    And with these words, good Justin and his brothers   425
Took their leave, and each one to all others.
And having seen that this was meant to be,
They cleverly arranged that he and she—
The maiden, named for the merry month of May—
Would marry just as fast as she was able,   430
And then become good Mistress January.
This story would be longer, if I tarried
Over each dull document and bond
Which gave her co-possession of his lands,
And especially to tell you how she dressed.   435
But the day did come, however long expected,
When May and January to the churchyard went,
And then inside to receive the sacrament
Of holy marriage. The priest, with a stole on his neck,
Said she should be like Sarah and Rebecca   440
In wisdom and fidelity, and respect
For marriage. He chanted his prayers, as custom expects;
He made the sign of the cross, said God should bless them,
And tied the knot securely, with holiness.
    And so they were married, fully and formally,   445
And at the wedding dinner he and she,
With other worthy folk, sat on the dais.
Filled with joy and bliss was his small palace,
And also music-making, and splendid eating—
The tastiest food, and wine from first-rate vineyards.   450
They listened to instruments producing sounds
That neither Órpheús nor Ámphíon
Of Thebes had ever heard or ever played on,
And every course was served to minstrelsy
Far louder even than Joab ever decreed,   455
Or Theódomás the seer—and yet much clearer

Than Thebans heard, with their city much in doubt.
Perhaps Bacchus himself was pouring out
The wine, and Venus laughing at every man,
For January, now, was in her hand.   460
He'd proved his mettle, first, in liberty,
And now would prove it in marital purity.
The goddess held a flaming torch, in a marriage
Procession, dancing before the bride, her carriage
Entrancing. Even Yméneús, the god   465
Of weddings, never saw a man more sodden
With happiness. Be quiet, poet Márcian,
Who wrote a celebrated poem on the merry
(But allegorical) marriage of Mercury
And Physiológus, and the songs the Muses sang!   470
Your pen is far too small, and so is your song,
To even begin describing this festive wedding.
When tender and lovely youth is married to bent
Old age, the mirth is so odd that nothing written
Can tell it. Try it yourself, and become a witness   475
To whether I lie or speak the truth on this point.
        Sitting and watching, the gracious bride displayed
A face so gentle she might have been a fairy.
Queen Esther never turned so meek a face
To Áhasúerus, when she became his wife.   480
Who could describe such humble beauty? Try
As I may, not me. But I can let you know
She shone like a morning in May, brightly glowing
With enormous pleasure and more than a measure of beauty.
        January was carried away, not looking,   485
Merely, but ravished into a kind of trance.
His heart began to feel such intense enchantment
He knew, in the night to come, he'd hold her tighter
Than Paris ever held Helen. He was almost frightened,
Thinking how ferociously he meant   490
To attack this fragile, tender creature, and then
He thought, "Alas! you soft, you delicate being!
I pray that God will give you the strength you'll need
To deal with a rising ardor like mine, so keen
And overpowering. Realizing this, I mean   495

To hold myself back. You could not stand my might.
I wish to God it were already night,
And tonight was able to last for ever more.
I wish that all these people had already gone."
And then he set himself, with all the grace   500
And tact he could, to politely empty the place,
Subtly, to save his honor, firm and wisely.
      Dinner was done; people began to rise
From the table. Everyone danced, and drank with delight,
And finally went around the house, spices   505
In hand, spreading blissful marriage perfume—
And the only unhappy man in all the room
Was Damyan, a squire who carved for the knight,
So overwhelmed with love for his master's lady
That his passion was painful, and he was almost insane.   510
He stood at attention, but almost sank to the floor,
Half swooning with all the fire Venus had poured
In his heart, pointing her torch as she'd danced, before.
And as soon as he could, he took himself to bed.
You know enough of him, from what I've said,   515
So let him remain where he is, weeping and crying,
Desperate for May to have pity, for he was dying.
      O dangerous fire, beginning to burn in bed-straw!
O domestic foe, supposed to be serving, not warming!
O traitor squire, falsely acting true,   520
A hidden adder deep in the bosom, untrue:
May God preserve us all from knowing you!
O January, intoxicated by marriage,
Just see how your squire, Damyan, pledged to your service,
Now longs most passionately to throw away   525
His obligations and turn on you, betray you.
May God grant you a chance to discover the wretch!
Nowhere in the world can pestilence
Be worse than an enemy right in your presence.
      The sun had now performed its daily arc;   530
For in this latitude, the shining barque
Of light had reached the limits of its stay;
Night's dark mantle, barbarous, replacing
Day, spread slowly across the hemisphere,

And lusty people invited to this wedding 535
Feast departed, saying farewell to their host,
Then riding, hard and fast, back to their homes,
Where they can do whatever suits them best,
And when they choose, lie down and take their rest.
Not long thereafter, impatient January 540
Made ready for bed, he could no longer tarry.
Drinking down wine with sugar, spices, and honey,
Some of it hot and strong, he heated up his heart,
And then he swallowed herbs, of a medical sort,
The kind that Cónstantíniús, that monk, 545
Discusses in his book on fun in the dark.
This would-be lover never rejected an herb.
And then he rounded up his closest friends
(Still in the house), saying, "For the love of God,
It's time for everyone to show their regard 550
By leaving." The task was neither long nor hard.
And, finally, the curtains around the bed
Were drawn, the bride was brought in, as still as if dead,
The priest administered a nuptial blessing,
And all but the wedded pair turned round and left, 555
And January quickly embraced his freshest
May, his paradise, his longed-for woman.
He soothed her with caresses, he kissed her again
And again, rubbing across her tender skin
The thick, hard bristles growing on his face— 560
For he was freshly shaved (what he called shaving)—
Much like dogfish scales, sharp as briar.
And then he said, "Alas! My pretty wife,
This will hurt you, you'll be greatly offended
Before I roll over, and finally descend. 565
And yet, reflect on this: No workman," said he,
"However good at his art, how skilled he may be,
Can do his work both well and hastily.
This will be done at leisure, and perfectly.
It makes no difference, however long we take, 570
For we are truly married, mate and mate,
And marriage is blessed, this yoke that we are in,
For whatever we do, nothing we do is sin.

Men can do as they wish, alone with their wives,
As no one can hurt himself with his very own knife.   575
We two are licensed to do as now will be done."
And then he labored indeed, till he saw the sun,
And then he soaked some bread in his finest wine,
And sat straight up in bed, and began to sing,
Both loud and clear, and kissed and hugged his wife,   580
Acting as if he'd had the time of his life.
He bounced like a colt, he flirted and winked, he laughed,
As full of words as a magpie perched on a branch.
The slack old skin around his neck was shaking,
As he was singing, jabbering, chanting, cackling.   585
But only God perceived the thoughts in her heart
As May observed him, flapping around in his shirt,
His nightcap on, his neck crinkled and lean.
She did not praise the workman, watching him preen.
At last he spoke: "Now I'll go to sleep.   590
It's daytime, peaceful rest is what I need."
He lay down his head and slept till another morning.
And then, seeing it was time to wake,
He rose, but his bridal flower, fresh young May,
Kept to her bed, and stayed for four more days,   595
The usual custom for wives, and much for the best,
For every laborer must sometimes rest,
Or else he cannot possibly endure—
I speak, of course, only of living creatures,
Whether fish, or bird, or beast, or man.   600
          Let me now return to woeful Damyan,
Still languishing for love, as you will hear.
I'll speak to him directly, right in his ear:
"O foolish youngster, O Damyan, alas!
Ponder my questions, in this hopeless case.   605
How can you tell your sorrow to your lady May?
Whatever you're able to say, she'll say you nay.
Speak too loud, or too much, and you'll be betrayed.
O God be your helper! That is all I can say."
          This wounded Damyan, held in Venus' fire,   610
Burned so hot he almost died of desire,
And could not help but take a terrible risk:

Secretly, he borrowed a pen and swiftly
Set his sorrows down, in a composition
He wrote in poetic form, creating his vision 615
Of love for his fresh and beautiful lady May.
Sealed in a silken purse, he hung it, that day,
On his shirt, careful to lay it next to his heart.

    The moon had been in two degrees of Taurus,
The day of January's marriage to May; 620
It glided to two degrees in Cancer. Four days
Had past, with May still keeping to her bed,
As noble people will, and tradition bids them.
A bride must never eat in the dining hall
Until four days are gone (though three may be all 625
They take), and then she can feast however she likes.
The fourth day ended, counting from moon to moon,
Just as mass had been sung, and now was done,
And there, both cheerfully eating, were lady May
And her husband. She was like a summer day, 630
And he was January, and suddenly thought
Of his favorite servant, asking whatever brought
His absence: "By Mary! How could it ever be
That Damyan's not here, attending on me?
Is the fellow sick? Tell me just what's happened." 635
The other squires, standing there in back,
Explained he could not come because of sickness,
Which kept him, alas, away from his proper business.
Nothing else could interrupt his service.

    "I'm sorry," said January, "he's an excellent servant, 640
A gracious squire indeed, now by my faith!
Now what a shame, were death intending to take him.
He is as sensible, discreet, and private
As any man I know of, in the trade he thrives at,
A manly man as well as one who serves 645
Most honestly. I dare say better servants
Are hard to find. But after dinner, I say,
I'll visit him myself, along with May,
And offer all the comfort I possibly can."
They all were pleased, and blessed the kind old man 650
Both for his goodness and his high nobility;

Not every lord would be as kind as he was,
So readily willing to comfort a poor sick squire.
"Lady," he said to his wife, "now I require
That, after dinner, you and all your women 655
Join together and visit our Damyan,
As soon as all of you are ready and able.
Cheer him up, for he is a good young man.
And tell him I too will come and pay a visit,
Once I've had a chance to get a bit 660
Of rest. Don't stay too long, for I will lie
Awake until I know you're at my side."
And then he turned away and began to call
For the squire who served as steward of his hall,
Issuing certain orders, as he wished. 665
  May was not reluctant to pay this visit,
And, gathering all her women about her, hurried
To where the young man lay, as if sick in bed,
And began to comfort him, as well as she could.
Watching with utmost care till he saw the chance, 670
Damyan secretly put his purse in her hand—
In which purse his passionate poetry lay.
That was all he did; for a moment nothing more,
Except profoundly sighing, deep and sore.
And then he whispered (her head was close to his), 675
"Have mercy! And please, say nothing at all of this,
For, surely, I'd be dead if it were known."
She hid the purse in her bosom, under her gown,
And soon she left him. What can I add, right now?
She went directly to January's room, 680
And found him peacefully sitting, awaiting her coming.
He put his arms around her, kissed her in welcome,
Then turned and slept, dozing off in seconds.
She slipped away, pretending nature beckoned
And she had to go where sometimes everyone needs to; 685
And when she had read his passionate poem (she was reading
Fast), she tore it into tiny shreds,
And dropped it gently in the privy. But she'd read it.
  And now, who needs to consider, except fresh May?
She laid herself down, beside old January, 690

Who slept like a log until abruptly awakened
By a cough. He told her he wished she'd make herself naked,
For he felt, he said, a need for some moments of pleasure,
And all her clothing interfered beyond measure.
He did not ask what she wished, and she did as directed.   695
Over-fastidious folk would loudly object
If I told you what he did, so I dare not tell it,
Or whether to her it was paradise or hell.
In any case, I'll leave them where they were,
Till the evening bell had rung; it was time for dinner.   700
   Whether by accident or destiny,
Whether by nature or magic sorcery,
Or the stars were so arranged, at just this time,
That lovers' pleas to Venus were likely to find
Success—as clerics say, all things have their time—   705
And access to any woman was guaranteed,
I cannot say, but God who knows all things
Assures us nothing happens without a reason,
And that is enough: for the rest, I hold my peace.
And the truth is this: our fresh and pretty May   710
Had been so deeply moved the very first day,
That affectionate sorrow for Damyan stayed in her heart,
And driving this away was extremely hard.
"Clearly," she thought, "whoever might be displeased
Means absolutely nothing at all to me,   715
And here I pledge myself to love this fellow
Best of all, though he owns just a shirt and a pillow."
Ah, pity travels fast in a heart that's willing!
   Thus you can see how highly superior grace
Resides in women, closely inspecting each case.   720
Some people are tyrants, and we have many of them,
With hearts as hard as rocks, cold as stone,
And would have let him starve in that lonely place,
Rather than granting him a bit of their grace,
They take their pleasure, their joy, in cruel pride,   725
Indifferent to another's homicide.
   This noble May, flowing over with pity,
Sat down and wrote a letter immediately,
Granting him her very faithful grace.

Nothing was lacking except a time and place,   730
A when and where that May could satisfy
Desire, when all would be the way he liked.
The moment she saw the chance, once on a day,
To visit him, she went and slyly placed
Her letter under his pillow, where if he pleased   735
Damyan could read it. When no one could see her,
She grasped him by the hand and wrung it hard,
Without a word assuring she'd do her part.
She left him, saying she hoped he'd soon be well,
And went to January, as soon as he called.   740
      This Damyan was cured the very next morning;
Sickness and sorrow had passed away by dawn.
He combed and cleaned himself, he dressed to the teeth,
All to impress fresh May, to try and please her.
He went to January, bowing low   745
Like a dog trained to an archer's hunting bow.
He showered pleasantries on every man
(Art is everything, for he who can
Abuse it), so all would speak of him in good
And favorable terms. Now let him do what he needs to,   750
And I will turn to my tale, and let it proceed.
      Clerics sometimes argue that felicity
Is based on material things, and certainly
Our noble January, with all his might,
In honorable ways befitting a prosperous knight   755
Arranged his life for living luxuriously.
His house, his clothing, and everything that he
Possessed was respectable, noble as a king's.
And among the other highly honorable things
He built was a garden, walled around with stone,   760
Fairer than any garden I have known—
Without a doubt, I certainly suppose
That even he who wrote *Romance of the Rose*
Could not have planned, or invented, such natural beauty,
And neither could Príapús, for all his duty   765
Serving as god of gardens; neither could tell
The amazing beauty found in garden and well
Standing beneath a laurel perpetually green.

How many times Pluto, along with his queen,
Prosérpiná, and all their circling fairies, 770
Amused themselves, and sung their melodies
And danced around that well, as men have told.
     This noble knight, our January, though old,
Took great delight in strolling there, and playing,
Though no one was permitted to carry the key 775
Except himself—a dainty silver thing,
Which locked and unlocked the gate, and which he would bring
Whenever he wanted to pleasure himself, or yet
Still better, desired to pay his wife her debt.
In summer season, this was where he would go, 780
Along with May, no one but just these two,
And what had not been done in their marriage bed
He did in the garden, performing outside instead.
And in this manner, for many a merry day,
January lived, and with him fresh May. 785
But worldly pleasures can't be enjoyed for ever,
Neither by January nor any creature.
     How swift is Fate! O you, unstable Fortune,
Deceitful, more dangerous than scorpions,
Smiling your attention before you sting! 790
Your tail, too, is death by poisoning.
O fickle joy! O sweet and artful venom!
O monster, knowing how to subtly paint
Your gifts in shining colors—but O! how tainted,
Your unreliable presents to everyone! 795
Why choose this January for deceit,
Who thought you a friend, someone he believed in?
And now, what you took from him is both his eyes,
And given him such sorrow he wishes to die.
     Alas! This gracious knight, this January, 800
Steeped in delight and high prosperity,
Has now been blinded by a sudden flicker
Of fate. He weeps and wails, his heart is sick
With pity for himself, and the fire of jealousy,
Frightened his wife might pursue some artful folly. 805
His heart was so aflame he almost longed
For someone to kill himself and his wife, so strong

Is jealousy. He could not accept that either
After his death, or in his life, she might be
Lover or wife to anyone else, but live   810
As widows should, wearing the blackest dresses,
Alone as turtles deprived of their mates. There are blessings
In time, and little by little, in a month or two,
His sorrow lost a bit of its bite, for in truth
He began to see that this was how it would be,   815
And so began to accept his adversity—
Except, most certainly, he could not keep
From universal jealousy, asleep
Or awake, a jealousy so great and outrageous
That neither in their palace nor another house,   820
Nor any other place, was May allowed
To ride or walk or go, unless like a shroud
She could not take off, his hand was touching her body.
Loving Damyan so graciously,
These harsh restrictions often left her weeping   825
And feeling, certainly, she'd either fall dead
Or have him, as each one madly wanted. When
Or how it could happen, neither knew. So they waited.
    Damyan, too, was sorrowfully impatient,
A woeful man, who neither night nor day   830
Was able to speak a single word to May,
Nothing, at least, to the purpose, for January
Was always there, and he would certainly hear,
His hand perpetually on her, clutching somewhere.
But nevertheless, by writing to and fro,   835
And secret signs, intelligible to both,
They each were aware of the other's heart, and their oaths.
    O January, how would it help or avail,
If you could see as far as ships can sail?
A man's as good as blind, when he's deceived: 840
Deception is blindness, even for him who sees.
    Lo, the gods gave Argus a hundred eyes,
So he could see whatever men devised,
But he was deceived, like many others, God knows,
Who surely did not think that it could be so.   845
But let me escape from this, and say no more.

This fresh young May, of whom I spoke before,
Had pressed warm wax against the garden key
Which only January possessed, for she
Was bold, and watched for its availability, 850
And Damyan, of course, who knew precisely
How to, took a wax impression, and a key
Was made. What else can I say? Both she and he
Were anxious, something good was bound to happen,
Which you will hear, unless you sit there, napping. 855
    O noble Ovid, God knows you said it well:
No cunning trick, no matter how long or hellishly
Hot, is safe from love's quick prying hands.
Pyramus and Thisbee teach this lesson,
Though strictly guarded, they managed to find their blessing 860
By means of a hidden hole in the wall, that no one
Could have discovered except a pair of lovers.
    But back to my story. Before a week was over,
In the warming month of June, May had gotten
Her husband breathing hard, at the very thought 865
Of what they could do in the garden, just them alone,
So early one morning he said to her: "Come,
Rise up, my wife, my love, my fresh young one!
The turtle's voice has been heard, my sweet young dove,
And winter, with all his soaking rains, has gone. 870
Appear, O you with beautiful dove-like eyes!
Your breasts so much more beautiful than wine!
Our garden's well closed in, all round about.
Come forth, my fair white spouse! Come, come out,
You've struck my heart, it bleeds for you, my wife! 875
O faultless one, you've never spotted my life.
Come let us play, relishing our sport:
You are my choice for marriage and lasting comfort."
    Such old and untaught language came rolling freely
Off his tongue. May listened, then quietly 880
Gave Damyan a simple signal, so he
Should enter the garden before them, and hurriedly
He did just that, in secret and in silence,
So no one could see or hear him as he moved.
And then he sat beneath a bush, and waited. 885

Blind as a stone, warmed by sun and impatience,
Came January, leading May by the hand.
Into the garden they went, and then he slammed
The gate with a clatter, so no one could surprise them.
"Now wife, no one is here but you and I," 890
He said, "and you are the only woman I love,
For by the lord who sits in heaven above
I'd rather be stabbed to death by someone's knife
Than give you cause for offense, my own dear wife!
Remember well, by God, I made you my choice, 895
Surely not in greed, but obeying the voice
Of love in my heart, which knew at once what I needed.
And though I am old, and can no longer see,
Stay true to me, and I will tell you why.
There are three things, for sure, you'll win thereby: 900
Love of Christ, and honor to yourself,
And all you'll inherit, lands, and towns, and castles:
These will be yours, whenever you want the deeds—
Tomorrow, before it's dark, they'll be drawn as needed.
God thus wisely fills my soul with bliss. 905
To seal that bargain, I pray you, first, come kiss me.
I know I'm jealous, but I am not at fault,
For you are imprinted deeply down in my soul:
As I reflect on your compelling beauty,
And the aged unfitness that characterizes me, 910
I simply exist to be in your company.
Without your love I'd just as soon not be
At all—of this, my wife, there is no doubt.
So kiss me, first, before we roam about."

Fresh May, when all her husband's speech was heard, 915
Graciously answered him with pleasant words,
But before she spoke, she sobbed, and then she wept:
"I too," she said, "have a soul that needs to be kept
From sin, and I too think about my honor,
And about my wifely state—a tender flower— 920
Which I have pledged to you, and given my hand,
The moment the priest created the holy bond
Between us, giving you my body. My answer
Is, without objection, my lord so dear:

I pray to God the day will never dawn,   925
So long as I live, that I may bring upon
My family's head such loathsome, filthy shame,
Or that I ever, ever injure your name
By being untrue. And if I ever did,
Strip me, and let me be forever hidden   930
In a sack, drowned for good in the nearest river.
I am a decent woman, not a whore.
Why do you say these things? It's men who more
Deserve them, but women are always the ones they blame,
Though men so freely commit these very shames.   935
You men have always been thus, I firmly believe,
Treating women like immoral thieves."
    And as she spoke these words, she looked, and saw
Where Damyan sat beneath the bush. So she coughed
And with her fingers signed to him that he   940
Should quickly climb up in the nearest tree,
Hung heavy with fruit, and up at once he went,
Truly understanding all she meant,
No matter what sort of unusual sign she gave him,
Far better than January, her lawful mate—   945
For in a letter she had written it out,
Informing him exactly, and with no doubt.
Now let me leave him sitting high in a pear tree,
While January and May roam merrily.
    The day was bright, the firmament shone blue;   950
Phoebus had sent the golden beams he uses
To warm all flowers into happiness.
He was, just then, in Gemini, I guess,
And just a little from his declination
In Cancer, Jove's most noble, highest station.   955
And then, in bright and shining morning time,
There in that garden, on the farther side,
Pluto, the ruling king of fáeríe,
And many a lady in the company
Of his wife, the famous queen Prosérpina   960
(Whom he had roughly stolen out of Aetna,
As she was gathering flowers in the fields—
Cláudian Cláudiánus tells it: read

His book—and threw her in his grisly chariot).
Pluto had heard and seen what May was up to. 965
He set himself on a soft turf-bench, fresh green,
And then, immediately, he said to his queen:
"My wife," he said, "who can deny this scene?
Every day of our lives we see what it means,
Women brewing treasons to inflict on man. 970
There are ten hundred thousand tales I can,
But won't, repeat of lying and fickleness.
O Solomon, so wise, and richest of rich,
Seeing truth profoundly, steeped in glory,
How justly your words are kept in memory 975
By everyone of intelligence and reason.
Here's what he said, in this matter of female treason:
'Among a thousand men, I find just one
Who's good, but of all women I find not one.'
  "Thus spoke a king who knows your wickedness. 980
The author of *Ecclésiástes*—but him, I guess—
Offers women little reverence.
Let roaring fire and infectious pestilence
Descend on women's bodies this very night!
Look at this noble, good and honorable knight: 985
Because, alas! he's now gone blind, and is old,
His very own servant's going to make him a cuckold.
Just look at him sitting, that lecher, up in a tree!
But I will ensure, from the depths of my majesty,
That this same blind, and old, and worthy knight 990
Will now be given back his own eyes' sight,
Just as his wife is doing him injury.
Then he will understand her harlotry,
Of which all women are guilty, and not just she."
  "O will you?" said Próserpíne. "That may not be. 995
By my mother's father, Saturn, I hereby swear
I'll give her a more than satisfactory answer,
And, for her sake, to every woman thereafter,
So even when captured right in the guilty act
They'll have the courage to stand and make up facts, 1000
Deny the truth, and knock their accusers back.
No woman will be allowed to die for lack

Of words. A man may say what his eyes can see,
But women will always face it vigorously,
And weep, and vow, and scold most subtily,   1005
So you—all men!—will look as stupid as geese.
     "And why should I listen to your authorities?
I'm sure this famous Jew, this Solomon,
Found lots of fools in dealing with his women.
But though he never found a virtuous one,   1010
Other men have honored many of them,
Faithful women, good and kind and virtuous.
Look at those who lived at home with Jésus.
They proved their steadiness with martyrdom.
The *Gesta Romanorum* reminds you men   1015
Of many wives, faithful and truly honest.
But Pluto, my lord, you need not be offended,
For though this Solomon saw no good women,
You ought to note not just his words, but his sense,
For what he meant was goodness eternally,   1020
Residing in God, but never in human beings.
     "Consider! Our God is simply the only one—
So why rely so much on Solomon?
So he made a temple, constructed a towering house
For God! So he was rich and glorious!   1025
But also he honored pagan deities,
And what could be much worse than housing these
False gods? But pardon me: whiten his name
As you like, his lechery will always stain it,
His worship of idols—and in the end he spurned   1030
His God, and surely God would quickly have burned him
To death, except that his father, David, begged
For mercy, and God for his father's sake consented.
The things you write about women, in all your books,
Are flapping vapors, mere butterflies! I look   1035
At the world as a woman, I have a need to speak
My mind, or else my heart would swell and break.
Solomon saying we're idle talkers hurts
My soul, and as long as I'm alive my words
Will fight with him, show him no courtesy,   1040
For all he says about women is injurious."

"My lady," Pluto said, "don't be angry.
I give it up! But since I swore an oath
That he would surely have his sight once more,
My word must stand; I can't reject what I've sworn to.　　　1045
Being a king, my word must be inviolate."

　　"And I," she said, "remain in my queenly state!
She will have her answers, as I have stated.
Let's speak no more; our words contain no weight.
Truly, I wish an end to our being contrary."　　　1050

　　So let us turn again to January,
Who walks around the garden with his May,
Singing happy songs like swallows or jays:
"I love you best, and you alone, no other!"
Along the paths he goes, first one, then another,　　　1055
And finally comes to the spot where the pear tree grows,
In which this Damyan sits, adjusting his clothes,
Up in the branches, among the shimmering leaves

　　Fresh May, herself so glistening with sheen,
Began to sigh, and said, "Alas, my womb!　　　1060
O now, my lord, to keep myself from swooning,
I must have one of the pears hung on this tree,
Or I may die, I so much want what I see:
I must have one of these little pears to eat.
O Mary, mother of God, come and help me!　　　1065
O husband, a woman in my condition longs
For fruit so desperately, with urges so strong,
She truly might die, not getting what she wants."

　　"Alas!" said he, "that here I have no servant
Able to climb! Alas, alas," said he,　　　1070
That I am blind!" "No matter, my lord," said she,
"But if you're willing, for God's own precious sake,
To grasp the tree with your arms, then I will be safe
If I climb myself. For I know you never trust me,
But I can climb it well enough," said she,　　　1075
"If I can set my foot flat on your back."

　　"Why, yes," he said, "I couldn't object to that.
I'd gladly sacrifice my blood for you."
He stooped and bent, and on his back she stood,
And grasping hold of a branch, thus up she went—　　　1080

And, ladies, please, don't think yourselves offended;
I can't be prissy, or shy; I'm a country man—
But quickly, then, this eager Damyan
Pulled up her gown, and thrust himself right in.
    And Pluto, seeing this wretched, wrongful sight,   1085
Immediately gave January his eyes,
Letting him see as well as ever he might.
And seeing the world again, recovering his sight,
He blessed himself, thanked God, and was delighted—
But focused, as he always did, on his wife.   1090
From where he stood, he cast his eyes on the sight
Of Damyan dealing with her private parts
In a way that nearly broke his aching heart,
But cannot be described in my courteous art.
And he began to roar, and uttered a cry   1095
Much like a mother when her child has died.
"Out! Help! Alas! Harrow!" he began to cry.
"O bold and cruel lady, what are you doing?"
    She answered: "My lord, what is ailing you?
Keep patience and reason alive, in your tottering mind,   1100
For I've been up here, curing both your eyes.
On peril of my soul—and I'm not lying—
I'm doing what I was taught, to heal your eyes,
For nothing is better, for helping you to see,
Than struggling with a man up in a tree.   1105
God knows, I climbed, and that was all I meant."
    "You struggled!" he said. "Yet all the way in it went!
May God give you, and him, a shameless dying!
He was inside you, I saw it with my eyes—
Or hang me up in a tree, at the end of a rope!"   1110
    "My remedy," she said, "must then be flawed:
Without a doubt, if you could truly see,
You'd not be saying things like this to me.
Your vision's faint and flickering, you don't see right."
    "I see," he said, "as well as ever I might,   1115
May God be thanked! Both my eyes see true,
And God be praised, I saw what he did to you."
    "You're still in a daze, good sir," she then replied.
"Alas, that ever I tried so hard to be kind!

These are the thanks I have for making you see."
     "Now, lady," he said, "let that be history.
Come down, my love, and if I've been mistaken
May God assist me, for I am badly shaken.
But by my father's soul, I thought I had seen
Damyan do it with you, up in that tree,
The hem of your dress all up around his shoulders."
     "Ah yes," she said, "your thoughts get bolder and bolder.
But, sir, a man just wakened out of sleep
May not so easily know just what he sees,
And focus his eyes, and see what's truly there,
Until he's fully himself, and his sight's repaired.
And doubly so, with a man so recently blind,
Who cannot yet adjust his eyes and his mind:
He must wait a day or two for perfect sight,
And until your vision's settled for a while
There may be many people and things beguiling
You. Be careful, please, for by heaven's king
You're not the only man to be seeing things
Exactly the opposite of what they are.
And when you think wrong, your judgment's also flawed."
And with those words, she leaped down from the tree.
     And January? O how delighted was he!
He was kissing her, and hugging over and over,
First stroking, then caressing her rounded womb.
And after, still holding tight, he led her home.
I ask you all, my friends, to share his glee,
For that is the end of this tale of January.
May God bless all, and his mother, the Virgin Mary!

1120

1125

1130

1135

1140

1145

Epilogue to the Merchant's Tale

"O ay, God's mercy!" our Host declared, right then,
"Now such a wife I pray God keep me from!
Lo, what tricks and deceiving subtleties
Women can use! They're always busy as bees,
Buzzing and humming tales for men to believe,   5
And up and down, around the truth they weave,
Exactly as this Merchant's tale informs us.
It happens that I have a wife, at home,
Reliable as steel, though poor like me;
But she's a blabbing shrew, when her tongue is free.   10
Of course, she has some other vices, too—
No matter! Let us stick to our happy route.
But let me tell you, in strictest privacy,
I'm often sorry, being tied to such as she.
But were I, now, to add up all her vices,   15
I'd surely be a fool, so I won't try it.
And why? Whatever I say might be reported—
I won't say by whom—but people do tell stories,
And this is a subject I've finished and now I'm done with,
For women's ears detect the blabbing of dumb-wits,   20
Of whom I'm surely one. But I know enough
To shut my mouth when I need to, so enough of this stuff!"

Introduction to the Squire's Tale

"Come closer, Squire," said the Host. "We'll be obliged
If you talk to us of love. It's on your mind,
I know, you've certainly thought of it hard and long."
    "No sir," he answered. "But since I truly belong
To this company, I have no thought of rebelling,   5
You've called on me, and now I will surely tell
My tale. Please pardon me, if I speak amiss.
Do not be offended. And lo, my tale is this.

The Squire's Tale
[unfinished]

South of Ukraine, in the land of Tartary,
Once lived a king who warred on Russia. He
And his armies caused the death of many a man.
The name of this noble ruler was Cambéeyuskán,
Who in his time was famous, of such renown   5
And glory that no one then could have found
A lord surpassing this man in anything.
Indeed, his nature contained whatever a king
Requires. He followed Islam, the faith he was born to,
And strictly followed its laws, as he was sworn to.   10
This ruler's hand was strong; he was wise, and rich,
Observing justice, but also pitiful
To the helpless, a man much honored, and always honest
And kind. His steady courage was like a compass.
He was young, and fresh, and strong, and drawn to war   15
As fiercely as all young men quite naturally are.
He carried himself most handsomely; he was lucky;
He preserved his royal estate so well that such
Another could not be traced in the world of man.
       This gracious king, this Tartar Cambéeyuskán,   20
Had had two sons, by lady Elphéta, his wife,
The oldest bearing the name of Álgarsíf;
The younger was given the name of Cámbaló.
This worthy king was given a daughter, also,
His youngest child, whose name was Cánacée,   25
But I, alas, cannot describe her beauty,
It will not sit on my tongue, nor rest in my mind,

I dare not attempt descriptions of so lofty a kind.
And, further, my knowledge of English is insufficient:
This is work for an expert rhetorician,   30
Fully trained in all the verbal arts;
No one else could capture every part.
I am no rhetorician, I say what I can.
  And after worthy King Cambéeyuskán
Had worn his crown for twenty happy winters,   35
He had his servants announce to his citizens—
Just as he always did, from year to year—
That he would have a birthday feast, right there,
After the final Ides of March. A clear
High sky brightened the day, for Phoebus was glad,   40
Knowing that he approached the top of the ladder,
Right against Mars, and in his astral mansion
In Aries, which signified a fiery sun.
The weather was perfect, ideally fine for men
And birds and beasts, living again in a green   45
Season, and singing sweetly their great affection
For the sun, returned to offer them protection
Against the winter's sword, sharp and cold.
  This Cambéeyuskán, of whom I've already told you,
In royal robes was sitting high on a dais,   50
His crown on his head, there in the midst of his palace,
Presiding over a feast so rich and exalted
That worldly celebrations were none at all
Its equal; even attempting to describe it fully
Would take an entire day at the height of summer,   55
And surely no one needs to know the stunning
Total of everything eaten and drunk that day.
So don't expect to hear the unusual way
Feasts are presented, with heron soups, and dishes
Of swans, enormous platters of meat, sufficient   60
For armies to eat. And indeed, the knights of old
Report that strange and unusual table food
Is easy to find, there in that land, but the meat
We like is considered odd, and is not eaten.
It is not possible to clarify all this,   65
And so I won't delay you, time is precious,

And that would amount to time certainly wasted.
    After the third of their courses was served and tasted,
And the king, up high on his throne, in royal robes,
Was listening to minstrels playing before him,   70
Thoroughly enjoying cheerful tunes,
When suddenly appearing, and entering the room,
They saw a knight riding a horse of brass,
Bearing a very large mirror of polished glass.
His thumb displayed a ring of shining gold,   75
And by his side there hung a naked sword.
And up he rode to the very head of the board.
No one seated, there in that hall, said a word,
Amazed by this knight's appearance. They sat and stared,
Both young and old, yearning to learn who was there.   80
    This unknown knight, who'd come so suddenly,
Was heavily armored—except his head—and richly.
He greeted the king and queen, and all the lords,
In proper order, wherever they were in the hall,
With such humility, and courtesy,   85
In both his face and in his careful speech,
That even Gawain, famed for dignity,
Even returning out of Faerie,
Could not have improved or amended a single word.
Still standing there, at Cambéeyuskán's board,   90
He raised his manly voice and gave his message,
According to all the forms used in his language,
With no mistakes in consonants or vowels.
Indeed, to let his message grip your bowels,
His face reflected what his words intended,   95
Exactly as the art of speech was meant to
Be. I cannot capture his sound or sequence,
Nor climb to the top of such a towering fence,
But what I will write is surely the basic sense,
Pointing in the direction he intended,   100
If memory serves me right, and my feeble mind:
    "The king of the Arabs and of India,"
He said, "greets you, my lord, on this splendid day,
Salutes you as only my king both can and may,
And sends you, honoring your sumptuous feast,   105

A messenger, now standing at your behest.
I bring you this steed of brass, who smooth and fast
Can cover, in the course of a single day—
Or if you prefer, in four and twenty hours—
And take you, no matter the day, no matter if it showers,   110
To any and every far-off worldly spot
For which your heart may yearn. And you will not
Be harmed in any way, no matter the weather.
In fact, this horse can fly as high in the air
As an eagle's great wings, whenever he feels like soaring.   115
This steed will carry you forever more,
Calmly, safely, exactly where you wish,
Whether you sleep on his back, or simply rest.
Wriggle the proper pin, he changes course—
For he who made this steed made more than a horse,   120
Waiting for just the perfect constellations,
Enduring harsh and grueling negotiations.
     "This mirror, held in my hand, is another creation,
And has the power to let you look and see
If ever this, your home in Tartary,   125
Has undergone some hard adversity,
And shows you, also, any plans or plots
Against your person, and who is your friend, who not.
     "And in addition to this, a glance at this glass
Will show a lady the nature of the man she has,   130
And if he's unfaithful, she'll see it plain and clear,
Just who he's been unfaithful with, and where,
And all the secrets he's been trying to hide.
And so, in this high-blooming summer time,
The mirror, and also this ring—which you can see—   135
My master has sent to your daughter, Cánacée,
The shining young lady seated here at your table.
     "Let me tell you what this ring is able
To do. Its power goes to work if she wears it
Upon her thumb or if she only bears it   140
In her purse—and every bird that flies above
Will speak in a language she is mistress of,
And she will understand him, clear and plain,
And in his own language can answer him again.

And all that grows in the earth, sends down its roots,   145
She'll understand, and for whom its taste is good,
Even if swords have pierced him deep and wide.
    "This naked sword, hanging by my side,
Possesses such power that any man you strike
Will quickly have this blade carving and biting   150
Through his armor, even if hard as oak,
And any man who's wounded by your stroke
Will never be whole until you wish, by your grace,
To stroke him with the blade in precisely the place
He's hurt. Perhaps I can more clearly explain: 155
The blade that wounded him must stroke his pain,
The wound itself, and it will swiftly close.
This is exactly the truth; it is not a boast.
This sword will never fail you, held in your hands."
    Having told his tale, as his king commanded,   160
He rode right out of the hall, and swiftly alighted;
His steed, that gleamed like sunlight, and almost as bright,
Stood in the courtyard, as still as any stone.
Swiftly, the servants led this knight to a room,
Removed his armor, and fed him fully and well.   165
    Cambéeyuskán then ordered the sword and mirror
So royally sent, quickly carried up
To the highest tower, and this important job
Was assigned to special officers, and was done.
And the ring for Cánacée, the only one   170
Of its kind, was brought to her as she sat at table.
But the horse of brass, believe me, no one was able
To move, except the visiting knight, so it stood
Where it was, as still as if its hooves had been glued
To the ground. No windlass device, and surely no pulley,   175
Could move it an inch. They saw it was foolishness
To try, until the knight had taught them the craft
Of making it move, and so it stayed where he'd left it.
    The crowds that came, and were swarming to and fro,
Stood staring at this horse, frozen like snow,   180
For it was so high, both very broad and long,
And clearly made to be enormously strong,
Something like a steed from Lombardy,

And yet so gentle, with sensitive, shining eyes,
It could have been an Apúlian palfrey, for ladies. 185
And plainly, from his tail right up to his ear,
It seemed quite clear, to everyone standing there,
That neither nature nor art could have made him better.
But mostly, looking it over, people wondered
Just how a horse of brass could move those thunderous 190
Hooves. It had to be magic, from Faerie land.
Truly, no one was able to understand it,
No single explanation carried the day,
Each man saw it in a different way,
As many views as there were human brains. 195
They swarmed around it like a hive of bees,
Each man's mouth spouting its fantasies,
Rehearsing, point by point, old poetries,
Some saying this was like great Pegasus,
Who with white wings became a flying horse, 200
Or maybe even the wooden horse that Sinon
Devised, and the Greeks deployed, for Troy's destruction,
As people have been reading for centuries.
"And I," said one, "am afraid of creatures like these,
Worrying that men of arms are inside, 205
Planning to take this town by homicide.
All things like this require to be explained."
Another whispered softly to a friend,
"It's a lie. All of this is simply like
The shows put on by wizards wearing stripes, 210
Minstrels and players amusing folk at feasts."
And so they went, babbling their arguments
As ignorant people do, when they're presented
With matters their brains can't fully comprehend.
According to them, the world will soon be ending. 215
  Others focused solely on the mirror,
Now stored in safety in the highest tower,
Wondering what visions could be seen.
And others answered, yes, it might well be,
Quite naturally, by very careful arrangement 220
Of astral angles, and skilful manipulation,
And one such fellow, they said, was at work in Rome.

They talked of Álhazén and Wítilo
And Aristotle, those who'd written tomes
On cleverly managed mirrors and strange perspectives— 225
Showing, at least, they knew these authors' names.
     Others thought about the naked sword
That went through wood, and iron, and steel, and brought
Swift death. They talked of Télephús, wounded
By Achílles, wielding a similar weapon that hurt 230
And healed, except that wasn't a sword, but a spear.
They spoke of different methods for hardening metal,
And spoke of the liquids hammered into them all,
And how and when the hardening took place,
Of which I know naught, and am saying naught in this space. 235
     They also spoke of Cánacée's bright ring,
All agreed it was so wondrous a thing
That nothing like it had ever been heard of or seen,
Except that King Solomon, and David, had been
Renowned for working in those sorts of secrets. 240
So people said, and walked away. And yet
There were a few who said that fern-ash glass
Was never so clear, so this was something vastly
Different, but since such things had once been known,
So long ago, why bother because they were known 245
Again? People, they said, are dazzled by thunder,
Too, by tides and mists and floods. Why wonder
And wonder on all of this? Men are not wise,
Who only wonder. And so they went on advising
Each other, until the king decided to rise. 250
     Phoebus had left the angle we call merídional,
And still ascending there was that noble royal
Beast, the Lion, along with his star, Aldíran,
When this ruling Tartar king, Cambéeyuskán,
Rose from the table, where he, of course, sat highest. 255
Preceding him as he walked were all his very best
Minstrels, until he reached his reception chamber
Producing the lovely sounds that they could make
On all their varied and many instruments,
So those who listened felt themselves in heaven. 260
So go on dancing, all you children of Venus,

For there, up high in Pisces, is where that goddess
Lies, watching you with friendly eyes.

  The king ascended to his royal throne,
And the foreign knight was brought into the room,   265
Where he began to dance with Cánacée.
This is the kind of pleasure and jollity
No slow and stupid man could invent or frame:
He has to know love and fathom its sacred claim,
And be as fresh a dancer as the month of May,   270
And then he can please himself, and others, all day.

  How can I tell you the steps and styles of dances
So differently done than here in England, or France,
And so many fresh faces, as well as peeping glances
Of sly and subtle jealousies and prancing?   275
Lancelot could, but Lancelot is dead.
So I will leave these joys to those who had them,
And say no more, except that they were able
To dance until their supper was on the table.

  The steward ordered spices brought for their pleasure,   280
And wine, and music played on, without any measure.
Spices and wine were quickly and well brought on,
So waiters and other such attendants were gone.
They ate and drank, and when they reached the end
Straight to temple worship everyone went.   285
Religious services done, they went on eating
All day, exactly when and how they pleased.
Everyone knew, as everyone should, that a feast
Put on by a king had food and drink enough
For all, and other dainties: I'm ignorant   290
Of all this. After supper, this noble king
Went to see the horse of brass, with a crowd
Of curious lords and anxious ladies about him.

  Continued amazement surrounded this horse, a bustle
Not seen since the siege of Troy, ending in disaster,   295
Where men had stood and worried about a horse.
Some similar things were seen and heard, of course.
The king at last inquired of the knight
The power of the beast, and how to control his might:
In short, what was the system of governance?   300

The horse began to shake his hooves and dance
As soon as the knight picked up and held his reins,
Declaring, "My lord, there's nothing more to say:
When you decide to ride him anywhere
You need to turn a pin, fixed in his ear,   305
As I shall explain, but only to you, and in private.
You need to tell him the place where you would like
To go, or just the country you want to ride to.
And when you reach that place, if you're up in the air
Tell him you want to descend, and point out where,   310
Then turn another pin, and he'll do as you will,
And when he's standing on ground, he'll stay quite still.
The secret lies in turning the pins, just so.
Once he's at rest, nothing can make him go,
He won't allow himself to be carried off,   315
Though every man in the world declared he would.
But if you prefer to keep him hidden, for a time,
Trill this pin, here—he'll quickly vanish from sight,
And come again, whether by day or night,
Whenever you wish to call him back again,   320
By means, in another moment, I'll fully explain,
But of course, only to you. And then it is done:
Ride wherever you wish, be it late or soon."
        The king had surely heard whatever he needed
To know; a clear, precise image in his mind   325
Would let him do with the horse whatever he liked.
Enormously pleased, this brave and resolute king
Returned to his celebration, the dancing and singing.
The bridle was taken off the horse and borne
To the tower where jewels and valuables were stored.   330
The horse abruptly disappeared, I don't know how
Or why: I've told you all I can, by now.
So let us leave, in pleasure and jollity,
King Cambéeyuskán and all his partying,
Ending, at last, just as the dawn was springing.   335

PART TWO

The nurse of our digestion, known as sleep,
Began to shut his eyes, with a subtle but steep
Warning: a lot of drinking and dancing needs rest.
Yawning wide, the king addressed his guests,
Saying it was time for lying down   340
(The blood in his body was now in domination).
"Be careful of blood, it's nature's friend," said he.
They yawned and thanked him, by one, by two, by three,
And all began to take themselves to bed,
As sleep had told them, advice they took for the best.   345
    Their dreams do not deserve description, here:
Their heads were filled with stomach vapors, weird
And senseless, and so their dreams were meaningless.
Most of them slept till late in the morning; their rest
Required that much of the day. But Cánacée   350
Was moderate, as women tend to be,
And shortly after darkness fell, she
Had asked her father to let her take her leave.
Her face would otherwise have turned quite pale,
And when she rose she wanted to seem as gay   355
As a feast deserved. She took her sleep, but woke
At an early hour, her heart longing to look
At the ingenious ring, and also to see what the glass
Might show: even in sleep her mind ran fast,
And one of her dreams had clearly come from the lasting   360
Effect of the mirror. Before the sun was back
In the sky, she was out of bed and summoning
Her governess, who still was soundly sleeping,
And woke to the sound of Cánacée's soft voice.
    This ancient woman, like her young mistress, enjoyed   365
Gossip and news, and found this early rising
Too curious not to inquire, "But madame, why
So early? Where will you go, when the rest are sleeping?"
    "I wish to arise," was the answer, "having no need
For sleep. So I will go and take a walk."   370
    The governess arose and quickly summoned
Many others of her lady's women, and up

They rose, easily ten, or even twelve.
Fresh Cánacée quickly prepared herself,
As ruddy and bright as the gleaming early sun— 375
Who had not risen an inch when she was done—
And out she walked, strolling slowly along,
Her clothing light as the summer breeze, befitting
Light amusement, in that balmy season, and with her
Some five or six of her flock of serving women, 380
Traipsing along an alley cut in the woods.

  The early dawn had already brought out a mist,
Making the sun seem furry, perhaps star-kissed,
But all the same the scene was so fair a sight
The women's hearts were instantly gay and light, 385
Because of the season, because the day was dawning,
And because of how the early birds were singing.
And Cánacée now knew just what they meant
By their songs, in perfect detail and plain intention.

  Now, every tale has a reason that must be told 390
Before whatever passion drives goes cold,
And those who thought it a jolly story are bored,
Because the teller is telling more and more
And stretching matters out with prolixity.
And for the identical reasons, it appears to me, 395
I need to pay much more attention to my story's
Thrust, not letting this walk encourage snoring.

  Sitting high in a dried-out, chalk-like tree,
Where Cánacée was walking, you could have seen
A single peregrine falcon, which suddenly 400
Gave out a great and sorrowful cry, a scream
That echoed loud in every part of the wood.
Flapping both her wings as hard as she could,
She beat at her breast until a stream of blood
Came running all the way down the chalk-white trunk. 405
Continuing to shriek, she used her beak
To stab herself so wildly that any beast
Of prey, tiger or any other, in forest
Or wood, would surely itself have burst in tears
(If tigers and lions can ever weep), hearing 410
The terrible cries she uttered, so sad, so fierce.

No man who's ever lived, not here on earth,
Could possibly have seen a bird so fair
Of plumage, so beautifully, so nobly shaped,
A falcon of falcons in every single detail. 415
She had to have flown from foreign lands, so strange
She seemed. Perched on high, from time to time
She staggered, weak from loss of blood, and might
At any moment have fallen straight to the ground.
     Now Cánacée, this beautiful daughter of a king, 420
Was wearing her exotic magic ring,
Allowing her to understand the speech
Of each and every bird, and could then speak
Right back, in words the bird could comprehend.
Having listened right from start to end, 425
She was struck by waves of pity, strong and deadly.
She walked as fast as she could to the base of the tree,
Looked up at the falcon with sorrowing eyes
And stretched straight out the hem of her dress, to provide
Some safer landing place when the bird fell down, 430
As she thought it must, from high above the ground.
She stood, and patiently waited, for a very long time,
Until at last she spoke to the bird, in words
You are about to read, written right here:
     "Tell me why, if this is a tale for my ears," 435
Cánacée began, desperate to hear it,
"Why do you suffer these burning pains of hell?
Are you mourning someone's death, or under the spell
Of love? Such pain is usually from both
Or either of these, when noble hearts feel woe. 440
All other evils, plainly, need no discussion:
You're punishing yourself, which means that passionate
Anger or desperate fear are your only reasons,
For I can clearly see there's no one chasing
Behind you. Now, in the name of our holy gracious 445
God, take heed of yourself, or who may help you,
Or how? I look to the east, I look to the west,
And never see (and never saw!) a beast
Or bird fighting with itself so wildly.
You kill me with your grief, quite truthfully! 450

Compassion overwhelms me, watching you.
For God's great love, come down from the tree—please do.
I swear, as I am a princess, a great king's daughter,
Once I understand what huge disorder
Afflicts you, I will do my best to cure it,   455
However I can. You will not endure it
Longer than nightfall, this very day, as our God
Of mercy shows me the way, however hard
It runs. I know of many herbs to heal
Your wounds, if not the enormous sorrow you feel."   460
    And then the falcon shrieked, as if in greater
Pain than ever before, and all at once
Fell to the ground, as still as any stone.
Cánacée then put the bird in her lap,
And held her quietly there until she came back   465
To life. And then, as soon as her eyes were open,
In falcon speech, these were the words she spoke:
    "That pity rises swiftly in noble hearts,
Who feel all noble pain in themselves, like sharpened
Knives, is proven again and again for all   470
To see, or hear, or read, for what is noble
Is drawn to nobility, and perfectly knows it.
I knew at once that you were compassionate,
O noble Cánacée, driven by passions
Of deep and truthful woman-kindness, planted   475
Deep in your heart by Nature, when you were born.
I answer your questions, but not expecting more
For myself than knowing I honor your generous heart,
Perhaps establishing examples for others—
Just as we beat a dog to punish a lion.   480
And for those reasons, not any others, I'll try
To leave you satisfied. I know I'm dying,
But while I have the opportunity,
I wish to confess my sins for all to see."
    And then, as she went on, one of them spoke,   485
The other wept as if swiftly turned to water,
Until, at last, the falcon asked for her silence
And, sighing, went on to empty out her mind:
    "I cracked open my shell—alas, that I did so!—

And was nourished high on a towering marble-gray cliff.   490
And I was kept and cared for so tenderly
That life held nothing of any adversity
Until I learned to fly as high as I liked,
And met a great male falcon, who lived nearby,
Who seemed to me as noble as a bird could be.   495
Although he was steeped in treachery and lying,
He kept that hidden beneath humility,
And truthful words, and pleasant abilities,
And constant careful masking, covering over
Who and what he truly was, coloring   500
Himself like a woven cloth dyed in grain.
He hid himself beneath those flowers, snake-like,
Awaiting the moment when he was able to bite.
This so-called god of love, this hypocrite,
Beautifully pretended with all his wit,   505
Establishing himself as a noble lover.
Just as freshness, in tombs, must be above,
But corpses lie beneath—as everyone knows—
So was this hypocrite, both hot and cold.
And indeed he played it well, and got what he sought,   510
Only the Devil aware of what he was.
He wooed me, begging, whining, for many years,
Vowing fidelity and loving service,
Until my generous heart, true but senseless,
Completely unaware of his perfect malice   515
Worried—as I was—that he might die
Of despair, acting on his guarantees,
Offered him my love, on one condition,
Namely, that my honor, and noble position,
Would go unthreatened by private or public ambitions—   520
Meaning that I thought this monster deserved
My love, my heart, and all that lived in my mind
(God knows I'd never accept another kind).
I gave it, exchanging my love for what I believed
Was his. The ancient saying is well conceived: 525
'The mind of an honest man is not like a thief's.'
And when he saw that matters had advanced
So far, and my full love had now been granted

Him (as I have mentioned, earlier),
Giving him my loyal heart, as freely   530
As he had sworn he was giving his to me,
This secret tiger, filled with doubleness,
Dropped to his knees with holy humbleness
And such high reverence that, seeing his face,
You'd think him a noble lover, full of grace,   535
Enraptured, as it seemed, by sweeping joy
Greater than Argonaut Jason, or Paris of Troy—
Jason? No, not any man since Lamech,
Noah's father, the first man on the earth
To have two wives, according to the Bible—   540
Never since the very first male child
Was born in this world! No man could duplicate
A twenty-thousandth part of his artful faking;
No other man would be good enough to untie
His shoe, when it comes to deceit and subtle lying.   545
Absolutely no one could thank a woman
As he thanked me! Heaven opens to women
Loved by such a man, no matter how wise
They are, for he deployed his lying devices
With total perfection—his words, his face, his eyes.   550
I loved him for his perfect subservience,
And for the truth I thought ran deep within
His breast—loved him so much that any slight
To him, no matter how small, burned like a fire
In my heart, which twisted as if approaching death.   555
This tiger played with my heart, toyed with my breath,
Until my will became a tool of his—
In other words, whatever he wanted, I did,
In everything within the bounds of reason,
Always preserving my honor from any treason.   560
I'd never had a thing so lovely, nor a lover,
Like him—God knows! Nor will I, for ever more.
        "For a year, or was it two? I fed on this food,
And thought of him as nothing other than good.
But in the end, as Fortune turned her wheel,   565
He had to be spun as far away from me
As wings and a false and fickle heart could take him.

That I was overwhelmed is beyond debate:
I cannot fit my feelings into words.
But one thing I can say, without fear of correction:　　　570
This taught me at once, and for ever, the pain of death.
But he would never believe how my heart was bled.
So, just like that, he said farewell, and left,
Looking so sorrowful that I truly believed
He felt as injured by this sudden leaving　　　575
As I was. O how he spoke, his face changed hue!
And yet, I still accepted him as true,
And fancied he would surely come again,
Before too long—so addled was my brain.
And also, I told myself, he had to go　　　580
Because of his honor, as often it happens so,
And I would make a virtue of necessity,
And accept it all, because it had to be.
I covered up my sorrow as best I could,
And took him by the hand (so help me, God!),　　　585
And told him: 'Lo, I am forever yours:
Stay true to me, as I have been to you.'
Whatever he said, just then, needs no repeating,
For who can speak like him, and act like a beast?
He talked, and talked, and when he'd finished, it was done.　　　590
'So she requires a very long, thin spoon,
Before she dines with a devil': that much I heard.
And off he went, at last, flying hard
And fast. And eventually he came where he must
Have wanted, and folded his wings, and came to rest.　　　595
And I think the saying he probably had in mind
Was 'Every creature, coming home to its kind,
Is happy'—these are the sort of things men say,
Always searching for novelty, the way
That captive birds will do, in their golden cages.　　　600
For though they are fed, and nothing can make them afraid,
Their cages lined with straw as soft as silk,
And given sugar, honey, bread and milk,
The moment the little door is left ajar
They jump away from their bowl and fly as far　　　605
And deep in the forest as they can go; they dine

On worms, and enjoy it, for everything is fine
If it's new, for men delight in a wheel that's winding,
And never permit nobility to bind them.
    "And so it was with him, alas the day!   610
His blood was surely the best, he was quite unstained,
And handsome, happy, noble, and easy of mind.
He happened to see a vulgar hawk fly by,
And suddenly he loved this creature so
That love for me went rushing out the door—   615
And thus his loyalty was gone, he was false
To me. He serves, instead, that ugly hawk,
And I am abandoned, and have no remedy!"
And immediately the falcon began to cry,
Then fainted again, in the lap where she was lying.   620
    Cánacée and all her women wept
For the pitiful bird, and the sorrow it had met with,
But knew no way to make her happy again.
But Cánacée carried her home, wrapped in the hem
Of her dress, and softly swathed her in plasters and balms,   625
In places where her beak had done her harm.
And then there was nothing more to be done than digging
Herbs out of the ground, and making new mixtures
Out of these precious roots, beautiful
To see, and heal the falcon. From day to night   630
She worked at saving the bird, with all her might.
And beside her bed she made the falcon a coop,
Covered with velvet cloth, blue as a jewel,
A sign of faith and trust that women display.
This coop was painted green, as bright as day,   635
And all around it were images of malicious
Birds, like titmice, owls, and anything male.
Contemptuously, beside these birds were magpies,
To gawk and cry, and raucously to chide them.
    Now let me leave this Cánacée and her falcon.   640
I've said enough about her ring, for now,
But more will have to be said, describing how
The falcon was brought together with her love,
And he repentant (as the tale is told for us)
Solely by means of princely mediation   645

From Cámbaló, the king's own son, as I've told you.
But all these strains of my story are now on hold,
For I have adventures to show you, and battles to show,
Marvels greater than any you're likely to know.
    To begin, I'll bring you back to Cambéeyuskán,   650
Who in his time had many cities won,
And then I'll turn to handsome Álgarsíf,
And how he made great Théodóra his wife,
Because of whom he'd often been in peril
So vast that even the magic horse couldn't help him.   655
And then I'll tell you what happened to Cámbaló,
Who fought in formal duels for the right to be wooing
Cánacée, quite sure that he could win her.
And so at the point I left, I'll begin again.

PART THREE

    Apollo whirled his chariot so high   660
That he reached the realm of Mercury the sly—

[unfinished]

WHAT THE LANDOWNER SAID TO
THE SQUIRE, AND WHAT THE HOST
SAID TO THE LANDOWNER

"In faith, Squire, you have well acquitted
Yourself, and nobly. I've nothing but praise for your wit,"
The Landowner said, "in light of your obvious youth.
You choose your words most sensibly, in truth!
It seems to me that there is no one here   5
Who matches you, and if you live, no peer
In eloquence seems likely to appear.
May God give you long life, and endless good cheer!
Indeed, I take a deep delight in your speech.
I have a son, and you might easily teach him   10
A thing or two. By the Holy Trinity,
I'd give a parcel of land, rich and pretty—
Dropping out of the sky, into my hand!—

If he could be a man of understanding
Like you! The devil with owning acres of land! 15
Virtue is everything, virtue is all!
I've scolded my son, and again and again I shall,
For he refuses to think of virtue at all!
He loves to gamble at dice, and throw away
Whatever he has in his purse that very day. 20
He'd rather stand and chat with a servant or two
Than listening and talking with someone who
Might really show him what nobleness can do."

    "Who gives a straw for nobility?" said our Host.
"O Landowner, what? Pardon—but don't you know 25
That each of you is pledged to tell a tale
Or two, or else our common adventure will fail?"

    "I know it well, sir," the Landowner quickly said.
"Please you, don't look at me with any contempt
Because I share a few words with this young man." 30

    "Without delay, sir, tell your tale, as you can."

    "Gladly, our Host," he said, "I will obey you,
Right as you please. But listen to what I say:
I will not contradict you in any way,
At least as far as I'm able. I'll do what I may. 35
I pray to God you appreciate my tale,
For then I'll know for sure I haven't failed."

The Landowner's Prologue

The old and noble Bretons, in their time,
Celebrated their adventures in rhyme,
Using the very first language, here in this land,
And sang these tales as music, soaring and grand,
And surely read them, written so keen and fine.   5
And I have one in particular in mind,
Which I shall tell in whatever words I can.
But gentlemen, I am an ignorant man,
So here at the start, I'm forced to beg and beseech you
To keep in mind, and forgive me, my clumsy speech.   10
I've never studied, in England, France, or Spain;
Whatever I say is bound to be bare and plain.
I've never slept in the fields of Mount Parnassus,
Or parsed out Cicero, not even one passage.
Grammar, syntax, and rhetoric are shadows   15
To me. The only technical terms I know
I've learned in the marketplaces of Liverpool
And London, or out in the fields. I'm not a school man,
Nor do I wish to sit on a dunce's stool.
But if you like it, my tale will be told for sure.   20

The Landowner's Tale

In Armoric, the land of Brittany,
There was a knight who loved and treasured his lady,
Serving her as surely she deserved,
Laboring, for his love, in noble service,
Hoping in time to win her for his own.   5
For she was one of the fairest under the sun,
The finest daughter born to the noblest family
He knew, and for a time he did not feel free
To let her know his love, or his lover's distress,
And indeed she, seeing his worthiness,   10
And his patient, silent attentions, was drawn to pity
His pain. Without a word from him, she secretly
Let him know that she was more than ready
To take him for her husband, and their household's head
(If husbands truly lead, and are not the led).   15
She had not asked, but he swore as a faithful knight
That never in all his life, by day or night,
He'd never assert the slightest mastery,
Or oppose her will, or show his jealousy,
But simply obey her, and follow along in her dust   20
(As any lover, with his lady, must),
Except the title of lordship must be in his name,
Or otherwise his knighthood would turn to shame.
    She thanked him, and answered with great humility,
"Sir, because you've offered, so generously,   25
To yield me such a wide and ample reign,
May God preserve us both from war or strife.

Sir, I will be your true and humble wife.
Accept my pledge, which lasts as long as my life."
And then they both were quiet, each in his way.   30
      And, gentlemen, I think it's safe to say
That friends exert no power, but only obey
Each other, if they mean a friendship to last.
Love is completely free of slaves and masters.
When mastery makes his entrance, the god of love   35
Just beats his wings, and whoosh! away he's flown!
Like any spirit creature, love is free.
Women, by nature, long for liberty,
And never wish to be constrained or bounded.
Neither do men, and is that any wonder?   40
Consider the man most patient in his love,
And see how clearly this stands out above
All others. The virtues of patience rank with the highest,
For they can conquer, wise men recognize,
Obstacles that harshness cannot attain.   45
A man must be careful not to scold or complain
At every word: endure, and suffer, or you must
Be taught this lesson at long and terrible cost.
For surely, in this world, we're all imperfect;
Our words, our actions, sometimes show our defects.   50
Anger, sickness, turbulent constellations,
Wine, or woe, or internal rearrangements,
Often make us say or do things wrong,
And no one can be judged too quick, too long.
So take all situations one by one,   55
And almost every battle can be won.
Ensuring that his life could flow in ease,
This wise and worthy knight so pledged, so pleased
And patient, that she responded well, swearing
He'd never find those virtues lacking in her.   60
      Thus men can see a humble, wise accord;
Thus she accepts her servant and her lord—
Servant in love, lord in terms of marriage,
For he achieved his lordship by offering service.
Service? Yes, but lordship even more,   65
Having his lady and his love, both sworn to.

His lady, without a doubt, but also his wife,
The laws of love approve this, thus reconciled.
And having achieved this wonderful success,
He took his wife and traveled home to his blessèd 70
Country home, in Penmarch, in Brittany,
Where he could live in delight, and so could she.
      Only a man who's married will ever see
The joy, the ease, the loving prosperity
Existing between a husband and his wife. 75
He spent a year or two in this blissful life,
And then this knight—the ancient books have told us
He came from Karrú, his name was Arvéragús—
Decided to go and live, for a year or two,
In England, also known as Britain. True 80
To his knightly vows, he hoped to win himself fame
And honor, for these were the heights he longed to attain.
And there he stayed for a year or two, say the books.
      Here I leave him, for a time, and turn my look
And my story to Dórigén, his lady and wife, 85
Who loved her husband as her true heart's life.
How she wept for his absence, how she sighed,
Which noble wives will do, when they desire to.
She lay awake, mourning, she fasted, she cried,
Complained, so tightly gripped by wanting him there 90
The rest of the world seemed nothing at all to her.
Her friends, who knew how heavy her thoughts had become,
Offered her comfort, as friends have always done.
They preached at her, they told her, day and night,
She had no reason to hurt herself; the sight 95
Alarmed them, but nothing helped, whatever they tried
For consolation was washed away by her tears,
So they were helpless: she was consumed by fears.
      In time, as you already know, trying
To engrave a stone eventually leaves signs, 100
Produces pictures, makes sense to a grieving mind.
They stayed, and gave her comfort for such a long time
That, in the end, hope and the power of reason
Imprinted on her heart some consolation,
The tempests and fires of sadness began to lower, 105

For passionate sorrow cannot burn forever.
    And during all this woe, Arvéragús sent
Her letters, describing how well his journey went,
Assuring her he'd hurry back as fast
As he could, knowing how hard she took his absence.   110
    Her friends could see her sadness ebb and slack,
And begged her, on bended knee, for God's own sake,
To enjoy their company, and use delight
To drive the darkness out of her weary mind.
And in the end she granted their request,   115
Seeing very well it was for the best.
    The castle had been erected close to the sea,
And there they often walked, her friends and she,
Enjoying the view from high on the sloping sand,
Tracking passing ships from many lands,   120
Sailing back and forth, wherever they pleased.
But that was part of her pain as well as her leisure,
And often she asked herself, "Alas, is there
No ship, of all the many passing here,
To bring me home my lord? That would cure   125
This bitter pain my heart can barely endure."
    At other times she'd sit alone and think,
Looking down, not seeing so far as the brink.
But then she saw the horrible rocks, so black
That sudden fear would rise, and her heart would quake   130
So hard that, were she standing, she would have fallen
Down. And sitting there, high on the grass,
Her eyes would wander out to sea, her glance
Would rouse a silent prayer, in words like this:
    "Eternal God, whose power and knowledge give   135
Our world a fixed and loving future, your gifts
Are many, and nothing you do is ever in vain.
But Lord, these evil rocks loom up in disdain of
Your perfect work; they seem a foul confusion,
Unlike the rest of this, your fair creation,   140
Shaped by a kindly God, eternally balanced.
Why have you constructed this black, irrational
Thing? Look south, or north, or west, or east,
And nothing benefits, no man, no beast,

No bird. All these rocks can do is destroy. 145
A hundred thousand men have lost their joy
And their lives, broken and battered to bits, or drowned.
If men are truly so carefully framed and bound
By you, that all of us reflect your likeness,
Why are these men destroyed in such a frightful 150
Fashion? Your heart apparently opens to men:
Why have you made such dreadful deaths for them?
Nothing good can come from sad destruction,
Evil by nature, intending no good, an obstruction
Solely designed for mankind's soaring sorrow. 155
I understand that priests will say, tomorrow
And always, that everything is meant for the best,
Mere man can never fathom his destiny.
But you, O God, who cause the wind to blow,
At least preserve my lord! That's all I know: 160
Let clerics rage and write; I have my woe.
But how I wish, O God, that these black rocks
Would drop right down to hell, and he'd come back!
They make me shake with fright, and quiver with fear."
      This was her prayer. And then she shed more tears. 165
Her friends could see there was no entertainment
For her, along the shore, and thus arranged
For fun and games in many other places.
They took her out to rivers, springs, and brooks,
And other spots she found less woeful looking. 170
They danced and played at chess, and at backgammon.
      One day, a little after the break of dawn,
They took her to a garden, there beside
Her castle, in which they'd carefully provided
Food and drink, and furnishings quite fine, 175
And in that garden they sang and danced and played
The entire time. It was the sixth of May,
And the first five days of that month had brought them showers,
Which softly painted leaves and bright new flowers;
The clever hands of men had skillfully dressed 180
All manner of things in this garden, giving the impression
That nowhere in the world was a better sight
To be seen, and this was truly paradise.

The scent of flowers, the brightly rising light
Would surely have quickened hearts, and lightened woes,   185
Except for people too sick to see, and those
Whose sorrows held them fast in sore distress—
For here was beauty and pleasure, God's own blessings.
They took their dinner and everyone went dancing
And singing, except for Dorigen alone,   190
Lost in lamentation, and grief and moaning.
Looking at the dancers she could not see
Her husband, and her love, without whom she
Was woeful. But she was patient, she did not leave them,
Hoping that time would help her, and end her grieving.   195
      And in this dance, among the other men,
There was a squire not known to Dorigen,
Fresher and jollier in every way
(According to me) than even the month of May.
His singing, and his dancing, surpassed all men   200
Alive or dead, since ever the world began.
Along with this, to show him as he deserved,
He stood among the handsomest men on earth,
Young and strong, virtuous, rich, and sensible,
Well beloved, his reputation excellent.   205
And let me add, to tell the entire truth
(Dorigen thought little about this youth),
This joyful squire was pledged to worship Venus
(His name, I ought to say, was Auréliús),
And he had fallen in love with Dorigen,   210
Two years before; he loved her best of all women,
But never dared to tell his long-grown passion,
Drinking, without a cup, great draughts of depression.
His cause seemed hopeless, he could not say a thing,
Except in songs, sometimes, he tried to sing her   215
News of his woe, but only in general terms,
Describing himself as loving, unloved in this world.
And this was a subject to which, in song, he returned
Again and again, beautiful phrases and words
Explaining what no one knew, for he'd never tell it,   220
But go on suffering like a spirit in hell,
And he would certainly die—like ancient Echo,

Loving Narcissus, not daring to tell her woe,
The kinds of expression I've told you were the only ways
He spoke to her, not ever daring to betray 225
Himself—although, of course, sometimes at dances,
When younger folk exchange their careful glances,
It may well be he would have looked at her face
The way a man will look, when seeking grace,
But she could never have understood his intentions. 230
And yet, because they both quite often went
To dances, and after all he was her neighbor,
And known to be a respected man of honor,
And she had learned his name some time before,
They started to chat and, quickly, more and more, 235
Auréliús led their talking toward his purpose,
And as soon as he saw his time, he said to her, thus:
    "Madame," he said, "in the name of God who created
This world, I wish, somehow hoping to please you,
That on the very same day your Arverágús 240
Sailed out to sea, O, I, Auréliús,
Had gone somewhere and never come back again.
I understand my wooing is all in vain,
My only reward remains a broken heart.
Madame, have pity on my wounds, so sharp 245
And painful. A word from you can kill or save me.
I wish that, here at your feet, I could make my grace!
There's nothing, now, that I am free to say.
Have mercy, O sweet one, or I will surely die!"
    She stood a moment, studying his face. 250
"Is that what you want?" she said. "And you ask for grace?
I've never known that this was what you meant.
But understanding, now, your true intent
I declare, by God who gave me soul and life,
I never intend to be an unfaithful wife, 255
Neither in word nor act, as best I can.
I wish to be his, who now I truly am.
Accept this, please, as a final answer from me."
    But later she added, smiling playfully:
"Auréliús," she said, "by God above, 260
I also wish that I could be your love,

Now that I see your sorrow, and hear your pain.
The day that all along this coast and plain
You take away those boulders, rock by rock,
That keep all boats and ships completely blocked—   265
In short, when you have made the coast so clean
That not a single rock can still be seen,
Then I will love you best of any man.
This is a serious offer, as much as I can."
     "Is there no better grace in your heart?" said he.   270
     "No, by that Lord," said she, "who once made me!
Of course, I know this cannot ever take place,
So let such folly fly from your heart, and escape.
What law permits a man, here in this life,
To seek his pleasure with another man's wife,   275
Because her body is one he happens to like?"
     Auréliús stood silent, heavily sighing.
How painful was the answer he had heard.
At last, he started talking, and these were his words:
     "Madame," he said, "you seek an impossibility!   280
So I must die a sudden death, and horribly."
And with those words he turned away and was gone.
Then many other friends were coming and going,
Roaming along the pathways, first down, then up,
None of them knowing what had been the result,   285
But starting up their games and dances anew
Until the sun began to dim his hue,
Because the horizon was blocking off the light—
Which is to say no more than it was night!—
And home they went, in comfort and in pleasure,   290
Except, alas, for the wretched squire who'd measured
His chance, and missed, and walked with sorrowful breath,
Knowing he had no hope of escaping death.
It seemed to him his heart was already icy.
He stood and raised both hands to the darkening sky,   295
And in his raving passion spoke a prayer,
Out of his mind, wholly unaware
Of where he was and what he said, but praying
First to Apollo, god of the sun, then aiming
His words at every single one of the gods: 300

He began: "Apollo, governor and god
Of every plant, and herb, and tree, and flower,
Who according to each time and season showers
Light to each, always as they deserve
And as your home-star changes, duly swerving,   305
Lord Phoebus, cast your great and merciful eye
On wretched Auréliús, who stands before you forlorn.
O lord! The lady I love has now forsworn me,
Condemned me, innocent, to death. Have pity,
Lord, upon my dying heart, for it   310
Is clear you have the power—though less than my lady.
Send me some possibility for help,
Some way, somehow, to keep myself from hell.
    "Your sacred sister Lucína, moon-goddess bright,
Governing oceans and shining high at night—   315
Though Neptune, of course, is deity of seas,
She is an empress above him, it's he who must please—
You know full well, O lord, how happy she is
To be brought to light by fires burning in you,
And therefore follows after, pays you her due,   320
Just as the sea comes flowing after her,
For she is goddess both of sea and rivers,
All waters, great and small, here on this earth.
And so, lord Phoebus, this is my request—
Perform this miracle, or my heart will burst—   325
That when the next opposing alignment is reached,
There in the house of Leo, that sacred beast,
You ask your sister to bring so great a flood
That it will overpour, by five full fathoms
At least, the highest rock on our Brittany shore,   330
And let this flood endure two years or more,
So surely I to my lady can safely say,
'Do what you swore to, the rocks have gone away.'
    "Lord Phoebus, perform this miracle for me.
Ask your sister to measure her pace so we   335
Will see her, daily, coming along behind you,
And this will last for years, or at least for two,
And if she keeps this steady, even pace
That surging flood will stand both night and day.

And if, alas, this flood cannot be produced   340
(Thus letting me become a successful wooer),
Then ask her, I pray, to bury each and all
Of these rocks down in the darkest regions of hell,
Her shadow land, there where Pluto dwells.
Or else I'll never be able to win my lady.   345
I'll walk to your temple in Delphi, on barefoot feet.
Lord Phoebus, see the tears run down my cheek,
And let my sorrows and pains awake compassion."
And when he'd spoken, he fainted away in his passion,
And for a time lay still on the ground, in a trance.   350
     His brother, knowing this squire's mortification,
Found him, lifted him up, and brought him home
To bed. And there, but lying still, and moaning,
I now must leave this passion-ridden man.
It's up to him, you know, to do what he can.   355
     Arvéragús, now richer, returned in honor,
A knight of chivalry, and indeed its flower,
And came to his castle, he and his worthy men.
How merry you have become, O Dorigen!
You hold your happy husband tight in your arms,   360
Your handsome knight, your noble man in armor,
Whose love for you is everything in his life.
He does not think of asking if some man
Has offered words of love, here in this land
Of his, while he was away. This was a thought   365
That never came to his mind. He danced and brought her
Good cheer. In peace and happiness they dwell.
And I'll return to Auréliús, lying in hell.
     And there, in languor and torment, for two whole years
And more, wretched Auréliús lay, too weary   370
Ever to set his foot on uncaring earth.
In all this time the only comfort he got
Was from his brother, who happened to be a cleric,
And knew his brother's woe, and what had worked
His sorrow, but he was the only one who was told.   375
Auréliús could not breathe a single word
Of his passion to anyone else on this earth,
More silent even than ugly Polyphemus,

The cyclops, worshipping sea-nymph Galatéa.
The young man's appearance seemed sound, to a casual eye,   380
But deep in his heart lay the arrow of which he might die,
And surely you know that a wound healed on the surface
Alone will never cure: some competent surgeon
Must reach inside and pull the arrow out.
    His cleric brother wept, remaining in doubt,   385
Until one day he suddenly recalled
That during his studies in France, in Orléan's halls—
The university, where youthful clerics
Are known to investigate almost all theories,
Prying and digging into heresies—   390
He'd started to read a book, left on a desk
By another student (with one degree already).
Natural magic was what that text was about,
And why the other student had it was doubtful,
For much of what those pages dealt with, and described,   395
Concerned the twenty-odd astral houses allied
To the moon, and with a good bit more of that folly
Which now, in our time, is worth as much as a fly,
Since Holy Church, and our belief, our faith,
Does not permit indulgence in such vexatious   400
Matters. Recalling this book, his heart did a dance,
And silently he took a brave new stance:
"It won't be long before my brother's healed,
For I'm convinced this science is true, and real,
And men with knowledge can play extravagant tricks,   405
Exactly the way that magical men and witches
Do them—calling water and then a boat
Right into a hall, then climbing in and floating
Up and down. I've heard of lions appearing,
And flowers swiftly sprouting, then disappearing,   410
Or else a vine, with grapes both white and red,
Or even an entire castle, built on a meadow,
Solid stone that could melt away in a moment.
All who were there could see what magic showed them.
    "Which certainly convinces me that I might,   415
At Orléans, consult these scholars and find
The best one skilled in affecting the moon, or a mind

Devoted to other natural magics, above
The clouds, and let my brother have his love.
Scholarly knowledge permits magicians to make   420
Appearances seem real, and cover those rocks
Clean out of sight, and hold them away for a week
Or two, and ships could come to the coast, and go
To sea, and my brother would then be cured of his woe,
For she will be forced to honor what she swore,   425
Or else he'll shame her, or else do something more!"
    I will not make a longer tale of this.
But running to his brother's bed, he swiftly
Convinced Auréliús to come with him
To Orléans, and up he rose, with vim   430
And vigor, ready to wake the power of the heavens.
    But just before they reached that famous city,
Short by only a furlong, or two, or three,
They met a young cleric strolling along the street,
Who spoke to them in Latin, with a pleasant greeting,   435
And then went on to say a wondrous thing:
    "I know," he said, "the reason for your coming."
And then, before they rode another foot,
He told them, accurately, what they meant to do.
    Auréliús' brother inquired after men   440
He'd known, with whom he'd studied, and drunk, back then,
And learned that every single one of his friends,
Had died, which made him weep, as he mourned for them.
    But quickly, Auréliús came down from his horse,
And they walked beside the magician, straight to his home,   445
Where he made the brothers entirely at their ease,
Producing everything that might be pleasing
To his guests. A house equipped as well as this
Was something neither brother had ever glimpsed.
    And then, as they went to supper, he put on a show,   450
Scenes of forests, parks where wild deer roamed,
Stags with horns winding incredibly high—
Antlers longer than ever seen by the eye
Of man. A hundred of them were hunted and slain,
Driven by hounds, and struck by arrow, again   455
And again. And then they vanished, as if never there,

Replaced by falconers, beside a river,
Hunting heron to their deaths, with no bow or quiver.
    And then they saw armed knights, in tournaments,
And after this the magician conjured a sequence   460
In which they saw Auréliús' lady dancing,
And he was dancing too, he truly fancied.
And when this master of miracles saw the time
Had come, he clapped his hands, and they went to dine,
The miracles all vanished, as if swept from the house;   465
Music and dancing became as still as a mouse.
He took them into his study, their senses shaken,
And set them down for dinner, where no food had been made,
And only the three of them were there in the room.
    And then the master called his squire to him,   470
Asking, "And is our supper ready at last?
Almost an hour has vanished, gone slowly past,
Since you were ordered to set a good repast
For these two men and me, here in my study."
    "Sir," said the squire, "whenever you please. It's done,   475
And if you like, you three may dine right now."
    "Then we will dine," he said. "That seems to me best.
These amorous folk may soon require their rest."
    And having eaten, they turned to fiscal details:
How much should such a master of magic be paid   480
To wipe out all the rocks in Brittany,
Sweeping them off from Gironde to the mouth of the Seine?
    It was difficult, he said. By God's own wounds,
He had to be paid at least a thousand pounds,
And even for that he hesitated and wondered.   485
    But Auréliús had no doubt, and at once he thundered:
"A thousand pounds? Fie on a thousand pounds!
I'd gladly pay you the world (which is said to be round),
Had I been placed high on the earthly throne!
We have a bargain, by God; our business is done.   490
You have my word, the money will be yours.
But mind you, I cannot afford delay.
You must not keep us here for more than a day."
    "Agreed," said the cleric, "I'll do it right away."
    Auréliús lay down to sleep, whenever he pleased,   495

And slept like a baby, feeling much relieved.
Now his struggles were over, his fruitless hope,
His chains of woe and penance apparently broken.
    The very next morning, shortly after dawn,
They traveled to Brittany on the straightest roads,   500
The magician mounted behind Auréliús, on his horse.
And so they took their way, and soon arrived.
The year, as these old books make me remember,
Had reached the cold and frosty days of December.
    Phoebus was old, and copper-colored in hue,   505
Although, when lying in Cancer, he'd blazed in the blue
Hot sky, shining bright as heated gold.
But now, in Capricorn, he drooped, and was cold,
Pale and hoary, for waning stars grow old.
Bitter frosts, with sleet and freezing rain,   510
Had wasted all the vegetation and grain.
Old Janus, with his double beard, stayed close to
The fire, drinking wine from his bugle horn,
In front of him the roasted flesh of a boar,
And every jolly fellow crying "Noel!"   515
    Auréliús did what he could to help,
Showering the master of magic with reverence,
And urging him to work with diligence
And free him from his wounds, which throbbed and smarted,
Or he would take a sword and slit his heart.   520
    The wondrous magician had so much pity for this squire
That night and day he worked as if on fire,
Trying to reach a fixed and definite time
For conjuring what he wanted people to see,
Using appearance as the tool of his jugglery—   525
Or whatever he did: I know no astrology—
So Dorigen and all in Brittany
Should think and believe the rocks had gone away,
Or else that they had sunken underground.
And when, at last, the definite time was found,   530
For playing his clever games and wretchedness,
His feats of superstitious wickedness,
He took the charts once made for a king in Toledo—
Corrected, of course, and marked with heavy thought,

Filled with his past experience, the years he brought   535
To this work, his tables of planetary bases,
And angles of movement, lines, and starry traces,
His calculations, by month and day, of planet
Centers, and arcs and angles and arguments,
And all the deviant fractions he needed to use   540
In his equations for astronomical houses
And equinoxes, and stars of influence—
And saw that Alnath, the moon star now in Aries,
Enabled him to fix the final spheres
He needed to know, the eighth and ninth. He steered   545
His calculations carefully and clearly.
     As soon as he located the very first mansion,
He figured all the rest by straight proportion.
Knowing exactly when the moon would rise,
And in which face of the zodiac he could find   550
The different unequal divisions, and everything else.
These central solutions were shaped and in his hands;
Everything would work exactly as planned,
And he could create the accidents and illusions
So common to heathen folk, in their confusion.   555
And there he was, needing no more delay,
So he did his magical work, and the rocks went away—
Or seemed to, in people's eyes; they stayed where they'd gone
For at least a fortnight, perhaps for even a month.
     Auréliús had watched with aching despair,   560
Not knowing what would happen, or how he would fare,
Hanging, night and day, at the edge of this miracle.
But seeing the cleric had now surmounted all obstacles,
And every one of the rocks had vanished from sight,
He threw himself down at the cleric's feet, crying,   565
"O, I, a woeful wretch, Auréliús,
Give thanks to you, and to my lady Venus,
For lifting me completely out of woe!"
And quickly, he set out along the road
To the temple, where he knew Dorigen would be,   570
And when he saw his chance, both happily
And in dread, he quickly approached and spoke to her,
His sovereign, sole, and lovely lady dear:

"My one true lady," said this woeful man,
"Whom I most dread and love as best I can,   575
And most reluctantly would ever displease,
Except that you have brought me such unease
That I will soon be lying dead at your feet—
But I have no desire to say how I feel
(Though certainly I either die or complain),   580
For you are innocent, and meant me no pain.
And if my death, perhaps, brings you no sorrow,
Do reconsider, before you break your oath.
Repent, in the name of holy God above,
Before you kill me because it's you I love.   585
Madame: you know precisely what you pledged,
Though I claim nothing because of the words you said,
My sovereign lady: I'm seeking only your grace.
Yet still, in a garden there, right in that place,
You surely recall the promise you gave to me,   590
And though you only gave it conditionally,
You swore you'd love me best—God knows, you said it,
Though I am wholly unworthy ever to have it.
Madame: I'm speaking, now, on behalf of your honor,
Far more than to save myself, today or tomorrow,   595
For I must do as you commanded me.
Madame, if you are willing, please go and see.
It's yours to decide, but keep your promise in mind:
Alive or dead, I won't be hard to find.
It's up to you. I'm dead or not, as you say.   600
But I can see the rocks have gone away."
          He took his leave. Right there, in astonishment
And terror, she stood, her face as pale as death.
She'd never expected to fall in so ghastly a trap.
          "Alas!" she said, "that this could ever happen!   605
I never considered the possibility
That such a monstrous miracle could be!
Yet this defies the deepest laws of nature."
And, slowly, home she went, a woeful creature;
Incredible fear half paralyzed her feet.   610
She wept and moaned, for a day or two at least,
And fainted, too. It was pitiful to see.

But no one was told what caused her sorrow and pain,
For her husband was out of town, and she was alone.
So she spoke to herself. Here is what she moaned,   615
Her countenance pale white, her lips tight drawn,
Addressing herself to Fortune, her words well chosen:
    "Alas," she said, "O Fortune, it's you I complain to,
It's you who tied me, innocent, in your chains,
From which I see no chance of ever escaping: 620
Either death or dishonor must be my fate.
These are the painful choices from which I must choose.
Yet clearly, having a choice, I'd rather lose
My life than put my body to terrible shame,
Knowing myself as false, disgracing my name,   625
Though death, I think, may be a road to redemption,
For many noble wives, I recollect,
And young girls too, have killed themselves, alas!
Rather than give their bodies to such transgressions.
    "Surely, yes, these stories stand in witness.   630
The Thirty Tyrants of Athens, Sparta's tools,
Murdered Phidon, who lay in pools of blood.
They dragged in all the dead man's daughters, fiercely
Stripped them naked, and lustfully and weirdly
Forced these girls to dance along the pavement   635
Right in their father's blood. Their maidenheads
Meant more to them than life: they found a well,
Jumped in, and drowned themselves, as old books tell us.
    "The ancient Mycynaeans required of Sparta,
Every year, a shipload of pretty girls,   640
Fifty in number, to indulge their lechery.
But not a one of all that company
Escaped the sword, choosing, with sacred intentions,
Immediate death, rather than ever assent
To cruel violation of their maidenhead.   645
Why then should dying seem to me so dreadful?
Consider, too, the tyrant Aristóclidés,
Who fell in love with a girl, Stymphálidés,
And when the tyrant killed her father, one night,
She ran to Diana's temple, heading straight   650
For Diana's image, clutching it so hard

That idol and girlish hands could not be parted.
No one could ever pull her hands away,
Until they fell, as she did, murdered that day.
    "And since these virgins are filled with such defiance,   655
Determined not to be fouled by bad men's violence,
A married woman should never hesitate
To kill herself, to keep from being raped.
What can be said of the courage of Hásdrubal's wife,
Who watched the battle of Carthage and took her own life,   660
Seeing Romans had finally won the town.
Her arms were holding her children, as she jumped down,
Leaping into the fire, choosing to die
Rather than letting Romans befoul her body.
And did not Lucretia kill herself, alas?   665
In Rome, when she was raped by Tarquíniús,
It seemed to her too raw and cruel a shame,
Living on when she had lost her name.
And also the seven maidens of Asian Melétus,
Killed themselves, in genuine fear and pain,   670
To keep Galatian soldiers from befouling them.
O, I could summon a thousand stories, or more,
Remembering tales of ravishment and war!
When Ábradátes, husband of Pánthee, was slain
By Egypt's warrriors, she took a sword and aimed it   675
At her heart, letting her blood go dropping
Into his wounds, saying, "This will stop
My body being fouled by anyone else."
    Why do I need to go on like this, telling
These tales, when so many women have killed themselves,   680
Rather then letting their bodies be befouled?
I have no choice, when so many women, proud
Of their reputations, have killed themselves. Enough!
I will be true to my husband, Arvéragús,
Slaying myself in one way or another,   685
As did Demócion's dearly beloved daughter,
When her betrothed was taken away by death.
And O, Sedásus, it takes away my breath
To think of how your daughters died, alas!
Killing themselves—and thus another case.   690

And pity runs as strong, or even stronger,
For the death of an unnamed Theban girl, for whom
Nicánor, Alexander's warrior, was the cause.
And yet another Theban girl, raped
By a Macedonian soldier, sought to erase   695
Dishonor by putting an end to her broken life.
But what can I say of Nícerátes' wife,
Her husband killed by the dreaded Thirty Tyrants?
And what of Álcibíadés, killed in Phrygia?
His lover kept his body always beside her,   700
Refusing to put her beloved down in the ground.
And what a wife was Alcéstis, who went underground
For her husband! And Homer's noble Penélopée?
Every Greek is proud of her chastity.
Of Láodámiá it is written thus: 705
Fighting at Troy, her husband, Prothéseús,
Was killed, and she was unwilling to live without him.
And I can say the same of Portia, proud
Good wife, who could not live with Brutus gone:
Her heart could not conceive of life with anyone   710
Else. The perfect wifehood of Ártemésia
Is honored everywhere in Barbary.
O Illyrian queen, Teuta! Your chastity
Is a mirror for wives to look in, and hope to see
Themselves. And so it is with Bílyá,   715
And Rhódogone, and also Valeria."
    Thus Dorigen sorrowed and moaned and wept for a day
Or two, always intending, sooner or later,
To kill herself. And then, before the third night,
Home came Arvéragús, that worthy knight,   720
Who wondered why he found her weeping so sore,
At which she began to wail, and wail, much more.
"Alas," she said, "that I was ever born!
Thus have I said, and thus, as well, have I sworn"—
She told him everything you've heard before;   725
I feel no need to rehearse this any more.
Her husband, smiling, asked in a cheerful style,
Answering her as I will now describe:
"And there is nothing else, my dear, but this?"

"No, no," she said, "God help me, so it is!   730
I'm overwhelmed, I know it is God's will."
     "Yes, wife," he said, "let things that sleep lie still.
It may be right, perhaps this very day,
You'll keep the oath you've sworn, now by my faith!
May God on high shed down his mercy on me,   735
But I would rather be stabbed for the love I feel
In my heart, which only belongs to you, my dear,
Than have you break an oath so solemn and clear.
An oath is the noblest thing a man can honor"—
And then he began to weep, and his tears fell on her.   740
"Don't," he said, "never, on pain of death,
Never, so long as your life may last, and your breath,
Never tell a person on earth this thing
(As best I can, I'll bear my suffering),
And never show an affliction of heaviness,   745
So people may think you troubled, and try to guess it."
     And quickly he summoned both a squire and a maid.
"Walk out, and now, with Dorigen," he said,
"Bring her where she's going, depart at once."
They took their leave, and in a moment were gone.   750
But why they were going there, they did not know.
He wanted no one told, so no one would know.
     Perhaps, my readers, many of you (I think)
May suspect his motives, setting his wife on the brink
Of what you suppose is serious jeopardy.   755
But please read on, before you make him guilty.
She may have better luck than you expect:
Read the story before you try to predict it.
     That lovelorn man, whose name was Auréliús,
Whom Dorigen had caused to be so amorous,   760
Came over to her, as if by chance, as she walked
Across the town, taking the shortest road
To the garden where she had sworn her impossible oath.
He knew, of course, the direction she was going,
For he had kept an endless watch on her movements,   765
Aware of every visit on which she went,
No matter where, and also no matter when.
This makes no difference, it looked like an accident.

He welcomed her, with a bright and cheerful greeting,
Asking where she was going, as they were meeting.   770
Her answer, spoken like someone already half mad,
Was, "Toward the garden, as Arvéragús has bade me,
To honor the oath I made, alas, alas!"
        Auréliús suddenly doubted the situation,
Feeling in his heart intense compassion   775
For her, and all her pitiful lamentation,
But pity for Avéragús, a knight
So worthy he had sent her out, that night,
To honor her promise—the oath worth more than their lives!
His heart was wrenched, pity overwhelmed him,   780
Wondering what would be best for them;
Perhaps desire ought to be held in check,
Rather than acting with brutal wretchedness,
Defaming honor, nobility and worth.
And so he spoke these simple, honest words: 785
        "Madame, tell your noble, honest lord
That seeing the strength of his gentility
Toward you, as I can clearly see your grief,
Knowing he would rather be shamed (O pity!)
Than have you dishonor your oath, in spite of his pain,   790
I'd rather go back to suffering again
Than separate two lovers like you and him.
I hereby release you, madame, from everything
You swore to, now and forever afterward.
And I promise, further, never even to breathe   795
A word of protest. And so I take my leave
Of the truest, most worthy, noblest and honest wife,
That I have ever known, in all my life."
        Let married women beware of making vows!
Remember Dorigen; think of her now.   800
        And so a squire performed a noble deed
As well as any knight—may we take heed!
        She fell to her knees, and thanked him in fervent words,
Then hurried home to the husband for whom she yearned,
And told him everything, as you have heard it.   805
You may be sure he was so happy to hear it
His joy is something more than I can inscribe.

And why should I struggle for what I need not write?
    Avéragús and Dorigen his wife
Conducted, in sovereign bliss, the rest of their lives.   810
Never thereafter was any anger seen.
He cherished her as if she were a queen,
And she was faithful to him for ever more.
And of this couple you'll hear from me no more
    Auréliús, who'd thrown away his stormy   815
Labors, cursed the time when he'd been born.
"Alas," he said, "alas, that I have sworn
To give a thousand pounds of purest gold
To this wise and useless cleric! What shall I do?
I see that now I am completely ruined;   820
I'll have to sell my whole inheritance,
And turn to begging. I can no longer plan
On living here and shaming all my family,
Unless my cleric can make it easier for me.
I'll have to try persuading him—paying   825
Some portion, year by year, on a regular day
Agreed on. He went far out of his way for me;
I'll surely thank him for his courtesy.
And he will be paid: my word is a certainty."
    His heart was sore, but he opened his money chest   830
And brought the cleric gold, the very best
He could do, perhaps five hundred pounds, I guess,
Beseeching him, for all his worthiness,
To give him time for raising all the rest,
Saying, "Master, I still can truly boast   835
That no one, ever in my life, has lost
When I've sworn to pay him back. Most certainly,
My debt to you will be paid, whatever may be,
Even if I go begging, with nothing to wear
But my shirt. Please give me two or three years to spare,   840
And I'll guarantee your payment. Or else I'll sell
My inheritance. There's nothing more to tell."
    The cleric answered him most steadily,
Hearing these words, and this is what he said:
    "Have I observed the terms of our agreement?"   845
    "Most certainly, truly and well," he said.

"Have you enjoyed the lady for whom you were longing?"
"No, no," he said, and his sigh was deep and long.
"And for what reason? Tell me, if you can."
And Auréliús slowly his tale began, 850
Explaining what you know and already have heard,
So I will not explain it any further.
He ended: "Avéragús, in his worthiness,
Preferred to die in sorrow and in distress
Rather than let his wife be false to her vow." 855
He also told him Dorigen's great sorrow,
How loathsome she thought it, becoming a wicked wife,
Wishing she could simply have lost her life,
And saying she'd sworn in utter innocence,
Never having heard of magic appearance. 860
"I listened; she made me feel such terrible pity,
That just as freely as he had sent her to me,
So freely sent she was, to him from me.
And this is everything. I can say no more."
    The cleric answered: "And so, my dearest brother, 865
All of you were gracious to each other.
You are a squire, and he is above you, a knight.
But God forbid, in all his blissful might,
That a simple cleric can't do noble deeds
As well as either of you, in my belief. 870
    "So, sir, I hereby forgive your thousand pounds,
As if you'd suddenly popped up from the ground
And never in all your life had come to know me.
For, sir, from you I will not take a penny
For this bit-work, or the heavy learning that made it. 875
You've paid me well for everything I ate.
That is enough, farewell, have a good day!"
He took his horse, and off he went on his way.
    Now, gentlemen, I ask of you, if I may,
Who you think was more generous, I pray? 880
Let me hear your answers, before we go on.
That's all I can say, my tale is truly done.

THE PHYSICIAN'S TALE

There was, according to Titus Líviús,
A knight who bore the name Virgíniús,
Heaped with honor, known for his worthiness,
With many friends, and blessed with abundant riches.
The only child he had was a daughter; his wife   5
And he were blessed with no others, all their life.
However, this child was given outstanding beauty,
Far above the girls one usually sees.
It seemed as if Nature, with sovereign diligence,
Intended to give her such high excellence   10
As if to say, "Lo! I am Nature,
And I can form, can shape each of my creatures
However I like. Who can imitate me?
Pygmalion could not, working hard as he may,
In metal, clay, or canvas, however he played,   15
And even Ápellés or Zeuxis would deceive
Themselves, trying to equal what I achieve,
No matter how hard they work, or what choices they make.
For He who was and is creator of all
Appointed me his vicar general,   20
Gave me the making of every earthly creature
In any way I choose, then setting them here
Beneath the moon, which goes on waning and waxing.
I'm never paid, nor do I ever ask.
My principal and I remain in accord.   25
And this one girl I shaped to worship my lord,
As of course I do with every one of my creatures,

No matter their qualities, or other features."
These are the words I think Nature would say.

    This girl had grown to the youthful, blooming age   30
Of fourteen, and clearly was Nature's own delight.
For just as she can paint a lily white,
And a rose all red, just so, with perfect painting,
She fashioned forth this bright and noble maiden—
Working before her actual birth, free   35
From restraint, deciding what the girl should be.
Her hair was long, and Phoebus dyed it, neatly,
To look like streaming rays of his great heat.
Beautiful she was, a very great beauty,
But a thousand times more virtuous was she.   40
Nature gave her every capacity
Worth praise, sound moral wisdom especially.
In spirit and in body living most chastely,
And therefore flowered bright in virginity.
Humility helped guide her, and abstinence,   45
Rational restraint, and high-born patience,
Balanced both in bearing and appearance.
She always answered questions with great discretion.
Though wise as Pallas (I think it fair to claim),
Her eloquence was womanly, and plain,   50
Without pretentious words to make her shine.
And every word she used, her terms both high
And low, were always shaped in fine straight lines
Productive of goodness, virtue, and gentility.
And she was modest, as a girl should be;   55
Her heart was steady, and always actively
Engaged in keeping her from slothfulness.
Her mouth was closed to Bacchus, he had no access
To her, since youth and wine may heighten Venus
Much as men can heighten fires with grease.   60
No one had said a word, but on her own
She often pleaded sickness and abandoned rooms
Where feasts and revels and dancing go out of hand,
And foolish happiness can turn to a brand
Of folly more serious, and end in sorrow.   65

Situations like that, today or tomorrow,
Let children turn too ripe too soon, and bolder
Than children ought to be, and as we older
Folk well know, nothing could be more dangerous.
A girl too hardened and bold will not be an angel,   70
When she grows a little more and becomes a wife.
      And you who are governesses, older in life,
Charged with the governance of noble daughters,
You should not be offended. Don't be good sports,
For you are hired to do your governing   75
Of lordly daughters only for two good things:
Either you've earned respectability,
Or else, though fallen before, in frailty,
And well acquainted with the timeless dance,
You've since rejected all such low mischances   80
Forever more. And so, for Christ's own sake,
Teach them virtue and not your old mistakes.
      A crafty poacher of deer, who later abandons
His greedy ways, and all his ancient crafts,
Is a better forest ranger than any man.   85
Keep things straight, for if you want to, you can.
Be careful that vices never have your assent
For fear of being damned for evil intentions,
And you would be a traitor, certainly.
So listen carefully to what I say: 90
Mankind suffers many treasons, today,
But of all our treasons, the sovereign pestilence
Is when a man betrays young innocence.
      You fathers, and all you mothers too, as well,
Are chargeable with all your children's surveillance,   95
As long as they are under your governance.
Be wary, watch that neither your way of living,
Or worse, your negligence in full chastising,
Make them fall. For that, you'd dearly pay.
A shepherd, weak and negligent, today,   100
Puts many sheep and lambs in the wolf's sharp jaws.
      But that's enough, my preaching words must pause,
For I must to move my story faster, and forward.
      This maiden, whose portrait I've tried my best to present,

So kept herself she needed no government: 105
The life she led was one where every maiden
Can read, as in a book, all the good deeds
And words a virtuous girl can ever need,
So prudent she was, also so kind and good.
Her reputation spread on every side,   110
Both for her beauty and her charity,
That everywhere they praised her, deeply respectful,
If they were lovers of virtue—envy excepted,
Of course, for envy regrets what's good for others,
Rejoicing in sorrow and sickness. (I am a doctor,   115
Please remember, writing this description.)
    Along with her mother, one day, the girl made a visit
To a temple in town, walking quite properly
Together, no sight extraordinary to see.
A judge was serving, in that Italian town,   120
As governor of the entire region.
And so he happened to see the women passing
By: the girl caught his attention, fast
And hard, as she and her mother went slowly past him.
His eyes were fixed, his heart beat wonderfully fast,   125
Profoundly taken by the girl's great beauty,
Saying to himself, "My civic duty
Commands, declares, insists I have this girl!"
    The devil leapt to his heart, seeing his turn
Had come, and quickly advised the judge of the paths   130
Available and ready to his hand,
For surely, neither force nor bribery
Could ever do the trick, or hope to succeed,
Since she was widely known, with many friends,
And a perfect reputation for holy deeds.   135
After long and sober meditation
He sent for a rascal, good in such situations
And a man he knew was clever as well as bold.
In private, of course, this rascal was quickly told
The judge's problem, having first been sworn   140
He'd never say a word to another man,
For if he did the judge would have him hanged.
The rascal agreed to help, and the judge was pleased,

Pouring wine for this handy man and thief,
And giving him good gifts, expensive and fine.   145
     Their plan, as then developed, perfected in time,
Point by careful point, was obliged to be
Centered around disguising lechery,
As you will quickly hear, quite openly.
The rascal's proper name was Claudius,   150
The wicked judge, as we are told the story,
Was Ápius (for this is history,
Not fable, often told and never doubted,
Known to be truthful facts, and tightly founded).
Ápius had no interest in wasting time,   155
For lechery with the girl had filled his mind.
As soon as he could; high in judicial chambers,
Dispensing justice however he was able,
Passing judgment on one case after another,
At last he saw the rascal before him, in court,   160
Pretending outrage and urgent legal need,
Bowing and scraping, whining, then swiftly pleading,
"My lord, if Fortune makes it your lordship's will,
I beg your swift approval of this plaintive bill,
In justice as in right, which I present   165
Against the knight Virgíniús, and when
He sees it, he will say it's falsely presented,
But I will prove it, and I have witnesses
Who'll testify to the truths this bill expresses."
     The judge then answered: "No definitive sentence   170
Is possible, so long as he is absent,
So let him be called to court, and I will hear you:
I represent justice, no wrongs will emanate here."
     Virgíniús was sent for, and he appeared,
And immediately the rascal's bill was heard,   175
The thrust of it was what you now will hear:
     "To you, my lord, Judge Ápius so dear,
Attends your impoverished servant, Cláudiús,
Showing how a knight, Virgíniús,
Against the law and all of equity,   180
Possesses my servant, taken away from me
Against my will, stolen away by night

Although the girl is bound to me by right.
He took her when she was young; she now is grown
And he pretends to be her father, a known   185
And provable falsehood: the truth will here be shown.
And so, my lord and judge, I ask that you will
Return my servant to me. And now I'll be still."
This was indeed the thrust of his cursèd bill.

    Virgíniús was stunned to hear and behold this,   190
But quickly, before his truthful tale could be told
And be proved—he, a noble, honest knight—
Supporting his word by witnesses, and by right,
That every word in the bill was falser than hell,
The wicked judge declared he could not tell it,   195
And without allowing a word from Virgíniús
Rendered his final judgment, saying at once,

    "Complainant, I rule, deserves to have his servant,
And you, sir knight, cannot keep her. Observe
The law, bring her here, and we will hold her.   200
Complainant must have his servant, and thus I award."

    And then this worthy knight, Virgíniús,
Forced by the sentence of this justice, Ápius,
Would have to make his dearest daughter a gift
To the judge, to be held in his house and then to live in   205
Lechery. He went home, he sat in his hall,
And then, at last, he had his daughter called.
And there was her humble face for him to behold,
But he looked dead as ashes long gone cold.
A father's pity was cutting through his heart,   210
But he had no choice, he had to play his part.

    "My daughter," he said, "my dear Virginia, by name:
There are two roads, one death, the other shame.
These are your choices. Alas that I was born!
Nothing you've ever done deserves this turn   215
Of events, death by sword or by a knife.
O dearest daughter, this ends my happy life.
You have been raised in peace and perfect pleasure,
Never out of my mind or memory!
O daughter, you are now my final woe,   220
As you're the final joy of my life, also!

O gem of chastity, take death with patience,
Because this terrible death has been made your sentence.
Because of love, not hate, you must be dead;
My pitying hand must now cut off your head.   225
Alas, that Ápius ever saw your face!
Alas, he lied, and falsified your case"—
And then he told her what had happened that day,
Of which you've heard, I think, enough already.
            "O mercy, father dear!" exclaimed this maiden,   230
And with those words she raised her arms and laid them
Around his neck, as she had done so often.
Tears came bursting down on his weary chest.
"Good father," she said, "must I truly die?
Is there no possible grace, no remedy?"   235
            "No, certainly not, my dearest daughter," he said.
            "Then give me a little time, dear father," she said.
"I need to mourn my unexpected death.
Even Jeptha allowed his daughter breath
To mourn with, before he had to kill her, alas!   240
God knows, she did no wrong, but hurried fast
To be the first to see her father's return,
Not knowing the fatal effect of firm-sworn words."
And as she spoke, she fainted dead away,
And then, come back to herself, she solemnly said,   245
"Blessèd be God, that I shall die a maiden!
Give me my death, I could not bear the shame.
Do with your child as you wish, in God's great name!"
            And then she said, over and over again,
She hoped his sword could cut with a gentle stroke,   250
And then she fainted, knowing there was no hope,
And so her father, resolved but filled with pain,
Struck off her head and brought it to the place
Where the judge was holding court, that very day,
And set it right in front of that startled man.   255
And as the story goes, the judge commanded
The knight be hanged immediately, or faster,
But a thousand people or more burst into court,
Demanding this execution come to a halt,
Their pity and sorrow raised to such a pitch   260

Because they'd learned the judge was false to his oath.
And having long believed he was a lecher,
They'd realized this was a plot to get her
Into his hands, and Claudius was his accomplice.
Crowds had gathered, and gone to the seat of justice   265
To seize this Ápius and throw him in prison,
Which now they did, arriving just in time.
In jail, the judge committed suicide,
And the people wanted Claudius quickly hanged,
But were stopped by the knight, worthy Virgíniús,   270
Who intervened, as ever kind and gracious.
They sent this Claudius rascal into exile,
Believing he had probably been beguiled.
But everyone else, both high and low, involved
In this crime, were well and surely hanged, by God!   275
      Here you can see that sin is bought at a price.
Be warned, for no man knows who God will strike,
Nor do we ever know just when, or how,
The worm of conscience will shudder, and somehow show
Wickedness its face, which may well be   280
Hidden from all the world but God and he.
For whether you are ignorant or learnèd,
You can't predict when you'll be struck by fear.
So I conclude by giving this advice:
Give up sin, or sin will leave you dying.   285

Introduction to the Pardon Peddler's Tale

Our Host began to swear as if he were mad:
"Good God!" said he, "by nails and, yes, by blood!
This was a crooked rascal and a vicious judge,
Both deserving shameful deaths—and I could
Invent some! Death to such judges and those who approve them!   5
And still, this innocent girl is dead. God move them—
But, O, she paid too dearly for her beauty!
I've always said how easy it is to see
That Fortune's gifts, and those of nature as well,
Can lead to heaven or else the depths of a well.   10
Her beauty was all that caused her death, I say.
Alas, how pitiful that she was slain!
Fortune's and nature's gifts can do more harm
Than good, I say; leave such pleasures alone.

   "But truly, doctor, our learnèd man right here,   15
This is a pitiful tale for us to hear.
But let's move on, no one truly minds.
May God allow you whatever health you find,
And bless your urinals and chamber pots,
Your wine-spiced cordials, and the herbs you've got,   20
And all your pastes and powders and herbs and such.
The Lord should bless them, and also his dear mother!
Now may I prosper, but you're a handsome man,
Just like a bishop, I swear by Saint Ronyán!
Is that all right? Men of my kind can't speak   25
Like doctors, but you have caused my heart to squeak
So much, I nearly caught a cardiac.

By God's own bones! Someone massage my back,
Or else I'll take a draught of corn-ground ale—
Or else, by God, I'll hear a merry tale: 30
My heart still churns for pity of this maiden.
My *bel ami,* you Pardon Peddler," he said,
"Quickly tell us something with joy and jokes."
        "I'll do it," he said, "in the name of Saint-what's-his bloke.
But here's an inn, and first I need a drink."   35
        Then all the high-toned pilgrims began to complain:
"Don't let him tell us any ribald tales!
Give us a moral story, so we can learn
A bit—and then we'll gladly listen and hear."
        "All right, all right," he said. "I need to think   40
Of some moral thing, standing here and drinking."

The Pardon Peddler's Prologue

Radix malorum est cupiditas, *"For the love of money is the root of all evil."*

—Timothy 1:6

"Gentlemen, in churches, when I preach,
I push my voice, so I can always speak
Right out, both loud and clear, just like a bell,
For I have memorized whatever I tell them.
My text is always the same, as it always was: 5
Radix malorum est cupiditas.
        "First I announce where I have been, and come from,
And then I show my papal bulls to one
And all, and then the bishop's seal on my license:
These things are necessary, to protect myself,   10
So no one will be bold—no priest, no cleric—
And interfere with me, in Christ's great work.
And then I start in telling a few of my tales.
I show them bulls by popes and cardinals,
And talk of patriarchs, and bishops, too,   15
And I speak some words in Latin, just a few,
To give a certain flavor to my sermon,
And also to rouse them up, raise their devotion.
And then I take out cases of crystal glass,
Crammed with rags, and bones of those who have passed   20
Away—holy relics, they're supposed to think.
And then I have a shoulder bone, in zinc
And copper, from a holy Jewish sheep.
'Good men,' I say, 'listen, and you may reap.
Take this bone and wash it in any well,   25
And then if an animal begins to swell,
From eating worms, or being bitten by snakes,

Wash that animal's tongue with water you take
From that well, and it's healed at once. And furthermore,
A sheep with pox or scabies, or any sore,   30
Will surely be healed directly, drinking a draught
From this well. And let me tell you something more:
Let a good man, he who happens to own
These beasts, drink a draught from this same well
Just once a week, before he eats, or the bell   35
Has rung, just after the cock is crowing, a spell
Will be cast (as that old Jew and our elders taught us):
His animals, and his gold, are bound to grow.
    " 'And sirs, it cools down jealousy as snow
Cools grass, for though a jealous man is raging,   40
One draught of this and he is calm and patient,
And never worries whether his wife is faithful,
For even if she is, and he knows it, who cares
Whether she's making love with priests, in pairs?
    " 'Here is a fingerless workman's glove, as you see: 45
Putting your hand in this glove works mysteries,
Multiplying your grain, how many times over!
(Whether what you've sown is wheat or oats)—
But you must offer pence, or else good groats.
    " 'Good men and women, one thing I must warn you: 50
Anyone sitting in church, cozy and warm,
Guilty of several sins so awful he
Dares not, for shame, confess and pray for mercy,
Or any woman, whether young or old,
Who's made her husband a true and sad cuckold—   55
These people, be there any here, are not
Permitted offerings to my relics. Not a jot!
But to him who comes and offers what he's got,
Not being guilty of such crimes, I grant
Eternal forgiveness, pursuant to the grand   60
And powerful bull issued expressly for me.'
    "Using these pretenses regularly,
I've earned at least a hundred pounds a year.
I stand like a cleric in his pulpit, so appearing,
And when the ignorant people are seated, they hear   65
Me preach as I have been doing, just before,

And telling a hundred lies, and maybe more.
I work quite hard at stretching out my neck,
Including people east and west in my beckoning,
And looking much like a dove perched on a barn.   70
My hands and tongue are always working so hard
It truly is a joy to be watching me.
Greed, and associated cursedness,
Is all I ever preach, to make them free
To give their money, and especially to me.   75
My entire purpose is geared to nothing but profit:
I don't say a word about sin, or trying to stop it.
I'm not concerned that, after they're in the ground,
Their souls may be lost, wandering forever around.
And certainly, a lot of oratory   80
Is badly intended, for pleasing and flattery,
Trying to get ahead by hypocrisy,
Or else for empty glory, or even hate.
And when there's someone I cannot beat by debate,
I still can sting him with my bitter tongue,   85
In a sermon, which he cannot claim is wrong,
Nor say that he has been defamed. How strong
My holy order is, and I protect
My fellows, too, and though I stick no name
On a guilty man, it's still exactly the same,   90
For people know the signs and circumstances.
That's my revenge, when others dare attack us.
I spit out all my venom, using the hue
Of holiness, so I seem holy and true.
        "I'll tell you my purpose, now, in a word or two: 95
All I preach about is greed, and true
To my theme my motto is, and always was,
Radix malorum est cupiditas.
Accordingly, I'm preaching against a vice
I'm guilty of myself, namely, avarice.   100
But just because I'm guilty of that sin,
I'm able to show most others how to flinch
Away from it, and then help them repent.
But that is not my principal intention.
Any time I preach, it's only for greed.   105

And that should give you all the facts you need.

    "And then I give them lots of examples, drawn
From ancient stories, told us long ago.
Ignorant people like their stories old,
Being things they can understand and take hold of.   110
Listen, why should anyone hear me preach,
And get the gold and silver I earn by teaching,
And think I'm likely to choose the life of the poor?
No, no, I never ever thought it, truly!
I'll preach and beg in England, and other lands,   115
But why should I ever labor with my hands,
Making baskets, and living on what I sell?
I'm living pretty by begging, let me tell you!
Why should I choose to act like Paul and Peter?
I want good money, good clothes and cheese and wheat,   120
No matter whether it comes from a serving maid,
Or the poorest widow, freezing while she prays,
Who needs the money to keep her children alive.
Me, I like to water my throat with wine,
And have a frisky wench in every town.   125
    "Now, gentlemen, I've come to my conclusion.
I understand you want me to tell a tale,
And now that I've had a jug of corn-bred ale,
By God, I think I'm ready to tell you things
That should, in reason's name, be much to your liking.   130
Despite the fact that I'm an immoral fellow,
I can tell a moral tale, and what I'll tell you
Is one I like to preach when I smell good profit.
So hold your tongues! Here my tale begins."

THE PARDON PEDDLER'S TALE

In Flanders, once, young people in a crowd
That liked fast living, prancing up and down
The town, in brothels, gambling houses, and bars,
Accompanied by lutes, small harps, and guitars,
Dancing and rolling dice both day and night,   5
Stuffing stomachs and drinking till they're tight,
All of which amounted to worshipping devils,
Sacrificing souls on altars of evil,
Overindulging to the point of abomination.
The curses they threw about achieved damnation,   10
So grisly and ghastly it was, hearing them swear,
Tearing our Lord's poor body to bits and tatters,
As if the Crucifixion had been too easy!
And how they laughed, finding sin so pleasing,
Often surrounded by female acrobats,   15
Shapely, slender, and gracious, and girls who acted
And sold fruit, some who sold women, or songs, or cakes—
Truly helping the devil, down in Hádes,
With kindling to fire the heat of lechery,
Which always burns together with gluttony.   20
I take the holy Bible for my witness
That lust's hot bed is heated by drunkenness.
        Remember drunken Lot, unnaturally
Sleeping with his daughters, not knowing what he
Was doing, too drunk to understand himself.   25
        Herod—read the books and see for yourself—
Sat at his table, feasting, drunk to the ears,

And gave the fatal command to his officers,
Who slaughtered Saint John the Baptist for no good reason.
      And see what Seneca said, always in season,   30
Seeing no difference at all, that he could find,
Between a man who's simply out of his mind
And a man descended into drunkenness,
Except that insanity, in any poor wretch,
Lasts longer by far than any drunkenness.   35
O gluttony, the height of wickedness!
O primal cause of mankind's utter fall!
O first and original sin that damned us all
Till Christ redeemed us with his own dear blood!
Consider that sacrifice, paid for our good,   40
And how far, once more, we've fallen to villainy!
This world is putrified in gluttony.
      Our father, Adam, and also Eve, his wife,
Were driven out of the Garden of Paradise
For just that sin, and now we work for our lives.   45
For as long as Adam fasted, which is how I read
The story, they could remain, but as soon as he
Ate the forbidden fruit from off the tree,
He turned an outlaw at once, in woe and pain.
O gluttony, how right we are to complain!   50
Surely, a man who knew the maladies
That follow excess, would think of gluttony
And make himself more careful with his mouth,
Of what he ate, and how much, as he lay on his couch.
Alas! How short our throats, how soft our mouths,   55
Requiring—in all directions, north to south,
In earth, in air, in water—mere men to sweat
So gluttons can eat and drink what they like best!
Saint Paul is worthy reading, on points like this:
"Meat goes to belly, and belly turns into meat,   60
And God destroys them both." Go and read it
Yourself. How foul it is for us to see this,
But what is even worse is the very deed,
Man guzzling wine till he is lost in a tizzy,
Making use of his throat as he uses a privy,   65
All because of this cursed, foul excess.

Paul himself, while weeping, says just this:
"For many walk, of whom I've told you often,
And tell you, now, even as tears are pouring,
That they are enemies of her Holy Cross, 70
And they will end in destruction, whose God is their belly."
O stomach! O belly! O stinking bag of jelly,
Filled with dung, and reeking with corruption!
From either end of you come foul eruptions.
How costly, how hard, the world must work to find you! 75
See cooks and how they stamp, and strain, and grind,
Turning reality to mere appearance,
Appeasing greed at a price both awful and fearsome!
They pound on narrow bones, knocking out
The marrow, for nothing gets cast away that might 80
Make passage through the gullet soft and smooth.
The sauce is spiced by leaves, and bark, and roots,
And turned into a thing of great delight,
To give the glutton a stronger appetite.
But certainly, indulgence in such rites 85
Is fatal: men are dead who live in vice.
     Wine is a lecherous thing, and drunkenness
Is full of quarreling and of wretchedness.
O drunken man, with your disfigured face,
Your breath is sour, you're stinking foul to embrace, 90
Your drunken nose emits an ugly sound
That almost seems to say, "Samson! Samson!"
And yet, God knows, Samson never drank wine.
You slip and fall much like dying swine.
You've lost your tongue, and all your self-respect, 95
For drinking turns a man into an object
Devoid of wit, deprived of all discretion.
Any man who suffers the domination
Of drink can never be trusted with secrets.
Drink white? Drink red? You're better off with neither, 100
And never fortified wines, product of Spain,
Sold by the barrel here in London lanes.
Such low-priced vintage from Iberia
Comes creeping into wine from ports still nearer,
Freely giving off such vicious fumes 105

That once a man has had as little as three
Of these cups, and thinks he's sitting here in Britain,
He's gone to sunny Spain, and there he's sweating—
No, no, he's not in London, he's not in Bordeaux,
And all he's able to say is "Samson! Samson!"   110
    But listen, gentlemen, one word, I pray:
Please note that all the greatest deeds, I say,
Recording victories in the Testaments,
Through God's own actions, he the omnipotent,
Took place in abstinence and constant prayer.   115
Go read the Bible, for sure you'll find that there.
    Consider Attila, the greatest of conquerors,
Dead in his sleep, in shame and sad dishonor,
Bleeding from the nose in drunkenness.
A general must live in soberness.   120
And in addition to this, consider well
What was commanded unto Lamuel—
Not *Sam*uel, but *Lam*uel, I said.
Read Proverb thirty-one, in so many words
Expressly forbidding wine to those who are leaders.   125
Enough. Perhaps I can turn some men into readers.
    And since I have dealt at length with gluttony,
Let me warn you, too, of gambling's history.
Gambling should be known as the mother of lies,
And cheating, and vicious, cursèd perjuries,   130
Blaspheming Christ, and causing murders, and also
Wasting both time and property—and more,
Because it attacks its opposite, which is honor,
The reputation of gamblers is well deserved.
Scanning up and down, at lords and servants,   135
You find that he who's highest falls the furthest,
Dropping into dissolution, deserted.
Any prince who takes the risk of gambling,
Especially in matters large and dramatic,
Will find that, everywhere, the clear opinion   140
Paints him negative in reputation.
    Chílbon, known as a wise ambassador,
Was sent from Lácedómiá to far-off
Corinth, to seek a possible alliance,

And when he arrived, it happened, purely by chance,   145
He found the noblest men in all that land
Down on their knees, rolling dice and gambling.
After which, as soon as he possibly might,
He sailed back home. His words were simple, forthright:
"I cannot take on myself the bitter shame,   150
And abandon the reputation of my name,
Allying my country to a land governed by gamblers.
Let some other ambassadors go there,
For, frankly, I would rather be hanged and die
Than have you take on gamblers as your allies.   155
This country has stood so long, and soared so grandly,
It seems to me we have no business with gambling,
And I, as well as you, should have no part
In it." And thus he spoke, straight from his heart.
    Consider King Demetrius, of Syria,   160
Once, when the Parthian king sent him a pair of
Dice, contemptuously, purely in scorn,
Because Demetrius had gambled before,
Thus signifying to all the world, and more,
He was indifferent to fame, and honor, and glory.   165
Surely men of such high station can play
At other games, to wile the time away.
    Now I turn to the subject of villainous swearing,
Discussed in many books by men of learning.
Swearing is surely something heinous, atrocious,   170
But constant swearing, completely uninterrupted,
Is infinitely worse. God forbade all swearing,
Saint Matthew tells us, but there is special learning
In words left us by Saint Jerome, the holy:
"If you utter an oath, make sure it's true; don't lie,   175
And utter it in judgment, and properly."
But casual swearing is impropriety.
Behold that even in the Ten Commandments,
Which God gave Moses to show to other men,
The second of these holy, sacred ten   180
Declares: "Don't take the name of the Lord in vain."
Notice: condemning oaths that use his name
Was more important than murder and other such things.

I'm talking about the order God framed, to bring
His prohibitions to our minds. This is nothing 185
Accidental, arranged by our heavenly king.
And furthermore, allow me to tell you, outrageous
Oaths and constant swearing will bring the plagues
Of Egypt down on your house. Our God is vengeful.
"By God's own precious heart," and "By his nails," 190
"By the blood of Christ, preserved in a vial at Hailes,
Seven's the number, and yours are five and three,"
"By God's great arms, if you try cheating on me,
This dagger will be planted right in your eyes!"
These are fruits from the cursèd pair of dice— 195
Swearing, anger, cheating, and homicide.
Now for the love of Christ, who came and died
For us, leave off your swearing, one and all.

    And now, good gentlemen, I'll tell my tale.

    These riotous youths could be found, soon after dawn, 200
Sitting in taverns, and cheerfully guzzling down
Their drinks, and on this morning when my tale begins
They heard, as they sat, the sound of bells clinking
Out in the street, as a corpse was carried to his grave.
One of the drinkers looked up, and sharply said 205
To his servant, "Run on ahead, and quickly ask
Who is this corpse that's passing on so fast—
Get his name right, and let me hear it at once."

    "Sir," said the boy, "No one needs to run.
I heard them speaking of him, two hours before 210
You came. He used to be a friend of yours,
And he was killed last night, given no notice,
Sitting straight up, dead drunk, without any motive.
Some sly old fellow, a famous thief called Death,
Who's known to close forever everyone's breath, 215
Here in our country, just cut his heart in two
With a spear, and left him. There was nothing to do.
They say a thousand people have died in this plague.
And master, before you meet him, along your way,
It seems to me it might be necessary 220
To watch and be careful of such an adversary.
Always be ready to meet him, for he'll always come.

My mistress taught me that. My speech is done."
"By holy Mary!" the tavern keeper declared,
"The boy is speaking truth, for just this year, 225
Not much more than a mile away from here,
In a good-sized village, he's taken laborers,
And children, servants and lords, men and women.
Maybe that's the place where he makes his living.
That sounds like good advice, the boy has given, 230
To be ready before this fellow does you dishonor."
    "By God's own arms!" declared the rioter,
"What makes this fellow so dangerous to meet?
I'll look for him on highways, I'll look on streets,
I swear I will, by God's eternal bones! 235
Now listen, my friends, we three have always been one,
Let's raise our hands and demonstrate to each other
That each of us are now the others' brother,
And we together will kill this traitorous Death.
He who has slain so many, will now be dead, 240
By God, before this day has turned to darkness!"
    And then these three took oaths and pledged their hearts,
And swore to live and die, each for the other,
As if each man was every other's brother.
And up they jumped, full of drunken anger, 245
And off they went to the village, indifferent to danger,
Still swearing a host of truly grisly oaths,
And ripping apart Christ's blessèd body, both
The corpse and all its sacred parts. O Death
Would soon be dead, when they met up with him! 250
    They hadn't gone too far, perhaps no more
Than half a mile, when coming toward them they saw
An exceedingly old and poverty-stricken man,
Who greeted them as humbly as anyone can,
Saying, "Young lords, may God protect you three!" 255
    The haughtiest rioter was much displeased,
Replying, "What, you peasant with dismal manners!
Except for your face, you're wrapped like a bundle of banners.
Why do you bother staying alive, at your age?"
    The old man stood and peered straight at his face, 260
And answered, "Because I'm quite unable to find

A man, no matter how far I walked or climbed—
Not in this village, or any other, or a city—
Who'd trade his youth for my age. Not willingly!
And so I have to stay as old as I am,   265
For as long as God is pleased to keep me a man.
And Death, alas! is unwilling to take my life,
So I keep on walking, too old for death or strife,
And on the ground, which is my mother's door,
I knock with my staff, and knock forever more,   270
And say, 'Dear mother, come and let me in!
See how I'm shrinking, flesh, and blood, and skin!
Alas! When will my bones have found their rest?
Mother, I want to exchange my coat and vest,
So long my wrapping, so long it seems they will be,   275
For a winding sheet, in which they'll be wrapping me!'
But she remains unwilling to grant me that grace,
And that has left me with this withered face.
  "But gentlemen, you show no courtesy
To speak to a man my age so nastily,   280
When I have spoken no word, and done no deed,
Against you. For in the Bible you may read:
'Meeting an old man, gray upon his head,
You must rise and bow,' and in truth it may be said
You must not injure a man of my great age,   285
No more than you may wish, at this same stage,
To be welcomed with, if you happen to live that long.
So God be with you, wherever you're going now!
I have to leave you, and go where I have to go."
  "No, old wretch, you won't, till we tell you so,"   290
Declared another of these drunken rioters.
"It isn't so easy to get away from us!
You mentioned that traitor, Death, a moment ago,
He who has slaughtered so many people we know.
It seems to me you're likely his own spy,   295
So tell me where he is, or you will die,
By God and by the holy sacrament!
You're surely someone Death has truly sent
To help him kill us young folk, you lying thief!"
  "Gentlemen," he said, "if it will please you   300

To meet with Death, turn up this crooked way,
For there in that grove I left him, by my faith,
Under a tree, and there he intends to stay.
Boast as you will, nothing will make him hide.
Do you see that oak? That's where you can find him.   305
God save you, he who once redeemed mankind,
May he reform you!" So spoke this ancient man,
And each of these rioters immediately ran
Till they came to the tree, but what they all of them found
Was a hoard of golden coins, so fine and round,   310
And as many bushels, it seemed to them, as seven
Or eight. And each of them believed this was heaven,
And chasing after Death was at once forgotten
As they contemplated the lovely, gorgeous sight
Of all those golden coins, which shone so bright.   315
They seated themselves beside this precious hoard.
The worst of the three was the first to speak a word.
          "Brethren," said he, "Listen to what I say.
My brain is sharp, although I jest and play.
This treasure comes from Fortune, we've had it given   320
So mirth and lust can be the joys we live in,
And lightly as it comes, so too we'll spend it.
Ah, God's own dignity! Who would have expected
That we'd be blessed, today, with such good grace?
I think we ought to remove it from this place   325
And bring it, perhaps, to my house, or to yours—
For all this gold, of course, is entirely ours—
And then we'd be in high felicity.
And yet, until it's dark, this cannot be
Accomplished. People would call us highwaymen,   330
And because of our treasure they'd hang us, there and then.
This treasure has to be carried away by night,
As carefully, in secret, as ever we might.
So my advice is draw the cut. We'll all
Take straws and see on whom the draw will fall.   335
And whoever gets it, he must run to town
And bring us bread and wine, without a sound.
The other two will keep a clever watch
To preserve this gold, and if he hurries back

Here we'll stay till dark. Whatever the best   340
Of places, we'll take it there, by one assent."
So one of them went and brought a fistful of straws,
And then they took their chances, to see who it was
That would go. It fell on the youngest among the three,
And off to town he went, most happily.   345
And watching till they saw that he had gone,
One of them turned and spoke to the other one:
"Now you are sworn, you know, to be my own
Dear brother, so let me tell you a good thing to do.
It's just as well that he has gone away.   350
Sharing this gold can be done in several ways,
And if we manage it right, we might agree
That two divisions are even better than three.
That's sound advice, by God! It's sound and friendly!"

    The other answered: "Yes, but how can it be?   355
He's well aware that you and I are holding
The treasure here. How can we keep this gold?"

    "You want my advice?" the first of the rascals said.
"I'll tell you how, without much waste of breath,
And pretty simply, we'll bring this thing about."   360

    "I'll bet you can," said the other. "I have no doubt.
And as I've sworn, you won't be betrayed by me."

    "You know quite well," the first man said, "that we
Are two, which makes us stronger than one alone.
As soon as he sits down, stand up as though   365
You feel like wrestling, and then position him so
That, while you're wrestling, both of you to and fro,
I'll quickly stick him right in the side I'm facing,
And you can use your dagger any place
You like. And then this pile of golden plenty,   370
My dearest friend, belongs to you and me."
And thus these rascals agreed, in so little a time,
To rid themselves of the third one. It struck them as fine.

    The third and youngest, he who had gone to town,
Kept hearing the sound of gold coins rolling around,   375
Those precious florins shining bright and new.
"O Lord!" he thought, "what can I possibly do,
To keep this golden treasure for myself alone?

No man living under God's high throne,
Could ever live as happily as I would!"   380
And then the devil, our ancient enemy,
Put in his head the help that poison might be.
Why, he could kill those others so easily!
(Finding him already living in sin,
The devil, of course, had license to haul him in.)   385
Happily, his heart concurred with his mind:
Kill them both, and never look behind you!
And so he fairly ran, straight to the town,
And hunted up a druggist, and swiftly found one,
And sought some poison to kill his rattlesnakes,   390
For which he was satisfied and ready to pay.
And if there was something more he was able to buy
To kill a skunk, who raided his yard and preyed
On his precious chickens, but since it always raided
In darkness, and he could not be watching all night,   395
He asked for another poison, if that was all right.
        The apothecary answered, "Ay, you'll have
A thing that, in the name of God that saved us,
No creature living in this world of ours
Can eat or drink, in just the smallest dose,   400
That will not fall on its face and breathe its last breath.
It doesn't take long: this poison brings on death
In less than the time it takes you to walk a mile.
This is a poison that's strong and violent!"
        This cursèd fellow took the box in his hand,   405
Then searching about he found another man
Who sold him three of the largest bottles in town.
He poured his poison into two of them,
Reserving the third for himself, and the wine he would drink.
He'd need that wine, he was inclined to think,   410
For carting all that gold to a safer place.
And when this rioter, God spurn his face,
Had loaded each of the bottles with fresh, new wine,
He rejoined his comrades, knowing just where to find them.
        And now, why do I need to preach any more?   415
For just as they had decided, long before,
They killed him; the process didn't take too long.

And when it was over, one of them said to the other:
"And now let's sit and drink, and make us merry,
And afterward we'll dig a hole and bury him."   420
Inevitably, he chose a poisoned bottle,
And passed it back and forth with his fellow rascal,
And for a while they had a jolly time,
Until they fell on the ground, and both of them died.

   I'm sure that Avicenna never wrote   425
A treatise covering all the symptoms they both
Presented, elaborating how and when
This pair of wretches finally came to their end.
Thus both the murderers were finished off,
And the traitor relying on poison got more than enough.   430

   O cursèd sin beyond mere cursedness!
O homicidal traitors, O wickedness!
O gambling, gluttony, and luxuriance!
You blasphemers of Christ, in evil phrases
And monstrous oaths, money lusts, and crazes!   435
Alas! O humankind, how can you do it,
Faithless to our Creator, who died so truly,
Expressly for you, redeemed by his dear blood,
And you so false, not worthy of such goodness?

   Now, you good men, may God forgive your sins,   440
And keep you away from lust and avarice!
These holy pardons I offer may bring you salvation,
Provided you requite me with coin of the nation,
Silver or gold, jewelry, spoons or rings.
Bow your head in the name of this holy bull!   445
Come up, you married women, bring me your wool!
I'll swiftly set your names here on my roll,
And into the bliss of heaven you will go
By my high power invested. I can restore you,
Make you as clean and clear as the day you were born.—   450
And this, my fellow pilgrims, is how I preach.
And Jesus Christ, who has our souls in keeping,
I trust will offer the pardon your souls are seeking,
For that would be best, and I mean no more deceiving!

   But gentlemen, one thing I forgot to tell you: 455
Here in my pouch I have both pardons and relics,

As worthy and good as any man's in England,
Bulls, indeed, I have from the pope's own hand.
If any of you would like, in high devotion,
Come see, and offer, and take my absolution.   460
Quickly, come forth, and kneel yourselves on down,
And humbly accept my powerful, perfect pardon,
Or else be pardoned all along the road,
All fresh and clean at each of our new mileposts,
As long as you pay me (new receipts for newness)   465
Whatever money you have, if it's been minted true.
All of you are honored to have right here
Someone so competent as a pardoner,
Anointed here as you ride, in the country-side,
For disasters always happen, all the time.   470
One or two of you may fall from your horse,
And snap his neck, or even something worse.
Consider the perfect assurance for you all
That I, these times, will be at your beck and call,
Saving the souls of people both less and more   475
When death comes knocking at that person's door.
It seems to me our Host should rightly begin,
For he, of us all, is most enveloped in sin.
Come forth, sir Host, and make the very first offering,
And you can kiss the relics, the bones and rings,   480
For half a penny! So open up your purse."
      "Oh no," said he. "For that I'd earn Christ's curse!
Give up," he said, "I'm not someone to be preached at!
You'd make me kiss your dirty, stinking breeches
And swear they were some relic of a saint,   485
Although your asshole made the fragrant stain!
But by the cross Saint Helen the holy found,
I wish I had your balls here in my hand,
Instead of relics and all the stuff you carry.
Let's cut 'em off, and I will help you cart 'em,   490
Enshrined, most properly, in a pig's high farting!"
      This Pardoner said nothing, too angry to talk,
Too churning and dumbstruck to assert his potent faith.
      "Ah now," said our Host, "here I stop my playing
With you, or any other angry man."   495

The worthy Knight was swift to intervene
As laughter broke and became an angry scene.
"No more of this, however funny, I say!
Now, Pardoner, good cheer for a happy face,
And you, sir Host, you're in my heart, and dear,   500
So please come over and kiss this Pardoner,
And Pardoner, I pray you, close up here,
And as we've done, let's all just laugh and play."
And kiss they did, then rode along their way.

The Shipman's Tale

A merchant used to live in Saint-Denise,
A man of wealth, whose life was light and easy.
He had a wife, a woman known for her beauty,
Who loved to make merry, being in company—
Which always ends by making more expense   5
Than income, despite the smiles and reverence
Bestowed on beauty by men, at feasts and dances.
Such words and gestures, and cheerful countenances,
Are much like shadows passing on the wall—
But woe is he who's paying for it all!   10
"The foolish husband always does the paying.
He has to clothe us, furnish our display
Of jewels, to keep his social credit high,
And we will wave at him as we dance by.
And sometimes, if he has a change of mind,   15
Or cannot make the necessary payments,
Or doesn't desire an outlay he thinks is heinous,
Money thrown away, wasted and lost,
Then someone else will have to pay our costs—
Or lend us gold, which can be hazardous."   20
      This noble merchant kept a splendid house,
And felt himself full well paid back for these sums
Of generous spending (truly no thing to wonder
At, since his wife was a beauty)—but here is my tale.
His house was visited by many and all,   25
One of whom was a monk, handsome and bold—
I think he was some thirty-odd years old—

Constantly drawn from Paris to this wide-open place.
A youngish monk, with a very handsome face,
He'd known the wealthy merchant, prince among men,   30
Ever since his human knowledge began,
Consorting on the kind of familiar terms
That friends who value friendship always yearn for.

    And since the worthy merchant, of whom I've spoken,
And also this monk, for whom this tale has opened,   35
Had both been born in the very same location,
The monk had claimed the merchant for a true relation,
Nor did the merchant ever once deny it:
It pleased him deeply, left him feeling requited.
Thus they were tied, or tied themselves in a knot   40
Of brotherhood and cozy reassurance
For the rest of their lives, no matter the circumstances.

    The monk, Don John, was free, especially
At spending, giving pleasure and making friends
Of everyone who served his wealthy cousin.   45
He never failed to tip the lowest servants,
And in his way, according to his resources,
He gave his host some pleasant, dainty morsels
Which helped to make him a very welcome guest,
Considered, up and down the scale, the best—   50
Much as the cock is pleased to welcome the sun.
Enough of this: this part of my tale is done.

    And as it happened, the merchant, one fine day,
Began to ready matters for going away
To Bruges, in Belgium, where he intended to buy   55
A quantity of salable merchandise.
Before he left, he sent a messenger
To Paris, inviting Don John to visit them
(He and his wife) for mutual entertainment
A day or two before he went on his way.   60

    This noble monk, of whom I've now informed you,
Had gotten permission from his abbot to go
Where and when he liked, for he was known
As a man of prudence, an administrator of sorts,
Often inspecting granaries and barns,   65
So off to Saint-Denise, and joy, he went at once.

No guest was ever so welcome as was Don John,
A dear-loved cousin of flowing courtesy.
He brought a handsome jug of good sweet malmsey,
And a second, filled with strong and bubbling Italian 70
Wine, gifts of the sort this pleasant man
Would usually bring. Now let them eat and drink
And play, before the merchant had to leave.

The third day came; the merchant rose with the morning
And got to business at once, assessing how strongly 75
He needed this, and didn't require that,
And how his reserves were holding, and how his capital
Stood, for the year, and if it had grown, how much.
The sacks of money were set on his counting
Board; receipts, and bills, and books were mounted 80
In piles. The state of his affairs was good,
Which no man ever knew, or ever could,
Except himself, for the counting door was shut
And locked, and never opened by anyone
But him. He sat some hours, adding, subtracting, 85
Deciding what, in Bruges, he'd be contracting.

Don John had risen early, as he always
Did, and walked about the garden pathways,
Saying prayers and devotions with perfect ease.

The merchant's wife, aware of him and pleased 90
He was there, slipped quietly into the garden, where
The monk was strolling, and greeted him, as often
Before. A servant girl came with her, not more
Than ten years old, an age which does as it's told.
"O my dear cousin," she said, "my dear Don John, 95
You're very early today. Is something wrong?"

"Niece," he said, "five hours of sleeping ought
To be enough for ordinary men,
Except for weakened, older fellows, whose bed
Is like a rabbit's burrow, in which they hide 100
And cower, as if set on and all surrounded
By barking packs of howling, scratching hounds.
But my dear niece, I wonder why I've found you
So pale? It surely must be that our good man
Has had you working hard, since night began, 105

And now you're sorely in need of sleep and rest."
And then he burst into laughter, deep in his chest,
And what he was thinking made his face go red.

    This beautiful married woman shook her head,
And replied: "O God who knows it all!" said she,   110
"My cousin, no, it isn't like that with me,
For by that God who gave me soul and life,
In all the realm of France there is no wife
With less desire for such enfeebled games.
And though I sing 'alas and wellaway   115
That I was born,' no one living," said she,
"Will ever hear how that stands—no, not from me!
Sometimes I think of running away from France,
Or else of ending all my foolish plans
And my life, as full as it is of worry and care."   120

    The monk was silent a moment. He stood and stared,
Then said, "Alas, my niece, may God forbid
That you, no matter the sorrow, whatever your dread,
Might kill yourself. Tell me your grief, instead.
Perhaps, whatever your misfortune, I may   125
Be able to help or advise you. Tell me, I pray,
The cause of your sorrow. And know, whatever you say
Is secret, for on my prayerbook I solemnly swear
That never in my life, for love or hate,
Will I reveal your words. I'll never betray you!"   130

    "I say the same to you," she said. "I affirm
By God, and on your book of holy words,
That men may declare they'll truly tear me to shreds,
But I'll not betray a single thing you've said
(For liars, surely, go straight to hell when they're dead).   135
And this I do not swear for family relation
But strictly and solely for love and in good faith."
They made their oaths, and thereupon they kissed
And spoke to each other exactly as they wished.

    "Cousin," she said, "if I had some private space—   140
And I have none, especially in this place—
I'd like to give an accounting of my life,
And all that I have suffered, being a wife
To my husband, despite his being your trusted cousin."

"O no," said this monk, "by God and by Saint Martin,   145
Your husband is no more closely related to me
Than this leaf, right here, hanging on this tree!
I call him so, by Denys, our Saint of France,
Only because it gives me a better chance
To be with you. I love you especially,   150
Far above all women—most certainly.
I swear this on the vow I made, the day
I became a monk. Tell me your sorrow, I pray you,
Before he appears. Hurry, so I can hear it."
     "My dearest love," she said, "O John, my spirit,   155
My love! These are things I'd rather keep hidden—
But out they must come, no matter how hard and forbidden.
For me, my husband has been the most useless man
There ever was, since first the world began.
Yet I am his wife, and it cannot be for me   160
To break the sacred seal of our privacy,
Neither in bed or any other place.
God forbid I tell it, for his great grace!
A wife is not supposed to speak of her husband
Except in honor, or so I understand it.   165
But just to you, this much I need to convey:
So help me God, by night and even by day
He's just as worthless as a hopping flea.
And still, what irks me most, is that he's stingy—
And surely you know most women, naturally,   170
Want six things from their husbands, as do I:
Women who marry want their husbands to be
Strong, and wise, and rich, and never stingy,
And humble with his wife, and active in bed.
But by Lord Christ, who let himself be bled   175
For us, in order to dress myself as my husband's
Honor requires, on Sunday next my hands
Must offer a hundred francs, or I go under.
I'd rather be burned to death by lightning and thunder
Than slander my name, my reputation stained,   180
And if my husband should ever discover this claim,
I'd be as good as lost. And therefore, I pray you,
Lend me this sum, for otherwise I might

As well be dead. O dear Don John, I cry:
Lend me these hundred francs! By God on high,   185
You needn't worry, you'll always have my thanks!
And if you decide to grant me what I'm asking,
Just set a date, and I will pay you back,
And in the meantime, whatever service or pleasure
You want from me, I'm more than willing to offer.   190
And if I refuse you, let God on high take vengeance
As awful as Ganelon received from France."
      This courteous knight replied in his soft manner:
"Now truly, my own lovely lady dear,
My pity for you is enormous, and so I swear   195
That as soon as your husband takes his trip to Bruges,
I'll free you completely from this burden, your hugely
Troublesome debt. You'll have your hundred francs."
And saying this, he caught her by the flanks,
And hugged her hard, and kissed her many times.   200
      "Go on your way," he said, "and give no sign,
And, if you please, arrange for us to dine,
For by my pocket sundial I know it's time.
Go now, and keep your word as well as me."
      "May God forbid I shouldn't, sir!" said she,   205
And off she went as merry as any lark,
And told the cooks they'd better work much harder,
For men were hungry, waiting to test their larder.
And then she went to her husband's counting chamber,
And rapped on the door as if the world were in danger.   210
      "*Qui là?* Who's there?" "Peter! You know who it is,"
She said. "How long do you mean to stay at your business?
How many times do you need to add and subtract?
Do you give a thought to eating? That too is a fact
Of life. O give the devil a share of your counting!   215
By God, you've more than enough, you're truly wealthy!
Wouldn't you be ashamed that good Don John
Has stayed here, fasting, as the day rolls on?
What! Let's hear a mass, and then go dine."
      "Wife," he said, "how little you have divined   220
This subtle business I am deeply engaged in—
For merchants and traders like me, and may God save us,

And also Bishop Saint Yves, that Persian genius—
Just one or two of any ten of us
Can stay afloat, lasting as long as I   225
Have now. We may make merry, we may look fine,
But either we keep this world rolling ahead,
Never disclosing the number of fish in our net
Until we die, or else we leave, pretending
A pilgrimage calls, or else we just disappear.   230
This cunning world would keep me forever in fear,
Unless I worked this hard at keeping things clear.
This is what a merchant's life is about.
    "Tomorrow, I leave for Bruges, at dawn, no doubt,
But when I'll return is something I cannot say.   235
So you, dear wife, will now assume, I pray,
The duty of keeping this house in proper order,
Watching with careful eyes that peer around corners,
Attentive to servants, none too slow or too forward,
And you in comfortable charge, with humble deportment,   240
Letting honesty rule. The house is well stored
With the food you'll need; your purse has silver enough
To purchase anything else you may require."
And so he shut the door behind him, with a sigh,
And a mass was rather hastily said, and the tables   245
Were laid, and then they ate what the cooks had made,
And the monk ate more than the other two combined.
    After dinner, John took his host aside
And spoke to him in a manner clearly private,
Saying: "Cousin, this is, as far as I know,   250
The plan. You, I see, are ready to go
To Bruges. May God and Saint Augústine guide you!
I trust, my cousin, that you will safely ride.
Be careful how and what you eat, especially
Now, in this heat: a temperate diet will be   255
The best. Nothing is foreign to the two of us.
So farewell, cousin! God shield you from all fuss
And worry! Anything that may occur,
By day or night, in which I might be of help,
You only have to ask and I'll do it, as long   260
As I'm able, and do it however you wish it done.

"One favor, before you leave, I'd like to ask
Of you. At the monastery, one of my tasks
Involves the purchase of livestock, and I will need
An unexpected hundred francs for these beasts,   265
And if you can I'd like to borrow that sum
From you. I'll store these creatures; the money will come
In a week or two; you'll have it the very same day.
Not for a thousand francs would I delay you!
But keep this secret, please, if you don't mind,   270
For later tonight is when I'll need to buy them.
Again, farewell, my own and very dear cousin:
Do well, your profits should grow by dozens of dozens!"
        The merchant's reply was gracious, and given at once.
He said, "My dear good cousin, my good Don John,   275
Surely this is a simple and small request.
My gold is yours, whenever you think it best,
And not just gold, but also my very own goods.
Take what you wish, may God protect what you don't.
        "But let me mention, although you know it already,   280
My business requires money as a necessary
Tool. Our reputation allows us to borrow,
But when gold's lacking, there's no today or tomorrow.
Yet pay it back whenever you find it easy;
I always prefer, when I can, to quietly please you."   285
        And then he fetched the hundred francs at once,
And no one noticed, as he passed the purse to Don John.
No one else in the world knew of this loan,
Only the merchant and ever-faithful Don John.
They drank together, and chatted, strolling in the grounds,   290
Until Don John rode off to his holy home.
        Next day, at dawn, the merchant also went riding,
Headed for Bruges, his apprentice carefully guiding,
And a trip so swift he merrily arrived,
Quickly set to work, and was deeply busy,   295
Not playing games of dice, or hopping and dancing,
But doing what was needful for commerce to happen,
Since he was a merchant. And there I'll let him dwell,
Leading his life, which I'm not equipped to tell you.
        On Sunday next, the merchant still away,   300

Don John was off to Saint-Denise, that day,
His head and also his beard freshly shaven.
Even the smallest, youngest, rawest servant
Was happy to see him, glad to be of service.
To get to the point, not beating about the bushes, 305
He and the merchant's wife arranged their business,
And for the hundred francs he'd receive, that night,
Her in his arms, in her bed—and they did it, all right,
Leading a busy, active, nocturnal life,
This honest monk and the merchant's faithful wife. 310
At dawn Don John went riding on his way,
Telling them all, "Farewell, have a good day!"
And none of them, nor anyone in town,
Had the slightest suspicious inkling about Don John.
So off he rode, back homeward to his abbey— 315
Or wherever he wanted: of him, there's no more to say.
    This merchant, hustling and bustling finished and done,
Turned his horse around and rode back home,
Relaxing with his wife, in feasting and good cheer.
He told her his business had been so very intense 320
He'd had to borrow thousands of francs (the expense
Was necessary, and worth it), and to pay this back
He'd travel to Paris, and from his friends and backers
He'd get what he needed, though much he already had.
And then, in Paris, for sheer good cheer and affection, 325
He went to visit Don John, with love and respect
But neither to ask for or borrow any gold,
But only to see for himself the monk's own home,
And tell him stories of business dealing in Bruges,
As friends will do, when they have time to lose. 330
His greeting from Don John was cheerful and merry,
And the merchant recounted, in some detail, how very
Well his business had gone—may God be praised!—
Except that commercial traffic had run so fast
He'd had to borrow gold (no difficult task, 335
Given his credit) and once he'd paid that back
His life would settle down in joy and rest.
    Don John then answered: "Surely, I am glad
That such good health and spirits have followed you back.

And were I rich—by God's high bliss that I hope for—   340
I'd heap ten thousand coins on your broad shoulders,
Blessing you for your kindness, the other day,
In lending me gold. As warmly as I'm able
I thank you heartily, by God and my faith!
In any case, I brought those hundred francs   345
—Indeed, the same gold coins, in sober fact—
To your wife, at home. They're lying on your bench.
She can identify these coins, I think,
By markings I can explain, if indeed she needs them.
Now cousin, with your pardon, I'm forced to leave you: 350
Our abbot's riding out, and I'm going along
At his request, and he needs me there at once.
Greet your lady, my own delightful niece.
And farewell, cousin dear, until we meet!"

      This merchant, a trader prudent and wise, proceeded   355
To borrow the funds (as he'd said he could) that he needed,
Then paid an Italian debt by gold in hand,
Took his receipt, and homeward swiftly cantered,
Singing like a bird, for this arrangement
Was likely to leave him a thousand francs ahead   360
Of the game, with all his assorted costs included.

      His wife, expecting him, was there at the door,
Waiting, as always, to welcome him back home.
And all that night they spent in celebrating,
For he was rich, and all his debts were paid.   365
At dawn, this merchant once again embraced her,
And started up, kissing her on the face
And then went at it again, both long and hard.

      "No more!" she said. "By God, you've had enough!"
And then, voluptuously, she worked it with him,   370
Until he was done and ended love's good rhythm.
"By God," he said, "wife, I must confess,
Although I hate to, I'm worried in one respect.
Do you realize why? By God, I have to guess
You've caused some sort of real unfriendliness   375
Between myself and my dear cousin John.
You should have warned me, before I'd ridden on
To Paris, that he had paid you a hundred francs

In gold, and felt himself distinctly unthanked
When I spoke to him of borrowing and paying.   380
I thought I saw it, distinct and clearly, in his face.
In point of fact, by God, our heavenly king,
I wasn't asking him to pay me a thing!
I beg you, wife, not to do this again:
Always tell me, when I leave you, now and then,   385
If any debtor, in the time that I am absent,
Has paid, to keep me from seeming negligent
And troubling him for something already paid."
    His wife was neither troubled nor afraid,
And boldly answered, as ever ready at once: 390
"By Mary, I curse that lying monk, Don John!
I didn't keep a penny of what he left me.
Yes, he brought some gold, the wicked thief—
What! Bad fortune fall on his evil snout!
Because I understood, without a doubt,   395
That what he gave was all on account of you,
Acknowledging the debt that we were due,
On family grounds, and entertainment, and to do
Me honor for everything he was given here,
So many times of extravagant good cheer.   400
But since you've put me in this situation
I'll answer you, in the straightest, truest fashion.
You deal with delinquent debtors worse than me!
For I will pay you hard cash, and willingly,
Day after day, and any time I fail   405
Go charge it up against my ready tail,
And you won't need to wait, you'll get the rest.
As a matter of fact, none of that gold was wasted,
I spent it, every cent, on beautiful dresses,
And that is money at work in your honor, expressing,   410
I say, what God has meant me to do, each day.
So don't be angry. Why not just laugh and play?
Certainly, you have my body ready
To serve you, but the only place I'll pay is in bed,
By God! Forgive me, my own husband, my dear,   415
Turn toward and not away from me, right here."
    The merchant understood there was nothing to do,

And scolding her would only be stupid, too,
Since what had been done was done, there was nothing to say.
"Now wife," he said, "Of course I forgive you. I pray 420
That in the future you may not spend so freely.
Take care of my fortune. But use whatever you need."

And so my tale is done. May God send us
The tail we want, until our lives have ended.

Amen. 425

The Host's Merry Words to the Shipman and the Prioress

"Well said, by God's own body," said our Host.
"And long may you go sailing along the coast,
Sir noble captain, gracious márinér!
God should bless the monk with a thousand bad years!
Ah ha, fellows! Watch out for all such games!   5
Inside the husband's hood, the monk put an ape,
And he also did the wife, by Saint Augústine!
Allow no monks to open your door and walk in.

   "But let's move on. Let's see who's next in line
For telling another tale, something fine   10
Enough to please us all." And then he said,
As graciously as any shy young maiden,
"My lady Prioress, and by your leave—
Because I'd never want to cause you grief—
I'd like to ask if you might like to tell us   15
A tale? Would you agree, my lady dear?"
   "Gladly," she said, and told what you'll now hear.

Prologue to the Prioress's Tale

Domine dominus noster, Lord, our Lord

"O Lord, our Lord, how very marvelously
Your name is spread throughout the world," said she.
"Not only is your precious praise-song sung
By men who run the world, and also this country,
But children know your generosity   5
And goodness, sometimes learning as they suck
The breast, to celebrate your sacred presence.

"So too I try to praise, as best I can,
You and the virgin lily flower who bore you,
Though never known by any mortal man.   10
The story I've chosen for this holy labor
Cannot increase your noble mother's honor,
For she is honor itself, and next to her son
The very root of bounty and help for the soul.

"O virgin mother! O noble maternal maiden!   15
O burning bush that would not ever burn,
In Moses' sight, speaking God's own words—
O Mary, humility on fire, lighting
God's great power, in you illuminated,
Born in God's eternal magnificence,   20
Help me adorn this story with your reverence!

"Lady, your goodness, your open-handed virtue,
Your high, magnificent humility,
Is more than we can say in mortal speech.

Even before a man can pray to you 25
You often come, O maiden made so kindly,
Bringing with you light from the prayers we seek,
To guide us near your son, O mother so meek!

"My mind is far too weak, O blessèd queen,
To ever state your endless worthiness; 30
I lack the strength to tell of your esteem,
Much like a babe of twelve months old, or less,
A child unable yet to even express
A single word. And so to you I pray:
Come guide the story I will tell today." 35

The Prioress's Tale

In Asia, once, and in a very great city
Filled with Christian folk, there was a Jewery,
Maintained and used by a lord who lived in that country
For the foulest usury and profit of greed,
Hateful to Christ and his society.   5
Men could ride or walk straight through that street,
For it was wide and open to anyone's feet.

And at the farther end there was a little
School, for Christian folk, crowded with
The children of workmen, all of Christian blood,   10
And year by year these little children were pupils
There, learning the skills children are taught,
Especially to sing and also read,
As little children do during childhood.

One such little child was a widow's son,   15
Barely seven years old, a boy who spent
Day after day learning in school, and then
Went walking home. Everywhere he saw
The image of Mary, Christ's dear mother, he bent
His knees and said the *Áve María,* as taught   20
To him by his mother: "Hail Mary, full of grace."

This honor for our blessèd lady, mother
Dear of Christ, devoutly worshipped, was never
Out of this little child's heart; he never forgot her.

And I myself, whenever I think of this matter,   25
Reflect on Nicholas, the patron saint
Of children in school, who even in his cradle
Showed reverence for Christ, and for Christ's mother.

And as he sat in school, holding his primer,
This little child, learning his little book,   30
The older children sang *Alma redemptoris,*
Studying the hymns in their anthem-book.
Closer and closer he went, to hear the words
And follow each moving note as each one took
Its path, until the whole first verse was learned.   35

He had no way of knowing what was said;
He knew no Latin, being too tender and young.
But soon he found a boy with an older tongue,
Asking him what message these words were meant
To convey, and why this hymn was always sung.   40
He begged him, on his knees, completely bare,
To teach him the tender sense this song declared.

The bigger boy, though older, knew little more,
And answered: "I've heard it said this song we sing
Was made to celebrate our mother of all,   45
The blessèd Mary, begging her to bring us
Help, when we come to the end of everything.
I cannot tell you any more than this:
I've learned the song, my knowledge of grammar is thin."

"So this is a song," the innocent child observed,   50
"Made in reverence of Christ's dear mother?
Now surely I will put myself to work
And try to learn it before our Christmas service.
And even if I'm scolded, not learning my primer,
And even beaten three times in an hour,   55
I'm going to learn it, in our Lady's honor!"

The older boy walked with him, going homeward,
And taught him, day by day, wholly by rote,

All the words and also the musical notes,
Until the child could sing it, clear and bright.   60
And twice each day, homeward and back, his throat
Rang out this hymn, sung boldly and sung right.
Christ's mother would hold his heart until it broke.

To and fro he walked, as I have said,
Along the Jewery street, and always singing   65
This hymn, merry and loud, as he knew it went,
O *Alma redemptoris*, the air would ring.
His heart so pierced by her eternal sweetness,
The mother of Christ herself, that heavenly being,
That nothing could have stopped his childish singing.   70

Now our original foe, the serpent Satan,
Who'd planted his evil wasp's nest among the Jews,
Raised his voice, and cried, "O Hebrew people!
How can this seem an honorable thing to you,
That such a boy is allowed to so offend you,   75
Singing such a song, and so offensive?
This is against your every sacred truth!"

And from then on, in secret, the Jews began
To conspire, wanting to chase this innocent child
From our world. They hired a brutal murdering man,   80
Who had a hidden room in an alley, and while
The little boy, still singing, was passing by
This cursèd Jew took hold, and held him fast,
And slit his throat. Then into a pit he cast him.

This pit was under a privy, where all the Jews   85
Emptied out their bowels. These were Herod's
People, Herod dead but born anew.
O cursèd people, who think that they can do
Such things in secret! Murder will always out;
God will make sure of that, without a doubt,   90
For God is honored, and blood will cry from the ground.

O little martyr, never now to grow,
But singing on in heaven, taking the path
Of our white celestial lamb, Christ as we know him,
He of whom Saint John declared, with passion,   95
That those who walked with him, singing a new song,
Were virgins, too, as Christ himself had been.

The poor young widow waited up all night,
And watched for her child. The boy never arrived.
And so, as soon as nighttime turned to light,   100
The mother, pale, with ever anxious mind,
Went searching for her missing little child,
And finally learned that, when last seen, he
Was walking home along the Jewery.

Motherly sorrows were welling in her breast;   105
She hurried, half senseless, her mind not fully controlled,
Searching wherever, for any reason, she supposed
Her little child could have gone, without success.
Continually she cried to our heavenly mother,
Weeping, until at last she focused her thought   110
On the Jewery, where at last she went to seek him.

She asked and inquired, and pitifully she prayed,
But every Jew who dwelled in that foul place
Denied the boy had been seen by anyone there.
They all said "no," but Jesus, ever gracious,   115
Seeing her wandering, crying out for her son,
Soon planted the subtle thought that, truly, where
She needed to look was deep in the pit where he was.

O noble God, who deserves the praise he receives
From the mouths of innocents, this is your power!   120
This jewel of chastity, this emerald flower,
And also the bright red ruby of martyrdom,
This child lay upright, and from his throat, slit open,
Alma redemptoris he started to sing,
So loud and strong the place began to ring.   125

Christian people walking along that street
Came in to stare and marvel at this thing,
And quickly sent for the local magistrate.
He came immediately, without delay,
And uttered praises to Christ, our heavenly king, 130
And she, the world's great honor, Christ's own mother,
And then the Jewish suspects were tied together.

The child was carried away, his bearers weeping
Piteously, but the corpse continued singing,
And with an honored, sorrowful procession 135
The body was brought to the nearest monastery.
His mother lay beside the bier, fainting,
And those who took this weeping mother away
Held her in gentle hands, all of them praying.

The magistrate took care of the Jews' last breath, 140
With rigorous torture, and a final shameful death:
Those who knew what was done were quickly killed.
Death was deserved for all such cursedness:
"Those who do evil, will surely be evilly served."
He had them drawn apart by untamed horses, 145
And then he hanged them, in the name of law and order.

As mass was being sung, the innocent child
Lay in front of the altar, and then the abbot
And all his monks hurried the pitiful body
To its final resting place, here on this earth. 150
And when the holy water was duly spread
On his grave, from under the ground his voice was heard,
Singing *O Alma redemptoris mater!*

This abbot was in truth a holy man,
As monks may be—and surely always should— 155
And sacred messages this abbot began
To send to the child, asking, "I beg you, my son,
By powers vested, in the name of the Trinity:
Tell me why we still can hear you singing
With your throat so cut, and you are dead, as we think?" 160

"My throat is cut as far as the bones of my neck,"
The child replied, "and surely, yes, I ought
To have died long since, by any proper reckoning.
But Jesus Christ, as men have often thought,
Wishes his glory to last, and be kept in mind, 165
And so for his mother's honor, so gentle and kind,
He lets me go on singing, clear and bright.

"This reservoir of mercy, Mary so sweet,
I always loved; my mind had followed her feet.
And when she saw that life would leave me behind, 170
She came to me, and ordered me to sing
The *Alma redemptoris* as I died,
As you have heard, and as I sang this song
It felt as if a pearl was laid on my tongue.

"And so I keep on singing, and ever shall, 175
In honor of that blessèd virgin, until
That pearl is taken off my tongue. And I will
Sing on. But then she also said to me:
'My little child, I'll come and bring you to me,
When that pearl is taken away. Do not fear. 180
I will not abandon you, you're much too dear.'"

This holy monk—the abbot, I mean to say—
Bent down and lifted his tongue, the pearl was taken
Away, and the child, as gently, gave up the ghost.
Seeing this miracle, hot tears came down 185
Like rain, from the abbot's eyes. He fell on the ground,
Lying flat on his face as if he were bound,
Alive but frozen still by what he'd seen.

And all the other monks prostrated themselves,
Weeping, and praising the holy mother Mary, 190
And then they all of them rose, and prayed as they went,
Bearing this little martyr away from his bier,
Erecting a tomb of translucent marble stone.
And there they shut his precious little body.
And there he remains. May God permit us to see him! 195

O little Hugh of Lincoln, also slain
By cursèd Jews—a fact I think worth mention,
For that took place not many years long gone—
Please pray for us, we folk of weak intention,
That God, so gracious, bountiful of his mercy,   200
Will let his eternal mercy continue to flow,
To honor Mary, his sweet and gentle mother.
                              Amen.

Prologue to Sir Thopas

This miracle story told and done, each man
So still and somber it was a wonder to see,
Our Host, as he liked to do, smiled and began
His joking. Abruptly looking up, he saw me,
And said: "What sort of man are you?" said he.   5
"You seem as if you're always hunting a hare.
Your never look up. The ground is all you stare at.

"Come over here, and let me see you smiling.
Get out of his way, my friends, let him approach!
His belly echoes the rounded shape of mine: 10
This would be a good stuffed doll for a woman
To hug, if she were small, though beautiful.
His face resembles, I think, a dwarf or an elf:
Like them he lingers out of sight, by himself.

"But now you have to talk, as others have done.   15
Tell us something funny, you look like someone
Who can." "Host," I said, "don't be offended,
Because I'm not the storytelling type.
The only tale I can tell is an ancient rhyme
I learned long ago." "That's good," he said. "We'll hear it.   20
This might be something special, I smell good times."

SIR THOPAS

Listen, my friends, with open ears,
And I will tell a tale of good cheer
    And in truth, also of solace,
About a knight, handsome and fearless
In battle and also in tournament lists,   5
    His name being Sir Thopas.

Now he was born in a distant country,
Flanders, lying well beyond the sea,
    Poperinghe was the place.
His father was of the nobility,   10
The lord and ruler of that country,
    As God had given him grace.

Sir Thopas was a valiant squire,
His face as white as bread baked fine,
    His lips were red as roses,   15
Complexion as scarlet as cloth well dyed,
And I will tell you what can't be denied:
    He had a well-shaped nose.

His hair and beard were the color of saffron,
Both reaching his belt, and hanging down;   20
    His shoes were Cordovan leather.
His stockings were made in Bruges, and brown,
He wore a very expensive gown
    That cost a lot of silver.

He knew the art of hunting deer,   25
And ducks, and other swimming birds,
　　With a goshawk on his hand.
He drew a bow like a genuine archer;
In wrestling, no one could be his peer,
　　Whenever the prize was a ram.   30

　　Many maidens, bright in their bowers,
Dreamed he would be their paramour,
　　Though they'd do better to sleep,
For he was chaste, not lecherous,
And sweet as the wild rose-bramble flower,   35
　　Sprouting above red leaves.

　　And so it happened, one fine day,
Because you know, as I must say,
　　Sir Thopas went out riding.
He climbed up on his steed (it was gray),   40
His lance that was made for high display,
　　And a long sword by his side.

　　He spurred his horse into a forest,
Containing many of the wildest beasts,
　　Hares, and also stags,   45
But as he galloped north and east,
Let me tell you, right there he almost
　　Had an accident.

　　Herbs were growing, great and small,
Licorice and flowered setwáll,   50
　　And lots of gillyflower cloves,
And nutmeg used in mugs of ale,
Whether it be fresh or stale,
　　And also for laying in coffers.

　　The birds were singing, as they do all day,   55
The sparhawk, the parrot popinjay,
　　And what a joy to hear!
The proud male thrush sang in his way,

As did the woodcock dove, as it swayed
  In the branches, singing away.   60

  Sir Thopas fell into high love-longing,
Hearing the woodcock dove's loud singing,
  And spurred his horse like mad.
His excellent horse, because of his spurring,
Sweated so hard he could have been wringèd,   65
  His sides were soaked with blood.

  Sir Thopas became so langorous,
With all this dashing across soft grass,
  His heart was really that mad,
And so he lay him down in that place,   70
To give himself and his horse some solace,
  Turning the horse out to grass.

  "O heavenly mother Mary, have mercy!
Why is this love so angry at me
  That it gives me such distress?   75
Last night I kept on dreaming, in sleep,
That soon an elf-queen ought to be
  My lover, and sleep in my tent.

  "I'll fall in love with an elf-queen, by God,
There's not a wordly woman to be had   80
  Worthy of being my mate
    In this town.
  All other women I'll forsake,
And with an elf-queen I will mate,
  By dales and, yes, by downs!"   85

  Up in his saddle he went at once,
And galloped his horse over fences and stones,
  Watching for such a queen,
Until he'd ridden so far-away gone,
That in a secret place he found   90
  The country of Fáeríe,
    Still unseen,

For nowhere in that country was one
That could confront him, riding head on,
    No man, or boy, or queen,   95

    Until there appeared a monstrous giant,
Whose name was Lord of the Elephants,
    A dangerous fellow, indeed,
Who said, "Now boy, by Termagaunt!
Unless you ride right out of my haunt   100
    I'll quickly kill your steed
        With my club.
    This land belongs to the queen of fairies,
With harps, and pipes, and other harmonies,
    And here she lives, by God."   105

    Sir Thopas said, "You might be dying;
Tomorrow I'll meet you, and we can try it,
    Once I'm wearing my armor.
    And yet I'm hoping, by my faith
That when you deal with this lance, you'll play   110
    A very sorry game.
        Your brains
Will break into bits, I hope, I pray,
Before the dawn has turned full day,
    And here is where you'll be slain."   115

    Sir Thopas rode away quite quickly,
For the giant hurled stones that barely missed him,
    Using a wicked sling.
But young Sir Thopas escaped at last,
Saved by the power of God's great grace,   120
    And his own noble upbringing.

    Now listen, gentlemen, to my tale
So much more merry than a nightingale,
    For now I'll talk about
Just how Sir Thopas, whose size was small,   125
Went riding over hill and dale
    Until he was back in town.

And his merry men, he commanded, then,
To play their games and entertain him,
    For he would soon be fighting   130
A giant who had three heads on one neck,
For love and joy and other requests
    From she who shone with brightness.

"Do come," he urged, "musicians all,
And also my jesters, to tell me tales   135
    As I put on my armor,
Tell me about romances royal,
And popes, and also cardinals,
    And all other good humors."

At first they brought him good sweet wine,   140
And honey mead in a bowl,
    And what royal spices they could find,
And gingerbread, so truly fine,
And licorice, and excellent cumin,
    And first-class sugar in all.   145

Then he wrapped his white flesh in white,
With linen cloth that was fine and bright,
    Breeches, and also a shirt,
And over his shirt a padded jacket,
And heavy breastplate over that   150
    To stop a spear's fierce piercing.

And then the heavy plate mail, made
Most properly by Jews,
    The best plate in the world,
And over that his coat of armor,   155
Shining white as a lily flower:
    He'd fight with what he was wearing.

His shield was the purest, reddest gold,
A boar's head painted, for men to behold,
    An eight-point star beside it.   160

And so he swore, on ale and bread,
The giant would soon be lying dead,
For he was resolved and decided.

His leather leg armor, stiff and hard,
His ivory sword-sheath: how long? One yard. 165
And a helmet of brass: exceedingly bright.
His pommel carved of true whale bone,
His saddle bright as a true sun shone,
Or maybe white moon light.

His spear was made of well-trimmed cypress, 170
A war-like image, not very peaceful,
And a spear-head to cut you to pieces.
His steed was dapple gray all over,
And knew how to amble along a road,
Up went his hooves, then down, 175
Unceasing.

And, gentlemen, see, we have one part!
If you want some more it won't be hard
For me to find it.

PART TWO

But hold yourselves quiet, easy, not free, 180
Knights who are he, and ladies, she,
Just listen to me as I chatter
Of battle and of chivalry
And ladies doing love's duty:
I'll get there when I have to. 185

Some romances are worthy, pricey,
King Horn, for one, and Ypotis
The converter, and Beves, Sir Guy and Sir Bevis,
The Fair Unknown, and He Full of Love—
But Thopas always shines above them 190
In royal chivalry.

He sat on his horse, and stayed on his horse,
And rode along, no matter the road,
    As fast as a flying spark.
His helmet's crest was tall as a tower,   195
And in that plume he'd stuck a flower.
    I hope he doesn't get hurt.

    And since he was an adventurous knight
He would not sleep in a house, at night,
    But wrapped himself in his cloak.   200
His handy helmet served as a pillow.
Close by, his horse ate weeds and willow,
    And also herbs that were good.

    He himself would drink from a well,
As did that knight, Sir Perceval,   205
    A very worthy gallant—
And then, one day—

THE HOST STOPS
CHAUCER'S NARRATION

"No more of this," said our Host, "for the dignity
Of God. Your storytelling is making me
So terribly weary of your stupidity
That, really, as I hope some day to be blessed,
My ears are aching from your utterly senseless   5
Blather. Send such poetry to the devil!
Whatever you call it, it's stuff of the lowest level."

    "But why?" I asked. "Is my storytelling so awful
That I can't go on, like every other man?
Believe me, Host, I'm doing the best I can."   10

    "By God," he said, "to put it in a word,
Your awful rhyming isn't worth a turd!
To put it bluntly, sir, your rhyming is over.
Try a romance, one that's told in prose,
But let it be prose, O please, whatever you choose,   15
With a hope of laughter, or a word or two of truth."

    "Now gladly," I said, "in the name of the crucifixion!
I'll tell you a little tale in prose, a fiction
You ought to like. It's more traditional,
And if you disapprove, you're over-critical,   20
For what I'll tell you, now, is a moral tale,
Though different people tell it different ways,
As I will now expound and try to explain.

    "You know that each of the four Evangelists,
Who tell us the sorrowful tale of Jesus Christ,   25
Never tell us a thing as the others do.
But yet what all are telling is absolute truth,

And to the extent that meaning is our concern
They speak one sense, though using different words.
Some tell us more, and others tell us less, 30
As they recount his dying, and do their best—
I'm speaking of Mark and Matthew, Luke and John—
But who can doubt their sense is spoken as one?
So therefore, gentlemen, I ask and beseech you,
Don't think I'm changing things, as you hear me speaking— 35
For instance, if I am using somewhat more
Of proverbs than you, perhaps, have heard before,
In matters I will be dealing with, right here,
Trying to make my presentation forceful,
Or if you observe my choice of language, say, 40
Is somewhat off, from all of you I pray
Indulgence, not blame, simply because I vary
My language. The *meaning* here is the same, and this merry
Little story is just as honest as true.
So listen carefully to what I say— 45
And this time let me finish my tale, I pray you.

The Tale of Melibee

A young man called Melibee, who was powerful and rich, had a daughter by his wife, who was named Prudence, and the girl was named Sophie.

One day he went hunting, out in the fields. He left his wife and daughter inside his house, all the doors of which were shut and locked. Three of his ancient enemies had seen him leave and, setting ladders up against the house, entered through the windows, beat his wife, and gave his daughter mortal wounds in five different places—namely, in her feet, her hands, her eyes, her nose, and her mouth. They left her for dead, and went away.

When Melibee returned to his house, and saw all this evil work, like a mad man he ripped his clothes and began to weep and cry.

His wife, Prudence, tried, as hard as she dared, to persuade him to stop, but nevertheless he began to cry and weep even more.

Prudence, this noble wife, remembered what Ovid had said, in the book called *The Remedies of Love:* "He is a fool who tried to prevent a mother from weeping over the death of her child, until she has wept her fill, however long that may be, and then a man must try as hard as he can to find loving words with which to comfort her, and begging her to stop her weeping." And so Prudence did not intervene, letting her husband cry and weep for what seemed to her a proper interval, and when she saw her time she said to him: "Alas, my lord, why act as if you were a fool? No wise man, surely, would create such a fuss. Your daughter, with the grace of God, will recover and be well. And even if she were in fact dead, right now, her death should not cause you to destroy yourself. Seneca says: 'A wise man will not be overly sorrowful, because of his children's death, for surely he should endure it patiently, exactly as he would endure his own death.'"

Melibee quickly answered: "What man," said he, "should stop his weeping when he has so much good reason for tears? Jesus Christ, our Lord himself, wept for the death of his friend, Lazarus."

Prudence answered: "Surely, I'm well aware that reasonable weeping is not forbidden, when someone is among others who are sorrowing; weeping in such cases is certainly permitted. In the Apostle Paul's "Epistle to the Romans," he writes, 'Rejoice with them that do rejoice, and weep with them that weep.' But though reasonable weeping is allowed, excessive weeping is certainly prohibited. The degree of weeping must be considered, according to the law Seneca teaches: 'When your friend has died,' he says, 'do not allow your eyes to moisten too much, but do not completely withhold your tears; if tears come to your eyes, do not let them fall; and having lost your friend, actively seek another one, which is better than weeping over him, for that is of no help whatever.' Accordingly, if you are guided by wisdom, wipe sorrow out of your heart.

"Remember what Jesus, son of Sirach, has said: 'A man who is joyous and glad of heart flourishes until he is old, but in truth a sorrowful heart dries your bones.' He also says that keeping sorrow in your heart has killed many men. Solomon says that just as moths in a sheep's fleece is injurious to clothing, and small worms are injurious to trees, just so is sorrow injurious to the heart. So we ought to be patient, after the death of our children, just as we are patient when we have lost our worldly goods. Think of patient Job. When he had lost his children and his earthly wealth, and his body had endured much grievous tribulation, he still said, 'Our Lord gave it to me; our Lord has taken it away from me; whatever our Lord wishes is done; blessed be the name of our Lord.' "

In answer to what she had said, Melibee said: "Everything you say is true, and therefore useful, but in fact my heart is so sorely and grievously troubled that I do not know what to do."

"Let us assemble," Prudence said, "all your true friends, and the wise members of your family. Then state your case and listen to the advice they give, and follow that advice. Solomon says, 'Everything should be done only after consultation, and then you will never regret what you do.' "

Following his wife's advice, Melibee called a large assembly of people, including surgeons, physicians, people old and young, and some of his old enemies, apparently reconciled; they were joined by some of his neighbors, who acted more in fear than out of love for him, which is not unusual. A good many clever flatterers came as well, and also some wise and learned lawyers.

And when all these people had assembled, this Melibee sorrowfully told them his situation. The manner of his speech made it seem that he bore savage anger in his heart, ready to wreak vengeance on his enemies, and suddenly longed to take action against them, and yet was asking their advice. A surgeon, generally acknowledged to be wise, stood up and said to Melibee what you will now hear:

"Sir," he said, "surgeons are pledged to do the best we can for everyone we deal with, once we have been retained, and that we be careful not to worsen a patient's health. It often happens that when one man has wounded another, the same surgeon heals them both, since in our art we have no need to take sides. But surely, when it comes to healing your daughter, no matter how seriously wounded she may be, we are obliged to be as diligently attentive, both day and night, so that by the grace of God she may be cured and sound as quickly as possible."

The physicians said almost the same thing, except that they added a few words, saying that, just as illnesses are cured by balancing one of the body's humors against another, so too men ought to cure war by the use of vengeance.

His neighbors, who were full of envy, as well as those of his enemies who were pretending to be his friends, and also his flatterers, acted as if they were weeping, and in the process often interfered with and even aggravated the situation, praising Melibee's virtue, his influence, his power, his wealth, and his many friends, speaking scornfully of his enemies' power, and saying plainly that he ought to revenge himself on them, and begin to make war.

Then a counselor stood up, after consulting with those who were wise, and said: "Gentlemen, the reasons for our being assembled in this place are truly serious matters, both because of the wicked wrongdoing that has occurred, and also because of the great damage that may, in the future, occur because of the same actions, as well as because of the great wealth and power of both sides, for all of which reasons it would be very dangerous to give bad advice. Accordingly, Melibee, this is the advice we have agreed upon. Firstly, and most important, we advise you to take good care of yourself, arranging for sentries, guards, and spies. Secondly, we advise you to so garrison your house so that both you and the house may be defended. But to start a war, or in any way to suddenly take vengeance, seems to us a matter we cannot so quickly decide upon, and therefore we ask that you provide us with the time necessary for due and proper deliberation. As the common proverb says: 'Whoever quickly judges will quickly regret it.' And people also say that a good judge is capable of quick understanding and leisurely judgment, for although having to wait may be annoying, it is not intended to deprive anyone of either a firm decision or the taking of vengeance, when there is sufficient and reasonable cause. This is exemplified by our Lord, Jesus Christ, who when a woman taken in adultery was brought before him, to determine what should be done with her, although he himself was well aware of what answer he was going to give, he refused to speak too quickly and insisted on being deliberate, and accordingly paused and wrote something on the ground, then paused and wrote again. This is the justification for leisurely deliberation, for then we shall, by the grace of God, give you advice which will be useful."

All the young people jumped up, and so too most of those who were scornful of this wise old man. They made a great deal of noise, asserting that men should attack when the iron was hot, and take vengeance when the wrongs done to them were fresh and new, crying loudly and often, "War! War!"

Another wise old man stood up, indicating with a raised hand that people should be quiet and listen to him. "Gentlemen," he said, "there are very many men who cry out 'War! War!' who know very little about the nature of war. When war begins, men flock to it as easily as they please, but it is not easy to predict what will happen. Surely, once war begins many a child, as yet unborn, will by reason of this war die young, or else live on in sorrow and wretchedness. And therefore, before a war is started, men must most seriously deliberate and sit in counsel." And when this old man tried to strengthen his argument, giving reason after reason, virtually everyone stood up, in order to stop him, saying that he had been talking for too long. Truly, whoever preaches to people who are not listening, and do not hear his words, annoys those people. As Jesus of Sirach says, "Music is noxious to weeping," meaning that it is just as useless to speak to people who are annoyed at you as it is to sing while a man is weeping. Seeing that he in truth had no audience, this wise old man took his seat once more. As Solomon says: "Do not speak when you have no audience." "I see quite clearly," this wise man remarked, "that the common proverb is correct: 'good advice is missing exactly when it is most needed.'"

And Melibee still had many people whispering one kind of advice in his ear, while in public taking the opposite view.

Seeing that most of his advisors agreed that he should go to war, he quickly indicated that he fully accepted their advice. Then Lady Prudence, seeing how her husband was readying himself to take vengeance on his enemies, said to him, in the humblest manner: "My lord," she said, "I beg you as sincerely as I dare and am capable of, not to go quite so rapidly, and for the sake of God please listen to me. As Petrus Alphonsus says, 'When someone either hurts you or helps you, do not respond too quickly, for this will preserve friendship and keep your enemy fearful.' The proverb says, 'He hurries best who waits the longest,' and there is no profit in disastrous haste."

Melibee answered his wife: "I don't intend to take your advice," he said, "and for many good reasons. Surely, everyone would then think me a fool, were I, because you had so advised me, to change decisions reached and affirmed by so many wise men. Secondly, I tell you that all women are bad, and none of them are good. As Solomon says, 'I have found a good man, but most certainly have never found a good woman.' Furthermore, were I to allow myself to be governed by your counsel, it would appear that I had surrendered my mastery to you, which God has forbidden! For as Jesus of Sirach says, 'Were the wife to be the master, she would stand in opposition to her husband.' And as Solomon says, 'As long as you live, never give power over yourself to your wife, nor to your child, nor to your friend, for it is better that your children ask you for things they may need than for you to see yourself in your children's hands.' And if I were to follow your counsel, surely there will be times when my counsel must stay secret, until it is proper to let it be made known, and this is impossible. For it is written that women's chattering cannot hide anything except what they do not know. And in addition, says the philosopher, 'Women defeat men, when it comes to bad advice.'"

Listening to this with gracious patience, and having heard everything her husband wanted to say, Lady Prudence asked for his permission to speak, and said: "My lord," she said, "surely, your first objection is easily replied to. I say, to the contrary, that it is not foolish to change advice when the thing itself has changed, or when the thing comes to be seen differently. And, moreover, I say that although you have sworn and promised to perform this enterprise, at the same time you have neglected to ensure that you perform it by just cause. If then you change your plans, no one can charge you with being a liar or with having broken your oath.

Because Seneca says that 'a wise man is not guilty of lying when he turns his heart to better things.' And even though your enterprise may begin and be planned by a great many people, what you will be fulfilling is not their plan but your own desires. Truth and usefulness are usually established by a relatively few, who are wise and full of good reason, while the multitude is full of folk, each and all crying and clattering whatever they happen to like. Truly, it cannot be said that such a multitude is honorable or respectable.

"And as for your second reason, in which you claim that all women are bad: I beg your pardon, but you certainly are contemptuous of all women, and 'he that looks down on everyone, displeases everyone,' as the book says. Seneca says that 'a man who wishes to act wisely must look down on no one, instructing without pride or presumption; whatever he knows he does not know, he must not be ashamed to learn, inquiring even of people less honored than himself.' And, sir, that there have been many good women is easily proved. Surely, sir, our Lord Jesus Christ would never have come to earth to be born of a woman, if all women had been savage and barbarous. And note the greater virtue of women in the fact that, after rising out of death, he did not appear before his apostles, but to a woman. And even if Solomon says he never found a good woman, it does not follow therefrom that every woman is bad. He may not have found a good woman; surely many other men have found many women very good and very faithful. Or perhaps what Solomon really meant was this: since he found no sovereign, supreme bounty in any woman may indicate that in fact no one has supreme bounty except God himself, as has been recorded of Christ by Saint Matthew and Saint Luke, in their gospels. No one is so completely good that he is not imperfect, as God, who is his maker, is perfect.

"Your third reason is that, should you follow my advice, it would seem as if you had given me mastery and lordship over you. Pardon me, sir, but that is not true. If it were true that a man must only be given advice by someone having lordship and mastery of his person, there would be very little counseling at all. Truly, a man who seeks counsel for some reason, still has the right and the freedom to accept that advice or not.

"And as to your fourth reason, where you say that the chattering of women cannot keep a secret unless they do not know anything about it, as if you were saying that a woman cannot hide what she does know: sir, these words have been noted and understood about women who are indeed bad, and who are indeed chatterers. Men say of such women, in observing that there are three things which drive a man out of his own house: smoke, rain coming through the roof, and bad wives. Solomon says of such women that 'it would be better to live in a desert than to live with a wild woman.' Sir, by your leave, I am not such a woman, for you have often proved my capacity for silence and for patience, and also how well that I can hide and cover things that men need to keep secret.

"And as for your fifth reason, truly, in which you say that in the giving of bad counsel, women defeat men, God knows perfectly well that this will not stand up to scrutiny. Understand: you seek advice in order to do a bad thing, and if your wife restrains you in this bad purpose, changing your mind by good reason and good advice, surely your wife ought to be praised rather than blamed. This is how you ought to understand the philosopher who argues that 'in the giving of bad counsel, women defeat men.'

"And insofar as you attack all women and their capacity for sound reasoning, I will show you by many examples that many women have been extremely good, and many still are, and their counsels have been sound and useful. So too there are men who say that women's advice either costs too much, or is worth too little. Yet though there are many bad women, whose counsel is vile and worthless, men have also found many good women, deeply sagacious, and who give wise advice. Lo, Jacob, because of the good counsel of his mother, Rebecca, won the blessing of Isaac, his father, and lordship over all his brothers. Judith by her good counsel liberated the Israeli city of Bethulia, in which she lived, from the hands of Hóloférnes, who had besieged and would have destroyed it. Abigail delivered Nabal, her husband, from King David, who would have killed him, appeasing the king's anger by her intelligence and good advice. Esther, by her good counsel, enhanced the standing of the people of God, during the reign of King Áhasúerus. The same prowess and worth in women can be testified to by many men. And moreover, when our Lord created Adam, our first father, he said: 'It is not good for a man to be alone; to help him, we will make a being like himself.' From this you may see that if women were not good, and their counsel good and useful, our Lord God would never have made them, nor termed them man's helper, but rather man's ruin. And a cleric once said, in a pair of verses, 'What is better than gold? Jasper. What is better than Jasper? Wisdom. And what is better than wisdom? Woman. And what is better than a good woman? Nothing.' And, sir, there are many more good reasons for seeing that many women are good, and their counsel good and profitable. And therefore, sir, if you will trust my advice, I will restore your daughter to you, whole and sound. And I will do so much more that you will be blessed with honor, in this cause."

Having heard the words of Prudence, his wife, Melebee said, "I see that Solomon has spoken truly. He says, 'Words that are spoken sweetly and rationally are like honeycombs, for they give sweetness to the soul and health to the body.' And, wife, because of your sweet words, and also because I have tested and proved your great wisdom and truthfulness, I will allow myself to be governed by your advice in all things."

"Now, sir," said Lady Prudence, "since you agree to be governed by my counsel, let me advise you how you ought to act, in choosing your counselors. In all that you do, you should start by humby beseeching God that he will be your counselor, and prepare yourself so that he will indeed give you counsel and comfort, as Tobias taught his son: 'At all times you must bless God, and pray that he will set your ways in good order; be careful that for evermore all your counsel will be found in him.' Saint James says the same thing: 'If any of you are in need of wisdom, ask it of God.' And afterward you can counsel yourself, considering such thoughts as you think best and most fruitful. And then you must banish from your heart three things that are in direct opposition to good counsel: to wit, anger, greed, and hastiness.

"To begin with, he who asks counsel of himself must certainly do so without anger, for a great many reasons. The first is this: he who has great anger and wrath in himself always believes that he is permitted to do things that in fact he may not do. And secondly, he who is angry and wrathful cannot make sound judgments, and he who cannot make sound judgments cannot give good counsel. Thirdly, he who is angry and wrathful, as Seneca says, can only speak in censorious terms, and with his foul and mistaken words he will stir other people to anger. In addition, sir, you must drive greed out of your heart, for the Apostle Paul says that greed is the root of all evil. And believe most profoundly that a greedy man can neither judge nor think, except to meet the demands of his greed, and certainly that can never be done with, for the more riches he possesses, the more he wants. And, sir, you must also drive hastiness out of your heart, because surely a hasty thought, falling into your heart, may not encourage you to your best judgment, unless you keep testing it. For, as you have heard before, the common proverb says, 'he who judges quickly, will repent quickly.' Remember, sir, that you may not always be in the same frame of mind and, certainly, that which seems good to you at one time may at another time seem exactly the contrary.

"When you have counsel of yourself, and by sound deliberation have come to a decision which seems to you best, then I advise you to keep it secret. Don't entrust your counsel to anyone, unless you feel absolutely sure that giving away your secret will prove more useful to you. For Jesus of Sirach says, 'Don't disclose either your secret or your folly to either a friend or an enemy, for in your presence they will listen to you, and seem to approve, and give you their support, but in your absence will scorn you.' Another cleric says that 'you will scarcely find anyone who is capable of keeping a secret.' The book says, 'As long as you keep your counsel in your heart, you have it in your prison, and when you betray it to anyone, he holds you in his snare.' And therefore it is better to hide your counsel in your heart than to beg him to whom you have disclosed it to keep it silent and hidden. For Seneca says, 'If you cannot keep your own counsel, how can you possibly believe that anyone else can keep your secret?' But nevertheless, if you are certain that telling your counsel to some particular person will improve your position, proceed to tell him, but in the following fashion. First, do not indicate any bias, whether for peace or for war, or for this or for that, and do not indicate what it is that you want or are prepared to do. For trust it well, usually counselors are flatterers, and especially the counselors of great lords, for they always exert themselves to speak pleasant words, leaning in the direction they know the lord desires, rather than words that are either true or useful. And therefore it is said that a rich man seldom obtains good counsel, unless he gets it from himself.

"And then you must consider both your friends and your enemies. As for your friends, consider which are the most faithful, the wisest and oldest, and the most tested, and ask them for their advice, as the particular case requires. I have said that you should first consult your true friends. For Solomon says that 'just as a man's heart delights in a sweet taste, so does the counsel of a good friend give sweetness to the soul.' He also says: 'Nothing can be compared to a true friend, for surely neither gold nor silver are worth as much as the goodwill of a true friend.' And again he says: 'A true friend is a strong defense; the man who finds it has certainly found a great treasure.'

"And then you need to consider if your true friends are also discreet and wise. For the book says: 'Always seek the counsel of men who are wise.' And for this same reason you should summon counselors who are older, those who have seen and been active in many things and been tested in their advising. For the book says that 'wisdom lies in older men, and prudence lies in long experience.' And Cicero says that 'great things have never been accomplished by strength, or by bodily agility, but by good counsel, by individual moral supremacy, and by knowledge, three things that are not enfeebled by age, and indeed are strengthened and increased, day by day.' And you should hold to this as a general rule: call as your counselors a few of your friends who have been pre-eminent, for Solomon says, 'You may have many friends, but among a thousand of them choose only one to be your counselor.' For although you may at first speak of your decision only to a few, you may tell them to more people, later on, if that proves necessary. But always keep in mind that your counselors meet the three requirements that I spoke of, before, that is, that they be faithful, wise, and of great experience. And do not turn to just one counselor, in different situations, for sometimes it is necessary to consult with many. For Solomon says, 'The best guarantee of success is where there have been many counselors.'

"Now that I have told you by whom you *should* be counseled, let me tell you what sort of advice you must avoid. First, you must shun the advice of fools, for Solomon says, 'Accept no advice from a fool, for the only counsel of which he is capable stems from his own desires and emotions.' The book says that 'the basic characteristic of a fool is this: he is easily convinced that another man is dangerous, and just as trusting in his own goodness.' You should also shun, more than any others, the advice of all flatterers, people who are primarily concerned with praising you by flattery, rather than telling you the truth about things. For that reason, Cicero says: 'Of all the plagues of friendship, the greatest is flattery.' And that is why it is imperative that you avoid and fear flatterers above all others. The book says: 'Choose to avoid and fear the sweet words of flattering sycophants, but not the sharp words of a friend who tells you the truth.' Solomon says, 'A flatterer's words are a snare, employed to catch innocents.' He also says that 'he who speaks sweet and pleasant words to his friend is setting a net in front of his feet, with which to trap him.' And therefore Cicero says, 'Don't listen to flatterers, and pay no attention to what they say.' Cato, too, says: 'Be very careful, avoid sweet and pleasant words.' So too you must avoid the advice of old enemies who have been brought back into your friendship. The book says that 'No man returns safely and securely to the favor of his old enemy.' And Aesop says: 'Do not trust those who have at one time or another fought with you, or been your enemy, and do not take them into your confidence.' And Seneca explains just why: 'It is impossible,' he says, 'that wherever a great fire has burned for a long time, there does not remain some degree of heat.' And so Solomon says, 'Never trust your old enemy.' Surely, although your enemy may have been reconciled, and speaks pleasantly and humbly to you, bowing his head, never trust him. For certainly he behaves with such pretended humility more for his own profit than out of love for you, thinking that he may conquer you by such pretenses, as he might not have been able to do by fighting or by war. As Petrus Alphonsus says, 'Do not enter into fellowship with your old enemy, for any kindness you show them will be seen by them as wickedness.' So too you must avoid the counsel offered by those who have been your servants, and who hold you in great reverence, for perhaps they speak from fear rather than from love. And therefore a philosopher says: 'There is no one who can speak entirely truthfully to someone of whom he is deeply afraid.' And Cicero says: 'The might of no emperor can long endure, unless his people love him more than they fear him.'

"You must also avoid the counsel of drunkards, for they can never keep a secret. For Solomon says: 'There can be no confidentiality anywhere that drunkenness flourishes.' Be wary of advice given by those who say one thing behind your back, and openly advise you to the contrary.' For as Cassiodorus says, 'It is a trick employed to harm and hinder you, when someone openly advises one thing and privately strives to do the exact opposite.' Be wary, too, of the advice given by people of bad character. For as the book says, 'The counsel of wicked and depraved people is always fraudulent.' And David says: 'Happy is the man who has not followed the advice of men disposed to evil.' You must also shun the advice of young people, for their counsel is not mature and fully developed.

"Now, sir, since I have shown you from whom you ought to take counsel, and whose counsel you should follow, I will show you how to test that counsel, according to Cicero's doctrine. In order to judge your counselor, you need to take into account many things. First and foremost, you must consider whether what you are trying to accomplish, and as to which you are seeking advice, has been carefully and honestly presented—that is, you need to have told the truth. For he who tells lies cannot be well counseled. And next you must consider if what you are proposing to do is rational, and if your resources are sufficient to accomplish it, and if most of your better counselors do or do not agree with you. And then you must consider what the results of your proposed action will be—that is, hate, peace, war, gratitude, profit, or damage, and many other things. And you must choose the best of all these things, and decline the others. Then you should consider from what root your counsel stems, and what fruit it may create. And you should, similarly, consider the roots from which the various results may spring.

"And when you have tested your counsel, as I have said, and which portion thereof is the better and more profitable, and this has been approved by many wise old people, you must then decide if you can accomplish your goal and bring it to a successful conclusion. Surely, reason requires that no man ought to begin a thing unless he is able to perform it as it ought to be; no one should undertake a responsibility so heavy that he may not be able to bear it. For the proverb says: 'He that tries to grasp too much, takes up very little.' And Cato says: 'Try to do things that you have the power to do, lest the burden press upon you so heavily that you are obliged to abandon the thing you have begun.' And if you are in doubt whether you are able to do a thing, choose to wait patiently rather than to begin. As Petrus Alphonsus says, 'If you have the power to do something of which you will surely repent, "no" is better than "yes."' This means it is better to stay silent than to speak. You will then understand, applying stronger reasons, that rather than perform a work you are sure to regret, you should endure the situation rather than begin what you have considered doing. Those who warn against doing something which seems doubtful to you, and advise that you test it before taking action, are giving good advice. Finally, once you have tested your counsel, as I have said before, and are sure that you can in fact perform it, validate it and soberly proceed until the end.

"Now it is reasonable and appropriate that I show you when and why you can change counselors without being shamed or disgraced. Certainly, a man is allowed to change his goals and his advisors if the cause vanishes, or if a new cause comes into existence. And Seneca says: 'If the advice you are given becomes known to your enemies, change your advisors.' You can also change your counselors if you discover that, by error or for any other reason, harm or damage might result. Also, if your counselor is dishonest, or is associated with some dishonest cause, change your counselor. For the laws state that 'all vows and promises which are dishonest are worthless,' and the same is true of something which it is impossible to do, or may not decently be performed.

"And take this for a general rule: every counsel affirmed so strongly that it cannot be changed, no matter what happens, I say that counsel is bad."

This Melibee, having heard the instructions given by his wife, Prudence, answered her as follows: "Lady," said he, "until now you have shown me, well and properly, how I should govern myself in the choosing and removing of my counselors. But now I wish, in particular, that you be willing to tell me how you like, or how you feel about, the counselors we have chosen in our present need."

"My lord," she said, "let me beseech that you will not stubbornly attack my reasoning, or upset yourself, if I say things that displease you. For God knows that, as far as my intentions go, I speak only for your best, for your honor, and also for your profit. And, truly, I hope that your kindly disposition will accept with patience what I have to say. Trust me," she said, "but your counsel in this case ought not, to speak properly, be called 'counseling,' but the movements and actions of folly, in which you have erred in very many assorted ways.

"First and foremost, you have erred in the calling together of your counselors. For you ought to have begun by assembling only a few advisors, and called upon more only later, if necessary. But without a doubt, you abruptly assembled a great multitude of people, burdensome and annoying to hear. And whereas you should only have called together your old and wise true friends, you have mistakenly summoned unfamiliar people, young people, lying flatterers, and reconciled enemies, and people who bow to you without love. And you have also erred in coming to this assembly with anger, greed, and hastiness in your own heart, which three things stand in opposition to every honest and profitable consultation, nor have you nullified or destroyed these three things, either in yourself or in your counselors, as you should have. You have also erred, showing your inclination to war and your desire to do so at once, and make vengeance. They were informed by your words as to what you were inclined toward, and they therefore advised you toward what you wanted, not what was the best thing for you to do. You have erred, yet again, for you seemed to be satisfied, having been counseled, and that scantily enough, only by these men, whereas in so great and high a need there should have been more counselors and more deliberation about doing what you proposed. You have erred also because you did not test your counsel, as stated earlier, and as the situation required. You have erred also, by not making any distinction between and among your advisors—that is, between your true friends and your deceiving counselors, nor were you informed as to the views of your true friends, old and wise, but have simply cast all their words into a jumble and bent your own heart toward the larger and more numerous portion, and agreed with that. And since you know very well that there are always a greater number of fools than wise men among a body of men, and your advisors were assembled in great numbers, in which more attention is paid to the weight of numbers than to the wisdom of those who speak, you can easily see that in such counseling fools will lead the way."

Melibee answered her once more, saying: "I admit that I have erred, but since you have already informed me that a man is not to be blamed if he changes his counselors in a specific case, and for right and proper causes, I am now ready to change my counselors exactly as you will advise me to do. The proverb says, 'Human beings will always sin, but to persevere long in sin is the devil's work.'"

Lady Prudence immediately replied: "'Test your counselors,' she said, "with a critical eye, and let us see which of them has spoken most reasonably and given you the best advice. That testing process being now required, let us begin with the surgeons and physicians, who were the first to speak. I say that the surgeons and physicians have counseled you judiciously, as they should have, saying with great wisdom that their office is to do honor and good to everyone, and to harm no one, and in their medical practice to be diligent in curing their patients. And, sir, just as they have spoken honestly and judiciously, I say that they should be rewarded for their noble words, and should be the principal parties working toward your dear daughter's cure. Although they are your friends, you must not permit them to serve you without reward, and you ought to praise them and show them your generosity. As for the statement they put forth— that is, that in sickness one extreme can be conquered by an opposing extreme—I would like to know how you understand this text, and what you think of it."

"Surely," said Melibee, "I take it like this: just as my enemies once acted against me in their way, I should act against them in mine. For just as they have avenged themselves on me, and done me wrong, so too I ought to avenge myself on them and do them wrong. I will then have cured one contrary by another."

"Lo, lo," said Lady Prudence. "How easily all men are inclined to their own desire and what will please them. Surely," she said, "the physicians' words should not have been understood in this manner. In fact, evil is not the opposite of evil, and vengeance is not the opposite of vengeance, for they are similar. And therefore one vengeance is not cured by another vengeance, nor one wrong by another wrong, but each of them increases and worsens the other. Rather, the physicians' words should have been understood as follows: good and evil are two opposites, like peace and war, vengeance and forbearance, disagreement and agreement, and so on. Surely, wickedness can be cured by goodness, disagreement by agreement, war by peace, and so forth. And here the Apostle Paul has often adopted these views. He says: 'Don't pay back one harm for another, or one wicked speech for more wicked speech, but do well to him who does you harm, and bless him who speaks evilly toward you.' And in many other places he advocates peace and agreement.

"But let me now speak to you about the counsel given you by the lawyers and the wise men, who all advocated the same things, as you have yourself heard, namely, that more than anything else you ought to be careful about your own life and the protection of your house, working in these matters according to careful counsel and after great deliberation. And, sir, as to their first point, dealing with care for your own life, you must understand that whoever wages war must continuously, humbly, and devoutly pray that Jesus Christ, for his mercy, will protect him and be the supreme help for all his needs. Certainly, no man in this world can be counseled nor kept safe without the protection of our Lord Jesus Christ. The prophet David agrees, saying, 'If God does not protect the city, it is a waste of time for any man to try to preserve it.'

"Now sir, you must commit the protection of your person to your true friends, those who are tested and known, and to them must you turn for help in this matter. For Cato says: 'If you need help, ask it of your friends, for no physician is as good as a true friend.' And then you should avoid all unfamiliar people, and stay away from liars, who must always be regarded with suspicion. For Petrus Alphonsus says: 'While traveling along, do not casually fall into conversation with an unfamiliar man, unless you have known him for some longer time. And if he himself starts a conversation with you, without your agreeing thereto, examine what he says as carefully and closely as you can, and learn as much as you can of his life before that point, and disguise the direction in which you are in fact going; say that you are going somewhere, when in fact you are going someplace else; and if the man is carrying a spear, stay on his right-hand side; if he is carrying a sword, on his left-hand side.' In addition, as I have said before, you should avoid all such people, shunning both the person and his counsel. And also, no matter how strong you think you are, do not underestimate or fail to take fully into account the strength of your adversary, or you will be neglecting to take proper care of yourself, for every wise man fears his enemy. And Solomon says: 'Lucky is the man who is fearful of everyone, for surely a man who allows his brave heart and a good deal of strength to think the less of his enemy has presumed too much, and bad things will happen to him.' And although you seem to be in a safe and secure place, remain always diligent in watching out for yourself. Or, to put it differently, do not focus all your attention on your greatest enemy, but also be careful of your least enemy. Seneca says: 'A deliberate and prudent man is afraid of his least enemy.' Ovid says that 'the little weasel can kill a huge bull and a savage stag.' But nevertheless, I am not saying that you ought to be such a coward that you worry where there is absolutely no reason for fear. The book says that 'some people are extremely eager to deceive, but are desperately afraid of being deceived themselves.' But you must remain fearful of being poisoned, as you must avoid the company of scornful people, for as the book says, 'Avoid scornful people, flee from their words as you would flee from venom.'

"Now, as to the second point, your wise counselors warning you to diligently protect the safety of your house. I'd like to know how you understand these words and what is your opinion of them."

Melibee answered, saying, "I understand it clearly, as follows: I must fortify my house with towers, as there are on castles and other similar edifices, and by means of them I will be able to so maintain and defend my house that my enemies will be fearful of approaching it."

Prudence immediately replied to her husband's opinion: "Fortification, by means of great towers and buildings, is sometimes a matter of pride. And men pay a great deal to make high towers and great buildings, which are laborious to build, and when they are completed they are not worth a straw unless they are manned by true friends, old and wise. And you must understand that the greatest and strongest garrison a rich man may possess, in order to preserve both his person and his wealth, is that he be beloved by his subjects and by his neighbors. For as Cicero says, 'There is only one garrison that no man can conquer or defeat, and that is a lord who is beloved by his citizens and his lesser subjects as well.'

"Now, sir, as to the third point, bearing on the advice of your old and wise counselors that you ought not to proceed suddenly or in haste, but rather that you prepare and provision yourself in advance, and do so with great diligence and thoughtfulness. Truly, I believe that they have spoken very wisely and most truthfully. For as Cicero says, 'In every necessity, before you begin it, provision and prepare yourself with great care.' I add that in taking vengeance, in war, in battle, and in fortification, you always prepare yourself in advance and after much deliberation. For Cicero says, 'Long preparation before a battle makes for quick victory.' And Cassiodorus says: 'The garrison is stronger when it has been thoroughly prepared in advance.'

"Now let us speak about the advice given you by your neighbors, people who bow to you but do not love you, and also by your reconciled enemies, your flatterers, all of whom gave you one sort of counsel in private, and in public advised you to the contrary, and let us add, here, the young people, who advised you to take your vengeance, and go to war at once. And certainly, sir, as I have said before, you made a grievous error in inviting such people to your assembly, those wrongly chosen counselors having been sufficiently censured, for all the reasons previously set forth. But nevertheless, let us deal with individuals. First, you ought to proceed according to Cicero's doctrine. (Of course, there is no need, here, to look into whether or not this thing happened, or what counsel it was based upon, for it is perfectly clear who it was that did this invasive injury to you, and how many of them there were, and how they did what it was that they were determined to do.) But then you need to look into the second condition that Cicero sets forth. He refers to something he calls 'consent,' which means exactly which people, and how many they were, who gave their consent to your having been counseled to take immediate vengeance, and also to your willingness to follow that advice. And we must follow the same approach as we consider those who counseled your enemies. Surely, as to the first issue, it is clear who consented to your hastily, wilfully taking vengeance, for without a doubt those who gave you such advice neither were nor are your friends. So let us turn to what they are like, those you consider your personal friends. You are certainly powerful and rich, you are relatively alone, for the only child you have is a daughter, you have no brothers, no first cousins, nor any other close relatives, because of whom your enemies might be afraid to wrangle with you, or to kill you. You also know that your riches would have to be divided among different recipients, and when every man has his share, there won't be much left to revenge your death. But you have three enemies, and they have many children, brothers, cousins, and other relatives. And though you might kill two or three of them, there would still be enough of them to revenge their deaths and to kill you. And even if your kinfolk are more dependable and steadfast than your adversaries' kin, nevertheless they are very few in number, and they are not closely related to you, but your adversaries' kinfolk are closely related. And surely, without any doubt, in that respect their position is better than yours.

"Then let us consider, in addition, whether the advice of those who urged you to take sudden revenge is reasonable. And surely you know that it is not. By the rules of law and of reason, no man may decide to take vengeance on anyone until the judge who has jurisdiction of the affair grants him the right to vengeance, immediately or after due consideration, as the law may require. Furthermore, consider once more the word that Cicero calls 'consent,' and whether your resources and your strength allow you to consent, and are sufficient, when you propose to do as you wish and as your counselors have advised you to do. And, once again, you surely have to say 'no.' For without a doubt we cannot do anything, to speak correctly, except things which we are permitted to do rightfully. And your own authority is insufficient to permit you to revenge yourself. Thus you can see that your strength neither can consent to, nor does it accord with, your wilfullness.

"Let us now test the third point, which Cicero calls 'consequences.' You must understand that the vengeance you propose to take is a consequence, and from that there arises another consequence, danger and war, and numberless other harmful matters which, as of now, we do not even know of.

"And as for the fourth point, which Cicero calls 'engendering,' you must understand that the wrong which has been done to you has arisen from your enemies' hate, and vengeance taken for that wrong would engender yet another vengeance, and a great deal of sorrow and waste of riches, as I have said.

"Now, sir, as to the point which Cicero calls 'causes,' this being the last of his points. You must understand that the wrong you have received has certain causes, which clerics call *oriens*, 'origin,' and *efficiens*, 'effect,' and *causa longinqua*, 'distant cause,' and *causa propinqua*, 'immediate cause.' The distant cause is almighty God, who is the cause of all things. The 'immediate' or 'closer' cause is your three enemies. The subsidiary cause was hate. The substantive cause was your daughter's five wounds. The formal cause is their carrying ladders and climbing in at your windows. The final cause was to kill your daughter. This did not occur, though they tried and failed. But to deal with the distant causes, and what end, in time, they will finally arrive at, I can only conjecture and imagine. Surely, we must suppose they will come to a bad end, because the Book of Death says: 'Seldom or only after great suffering, have causes been brought to a good end when they have been begun badly.'

"Now, sir, if I am asked why God permitted men to do these evil things to you, truly, I cannot answer. For the Apostle Paul says that 'the knowledge and the judgments of God almighty are profoundly deep, and no man can understand or search them out.' Notwithstanding, using certain presumptions and conjectures, I maintain and believe that God, who is full of justice and righteousness, has allowed this to happen for a just and reasonable cause.

"Your name is Melibee, which means 'a man who drinks honey.' You have indeed drunk much honey of sweet worldly riches, and the delights and honors of this world, so that you are intoxicated, and you have forgotten Jesus Christ, your creator. You have not honored and reverenced him as you should have, nor have you listened to Ovid's words, saying, 'Under the honey of bodily goods there lies hidden a venom which kills the soul.' And Solomon says: 'If you have found honey, eat as much of it as is sufficient, for if you eat more than enough you will vomit out again,' and be in need, and poor. And perhaps Christ feels contemptuous of you, and has turned away his face, and his ears which hear the sounds of misery, and thus has permitted that you be punished according to the degree of your sins. You have surely sinned against our Lord Christ, for mankind's three enemies—that is, the flesh, the fiend, and the world—have been admitted into your heart, willingly, through the windows of your body, and you have not adequately defended yourself against these attacks and temptations, and allowed your soul to be wounded in five places. This means that your five senses have conducted these sins to your heart. So our Lord Christ has wanted and permitted that your three enemies enter your house through its windows, wounding your daughter as they have."

"Indeed," said Melibee, "I see perfectly well how you press words on me, trying to overwhelm me, and get me to not take vengeance on my enemies, showing me the perils and the evil that might be caused by this venture. But if we are always to consider all the perils and evils that might be caused by taking vengeance, no one would ever take vengeance, and that would be bad, for vengeance separates the wicked men from the good ones, and then those who want to do evil things are obliged to restrain themselves, when they see the punishment and the disciplining of wrongdoers."

Lady Prudence replied to this answer as follows: "Certainly, I grant you that much good as well as much evil comes from vengeance, but the taking of vengeance is a matter that falls under the authority of judges, and others who have proper jurisdiction over the trespassers. And I have still more to say about this, for just as one individual sins in taking vengeance, so too the judge commits a sin if he does not permit vengeance against someone who deserves it. For Seneca says: 'A master is good if he combats evil folk.' And as Cassiodorus says, 'A man fears to commit outrages when he is well aware that this displeases judges and kings.' And Saint Paul the Apostle says, in his Epistle to the Romans, that 'judges do not take up the spear for no reason, but use it to punish the wicked, and in order to defend good men.' When you want to take vengeance on your enemy, you must seek out the judge who has jurisdiction over them, and he will punish them as the law provides and requires."

"Ah!" said Melibee, "this sort of vengeance does not please. I think how, from childhood on, Fortune has nourished me, helping me to overcome many powerful barriers. Now I propose to test her, trusting, with God's help, that she will help me be revenged for my shame."

"Indeed," said Prudence, "but if you choose to follow my counsel, you will not put Fortune to the test, nor will you bend or bow to her, for as Seneca puts it, 'things that have been foolishly done, in hope of Fortune's aid, will never come to a good end.' And this same Seneca also says, 'When Fortune shines clearest and brightest, the more brittle she turns out to be, and the sooner broken.' Do not put your trust in her, for she is neither reliable nor stable, and when you think you are the safest and the most sure of her help, she will fail and deceive you. You may say that Fortune has nourished you, from your childhood on, but I say that so much the less you ought to trust her, now. For Seneca says: 'When a man is nourished by Fortune, she makes him a great fool.' Now then, since you desire and ask for vengeance, and the law's variety of vengeance and also its judges do not please you, and vengeance which depends on Fortune's aid is perilous and uncertain, you have no recourse but to turn to that Sovereign Judge, on high, who takes vengeance on all wrongs and evil. And he will revenge you as he himself has testified, having said, 'Leave vengeance to me, and I will do it.'"

Melibee replied, "If I do not take revenge for the evil deeds done to me, I notify those who have committed those evil deeds, and all others, that they should commit more evils against me. For it is written: 'If you do not take vengeance for an old evil, you notify your adversaries that they should commit more evils against you.' And also, because of my patience men will do me so much evil that I will not be able to endure or survive it, and thus I will be brought too far down. For men say, 'When you bear up under much misfortune and suffering, many things will happen to you which you ought not to endure.' "

"Of course," said Prudence, "I grant you that excessive patience is not good. But it does not follow, from that, that every man against whom evil has been done is required to take vengeance thereof, for that is the business, and only the business, of the judges, who are required to take vengeance against evil deeds and injuries. And so the two authorities you have just cited are relevant only for the judges. For when judges allow too many wrongs and evils to go without punishment, they not only call on men to commit new wrongs, but they absolutely command them to do so. As a wise man has said, 'The judge who does not rebuke a sinner, is asking and commanding him to sin.' And if judges and kings are too patient with rascals and evildoers, in due time the bad men will become so powerful that they will turn the judges out of office, and overthrow the kings.

"But let us now assume that you have been given permission to revenge yourself. I must tell you that, as of now, you do not have the strength and power to take vengeance, for if you compare your might with that of your adversaries, you will see that in many ways, as I have previously shown you, their position is superior to yours. And so I say that, as of now, it is good that you endure and be patient.

"Furthermore, you are well aware that, as the common saying goes, 'A man is crazy to fight with a man stronger than himself, and even to fight with a man of equal strength is dangerous; to fight with a weaker man is foolishness.' Accordingly, a man should avoid fighting as much as he can. As Solomon says: 'It is greatly to your credit, if you can keep a man from noise and fighting.' And if it happens that a man of greater might and strength causes you some grievance, try to relieve that grievance, rather than to take revenge for it. For Seneca says, 'He who fights with a man greater than himself is putting himself in danger.' And Cato says: 'If a man of higher status or position angers or does grievous things to you, be patient with him, for he who has hurt you may, at some other time, help and relieve you.' Still, assuming you have both the strength and the license to take revenge, I say that there are many things which ought to restrain you and make you inclined to be patient. First and foremost, you consider your own defects, because of which, as I have said, God has permitted you to bear these sorrows. For the poet says that 'we should patiently accept the tribulations which come to us, if we think and consider that we have deserved them.' And Saint George says that 'when a man thinks soberly and well how many defects he has, and how many sins he has committed, the pains and tribulations he suffers will not seem as hard to bear, and the more he reflects on his own heavy and grievous sins, the lighter and easier to bear will his pain seem.' And you also ought to bend your heart, in order to receive the patience of our Lord Jesus Christ, as Saint Peter says in his epistles: 'Jesus Christ,' he says, 'has suffered for us and shown every man a model he ought to follow and imitate, for he never sinned, nor did a wicked word ever come from his mouth. When men cursed him, he did not curse them back, and when they beat him, he did not threaten them.' There is also the great patience shown by the saints, now in Paradise, throughout the tribulations which they suffered, though neither deserving them nor being guilty of anything, and that ought to seriously influence you toward patience. Furthermore, you ought to require patience of yourself, viewing the tribulations of this world as insignificant, so long as they endure, and they pass quickly and are gone, while the joy that a man seeks in patience is eternal, as the Apostle Paul says in his epistle: 'The joy of God is eternal,' meaning that it does not wear away. Also trust and believe steadfastly that a man who does not have and will not receive patience has not been properly brought up or taught. For Solomon says that 'the beliefs and intelligence of a man are known by his patience.' In another place, he says that 'a man who governs himself by patience is a very prudent man.' And this same Solomon also says, 'An angry, wrathful man makes a great deal of noise, and the patient man calms himself and is silent.' And again he says: 'It is more valuable to be patient than to be very strong, and he who controls his own heart is more praiseworthy than he who, by great strength or force, takes great cities.' Accordingly, Saint James in his epistle says that 'patience is one of the great qualities of perfection.'"

"Yes," said Melibee, 'Lady Prudence, I grant you that patience is one of the great qualities of perfection. But not every man can possess the perfection you are seeking, nor am I one among the number of truly perfect men, for my heart can never be at peace until it has been avenged. Even though it was highly dangerous for my enemies, taking their vengeance on me and doing me a great wrong, they took due note of the danger and accomplished their evil intent and did what they longed to do. With that in mind, I do not think I ought to be censured, even though

I incur some degree of danger in avenging myself, nor ought I to be considered highly excessive, insofar as I revenge one outrage by another."

"You're always talking about your will and your desire," said Lady Prudence, "but for no reason in this world should a man be intemperately violent, or go to any extremes, in order to revenge himself. For Cassiodorus says that 'a man who avenges himself by intemperate violence is as evil as the man who commits intemperate violence.' Accordingly, you ought to revenge yourself by doing right, which means following the law, and not by doing wrong. Further, if you long to take revenge for an outrage, and intend *not* to follow the right way, you are a sinner. Which is why Seneca says that 'a man must never revenge wickedness by being wicked.' And if you say that right and justice require a man to defend against violence by being violent, and to defend against fighting by fighting, of course you speak the truth, but when a man defends himself with no interval between the attack and the defense—that is, it is a defense and not an act of vengeance. And a man must still so temper his defense that no one can accuse him of being excessive or outrageous, which would be against reason. Excuse me, but you are well aware that you are not now engaged in self-defense, but thinking strictly in terms of revenge, and that is why you have no interest in moderation. I believe that patience is a good thing, for Solomon says that 'he that is not patient shall endure great injury.' "

"Yes," said Melibee, "I grant you that when a man is impatient and angry about things that don't directly involve him, it is no wonder that it harms him. For the law says that 'he is guilty who involves himself or meddles with things as are none of his business.' And Solomon says that 'he who involves himself with the cries or the fighting of another man is much like the man who tries to lift a hound by the ears.' For just as a man who grabs by the ears a hound who does not know him is often bitten by that hound, so too it is reasonable that he who meddles in the loud affairs of another man is likely to be injured. But you know perfectly well that my grief is a matter that touches me closely. And therefore, though I am indeed angry and impatient, that should not be surprising. Please forgive me, but I cannot see how vengeance will greatly harm me. For I am richer and stronger than my enemies, and you are well aware that money and possessions govern all worldly affairs. And Solomon says that 'everything is obedient to money.' "

Hearing her husband boast of his wealth, and deprecate his adversaries' power, Prudence spoke as follows: "Certainly, my dear sir, you are indeed rich and strong, and that wealth is useful to those who have rightly acquired and properly use it. Just as a man's body cannot live without his soul, neither may it live without worldly goods. And great riches can lead to great friends. And therefore Pamphilius says: 'If a cowherd's daughter,' says he, 'is rich, she may choose which of a thousand men she will take for her husband, for not one in a thousand will refuse or abandon her.' And this Pamphilius also says: 'If you are justly happy— that is, if you are justly rich—you will have a large number of friends and companions. And if your fortune changes, and you become poor, then farewell to friends and companions, because you will be alone and without any company but other poor people.' And still he also says: 'Those whose lineage is composed of servants and bondsmen are suddenly made dignified and noble because of their riches.' And it is true that many good things come of being rich, just as being poor brings many bad things. For intense poverty can oblige a man to do many bad things. And therefore Cassiodorus calls poverty the mother of ruin—that is, the mother of being cast or falling down. And thus Petrus Alphonsus says: 'One of this world's greatest hardships occurs when a man, fully at liberty either by birth or heritage, is obliged by poverty to eat his enemy's alms.' So too says Innocent in one of his books, observing that 'sorrowful and unhappy is the state of a poor beggar, for if he does not ask for food he will die of starvation, and if he asks he dies of shame, and necessity always forces him to ask.' And Solomon says that 'it is better to be dead than to be beggarly poor.' As Solomon also says, 'It is better to die than to live in such poverty.' Because of all these reasons, and many more that I could cite, I concede that riches are a good thing for the man who rightly has and uses them. And now I will show you how you ought to behave, as you gather in your riches, and how you should use them.

"First, you must acquire riches without excessive desire, and leisurely, gradually and not too hastily. For a man who is too anxious to gain riches gives himself over to theft, and to all other evils, and therefore Solomon says: 'He who works too rapidly at acquiring riches cannot be an innocent man.' He also says that 'the wealth that comes quickly to a man, soon and easily leaves a man, but wealth acquired bit by bit always grows and multiplies.' And, sir, riches should be gained by your intelligence, and your profitable labor, and without doing harm, or committing any improper deeds, to anyone else. For the law says that 'no man shall make himself rich by harming anyone else.' This means that nature forbids a man from making himself rich at another man's expense. And Cicero says that 'no sorrow, no fear of death, nor of anything else that can fall to a man, is so much against nature as a man increasing his own profits by causing harm to others. And if the great and the powerful become wealthy easier than you, you ought not to be lazy or slow at making money, for you must under any and all circumstances flee from idleness.' For Solomon says that 'idleness teaches a man many evils,' and he also says that 'he who works, and keeps himself busy, at tilling his land, will eat bread, but he who is idle, and throws himself into no business or occupation, shall fall into poverty and die of starvation.' And he who is lazy and slow can never find the time to make money. There is a versifier who says that 'the lazy man excuses himself in winter, because of the great cold, and in summer by reason of the great heat.' For these reasons, says Cato, 'Wake up and stay awake, don't indulge yourself with too much sleep, for too much is the cause and inciter of vices.' And so Saint Jerome says: 'Do good deeds, in order that the devil, who is our enemy, may not find you unoccupied.' For the devil is not disposed toward trying to tempt those he finds occupied in good works.

"So there, in getting rich, you need to flee idleness. And then, afterward, you must use the wealth which you have gotten, by intelligence and hard work, in such a way that men do not think you too stingy or sparing, nor too foolishly generous, which means not too free and loose with the spending of your money. For just as men criticize an avaricious man because of his stinginess, so too he is to blame who spends more than he should. So Cato says: 'Use your riches so that no one is likely to call you either a wretch or a miser, for it is dishonorable for a man to have a poor heart and a fat purse.' He also says: 'Your possessions should be used temperately,' for those who foolishly waste and throw away what they have, when they have no more of their own, are likely to try taking things that belong to some other man. So I say that avarice, too, should be shunned, using what you possess in such a fashion that men will not say that your wealth has been buried, but see that you both own and control your riches. For a wise man reproves men who are avaricious, criticizing them in two verses: 'Why does a man bury his wealth, out of sheer avarice, when he knows perfectly well that he too will have to die? For in this present life of ours, death is the end of every man.' For what reason can he so knot and tie himself to his possessions that his mind is unable to separate him from what he owns, knowing well—or at least ought to be knowing—that when he is dead he will take nothing worldly out of this world with him? And therefore Saint Augustine says that 'the avaricious man can be compared to hell: the more bloated it becomes, the greater its desire to swell larger and devour more.'

"And just as you should keep yourself from being termed stingy or a miser, you ought equally well to act so that no one calls you a spending fool. Cicero says, accordingly: 'What you possess, and keep in your house, should never be hidden away, nor guarded so closely that pity and generosity cannot make them available,' which is to say, giving them to those in great need. In both the getting and the using of your wealth, you need to keep three things in your heart: our Lord God, your conscience, and your good name. God must be first, and to attain riches you must do nothing which may in any fashion displease God, for he is your creator. And according to Solomon, 'It is better to own less, and have the love of God, than to own many things and lose the love of the Lord our God.' And the prophet says that 'it is better to be a good man, and have few possessions and treasure, than to be considered wicked and have great wealth.' And yet I say more than this, for you should always work toward wealth, but only with a good conscience. And the Apostle says that 'there is nothing in this world which should bring us such great joy as when our conscience testifies in our favor.' And the wise man says, 'A man is as well as he can be when there is no sin on his conscience.' As you go about acquiring wealth, and using it, you must take great care that your good name is properly maintained. For Solomon says that 'it is better for a man, and helps him more, if he has a good name, as opposed to having great riches,' and thus he also says: 'Be careful about keeping your friend and your good name, for it will last longer than any treasure, no matter how precious it may be.' And surely a man should not be called a gentleman if, aside from God, he does not do his very best to preserve his good name. And Cassiodorus says that 'it is the sign of a noble heart when a man loves and wants to have a good reputation.' And so Saint Augustine says, 'There are two required and necessary things, namely a good conscience and a good reputation.' And a man who trusts too much in his good conscience will become unpleasant and turn his good reputation to nothing, and a man who does not care whether he keeps his good name is nothing but a savage rascal.

"Sir, now I have shown you how you ought to acquire riches, and how you ought to use them, and I can see quite well that because you trust in your riches you are disposed to war and battle. I advise you not to begin a war because you so trust in your wealth, for it is not enough to sustain a war. And so a philosopher says: 'A man who always longs for and enters into war will never have riches enough, for the richer he is, the more he will need to spend, if he desires victory and honor.' And, dear sir, despite the fact that, because of your riches, you have many servants and retainers, it is neither good nor is it necessary for there to be war, when you can by acting differently have both honor and profit. For victory in this world's battles does not stem from a great number of soldiers, nor in any man's qualities, but stems from the will, and lies in the hand of our Lord God Almighty. And so Judas Maccabeus, who was God's knight, when he had to fight against an adversary with much greater strength and a greater number of soldiers, still offered words of comfort to his little band, saying, 'Just as easily,' said he, 'might our Lord God Almighty grant victory to a small army rather than to a large one, for victory in a battle comes not from mere numbers but from our Lord God in heaven.' And, dear sir, since no man can be certain that God thinks him worthy to be granted victory in battle, just as no one can be certain that he deserves God's love, or that God neither loves him nor will grant him victory, as Solomon says, it is necessary that a man should greatly fear to begin a war. And because there are many dangers in warfare, and it sometimes happens that a great man is slain, just as little men are slain, so it is written in the second book of Kings, 'battle is risky and dangerous, and never certain, for one man can be hurt by a spear as easily as another.' And since there is such risk and danger in battle, a man should flee from and avoid war, to the extent he possibly can. For as Solomon says: 'He that loves danger will die of danger.'"

Having heard Lady Prudence's words, Melibee answered: "I can see perfectly, Lady Prudence, by the fine words and well-chosen reasons you have shown me, that you have no fondness for war, but I still have not heard your advice as to how I shall act in this urgent emergency."

"Surely," she said, "I advise you to come to some agreement with your adversaries, and that you come to a peace with them. For Saint James says in his Epistles that 'by agreement and peace, small riches grow into wealth, and by argument and disagreement great riches fall to the ground.' And you are well aware that one of the greatest and most sovereign things in this world is unity and peace. And therefore our Lord Jesus Christ said to his apostles: 'Those who arrange for peace are extremely happy and blessed, for they are called the children of God.'"

"Ah," said Melibee, "now I can see perfectly that you do not love my honor or my reputation. You are certainly aware that my adversaries have, by their outrageous attack, begun this argument and fighting, and surely you see that they have neither asked nor inquired about peace, and further that they do not seek reconciliation. Do you want me to humble myself and subject myself to their will, crying to them for mercy? Truly, that is not my reputation. For just as men say that 'too much familiarity is offensive,' so too they speak of excessive humility or gentleness of spirit."

Then Lady Prudence showed signs of anger, and said: "Certainly, sir, with your permission, I love both your honor and your gain and benefit as I do my own, and always have. Neither you nor any other man has ever spoken to the contrary. Yet still, if I had said you ought to have arranged for peace and reconciliation, I would have spoken accurately, on the whole. For the wise man says: 'Let the argument be begun by another man, and the reconciliation begin by you.' And the prophet says, 'Flee from wickedness, and do that which is good; seek peace and follow it, as much as you possibly can.' I am quite sure that, stubborn as you are, you will do nothing simply because I tell you to do it. And Solomon says, 'A man who is too stubborn will, in the end, plan wrongly and do wrongly.'"

Hearing how angry Lady Prudence was, he said, "Lady, please don't be annoyed by the things I say, for you know very well that I am angry and out of sorts, and that should not be surprising, and people who are angry do not fully understand what they are doing or saying. Therefore the prophet says that 'troubled eyes cannot see clearly.' But speak and advise me as you think best, for I am ready to do whatever you want. And if you scold me for my foolishness, I am the better disposed to love and praise you. For Solomon says that 'whoever scolds a fool for his folly will find more grace than someone who deceives the fool with sweet words.'"

Then Lady Prudence said: "I am only angry because what I seek is your benefit. For Solomon says: 'A man is worthier for scolding or criticizing a fool for his foolish deeds, and displaying anger, than he would be if he supported the fool, praising him for his misdeeds, and laughing at his folly.' And this same Solomon also said that 'by the sorrowful face of a man, the fool corrects and reforms himself.'"

Then Melibee said, "I will not have answers to many of the fine reasons you have set out for me. Tell me in a very few words what you wish and what you advise, and I am entirely prepared to accept and perform it."

Then Lady Prudence was entirely open with him, and explained exactly what she had in mind, saying, "I counsel you, above all other things, to make peace between God and you, and that you be reconciled to him and to his grace. For, as I have said before, God has permitted this tribulation and discomfort to come to you because of your sins. And if you do as I tell you to, God will send your adversaries to you, and make them fall on their knees in front of you, ready to do what you want and command. For Solomon says, 'When the state of a man's heart is pleasant and pleasing to God, he changes the hearts of the man's adversaries, obliging them to seek peace and God's grace.' And so I ask you to let me speak with your adversaries in some private place, for they should not know that this is what you wanted and what you have agreed to. And then, when I know what they wish, and what they intend, I will be able to advise you with more certainty."

"Lady," said Melibee, "do as you wish and like, for I put myself completely under your control and command."

Then Lady Prudence, seeing her husband's goodwill, began to consider most deeply, weighing all the circumstances, and wondering how she might best deal with this pressing emergency, bringing it to some good conclusion. And when she had decided what needed to be done, she sent for these adversaries, asking them to meet her at a private place, and there she showed them the great advantages that could follow on peace, and the great damages and dangers that could follow from war, and said to them, in a very gracious way, that they needed to be profoundly repentant for the injuries and damages they had done to Melibee, her lord, as well as to her and to her daughter.

And hearing the gracious words of Lady Prudence, they were so startled and entranced, and felt so joyful, that it was remarkable. "Ah, lady," they said, "you have shown us the blessing of sweetness, according to the sayings of David the prophet. We have been totally unworthy to have a reconciliation with your husband, but we should now seek it with great contrition and humility, as you in your great goodness have presented it to us. Now we understand that Solomon's knowledge and cleverness is validated. For he says that "sweet words cause friendships to multiply and increase, and make vexatious, wicked men turn kindly and meek.

"Yes," they said, "we put this entire affair under the charge of your goodwill, and we are ready to do as my lord Melibee asks and commands. And therefore, dear and kind lady, we request of you, beseeching you as meekly as we know how, that you turn your words of great goodness into deeds. For we believe, and acknowledge, that we have beyond measure offended and grieved my lord Melibee—and so outrageously that it is not in our power to make the amends he deserves. Accordingly, we hereby commit and oblige ourselves and our friends to do whatever he likes and asks us to do. But perhaps he feels such sorrow and such wrath toward us, that he might lay upon us such pain that we could not bear to perform it. Consequently, noble lady, we appeal to your womanly compassion to consider, for this difficult situation, proposing such counsel that neither we nor our friends will be disinherited or destroyed by our folly."

"Certainly," said Prudence, "it is extremely difficult, as well as decidedly dangerous, for a man to put himself completely under the decisions and judgments, as well as in the power, of his enemies. For Solomon says: 'Trust me, and believe what I will say to you. I say,' he said, 'that you people, all of you, and the governors of the church, and your sons, and wives, and friends, none of you must ever give anyone power and control of your body, for as long as you live.' Now since he forbids giving power over his body either to his brother or to his friend, for still stronger reasons he forbids a man to yield himself to his enemy. Nevertheless, I advise you not to mistrust my lord, for know very well that he is gracious and merciful, generous, courteous, and neither interested in or anxious to possess other people's property or their wealth. For there is nothing in the world he wants, except respect and honor. Furthermore, I know perfectly well, and am totally convinced, that he will not act in this matter without my advice, and I will see to it that, by the grace of our Lord God, you must and shall be reconciled with us."

Then they said, speaking with one voice, "Honorable lady, we put ourselves and our property completely in your hands, and we are ready to appear, on whatever day it pleases your graciousness to fix and assign to us, to formalize our obligations, under however strong a bond of security as your goodness is pleased to set, in order that we can fulfill your desires and those of my lord Melibee."

Having heard these men's answers, Lady Prudence told them to leave, as they had come, privately, and then she returned to her lord Melibee and told him that she had found his adversaries fully repentant, acknowledging most humbly their sins and their transgressions, and that they were ready to endure any suffering required of them, asking only for his pity and mercy.

Then Melibee said: "The man who admits but does not excuse his sin is deserving of pardon and forgiveness, since he regrets it and asks our indulgence. For Seneca says: 'When there is confession, it is accompanied by remission and forgiveness,' for confession is a neighbor of innocence.

And Seneca says, in another place, that 'he who is ashamed of his sin, and acknowledges it, is worthy of forgiveness.' And I therefore agree and consent to there being peace, but it is important that we do not do so without the agreement of our friends."

Then Prudence was very glad, and joyful, and said: "Certainly, sire, you have answered well and decently, for just as by the counsel, assent and help of your friends you have been brought to take your revenge and make war, so too without their counsel you must not agree nor should you formally make peace with your adversaries. For the law declares: 'There is nothing so intrinsically good as to have something unbound by him who bound it.'"

And then Lady Prudence, without hesitation or delay, swiftly sent messages to her relatives, and to those of her old friends who were both faithful and wise, and explained to them, in Melibee's presence, and at his command, everything that has been just set out and declared, asking them for their advice and counsel as to what it was best to do next. And when Melibee's friends read the advice she had given, and the deliberations which had occurred, and considered the entire matter with great care and diligence, they gave their full consent to instituting peace and calm. Melibee, they said, ought with a good heart to admit his adversaries into forgiveness and mercy.

And when Lady Prudence had heard her lord Melibee's assent, and also that his friends' advice was in accord with her desires, and her intentions, her heart was wonderfully glad, and she said, "There is an old proverb," said she, "which declares that 'whatever goodness you are able to do today, do it, and do not delay until tomorrow.' And so I counsel you to send your messages to your adversaries, in judicious and wise terms, and letting them know that, as far as you are concerned, if they want to negotiate peace and conciliation they should, without delay, come to us for that purpose."

And that was what was done. And when these adversaries of Melibee heard the messages sent to them, they were very pleased and happy, and answered with great courtesy and graciousness, sending blessings and thanks to their lord Melibee and to all his people, and preparing themselves to go back with the message-bearers, following the command of their lord Melibee.

Which they did immediately, bringing with them some of their friends, to support and testify to their good faith, and to provide guarantees. And when they came into Melibee's presence, he spoke as follows:

"Here is how things stand," said Melibee. "Truly, without cause or reason you have done great wrongs, and done great injuries, to me and to my wife, Prudence, and also to my daughter. You broke into my house, and you have committed such outrageous deeds that all men know you deserve to be put to death. And so I would like to inquire, and learn from you, whether you will allow your punishment to be decided by me and my wife, Prudence, or if you will not?"

Then the wisest of the three adversaries answered for them all, saying, on bended knees, "Sir," he said, "we know that we are not worthy of making an appearance in the court of a lord so great as yourself. For we have so greatly erred, and we have been offensive and done wrong against your high lordship, so much so that indeed we have deserved to be put to death. But, because of the great goodness and graciousness that all the world knows you possess, we hereby submit ourselves to the dignity, wisdom, and kindness of your gracious lordship, and are prepared to obey all your commands, beseeching you that, on account of your merciful compassion, you will take into account our great repentance and humble submission, and grant us forgiveness for our outrageous crimes and offenses. For we are well aware that your generous grace and mercy reach even further into goodness than our outrageous guilt and offensiveness reach into wickedness, even though, damnably and cursedly, we have sinned against your high lordship."

Then, in most kindly fashion, Melibee raised him from the ground, and accepted their oaths and bonds, sworn to by others in support of their pledges and guarantees, and gave them a fixed date upon which to return to his court, to accept and receive the pronouncement and judgment which Melibee would then impose upon them, for the causes aforesaid. When these things had been done, everyone went home.

And when it seemed to her appropriate, Lady Prudence asked her lord Melibee what vengeance he planned to take on his adversaries.

To which Melibee answered, and said: "Surely," he said, "I plan to fully disinherit them, taking away everything they have, and to send them into permanent exile."

"Certainly," said Lady Prudence, "this would be a cruel punishment and very much against sound reason. For you are rich enough, and do not need other men's goods, and you all too easily acquire for yourself a name for greediness, which is a depraved thing that should be avoided by every good man. For as the Apostle declares, according to an old saying, 'Greed is the root of all evils.' And therefore it would be better for you to lose a great deal of your own riches, than to take away theirs, in this fashion, for it is better to suffer an honorable loss of property than it is to acquire property with wickedness and shame. And all men need to work as hard as they can to acquire a good reputation. And still, though he has in fact worked to get such a reputation, he should always be on the lookout for an opportunity to refresh and renew his good name. For it is written that 'a man's former good reputation soon fades into nothing, if it is not renewed.' And as to the matter of exiling your adversaries, that too seems to me against reason and far out of proportion, considering the power over themselves that they have given you. And it is written that 'a man deserves to lose his privileges if he misuses the power he has been given.' And, hypothetically, you might lay that punishment upon them, invoking right and law (and as I hope you will not do), you might perhaps be unable to enforce that sentence, and then we would be right back to where we were before, and fighting. Accordingly, if you want men to obey you, you must exercise your judgment more graciously—that is, you must pass lighter sentences and judgments. For it is written that 'the man who commands most courteously is the man most other men will obey.' And therefore, I urge you, in this urgent time of need, to overpower your heart. As Seneca says: 'He that can overpower his heart, will overpower not once, but twice.' And as Cicero says, 'There is nothing so commendable about a great lord as when he is gracious and gentle, and punishes lightly.' And I urge you to forbear vengeance, now, so you may keep and sustain your good name, and men may have reason, and facts, to praise you for your compassion and mercy, and you yourself will not have any reason to repent what you have done. For Seneca says: 'He who repents his victory is a vicious conqueror.' Accordingly, I urge you once more to allow mercy into your heart, so that God almighty may have good reason to have mercy on you, at the Last Judgment. As Saint James says in his epistle, 'Judgment without mercy shall be passed upon a man who displays no mercy for other men.' "

After hearing Lady Prudence's well-reasoned criticism, and her wise quotations and examples, his heart began to bend toward her desires, and he examined his heart, to learn his true intentions, and changed his proposed punishment accordingly, and agreed to completely follow her advice, and he thanked God, from whom comes all virtue and goodness, for having sent him a wife of such immense wisdom and discretion. And when the day arrived, and his adversaries appeared before him, to learn their punishment, he spoke most courteously to them and said as follows:

"Even though your great presumption and foolishness, and your negligence and ignorance, have misled you into offending against me, because I can see your genuine and deep humility, and that you regret and repent your misdeeds, I am obliged to deal with you easily and mercifully. Accordingly, I accept you into my favor and forgive you entirely for all the offenses, injuries, and wrongs that you have perpetrated against me and mine, and may God out of his boundless mercy forgive us our sins, when we die, and our offenses against him in this wretched world. For without a doubt, if we regret and repent the sins and offenses we have committed, directly in the sight of our Lord God, he is so generous and merciful that he will forgive us for our sins and bring us to the bliss which is eternal and never ends. Amen."

The Prologue of the Monk's Tale

When I had finished this story of Melibee,
And also of Prudence, her wonderful and kindly
Ways, our Host declared: "As I am a man
Of Faith, and by our precious Madrian,
I'd choose, instead of a barrel of first-class ale,   5
That Goodleaf, my wife, be here to hear this tale!
For she is not endowed with the kind of patience
That Prudence, Melibee's wife, has here displayed.
By God's own bones! When I start beating my servants,
She runs and gets me a stick as broad as Mars   10
And cries, 'Now kill the dogs, each one and all,
And break their backs, and every bone they own!'
        "And any neighbor of ours, who will not bow
To my wife, in church, for reasons I neither know
Nor care, or dare to give her any offense,   15
When she comes home she screams straight in my face:
'You traitorous coward, go take revenge for your wife!
By Christ's own bones, I'll live your manly life
And you can have my spinning wheel, and stay home!'
From morning to night she cries and yells and moans.   20
'Alas!' she says, 'that I was ever made
To marry a milksop, a squirming cowardly ape,
Overwhelmed by any mannish shape!
You're far too frightened to stand behind my rights!'
        "And that's my life—except that, if I fight,   25
She'll push me out of the house, by day or night,
And then I'm ruined, unless I make myself

As wild as a lion, and fight at any expense.
Some day, I know, she'll make me kill a neighbor,
And then I'll have to leave and run away—   30
Because I'm dangerous, with a knife in hand,
Despite the fact that she's the one commanding,
For she has muscles all over her arms, like a horse,
As people learn, who ask for a show of force.
     "Enough of that, let's leave such things behind us.   35
My lord, the Monk: I hope I find you smiling,
For here we are, approaching Rochester,
And you must tell us a tale, a proper one!
Ride on, my friend, and keep our stories flowing.
But how can I address you, not knowing your name?   40
Now what should I call you? My lord, the good Don James?
Don Thomas, perhaps? Or maybe good Don John?
What house do you ride from? Where do your people belong?
I swear to God, your skin's as nice as dawn.
A hide that good is fed on handsome fodder: 45
You can't be fasting, you're no spirit father.
You've got some pleasant rank, something fine,
In charge of the garden, or maybe a cellar of wine—
Whatever you are, I swear by my father's soul
It's got to be good, you must be a master, at home,   50
Not shut in a cell, and not a novice, either,
But a man in control, not chained to anyone's tether,
And a strong-looking man, built with blood and bones,
And handsome, too, though a bird that hasn't flown.
May his head go spinning around, who put you in church!   55
I'll bet you could have been sold as a better purchase:
If you were set in a yard with a flock of hens,
You'd turn out lots of brand-new bouncing chickens.
You dress quite well, aside from that flapping cowl,
And were I pope—oh my!—I swear by my soul   60
I'll guarantee that every potent man
—Not only you, but all the monks of your clan—
Would have to have a wife, for the world's deprived!
Religion's taken all the men most lively,
Compared to whom the rest of us are dwarves.   65
The shoots of scrawny trees are pale and awful.

All our heirs and descendants are thin and feeble,
And their descendants are wasting, waning people.
That's why our wives go chasing after religious
Folk: you men are patently prodigious 70
At paying Venus' debts. We cannot match you.
God knows, when you're in bed you're not stone statues!
But don't be angry, my lord: I'm only playing—
Though jesting words are often truthful sayings!"

    This worthy Monk heard everything with patience, 75
Saying, "I'll try to show the diligence
Of a man committed to earthly honesty,
And tell you a tale, or two, or even three.
And if you care to listen as we ride,
I'll tell you the tale of good Saint Edward's life, 80
Or better still, perhaps instead I'll tell you
Tragedies, which line the shelves in my cell.
Tragedies are fixed, historical stories
Which ancient books restore to memory,
Tales of those who lived in prosperity, 85
Then tumbled down to wretched misery,
Fallen from what was once great height. Now these
Are often told to us in rhyming verse
Of six metrical feet, or hexameter.
But some are told in prose, however they happen 90
To be, all in different, varied patterns.
But that's enough of this high scholastic chatter.

    "Now listen, please, if you're interested in hearing.
But let me warn you, first, that this will clearly
Be a disordered sequence, all out of order, 95
Emperors, popes, or kings will all spill forth,
But hardly year by year. They come from my mind
However my memory gropes around and finds them,
Jumping back and forward, out of time.
Excuse me, please, as I walk this crooked line." 100

The Monk's Tale
De Casibus Virorum Illustrium
[the fall of illustrious men]

I will lament what we see in tragedies,
The sorrows of those who stood in high degree
And fell so far there was no remedy
To bring them back from their adversity.
For surely, once wild Fortune turns and flees   5
No living man can hope to block her road.
Let no one trust in blind prosperity:
Be warned by these examples, true and old.

LUCIFER
I start with Lucifer, an angel born
And not a man. Though even Fortune never   10
Attacks God's angels, Lucifer fell because
He sinned, fell all the way to hell, and there
Remains, burning in that fiery darkness.
No angel shone like Lucifer, above,
Who now is Satan, in misery forever,   15
Fallen from heaven's light and God's great love.

ADAM
Lo Adam, shaped by the very fingers of God
From desert earth and gleaming Syrian sand,
Not spawned by sinful sperm of any man,
The Lord of Paradise, except one tree.   20
No man on earth enjoyed such high degree
As Adam, banished from prosperity

For bad behavior and misgovernment,
To labor and sweat, who then to hell was sent.

SAMSON

    Lo Samson, whom an angel loudly proclaimed   25
Long before his birth, as consecrated
To God Almighty, intended and made to be
Of noble state, so long as he could see.
No man would ever exist, as strong as he,
Tireless, powerful, with courage to spare,   30
Until he told his wife his strength was his hair,
And then he killed himself in adversity.

Samson had been a mighty, noble champion:
Fighting without any weapons, only his hands,
He killed and tore apart a savage lion,   35
Spotting the beast while walking toward his wedding.
His wife, a subtle, lying cheat, begged
And begged, until she had his secret, then shed him,
Immediately, and had his secret sent
To his enemies, then married another man.   40

An angry Samson caught three hundred foxes,
Twisted all their tails to one, like a rope,
Woven together with brands and smoldering torches,
Then lit a fire, and let the foxes go.
And they went running into fields and orchards,   45
Burning vines, and olive trees as well,
And all the corn. A thousand men he felled,
His only weapon a bone, an ass's jaw.

And when those men were dead, he was torn with thirst,
And nearly died himself, but prayed to God   50
For pity, for only Almighty God could work
A miracle, on that parched and desert sod.
And from that ass's jaw, a dried-out bone,
A molar-tooth, was suddenly a flood
Of water, a crystal well from which he drank,   55

Then offered God his sated, prayerful thanks.
Fighting in Gaza, one night, a city held
By his Philistine foes, no one dared oppose him.
He pulled the city's gates apart, throwing
Massive heaps of wood on his back and going 60
Up a steep hill that was near the city, and there
He left them. O noble Samson, beloved and dear,
If only you had not betrayed yourself,
In this whole world no one would be your peer!

This Samson never drank fermented cider 65
Or wine; no razor or scissor blade had ever
Come near his head, for the angel had told him never
To trim away his strength, for it lay in his hair.
For two full decades, twenty bountiful years,
He ruled in Israel, a man much feared. 70
But then his strength came pouring out in tears;
He'd put his trust in a woman, and she destroyed him.

Delilah was her name, and to her he told
His hair contained his strength, for there it lay.
And quickly she betrayed him, swiftly sold him. 75
He slept, soft, in her bosom, one fine day,
She took a shears and cut his hair away,
And carried his secret into his enemies' lair.
They came and saw him helpless, there where he lay,
And so they tied and chained him, and put out his eyes. 80

Before those shears had cut away his hair,
No ropes or chains could ever have bound him fast.
But now he lay in a cave, their prisoner,
Reduced to turning a grind-stone, a donkey at last.
O noble Samson, the strongest man in the world, 85
O once a judge, living in glory eternal!
Now weep, weep, with those eyes that cannot see,
Fallen as low as a living man can be.

The end of this wretch will now complete this tale.
His enemies had made a feast, one day, 90

And forced blind Samson to juggle, and fetch, and play
Their fool, all of this on a temple stage.
But he finished foolishness in a burst of rage,
Shaking two pillars till their stones went sprawling,
And down came the roof, the temple, the people and all,   95
And dead lay Samson, with every enemy fallen,

Princes and priests and kings: his foes lay dead,
Three thousand enemies destroyed at a stroke,
Buried under the temple's broken stones.
Nothing more of Samson needs to be said.   100
Profit from this example, old and plain:
No matter how your wives may weep and complain,
Tell them nothing of what they wish had been said,
Except for trifles, that will not cause you pain.

HERCULES
Hercules was the greatest of conquerors,   105
Celebrated, covered with ancient honor,
For in his time he was the brightest flower.
He slew a lion, and skinned him bald as a baby.
He killed two centaurs, who'd offered to treat him badly.
He slew the fearful harpies, birds of hell.   110
A dragon's golden apples he snatched as they fell.
Three-headed Cérberús he dragged to sunlight.

He killed the savage tyrant, Búsirús,
And forced his horse to eat him, flesh and bones.
He slew a flaming dragon, full of poison.   115
Áchelós, a river god, had fought him
In the shape of a bull, but lost one of his horns.
He killed Cácus, Vulcan's son, for stealing
His oxen, and giant Ántheús, and held
The world on his shoulders, while Atlas went apple-peeling.   120

No one ever since this world began
Killed so many monsters as did he.
Across the length and breadth of this earth ran
His name, famous for strength and generosity,

And he too roamed the world, anxious to see it: 125
No man existed strong enough to stop him.
At either end of the earth, reports Trophee,
He set a pillar, instead of a boundary.

This champion fighter had a wife, and loved her,
Díaníra was her name, as fresh 130
As May. Ancient writers always mention
How she sent him a shirt that fit like a glove
But, alas! A dying centaur had his revenge:
He'd given Díaníra some of his blood,
And said it was healing. Hercules put the shirt on, 135
That blood began to peel away his flesh.

The ancient clerics say she had not known;
Hercules had killed that centaur, Nessus
By name, and he had known quite well. I guess
That might be true, I cannot lay the blame. 140
But certainly this hero writhed in pain,
His skin turned black, his flesh fell off, and sensing
Nothing could stop this poison, he rolled in the flame
Of burning coals, refusing to let himself die
In the grip of witchery and a poisoner. 145

And that was this worthy, mighty champion's death.
O who can turn his back on Fortune, forever
Shifting? Moving through this bustling earth
Of push and pull, no man can expect—ever!—
To know when the blow will fall. Knowing himself 150
Is more than enough! When Fortune intervenes
No one can see her coming, or what is held
In her hands. Death can never be foretold.

NÉBUCHADNÉZZAR
How mighty his throne, what rare and precious treasures,
His glorious scepter, and the royal majesty 155
Of the king named Nébuchadnézzar can't be measured
In words, nor ever pictured entirely.
Twice he captured Jerusalem, the city

Of cities, and took away the Ark of the temple.
Babylon was where his capitol sat,   160
And where his glory and his pleasures were at.

The handsomest children of Israel's royal blood
He quickly emasculated, and every one
Of them became his slaves. And one of these
Was Daniel, by far the wisest child of these people,   165
Or any other. The king had elaborate dreams
Which only Daniel could understand. Chaldéan
Priests could never explain their hidden meanings.
But Daniel could, and did, and won the king's favor.

This haughty king had ordered a statue of gold   170
To be built, sixty cubits long and seven
In width, and then commanded that young and old
Must bow to this golden image as God in heaven,
And he who refused this order would die in a furnace
Burned by a roaring fire: "Obey me, or perish!"   175
But Daniel, and two of his friends, would never comply,
Sure that God would never let them die.

This king of kings was proud and arrogant,
Convinced that even God, who sits in heaven,
Could never force him from his royal throne.   180
Then, suddenly, completely gone was his rank
And even his human dignity. He chewed
On hay like an ox, and lay on the ground when it rained;
He walked with the other beasts, both wild and tame,
And this endured for a certain but endless time.   185

His hair had come to growing like eagle feathers,
His nails had turned to arching vulture claws,
Until he was released by God in heaven,
Who gave him back his mind. The king shed tears
As he thanked our God, then lived his life in fear   190
Of angering God again, or doing wrong,
And so he stayed until he lay on his bier,
Knowing the might of God, and also his grace.

BALTHASAR
Nébuchadnézzar's son, named Belshazzar,
Ascended to his father's throne when the old   195
King died. But nothing his father knew, or told him,
Mattered, now that he was king, too proud,
And from the beginning he always worshipped idols.
Holding the throne, he reveled in his pride.
But Fortune threw him down. He could not rise,   200
And so his kingdom began to split and divide.

He gave a banquet to all his subject lords,
And told them they should rejoice, as so did he,
And then he called his palace servants to the throne:
"Go, and fetch the gold and silver vessels   205
My father took, in his prosperity,
From Jerusalem, the temple in that city,
And may we, then, do honor and give high praise
To everything our elders give to our days."

His wife, his lords, and all his concubines   210
Drank as much as they wanted, using these vessels,
Contaminating these sacred things with wine.
And then the king looked up, and saw, on a wall,
An armless hand that wrote, in a rapid scrawl,
And made this king so fearful he shook inside.   215
The hand had written, making the king afraid,
Mané, tekel, ufársin: "Numbered, weighed, and divided."

No one in that land, magician or scholar,
Could understand and explain these simple words;
Only Daniel saw and understood   220
At once: "King, your father, by the grace of God,
Was given glory and honor, his throne, his wealth.
But he was proud, and unafraid of God,
And therefore wretchedness was what God sent him,
Throwing him to the ground, as the beast he was.   225

"There was no place for him, with other men,
He lived with donkeys, made his home with them,
And fed like a beast, no matter wet or dry,
Until he finally knew, by grace and reason,
That God is supreme in every time and season   230
And over every creature and every kingdom.
And God looked down on him and had compassion,
Making him human again and restoring his throne.

"And you, his son, are a man equally proud,
And surely know these things from your father's mouth,   235
And challenge God, turn him into your foe.
You boldly drank from these sacred vessels, knowing
What you know. So did your wife and wenches. You all
Drank wine after wine from these golden vessels, too holy
For men. You praised false gods, exalted them.   240
And God has now replied with this penalty.

"God sent this hand, and had it write on the wall,
Mané, tekel, ufarsin. Believe what I say:
Your reign is done, you're king over nothing at all.
This kingdom will be divided, and ruled, from this day,   245
By Persians and Medes." And what he had said was the way
It happened. That very same night the king was slain,
And Dáriús, the Persian, took his throne,
Having no rights, but unconcerned with law.

Gentlemen, you learn from this example   250
That lordship never has security,
For Fortune, when she wants to, raises her hand
And takes away a kingdom and all its wealth,
And a lord's friends, of every age and degree.
If friendship comes from Fortune, Fortune can stamp   255
Them down again, or make them enemies.
This is a common saying, and full of truth.

ZENÓBIÁ

According to the Persian histories
Zenóbiá, the queen of Palmaree,
Was such an expert fighter, so daring, so bold   260
That no mere man surpassed her fierceness in war,
Nor in family or matters of courtesy.
Her family began as ancient Persian kings.
I cannot say that she was fairest of all,
But nothing could have made her body more lovely.   265

Old stories tell us that even as a child
She ran away from women's work, fled
To the forests, killing even the largest, wildest
Stags, pierced by arrows her strong arms sped
To their hearts. No deer could escape her, for all their quick legs.   270
And when she was older she cut lions to pieces,
As well as leopards and bears, and also succeeded
At wrestling bears to the ground, using no weapons.

She had the courage to enter the dens of these beasts,
And often lingered in mountains the whole dark night,   275
Sleeping under a bush. She wrestled young knights
And beat them, no matter how strong. So great was her might
That nothing she was able to grasp in her arms
Was able to escape, unless and until she released it.
No man could ever take her maidenhead;   280
She had no interest in being ruled by men.

But in the end her friends did marry her off
To Ódenák, a prince of that country's royal
Lineage, although his wait was long.
But you must clearly understand that he   285
Was gripped by much the same desires as she,
And once they joined in tight-knit marriage bonds
They lived in joy and great felicity,
Each one loving the other, in firm affection,

Except for a thing that she would never agree to,   290
For she was absolute: she said he could lie
With her just once, and then they had to wait.
She truly wished to live and multiply,
And if she saw that she was not with child,
She lay with him once more, but only one time.   295
This was a process based on firm belief.
She slowly had her children; he had no relief,

For while she carried a child, for forty weeks
He had to wait again. Argument
Was completely in vain: each time that she was pregnant   300
He went to purgatory, however he pleaded.
Her rules, as she explained them, were based on sense
And efficiency, for if a wife went wild
And let her husband have his way, shame
And lechery would prevail, and the wife would be blamed.   305

She had two sons by her husband, Ódenák,
And kept them virtuous and busily learning.
But now the wheel revolves, our story's turning.
She was, remember, a deeply honorable creature,
And sensible, believing in moderation,   310
Fierce when she fought in war, but courteous too—
She never wearied of fighting, but stayed at her station
As calmly ferocious as if she were only playing.

So rich was her household, words could never tell you;
Her clothing and her tableware were equally   315
Fine, and over her dress she wore bright gems
And precious jewels. She never gave up hunting,
But learning languages was hardly neglected,
Whenever she had time; she went on reading
All the many books she kept collecting,   320
Above all wanting to live her life in virtue.

To trim this story down to proper size,
I'll simply say that she and her husband fought

So bravely and well that they were conquerors
Of many famous oriental cities 325
And kingdoms, often linked to the power of Rome,
And once they had them, were not overthrown.
No armies were strong enough to make them run,
As long as Ódenák was there at her side.

Their splendid battles, for those who might inquire, 330
Against the like of Shapur, the Persian king,
And all the details, why they fought each fight,
And who she conquered, whether wrong or right,
And what resulted, what her worries were
And sorrows, too, how she was besieged and taken— 335
Go read my master Petrarch, whose many words
On these great themes await you (if I'm not mistaken).

After Ódenak's death, she carried on herself,
Holding on to their conquests with powerful hands
And fighting each of her foes so savagely 340
That none of the princes and kings in other lands
Regretted her choice, if she chose to leave them alone,
Making alliances to keep her in peace,
Binding her to her hunting and the books she owned,
Rather than leaving her free to destroy their realms. 345

Claudius, the mighty emperor of Rome,
Nor Gálién, who ruled the world before him,
Had never thought of being so courageous;
No more had the Armenians, or Egyptians,
Nor Syrians, or the fierce Arabians— 350
None would come to the field of battle with her,
Afraid her steady hands would surely slay them
Or that their armies would break, and flee from her men.

Both her sons were always royally dressed,
The heirs of many lands, their father's conquests; 355
Their names were Tímaláo, and Hérmanó
(At least, the ancient Persians called them so).

But Fortune's honey always hides its gall:
This mighty queen would soon be ready to fall.
Fortune would topple her jeweled and golden throne,   360
Drop her to wretchedness, diamonds and all.

Roman Aurélián, as soon as he came
To power, began to plan a fierce campaign
Of vengeance, then launched it, hot and hard. His legions
Marched against Zenóbiá, and I'll waste   365
No words, the Romans beat her, and Aurélián
Caught her, as she and all her armies ran.
The queen was put in chains, and also her sons;
Then he went back to Rome, the battle won.

Among the other trophies he took home   370
Was her bejeweled and shining, golden throne,
Which this great Roman, Aurélián, made sure
Was shown for every curious eye to see,
And in the front of his victory march walked she,
Now wearing golden chains around her neck,   375
And a crown on her head, as an empress ought to be,
Diamonds and sparkling jewels all over her dress.

Alas, for her fortune! She before whom kings
And emperors trembled and shook, full of fear,
Was now a victory token, a decorative thing!   380
She who had worn a helmet and fought like a bear,
Defeated armies, and conquered mighty towns
And cities, her crown will be a paper cap;
She who had carried a scepter, bright with flowers,
Would spin coarse cloth, an apron on her lap.   385

   DE PETRO REGE ISPANNIE [*Peter, King of Spain*]
   O noble, worthy Pedro, glory of Spain,
Lifted by Fortune into lofty heights,
How men should mourn your death, and loudly complain
Your pitiful end, driven out of your reign,   390
Fled but followed, stalked and then betrayed,

Led to darkness inside your brother's tent
And there, immediately, stabbed by the knife
In his brother's hand, taking kingdom and life.

He who brewed this wickedness and sin,   395
He whose colors were snow and an eagle in black,
Snared by a lime twig red as burning fire,
He laid this trap for you, O noble king,
Led you where you never expected to be.
This was not Charles Oliver, who heeded   400
Honor and truth, but an Oliver Breton, bribed
To make a corpse of this worthy Spanish king.

    DE PETRO REGE DE CIPRO [*Petro, King of Cyprus*]
    And Petro, King of Cyprus, he also,
Who conquered pagan Alexandria   405
And gave its pagan fighters fields of woe,
Which filled your faithless followers with envy,
And only for your brilliant chivalry
They stabbed you in your bed, at early dawn.
Thus Fortune turns and spins her fatal wheel,   410
Reclaiming joy and bringing men to heel.

    DE BARNABO DE LOMBARDIA [*Barnabo of Lombardy*]
    Great Bárnabó, a Viscount from Milan,
Prince of pleasure and scourge of Lombardy,
Why should I refrain from telling your   415
Misfortune, you who climbed so very high?
Your brother's son, and doubly your ally—
Both your nephew and your son-in-law—
Threw you in his prison, where you died,
But how, or why, I never knew or saw.   420

    DE HUGELINO COMITE DE PIZE [*Count Ugilino of Pisa*]
    The suffering of Ugilino, Count
Of Pisa, is almost too pitiful to recount.
Not far from Pisa, now, there stands a tower
In which he was imprisoned—not only he,   425
But also his little children, of whom there were three,

The oldest barely five. This cruelty
Was immense, O Fortune! Locking tiny birds
In such a gruesome cage, at such young ages!

Roger, then bishop over all of Pisa,   430
Had brought about this grisly sentence of death,
Falsifying horrific accusations
Which caused his people to want their ruler dead,
And Roger devised a wicked situation
In which the Count, imprisoned, was only fed   435
Enough to ensure a slow and painful death—
Too little food, and hard to swallow, at best.

And then there came a day, and a ghastly hour,
When food had regularly been brought to the tower,
And Ugilino heard the jailer loudly   440
Slamming closed the doors; he locked them from outside.
He heard but did not speak, for in his heart
He knew that they would die, that they would starve.
"Alas!" he finally said, "that I was ever
Born!" His eyes filled up and tears fell over.   445

His middle son, whose age was all of three,
Said, "Father, why do I see you weep so freely?
When will the jailer come and bring us food?
Don't you have a bite of bread hidden
Somewhere? I'm very tired, and if I could   450
I would sleep, but hunger bites me too hard. I would
That I were dead, rather than be so hungry!
All I really want is bread for my belly."

Day by day this tiny child lay still
And cried, lying against his father's heart,   455
And saying, "Father, father, I'm ready to die!"
And kissed his father, then died, both slow and hard.
And seeing his son was dead was such a blow
That he started biting his arms, for sorrow and woe.
"Fortune," he said, "your wheel is grinding me now."   460

It ground away till, desperate, he died.
And that was the end of the mighty Count of Pisa,
For Fortune carved him out of his life of ease
But that is enough of this grisly tragedy:
Whoever wants any more can read it in Dante,   465
Italy's great poet, who writes of evil
And good as no man then or since, writes
Exactly so, word by word, and right.

  NERO
  Although this Nero surely was as vicious   470
As any fiend who's lurking under ground,
He still, we're told by good Suetonius,
Was ruler of this world, both wide and round:
East and west, south and north, were his subjects.
Rubies, sapphires, pearls of peerless white   475
Decorated his garments, up and down,
For jewels gave him infinite delight.

He wore much lusher, brighter, pretentious clothes,
More arrogant than any emperor of Rome:
He wore a garment one day and no one saw it   480
Ever again. For fishing in the Tiber
His nets were golden thread, of every size
And in plenty, so he could fish all day, if he liked.
His pleasures became enforced by Roman law,
For Fortune, his friend, then did as she was told.   485

He burned down Rome, for the beautiful fire it made.
One day he slaughtered Roman senators
To see how men would scream and weep and cry.
He killed his brother, and with his sister lay.
He murdered his mother in a frightful way,   490
Slicing open her womb so he could see
Where he was conceived, one great, stupendous day.
He valued his mother just that much, no more.

Watching her die he never shed a tear,
Remarking only "How fine a woman she was!"   495

How strange a comment, how strange a man who does
Such things, and then discusses a corpse as "fine."
He ordered his servants to bring him a cup of wine,
Which he drank—in woe or celebration, who knows?
When power is linked to savage cruelty,   500
Alas! how deeply the venom invades, and stays.

The youngster Nero had been taught by Seneca,
Brought to knowledge of books and courtesy,
Until for words of formal morality
He outshone his time (unless our sources lie).   505
And following his teacher's subtle mind,
Nero became a master so supple, so fine,
That setting the dogs upon him took a long time,
And visible vices only slowly entwined him.

Seneca, indeed, kept the youthful emperor   510
So closely in hand that Nero truly feared him,
And the scoldings he gave, so vices couldn't go near him—
So softly, discreetly, Seneca gave him his laws:
"Sir," he would say, "an emperor should always be
A man of virtue, scornful of tyranny"—   515
So Nero laid him in a tub, to bleed
From both his arms, until at last he died.

Even when younger, Nero had a habit
Of fiercely throwing off his teacher's reins,
Believing reins had nothing to do with him.   520
And so his teacher was killed, as I've described.
Seneca was truly wise; he climbed
Down in that tub, choosing the way he died
And not some different, tortured, terrible end.
The choice was a good one, once Nero wanted him dead.   525

But Fortune began to worry about his pride,
And lost her interest in keeping him on high.
Although he was strong, of course her powers were greater.
And she said to herself: "By God! It makes no sense
To set a man with such enormous vices   530

On Rome's great throne, and lend him the title of emperor.
By God! I'll lift him out of that royal chair.
He won't expect it, but down he's got to go."

The Roman people rose against him, one night,
Because of his crimes. And seeing this frightening sight   535
He slipped, alone, out the back of his palace,
And hurried to those he thought were on his side.
He started knocking; the harder he knocked, the faster
They locked their doors. The world had become a disaster,
He stopped his calling. It was done, he realized,   540
He'd gone all wrong, he was no longer master.

People were shouting, rumbling up and down.
He heard quite plainly what they kept on saying:
"Where is this tyrant, this traitor, this lying Nero?"
He was overwhelmed, and terribly afraid,   545
And to his gods most pitifully he prayed
For help, but help, he saw, was not forthcoming.
Fear drove him, running, into a garden he passed,
Hoping, somehow, to keep himself in hiding.

And here in this garden he saw a burning fire,   550
And seated at it, a pair of simple servants.
He begged them, then, to do him a final service:
Kill him, and carefully cut off his head,
To protect his body, after he was dead,
From vile mistreatment (knowing he deserved it?).   555
They stared, unmoving, so Nero killed himself,
And Fortune laughed, pleased by the end of this joke.

    HÓLOFÉRNES
    No general, subjected to a king,
Was ever held so tightly by the reins,   560
Or in his time could work a battlefield
With such success, or gained a greater fame,
Or stood more pompously in high presumption
Than Hóloférnes, who was wantonly

Embraced by Fortune. She led him up and down,   565
Until his head came off, before he knew it.

It wasn't simply fear of the man, who was known
For clutching other men's gold, or taking their freedom,
But also because he made men give up religion.
"Nebuchadnezzar is God," he would intone.   570
"No other god is worshipped, where I'm in charge."
No one dared to openly oppose him,
Except in Bethulia, a strong and Jewish city,
Where Éliáchim was the rabbi in charge.

Now listen to how this Hóloférnes died: 575
In the midst of his army, one night, he lay on his bed,
Dead drunk, inside his huge and sprawling tent,
And yet, for all his pomp, and all his strength,
A woman, Judith, while he lay on his back,
Snoring, picked up his sword and cut off his head,   580
Then quietly, and safely, went out of that tent,
And carried his head to Bethulia, where people rejoiced.

    DE REGE ANTIOCHO ILLUSTRI [*Renowned Ántióchus, King of Syria*]
     Who needs, by now, to speak of Ántióchus
And tell the world how royal a king he was,   585
How arrogant, and also how venomous?
No one else is like him, in history.
Read the apocryphal book of the Maccabees
And hear the arrogant words he dared to say,
And why he fell from high prosperity,   590
And on a hill how wretchedly he died.

Fortune had so puffed up his booming pride
That, truly, he thought he'd leap and touch the stars,
Turning in every direction, on every side,
Weighing each mountain with his balance bars,   595
Pushing the sea away from any shore.
And Jews, the people of God, he hated most,
Longing to hurt and kill them, with passionate lust,
Believing that even God could never stop him.

And when his generals, first Nichanor,   600
Then Tymothee, were badly beaten by Jews,
His hatred for Jews then swelled so gross, so huge,
He ordered his chariot readied for instant use
And swore, declaring most contemptuously,
That he would be in Jerusalem in a moment,   605
And there would avenge his anger most cruelly—
But his plan was foiled, and he was stopped quite soon.

Because of his threats, God struck him down with invisible
Wounds, that nothing could ever possibly cure,
And the pain, as his guts were punctured, cut and bitten,   610
Was overwhelming, unendurable.
This was surely an honest, direct revenge,
For he had twisted and torn many men's guts.
And still, despite the pain, he meant to continue,
Fulfilling his damnable plan to the bitter end.   615

But his army's equipment defected, his chariot faltered,
And suddenly, without a hint or warning,
God smashed his pride and boasts, threw him to the ground,
Tossed from his chariot, landing quick and hard,
Ripping and tearing his arms, his legs, his skin.   620
He could not ride, and surely could not walk,
So they had to make a litter to carry him in,
Bruised and bleeding on every side, and in back.

God's revenge now struck him cruelly,
As vicious worms began to creep all through   625
His body, and made him stink most horribly,
So none of those who served him could stand the stench,
Whether he slept or not, and so they left him,
Completely unable to serve him any longer.
He wailed and wept for these calamities,   630
And learned that God, not him, was ruling the world.

His flesh became so loathsome, putrefying,
That he as well as his men couldn't stand the stench.
No one approached him, now, no one could carry

This living corpse, that stank and rolled in its pain.   635
He starved to death, left to die on the side
Of a mountain. And so this thief, this grossest of killers,
Who'd driven so many men to painful ends,
Received a reward most fitting to such foul pride.

    ALEXANDER THE GREAT   640
   Alexander's story is so familiar
That a man who knows how one thing differs from
Another has heard some part of the glory he won.
To put it all in a word, he conquered the world,
Took it by strength, or because of his great renown,   645
As kings surrendered and gave him whatever he wanted.
The greatest pride and noblest strength, fell down
At his feet wherever he went, until it ended.

No other conqueror in history
Has ever been compared, or ever will be: 650
Fear of him went running around the world.
Knighthood's flower, the peak of nobility,
Fortune made him her heir, lent him her honor.
Only wine and women gave him an hour
Or two away from war, his constant labor,   655
Full of courage like the fiercest lions.

How much would it be worth to him, were I
To tell you of Dáriús and the hundred thousand
Other princes and kings, and dukes, and earls
Whose kingdoms and thrones he threw flat on the ground?   660
If I say: as far as any man can ride
The world was his, what more can I say or describe?
Whoever tries to lengthen out the tale
Of his glory, more than likely is bound to fail.

Ancient books declare he reigned twelve years,   665
Beginning as king of Greece, the entire country.
Philip of Macedonia was his father.
O worthy, noble Alexander, alas!
That such a thing should ever come to pass!

Poisoned by Greeks, some of your very own men,   670
Fortune turned your dicer's *six* to a *one,*
And never shed a tear when you were dead.

JULIUS CAESAR
    Driven by manhood and wisdom, and laboring hard,
Julius Caesar, the greatest Roman conqueror,   675
Rose to the heights, after a humble start,
Winning the west of Europe, by land and sea,
Either by strength of hand or else by treaty,
Subordinating nations to the power of Rome.
And then, it is written, he sat on the Roman throne,   680
Until fair Fortune became his enemy.

O mighty Caesar, who drove through Thessaly
Against Pompey the Elder, your father-in-law,
Whose armies were filled, as day began to dawn,
With all of eastern knighthood and chivalry: 685
You beat them down, killing almost all,
Except a few who fled at Pompey's heels,
And all the eastern kingdoms stared in awe.
You thanked fair Fortune, who lent you strength and speed.

But let me step aside and mourn, a while,   690
For Pompey, Roman governor, and noble,
Forced to flee this battle by Caesar's might.
One of his men, as false as every traitor,
Cut off his head, hoping to win himself favor
From Caesar, to whom he carried the bloody head.   695
Alas, O Pompey—victor, once, of the east—
That Fortune prepared this banquet for your victory feast!

Julius returned to Rome, staged a triumphal
Parade, hero in every Roman's eyes,
Except for Brutus Cassius, who watched for his time,   700
For many long years jealous of Caesar's rise.
Taking great care, in utter secrecy,
Brutus prepared his plot most subtly,

Fixing the spot where Caesar was meant to die
By close-in dagger thrusts, both low and high. 705

And Caesar went to the Capitol, that day,
As he was accustomed to do, and there this traitor
Brutus and all his friends surrounded Julius,
Drew their daggers and stabbed him, again and again,
Then watched him fall to the ground, and die in silence, 710
Having made no sound, the old books say,
At any dagger thrust, perhaps at one,
Or two at most, according to these reports.

So thoroughly was Caesar a man at heart,
So deeply committed to noble modesty, 715
That even in deadly pain from dagger strikes
He pulled his tunic tightly around his hips,
So no man could glimpse him naked, and especially
His manhood. He lay there, still half conscious, dying
And knowing he'd soon be dead, but still aware 720
Of modest, decent respectability.

For the rest of this story, go read Lucan, the poet,
Valerius Maximus, and Suetonius,
All of whom describe how Julius
Lived, and was killed, and by whom. Fortune had once 725
Been his friend, for a time, and then his foe.
No man can ever expect her favor to last:
Watch her closely, let your eyes stay open.
Strength and power are gifts, and at length they go.

CROESUS 730
    This rich man, Croesus, was once the king of Lydia,
Immensely feared by Cyrus, the Persian emperor,
Nevertheless was caught in the flush of pride
And burned in the fire to which he expected to take
Others. And then the skies fell open, and rain 735
Poured down, the fire was quenched, and he escaped.
But yet, this wasn't enough, he did not repent
Till Fortune hung him high on the gallows, and he gaped.

Running from fire, he was barely able to wait,
And started, at once, to prepare a brand new war. 740
He felt himself blessed, because the rain had freed him,
And clearly, he felt, Fortune now was smiling,
And never again could his enemies have him slain.
And also he had a dream, as he slept one night,
Which swelled his pride, and made him terribly happy, 745
That nothing but vengeance filled his busy mind.

For in his dream he was sitting high in a tree,
And Jupiter himself was bathing him, his back
And his sides, and Phoebus, God of the sun, asked
If he'd like a towel, and brought one, and his pride expanded. 750
Knowing his daughter was wise in many ways
The very next day he told her the dream, and inquired
What this strange but wonderful fable might mean.
And without a bit of hesitation, she answered:

"The tree," she said, "must signify the gallows; 755
Jupiter must indicate both snow
And rain; and Phoebus offering you a towel
Must represent bright sunbeams shining down.
Father, your death will be by hanging, no doubt.
Rain will wash you, and then the sun will dry you." 760
His daughter's words were brutally flat and plain.
And what did he do? Nothing, once again.

So Croesus, the proudest of kings, was hanged by the neck.
His royal throne was not the slightest help.
As tragedies are always trying to tell us— 765
Not that crying aloud or the deepest wailing
Will do any good—Fortune always prevails,
Forever unexpected by proudest reigns,
For when men trust her, she may turn her tail,
And run, hiding her face behind a cloud. 770

The Prologue of the Nun's Priest's Tale

"Ha!" said the Knight, "good sir, no more of this!
You've told the truth, for sure, but not much bliss
Stems from your stories. A little heaviness
Is more than enough for the likes of us, I guess.
Speaking for myself, there's little comfort   5
In hearing how men of wealth are spread on the floor,
Or so to speak, quickly, without warning.
But joy, and solace, and much that's nicely warming
Glows when a man can rise, suddenly rich,
And those are the kinds of stories we rejoice in: 10
Such tales are always welcome, and gratefully heard."

    "Yes," said our Host. "By great Saint Paul's long beard!
You're exactly right. His tongue wagged good and hard,
He spoke of Fortune covered up with clouds,
Or something like that, and much about tragedies,   15
But what you heard, by God, had no remedies,
But only people wailing, and others complaining
At what's been done, and frankly it's plain painful,
Just as you said, to hear such heaviness.

    "Sir Monk, no more of this, so God you bless!   20
Your tale afflicted all this company.
Such talking isn't worth a well-squashed flea,
It offers no good cheer, it isn't fun.
I wish, and very earnestly, you'd told us
Something else. Without the clinking bells   25
Hanging down your bridle on either side,
By heaven's king who for us all once died,

I might have fallen off my horse while sleeping,
And I see the ditches here are very deep.
All your tales would then have been in vain, 30
For surely, as these clerics forever say,
A man without a listening audience
Might just as well be silent. It makes no sense.
  "For when I'm listening, I catch the meaning just fine.
Anything worthy that's said, it sticks in my mind. 35
So sir, just talk about hunting instead, I pray you."
  "No," said this Monk, "I have no interest in playing.
Let someone else tell a tale, as I have done."
  Then speaking rugged words, the Host picked on
Our Nun's good Priest, calling, rough and loud: 40
  "Come closer, you Priest, come here now, you, sir John!
Tell us something to lift our hearts so we laugh.
Your horse may be awful, but that doesn't mean a damn.
You can be cheerful, no matter what you're crammed on.
Who cares if a horse is shambling, dirty and lean? 45
If he does your job, wining's not worth a bean.
Take care that your heart is merry for ever more."
  "Yes, sir, yes Host, that's how I have to go.
Unless I'm merry, I'll certainly get blamed."
He started his tale, careful to keep it plain 50
And happy, as he spoke to us all, each one,
This pleasant priest, this worthy man, sir John.

The Nun's Priest's Tale of Cock and Hen, Chauntecleer and Pertelote

A widow, poor and somewhat advanced in age,
Was living, some time ago, in a tiny cottage,
Close to a cluster of trees deep down in a valley.
She is the center of this story I will tell you,
And since the end of the days when she was a wife   5
She'd led, most patiently, a simple life,
Owning little, and earning not much more.
By cultivating whatever God provided
She kept herself, and her two daughters, alive.
Her sty held three large sows, and that was all,   10
And three milk cows, one with the name of Moll.
There being no chimney, her house was sooty inside,
And here she slept, and ate what she could, and thrived.
She used no tangy sauces, her appetite
Was keen, no dainty morsels went down her throat.   15
Her diet was much the same as her scraggly cottage:
Overeating would never make her sick,
A modest diet remained her only physic,
Plus exercise, and an easy, happy heart.
She danced when she could, having no goutish parts,   20
And apoplexy never entered her head.
She drank no wine, neither white nor red.
Mostly, her table was set in white and black:
Milk and dark bread (she did not think it lacking),
Scraps of bacon, sometimes an egg or two,   25
For she was, more or less, a dairy woman.
    She had a yard, with sticks set all around it,

And also a dry-ditch, where her cock could be found,
As fine as his perfect name, which was Chauntecleer.
When it came to crowing, no cock could be his peer. 30
His voice would gurgle more gloriously than an organ,
Happily playing in church, as the mass went on—
Crowing, comfortably erect in his ditch,
Clearer than clocks in a tower, steady in pitch.
His body felt and understood each hour 35
Passing across his ditch; he seemed to count them.
When fifteen degrees of the equinox had risen,
He crowed: that was an absolute decision.
His comb was redder than even the finest coral,
And notched as if it were a castle wall; 40
His bill was black, and just like jet it shone;
His legs were azure blue, as were his toes;
His nails were whiter than any lily flower;
And smoky yellow, like gold, was the rest of his color.
This noble cock was the unmistakable ruler 45
Of seven hens, for whom he regularly tooled
Away; they were his sisters and his lovers,
And looked like him, feathers of similar color.
The fairest of all, with a dazzling, gleaming throat,
Was always called "my Lady, Pértelóte." 50
Discreet she was, and civil, but also gracious,
And friendly; she walked like a queen from outer space,
And always had, since she was seven nights old.
And truly she possessed the heart and soul
Of Chaunticleer, her every movement tolled 55
In his heart and his limbs: he was happy to hold her.
And such a pleasure it was to hear them sing,
As the brightening sight of sunlight began to spring!
They harmonized "My Love Has Gone Away"
(A popular song, for people always say 60
That once both birds and beasts could speak and sing).
      And so one day it happened that, at dawning,
As Chaunticleer and his seven wives were all
In place, he on his perch, which was in the hall,
And next to him his pretty Pértelóte, 65
This Chaunticleer began to groan in his throat,

Like a man who's dreaming, and troubled very sorely.
And Pértelóte, hearing how he was roaring,
Was frightened, and said at once, "My dearest heart,
What's wrong with you, to groan so sad, so hard? 70
You're really quite a sleeper. Fie, for shame!"
  He answered her like this: "My Lady, Dame,
Please do not take a dream as such a grievance.
I dreamed, by God, of sudden circumstances
Perfectly fearful. Indeed, my heart is frightened 75
Still. O God, please let this turn out right,
So I won't really be a prisoner!
I dreamed that I was roaming in our yard,
And saw a beast that could have been a hound,
And he was trying to catch and carry me off, 80
And if he caught me, I knew I'd soon be dead.
His color was something neither yellow nor red,
With a tuft at the end of his tail, and both his ears
Were black, unlike the rest of his body's hair.
His snout was slender, his eyes were glowing bright: 85
I nearly died, I felt so terribly frightened,
Which well accounts for my heavy groaning, I'm sure."
  "Good God!" said she. "Your dream is sorely impure!
Alas!" she said, "for O, by God above,
You've broken my heart and thrown away my love, 90
For I cannot love a coward, by my faith!
For surely, whatever a woman likes to say,
What we all want, if it can be obtained,
Are generous husbands, wise, but also brave,
Discreet, not niggardly, and never a fool, 95
Or ever a male afraid of the deadly tools
Of war, and not a boaster, by God above!
How dare you say—for shame!—to your lady love
That anything on earth could make you afraid?
Is your heart a man's? Why do you have a beard? 100
Alas! But how can you be afraid of a dream?
They're worthless, by God, empty, puffy, streams
Of nothingness, born from stuffing your belly,
And stomach gases, and most especially
From a body too torn by different-crossing humors. 105

It seems to me this dream of yours is surely
Caused—please pardon me for saying—by the excess
Of red on your body: it causes restlessness,
And dreams of arrows, and fires with great red flames,
And reddish beasts, who chase and try to bite them,   110
And fighting, and also puppies, dark and light.
Just as melancholic humor often
Causes deeply sleeping and dreaming men
To shout for fear of great black bears, or blackish
Bulls, and also devils, extremely black,   115
Who try to drag them to hell. And thus it goes
With other humors, which give men sorrow and woes.
I'd say much more, but I'll put the matter aside.
Remember Dionysius Cato, that wise,
Wise man, who said, 'There's nothing real in dreams.'   120
      "Now sir," she said, "when down we come from these beams,
For the love of God, please take some laxatives.
I swear by my soul, and also by my life,
I've given the best advice, and I never lie:
These herbs will purge you clean of melancholy,   125
And more. And so you needn't have to tarry
(There being, in this town, no apothecary),
I'll take upon myself the task of teaching
You what herbs you need, instead of preaching,
And in our yard I'll search out those just right   130
For curing you, avoiding silly fright.
They'll purge you out from behind, and also above,
And don't neglect this, for God's own watchful love!
Indeed, I see you're over-red in complexion:
Beware of the sun, when he makes his high ascension,   135
Or you may have too many humors, hot
And dry, and if you do, I'd bet a bean
You'll then develop a fever tércyéen,
Or even an áygue, which might well cause your death.
For a day or two, I'll give you herbals meant   140
To drive out worms, before your laxatives,
Including cornflower, laurel, fumitory,
Perhaps some hellebore, which grows right here,
Or caper spurge, or even dogwood berries

And ivy leaves, also grown in here. 145
Feel better, husband! Pick them up and eat them!
Be merry, by your father's family's kin!
And no more dreams! I cannot tell you more."
    "My lady," he said, "congratulations on your lore.
But nevertheless, as far as Cato goes 150
(Whose reputation for wisdom everyone knows),
He may have said that bad dreams shouldn't be feared,
But many ancient books assert, most clearly,
Contrary views, from higher authorities,
With very much greater reputations than his— 155
Indeed, taking flatly the opposite stance.
And men have clearly learned from experience
That dreams are indications of joy, often,
As well as pointed predictions of trouble to come,
Disasters we all must endure, living our lives. 160
No argument is needed, my learnèd wife:
Experience is more than proof enough.
    "One of the greatest of authors tells it thus:
Once, two fellows joined in a pilgrimage,
Each of them filled with good intentions and courage, 165
And as it happened, they walked into a town
So crowded with visiting people, and so little room
For more, that lodging anywhere together
Was out of the question, they had to sleep wherever
They could, alone. They had no choice at all, 170
But took their lodging however it happened to fall.
One was able to sleep in a backyard stall,
Along with the oxen who pulled the landlord's plow;
The other's lodgings were in a well-kept house,
Fortune having so decided, exactly 175
As Fortune will or will not—and that's a fact.
    "And then, quite long before the light of day,
The one with a bed was dreaming, there where he lay,
He heard his fellow urgently trying to call him,
And saying, 'Help! I'm in an ox's stall, 180
And here, tonight, they'll kill me where I lie.
So help me, my dear brother, or else I die.
Come to me as fast as you can!' he said.

The sleeper started up, with a whirling head,
But then, when he was fully awake, he went back   185
To sleep, since dreams were vapors, sadly lacking
Reality. He dreamed the same dream twice more,
And then, the third time, it seemed to him he saw
His fellow's unmoving body. 'Behold!' the corpse
Declared. 'I'm dead! See my bloody wounds!   190
Rise up early, tomorrow, and go to the town's
West gate, and there you'll see a cartload of dung,
Under which my corpse was secretly flung.
They killed me for my gold, the deed has been done,
But stop them there, do not let them escape.'   195
And then he told exactly how it was staged—
And O how pale, how pitiful his face.
The sleeper awoke, much less inclined to scoff.
So early in the morning he headed off
To where his fellow was supposed to spend the night,   200
And standing near the dirty oxen stall
He loudly called to his fellow, and called, and called.
        "The man who owned the place at last appeared,
And said, 'Your fellow got up and disappeared.
He took the road that leads straight out of town.'   205
        "Doubting, now, that his friend had truly gone—
The dreams had been too clear, and seemed all true—
He made up his mind to see what he could do,
And hurrying to the western gate he found
A dung-cart wending its way to foul dung-land,   210
And looking exactly like the clear description
His fellow, in the dream, had provided him.
And boldly, like an honest friend, he cried
Out loud for justice in this felony:
'My fellow, sleeping here, was murdered last night,   215
And now he's lying in there, his face to the sky.
Call out the magistrates, I say!' said he,
'Whoever enforces laws in this crowded city!
Harrow! Alas! Here lies my fellow, slain!'
There isn't much more of this story I need to say.   220
People jumped up, threw the cart to the ground,
And underneath the dung the body was found,

Not long dead, murdered the night before.
    "O blessèd God, source of holy grace,
Who always exposes murder and shame—always! 225
Murder will out, we see that day by day,
Disgusting murder, filthy, abominable
To God. It seems entirely reasonable
That hidden crimes are never allowed to stay hidden,
Though a year may pass, or two, thus it is bidden: 230
Murder will out. This is my conclusion.
And quickly, the magistrates in charge of that town
Arrested the carter and tortured him so hard,
And also the renter, half pulling him apart,
That what they'd done was quickly fully confessed, 235
And both of them were swiftly hanged by their necks.
    "This shows quite clearly: dreams must be taken to heart.
Indeed, in the very same book, the very next part,
Immediately in the chapter after that one—
This is no lie, this is simple fact— 240
I read of two men, traveling over the sea,
Headed on business to a very distant country,
And would have reached it, except for a contrary wind
That blew them here and there, and back again
To a harbor, near an exceedingly pleasant place, 245
Where they waited. That night the wind began to change
As they'd hoped, so they went to sleep, expecting to sail
In the morning. But during the night, one of the men
Dreamed that a man appeared, and stood by his bed,
Directing him to give up sailing again 250
That next day, 'for if you do, I tell you,' he said,
'You'll die a watery death.' And then the dream ended.
He woke, and told his friend what he had dreamed,
And begged him to stay just where he was, and not leave
The next day, for he himself would not be sailing. 255
Lying in bed, his friend replied most gaily,
Laughing, and calling the dreamer a silly fool.
'No dream,' he said, 'is fearful enough to rule
My coming and going. These are matters that I
Decide for myself. Yes, you can change your mind, 260
If you wish, but to me these dreams are empty vapors,

Delusions better fitting for the owls and apes
Men often dream of, falling into that maze
Of nonsense. No dream is true, or ever will be.
You can do, of course, just as you please,   265
And wilfully waste the hours, lying at ease,
Which I dislike. Farewell to you, and good day!'
And so he took his leave, and went his way.
But before his ship had sailed one-half its distance,
I don't know why, or what was the true mischance,   270
But something, somehow ripped the bottom open
And ship and man were dropped deep in the ocean,
In sight of other ships sailing nearby,
Outgoing vessels taking the very same tide.
    "Accordingly, fair Pértelóte, my dear,   275
These ancient examples, I pray, will help you learn
That no one should ever be so rashly heedless
Of dreams, for let me tell you a truth that, needless
To say, I believe in: dreams are things to be dreaded.
    "Lo, in Saint Kénelm's life, a book I have read   280
(Kénelm, Kenúlphus's son, Mercia's old king),
One day, it appears the boy had dreamed a thing
Horribly prophetic: that he would be murdered
By treasonous hands. His nurse (who was not his mother)
Explained each part of the dream, told him its meaning,   285
But he was only seven years old, and dreaming
Really meant nothing to him, his heart was so holy.
By God! I wish you had read this book, wholly
And well, and you would know this, as indeed do I.
    "My lady Pértelóte, I tell you truly,   290
Macróbiús, who recorded the vivid dream
Of Scípio Áfricánus, of Roman fame,
Validates dreams, declaring that what they are
Is notice in advance, explicit warning
Of what will come. And also, I pray you, look well,   295
In the older testament, at the story of Daniel,
And see if he thought dreams were merely empty.
And read about Joseph, and there, good wife, you'll see
If dreams can sometimes—I do not say they're always
True—be warnings of things that surely will fall.   300

Consider Pharaoh, the noble king of Egypt;
Remember the dreams of his butler, and also his baker,
And whether or not these dreams had God for their maker.
Read the histories of various realms
And learn the wondrous things that dreams have done. 305
Lo, Croesus, once the king of Lydia:
Did he not dream of sitting in a tree,
Which signified that very soon he'd be
Hanged? Or Andrómaché, Hector's wife,
Who knew the day that Hector lost his life 310
Before that happened, dreaming, the night before,
That he would die tomorrow, if he went to war.
She warned him, but her words were said in vain,
He went back out to fight the Greeks again,
And fought with Achílles, and died, there on the field. 315
But there's a tale that's all too long to review—
And now it's almost dawn, I have work to do.
Let me just say, in a word, it's my conclusion
That adversity will come of this night vision—
And further, I put no store in laxatives, 320
For they are venomous, I know that well,
And I won't take them; let them go to hell!
      "So let us speak of delight, and stop all this.
My Lady Pértelóte, as God may bless me,
He has sent me a thing of precious grace, 325
For when I see the beauty of your face,
You shine so scarlet red around your eyes
You kill what's left of my fear, it flees, you drive it
Away, for just as certainly as *In*
Principio mulier est hominis confusio— 330
Lady, the meaning of this Latin is,
'Woman is all man's joy, and his great bliss.'
For when I feel, at night, your soft, smooth side,
Although, my dear, I cannot manage to ride
On you, because our perch is narrow, alas! 335
Yet I remain so full of joy and solace
That here and now I give up both dreaming and dreams."
And with those words he flew right down from the beams,
For day had dawned, and there on the ground, for all

To share, he'd found some corn, and he clucked and called,   340
And the hens came running to him, out in the yard.
Now he was royal, not afraid any longer.
Wrapping his wings around his Pértelóte
Full twenty times, he trod her just as often,
Before the sun was high. He looked like a lion,   345
Tripping along on his toes, both up and down:
He never so much as touched his foot to the ground.
Each time he found some corn he clucked out loud,
And his hens came running, as if attending a ball.
Thus royal, exactly like a prince in his hall,   350
Let me leave Chaunticleer in his feathered pasture
And as I go along I'll tell his adventure.
        Now when that month of the year, when the world began,
Which we call March—the month when God made man—
Had passed and gone, and thirty-two days after   355
March were over and done with, one-tenth of a year,
It happened that Chaunticleer, filled with his pride,
Was strolling, his seven wives bobbing beside him,
And he glanced up high, at the brilliant-shining sun,
And saw that the sign of Taurus, the bull, had run   360
Twenty-one degrees and a little bit more,
And knew by his nature, and not by learnèd lore,
That this was the day's first hour. He crowed the time.
"The sun," he said, "has now been climbing high
In the heavens, forty-one degrees, precisely.   365
My Lady Pértelóte, my worldly bliss,
Hear the happy birds singing like this,
And see the fresh new flowers growing like grass.
O how my heart is overflowing with peace!"
Then suddenly his world was shattered in pieces,   370
For the other end of joy is always woe.
God knows, our worldly joy is quickly over,
And if a rhetorician was able to more than say it,
He'd surely know how to write a book, and safely
Claim he'd recorded a notable, worthy fact.   375
Let every wise man join me: here, I tactfully
Swear this story I'm telling is just as correct
As that of the famous Lancelot of the Lake,

To which all women, by nature, are dedicated.
But back to my story, which most politely has waited.　380
　　　A black coal-fox, a master of sly deceit,
Had come to live in the grove, two or three
Years back. He was clever enough to see
How handsome Chaunticleer was fond of parading,
Beside his wives, strutting away the day.　385
He lay most perfectly still, in a cabbage bed,
Awaiting his chance to spring at the rooster's head,
Joyfully working his subtle, murderous plan,
Leaping out to slay an innocent man.
　　　O treacherous killer, lurking in your den!　390
Judas Iscariot and Gánelón again,
O liars, thieves, inventors of Trojan horses,
Toppling down those great, unbreakable walls!
O Chaunticleer, accursèd be that call
That sent you flying down, that morning, from the beams!　395
You'd had a clear and potent warning dream
That this would be a dangerous day for you,
But clerics tell us, as clerics like to do,
That what God knows is sure to actually happen.
Any cleric will tell you this, by habit,　400
Adding that schoolmen continue altercating
These points, and telling you their deliberations,
Which pour from a hundred, maybe a thousand men.
But I can't possibly sift the chaff from the bran,
After the style of Doctor Áugustíne,　405
Or Boethius, or Bishop Bradwardine,
Or even determine if God, with his future knowledge,
Obliges me to go where his knowledge knows.
I work my path by simple necessity.
They say that freedom of choice has been granted me,　410
So I can do my thing, or refuse to do it,
Despite God's knowledge—in any case, I'll rue it!—
If even God escapes from necessity,
Which may, or may not, then be granted me.
I do not touch such stuff, whatever it be:　415
This tale is about a cock, not you or me—
Although, like us, he took his wife's advice

And came to regret it, walking out on a nice
Calm day, ignoring his dream and what it was saying.
Women's advice is very often fatal. 420
Women's advice brought us original woe,
Requiring Adam to pick up his sticks and go
Right out of Paradise, where he'd lived so easy.
But do not take these words too seriously:
I do not accuse either Adam or Eve. 425
Ignore these passing words, if they displease you.
Go read the writers who write this awful stuff,
And learn, of their feminism, more than enough.
(And those were Chaunticleer's words, not truly mine:
I think that women are perfect, even divine.) 430
　　　Looking lovely in sand, Pértelote scratched,
She and all her sisters, in their fenced-in patch
Of ground, sun-bathing while her husband sang
More nobly and entrancingly than mermaids—
Of whom Phísiológus reports that they made 435
Such merry music that men were happy to hear it.
And Chaunticleer became aware that, near him,
In a vegetable bed, a fox was crouching down.
Though this was nothing to crow about, he shouted,
"Cock, cock!" and quickly got himself ready to flee, 440
Frightened as any sensible beast should be,
Sighting an animal surely an enemy,
Though nothing like it had he ever seen.
　　　And fly away he would have, but the fox
Addressed him, using the courteous voice of logic 445
And reason: "Good sir, why should you run from me?
Afraid of someone as friendly as friends can be?
Surely, I would be worse than even a devil
If I behaved toward you in the way of evil!
I haven't come here to spy on how you live, 450
But honestly, because of the joy it gives me
To hear you singing, the way you were just now.
It's simply true: no human voice knows how
To sing like that, so merry a vocal organ
That comes to my ears like angel sounds, not man's. 455
The things I hear in your music do not ring

In Boéthiús, or any other singer.
My lord, your father—God has surely blessed him!—
And also your noble mother, both of them,
Have visited my house, and been at ease,   460
And you too, sir, I'd very gladly please.
People speak of singing, but I must say—
I swear by my very eyes, as I use them today—
Except for you, I've never heard such singing
As your father always gave us, morning by morning.   465
He must have sung straight from the very heart.
To strengthen his voice, he chose a singular, hard,
But successful maneuver—namely, he always closed
His eyes, singing full voice, as he always chose to,
And standing high as he could, on his very toes,   470
Stretching out his neck and raising his face.
O, he could sing with such immense good taste
That no one else in this good and jolly land
Could sing, I think, at his level, much less surpass him!
And I have read, in *The Mirror of Fools*, about   475
A priest's young son who took a stick to a cock,
During the fooling years of childhood, and when
The son was a priest and offered a benefice living,
The cock refused to crow, and he overslept,
And the living was lost. This tale does not reflect   480
On your father's wisdom and his pointed sense of discretion.
So now, sir, sing for the sake of charity.
Let's see if you're your father's son indeed."
    Chaunticleer began to beat his wings,
Like a man so duped he cannot see a thing,   485
Deceived by flattery, and aware of nothing.
    Alas, O lords, some of you have in your courts
Deceivers, too, lying and cheating frauds
Who actually please you more, I say by my faith,
Than he who knows the truth and actually says it.   490
Read Ecclesiastes, on flattery,
And be warned, you lords, of subtle treachery.
    So Chaunticleer stood high upon his toes,
Stretching his neck; his eyes he kept tight closed;
He started crowing as loud as a cock can crow.   495

And Russell the fox leapt like a frightened deer
And by the neck took hold of Chaunticleer,
Swung him onto his back, and headed home
To the woods, and no one so much as threw a stone.

     O Destiny, that may not be avoided!   500
Alas, that Chanticleer flew down from the beams!
Alas, that his wife paid no attention to dreams!
And of all of these disasters fell on a Friday.

     O Venus, you, the goddess of every wife,
Seeing the service gotten from Chaunticleer,   505
Who, acting for you, did everything in his power
(More for his pleasure, indeed, than to multiply),
Why did it happen that on your day he died?

     O Geoffroi, sovereign master of poets in rhyme,
Who wrote so feelingly of the death of Richard   510
The king, as little children read in their primers,
Why haven't I your learning and sharp-tongued insight,
Scolding Friday itself, as you did chide it?
Richard too was slain on a Friday night.
Ah, then I could have shown you how I'd regret   515
Chaunticleer's pain, as well as his utter dread.

     But surely, no equal volume of lamentation
Poured from female throats at the devastation
Of Troy, and Pyrrhus wielding a sharp-edged sword
Took Hector's father, King Priam, by the beard   520
And killed him, as we can read in Virgil's *Aeneid*—
Nothing compares to the cries of hens in the yard,
Seeing Chaunticleer captured and swept off to death.
But sovereign Lady Pértelóte cried higher
And louder than, in Carthage, Hásdrubal's wife,   525
Having heard her husband had lost his life
And Carthage itself was burned to the ground by the Romans.
Pértelóte was so full of rage and torment
That all at once she threw herself in the fire
Totally determined to burn till she died.   530

     O sorrowful hens, so fully you once cried
As senators' wives, in Rome, when Nero fired
The city, and all of them knew their husbands were dead—
None of them were guilty of any deed

Whatever, but Nero killed them in his fury.   535
And now I'll go back and finish up my story.
     The innocent widow, and both her daughters, too,
Heard how the hens were crying (as women will do)
And hurried out the door as fast as they could,
And saw the fox go hurrying into the wood,   540
With Chaunticleer stretched out across his back.
"Out!" they cried. "Our cock is gone, alack!
O O the fox!" and after him they ran,
And bearing sticks came many another man.
The widow's dog ran too, and Talbot, and Gerland,   545
And Malkyn with her spinning staff in hand.
The cows were running, and calves, and even the hogs,
All terrified by the furious barking of dogs
And the shouts and yells of men, and also the shrieking
Of women, all running as if their hearts were breaking.   550
The roaring sounded much like fiends in hell;
The ducks were quacking as if they were being killed;
Terrified geese were flying over the trees;
And out of the hive came a solid swarm of bees.
So hideous was the noise—ah, may God bless me!—   555
That even Jack Straw and all his breakers of peace
Could never muster shouting half so shrill
When they were hunting up a Fleming to kill,
As the waves of sound that followed after the fox.
They carried trumpets of brass, and also of boxwood,   560
And horns, and great bones, in which they blew and puffed,
And shrieking they came, and whooping more than enough.
It truly seemed the heavens were likely to fall.
     And now, good men, allow me to ask you all:
Can you see how Fortune swiftly turns again   565
And defeats the hopes and pride of wicked men?
This cock, still lying across the fox's back,
Shaking with fear, cleared his throat and spoke:
"Sir, if I were you, and you were me,
I'd feel like saying—O mighty God, please help me!—   570
'Go back, you lumping, puffed-up, red-faced peasants!
A plague on you, and one deeply unpleasant!
Here I am, at the very edge of the wood,

And in spite of you I've got my dinner food
And I will eat him, by God, without more ado!' "	575
    The fox replied: "By God, that is what I'll do."
As soon as he opened his mouth and spoke, the cock
Broke out of his grip and, flapping his wings, went aloft,
Perching himself on a branch in a nearby tree.
And seeing the cock escaped, and suddenly free,	580
    "Alas!" said the fox. "O Chaunticleer, how sad!
I've sinned against you, I've done what seemed to you bad,
For I frightened you by the way I took you home.
But sir, I never meant to do you harm.
Come down, and I will tell you just what I was thinking.	585
God help me, I will speak true, there'll be no shrinking!"
    "O no," said the cock, "for then I'd curse us both,
But mostly I'd curse myself, I say by my oath,
If you were able to trick me more than once.
Your flattery fooled me once; it won't any more.	590
You got me to sing, while keeping my eyes tight closed.
But he who will not look, when he knows he must,
May God give him a terrible string of bad luck!"
    "Ah," said the fox, "may God give him bad fortune,
Who has so little control, when something's important,	595
That he chatters away when he ought to hold his peace."
    Indeed, and this is what it means to be heedless
And negligent, and put your trust in flattery.
    But you who think this tale could never have happened,
Not between a fox, and a cock and a hen,	600
At least approve the story's moral, good men:
As Saint Paul says, whatever appears on a page
Is written for the Church, all through the ages.
So take the fruit, and leave the chaff where it is.
I pray to God that he, in all his wisdom,	605
Consents to making all of us good men,
And bringing us to eternal bliss! Amen.

Epilogue to the Nun's Priest's Tale

"Good sir, Nun's Priest," our Host declared at once,
"May your thighs be blessed, and also both your balls!
This was a merry tale of Chaunticleer.
But if you weren't a priest, were secular,
You'd be a treading-fowl, by God's own towers.   5
For if you had desire, as you have power,
The number of hens you'd need, it seems to me,
Is seven multiplied by seventeen.
Just look at the muscles on this noble priest,
So strong a neck, and what an enormous chest!   10
Turning his eyes your way, he looks like a hawk.
He doesn't have a priest's pale face, like chalk.
But sir, we thank you for your handsome talking."
    And after that, with a cheerful, smiling face,
He said to another pilgrim—Please turn the page!   15

The Second Nun's Prologue

The minister and nurse of all our vices,
Called in our English language "idleness,"
The porter who stands at the door to all delights,
He must be shunned, and kept by force in his place—
Which means, in a word, by loving, active faces, 5
At work for the Lord, who deserves to have our hearts,
Or idleness will draw us down from light.

For he who wields a thousand webs and nets,
Always waiting to catch us unawares,
The moment he finds a man in idleness 10
He snatches him, all ready, fully prepared
To haul him down by the hem or by the hairs,
So light of touch his captive never knows it.
And so we need to work, or else we go there.

And though men never think ahead to death, 15
They're capable of seeing, still, how obscene
This idleness is, mere tainted laziness,
Adding nothing to our lives, increasing
Only sin, led about by a leash
With sloth at the other end, and seeking sleep, 20
And food, and drink, existing only to eat.

To help us put away such idleness,
Which causes us to slowly ruin ourselves,

In all good faith I've written here, as best
I can, the sacred tale I'd wish for myself   25
But belongs to Saint Cecilia, her glorious life
And suffering—she, with her garland of roses and lilies,
She, both maid and martyr, Saint Cecilia.

Prayer to the Virgin Mary

You are that flower of earthly virgins, of us all,
You of whom Saint Bérnard loved to write,
So here as I begin, Mary, I call
To you, comfort of maidens in sorrow, to right
My wrongs and help me tell this tale of death   5
That ends in heaven, with Satan well defeated,
As those who follow my story will surely see.

Mary, maid and mother, your own son's daughter,
O well of mercy, cure of sinful souls,
God's kindness came to you, your son your father,   10
O humble, humble, but higher than us all,
How you ennobled us, becoming his mother,
For God had no concerns, in choosing you
To bear his son, and care for Jesus, too.

Protected by the shelter of your body,   15
Eternal love and peace took human shape,
Lord and guide of heaven, earth, and sea,
Endlessly shifting threefold unity,
All hail! And you, O spotless virgin-she,
Gave birth from your body—still a virgin, and pure—   20
The high Creator of every living creature.

Joined in you, united in your soul,
Are merciful compassion, goodness, and pity,
And you, containing more majesty than all

Of earth, who answer prayers for help so kindly,   25
But also aid to those who've never known you,
And generously, before they know they're needy,
You come to them and save their eternal souls.

But now do help me, gracious, blissful maid,
For I am an exiled wretch in a desert of gall.   30
Remember the Canaanite woman, she who said
That hungry dogs can eat a little, from all
The crumbs that, from their lord's great table, may fall.
And though I am an unworthy daughter of Eve,
And sinful, I hope you will accept my devotion.   35

And also, because all faith is dead, without deeds,
Breathe on me the intelligence and time
To keep myself from that place where devils breed.
O you, so beautiful and full of grace,
Become my advocate in that high place   40
Where songs are sung, without an end, to your praise!
O mother of Christ, daughter of Anne, come save me!

Send down, set into me, some glow, some light,
For my soul is agitated by my body's load,
Pressed down by the heavy weight of earthly desires   45
And false, deceiving indications of love.
O haven of refuge, hope of all salvation
For those who live in sorrow and distress,
Come help me: this work must now be truly addressed.

But you who read what I am writing now,   50
Forgive me for writing this tale, although I know
I lack the skill to tell it properly.
But still, I've read the many words of he
Who, originally, had written down the story,
Honoring the saint, showing her glory,   55
And if I've written it wrong, let someone inform me.

COMMENTARY ON THE NAME "CECILIA," BY JACOBUS JANUENSIS [*VORAGINE*], AUTHOR OF *THE GOLDEN LEGEND*

Let me expound on Saint Cecilia's name,
As you encounter it in the course of the tale.
In English it simply means "lily of heaven,"
Because of her purity in work and faith,
But also because of her gleaming honesty,   5
And the strength of both her conscience and reputation,
And this may be the cause of her appellation.

Or perhaps it comes from *caecis via,* "the blind man's
Way," for she has taught us to take the right road.
Or else "Cecilia" may be a combination,   10
Subtly composed, of *caelum,* a signification
Of "heaven," and "Lia" (for "Leah"), the initial one
For perfect holiness in all her thought,
And the second to honor all the deeds she wrought.

Or else, by another turn, we can take the name   15
In the sense of "lack of blindness," for the woman came
To wisdom early in life, and the clarity
Of her virtues. And also—Lo!—it might well be
That this shining name proceeded, instead, from *leos,*
Greek for "people," and "heaven": "the human heaven,"   20
Combining good and wise deeds under one banner—

We are not Greeks, but *leos* in English is "people"
—Just so!—and men themselves can see in the heavens
A sun and moon and stars in every direction,
Right as we find in this maiden a spiritual leaven,   25
A force of faith and magnanimity,
As well as wisdom of perfect clarity,
And deeds that shine with holy excellence.

And just as clerics, speaking of heaven, describe it
As swift and circular, round and burning,   30

The same can be said of Cecilia, fair and white,
Forever doing deeds of wonderful working,
Round and whole in always persevering,
Forever burning in charity as bright
As the sun. And thus we have the name I write of.   35

The Second Nun's Tale

This shining maiden, Cecilia (as her life will show us),
Was a Roman, born into a noble clan,
And from her childhood on was taught to know
And acknowledge Christ, and what his doctrines demanded.
All sources agree she carried on in this way,   5
Loving and fearing God, and always praying,
Beseeching him to let her remain a virgin.

And then a marriage for her was arranged, the man
As young as herself; his name was Valérian.
And when the wedding day at last arrived,   10
She wore the golden robe, as the rite required
But under that robe, which glittered and shone on the bride,
She wore against her flesh, and wore with pride,
A stiff and brittle shirt of horse's hair.

Day became night, and she was obliged to sleep   15
With her husband, as brides have always done, but she
Whispered to him, in private: "My dear, my sweet
Belovèd husband, I have a divine instruction,
And I would dearly love to tell it to you,
If you would like to hear those holy words,   20
And promise never to betray my secret."

Valérian at once declared that never,
Under any circumstances, would he
Betray her trust, in this or anything.

And then she said, most confidentially: 25
"I have an angel from heaven, and he loves me
With such great love, that whether I wake or sleep
It hovers, always ready, at need, to protect me.

"And if he sees, and feels with foreboding fear,
That you are touching me, and planning carnal 30
Intercourse, he'll kill you then and there,
And you're too young to die, my sweetest dear.
So if you'll love me sweetly, and leave my body
Untouched, he'll come to love you as he loves me,
Revealing to you his brightness and his joy." 35

Valérian, his mind set right by God,
Answered again: "If I'm to trust your words,
Let me see that angel, watch and behold him,
And if an angel is what he seems to be
Then, yes, I'll do what you have asked of me. 40
But if you love another man, in truth
I'll use this sword and quickly kill you both."

Cecilia made a quick response, and advised:
"If that is what you want, you'll see the angel,
So you can believe in Christ, and be baptized. 45
Go out to Vía Ápiá," she said,
"Just three short miles away from where we stand,
And tell the impoverished people who live on that land
Exactly what I tell you needs to be said.

"Say that I, Cecilia, I have sent you 50
To them, and you are to see Urban the old,
On secret business, and your intentions are good.
And when you see our Urban, a holy saint,
Tell him exactly the words that I have said,
And when he's cleansed your soul from worldly sin 55
You'll see that angel, before your visit ends."

So Valérian went to the place that he'd been told to,
And just as he'd been promised he was soon beholding

Sainted old Urban, down in the catacombs,
Among the hidden burial places of other   60
Saints. Valérian promptly and clearly told him
His message, and as soon as Urban heard his words
The old man joyfully lifted up his hands.

His ancient eyes let tears begin to fall.
"Almighty Lord, O Jesus Christ," he said,   65
"Sower of celibate thought, guide of us all,
The fruit of that lovely seed of chastity
You sowed in pure Cecilia has now been grown.
Like a busy fertilizing bee,
Your loyal servant serves you—O Cecilia!   70

"See how the husband she's taken to her heart,
A wild and raging lion, and sent him here,
Now as meek as a lamb. Saint Paul, appear!"
And immediately another old man was there,
Wearing clothes of the purest, thinnest white linen,   75
And in his hands he held a book, lettered
In gold, and stood there, facing Valérian.

Valérian came close to fainting from fear,
Seeing so strange a vision, but he held himself
Together, and began to read the golden letters: 80
"O Lord, O faith, O God, and no thing other,
O Christendom, the father of us all,
Above us all, above all everywhere."
These were the words he saw, written in gold.

When this had been done, the old man spoke these words: 85
"Do you believe what you've read? Say yes or no."
"Yes, I believe it all," said Valérian.
"It seems to me that this is all we can say,
And under these heavens no one can disagree."
The old man vanished, but where or how unknown.   90
And Urban, the pope, christened him at once.

So Valérian went home, and found his wife
Standing in their bedroom with an angel,
Holding in his hands a pair of crowns,
Woven of roses and very whitest of lilies. 95
The sources say the first crown went to Cecilia,
And afterward he solemnly gave the second
To Valérian, her newly wedded husband.

"Be careful of these crowns," the angel said,
"Wear them with thoughts of the purest pure, and hearts 100
Of the chastest. I bring them to you from high in heaven:
No petal will rot or ever rust away,
Or lose their fragrance. This is the truth, I say.
But no one's eyes can ever see these crowns,
Unless they're chaste, impurity held at bay. 105

"And you, Valérian, because you so soon assented
To good advice, shall have whatever you want:
Just tell me what it is, and you will have it."
And then Valérian said, "I have a brother,
And in this world of ours there is no other 110
I love so much. I ask you to give him the grace
Of knowing truth, as I do, here in this place."

The angel said, "God approves your request,
You both will have the honor of martyrdom
And rise to heaven, and sit at his blissful feast." 115
And then the brother, named Tibúrce, did come,
And when he perceived the perfume of heavenly flowers,
Spread around the room by roses and lilies,
Silently, but deeply, he began to wonder,

And said, "I am astonished, this time of year, 120
To sense that sweet perfume I'm finding here,
Roses and lilies, which should be out of bloom.
Even holding them tight in my hands, I could
Not feel the savor more deeply than I do now.
This scented sweetness has gone to my heart, I find, 125
And changed me into a different human kind."

Valérian said, "We're graced with a pair of crowns,
Snow white and rose red, gleaming bright and clear,
But which your eyes, as yet, cannot behold.
You smell them only through my silent prayer, 130
And you will see them, my brother, beloved and dear,
If so you wish it, without the slightest delay,
If you accept the truth, right here, today."

Tibúrce then answered, "Are you speaking to me,
Truly, right now, or am I only dreaming?" 135
"In dreams," Valérian said, "is where we have been
Till now, my brother: our seeing has been mere seeming.
In truth, we now know where we have been dwelling."
"How do you know this? And where is this message from?"
"That," Valérian said, "is now what I'll tell you. 140

"The angel of God was here, and taught me the truth,
And you too will see it, if you'll reject all idols
And be chaste and pure, and never anything else."
Saint Ambrose, in his preface to the book I follow,
Explains the miracle of this pair of crowns, 145
And with great reverence he sets it down,
This noble cleric, and I will copy it out:

" 'Receiving the gift of holy martyrdom,
Blessèd Saint Cecilia to God had come,
Renouncing the world and also the bed in her room, 150
In witness of which, now see the brothers' conversion,
And holy God will assign two further crowns,
Fragrant, exactly as sweet as the very first,
And the angel's task will be to bring them down.

" 'The maiden has brought these men to eternal bliss, 155
And the world is learning how much it's truly worth
To dedicate yourself to chastity.'
And then Cecilia showed her brother-in-law,
Speaking plainly, how each and every idol
Is empty, and dumb, and consequently deaf, 160
And told him all his idols should now be left.

"Whoever won't believe it is simply a beast,"
Tibúrce then said. "I cannot lie about this."
Hearing these words, Cecilia kissed his chest,
Delighted to have her truth accepted so quickly.   165
"Starting here and now, you're my ally,"
Said this blessèd, beautiful young maiden.
And then she continued, in words that follow now:

"Lo," she said, "just as the love of Christ
Has made me truly your dear brother's wife,   170
Just so I join my hands with yours, seeing
You spurn the idols you used to recognize.
Go with your brother, now, and be baptized,
And let your soul be purged, and then you'll be
A proper Christian and see the angel's face."   175

Tibúrce then said: "Dear brother, tell me, first,
Where I need to go, and who I will meet."
"To whom?" was the answer. "Come, and you will be blessed
By Urban, our pope, and I will lead you, now."
"To Urban? O, Valérian, my brother,"   180
Tibúrce exclaimed, "to him, and not some other?
That would be a wondrous thing indeed.

"You don't mean, do you, the Urban I have heard
So much of, he so often condemned to death,
Living in corners and cracks, forever in motion,   185
And never ever daring to show his head?
He would be burned in a flaming fire, red
And hot, if he were ever found, and we
Who were with him would meet the same bad ending.

"And we who seek this secret divinity,   190
Hidden in heaven, which only we can see,
We will always be burned, in this world of ours!"
Cecilia answered with quick and fervent courage:
"You're surely right, my brother, for men should be cautious
Before they give up their lives, my own dear brother,   195
If this were our only life, and there were no other.

"But there is another life, in a better place,
And that life lasts forever, so have no fear,
For God's own son has told us, by his grace,
And he is our creator, the world's true maker,   200
And he has worked with skilful heart and hands,
Sharing with the Holy Ghost and his Son,
Both of whom, in heaven, he blessedly made.

"By miracles and words, High God's own Son
Declared, when he was in this world, that life   205
Went on in heaven, a holy life to be won."
Tibúrce then answered, "O my dearest sister,
Do I hear you right? You're saying that God is not one,
But truly divided into three. How
Can it be, and how can you know this thing was done?"   210

"I will tell you," she said, "before I go.
Just as a man has three clear powers to guide him,
Memory, imagination, and mind,
So too a holy being, blessed and divine,
Can turn himself to three, which is how we find him."   215
And then, most earnest and actively, she preached
Christ's coming; his sufferings, too, were part of her teaching,

And, especially, parts of his crucifixion:
How God's own Son was allowed to come to our world
To save our sinful souls, which needed forgiveness,   220
And show us mercy, despite our lack of compassion:
This, and much more, was the theme of her passionate words,
And then, his heart and mind much clearer, he
And his brother traveled the hidden road, to see

Pope Urban, who welcomed them with thanks to God,   225
And then he christened Tibúrce, with a happy heart
And saintly light, completing his knowledge of Christ.
And after this, Tibúrce was blessed with such grace
That now he could see, at every time and place
God's angel, and whatever he asked the angel to do   230
Was swiftly done, and he was a man made new.

Categorizing the wonders Jesus worked
For them would be a task too much for me,
But finally, to make this business short
And plain, the Roman police appeared and caught them,   235
And had them taken before the magistrate,
Who questioned them (knowing their answers already),
And sent them to the statue of Jupiter the great,

Declaring, "Whoever will not sacrifice
Must have his head chopped off: this is my verdict."   240
These martyrs, the men and women I here describe,
Were put in charge of Maximus, one
Of the magistrate's officials, and his assistant,
And when he took these saintly Christians from court
He wept, for the pity felt in his heavy heart.   245

And hearing the truths these Christians soon had told him,
He managed to get the torturers' permission
To take these people out, bring them to his home,
And before it was dark, they spoke so warmly with him,
Succeeded so well in their christianizing mission   250
That he, the torturers and all their families
Gave up false faith, believed in God alone.

Then Cecilia came, when day had turned to night,
Bringing priests who christened them all together,
And afterward, when darkness was turning light,   255
Cecilia told them, with bold, encouraging heart:
"All of you are now Christ's much belovèd
Knights. Cast off the works of pagan darkness,
Armor yourselves in purest Christian brightness.

"Truly, you've fought a tremendous battle, and won;   260
You've won the race, your faith is safe forever.
Accept the crown eternal, from the one
And only judge, whose service you have entered.
And you will have that crown, for you deserve it."
And after this, which happened as I describe it,   265
They all were led to the place of sacrifice.

But once Valérian and his brother, Tibúrce,
Were there, to tell you how this process ended,
They both most firmly, courageously refused
To make a sacrifice, and fell on bended   270
Knees, their hearts all humble, in solemn devotion,
And both their heads came off, in rapid strokes.
Their souls ascended to heaven and the king of grace.

And Maximus, seeing these things had happened,
Wept and declared, immediately, that he   275
Had seen their souls fly high, the white wings flapping
Among a flock of angels, shining bright,
And with these words alone converted many
Unbelievers, for which the judge had him
Well beaten with leaden whips, until he died.   280

Cecilia came and took his body away,
Gently placing him in the ground beside
Tibúrce and Valérian, under a stone,
And hearing of this, the judge at once decided
To have his officials bring her before him, in court,   285
In order to have her, right there and in his presence,
And make a sacrifice, while burning incense.

But all these officials, converted by her wisdom,
Wept hot tears, believing what she'd told them,
And went on crying more and even more: 290
"Christ, God's Son, an equal part of godship,
Is truthfully God, and so we must inform you
That Maximus was a worthy servant of God.
We speak with one voice, and truly. We'll die if we must!"

Learning these troublesome events, the judge   295
Gave orders to bring Cecilia into court,
And the very first question asked of her, was, Lo!
"What sort of woman are you? How do you live?
"I am of noble birth, and a Roman," said she.
"I am obliged to ask you, please pardon me,   300
About your religion. Tell me your beliefs."

"But you began by foolish questioning,"
She said, "making me answer twice when the thing
You wanted was hidden at first. Was that not foolish?"
And now the judge replied with the tone she'd used: 305
"Where did you learn to answer questions so rudely?"
"Where?" she answered, repeating his foolish question.
"From conscience and good faith, honestly proven."

The judge replied: "Are you aware of my power?
Do you take it as nothing?" And this was the answer she gave him: 310
"I see no reason to fear your power," said she,
"For all and any mortal power must be
Like bladders full of air. Most certainly,
A needle point, stuck in the outside skin,
Can make them blow away, just like wind."   315

"Your very first answers," he said, "are stubbornly wrong,
And it is doubly wrong to persist in such things.
Do you know that all our generous princes
Have made it the law, which we've enforced ever since,
That all you Christian people shall be forgiven   320
Simply by leaving this Christian belief behind?
The law will step aside, if you'll deny it."

"Your princes are wrong, as all your noblemen are,"
Cecilia replied, "creating a lunatic law
To make us guilty, on premises all false.   325
For you are well aware of our innocence,
And what we've done is express our reverence
For Christ. And because we carry a Christian name,
You make us criminals, and try to shame us.

"But we who know the virtues in that name   330
Cannot, in faith, deny the truth we know."
The judge replied: "You have your choice of two ways
To freedom. Make sacrifice, or deny your religion.
These are the only pathways for your escape."
At which the holy, blessèd, and beautiful maiden   335
Laughed, and then replied to the judge, saying:

"O judge, bewildered in your foolishness,
How can you want a denial of innocence,
To turn me into a road of crime? Nonsense!
See how he pretends, in a public place, 340
Staring, and sometimes raving, out of his senses!"
To which he answered, "O, you miserable wretch,
Have you any notion how far my power stretches?

"Surely, you know our princes bestowed me,
Lo! the power and authority 345
To let you live or sentence you to death?
How can you be so arrogant to me?"
"I've only spoken steadily," said she,
"Not proud, for let me say the truth on my side,
We Christians hate the deadly sin of pride. 350

"And if you're not afraid of the power of truth,
Then let me make it publicly known, by right,
That you have told enormous lies, in this room.
You say your princes have given you the might
Both to kill and also revive our lives. 355
But all you can do, and I tell you this most truly,
Is kill us. Only that can your power decide.

"Your princes have only made you minister
Of death. You cannot make a claim for more,
And if you do, you lie, for not an inch further 360
Can your power go." "Enough of your boldness. The law
Says sacrifice to the gods, before you leave.
It makes no difference to me, what you blame me for;
I can endure that, being a man of learning.

"But you go too far, when you attack our gods, 365
And that I cannot allow," the judge then said.
Cecilia answered: "You speak like a foolish sod!
Not a word you've said, since I've been here,
Has been untainted by your silly mind,
Showing you in every way, I find, 370
An ignorant official, afflicted with pride.

"Your outer eyes, so far as I can tell,
Are hardly blind. And when we see these stones,
Which you believe are gods, it's easily known
That stones are stones, no matter what you call them.   375
O judge, if you allow your hand to fall
On one, then lick your hand, I know that all
You'll taste—if you taste it truly—is nothing but stone.

"Try your tongue, if you cannot use your mind.
The people scorn you, laughing at your folly,   380
For all men know, as you might easily find,
That almighty God is up in heaven so high,
And all these images, it's plain to the eyes,
Are nothing, and give you nothing, and cannot try
For more—worthless lumps of stone, where they lie."   385

This, like everything else Cecilia said,
Infuriated the judge, and he ordered her led
Home to her house, "and in her house," he said,
"Burn her to death in a bath of flaming red."
His officers did everything he'd ordered,   390
Bringing her home, locking her in her bath,
And setting underneath her the fires of wrath.

For one whole night, and then the day that followed,
Despite the fire and overpowering heat
She sat as cool as ice, untouched by woe.   395
Her body declined to show a drop of sweat.
But in that bath, she'd have to meet her death,
For the judge was determined, and wickedly he sent
A court official to accomplish what he intended.

Three times he swung at her, right in the neck,   400
This torturer, but the law would only permit him
Three strokes, and so he could not cut her through.
The law was absolute, and had its effect:
No one could offer such a punishment
As a deadly fourth stroke, be it gentle or hard,   405
And having done what he did, he could not do more.

So half alive, half dead, her neck half chopped
Apart, he left her lying, and went on his way.
The Christians gathered all around her sopped up
Blood with sheets, but could not do much more. 410
She lived three days, in torment fierce and strong,
But went on giving them the holy teaching
She'd begun, and so she went on preaching.

All her possessions, she said, should go to these people.
And this was done; they brought them to Pope Urban. 415
And she said: "All I asked of the king of heaven
Were three more days on earth, and not another
More, but the better to do the work of saving
Souls, performing the holy deeds our savior
Began, may this house of mine become a church." 420

Saint Urban, with his deacons, secretly brought
The body, and buried it, in the darkness of night,
Where all the other saints had truly been laid.
Her house was named the church of Saint Cecilia,
And Urban hallowed it, as well he might, 425
And there, in noble fashion, men continue
To worship Christ, honoring this saint.

Prologue of the Cleric-Magician's Servant

By the time we came to the end of this good saint's life,
Not having ridden, as yet, a full five miles,
At Boughton, near the forest of Blee, a rider
Overtook us, dressed in black, a surplice
White as snow under the rest of his clothes.   5
His hackney horse, dappled gray from its nose
To its tail, was dripping wet from his gallop—three
Hard miles, at least—and a wonderful sight to see.
In fact, this hard-worked horse might well have been
On its last legs, by the time we got to see him: 10
The foam that dripped from its mouth stood high on its chest,
And flecks of foam had flown and stuck to the rest
Of its body. A double-folded bag was lying
Flat on its back: the man was traveling light,
For the summer. He seemed a truly significant man,   15
But in my heart, already uneasy, I began
To wonder what he was, till I understood
His cloak, not hanging free, was sewn to his hood,
From which, upon some heavy consideration,
I realized he had taken ordination.   20
His hat was hung by a cord, right down his back,
For he had clearly been riding very fast—
Steadily prodding his horse like a man gone mad.
He'd tucked a burdock leaf under his hood,
To hold off sweat and keep his head from heating   25
Up. But what a pleasure to see him sweat!
His forehead dripped like a boiling potted distillery,

Herbs and medical plants almost ready
For use. And when he reached us, he began to cry,
"God save," he said, "this jolly company!   30
You see I've galloped hard, but for your sake,
Because I wanted badly to overtake you
And ride along in your merry company."
His servant, too, was full of courtesy,
Saying, "Gentlemen, this morning-time,   35
I saw you leaving your inn and then go riding
Away, and went to warn my sovereign lord,
Knowing he'd dearly love to ride with you,
For this is the kind of company he adores,
Full of merriment, people enjoying their sport."   40
     "My friend," said our Host, "may God send you his grace,
For warning your lord, and getting him to this place:
Your lord is a man of wisdom, or so I judge him,
And he likes his pleasure, in any dose but a smidgin!
Might he know a merry tale or two   45
That he can offer this company, when it's due?"
     "Who, sir? My lord? Yes, yes, and I'm no liar,
For he can hold his toes to a merry fire
Of wonderful heat. But, sir, please trust me, if you knew him
As well as I, and learned what he can do,   50
You'd see how hard and also how craftily
He's able to work—and how many things you'd see!
He runs from little projects right up to the mighty,
And no one riding here, take it from me,
Could do what he does unless my lord had taught him.   55
He dresses simply, and surely the horse who brought him
Here is a hack, but he is a man worth knowing.
Making an acquaintance of my sovereign lord
Would be to your benefit, I'd bet my purse,
And everything else I own. He is a person   60
Of high discrimination, and also of wisdom.
I warn you truly: this is a man among men."
     "Well," said our Host, "I pray you, tell me, then,
Is he a cleric, or not? If not, what is he?"
     "No, he's far above a cleric, in wisdom   65
And power," the servant said. "Let me tell you,

Host, a little of what this man can do.
   "My lord and master has such subtle ways
That all his powers, all his art, I can praise
But not report. I work with him, a bit—   70
So here's an illustration, just a little
Idea: take all this ground that we'll be riding,
From here to Canterbury. He could slide it
Upside down and pave it with silver and gold."
   And when this wildest of illustrations was told   75
To our Host, he exclaimed, "Now, God's great grace on us all!
This seems too marvelous a thing for a man
Like me to fathom, for if your master can
Indeed perform such wonders, I don't understand
How he can undervalue his appearance.   80
His cassock, now, has been worn to disappearance—
And I say this truthfully, despite his worth.
It's also torn and stained, impossibly dirty.
How can your lord go riding about like this,
Having the power to put himself in bliss,   85
If now, in fact, these powers lie in his hands?
Tell me that, so I can understand."
   "Why?" asked the servant. "Is that a question for me?
By God, I doubt he'll ever let himself be
In public what his arts would. (I tell you this   90
In private, and in secret, and would never dare admit
I told you!) He's more than wise enough to know
Too much is dangerous: for him to show
His power would surely be seen as a sin, a vice.
It often happens to men with too much mind   95
That wisdom denies them all hope of paradise.
In that, I think, he's far too foolish and artless—
Which grieves me, seeing him throw himself away.
May God preserve him! I've nothing more to say."
   "That's fine, my very good man," declared our Host.   100
"But since you work with him, and do your best,
Tell us his path of life, from day to day,
Being so clever and skilled in such various ways.
Where do he and you live, if you can say?"
   "Off in the outskirts of a town," he replied,   105

"Lurking in nooks and crannies, exactly like
Men who are thieves and robbers, and all that kind,
Afraid to show their faces except in the dark,
Hiding in shabby houses, well set apart.
That's our way of life, to tell you the truth."   110
        "And now," said our Host, "allow me to ask you, forsooth:
Why is your face discolored, your skin so mottled?"
        "Saint Peter!" he answered. "It doesn't come from a bottle.
I spend long hours over a fire, blowing,
And that has surely changed my color, I know.   115
I'm not the sort who's always looking in mirrors;
I work and study too hard to think of appearance.
We're always making mistakes, watching these fires,
And never really getting what we desire.
We always seem to end in total confusion.   120
We please a lot of people, creating illusions,
Then borrowing gold, a pound or two at a time,
Or ten, or twelve, however we're inclined,
And telling them to believe we can transform
One pound to two, or maybe even more.   125
It's always a lie, but we are always in hope
Of making it work, and success is what we grope for.
And yet that knowledge is far too advanced for us,
We cannot do it, and we betray our trust:
We're running hard, but it slides away so fast   130
It's out of our hands. We'll be beggars at last."
        And as his servant was chattering on and on,
The master rode closer, hearing suspicious sounds
From his trusted servant, since he was always concerned
When men were talking. And we have surely learned   135
From ancient texts that a man who is truly guilty
Thinks, whenever men speak, that it is he
They're speaking about. And thus the master drove
His horse to his servant's side, carefully lowered
His voice, and said, "Now hold your peace, I permit   140
No conversations like this. You will regret it
If, here in this company, you say a slanderous
Thing of me, words that are dangerous,
And secrets about me that never should be told."

"Ah," said our Host, "go on, and be as bold   145
As you like. What do all his threats amount to?"
        "In truth," said the servant, "I've little left to recount."
        And when the cleric saw it was no use,
His servant was going to tell what he might choose to,
He turned and galloped away, for sorrow and shame.   150
        "Ah ha!" said the servant, "now we're into the game,
And I can tell you everything I know,
With him gone. I'll never lose a minute around him,
Never again, neither for penny nor pound.
He led me into that lying, cheating game,   155
And before he dies I wish him sorrow and shame!
I mean what I say, I tell you, by my faith;
I'm sure of my ground, whatever anyone says.
But I admit, despite my pain and grief,
And all my wasted labor, I'd never leave it,   160
No matter calamities or even disasters.
How I wish I knew enough of my master's
Art to tell you everything about it!
But I can tell as much as I've found out.
My lord having fled, I'll say whatever I can;   165
You'll hear as much, truly, as I understand."

Tale of the Cleric-Magician's Servant

I've lived and worked with this man for seven years,
And cannot say that his art is any clearer
To me than it was. All I ever owned
Has been lost, and I'm surely not the only one.
God knows, I was then well dressed, both fresh and fine   5
In all I wore and carried with me. Times
Were good. And now I cover my head with stockings;
My face was ruddy, my whole complexion bright,
But now it's wan and of a leaden hue—
Which is what alchemy will do to you!   10
Wherever I go, my eyes are always bleary—
Another advantage of magic arts and theories!
That slippery science has stripped me down so bare
I own flat nothing except the clothes I wear.
Indeed, these magic arts have me so deeply   15
In debt, with all the gold I've borrowed at steepest
Rates, that as long as I live I'll never be out
Of debt. Let others learn from me, by God!
Whoever jumps in the waters of alchemy,
And keeps on swimming, is doomed to poverty.   20
So help me God, no one wins in that game,
Only empties his purse, and purges his brain.
Caught in that web, through madness and desperate folly,
He loses what he has, he takes too many
Risks, and urges others to do the same,   25
So they can see their gold run down the drain,
As his did. Rascals are always wonderfully pleased

To treat their friends to pain and misery.
A priest once taught me that. But what's the difference?
My subject is alchemy, and not good sense.   30
     There in our laboratories, exercising
Our elfish craft, we seemed incredibly wise,
Our language was so priestly, wonderfully clever.
I blew those fires until my heart felt feverish.
Why should I describe our measurements   35
For all the things we worked upon, and spent—
Like five full ounces of silver, or maybe six,
Or more, or less, depending on the mixture—
And busy myself recounting all the names,
Like arsenic, burned bone, and iron flakes,   40
All ground to perfect powder, fine and small,
Which then goes into an earthen pot, and all
The ingredients are mixed with salt, and pepper,
And everything is fully blended together,
Then covered over by a sheet of glass—   45
And many other steps are taken, by God—
Until, at last, the pot is totally sealed,
So nothing might escape out in the air;
And then the fire underneath it all
Was made to be brisk, the flames were even and tall—   50
And all the difficulties we were forced
To deal with, subliming and other alchemic courses,
Amalgamation, and fusing mercury,
Quicksilver, it is called, until it's refined—
We failed, despite the endless tricks we tried.   55
Our arsenic, our mercury sublimed,
Our well-ground lead and powdered porphyry—
A measured dose, well made, it seems to me,
But nothing helped us, our work was all in vain,
Neither our gases, rising up, or the main   60
Materials, all fixed and heated in place,
Did absolutely nothing, our labor was wasted,
And all the great expense, in twenty devilish
Ways, was lost, and empty-handed we finished.
     Still, there are many other important things   65
That bear, and heavily, on our practicing.

Although I cannot list them in proper rank,
Because I remain, at best, an ignorant man,
Let me rehearse them, as they come to mind,
Even if left unsorted, as to their kind: 70
Medicinal earth from Armenia, acetate
Copper, borax, all sorts of vessels and plates,
All glass, chemical flasks, distilling retorts,
Vials, porcelain crucibles, vaporizers,
Distiller bottoms, alembic upper sides,   75
And other such things, expensive and much to be prized.
I see no need to tell you each and all—
Waters turning red, and liver bile,
Sulphuric brimstone, and sal ammoniac,
So many herbs we'd buy them by the peck—   80
Like agrimony, valerian, and moonwort,
And many more—but why waste idle words?
Our lamps were always burning, night and day,
To finally succeed, if only we may—
And then there was our furnace of calcification,   85
And one for removing color, by albumination
With unslaked lime, and chalk, and the white of eggs.
All sorts of powder, ashes, dung, and piss,
Waxed pots, saltpeter, clay, and iron sulfate;
Tartar salt, and sodium carbonate,   90
Our different fires, both of wood and coal;
And calcinated, burned-down things made whole;
And clay combined with human hair, or horse's,
And tartar oil, alum rock, and yeast,
And tartar crust that forms on wine in casks,   95
Arsenic of ratsbane, and liquifications,
And many different kinds of solidifications,
And yellowing silver so it looked like gold,
Fusing at roaring temperatures, and fermenting,
Ingots, and many tests and experiments.   100
       But let me tell you, as I was also taught them,
The spirits four, and metal bodies, seven
In number, as often I heard my good lord name them.
       The first of the spirits bears the name quicksilver,
The second is arsenic, the third, I never   105

Forget, is sal ammoniac, then brimstone.
The seven bodies, lo! and here they come:
Sol is gold; Luna is silver, we know;
Mars is iron; Mercury is quicksilver;
Saturn is lead; Jupiter is tin;   110
And Venus is copper—and that little list is finished!
    Trying to work at this most wretched craft
Is hopeless: no one's will, or gold, will last.
Any and every thing you spend on this
Is wasted, gone forever with a farewell kiss!   115
Whoever is stupid enough to make the attempt,
Let him come try, and watch his purse grow empty.
And he who's put some silver and gold away,
Can watch it dissolve, transformed in magic play.
You think this craft is easily acquired?   120
No, no, God knows, not even for monks and friars,
Or clerics and priests, or anyone else who tries it,
Not even sitting at books till their brains are fried.
Learning this foolish, elfin-magic craft
Is hopeless work. By God! The devil is laughing.   125
And teaching an ignorant man these subtleties?
Fie! That's nonsense, a trick that cannot be
Performed. Whether he has learning, or not,
It's all the same: instead of learning, he'll rot.
Whether your brain has multiplication down pat,   130
Or never saw it before, I'll tell you flatly,
From full experience, you come out the same—
In short, whatever way you're going to fail.
    Ah: I'm forgetting to tell you all about acids,
Which come in liquid form, or metallic filings,   135
And of iron and other metals made soft as wool,
And, equally, made infinitely harder, as tools.
Oils make baths for meltable metals—but all
The details would swell out larger than any Bible
In the world. And so I think it would be best   140
If I finished these iterations, and let it all rest.
You've heard enough from me, already, I guess;
You might call up a devil as a friendly guest!
    Ah, no! Enough! The magic philosopher's stone,

Talisman, elixir—we hunted it down   145
But never got that far. We would have been kings!
But God in heaven, I swear it, knows that nothing
Like that would come to us, not ever, no matter
What tricks we tried. We surely wasted and shattered
Our fortunes, spending everything we got   150
In the hunt, but never finding a thing—not
A single thing, which nearly drove us crazy.
Our hearts were passionate, we were not lazy
Or stupid. We knew what we wanted, and never got it.
Let me warn you: hope is never forgotten,   155
Men will continue chasing this magic stone,
Cutting themselves away from actual life.
This thing is bitter sweet, not hopeless strife,
For those who desperately want it. A man who owns
Nothing, who spends his days hunting this stone,   160
Who rolls himself in a sheet and tries to sleep,
And waking up, one morning, suddenly sees
A grubby brat in his house, would grab the child
And sell it, and get enough for one more try.
They cannot stop, if anything is left: 165
They'll take it, spend it, then walk about, bereft.
And forever after, wherever these men may go,
You'll recognize the sooty smell of brimstone;
The rest of the world will think they stink like goats
In heat, so rank, disgustingly intense   170
That even standing a mile away you can sense
Their odor, know who they are by their stink
And threadbare clothes, poor as a church mouse, I think.
If someone bothers to ask them, privately,
Why in the world they're dressed so very badly,   175
They'll whisper an answer, all right, close to his ear,
Explaining how they walk about in fear
Of being killed, because they know so much.
So help me. They've murdered their brains with herbs and sludge!
    Enough of this. Let me turn to my story.   180
When the pot is ready to leave the fire, still roaring
And bubbling with molten metals in quantity,
My master stirs it up, no one but he—

And since he has left us, I tell you this quite frankly—
He has a reputation for being wily.   185
I always knew that he was seen as clever,
And yet he made mistakes—and not just seldom.
How could that happen? Often it went like so:
The pot would break—and farewell! everything's gone!
Metals like this are so extremely violent,   190
And our containers lacked the needed strength;
Even when made of sturdy limestone and rock,
Metals burst through, and everything goes "pop!"
Some of them sink like water, right in the ground—
How many times we've lost pound after pound!—   195
And some will scatter everywhere around
The floor. Some leap to the roof. We never found
Him there, but I know the devil from hell was roaming
Up and down the room. He was quite at home:
Even in hell, where he is absolute sire,   200
There isn't more sorrow, or bitterness, or ire.
And when our pots got broken, as I have said,
We each complained, and wished the other one dead.
    Someone would say the pot was over-heated.
Someone said no, more blowing of air was needed,   205
And I was afraid, for I did the puffing and breathing.
"Nuts!" said the third one, "you're stupid, and also a fool!
It wasn't mixed according to all our rules!"
"No," said the fourth. "You people, listen to me:
It happened only because our wood wasn't beech.   210
That was the cause, you stupid son of a bitch!"
I can't remember how long we went on quarreling,
But we were always lost in argument.
    "Well," said my lord, "there's nothing more to be done.
These are problems we'll come to the end of, soon.   215
I'm certain that particular pot was cracked.
Whatever it was, we're talking after the fact.
As we usually do, quickly sweep up the floor,
And ease your hearts. And then we'll do it once more."
    The rubbage and muck was swept in a pile,   220
And then we spread out a canvas, and lifted it high,
And tossed our garbage into a great big sieve,

And sifted it, removing what bits it would give.
    "Hey, wait a minute," one said, "there's lots more metal
In there, we simply haven't gotten it all.   225
This piece, for example, is bent like the devil, sure,
But another time it may be a perfect tool.
All of these are things we've had to buy.
No merchant anywhere, I know, gets by
With no losses. You can't hold on to prosperity: 230
Some merchandise will sink deep in the sea,
And some will sail into port, all safe and dry."
    "Peace!" said my lord. "On the next attempt I'll try
To work from a different, perhaps a better plan,
And, fellows, if I don't, I'll be the man   235
To blame. Something was wrong, this time, I know it."
    Someone said, again, the fire was glowing
Too hot—but hot or cold, it seems to me
We went the wrong way every single time,
And in our madness whimpered and yelled and cried.   240
Though when we met together every man
Among us seemed to be a Solomon,
Everything you see that gleams like gold
Is not what it seems, as I have heard it told,
And every apple that pleases a human eye   245
Is not worth eating, no matter how we cry.
And that, right on the button, is apt for us:
He who seems the wisest, in the name of Jesus,
Is the worst of fools in fact—which is not belief!
And he who seems most honest is often a thief.   250
You'll see that for sure, before I finish and leave you:
This is a tale that's deeply steeped in grief.

PART TWO

    This priestly magician I'm telling you about
Could quickly infect an entire city—no doubt!—
Even ones as great as Ninevee,   255
Alexandria, Rome, and another three.
His tricks and bubbling-over bags of lies
Cannot be told, no matter how hard I try.

Even should he live a thousand years,
No one could match his falsehood, he has no peer. 260
For he will wrap himself in the slyest words,
And stupefy all men who live in this world,
Quickly turning wise men into fools—
As devils do, and he's a devil, for sure!
He's cheated, deceived and lied to many men 265
Already; he'll go on cheating, again and again.
And yet men travel a very long way to be cheated,
Not knowing how he lies, and thinking this creature
A man so well worth knowing he must not be missed.
And if you're willing to be my audience, 270
This is the horrid tale I mean to present.
     But let me be clear: I'm not attacking religious
Men, not anyone here, or wherever you choose,
Although my story is focused on a priest.
In every group, there must be rascals and thieves, 275
And God forbid that any assemblage of men
Are marred by one man's faults. Let him relent
Alone! Slander of priests is not what I meant:
Correction of wrongs and crime is my intention.
You're hearing this tale, but I'm not talking to you 280
Alone, but many others. Isn't it true
That even among the twelve Apostles of Christ
One was a traitor, focused on wrong, not right?
And why should all the others get the blame,
As guiltless as they were? And to you I'm saying 285
Only this, if you'll hear me: if you have a Judas
In any company or group, take steps at once
To throw him out. That's what I advise:
To stop disaster before it happens is a wise
Procedure. And no one here should be unhappy! 290
And here's the rest of my story, just as it happened.
     A London priest, hired for chanting memorial
Masses, had lived in that city for many years,
Always cheerful to the lady he boarded with,
So wholly ready to be, if he could, of service 295
To her, that she refused his payment for rent,
Or food, or the rest, no matter how much he spent.

So he had a purse all stuffed with silver and gold.
That doesn't matter. Let me return to my former
Lord, and tell how this man, doubly and triply 300
False, succeeded in ruining an innocent priest.

    The cleric-magician came, one day, to the priest's
Home chamber, the place he lived and slept in, beseeching
Him to make a loan of a certain sum
Of gold, which would be repaid when the time had come. 305
"Give me half a pound of gold, just for
Three days, and I will pay you back, for sure,
And if I haven't paid this debt in time,
Go hang me by this wicked neck of mine!"

    The chanter of masses immediately handed it over, 310
And the priestly magician thanked him for the favor,
And left, and on the day assigned, brought
The borrowed money back, and the lender thought
Him splendid, the whole transaction a wonderful thing.

    "Indeed," he said, "what pain can it possibly bring me 315
To lend a man a bit of gold, or whatever
Else I own, when he is careful never
To break the day assigned? To such a man
I cannot refuse a loan. I simply can't."

    "What?" said the crooked priest. "Should I break my word? 320
That is something I could never do.
My loyal word is something I will keep
Until the day I die, and go off creeping
To my grave. God is watching, He's not sleeping:
My word's as certain as holy Church's creed. 325
I'm grateful to God, for he has given me grace
To ensure that what is loaned me is repaid,
And no man ever passed me silver or gold
Who didn't receive it back on time, and in whole.
Now sir," he said, "I'll tell you a little secret, 330
Since you have been so very gracious with me,
And shown me kindness and generosity.
Perhaps I can pay you back in another way,
By teaching you, right now, this very day,
How I have been able to work in alchemy. 335
Listen well, for I think you soon will see

You've made yourself a master before I go."
"Yes," said the priest, "good sir, and will you so?
Indeed! Proceed, I beg you heartily."
"At your command, sir, I say to you most truly,"   340
Declared the magician, "or else may God forbid me!"
Lord, how this thief advanced himself as he pleased!
How true it is that service offered as this was
Stinks—as the very old saying goes. And I
Will verify it in this magician, the root   345
Of treachery, who sucked out others' blood—
His heart was every bit that devil-like—
And made himself happy, bringing others to ruin.
God save us from all such lying men as him!
The priest had no idea with whom he was dealing;   350
Imminent harm was not at all his feeling.
O foolish priest! O simple innocent!
Unseeing eyes are blinded by savage men!
You've lost God's grace, your mind is thick as stone,
You have no sense of what is going on,   355
Or what this slyest of foxes will do to you!
His clever tricks will pull you down to ruin.
In short, to underline your sad confusion,
Unhappy man, I'll come to my tale's conclusion
And try, as hard as I can, to show your delusion,   360
Your lack of brain, your utterly silly folly,
And also the total wickedness of this wretch—
At least, so far as my own mind can stretch.
This lying priest was my lord, you may be thinking?
Our Host, in truth, it must be some other being,   365
A different man, a better man, not he
Who displayed a hundredfold more subtlety,
Who betrayed the innocent with his clever hands—
For as I tell this, I find I cannot stand him.
Whenever I speak of how he cheated and lied,   370
My face grows hot, my cheeks go red, and my eyes,
So terribly red they almost seem to glow.
I have no redness left in my skin, I know,
And yet it happens. The metallic fumes I've inhaled
Have siphoned away my color. You've heard that tale   375

Before. I'm wasted away like a dried-out stick.
But now, take heed of this traitor's wickedness!
    "Good sir," he said to the priest, "let your servant go
And fetch quicksilver. We'll need it as we work.
And let him bring two ounces, or maybe three,   380
And when he's back, oh my! Then you'll see
A wondrous thing you've never thought or seen."
    "Sir," said the priest, "it will be done indeed."
He ordered his servant to quickly do the deed.
The servant was more than ready to go and fetch it,   385
And hurried out, and returned, bearing this wretched
Stuff, three ounces he had gone and bought,
Exactly as ordered, and gave the traitor what he sought.
The mercury was set down on the floor,
And then the magician ordered coal to be brought,   390
So he could proceed with what he planned to do.
    Once the coals were there, and ready to go,
The magician produced a half-size crucible, small
But effective, out of a pocket somewhere, and called on
The priest to use it. "This instrument, held   395
In my hand, take it in yours. Then take an ounce
Of this quicksilver, and then, by Christ, announce
The birth of your career in alchemy.
By God, there haven't been a lot of men
To whom I've shown this much of how I work!   400
For what you will see, and learn by experience,
For I will change, by means of my secret science,
This substance in the crucible—you put it
There yourself!—to silver just as fine
As anything in your purse, or any in mine,   405
Or anywhere, holding its shape and able
To be hammered hard. If not, you may, if you like,
Order me out of here, call me unfit
To appear in public. I have a powder here—
It cost me, let me tell you, very dear!—   410
And this will do the trick, for I designed it
So, and I have similar things in mind.
Send away your servant, let him stay out,
Then shut the door, and we will go about

Our secret business. No one ought to see us,   415
Or steal away our secret alchemy."
    Everything he asked, of course, was done.
It took a minute, and then the servant was gone.
His master quickly closed the door, and locked it,
And they began to perform their operation.   420
    The priest did everything that he was bidden,
Setting the precious crucible in the middle
Of the fire, and blowing on the coals, and puffing
Hard. And then the magician threw some stuff
In the crucible—whatever junk it was,   425
Powdered glass, or chalk, it makes no difference,
Its only purpose was the priest's deception—
And told the priest that now it was time to heap
The coals around the crucible, to keep
The fire hot enough to do what was needed.   430
"You see," this deceiver said, "in token of my love
For you, I carefully leave the final proof
For you to accomplish. You with your own two hands
Will fully perform each of the steps of this task.
You yourself control the operation."   435
    "My many thanks," said the priest, who glowed with elation,
And busied himself, heaping the silly coals.
And while he was doing this, that lying wretch,
That traitorous priest—O let the foul fiend fetch him!—
Slipped from under his shirt a beechwood coal,   440
In which most cleverly he'd drilled a hole,
Which then he'd filled with an ounce of silver filings,
And tightly closed the hole with a wad of wax.
Please understand, these are the sober facts
Of how he worked. Preparing these devices   445
Ahead of time, he brought them with him, devising
Ways of taking them out of hiding when the fool
To be cheated was being distracted, not as a rule
A difficult matter. Skinning such silly rabbits
Was easy enough, once you knew their habits,   450
And he was a thief with years and years of practice:
It makes me gloomy, telling his wicked tactics,
I'd love to smash his lies to little bits,

If only I knew how. But he's here, he's there,
He changes so fast he seems to be everywhere! 455
  But pay attention, gentlemen, for the love
Of God! He took the charcoal I mentioned, above,
And carried it closed in his hand, and as the priest
Was worrying over the coals, as I told you, briefly,
Before, this magic-maker said, "No, no, 460
You aren't doing it right. I'm sorry, it's all
Quite wrong. But I can fix it, I've done this before,
God knows. But my, how hard you're sweating, my friend!
You're truly heated. I have a cloth; accept it,
Please, and let it help you wipe the wet 465
Away." And while the priest, most gladly, dried
His face, this treacherous thief moved him aside
And taking his place, bent and quietly placed
His charcoal right in the middle, set his face
And blew like the wind, maintaining this rapid pace 470
Until the entire fire leapt and flamed.
  "Let's have a drink," this false magician suggested.
"It all goes well, everything's for the best.
Sit down, and let's be merry while we wait."
Meanwhile, his beechwood coal grew burning hot, 475
The wax was melted, and all the silver poured out
And trickled down to the bottom, as of course
It had to, being where and what it was,
Neatly set at the top, in the fire's middle.
But this, to the innocent priest, was all a riddle! 480
All the coals were alike, as far as he knew,
And how could he know the things a priest will do
To another priest, or anyone else, for gold
And silver? And seeing the job had been well handled,
The magician said, "Rise up, good priest, and stand 485
By me. Now since I know you have no mold
For casting silver in, let's sally forth
And find ourselves a chunk of good chalk stone,
And I will turn it to the shape and form
We need, if the stone is right and I'm not wrong. 490
Bring with you, too, a bowl or pan of water,
And we will use these tools to see a better

Thing than you expected. And I'll go too,
So I will not be alone with this, and you
Will have no reason for doubt, while you are absent.   495
This way, in truth, I'll never be out of your presence,
Going with you, first out, then in again."
They opened the chamber door, to put it plainly,
Then shut it, careful to take the key away.
They did their business, returning without delay.   500
Why should I stretch this out, the whole long day?
He took the chalkstone, quickly gave it the shape
Of an ingot mold—and here's how he achieved it.

　　He quietly shook his sleeve, and a smallish piece
Of silver dropped in his hand, exactly an ounce,   505
Hidden so well that no one could see it. Not frowning
Or laughing—giving no indication at all—
He quickly formed his piece of stone as a mould
Exactly the length and breadth of his silver, then hid it
Again; the priest, of course, never noticed.   510
And then he removed the silver he'd put in the crucible,
Fitted it into the mould and shaped it like new,
And threw it into the pan of water they'd brought,
And then invited the priest to take it out.
"See what's in there, put in your hand and grope.   515
Silver is what you're going to find, I hope.
What, the devil in hell! What else should it be?
A slice of silver is silver, according to me!"
At last the magician reached with his own hand,
And took out an ounce of silver, looking brand new   520
And shining fine. The priest didn't know what to do.
"God's blessings, as well as his mother's, fall on you,"
He said, shaking with joy in every vein,
"As well as all the saints, my friend and fellow
Priest. If there are maledictions, they're welcome,   525
Too! I tell you, teach me how this is done,
This noble craft of yours, and its subtleties,
And I am yours forever, whatever I be."

　　The alchemist said, "I'd like to try again,
A second time, so you can watch and see   530
The finer details of what we've done. You'll be

An expert, soon, and able to play this game
When I am somewhere else, and far away.
We'll take another ounce of quicksilver, here,
And see if you can do with that, perhaps,   535
What you did with the other—and not by mere chance."

    The priest was just as busy, this time, too,
Obeying every command. The fire he blew
As fast and hard as he could, not saving his breath,
Hoping to do as well, for best is best!   540
Meanwhile, this cursed magician was setting the stage.
He took up a hollow stick—you need to pay
Attention to this!—in the hollow end of which
He put an ounce of silver, not even a small bit
More, and fine as before, and then he sealed them,   545
Again, with wax, to hold them tightly concealed.
And while the priest was busily puffing and blowing,
The magician, once again, loudly informed him
That he was pouring in powder, just as before—
I hope the devil flays him out of his skin,   550
By God, for every single thing he did
Was a lie—and then he worked his wooden stick,
Filled in advance, as you well know, to stir
The coals and make them burn with vigor, faster
And hotter, until the wax—of course!—melted   555
And, just as every man who's not a fool
Could tell you, the molten silver poured right down,
And the lying rascal knew where it could be found.

    And, gentlemen, as you've been warned before,
The innocent, bedazzled priest was once more   560
Cheated. He was so thrilled I cannot express
His happiness, his joy at being so blessed,
And told the cleric-magician what he possessed,
Including himself, would now belong to his guest.
"I may be poor," said the traitor, "but you'll soon find   565
I know what I'm doing, and I have more in mind.
Tell me, can copper be had in this place?" said he.

    "Yes," said the priest, "I know quite well it can be."
"Then go and buy us some, as quick as you're able.
Go on, good sir: put copper right on this table!"   570

The priest went hurrying out (you cannot believe
His scurrying!), and was back as swift as a running thief.
The traitor took the copper, broke off a piece,
Then trimmed it down to exactly a single ounce.
    Truly, my simple tongue cannot pronounce,   575
Being the simple voice of my ignorant mind,
All the duplicities that we could find
In this man! Strangers always thought him friendly,
But in his work, and his heart, he was a fiend.
How tiresome it seems, re-telling his falseness,   580
But, dulling or not, it has to be expressed,
So other men can somehow be prepared
For men like him. That's all I care about.
    The crucible received an ounce of copper,
And swift as the devil's tale he had it set   585
On the fire, and threw in powder, and the priest was blowing,
Stooping over, just as he had before—
And everything was just a nasty joke.
One priest swindling another, tied and yoked!
And this time it was copper he shaped in the mold,   590
Then dropped into the bubbling pan of water,
And, later, when the magician again went fishing
In the pan, his sleeve contained (for he was missing
No tricks, believe me!) an ounce of powdered silver,
Slipped, on the sly, in the water, where it went sinking   595
Down to the bottom, and bubbles bounced it about.
But at the same time, this rascal was taking out
The copper ingot, and the priest knew nothing about it—
Then, suddenly, and very nearly shouting,
The magician reached over and grasped the priest's loose clothing: 600
"Stoop down, by God! You've missed the thing once more!
Give me a hand, as I helped you before.
Stick in a paw and see, by God, what's there!"
    The silver ingot, of course, was what was there.
The priest removed it, and said: "Let us now go,   605
With these three ingots, which you and I have wrought,
And show them to some goldsmith, to check their worth.
For by my faith, I'm willing to wager my shirt
That all of these are silver, fine and good,

And the smith will quickly say so, as of course he should."   610
    So off they went to the goldsmith's shop, where
The smith put all three ingots into the fire,
And then went hammering hard, and quickly declared
That these were silver, and he was ready to swear it.
    Who can have been more pleased than this besotted   615
Priest? No nightingale could welcome a day,
In the merry, sunny, glorious season of May,
And never gladder to sing his celebration.
No lady took more pleasure in caroling,
Or speaking graceful words on love and ladies,   620
No knight in arms performed courageous deeds
To serve his lady love, and also his needs,
Than did our priest, seeing this tattered craft.
And so he spoke to his fellow, immediately after:
"For the love of God, who died for all of us,   625
And as I may deserve it, from someone so gracious
As you, how much does this wonderful recipe cost?"
    "By our lady," the other replied, "a lot.
Let me warn you: except for me, and one friar,
No one else in England could even try it."   630
    "No matter," said the priest. "For God in heaven's sake,
Tell me, I beg you, how much this purchase will take?"
    "Well," said the other, "I warned you. It will be dear.
But since you want a price, you'll have one here:
Forty pounds in gold. That's that. Am I clear?   635
Except for the friendly loans you gave me, before,
Let me assure you, you would pay much more."
    Without a word, the priest immediately sought out
Forty fat and golden coins, and brought them
To this lying swindler, rewarding him for his fraud.   640
What he had done to earn them was—nothing at all!
    "Sir priest," he said, "I want no publicity
For my craft. I want it kept, as it's been, a secret.
So as you love me, let's have it stay that way.
By God, if everyone knew the game I play,   645
They'd hate me in their hearts, for jealousy,
And also detest my learning in alchemy.
I'd end up dead—and that's as clear as daylight."

"God forbid!" said the priest. "What are you saying?
I'd rather lose whatever I may own, 650
And my old heart would have to be of stone,
Making sure that you be treated that way."
    "And your good will," said the liar, "is clearer than daylight,
For you have your proof. And now I wish you good day."
He turned and left the priest, who never again 655
Saw him. Be sure, however, that when this fool
Attempted the trick, following the rules
His recipe taught him—poof! There'd be nothing in hand,
So totally deceived had he been. The grandest
Truths remain, when others may be toppling: 660
Thieving and lying are deadly, but who can stop them?
    Reflect, good gentlemen, that in every estate
Gold and men together cause debate
That runs like wind or water, without an end.
Alchemy and mathematics should be sent 665
To the devil, from whom they came—for what could cause
Such woe and troubles, disasters, deaths, and wars,
Except these two deceiving, devilish crafts?
When scholars speak of such things, it's better to laugh,
So mist-filled, dully stupid are all their words 670
(And who can understand their slippery terms?),
That no one, here and now, can read their pages,
Which sound to us like magpies making outrageous
Noise, or else, if we try to decipher and learn them,
There's no result, we'd do as well if we burned them. 675
Learning isn't worth the effort, don't try it.
You'll lose whatever you have. Just smile and go by it.
    There's so much profit in this pleasant game,
It turns our merriment to grief and shame,
Emptying out the heaviest of purses, 680
And making those who play it earn the curses
Of everyone who lent them goods or gold.
O Lord, how shameful! Having once been scalded,
Can't they turn and run from the fire's heat?
You who indulge, O why, O why can't you flee it, 685
Before it's too late? Better late than never,
And "never" will be your reward, alas, every

Time you try. Hunt as hard as you like,
It's not there. O, you're bold as Bayard the Blind,
A horse without fear, who never could see his danger;   690
Colliding with boulders and rocks was just as courageous,
For him, as ambling quietly down the road.
Your backs will be broken, hefting up that load.
And if, like Bayard, your eyes don't see quite right,
You'd better make sure your mind preserves its sight.   695
For you can stand and goggle, steadily stare
At an alchemist's fire, you'll never see anything there
But waste from what you've worked and fought to acquire.
If you want to keep it, take it out of the fire.
Have nothing more to do with that art, I mean,   700
For it will wipe your assets away, quite clean.
But, quickly now, I'll tell you what is written
In philosophical books, modern and ancient.
    Arnaldus de Villanova, a French physician
And alchemist, too, took the time to mention,   705
Setting us straight from the start, and O how truly!
"No one can change a pan of mercury
Without the help of our precious friend, good sulphur."
Hérmes Trísmegéstus, long before—
Since he was the very first of philosophy's fathers—   710
Explained that a dragon is born immune from death,
Unless you use his brother to slay him. He meant,
Of course, the dragon "mercury," and by
"His brother," he meant good sulphur, extracted, high
And low, by combining gold and silver—Sol,   715
The sun, being gold, with Luna, the moon, as silver.
"And so," he said—the proverb is worth your attention—
"Let no man ever try to test this convention
Unless he's studied, and very deeply grasped,
The questions philosophers broach, as well as their answers.   720
Anyone less who tries, is ignorant
And a fool," he said, "for this is what a man
Must know, to hold the secret of secrets in his hand."
    Once a disciple of Plato was rash enough
To ask his master about this secret substance   725
(*Seniorus Zadith*, a treatise of alchemy,

Records this), and very rash indeed was he:
"Tell me the name," he dared, "of the secret stone."
    And Plato gave him his answer, gave it at once:
"Start with the stone men label Thitáriós."   730
    "And which is that?" "They call it Mágnasía,"
Said Plato. "But sir," the disciple said, "what's this?
You seem to explain one unknown by another."
    "Magnasia is a liquid made, young brother,"
Said Plato, "of a combination of elements."   735
    "Tell me the basic facts, good sir, that you meant
To convey, I'm sure," the baffled disciple said.
    "O no, no." And Plato shook his head.
"I cannot. Those who have this knowledge are sworn
Never to tell its truths to any man born,   740
Or set its nature down on any pages.
For this is a secret beloved by Christ, for ages,
So dear to him, and beloved, that he wants it known
Only to those who have it, by his grace bestowed,
Employed by him as a tool in the sacred defense   745
Of those he prefers. This is the absolute end."
    So I, too, will conclude, since God in heaven
Expressly wishes alchemy's secrets unknown,
No man, of himself, can ever find this stone.
My own advice would be: leave it alone.   750
A man who turns his God to an adversary,
Trying to do what God prefers untried,
Will surely never succeed, will never thrive,
No matter how many years he remains alive.
And now I stop. I've reached the end of my tale   755
May God help every good man, whatever his ailment!

THE PROVISIONER'S PROLOGUE

Haven't you heard about the little town
Known in England as Bobbing-up-and-down,
At the edge of the forest of Blee, near Canterbury?
There our Host began to joke and play,
And said, "Gentlemen! Look, that horse behind us   5
Is lost in the muck. Don't tell me we can't find us
Some fellow who, either for prayer or else for payment,
Will amble back and get our friend awake?
He wouldn't be hard to steal from, meeting a thief.
He's bobbing up and down, he's fast asleep,   10
He'll fall! Is that our unlucky Cook from London?
Get him up here. He knows what must be done, then:
He'll have to tell a tale, and by my faith
He will, although it won't be worth a hay straw!
Wake up, you Cook!" he said. "God give you sorrow!   15
What's wrong with you, sleeping in the morning?
Have you had fleas all night—or are you drunk?
Or is it some whore who's had you up and pumping
So hard that, even now, your head is slumping?"

    The Cook, who was ghostly pale, with no color at all,   20
Replied to the Host: "Such heaviness has fallen
On me, by God, who still, I hope, will bless me,
That—who knows why?—I'd rather I were resting
Than drinking London wine and walking its streets."

    The Provisioner said: "If this idea will please you,   25
Sir Cook, and no one else will be displeased,
Of those who ride with us, in this company,

And our Host will oblige me, for his courtesy,
For now, at least, you'll be excused from your tale.
To tell the truth, your face is extremely pale, 30
Your eyes are watery and weak, I think,
And I know for sure your breath is sour and stinking.
In short, it's clear you are not well, today.
You cannot expect that I will explain it away.
Just look how he yawns! O this drunken fellow! 35
His mouth is open wide enough to swallow
Us all! Now close your mouth, my man, by your kin!
The devil from hell has gotten his foot therein!
Your cursed breath will have us all infected.
Ah, stinking swine! Have you no self-respect? 40
Now, gentlemen, just see this merry man.
O happy fellow, anxious to dance the can-can.
I see your limbs are fit and ready for prancing!
This is the time to jump and scratch like an ape."

    The Cook got angry at this, but found no words 45
He could say, though he tried, so he fixed his eyes and turned
His head, then suddenly he fell to the ground
And would have stayed there, except that others climbed down
And though it was not easy, they somehow got him
Back on his horse. He flopped and gaped, this rotting 50
Ghost of a cook, who should have stuck to his ladle.
He certainly had not stuck to his slippery saddle.
Shoving and pulling for all they were worth, they were able
To sit him upright, though he kept on swaying:
A drunken man, when you lift him, seems to weigh 55
A ton or more. The Host had this to say:
    "Since alcohol has taken domination
Over this man, I swear, by my salvation,
He'd likely tell a lewd and ignorant tale.
And whether he's drunk with wine, or fresh new ale, 60
His words appear to come straight from his nose,
And he's been snorting as if he had a cold.
    "Also, there's more than enough that has to be done
To keep himself and his horse out of the mud,
And if he topples off his horse again, 65
We'll all have more to do, we sober men,

Lifting his sodden, heavy self, like a corpse.
Provisioner, you tell a tale, of course!
  "And still, you know, your words were not too smart,
Scolding him so openly and harsh.   70
Some other day, who knows? he'll turn on you,
And take revenge, as he will think his due.
I mean, he'll edge around the work you do,
Finding fault with some of your accounting,
Which wouldn't be fun—indeed, which might be daunting." 75
  "No," the Provisioner said, "that would be bad.
That could be a problem I would rather not have.
In fact, I'd rather pay the hire for his horse
Than have to fight with him, perhaps in court.
Truly, I should not anger this drunken cook!   80
—Although I spoke in jest, a sort of joke—
I'll tell you what. I have a flask of wine,
Pressed from an excellent grape, properly ripe,
And I'll turn this thing around, in just a minute.
I'll offer him the flask, and we'll drink on it.   85
I'll bet my life he'll take a swig, and like it."
  And just as he said, to tell it as it happened,
The Cook accepted, drinking deep from the flask—
He couldn't have been dry, he'd drunk enough before—
And then returned to its owner this pleasant horn,   90
Saying, as well as words took shape in his mouth,
That this was a welcome gift, and broke his drought.
  The Host began to laugh, and wondrously loud,
Saying, "Now I can see how necessary
It is for travelers to always carry   95
Good drinks, for they turn rancor, and also discomfort,
To concord and even love, and that's what they're for.
  "O Bacchus, god of drinking, blessed be your name,
Easily subduing earnest into game!
Our worship and thanks to your great deity!   100
And on that subject, you'll get no more from me.
Tell on your tale, Provisioner, I pray you."
  "Well sir," he said, "now listen to what I say."

The Provisioner's Tale

When Phoebus, now Apollo, was living on
This earth, as ancient books have often mentioned,
He was the merriest of bachelors
The world had seen, and also the best of its archers.
He killed great Python, the serpent, where he lay   5
Sleeping in the sunshine, one fine day,
Performing many other noble deeds
As well, with his bow, as everyone may read.
      He played most beautifully on any instrument,
And sang so that it soothed the listener's senses   10
To hear the sound of so clear a voice, so sweet.
And surely, Ámphión, the king of Thebes,
Whose singing helped him build the wall of his city,
Could never make music even half as pretty.
And all in all he was the most handsome man   15
Who ever walked the earth, or ever can.
Why should that shining face need me to describe it?
Handsomeness like his you'll never find
Again—the epítomé of graciousness
And honor, the perfect height of worthiness.   20
      This Phoebus, of living knights the brightest flower,
Open-handed, chiválrous, lived happy hours,
Displaying, as a sign of his victory
Against the Python (this is told by the story),
Wherever he went or rode, he carried a bow.   25
      Now in his house, this Phoebus kept a crow,
Caged and fed by his own hand, every day,

And taught it to speak, as men have taught the jay.
This crow was white as any snow-white swan,
And imitated the speech of every man   30
He heard, telling any sort of tale.
And nowhere in the world could a nightingale
Sing so wonderfully merry, fantastically well—
Better a hundred thousand times, I'll tell you!

    Now Phoebus also had in his house a wife,   35
A woman he loved, in truth, more than his life,
Diligent both night and day to please her,
And show his love in ways that might have appeased her—
For there was a problem, a matter of some impact:
He was jealous, needing to keep her apart, and intact,   40
But only for himself, as most men do,
Although it never works, and that's the truth.
A wife who's good, and honest in thought and deed,
Should not be shut away, with lock and key.
And if she's somewhat perverse, disposed to be loose,   45
The husband's trying in vain, in simple truth,
Indeed, a foolish labor by a fool,
Trying to isolate and guard their wives.
Ancient books have warned us, all our lives!

    And so, back to my story, as I first began.   50
This worthy Phoebus was doing all one can
To please a woman, believing that, this way,
He guaranteed his manhood, night and day,
And no one else could ever come and replace him.
But no man ever succeeds in closing in   55
A being meant by God and eternal nature
To live its life as a freely loving creature.

    Take any bird, and set it in a cage,
Make it a friend, don't treat it like a stranger,
Feed it tenderly with meat and drink   60
And all the dainty tidbits you can think of,
Treat it artfully, as well as you may,
And though its golden cage will shine so gaily,
The bird would rather (twenty thousand fold!)
Live in a forest, however brutal and cold,   65
Eating worms and other such wretchedness.

A bird will always do his best to escape
From your cage, he'll never give up, he'll try all ways
He knows to live in freedom, night and day.
  Go take a cat, and feed him well with milk   70
And tender meat, give him a bed of silk,
But once he sees a mouse go by the wall
He abandons, at once, milk and meat and all,
And every dainty you keep for him in your house!
Hear me: desire will always dominate,   75
Discretion is always broken by appetite.
  She-wolves, too, are born with a villainous side:
A she-wolf's happy with the crudest male she can find,
When she's grown anxious to have herself a mate.
Other wolves may shun him, if they like; she'll take him.   80
  All of these examples deal with men
Actively unfaithful, none with women.
Men are born with a gift for lechery
With females of a baser kind than she—
So fair, so true—who happens to be his wife.   85
Lust is addicted to novelty. This life
Of ours provides clear evidence that virtue
Pales, in time, and men will change. It's true.
  Now Phoebus, who never expected to be beguiled,
Was shocked by deceit, for all his winning smiles.   90
She had another man, of a lower kind
And little reputation, who couldn't compare
With her husband, Phoebus. Do you think the lady cared?
One upper, one lower, is the usual situation,
Leading to trouble and dangerous irritation.   95
  As it happened, when Phoebus made himself absent
The lady wasted no time, but quickly sent
For her sweetheart. Her sweetheart? This is vulgar speech,
For which I hope you'll forgive me, I beseech you.
  Wise old Plato has said (you may have read it)   100
That words should truly match and express the deed.
If men are expected to properly tell a tale,
Their words must be tied to their story, like shells to snails.
I happen to be a rough, crude man, myself,
And I see no serious, honest difference   105

Between a wife with an ancient family tree,
If she is inclined, in fact, to harlotry,
And some nameless, poverty-stricken wench, but this—
Assuming they both are guilty of going amiss—
Except that the noble lady, of birth above 110
The filly, can still possess herself of a lover,
And the poor girl, born to lower, vulgar parts,
Has to be called a wench, or at best a sweetheart.
And let me remind you, O, my own dear brother,
Each man lies with a woman like any other. 115
      Just as a vulgar bandit, who becomes a tyrant,
Compared to an outlaw, or a thief who's on the run,
Is no comparison at all, but the same,
The only difference is simply the name.
This was told to Alexander the Great. 120
A tyrant's possessed of higher power and might;
With armies to back him, he can kill as he likes,
Burn houses and homes, level a town to the ground.
That's how he earns the title of General.
The outlaw, however, has many fewer men 125
Around him, cannot put cities down on their knees,
And so men call him an outlaw, or even a thief.
But since I'm not a scholar of ancient texts
I'll stop at this, and leave off all the rest.
Let me return to my tale, as I have started it. 130
When Phoebus's wife had notified her sweetheart,
They came together with a lust of very high voltage.
      The snow-white crow, hanging up in his cage,
Watched her at work, but never said a word.
But when he saw Phoebus, triumphant household lord, 135
Come home, the bird sang, "Cookoo! Cookoo! Cookoo!"
      "My bird!" said Phoebus. "Why are you singing that tune?
You used to make music, day after day, so happy
And long that my heart and soul would always be gladdened.
What's happened now? What kind of song is this?" 140
      "By God!' said the crow. "I never sing amiss.
Phoebus," he said, "despite your worthiness,
Despite your body's beauty, and your courtesy,
For all the music you make, and your lovely singing,

For all your watching and spying, you've still been hoodwinked   145
By a man with no reputation, compared to you
A bug, a gnat, with none of the reverence due
To a man of glorious fame, a man like you.
I saw them in bed, going at it hard."
    Do you need to hear more? All the rest was told   150
By the crow, in the strongest terms, with words as bold
As you'll ever hear, the details of all they did,
And how, and when. Thus Phoebus was duly defiled.
He'd seen this before, said the bird, with his very own eyes.
    Phoebus stalked off, turning away in anger,   155
Thinking his heart would break. But the only danger
Was hers. He bent his bow, mounted a dart,
And in anger shot it straight into her heart.
That is what happened, I cannot pretend it did not.
Grief then drove him to smash his guitar, and his lute,   160
His harp, and every musical thing he owned.
He broke his arrows, he even broke his bow,
And then he turned and spoke to his snow-white crow:
    "Traitor," he said, "who speaks with a scorpion's tongue,
It's you who've turned my peace to this confusion.   165
O God, why was I born? I should have died,
Instead. O gem of women, my dearest wife!
You who were so constant, so perfectly true,
Lying dead, your face so pale of hue—
And innocent, I swear it! I know it's untrue!   170
O rashest of men, what an evil thing to do!
O shaken mind, trembling with restless fury,
Hasty hand, acting as judge and jury!
Mistrustful fellow, full of false suspicion,
Where was your brain, where was your discretion?   175
O men of this world, beware of reckless action!
Believe no tales that have no witnesses.
Don't strike too soon, before there's been confession,
And never strike in anger, seek good advice
Before you execute your loving wife.   180
Alas! How many thousand men have killed
In anger, against their deepest, truest wills.
I ache! I wish it were myself I'd slain!"

He turned to the crow. "O shameful thief!" he said.
"I'll quickly take revenge for your lying tale.   185
You sang for me like a lovely nightingale,
But now, deceitful cheat, your song is gone,
Also your snow-white feathers—every one!—
And never again, so long as you live, will you speak.
In dealing with traitors, this is how men act.   190
You and your offspring forever will now be black,
Sweet songs you'll never again be heard to make,
But raucous, angry cries at storm and rain,
To show that you were the reason she was slain."
Fast and furiously, he jumped on the crow,   195
Pulling out white feathers, every one,
Turning him black, and taking away his song,
And also his speech. Then out the door he slung him,
Straight to the devil, and the devil took him in.
And crows have now been blackened, ever since.   200
        You've heard the story, and now, good sirs, I pray you:
Be careful, hold back on all the things you say.
Tell no man, ever, all the rest of your life
How any man has handled that man's own wife.
He will become your mortal enemy.   205
Old Solomon, and those who always repeat him,
Urge you to watch your tongue. This is their teaching.
But I, as I've said, am not at all a preacher.
And yet my mother taught me, all the same:
        "My son, remember the crow, in God's great name!   210
My son, restrain your tongue and keep your friends.
A wicked tongue is worse than even a fiend:
My son, high holy aid will always protect you
From fiends. Acting out of endless goodness,
God has walled your tongue with teeth and lips,   215
To help you keep close watch on what you speak.
My son, how many times has too much speech
Ruined a man! This is what clerics teach.
But how many men have fallen for saying little?
Only a few, so this should be habitual.   220
Always, my son, hold your tongue in check,
Unless you're honoring God, in deep respect.

The very first virtue, son, if you want to acquire it,
Is hold back your tongue, and learn the value of silence.
My son, great harm is done by flowing, unguarded   225
Speech, when fewer words would be enough.
This has been what I myself was taught.
In torrents of speech, sin can find what it wants.
Would you like to know what a reckless tongue produces?
Exactly what a knife or a sword cuts through—   230
An arm or two, my very dear son—so too,
A tongue can cut a friendship right in two.
A chattering man is one that God finds hateful.
Read Solomon, so wise and honorable;
Read David's Psalms, read ancient Seneca.   235
Say nothing, my son, but shake or nod your head.
Hearing a chatterer speak of dangerous matter,
Pretend to be deaf, ignore his clitter and clatter.
As Belgians say, and repeating it is blessed,
Peace drifts down when you give your tongue a rest.   240
My son, if wicked words are not what you say,
There's little reason to worry, you can't be betrayed.
But once you've said the wrong thing, allow me to say,
You cannot take your saying back again.
Whatever's said is said, and out it breaks,   245
Though you regret it, even find it hateful.
A man is pledged in service to the words he says,
And every tale has debts, which must be paid.
My son, be careful, don't be a bearer of news,
It doesn't matter whether false or true.   250
Wherever you come, with people high or low,
Hold in your tongue, and think about the crow."

The Parson's Prologue

And when, at last, the Provisioner had ended
His tale, the sun, in passing south, had descended
So low that it was barely, to my sight,
Twenty-nine degrees of astral height.
Four o'clock, or so, I had to guess,   5
Seeing my shadow extend, come more, come less,
To eleven feet, assuming I had a length
Of roughly six feet—a handy measurement
And not, I suspect, too badly out of proportion.
This is standard time for the moon's ascension—   10
Really Libra, the zodiac star, I meant—
And we had come, I believe, to the northern end
Of a village, and our Host, by whom we always were led,
And who was leading us now, turned and said:
"My lords, and ladies, gentlemen, and friends,   15
Our telling of tales has almost come to an end,
And I have almost completed, together with you,
Everything we pledged ourselves to do
Except for a single missing thing, a last
And final tale to wind up our affairs.   20
May God be guiding the teller, as he delight us.
        "Sir priest, are you a vicar, substituting
For some other? Or a parson? I pray you, tell us the truth!
Whatever you are, please don't disrupt our game,
For every person but you has told us a tale.   25
Unbuckle, will you, and show us what you have?
Just looking at you, I see some signs of grave

And deep, important matters that you could narrate.
Tell us a fable, please, by the cock's own bones!"
    The Parson gave it back, by God, at once: 30
"Fables aren't what you'll hear from me,
For Paul, the Apostle, writing to Timothy,
Scolds those people who live outside the truth,
Telling fables and other tales that hurt you—
And why should I sow chaff with my own hand?   35
I can sow wheat, and talk of things much grander.
So let me say, if you're inclined to hear
Morality and virtuous, holy matter,
Like the word of Christ, for whom I live in reverence,
And, expecting that, you'll listen to what I dispense,   40
I'll gladly give you the lawful pleasure I can.
Believe me, please, I am a Southern man,
I cannot play with 'rum, ram, ruf,' by letter—
Nor, by God, does rhyming fit me better.
And if you like ideas that wear plain clothes,   45
I'll tell a very happy tale in prose,
To wind up this long trip, and make an end.
I need Lord Jesus, for his grace, to send me
Thought and reason, to show you, on this voyage,
The road to that perfect, glorious pilgrimage   50
We call Jerusalem, but high in heaven.
And if you agree, the question is fully settled
And I'll begin my tale, and afterward, pray,
Tell me what you think. That's all I can say.
    "Still and all, this tale, or meditation,   55
May well, of course, require firm correction
By scholars, for I have little knowledge of texts.
I work with basic meanings, and leave the rest.
So let me repeat my initial protestation:
I'm well prepared for anyone's correction."   60
    We all consented, easily and soon,
For as it seemed to us, it would be good
To finish our journey on some religious theme,
And give this Parson our willing ears, and time.
And so we told our Host to say to the Parson   65
That we were all at one in what he wanted.

The Host then said as follows, and spoke for us all:
"Sir priest, let goodness descend and on you fall!
Tell us," he said, "your words of meditation.
But waste no time, the sun is running down.   70
Be fruitful, and multiply, but in little space,
And may God, surely, shower on you his grace!
Say what you like, and we will gladly hear."
And after those words, the Parson filled our ears.

The Parson's Tale

Thus saith the Lord, Stand ye in the ways, and see, and ask for the old paths, where is the good way, and walk therein, and ye shall find rest for your souls.

—Jeremiah 6:16

Our sweet Lord God of heaven, who wishes no man to perish, but wants all of us to come to the knowledge of him, and to blissful, eternal life, warns us through the words of the prophet Jeremiah, who says: Stand in the roads, and see and ask the old roads (that is, older writings and teachings) which is the good road, then walk in that road, and you will find refreshment for your souls. There are many spiritual pathways that lead men to our Lord Jesus Christ, and to the reign of glory. And among these many ways there is one that is completely noble and wholly appropriate, and which will never fail to any man or woman who, through sin, has wandered from the right and true way to celestial Jerusalem, and this way is called Penitence. And men ought to gladly listen and search out, with all their hearts, just what Penitence is and in how many different ways it can be at work, how many varieties of Penitence there are, and which things are proper and appropriate for Penitence, and which things are not.

Saint Ambrose says that Penitence is man's lamenting his sins, and ought never again do anything which he will later lament. And it has been said, by a learnèd cleric: "Penitence is a man lamenting his sins, and sorrowing for having committed them." Penitence, then, is in certain circumstances a man's full, honest, and sorrowful repentance for his sins. In order to be truthfully repentant, he must begin by lamenting the sins he has committed, and then resolve firmly, in his heart, to confess those sins and do penance for them, and never again do anything for which he would need to lament, and to proceed in the doing of good works, for otherwise his repentance will fail. For as Saint Isidore of Seville says, "he is a jester, and a boaster, and not an honest repentant, who then proceeds to do things he ought to repent." Weeping, without ceasing to be sinful, will not help. Of course, we must hope that whenever a man falls, no matter how often it happens, he may still rise by means of Penitence, if that grace is granted him—but surely, this is a doubtful matter. For, as Saint Gregory says, "he who is heavily burdened with sin can scarcely lift himself out of it." And so those who repent, who cease to sin, and abandon sin before it occurs, can be assured of their salvation by holy church. Even he who sins, but who at the end of his life honestly repents, even he, says holy church, can hope for salvation, through the great mercy of Jesus Christ our Lord, because his repentance is honest and true. But you should take the safer road to heaven.

And now, having told you what Penitence is, you must understand that there are three ways in which Penitence works. The first is what happens if a man is baptized after he has sinned. Saint Augustine says: Unless he is penitent for his former sinful life, he cannot begin the new, honest life. Surely, if he is baptized without being penitent about his former sins, what he receives is only the mark of baptism, but not the grace which accompanies it, the remission of those sins, which can only take place when he has truly repented. Another failure of that grace occurs if, after having been baptized, a man commits deadly sins. And a third failure of that grace occurs when, again after baptism, a man falls into the daily commission of less serious, venial sins. This is why Saint Augustine declares that the penitence of good, humble people is that which takes place each and every day.

Penitence takes three forms, the first being sacred and churchly, the second communal, or social, and the third personal and private. Sacred and churchly penance takes place when, for example, a man is barred from church attendance, during Lent, because he has slaughtered children, or done other similar things. Another instance is a man who has openly sinned, and his sinful reputation has become public knowledge, so that holy church imposes upon him the obligation to do open, public penance. Communal or social penance occurs when a priest sets limits upon social behavior, as for example barring nakedness, or walking barefoot, while going on pilgrimages. Personal and private penance is that which men perform all the time, making private confessions and receiving private penance.

Now you must understand what is absolutely necessary to true, perfect Penitence. It rests upon three things: Contrition in your heart, Confession by your mouth, and the doing of Penance. For as Saint John Christosom declares: "Penitence obliges a man to accept with kindness every punishment laid upon him, with a contrite heart, a clearly expressed confession, and penance, and—in everything he does—with humility." And this will be fruitful penitence in three matters which draw down on us the anger of our Lord Jesus Christ, namely, erotic thoughts, reckless speech, and wicked, sinful deeds.

And standing against these wicked sins is Penitence, which may be compared to a tree, the root of which is contrition, hiding itself in the heart exactly as tree roots are hidden in the earth. Out of this root of contrition grow the branches and leaves of confession, and the fruit of penance. And so Christ says, in his gospel: "Be worthy of the fruit of Penitence," for it is by this fruit that men can know the tree—neither by the root, hidden in men's hearts, nor by the branches and leaves of confession. And so our Lord Jesus Christ says, "By their fruit you must know them." From this root there also springs a seed of grace, which is the very mother of safety and security; this seed is pungent, and it is hot. The grace of this seed springs from God, reminding us of the Day of Judgment and the sorrows and suffering of hell. Solomon says of this that fear of God causes man to cease his sinning. The seed's heat is God's love, and our longing for eternal bliss. This heat draws man's heart to God, and makes him hate his sins. Truly, there is nothing that tastes so good to a baby as the milk he draws from the breast, and nothing disgusts him more than this same milk, if it is mixed with other food. So too the sinful man, in love with his sin, thinks of it as the sweetest thing in the world, but once he seriously loves our Lord Jesus Christ, and longs for eternal bliss, nothing becomes more revolting to him than his sins. Truly, the law of God is the love of God, which is why David, the prophet, says: "I have loved your law, and hated wickedness and hate itself." He who loves God observes his law and his words. This is the same tree which, in spirit form, the prophet Daniel saw, in King Nebuchadnezzar's dream, upon which he counseled the king to do penance. To those who receive it, penance is the tree of life; he who keeps himself truly penitent is blessed, exactly as Solomon said.

Man must understand four things about this Pentitence, or Contrition: namely, what Contrition is; what causes a man to become contrite, and also how he ought to be contrite; and the help which Contrition offers to the soul. As to what Contrition is: it is the true, honest sorrow that a man's heart feels, sin having been acknowledged, sorrow which is accompanied with a sober, determined intention to make a confession, and to do penance, and never to sin again. This sorrow, as Saint Bernard says, "must be heavy, and grievous, intensely sharp and piercing in the heart." This is because, first, man has sinned against his Lord and Creator, and becomes even sharper and more piercing because he has sinned against his Father in Heaven, and then it becomes still sharper and even more piercing, for he has angered his Redeemer, who with his precious blood has freed us from the bonds of sin, and preserved us from the devil's cruelties and the pains of hell.

There are six causes that should move a man to Contrition. First, he must keep his sins in mind, but be careful that this memory is not only unpleasant, but creates in him both great shame and sorrow. For Job says: "Sinful men do things that require confession." And so too says Ezekiel: "You must loathe yourself in your own sight, for all the sins that you have committed." And as God declares in the book of Revelations, "Remember therefore from whence you have fallen, and repent," since before you sinned you were the children of God, and a part of God's kingdom, but because of your sins you have become slaves, and foul, and a part of the devil's realm, hating angels, disgracing holy church, and the very food of the traitorous serpent—eternal coals for the fires of hell, and even more foul and disgusting, for you go on sinning as regularly as the dog who returns and eats his own vomit. And, indeed, you are fouler still, for how long and lovingly you have been a sinner, on account of which you have become putrid in your sin, like a dog rolling in his own dung. And it is thoughts like these which compel a man to feel shame for his sin, giving him no pleasure, just as God says, speaking through the prophet Ezekiel: "You must remember what you have done, and what you have done must displease you." Truly, sins are the roads that lead people to hell.

The second of the six causes that ought to move a man to Contrition is, as Saint Peter says, "He who sins is the slave of sin," and that is a very great slavery. So says the prophet Ezekiel: "I walked sorrowfully, contemptuous of myself." Certainly, a man should scorn sin, and remove himself from such slavery and wickedness. And lo, what does Seneca say about this? "Though I recognize that neither God nor man should have any knowledge of it, I want myself to be scornful of sin." He also says: "I have been born to greater things than being enslaved by my body, or to making my body a slave." Neither man nor woman can make a fouler thing of their body than to deliver it to sin. No matter how foul and worthless a slave or a woman may be, sinning makes them fouler and more worthless still, and yet more deeply enslaved. The higher the height from which a man falls, the more tightly is he enslaved by sin, and the viler and more disgusting to God and to the world. O gracious God, a man desperately needs to be scornful of sin, since starting from freedom, he has enslaved himself by his sin. And therefore Saint Augustine says: "If you scorn your servant, when he has been sinful, then be scornful of yourself when you, too, have committed sin." Consider the standard by which you make your judgment, so you do not befoul yourself. Alas! Those whom God, in his endless goodness, has set in high estate, or to whom he has given intelligence, bodily strength, health, beauty, prosperity, should certainly scorn themselves for being enslaved by sin, since he redeemed them from death with his own heart's blood, and they react so unnaturally to his kindness, reward him so villainously by slaughtering their own souls. O good God, you women of great beauty, remember Solomon's proverb: "Compare a beautiful woman, behaving like a fool with her own body, to a gold ring in a sow's snout." For just as a sow grubs about in dung of every sort, such a woman makes her body grub about in the stinking dung of sin.

The third of the six causes that should move a man to Contrition is fear of the Day of Judgment and the horrible pains of hell. For, as Saint Jerome says, "Every time I remember the Day of Judgment, I tremble, and whether I am eating, or drinking, or doing anything else, it seems to me that I hear the sound of God's final trumpet, calling, 'Rise up, all you dead, and come to judgment.'" O good God, how much a man should fear that judgment, "when all of us," as Saint Paul says, "will be standing before the throne of our Lord Jesus Christ." For he will make this a universal congregation, from which no man will be allowed to be absent. Surely, there will be no excuses, and no excusing. It will not be only our sins which will be judged, but the entire book of our lives, everything we have said and everything we have done, will be open and known. As Saint Bernard says, "No begging will be permitted, nor any tricks or deceptions: we will be judged by every single frivolous word."

And we will be facing a judge who cannot be either deceived or bought off. And why? For, surely, all our thoughts are known to him. Neither prayer nor bribery will turn his attention away from us. Which is why Solomon says, "God's anger will spare no one; no prayer and no bribe will avail." On the Day of Judgment, accordingly, there is absolutely no hope of escape. As Saint Anselm says, "Sinful people will be suffering terrible anguish: the stern angry judge will be seated high above them, and beneath him they will see the horrible pit of hell, open to destroy those who have not acknowledged their sins, which sins have been openly displayed for God and for everyone else to see. On his left side, there will be more devils than we can possibly imagine, to ravage sinful souls, drawing them down to suffer in hell. People's hearts will be pierced by the pangs of conscience, as all about them the entire world is in flames. Where, at that moment, can the sinful man flee, where can he hide? Surely, he cannot hide, he is obliged to come forward and show himself." As Saint Jerome says, "the very earth will cast him out, and the sea, and the air, which will be full of thunder and lightning." Truly, whoever reminds himself of these things would not, I believe, relish his sins, but feel great sorrow because of them, and for fear of the pains of hell. Which is why Job said to God: "Are not my days few? Let them end, and leave me, that I may take comfort a little, before I go from whence I will not return—to the land of darkness and distress and the shadow of death, without any order, and where the light is like darkness."

Here it may be seen that Job prayed for some respite, a little time of delay to weep and bewail his sins, for truly a single day of respite is better than all the treasure of this world. And since a man can clear himself of guilt in this world, by means of penitence, but cannot do so by gold and silver, of course he ought to pray that God give him some respite, to weep and wail for his sins. Certainly, however much sorrow a man may create, starting from the very beginning of the world, is as nothing, compared to the sorrows of hell. As to why Job calls hell the land of darkness, he calls it a "land," or earth, for it is stable and will never fail, and he calls it "dark" because, to he who is in hell, "light" as he has known it does not exist. For, surely, the dark light coming from hell's eternal fire must be painful to those who are forced to experience it, for it is by that light that the devils who torment him are able to see him. "The land of darkness and the shadow of death" refers to the miserable sins that a wretched man in hell has committed, which conceal from him, now, God's face, for without question the sight of God requires eternal life in heaven. "The darkness of death" means the very sins the man has committed, which blocks the sight of God, just as a dark cloud blocks us from the sun. It is "the land of distress" because there are three ways in which men in this world can fail, there being three ways in which men can prosper in our present life: honor, pleasure, and riches. Instead of honor, what they have in hell are shame and confusion: you know very well that we call "honor" the reverence a man shows for another man, but there is neither honor nor reverence in hell. Surely, in hell a king will receive no more reverence than a common rascal. Accordingly, God tells us, by means of the prophet Jeremiah, "Those who honor me, I will honor, and those who despise me will be despised in turn." Honor is also known as "great lordship," but in hell there will be no servants; injury and torment will be universal. Honor is also known as "great dignity and nobility," but in hell everyone will be trodden down by devils. God has said that "the horrible devils will walk to and fro, upon the heads of the damned." And, indeed, the higher their estate in this present life, the more shall they be beaten down, reduced and defouled, in hell. Instead of the riches of this world, they are forced to endure the distress of poverty, which poverty consists of four aspects: the replacement of treasure, as to which David says that "Rich people who embraced and linked themselves, with all their heart, to the treasures of this world, must now sleep the sleep of death, and in their hands there will be nothing of all their treasure." Further, the misery of hell will also involve the absence of food and drink, for God has said, through Moses: "They shall be burned and wasted with hunger, and devoured by the birds of hell, and dragon gall must be their drink, and dragon venom what they eat." And still more: their distress must be the lack of clothing, for they must be naked, clothed only in the fire which burns them, as well as by other filth; so too must they be naked of soul, devoid of all virtues, which are the soul's true clothing. Where then will be their bright robes, and their soft sheets, and their fine-textured shirts? Lo, God says of them, by the words of the prophet Isaiah, "they will lie upon beds of moth-scatterings, and their blankets will be the serpents of hell." And in addition, their misery will be the lack of friends, for he is not poor who has friends, but in hell there will be no friends, for neither God nor any creature will be their friends, and each of them shall hate all the others with deadly passion. "The sons and daughters will rebel against the fathers and mothers, and cousins against cousins, and they will scold and scorn each other both by day and by night," as God says by the prophet Micah. And their loving children, who once loved each other so sensually, when they had their bodies, would now devour each other, were they able to. Indeed, how could they love one another, in the midst of hell's pains, when in the prosperity of this life they had hated one another? For you must understand that their sensual love was in fact deadly hate, as the prophet David says: "He who loves wickedness hates his own soul." And, certainly, he who hates his own soul cannot love any other man. Accordingly, there is neither soul nor friendship in hell, but only still more sensuality among members of the same family, still more cursing of one another, still more scorn and bitterness, and still more deadly hate. And in addition, there will be a total lack of all pleasures, for surely pleasures come to us through the five appetites (sight, hearing, smelling, tasting, and touching). But sight, in hell, shall be full of smoke and darkness, and therefore full of tears, because what they hear shall be full of moaning and the grinding of teeth, as Jesus Christ has said. Their nostrils shall be full of stink and stench, and as Isaiah the prophet says, "what they taste will be bitter gall," and as for touching, their bodies will be covered with "fire that never is quenched, and with serpents that never die." Nor can they believe that their pain can kill them and allow them to escape, so they will fully understand Job's words, when he speaks of them as being "like the shadow of death." Now a shadow certainly looks like the thing that causes it to be seen, but it is not the same as that of which it is simply a shadow. So too the pain of hell: it is like death's terrible anguish, because it is everlasting pain, and though they may think they will die of it, they cannot. As Saint Gregory says, the occupants of hell can be compared to "wretched captives who experience death without ever dying, who experience an end that never ends, an emptiness that is never emptied. For them, death will always be alive, and their ending will forevermore be beginning." As Saint John the Evangelist says: "They will chase after death, but they will never find him, and they will desire death, and death will flee from them." And, as Job says, in hell there is no order. It is true, indeed, that God created everything, each in its right order and nothing without order, all things numbered and in their place, but those who are damned and in hell have no order, nor do they find order in anyone or anything else. The earth will never bear fruit for them. For as the prophet David says, "For them, God will destroy the fruit of the earth, and water shall give them no moisture, air shall not refresh them, and fire will not show them light." For, as Saint Basil says: "The burning fire of this world will be given to those damned to hell, but its light and clarity shall be given to his children, in heaven," just as a good man gives meat to his children and bones to his dogs. Having no hope for escape, as Saint Job says, for them "horror and grisly fear will be endless." Horror always stems from harm which we are afraid will come to us, but this fear will forever dwell in the hearts of the damned. And so they have no hope, for seven reasons. First, because God, their judge, will extend no mercy to them, nor can they appease him through appeal to any of his saints, nor can they ransom themselves, like captives in this world, nor do they have a voice with which to speak to him, nor can they flee from their pain, nor do they have in themselves any goodness which they can display, in order to deliver themselves from pain. And so Solomon says: "When a wicked man dies, he can have no hope of escaping from his pain." Anyone who properly understands these pains, and understands, too, that he has deserved them, for his sins, surely he should be more disposed to sigh and weep than to sing and dance. Because, as Solomon says, "Whoever knows enough to understand the pain commanded for sinners, ought to know enough to repent." "This is knowledge," says Saint Augustine, "to cause a man to moan and lament in his heart."

The fourth reason for a man to feel contrition is his sorrow and regret for all the good he did not do, when he was here on earth, and also all the good he has lost—truly, either good works performed before he fell into deadly sin, or else the good works that he performed, even while lying in sin. But, clearly, good works before a man falls into sin are killed, rendered powerless, dulled by his frequent sinning. Good works that he performed while lying in sin, as far as eternal life in heaven may be concerned, are utterly dead. Only honest penitence can revivify such goodness. And so God says, through the mouth of Ezekiel: "If a righteous man turns away from righteousness, and commits sin, shall he live?" No, there will be no memory of his good works, once he has died in sin. As Saint Gregory says, about this matter: "What we most of all need to understand is this: when we commit deadly sin, it is especially intended to make us think of the good works which, earlier, we had performed." Not that there is any direct relationship between the deadly sin, as we commit it, and good works we have done before; mere memory of good works will not earn us eternal life in heaven. But nevertheless, good works can be returned to life, and can enliven us, and help us toward the road to eternal life in heaven, if we are contrite. However, good works done by men actively engaged in deadly sin cannot be requickened, just as something which was never in fact alive cannot be made alive once more—nor can they help us to attain eternal life in heaven, or modify the pains of hell, or to acquire riches. God may still make use of them to illuminate the sinful man's heart, leading him to repentance, and they can also reduce the power over the sinful man's soul that his sins have given to the devil. Thus our gracious Lord Jesus Christ intends that no good work will be entirely lost; some good may well come of it. Therefore, a man who has never done any good works may well sing, in the words of a new French song, "*J'ai tout perdu mon temps et mon labour,* I have completely lost both my time and my labor." There is no doubt that sin deprives a man of both natural goodness and the goodness of heavenly grace. Indeed, the grace of the Holy Ghost flames up like fire, and dies down just as quickly, for a fire fails when it has finished burning, and grace fails when a man no longer seeks to obtain it. Thus, the sinful man loses the goodness of glory, which is promised only to good men who work to attain to it. Owing God for his life, so long as he has lived or will live it, a man may well be sorry that he has no goodness with which to repay his debt to God. You may trust in this: "He will take into account," as Saint Bernard says, "all the goods a man has been given, in this present life, and how he has spent those goods—and in such detail that not a single hair of his head, nor a moment, an hour of his life, will not be included in God's reckoning."

The fifth thing that ought to move a man to contrition is remembrance of what Lord Jesus Christ suffered for our sins. For, as Saint Bernard says, "For as long as I am alive, I will always remember the wearisome, oppressive hardships suffered by our Lord Christ, in his preaching—his fatigue, his temptations when he was fasting, the long periods of wakefulness, during which he prayed, his tears when he wept for the good people, the sorrow and the shame and the filth of what men said to him, the foul spitting in his face, the blows that men gave him, the contemptuous scowls, and the reproofs spoken to him—the nails with which he was nailed to the cross, and all the rest of the pain he suffered for my sins, having never himself been guilty of sin." You must understand that, when men sin, all order and proper governance is turned upside down. For it is the truth that God, and reason, and sensuality, and man's body have all been created so that each of these four things must be in control of the others: God must have control over reason, and reason over sensuality, and sensuality over man's body. And therefore, to the degree that man's reason will not obey God—his lord by right—reason then loses its control over sensuality, and also over man's body, which it ought to have. And why? For in those circumstances, sensuality rebels against reason, and against God, as also does man's body. And surely this disorderliness and rebellion is what our Lord Jesus Christ paid for, upon his dear, precious body, and listen to what this means: to the degree that reason rebels against God, man deserves to be sorrowful and to die. Our Lord Jesus Christ suffered these things for man, after having been betrayed by his disciple, Judas, seized and bound so tightly that, as Saint Augustine says, the blood burst out of the nails of all his fingers. Moreover, to the degree that man's reason refuses to control sensuality, when it is able to do so, man is again worthy to be shamed, as our Lord Jesus Christ was shamed when they spat in his face. And yet even more, to the degree that man's captive body rebels against both reason and sensuality, it deserves to die. This too our Lord Jesus Christ suffered on the cross, every part of his entire body experiencing great and bitter pain. This was all suffered by Jesus Christ, who had never sinned. So we may reasonably say, on behalf of Jesus Christ: "I have suffered too much pain that I never deserved, and been too much befouled for disgrace on account of which man deserves to suffer." And so the man who sins may well say, according to Saint Bernard, "My sin should be cursed for having caused so much bitter suffering." Certainly, Jesus Christ's pain and suffering were ordained by God because of the disorderliness and wickedness of men. For example, the sinful man's soul is betrayed, by the devil, into greed for worldly prosperity, as his soul is scorned when he chooses sensual pleasures, and as his soul is tormented by the impatience of adversity, and as it is spat upon by bondage to sin, and in the end it is killed. This disorderliness of sinful man was the cause of Jesus Christ being betrayed, and then bound—he who came to unbind us of sin and pain. And then he was scorned—he who should only have been honored, in all things and by all things. Then his face—which all of mankind should have desired to see, and at which angels long to look—was spat on. Then he was whipped, he who was entirely guiltless, and finally he was crucified and slain. Then Isaiah's words were fulfilled: "He was wounded for our misdeeds, and befouled for our crimes." And since Jesus Christ took upon himself the pain of all our wickedness, sinful man must weep and wail, for having caused God's son to descend from heaven and endure all this pain.

The sixth thing that ought to move a man to contrition is the hope for three things, namely, forgiveness for sinning, the gift of grace with which to properly accomplish this, and the glory of heaven, by means of which God will reward man for his good deeds. And since Jesus Christ extends these gifts to us, out of his munificence and his sovereign generosity, he is known as *Jesus Nazarenus rex Judeorum*, literally "Jesus of Nazarus, King of the Jews." But taken more largely, *Jesus* means "savior" or "salvation," he on whom men must hope to be forgiven for their sins, which is to say their salvation in spite of their sins. And so the angel said to Joseph, "You will call him Jesus, he who will save his people from their sins." And as Saint Peter also says: "There is no other name for any man on earth, by which a man may be saved, except the name Jesus." *Nazarenus* is virtually the same as "flourishing" or "thriving," in which state a man hopes that he who grants a man remission of his sins will also grant him the grace to do so properly. For in the flower there is the hope of fruit, in time to come.

"I stood at the door of your heart," says Jesus, "and called out to enter. He who opens his heart to me shall be forgiven for his sins. By means of my grace, I will enter and dine with him," meaning the good works which the man has performed, which good works constitute God's food, and "sup," meaning the great joy I will give him. This must man hope for, as a reward for his penitential works: that is, that God will allow him into his realm, as he promised to do in the gospels.

A man must understand the working of contrition. It must be universal and total. That is, a man must be truly repentant for all the sins he has committed by means of pleasurable thoughts, since pleasure is terribly dangerous. There are two ways of consenting to such things, one being called emotional consent, in which a man is moved to commit a sin and takes great and prolonged pleasure in thinking about that sin, and though his reason is well aware that this is a sin against the laws of God, his reason does not block or restrain such foul pleasure. But although his reason does not consent to his actually committing the sin, there are clerics who say that when such a pleasurable thought endures for a long time, it is deeply dangerous, no matter how trivial it may seem. And, it is said, a man must specifically repent for everything that he ever wanted to do, which was against the laws of God, and to which his reason consented, for there is no doubt that consent is, in and of itself, a deadly sin. For surely no deadly sin can occur without being, first, a thought in a man's heart, and thereafter a pleasure in his heart, and so on and so forth, straight into consenting and, at last, into actually doing the deed. There are many men who never repent such thoughts and such pleasures, nor do they confess them, but only repent and confess the great sins they have actually committed. Such wicked thoughts and pleasures, I say, are subtle deceivers, for men must be damned on account of these things. Not only that, but a man must repent his wicked words, as well as his wicked deeds. Surely, repentance for one particular sin, and not for all the others, or—in reverse order—repentance for almost all sins, but not for one particular one, will not be sufficient. Certainly, God almighty is completely good, and so he forgives either everything or nothing. Saint Augustine says, on this matter, "I know that God is the enemy of all sinners." How then can a man who continues to commit one particular sin be forgiven for his other sins? No, he cannot. And furthermore, contrition ought to be tremendously sorrowful, and full of anguish—and that is what God will reward by his mercy, for when my soul was in anguish I was thinking of God, and that my prayers would come to him. Indeed, contrition ought to be a continual process, man must be relentlessly confessional, and equally determined to amend his ways. Truly, when contrition is enduring, a man may always hope for forgiveness, from which comes a determined hatred for sin, which then destroys sin—and not just in him, but in others, so far as he is able to affect them. And so David says, "You who love God, hate wickedness." Trust this well: to love God means that you love what he loves, and hate what he hates.

The final thing that men must understand about contrition is this: what does contrition accomplish? I say that sometimes contrition can free a man from sin, about which David says, "I came to you, God, intending to confess, and I did, and you freed me from my sins." And just as contrition is ineffective without a sober intent to confess, if the opportunity is available, so too neither confession nor penance is worth anything whatever without contrition. Moreover, contrition destroys the prison which is hell, enfeebling the devils, and restoring the gifts of the Holy Ghost and all the good virtues, and it cleanses the soul of its sins, freeing the soul from hell's pains, and the fellowship of the devil, and from the servitude of sin, and bringing the soul back to the fellowship and communion of holy church. And yet more: contrition turns a man who was a son of anger into a son of grace—and all of these things have been proved by the Bible. Accordingly, the man who sets his mind on these things is truly wise, for during the rest of his life his heart ought not to turn toward sin, and he can give his body and his whole heart to the service of Jesus Christ, and in so doing give him the homage to which he is entitled. For truly, our sweet Lord Jesus Christ has so graciously spared us our follies that, had he not taken pity on men's souls, we might all be singing a very sad song.

HERE ENDS THE FIRST PART OF PENANCE, AND THE SECOND PART FOLLOWS

The second part of Penance is Confession, which is a sign of contrition. You must understand what Confession is, and whether or not it is necessary, as well as what things are appropriate to true Confession.

You must first understand that Confession means an honest narration of your sins to a priest. The word "honest," here, means that a man must confess, fully and completely, every aspect of every one of his sins, as far as he is able. Everything must be said, and nothing ought to be excused, or hidden, or disguised, nor ought a man to boast of his good works. Furthermore, it is necessary to understand from whence sins spring forth, and how they grow, and what they in fact are.

Saint Paul says, about the origin of sins: "Just as sin first entered the world because of a man, and so too came death, so death enters into all sinners." The man Saint Paul speaks of is Adam, by whom sin entered this world, because he broke God's commandment. And thus he that was at first so mighty, and not subject to death, became a creature who had to die, whether he liked it or not, and so too all his descendants, because of this one man's sin. Consider how, in their first estate of innocence, when Adam and Eve walked naked in Paradise, and were not ashamed of their nakedness, the serpent—cleverest of all the beasts God created—said to the woman: "Why has God forbidden you to eat the fruit of all the trees in Paradise?" The woman answered: "We eat," she said, "the fruit of the trees in Paradise, but truly, the fruit of the tree in the center of Paradise is forbidden to us, we must never touch it, because then we might have to die." The serpent then said to the woman: "No, no, death will not kill you, for truly God is very well aware that, the very day you eat the fruit of that tree, your eyes will be opened, and you will be like gods, knowing good and evil." The woman looked and saw that the fruit looked like something good to eat, and was fair to the eye as well, and delightful to look at. She plucked fruit and ate it, and gave fruit to her husband, and he ate it, and soon they both opened their eyes. And when they knew that they were naked, they took birch leaves and made breeches, to hide their sexual members.

From this you can see that their deadly sin had been initially suggested by the devil; afterward, there is clearly fleshly delight, as exhibited by Eve; and after that the consent of reason, as shown by Adam. Understand that, though the devil tempted Eve (which is to say, the flesh) and the flesh then took delight in the beauty of the forbidden fruit, not until reason (which is to say, Adam) consented to eating the fruit did he become guilty of sin. This is original sin, and we have it from Adam, since we are all descended from him, conceived and born out of vile and corrupt matter. And when the soul is put into our body, it immediately is infected with original sin, and that which was to start with only the painful crime of sexual desire, then becomes both a crime and a sin. And so we are all born as the sons of anger and eternal damnation, unless and until we are baptized, which cleanses away and removes our culpability. But in fact the crime remains with us, in the form of temptation, which is known as sexual desire. And sexual desire, when it turns in the wrong direction, or is so created from the start, makes a man covetous—that is, fleshly covetous, which is fleshly sin even when exercised only by the eyes, looking on earthly things, and also leads to covetousness of place, by prideful hearts.

Now, I will speak of the first covetousness, namely, sexual desire, as framed in the law of sexuality, since both men and women were created by God as sexual beings, and God is moved only by lawful and proper judgment. I tell you that, insofar as man is not obedient to God, who is his lord, then his flesh becomes disobedient to him by means of sexual desire, and this we call both the nourishing of sin and the doing of sin. Accordingly, when a man suffers from sexual desire, it is impossible for him, at one time or another, not to be moved to sin, by the action of his flesh. Nor will this disappear, for as long as he lives; it can be made weaker and even be controlled by baptism, and also, through penance, by the grace of God, but it can never be fully quenched except when he is cooled down by sickness, or by sorcery and magic, or by cold drinks. For here is what Saint Paul says: "The flesh lusts, in opposition to the spirit, and the spirit contends against the flesh, and between them they are so deeply in discord and combat that a man may not always act as he wishes to." This same Saint Paul, after his great penance, in water and on the land—in water by night and by day, in great danger and pain; on land, in hunger and thirst, in cold weather and without clothing, and once stoned almost to death—still declared, "Alas, I am a captive man! Who can free me from the prison of my captive body?" And Saint Jerome, after he had dwelled in the desert for a long time, with no human company, but only wild beasts, and having no food but herbs, and only water to drink, and no bed but the bare earth, because of which his flesh was burned as black as an Ethiopian, and almost destroyed by cold, still declared that "the fire of lechery still boiled in his body." All of which shows me that whoever says he has no bodily temptations is deceiving himself. Take witness of Saint James the Apostle, who says that "every man is tempted by his own sexual desires," which means that each one of us has both the flesh and the occasion to feed the sin that is in his body. Therefore, Saint John the Evangelist declares: "If we say that we are free of sin, we deceive ourselves, and there is no truth in us."

You must now come to understand how sin grows or becomes weaker in a man. The very first factor is that nourishing of sin, of which I spoke before, namely, sexual desire. And then there is the role of the devil, or to speak more exactly, the devil's belly, from which he blows into man the fire of sexual desire. And then a man thinks whether to commit, or not to commit, that which he is tempted to do. If a man stands firm, and opposes his initial fleshly enticement, no sin occurs, and when he does not commit the sin he will soon feel the flame of pleasure. But he must continue to be wary, and control himself well, or later on he will indeed consent to sin, after which he will indeed commit it, if there is time and place. And Moses shows us the devil speaking about this matter: "The devil says, 'I will chase and pursue man by wicked suggestion, and I will catch him by the stirring and working of sin. I will single out my prey, my prize, with careful consideration, and my own sexual desire will work together with his lust. I will draw my sword when he indicates consent (surely, just as a sword cuts a thing in two pieces, so giving his consent cuts man away from God), and then I will slay him with my own hand, right in the act of committing sin'; so says the devil." Surely, a man is then already dead in his soul. And so sin is accomplished by temptation, by pleasure, and by consent, and at that point it becomes actual sin.

Truly, there are two kinds of actual sin, either venial and trivial, or deadly. Indeed, when a man loves any creature more than he loves Jesus Christ our Creator, that is deadly sin. It is venial sin when a man loves Jesus Christ less than he ought to. But this venial sin is very dangerous, for it decreases, more and more, the love a man ought to have for God. And therefore, if a man loads himself with a good many venial sins, unless he rids himself of some of them, by confession, they can easily reduce away all the love he bears for Jesus Christ, and so venial sin can skip right into deadly sin. And therefore let us not be negligent about freeing ourselves of venial sins, for as the proverb says, "Many little things add up to a great thing." Hear this example. Out at sea, sometimes a great wave breaks over a ship with such violence that the ship goes under, and drowns. But sometimes this same result can occur from small drops of water, which leak into little cracks in the ship's hold, or its bottom, if the sailors are negligent in making necessary repairs. And so, although there is a difference between these two causes of a ship sinking, nevertheless in each case the ship goes down. So too does deadly sin work, and to the same end do smaller, annoying venial sins, when they multiply so greatly that his love for worldly things (in itself a venial sin) becomes as great as his love for God—or still greater. Love for anything, therefore, which is not founded in God, nor accomplished principally for God's sake, is a venial sin, although a man loves it less than he loves God. But it is a deadly sin when love for anything equals a man's love for God, or exceeds it.

"Deadly sin," says Saint Augustine, "occurs when a man turns his heart away from God, who is of a truly sovereign goodness which does not ever change, and gives his heart, instead, to something that may well change and fly away." And, surely, this is true of everything that is not of or from God in heaven. Truly, if a man gives the love he owes God to any creature, a love to which he should wholly dedicate his heart, clearly as much love as he gives to this creature he steals from God, which is sinful. He is in debt to God, but does not pay all of his debt, which is nothing less than his whole heart.

Since most men understand, in general, the scope of venial sin, it is appropriate that I speak more particularly about sins which a good many men may not think are in fact sins at all, and therefore do not mention them at confession, but they are very real sins. Truly, as many clerics have noted, this means (among other things) that every time a man eats or drinks more than he needs to sustain his body, he is certainly sinning. So too when he speaks more than necessary, that too is sinful. As it is, also, when a man will not listen, in kindly fashion, to poor people's complaints, or when, being in good health, he will not fast when other people do, without having any reasonable cause, or when he sleeps more than is needed, or when because of such oversleeping comes to church too late, or to other worthy and benevolent occasions. It is sinful, too, when he has sexual intercourse with his wife, not having a supreme desire to procreate, to the greater honor of God, or even because he wishes to pay his husbandly debt to his wife. It is sinful when he will not visit the sick, or prisoners, though he is well able to. It is sinful if he loves his wife or his child, or any other worldly thing, more than is required by reason. It is sinful if he flatters or fawns more than he is obliged to. It is sinful if he reduces or abandons the alms he gives to the poor. It is sinful if he prepares his food more deliciously than is necessary, or eats it too rapidly, out of his gluttony. It is sinful if he tells gossipy tales at church, or if he speaks empty, foolish, or villainous words, which he will be held accountable for, on the Day of Judgment. It is sinful when he promises to do things and does not do them, or when he, whether thoughtlessly or stupidly, slanders or acts scornfully toward his neighbor. It is sinful when he entertains wicked suspicions about something, having no knowledge of it whatsoever. These things, and more without number, are all sins, as Saint Augustine has said.

Men must understand that, although no man on earth can avoid all venial sins, it is possible to stay aloof from them by means of burning love for our Lord Jesus Christ, and also by prayers, and confession, and other good works, so little damage may be done. As Saint Augustine says, "If a man loves God so entirely that everything he does is done in Godly ways, or for the love of God, truly burning in his love for God: consider that if a single drop of water falling into a blazing furnace can be disturbing, or painful, that is precisely how much a venial sin will grieve a man who is perfect in his love for Jesus Christ." Men can also keep off venial sin by worthy reception of the precious body of Jesus Christ, in communion, and by receiving holy water, and by giving alms, as well as by ritual confession at mass and in the canonical hours just before going to sleep, and by the blessings of bishops and priests, and by other good works.

HERE ENDS THE SECOND PART OF PENANCE, WHICH IS NOW FOLLOWED BY A DISCUSSION OF THE SEVEN DEADLY SINS, AND THE SUBDIVISIONS, CIRCUMSTANCES, AND SPECIES THEREOF

Now it is necessary to discuss the seven deadly sins—the chieftains of sin. They all run on one leash, like a pack of devil dogs, but in different ways. We call them chieftains because they largely lead the way for all lesser sins. The root of them all is Pride, which is in general the root of all evils, from which spring specific branches, like Anger, Envy, Sloth, Avarice (called Greed, in common understanding), Gluttony, and Lechery. And each of these major sins has its own branches and twigs, as shall be explained in what follows.

Pride

Although no man can be sure of the exact number of twigs that spring from Pride, or the precise total of its evil deeds, I will describe some of them, so you can understand. There is Disobedience, Boasting, Hypocrisy, Contempt or Scorn, Arrogance or Self Importance, Impudence or Disrespect, Heart-swelling or Over-enthusiasm, Insolence or Haughtiness, Elation or Vainglory, Impatience, Contumaciousness or Stubbornness, Presumption, Irreverence, and many other twigs I cannot here describe. Someone who is disobedient scorns God's commandments, or his ruler's, or his spiritual guide. A boaster may boast of either the evil or of the good that he has done. An hypocrite hides his true nature, and shows a self that is not his own. Someone is contemptuous when they scorn their neighbor, a fellow Christian, or scorns to do what he is supposed to do. Someone is arrogant when he thinks he has virtues and qualities which he does not have, or who believes that he deserves more than he has, or thinks that he is something which he is not. Someone is impudent when he has no shame for his sins. Heart-swelling occurs when a man rejoices at the evil he has done. Someone is insolent when he considers other people inferior to himself, either in his worth, or his knowledge, or in his behavior. To be guilty of Elation, someone will not tolerate that anyone is either his master or his equal. An impatient man is someone who refuses to be taught or to accept criticism, and continuously fights against the truth and defends his folly. A contumacious man is he who is indignant at the authority or power that others, in higher station than himself, have over him. Presumption occurs when a man attempts to do something which he cannot or ought to do. Irreverence is when men do not bestow honor where they ought to, and expect to be reverenced themselves. It is Vainglory to be pompous, and to take pleasure in your own elevated status, glorifying yourself. Jangling or Chattering is when a man talks too much, as loudly and steadily as a turning mill wheel, but neither cares nor pays any attention to what he says.

And there is a secret sort of Pride, which waits to be greeted before giving a greeting, even if he is a person of lesser status, and also waits to be seated or to declare whether or not he desires to be seated, and exactly where, and where he will stand in a procession, and whether or not he wishes to be wafted by the incense bearer, or whether he wishes to be the first to kiss the tablet bearing a representation of the Crucifixion, or whether he or his neighbor should be first to make an offering at the altar, and other similar matters, in which he wishes to be given more attention than he deserves, except that his heart has such a lofty desire to be publicly made much of and honored.

There are two ways of exhibiting Pride, one being inside the heart and the other outside the heart. The things I have thus far spoken of, surely, as well as many other things, rise from inside a man's heart. But either one of these species of Pride is an indicator of the other, exactly as a lush bower outside a tavern is an indicator of the wine in its cellar. This applies in many ways, in speech, in facial appearance, and in outrageous clothing. Surely, had there been no sin in clothing, Christ would not so quickly have noted and spoken about the rich man's clothes, in the gospel. And as Saint Gregory says, "Expensive clothing is sinful because it is so rare, and for its excessive softness and strangeness, and its purely fashionable qualities." Alas! Can we not see, in our own time, sinful, costly displays of clothing, and particularly its extravagance and over-abundance, and sometimes its excessive scantiness.

As for the sin of too much clothing, its rarity and cost make it injurious to the public at large, not simply because of all the expensive embroidery, its flamboyant notching, decorations of bars, vertical stripes, coils, and bordering, and the obvious waste of cloth, out of pure vanity, but many of these gowns bear too much expensive fur trimming, so much black-punched and purely decorative designs, and unneeded holes and slits, as well as the overlong length of these gowns, trailing into the muck and dung, whether they go on horse or on foot, whether they are men or they are women, and all this trailing is truly wasted, consumed, made threadbare and rotten with dung, instead of it being given to poor people, much to the loss of the poor. The more cloth is wasted, the more expensive cloth in general becomes, and this too is a burden on common people. And even should such pierced and punched and slashed clothing be given to the poor, it would not be consonant with their estate to wear such garments, which cannot take care of their needs, for it cannot keep them from the distempers of the weather. From yet another perspective, let me speak of the loathsome, improper scantiness of much clothing, as for example these short-cut coats and jackets, or even brief jackets, that because of their shortness do not cover the shameful parts of the human body—intentional wickedness. Alas! Some of these garments actually and clearly show the swelling of such wicked parts, horribly swollen male members that look like dangling hernias, wrapped around by these men's stockings, and their buttocks go up and down like the rear end of a female ape, at full moon. In addition, because they wear stockings half white and half red, when they try to hide their wickedly swollen members under these stockings, it looks as if half these shameful private members have been cut off. And if they use still other colorings for their stockings—like white and black, or white and blue, or black and red, and so forth—the variations in color make it seem that half of these private members have been affected by Saint Anthony's fire, eryispelas, with its scarlet rash, or else by cancer, or some other ghastly disease. The sight of the back parts of their buttocks is simply ghastly. Surely, this is the part of their body through which they get rid of their stinking ordure, and yet they proudly exhibit this utterly foul part of their bodies, in open public, violating all the displays of decency which Jesus Christ and his followers and friends were careful to maintain throughout their lives.

As for the outrageous clothing of women, God knows that although some of their faces seem distinctly chaste and gracious, their clothing signals lechery and pride. I have no objections to women who dress decently, but those who wear too much or too little are most certainly in need of correction. The sin of adornment appears, too, in the horses some people ride, often maintained strictly for pleasure, rather than, as properly, for work—handsome, fat, and expensive animals, the care of which maintains a good many vicious rascals. And their elaborately crafted harnesses, and saddles, bridles, tail straps, breast shields, some of these things covered with precious cloth, and costly metal adornments, often of silver and even gold. As to which God has said, speaking through Zachariah, the prophet, "I will ruin and destroy the riders of such horses." Such people pay no attention to the way God's son, who came down from heaven, did his riding, here on earth. He rode on an ass, and had no harness other than his disciples' wretched clothes, nor do we ever read that he rode on any other sort of beast. I am speaking of the sin of excessiveness, rather than of simple decency, as reason may require it. Moreover, to be sure, pride is flagrantly signaled by the maintenance of a large company of servants and followers, who either do very little work or sometimes do no work at all. And when that large company displays the insolence of office, to the damage of common people, they have become criminal and dangerous. Surely, the lords of such men have sold their lordships to the devil in hell, by maintaining such companies. And there are other men, of much lower degree—as for example those who operate inns—who support the thievery of their clients, in a great range of frauds and false dealing. These are among the many men who are like flies following honey, or hounds that seek out carrion. The lords who follow such ways have, in spirit, strangled their lordships, as David the prophet has said: "Wicked deaths must fall upon such lordships, and God, I pray, will drive them straight down into hell, for their houses are filled with unrighteousness and wickedness, not with God. And surely, unless they reform themselves, God will curse them, just as he rewarded Laban for his treatment of Jacob, and Pharaoh for his treatment of Joseph. And pride for the table often shows itself, as rich men are invited to feasts, and the poor are driven away and rebuked. Pride can be seen, too, in the superabundance of particular varieties of food and drink, and especially foods which are baked, and those served in elaborate dishes, some of them with flames still burning in them, colored and decorated with paper castles—so excessive that it is perverse even to think of them.

The same is true of the vast expense wasted on musical instruments, which only leads a man still more to the pleasures of luxury. If these things make the heart think less often of our Lord Jesus Christ, they are certainly sinful, and, certainly, the pleasures given by such things might well be great enough to lead a man, without a thought, into deadly sin.

The species that arise out of Pride, especially when they stem from premeditated evil, or malice, considered in advance and planned, or else caused by habitual practices, are without any doubt deadly sins. When however they stem from unpremeditated weakness, sudden and abrupt, and are just as suddenly withdrawn again, although they are grievous sins they are not, it seems to me, deadly ones.

Now men might ask from whence Pride arises, and I say sometimes from the advantages and benefits of nature, sometimes from the gifts of fortune, and sometimes from the gifts of grace. The benefits of nature, certainly, are either benefits of the body or of the soul. Just as certainly, benefits of the body consist of health, strength, agility, outward appearance, good lineage, and freedom. And benefits of the soul are intelligence, sharp understanding, subtle ingenuity, natural virtue, and good memory. The benefits of fortune are wealth, high degrees of lordship, and popular acclaim. The benefits of grace are knowledge, the power to endure spiritual labor, generosity, virtuous contemplation, resisting temptation, and other similar matters. Now, with regard to all these benefits, it is surely total folly for a man to be prideful about any of them.

Natural benefits, God knows, sometimes come to us as much to our harm as to our gain. We can pass lightly over bodily health, which can be very quickly lost, and that loss is very often the cause of the sickness of our soul. For, God knows, the body is a tremendously dangerous enemy of the soul, so that the more healthy and potent the body is, the more likely is the falling away of our soul. The body fights with the soul, so that the stronger the body becomes, the more pained and distressed is the soul. In addition, bodily strength and worldly daring and endurance frequently put a man's soul in danger and lead to spiritual misfortune. To be proud of your high birth is a very great folly, for often the high birth of the body removes high birth from the soul, and surely we all come from one father and one mother, and we are all of the same human nature—rotten and corrupt, whether we are rich or poor. For, surely, there are praiseworthy aspects to high birth, and in particular when it prepares man's heart with virtuous and moral teaching and practice, making a man into Christ's child. You may well believe that when a man has become sin's master, sin is treated very harshly indeed.

There are broad-ranging signs of nobility, as for example the avoidance of vice and ribaldry and a refusal to bow to sin in speech, or in work, or in their general demeanor and behavior, and practicing virtue, courtesy and honesty, and being generous—but not over-generous, for that becomes folly and sin. Another thing that demonstrates nobility is the keeping in mind of what kindnesses a man has received from others. And still another is to be kind to his good subjects, of which Seneca says: "Nothing is more becoming to a man of high estate than graciousness and compassion. And so these flies who are called (but are not) bees, when they choose a king for themselves they choose someone who has no stinger to stick them with." Also, a man may exhibit his nobility by having a heart both noble and attentive, striving after things of high virtue.

For a man to pride himself on the benefits and gifts of grace is surely outrageous folly, for instead of these gifts turning him to goodness and self-improvement, they have turned him to venom and destruction, exactly as Saint Gregory says. A man who prides himself on the gifts of fortune is just as surely a great fool, for it has been known to happen that a man who is a great lord, in the morning, has become a servant and a wretch before nightfall, and sometimes a man's great wealth is the cause of his death, just as sometimes the pleasures in which a rich man indulges can cause the sickness which kills him. Without any question, popular praise can sometimes be lies, far too brittle to be trusted: one day the people praise, the next day they accuse. God knows, this desire for popular praise has also been the cause of death to many an industrious and diligent man.

The remedy for the sin of Pride

Now that you understand just what Pride is, and what different forms it takes on, and from whence it grows and arises, you must understand what is the remedy for Pride, which is humility, or meekness. This is a virtue by means of which a man can obtain truthful knowledge of himself, and consider himself neither the most worthy of men nor the most delightful or rare, constantly keeping in mind his weaknesses. There are three kinds of humility: one is of the heart, another is of the mouth, and the third is of deeds. Humility of the heart occurs in four different ways. One is a man who thinks himself not worthy to stand before God in heaven. The second is a man who does not look down on any other man. The third is when a man is totally indifferent to the fact that other men do not think him worthy. And the fourth is when he is not distressed by humiliation. Similarly, humility of the mouth occurs in four different ways. The first two involve moderate and humble speech, and the knowledge that what he says with his mouth is exactly what he thinks in his heart. And the next two are when he praises the kindness of some other man, and does not criticize it or complain of it. And humility of deeds, likewise, occurs in four ways. The first is when a man puts others ahead of himself. The second is when a man chooses the lowest possible place for himself. The third is to cheerfully assent to good advice. And the fourth is to gladly abide by the decisions of his rulers, or of others who are above him in degree. This is truly humility.

Here follows the discussion of Envy

Now I will leave off my discussion of Pride, and turn to the foul sin of Envy, which is what philosophy has called "sorrow for another's prosperity," and according to Saint Augustine, is "sorrow for a man doing well, and joy at a man suffering harm." This foul sin runs diametrically contrary to the Holy Ghost. Although every sin is against the Holy Ghost, nevertheless, since kindness and generosity are properly under the guidance of the Holy Ghost, and Envy rises up from malice, it is intrinsically opposed to the generosity and kindness of the Holy Ghost. There are two varieties of malice, which means hardness of heart in wickedness, or else that a man is so blind that he cannot believe he is sinning, or does not care whether or not he is sinning, which is indeed the hardness of the devil himself. Another form of malice is when a man fights against truth, even knowing that in fact it is true, and also when he opposes the grace that God has bestowed on his neighbor—all of this is Envy. Without a doubt, Envy is the very worst sin there is. Truly, all other sins are, at times, only transgressions against one particular virtue, but Envy is flatly opposed to all virtues and to all goodness. It regrets his neighbor's generosity and kindness, and thus differs from all other sins, for there is scarcely any other sin without some pleasure attached to its commission. Envy is the only sin completely and wholly wrapped in sorrow and anguish.

Envy has the following varieties. First, there is sorrow for another man's goodness and prosperity, and since prosperity is a natural cause of joy, Envy is thus a sin against nature. Second, Envy takes joy in another man's harm, which is directly drawn from the devil himself, who is eternally joyful at mankind's harm. And out of these two varieties of Envy comes backbiting, or detraction, which too has certain varieties. A man can seem to praise his neighbor, but only with malice aforethought, for at the end there is always a wicked qualification, a nasty complication, a nasty lump of sorrow. He always gets close to the end and says, "But . . . ," concluding with blame far weightier than any of his seeming praise. Another variety of backbiting occurs when some good man does or says something praiseworthy and good, and the backbiter turns it entirely upside down, nastily, intentionally. And yet another variety is to deprecate and make little of his neighbor's kindness and generosity. The fourth variety of backbiting is that, when a man is spoken well of, by others, the backbiter will say, "But, it seems to me, so-and-so is a lot kinder and more generous," in order to undercut the others' praise for him. The fifth variety is to enthusiastically endorse the negative things said of someone: this is an especially wicked sin, and the backbiter loves to whip up all the negative feelings he can. After backbiting comes complaining, or behind-the-back whispering, which sometimes springs from impatience with God, and sometimes with men. When a man complains about the suffering in hell, that is a complaint against God. So too when a man complains of poverty, or the loss of cattle, or against rain or storm, or else complains that rascals are too prosperous, or even that a good man is prosperous. All of these are things that a man must patiently endure, for they come by the rightful judgment and command of God. Sometimes complaining is born of avarice and greed, as Judas complained about Mary Magdalene, when she anointed the head of our Lord Jesus Christ with her precious ointment. Whispering behind other men's backs occurs when a man is doing a good deed, and at the same time complaining about it, and sometimes when other people are doing something good for their own cattle. Pride sometimes engenders complaining, as when Simon the Pharisee complained against Mary Magdalene, when she approached Jesus Christ and fell at his feet, weeping for her sins. Sometimes Envy engenders complaining, as for example when a man reveals a previously secret harm which another man has suffered, or accuses another man of something which he knows quite well the other man has not done. Whispering in the dark, so to speak, often occurs among servants, who complain when their masters order them to do perfectly permissible things, and since they do not dare to openly refuse their masters, they grumble and say bad things, and whisper among themselves, angrily, or as men call it, they recite the devil's *pater noster*, "Our Father" (the Lord's Prayer), though the devil, of course, has never had a *pater noster*, but ignorant, illiterate people give it that name.

Sometimes this occurs because of anger, personal and private, which feeds ill-feeling in the heart, as I shall explain shortly. This can lead to true bitterness of heart, by means of which a neighbor's every good deed seems bitter and tasteless, insipid. And then this leads to discord, which destroys all the bonds of friendship. Then comes scorn of his neighbor, though thoroughly undeserved, for the other man may in fact be doing very well. Next follows accusations, the accuser looking for opportunities to annoy his neighbor; this much like how the devil operates, who lurks and waits, both night and day, for his chance to accuse us all. And then there comes maliciousness, a man angering his neighbor by secret, malign deeds, if he can find the opportunity. And if he cannot, his wicked heart will not simply suffer in silence, for the man may proceed to secretly burn down his neighbor's house, or poison or otherwise dispose of his cattle, and do other things along these lines.

The remedy for the sin of Envy

Now I speak of remedying this foul sin of Envy. Love of God comes first and foremost, and loving his neighbor as he loves himself, for truly one of these two kinds of love cannot exist without the other. Believe me: you must understand that your neighbor is very like your brother, since without any doubt we all have the same earthly father and mother, namely, Adam and Eve, as we also have one spiritual father, who is God in heaven. You must love your neighbor, and wish only good things for him, for as God has said, "Love your neighbor as you love yourself"—which includes both his good in life, and the salvation of his soul after death. And in addition you must love him by your words, kindly admonishing him, when necessary, and comforting him in his afflictions, and praying for him with all your heart. And your deeds, too, shall show such love for him as you would wish to have done for you, in similar circumstances. Accordingly, you must never injure him by wicked words, nor do any harm to his person, or to his cattle, nor to his soul, by enticing him into sinful deeds. You must not desire his wife, or anything else that he owns. But you must also understand that the word "neighbor" also includes the word "enemy," and surely a man must love his enemy, as God has commanded, just as you must, in God, love your friend. Were it reasonable that a man should hate his enemy, truly God would not then be able to receive us into his love: as I said, a moment ago, love of God and love of your neighbor are inextricably joined, one cannot exist without the other, so that if we hate our enemy, we are also hating God.

When an enemy does one of three kinds of wrongs to you, you have three kinds of responses to make. Against hate and bitterness of heart, you must love him in your heart. Against bitter words, you must pray for your enemy. And against an enemy's wicked deed, you must act toward him in kindness and generosity. As Christ says: "Love your enemy, and pray for those who speak ill of you, and also, for those who chase and pursue you, you must do good things for them." Lo, thus commands our Lord Jesus Christ to respond to our enemies. Certainly, nature drives us to love our friends but, by my faith, our enemy is in far greater need of love than is our friend, and to those who are in need, surely a man must do good deeds, and equally surely, by so doing we will keep in mind the love of Jesus Christ, who died for his enemies. And because this is a harder love to bring to bear so too it is a worthier kind of love, because by loving your enemy you have routed the devil: just as the devil is overthrown and defeated by humility, so too he is wounded to death by the love we display for our enemy. Love is, very plainly, the healing balm which drives Envy's venom from man's heart

This is a subject I will return to, later.

The next subject is Anger

Truly, whoever envies his neighbor will usually become angry at him, and that anger will be expressed either by word or by deed. And just as Envy comes from Pride, so too does Anger, for indeed whoever is proud or envious is easily made angry.

This sin of Anger, according to Saint Augustine's description, is the wicked wish to be avenged, either by word or by deed. According to Aristotle, Anger is the burning, hot blood beating in a man's heart, by means of which he means to do harm to whoever it is that he hates. Surely, by heating and by rapid movement of his blood, a man becomes so agitated that he has lost all judgment and is beyond the reach of reason.

But you must understand that Anger takes two different pathways, one good, and the other wicked. Good Anger is a vehemence of goodness, by means of which a man is made angry with wickedness, and fiercely opposed to it, which is why a wise man has said that Anger is preferable to amusement. This variety of Anger is tinged with graciousness, and it is not bitter, nor is it directed at a man but at a man's misdeed, as the prophet David says, "Be angry, and do not sin."

The wicked form of anger has two different varieties. One is sudden, hasty, totally without forethought or any rational deliberation. That is, a man's reason does not consent to this sudden rage, and it is a venial sin. But the other variety is totally wicked, coming from a criminally minded heart, after full deliberation and definitely with forethought and a wicked determination to be avenged, to which the man's reason has consented: this is truly a deadly sin. This anger so displeases God that it disturbs all of heaven, driving the Holy Ghost out of a man's soul, and ravaging and destroying the image of God—that is to say, the virtue in a man's soul—and replacing it with an image of the devil, cutting man off from God, who is his rightful lord. This anger is an immense delight to the devil, for it is indeed the devil's furnace, heated by the fires of hell. For surely, just as fire is more likely to destroy earthly things than any other element, just so Anger has the power to destroy all spiritual things. Observe the fire in small coals, lying under the ashes and almost dead, will leap up again if they are touched by sulfur. Just so Anger, too, will flame up once again when it is touched by the pride lying inside a man's heart. Certainly, fire cannot come from nothing, except from things combustible by nature, much the way fire is drawn out of flints by the touch of steel. And just as Pride is often the matter on which the fire of Anger burns, and feeds, so too bitterness is the nurse and attendant of Anger. There is a kind of tree, Saint Isidore says, that when it is used to make a fire, men need only cover that fire with ashes and it will last for a year or even more. And this is also true of bitterness, for once conceived in the hearts of some men, surely, it will last even as long as from one Easter Day to another, or even longer. But without any doubt, during this entire period a man is far, far away from the mercy of God.

Three rascals work the forge of this furnace: Pride, which constantly blows on and increases the fire by scolding, wicked words; Envy, which stands, holding the hot iron against a man's heart, in a pair of long tongs made out of long bitterness; and next to them stands Rebelliousness, or fighting and quarreling, hammering and forging with villainous insults and cursing. This damnable sin is painful both to the man himself and also to his neighbor. Truly virtually all the harm any man does to his neighbor stems from Anger. Certainly, outrageous Anger does everything and anything the devil orders it to do, making no exceptions either for Christ or for Mary, his sweet mother. And in this outrageous Anger—alas! alas!—a man's heart cherishes wickedness toward Christ and all his saints. Is this not a cursed vice? Yes, certainly! Alas! it deprives a man of his intelligence and of his reason, and of that humble spiritual existence which is meant to preserve his soul. Surely, it also deprives him of God's proper lordship, which is man's soul and his neighbors' love. It constantly fights against truth. It shatters the peace and quiet in a man's heart, and upsets his soul.

Anger produces the following stinking dung: first, hate, which is cold anger; quarrelsomeness, by means of which a man is separated from an old friend that he has loved for a long, long time; and then war comes, and every kind of evil that man does to his neighbor or to his property. Also stemming from this cursed sin of Anger is manslaughter. But you must understand that murder, or homicide, takes different forms. Some forms of murder are spiritual, and some are bodily. Spiritual manslaughter is composed of six things. First, by hate, as Saint John says: "He that hates his brother is a murderer." Murder can also be accomplished by backbiting, about which Solomon says, "There are two swords with which a man slays his neighbors." Truly, it is just as wicked to kill a man's good name and reputation as it is to take his life. There is murder, too, in fraudulently giving wicked advice, as for example urging someone to impose wrongful forms of taxation. Solomon says of this: "Roaring lions and hungry bears are like cruel lords who reduce wages (or reduce the number of people hired), or who practice usury, or who withhold the alms of poor people." As to which the wise man says: "Feed those who are almost dead of hunger," for truly, unless you feed them, you kill them, and these are all deadly sins. Bodily murder can occur in other than direct attacks on a man's body; for example, you can kill a man with your tongue, or you can order someone else to kill a man, or advise someone to do so. Direct bodily murder has four different forms. One is by law, as for example when a judge condemns a guilty man to die. But the judge must be sure that he is correct, and that he is not giving the death penalty for the sheer pleasure of spilling blood. Another form of homicide is that which has become obligatory, as for example when a man has been attacked and kills his attacker in the process of protecting his own life. Surely, however, if he could have escaped without killing his adversary, and kills him anyway, he has sinned and must do penance for a deadly sin. Similarly, if a man happens to shoot an arrow, or throw a stone, and kills someone thereby, he is a murderer. If a woman negligently turns over, in her sleep, and smothers the child who is lying in bed with her, she is a murderer and has committed a deadly sin. So too if a man administers venomous herbs to a woman, because of which she cannot conceive a child, or else produces an aborted pregnancy and kills an as yet unborn child, or inserts things in her vagina which kills such an unborn child, or else if a pregnant woman has deliberately injured herself, and the unborn child is killed, that too is murder. What can we say about women who murder their children, born out of wedlock, because they are afraid of being shamed? That is surely a horrible murder. If a lecherous man has sexual intercourse with a pregnant woman, and the unborn child is killed, or if he deliberately hits her and thereby kills her unborn child, these too are murder and horrible deadly sins.

But Anger leads to many more sins, in thought as well as in word and in deed, as for example a man who accuses God of things for which he himself is guilty, or curses God and all his saints, as gamblers regularly do in many different regions. This cursed sin occurs when they feel intensely wicked, in their hearts, toward God and all his saints. And approaching the altar and treating the holy sacrament irreverently, as they also do, is so great a sin that it can scarcely be mitigated and forgiven, except that God's mercy surpasses all his creatures, being so great, and he so merciful. Anger also becomes poisonous, as when, during confession, a man is sharply reproached and told he must stop committing some particular sin, and he becomes angry and replies scornfully or angrily, or defends or excuses his sin as simply the weakness of humankind, or else says he did it to preserve his friendships with others, who were doing it, or perhaps he says that he was lured on by the devil, or else that he was too young to understand what he was doing, or else his temperament is so virile and forceful that he cannot refrain, or else that this is simply his destiny, as he puts it, to so act until he has reached a certain age, or else, he says, it comes from the nobility of his lineage, and so on and so on. Such people are so wrapped in their sins that they will not free themselves, for surely no one who insists on excusing himself from his sin can overcome and be forgiven for that sin until, most humbly, he acknowledges and confesses his guilt.

And then there is swearing, which is expressly against the commandment of God, and often develops out of Anger. God says: "You must not take the name of your Lord God in vain, or use it frivolously." And our

Lord Jesus Christ says, according to Saint Matthew, "You should not swear at all, neither in the name of heaven, for it is God's throne, nor by earth, for it is his footstool, nor by Jerusalem, for it is a great king's city, nor by your head, for you are unable to turn a hair either white or black. But when you mean to say 'yes,' say 'yes,' and when you mean to say 'no,' say 'no,' and when you say anything more, it is evil." That is what Christ says. So for Christ's sake, do not so sinfully swear, dismembering Christ's soul, heart, bones, and body. Surely you must think that the cursèd Jews did not do enough to the precious body of our Lord Jesus Christ, so you need to dismember him still further. And when the law compels you to swear, then swear according to God's law, as Jeremiah says, in his fourth book: "Observe three conditions: swear truthfully, in court, and righteously," for all lying is against Christ, he being truth himself. And remember this: every great swearer, not compelled by law to swear, injures his own household so long as he persists in this sinful practice. You must not swear because of envy, because of some favor, or for a drink, but only for righteousness, and to the worship of God and for aid to other Christians. And therefore every man who takes God's name in vain, or speaks false words and swears to them, or makes use of Christ's name as if it were his own, cannot be called a Christian man, living according to Christ's own life and to his teachings, so long as he continues to take God's name in vain. Take notice of what Saint Peter says, in Acts, book four: "Christ's is the only name under the heaven of this world which can save a man's soul." Notice, too, how precious the name of Christ is viewed by Saint Paul, in his Epistle to the Philippians, chapter four: "The name of Jesus ought to make every creature, heavenly or mortal, or of hell, bow down," for it is so noble and so honorable that even the cursèd devil in hell must tremble, simply to hear it pronounced. It must appear, accordingly, that those who swear so horribly by his blessed name must despise him even more than the cursèd Jews did, or the devil in hell.

Clearly, if swearing—unless lawfully required—is so totally forbidden, then perjuring yourself by swearing falsely is worse still, and, furthermore, is unnecessary.

What then do we say of those who take such pleasure in swearing, and consider it an aristocratic or a manly deed to swear great oaths? And what about those who never stop swearing great oaths about matters that are not worth a straw? Surely, this is a horrible sin. Swearing when surprised is also a sin. But let us turn, here, to the horrible swearing involved in exorcism and incantation, as practiced by pretended magicians, over basins of plain water, or over a shining sword placed in a circle, or in a fire, or in a sheep's shoulder bone. All I can say is that they are cursedly and damnably working against Christ and the entire faith of holy church.

What must we say of those who believe in divination, based on the flight of birds, or on their singing, or on beasts, or by the drawing of lots, or by black magic, or by dreams, or by the creaking of doors, or by sounds made by the boards, or by the gnawing of rats, or any other such wretchedness? Without a doubt, all this is forbidden by God and by holy church, and those who practice such things, until they abandon such filth, are accursed. When people say charms for wounds or sickness, whether of man or of beasts, and they seem to be effective, it may well be that under those circumstances God permits it, so that people will place more faith in, and give more reverence to, his name.

Now I will speak of lying, which is usually false words spoken to deceive fellow Christians. Some lies are told for no reason and accomplish nothing, and some are told for the profit and convenience of someone, and for the inconvenience and loss of another man. People lie to save their lives, or their property. But some lie for the pleasure of lying, and long tales are often wound around such lies, filled with precise details, although the entire tale is a fabrication. Some lying occurs in order to bolster something else the liar has previously said, and some lying is casual and utterly reckless, performed without a thought. And so on.

Let us now turn to the sin of Flattery, when it is involuntary but spoken out of fear or to gain something. Flattery is generally wrongful praise. Flatterers are the devil's nurse, feeding his children with the milk of lying. Solomon says, truly, that "flattery is worse than slander." Sometimes, indeed, slander can make a haughty man more humble, for he fears slander, though more usually it leads a man to raise up both his heart and the way he behaves toward others. Flatterers are the devil's enchanters, for they make a man think he is something that he is not. Flatterers are like Judas, betraying a man in order to sell him to his enemy—namely, the devil. Flatterers are also the devil's own priests, constantly singing "*Placebo,* I will praise you." I place Flattery among the vices of Anger, for men will often, when they are angry with another man, hunt up someone to whom they speak flattering words, in order to gain support in their quarrel.

Let us speak, now, of the kind of cursing that comes from an angry heart. Cursing in general may have a wide range of seriously negative effects, removing man from the realms of God, as Saint Paul says. And cursing often turns against the man who utters it, like a bird returning to its nest. Above all else, men should avoid cursing their children, as much as they possibly can, so they do not consign their offspring to the devil. It is certainly both a great danger and a great sin.

Let us speak also of scolding and the laying of blame, which are very serious wounds in a man's heart, since they rip open the seams of friendship. Surely, a man can hardly be expected to be intimate and comfortable with someone who has openly reviled and censured and slandered him. This is a deeply terrible sin, as Christ says in the gospel. And be very aware that a man who censures his neighbor usually threatens something causing bodily pain, calling him a filthy beggar, a crippled leper, or by doing something sinful to him. Threatening bodily pain brings this censure to Jesus Christ, because pain is something that comes from the righteous dispensation of God, and with his permission, whether it be leprosy, or maiming, or sickness. And to censure him, most uncharitably, of sin, using such language as "you lecher," "you drunken cripple," and so forth, that makes good sense only to the devil, who is always joyful whenever men sin. And to be sure, scolding can only come from a villainous heart. More often than not, a man's mouth speaks out of the fullness of his heart. And in a situation like this, a man must be wary of uncharitably censuring and scolding his neighbor, for if he is not careful he may all too readily kindle the fire of Anger, which in truth he ought to quench, not feed, and might well end by killing the man. How much better to criticize kindly! For as Solomon says, "An amiable tongue is the tree of life"— that is, of the spiritual life—and surely an unbridled tongue kills the spirits of both the man who waggles it and the man who is being reviled. Lo, hear what Saint Augustine says: "Nothing is so like the devil's child as a man who is always censuring others." Saint Paul also says, "God's servants ought not to revile other men." And although scolding is a villainous thing between all human beings, yet it is certainly extremely inappropriate between a man and his wife, for then there is no peace. And therefore Solomon says, "A house that has lost its roof, and is falling apart, is very like a scolding wife." When a house is falling apart, a man can avoid some of the places where things are falling, but wherever he goes there will be something falling on him. A scolding wife is like that: if she scolds her husband in one place, she will surely scold him in another. And therefore, as Solomon says, "a morsel of bread eaten with pleasure is better than a house full of delights and with scolding." Saint Paul says, in his Epistle to the Colossians, chapter three: "O women, be your husbands' subjects and subordinates, as God wishes you to be, and O you men, love your wives."

Next we will speak of scornful, contemptuous behavior, which is a wicked sin, and especially when the scorn is directed at a man because of his good works. Surely, such contemptuous people are like foul toads, unable to endure the sweet fragrance of a vine, when it blossoms out. Such scornful folk are the devil's companions, for they feel joy when he prevails, and sorrow when he loses. They are adversaries of Jesus Christ, because they hate what he loves, namely, the salvation of the soul.

And let us speak, also, of wicked advice, for the person who gives wicked advice is a traitor, deceiving the person who trusted him, as Achitophel did to Absalom. Nevertheless, the primary damage done falls on the person who gives wicked advice, and not the person to whom it is given. As the wise man says, "All deceitful lies have this effect: before the liar hurts another man, he first hurts himself." And a man must understand that he should not seek advice from liars, or from angry men, or from those who are oppressive to others, or people who are too much concerned with their own personal gain, nor to overly worldly people, and most especially in seeking advice on matters pertaining to the soul.

And now we turn to the sin of those who cause quarrels and discord among other people, a sin which Christ passionately hated. And that is hardly surprising, for he died in order to create peace. And those who sow discord shame Christ more than did those who crucified him, for God strongly desires people to be friendly to one another, valuing it above his own body, which he sacrificed in order to achieve earthly harmony.

And so we turn to the sin of those who speak with a double tongue, saying pleasant things openly, and in secret saying wicked things. Or else they pretend that what they are saying is meant well, or else is merely a joke or a game, though in fact their intentions are wicked.

We must mention the sin of betraying confidential advice, in order to defame someone. The damage thus effected is very hard to undo.

Then there is the man who menaces others, which is a plain folly, for a man issuing threats is not likely to be able to do all the menacing things he talks about doing.

And then there are frivolous words, spoken with no gain to the person saying such things, nor with any gain to the person who hears them. Frivolous speech can also be unnecessary speech. And although frivolous words can sometimes be a venial sin, men should beware of them, for we will have to account for them, before God himself.

And then there is babbling, which may often be sinful, though not always. And, as Solomon says, "It is an open indication of folly." And so a philosopher has said, when asked how to please others: "Do many good works, and try not to babble."

And so we reach the sin of acting like a clown, telling jokes and making impersonations. Such people are the devil's monkeys, making people laugh at their jokes and foolish actions, just as men laugh at a monkey's tricks. Saint Paul forbade such performances. Just as virtuous, holy words comfort those who are dedicated to God's service, so the sinful performance of jesters comforts those who serve the devil. These are sins that come from the tongue, and from Anger, and from other causes as well.

The remedy for the sin of Anger

The remedy for Anger is a virtue men call humility, or meekness, or graciousness and courtesy, as well as yet another virtue, which men call Patience or Forbearance.

Graciousness and humility restrain and rein in the stirrings and movements in a man's heart, in such a way that the man does not leap out in anger. Patience gently endures all the irritation and the wrongs a man may do to others. As Saint Jerome says: "It neither hurts nor threatens anyone; whatever hurtful things a man may say or do, the gracious and humble man does not grow excited, nor does he either act or speak against reason." This is sometimes a naturally occurring virtue, for as the philosopher says: "A man is a living being, by nature gracious and molded for goodness, but when such graciousness is enlightened by grace, it becomes more valuable."

Patience, yet another remedy against Anger, is a virtue that enables a man to deal easily and sweetly with every man's goodness, nor does he become angry whatever harm may be done to him. This is a virtue that makes a man resemble God and, as Christ says, makes him God's own dear child. This virtue will defeat your enemy, and therefore the wise man says, "If you want to conquer your enemy, learn to endure."

And you must understand that a man may have to endure four kinds of external grievances, against all of which he must have four different kinds of patience. The first such grievance is wicked words. Jesus Christ endured these very patiently, when the Jews scorned and scolded him, as they often did. You too must endure patiently, for as the wise man says: "If you struggle with a fool, whether the fool is angry or laughing, you will never have peace and quiet." The second external grievance is harm done to your property. There, once again, Christ endured most patiently, when everything he owned was taken from him, leaving him nothing but the clothes he was wearing. The third such grievance is harm to your body. And that too Christ suffered with great patience, when he was crucified. The fourth such grievance is the imposition of outrageous tasks. Accordingly, I say that when a man forces his servants into oppressive labor, or makes them work much past their time, as for example on holy days, a great sin is done. Here, once more, Christ endured patiently and taught us patience, bearing upon his blessed shoulder the cross upon which he was to suffer a shameful death. This can surely teach a man to be patient, for surely it is not only Christian men who have been patient, for love of Jesus Christ and for the reward of eternal blessedness, but without a doubt the ancient pagans, who were never Christians, both commended and practiced the virtue of patience.

Once, when a philosopher meant to beat his student, on account of some great transgression, which fiercely irritated him, he went and fetched himself a stick with which to beat the child and, seeing this stick, the child asked, "What are you going to do?" "I am going to beat you, to teach you a lesson." "Truly," said the child, "you first ought to teach yourself, you who have lost your patience because of a child's misdoings." "Truly," said the master, weeping, "you are right. You take this stick, my dear son, and beat me for my impatience." Obedience comes from patience, and teaches a man to be obedient to Christ, and to all others, in Christ, who deserve his obedience. Now understand this clearly: obedience is perfect when a man, gladly and swiftly, and with a fully good heart, does all that he ought to do. Obedience usually means following God's doctrines, and those of a man's rulers, to whom in all righteousness he is obliged to be obedient.

Now follows the discussion of Sloth

Envy blinds a man's heart; Anger disturbs and troubles a man; and Sloth makes him ponderous, moody, pensive, and peevish. Envy and Anger create bitterness in the heart, and this bitterness is the mother of Sloth, which removes the love of all goodness. Accordingly, Sloth is the anguish of a troubled heart, as Saint Augustine says: "It is vexation of goodness and pleasure in discomfort and evil." Surely, this is a damnable sin, for it wrongs Jesus Christ, because it removes men from the service they owe Christ, which ought to be diligently performed, as Solomon says. But Sloth knows nothing of diligence. It performs anything and everything with vexation, and peevishness, slowly and negligently and many excuses, as well as ineptly and with lack of pleasure, because of which the book says: "Accursed is the man who negligently performs God' service." Thus Sloth is the enemy to all men, whether they live in a state of innocence, as Adam did before he fell into sin, and in which state his duties were to praise and adore God; or whether they live as sinful men, in which state they are expected to pray to God for reformation of their sins, and from which, for his grace, God will free them; or in a third state, that of grace, in which a man is expected to perform penitent works. Certainly, Sloth is man's enemy in everything, for it has no affection for any work whatever. Surely this foul sin of Sloth is a great enemy to the body's livelihood, for it cannot organize itself to deal with temporal necessities, since it is slow and dilatory and without much energy, and ruins all worldly goods by indifference and carelessness.

Sloth is like those who are suffering in the pain of hell, wholly sluggish, profoundly heavy. Those have been bound so tightly that they cannot either do or even think about much of anything. Sloth vexes and irritates a man so that he is incapable of goodness, which is why God hates Sloth, as Saint John says.

Sloth cannot endure either rigor or severity, nor is it capable of penance. Indeed, Sloth is so soft and delicate, as Solomon says, that it disgraces and ruins whatever it touches. To combat this rotten-hearted sin of Sloth, men must oblige themselves to do good works, employing virtue and manliness to build in themselves the capacity to act, and to act well, reminding themselves that our Lord Jesus Christ rewards every good deed, no matter how small it may be. Labor is a very great thing, for as Saint Bernard says, it gives the laborer strong arms and tough muscles, whereas Sloth makes them weak and feeble. And slothful folk dread the thought of beginning to do any sort of good works, which seems to them too large to even contemplate, and thinking this way certainly tends toward sin. Sloth makes men believe that goodness is so painfully hard and so complicated that it requires more daring than they possess, as Saint George says.

Hopelessness and despair of God's mercy sometimes lead slothful folk to profound sorrow, and to great fear, believing that they have already committed so many sins that nothing will be able to help them, even if they should want to repent and stop their sinning. And this despair then leads them to abandon their hearts to every kind of sin, as Saint Augustine says. And this damnable sin, if it continues to the end of a man's life, is termed sinning against the Holy Ghost. It is a horrible sin indeed, and extremely dangerous, for a man in despair may not refrain from any and all crimes and sins, as Judas illustrates. Surely, then, this is of all sins the one most unpleasant to God, and most adversarial to our Lord Jesus Christ. Truly, a man in despair is like a cowardly fighter, who surrenders and cries "mercy! mercy!"—but all superfluously, because he does not need to admit defeat and has no need to despair. God's mercy is always available to a penitent man, and especially to the good works he performs. Alas! Why should a man be unable to think of the gospel of Saint Luke, chapter 15, in which Christ says, "The joy in heaven, when a sinful man does penitence, is equal to heaven's joy over ninety-nine righteous men who need no penance." And note, further, in the same gospel, the joy of the father who had lost his son, and the feast of celebration he gives, when that son, penitent, returns to his father. Can people not remember, also, that as Saint Luke reports, in chapter 23, the thief who was crucified next to Christ, says: "Lord, remember me, when you come into your kingdom." "I surely will," Christ replies. "I say to you, today you will be with me in paradise." Indeed, no sin a man can commit is so horrible that, during his lifetime, it may not be destroyed by penitence, by means of the crucifixion and death of Christ. Alas! Why does a man need to fall into despair, since Christ's mercy is so available and so great? Ask, and you shall have.

And then there is drowsiness, or sluggish slumbering, which makes a man heavy and dull, both in body and in soul. And this sin, too, comes from Sloth. And reason surely says that men ought not to sleep once the sun is up, unless there are special justifications. Certainly, early morning is the best time for a man to say his prayers, and to think of God, and to honor God, and to give alms to the first poor person who, in the name of Christ, seeks your help. Hear what Solomon says: "Whoever wakes in the morning and comes to seek me, he will find me."

There is also negligence, or recklessness, which does not care about anything. And if ignorance is the mother of all harm, surely negligence is its nurse. A negligent man does not care, when he is doing something, whether he does it well or badly. As to the remedy for these last sins, the wise man says that "whoever fears God does not neglect to do what he needs to do." And the man who loves God, he will be diligent in order to please God by his works, and give himself to his work with abandon, in order to do that work well. As for idleness: that is indeed the entrance door for all evil. A man who is idle is like a house without walls; devils can come in from any side, or shoot at him as if he is out in the open, and give him temptations on every side. Idleness is the disgusting wastewater bilge of a ship, in which all wicked and villainous thoughts can be found, and in which are also intermingled all jabbering and stupid noises, all foolishness and lying, and every variety of dung. Heaven is surely meant for those who labor, and not to those who are idle. And as David says, "they do not do men's work, so they ought not be whipped along with men"—in Purgatory, that is. If they do not do penitence, they should surely be tormented by the devils in hell.

Then there is the sin called tardiness, as when a man is late, or lingering, before he is willing to turn to God. And surely this is a great folly. Such a man resembles a fellow who falls in a ditch, and can't be bothered getting out again. This stems from a false, vain hope, namely, that he will live a long life and worry about God at some later time. That does not often come to pass.

Laziness is next. That is, a man who begins a good work and soon stops and leaves it, like those who are responsible for the control and guidance of another person, and stop being concerned about him at all, as soon as they find their responsibilities in any way annoying. These are the new-style shepherds, who cheerfully allow their sheep to run to the wolves, hiding in the bushes, and do not attempt to control even their own actions. Poverty and destruction are what this leads to, both in spiritual and in worldly matters.

And then there is a sort of coldness, which freezes a man's heart. And that leads to the loss of devotion, a man's heart being so blinded, as Saint Bernard says, that his soul turns languid, and he can no longer read or sing in holy church, nor hear or think about any devotion, nor put his hands to any good work, all these things seeming to him tasteless, unattractive, and boring. He grows slack and sleepy, and soon will become angry, and soon thereafter is inclined to hate and envy. Then there is the sin of worldly sorrow, called *tristicia* or sadness, which kills men, as Saint Paul says. For such sorrow surely leads to the death of the soul, and of the body as well, since a man comes to be irritated by his own life. And thus this sadness often shortens men's lives far beyond what they might naturally have expected.

Remedy against the sin of Sloth

Against this terrible sin, and all its branches, there is a virtue called *fortitudo* or strength, an emotion by means of which a man scorns irritating things. This is so powerful and so vigorous a virtue that a man so endowed can powerfully withstand, and wisely keep himself away from, all manner of wicked perils, and which enables him to wrestle against the devil's assaults. This virtue enhances and strengthens the soul, just as Sloth makes it decline and grow weak. This *fortitudo* can endure for a long time, aiding in the doing of many useful things.

There are many different kinds of this virtue, and the first is called magnanimity, meaning "great courage or fortitude." And certainly great courage is needed, in dealing with Sloth, in order to keep it from swallowing the soul with its sorrowfulness, or destroying it with hopelessness. This virtue allows men to take on, reasonably and of their own free will, tasks which are difficult and painful. And since the devil wages his battles against mankind far more by cleverness and tricks than by strength, men must fight back with wit, reason, and discretion, arming themselves with the virtues of faith and hope in God, and in his saints, which will bolster him in finishing the good works he means to continue. This develops security, and a man no longer doubts, then and in the future, that he can complete any good works he begins. And this develops glory, and a man performs great good works, which is indeed the reason why men should begin doing them, for their accomplishment results in this great reward. Associated with this glory is constancy, stability of heart, and it will be held in place by steadfast faith, and faithful words, and in the man's bearing and appearance, as well as in his deeds. There are also other more particular remedies against Sloth, in doing all sorts of good works, such as remembering both the pains of hell and the joys of heaven, and lacing your trust in the Holy Ghost's grace, and these will bolster a man in doing the good he truly wants to do.

Now follows the discussion of Avarice

Saint Paul says, in the Epistle to Timothy, chapter, 6, that "the root of all harms is Avarice." And truly, when a man's heart feels defeated, and is uncertain, and it seems as if God's comfort has been lost, the heart seeks fruitless satisfaction and comfort in worldly things.

According to Saint Augustine, Avarice is the lust for the acquisition of worldly things. Others say that Avarice occurs when a man purchases many things for himself, but gives nothing to those in need. You must understand that Avarice does not involve only land and other kinds of property, but sometimes involves knowledge, or glory, and every sort of excessive thing. Strictly speaking, however, there is a difference between Avarice and Covetise, the former involving the lust to hold on to property you already own, and the latter involving the lust to acquire what you do not already own. Avarice is certainly a damnable sin, for it is cursed in holy writ, where this vice is attacked, and because it wrongs Jesus Christ, depriving him of the love that men owe him, turning it away against all reason, and making an avaricious man have more hope from his cattle than in being of service to Jesus Christ. Which is why Saint Paul says, in the Epistle to the Ephesians, section 5, that an avaricious man has been enslaved by idolatry.

And the difference, arguably, between an idolator and an avaricious man, is that the idolator has perhaps two or three idols which he worships, while the avaricious man has many more. Plainly, every coin he adds to his coffers is his idol. Further, the sin of idolatry is the first thing forbidden by God, in the ten commandments: see Exodus 20: "You shall have no false gods before me, nor shall you make for yourself any images of gods." And so an avaricious man, who loves his treasure more than he does his God, becomes an idol-worshipper, by means of this cursèd sin of Avarice. Covetise, similarly, leads men to become harsh and severe lords, squeezing men by taxes, custom duties, and tolls, far in excess of what is required or reasonable. They set fines against their bondsmen, which might more reasonably be termed extortions. These fines and ransoms are claimed to be rightful, according to the stewards of these cruel lords, for according to them a bondsman truly owns nothing worldly, but everything he has belongs to his lord. But it is plainly wrong for lords to take away from their bondsmen things that their lords never gave them, as Saint Augustine says, in *The City of God,* book 9, that "it is true that the state of slavery in which a bondsman lives, as well as the primary reason for that state, is sin." And we can thus see that the sin deserves to be punished by slavery—but that slavery is not part of man's inherent nature. Accordingly, these cruel lords should not so glorify themselves in their lordships, since it is not nature which makes them lords over their slaves but the slaves' sin which brings them into slavery. Furthermore, when the law stipulates that the worldly goods of bondsmen are the property of their lords, that is to indicate only that all worldly goods belong to the king, and bondsmen are required to defend the king's property, but the lords are not entitled to rob their bondsmen. As Seneca says, "Kindness to your slaves is the wise way to live." Reflect on the fact that those you call your slaves are God's people; humble people, too, are Christians, and therefore your friends; they too are intimate to and known by the Lord. Lords spring from the same seeds from which slaves are born into this world; slaves have souls and they may be saved just as lords may be. The same death, in the end, comes to both lords and slaves. My advice is that you do right to your slaves, as you would wish your lord to do to you, were you in the slave's place. Every sinful man is a slave to sin. So I advise you, you lords, to try to have your slaves love you, rather than fear you. I know very well that there are differences in status, among men in this world, and it is right and proper that men do their duty as they owe it; but it is certain that extortions of your underlings, and displays of contempt toward them, are sinful and damnable.

And still further: understand quite clearly that conquerors and tyrants often make slaves of people born to blood every bit as royal as that of their conquerors. The very word "slavery" was unknown until Noah declared that his son, Canaan, must be enslaved to his brothers, because of his sins. What then do we say about those who pillage and force extortions upon holy church? Surely, the sword first given to a knight, when he is newly dubbed, is a sign that he must protect holy church, and neither rob nor pillage it, for who does so is a traitor to Christ. And as Saint Augustine says, "those who strangle Christ's sheep are the devil's wolves," and what they do is worse than wolfish. For it is true that, with his belly full, the wolf stops hunting sheep. And it is equally true that those who pillage and destroy the goods of holy church do not thus interrupt their activities, for they never stop their pillage.

As I have said, since sin was the initial cause for slavery, ever since there has been sin, this entire world has been in slavery and subjection. But ever since the time of grace has come, surely, God decreed that some people should be of higher estate than others, and some of lower estate, and that each should be dealt with in accord therewith. And in some countries, therefore, when slaves turn to the faith, they become free men. Lords are thus in debt to their men, just as their men are in debt to them. The Pope calls himself the servant of the servants of God, but if the estate of holy church is to be maintained, and community property preserved, as well as peace and quiet on earth, it is essential that God has ordained there to be men of both higher and lower status, and ordained the existence of sovereignty, to preserve and maintain and defend their subjects and underlings, within reason, as much as sovereignty is able to do such things—but not to destroy their subjects or underlings, nor shame them. Which is why I say that when lords become like wolves, when they wrongly devour the cattle or other possessions of poor people, without mercy or any restrictions, they must only receive Jesus Christ's mercy, according to the same standards they have applied to their treatment of poor people, if their behavior is altered.

Which brings us to the deceit employed by merchants against other merchants. You must understand that merchandise has a number of aspects, some bodily and material, some spiritual, some honest and trustworthy, some dishonest and untrustworthy. As to bodily merchandise that is trustworthy and honest, when a country has been ordained, by God's bounty, to be able to take care of itself and its people, then it becomes honest and trustworthy that, using their country's abundance, the men of that country may help those of another country, more in need. Merchants are thereby made necessary, to ensure that merchandise is brought from one country to another. But merchandise afflicted with fraud and treachery and deceit, with lying and false oaths, is cursèd and damnable. Spiritual merchandise ought to be termed simony—that is, traffic in spiritual things, the buying and selling of things which belong to the sanctuary of God and the saving of souls. If a man work at this trafficking, and have no desire to sin thereby, it is nevertheless a deadly sin, and if he is a man in holy orders, he is unfit to function in any sacred capacity. Simon Magus (see Acts 8, 9–13), for example, who wished to buy the gift that God had given, through the Holy Ghost, to Saint Peter and to the Apostles, was surely guilty of simony. From which you must understand that both the buyer and the seller of spiritual things are guilty of simony, no matter what the medium of exchange—whether it is by cattle, or procuring, or through urgings by others, whether friends or kin being irrelevant. Indeed, prayers said for someone who is not worthy of them constitute simony. And when either men or women seek clerical advancement, on the basis of sexual favors, that constitutes foul simony. On the other hand, when a man bestows spiritual things on his servants, it is not simony if the service is actually and honestly performed. But there must be no bargaining and the servants must be competent and qualified. For as Saint Damasus, who was a Pope, says, "Compared to this sin, all the other sins in the world, are like nothing." It is indeed the greatest of all possible sins, except for those of Lucifer and the anti-Christ, for it deprives God of the church and the souls that he bought with his precious blood when churches are handed over to those who are not worthy, putting into ecclesiastical posts, and power, thieves who steal Jesus Christ's patrimony. Such dishonorable priests and pastors cause ignorant men to feel less reverence for holy church's sacraments. Further, such unworthy appointments squeeze out the true men of Christ, putting in their stead the devil's own children. They sell the souls they are charged with, like lambs, straight to the wolf who will kill them. Such unworthy hands should never have any part of the lambs' pasture, which is itself a part of heavenly bliss.

Gambling enters, bringing its tools along with it, such as backgammon and dice, and from such activities come deceit, false oaths, quarreling, stealing, blaspheming and denying God, as well as hatred for one's neighbors, waste of property, and sometimes murder. Without a doubt, it is impossible for there to be gamblers who are free of sin. Avarice, which is associated with this sin, also produces lying, theft, false witnessing, and false oaths. And you need to understand that these are great sins, all of them expressly in violation of God's commandments, as I have said. Giving false witness is both a matter of words and a matter of deeds. In the matter of words, for example, it may amount to stealing your neighbor's good name, or his property, or his inheritance, nor does it make any difference whether your motivation in giving false witness is anger, or bribery, or envy, or deflecting guilt from yourself. Be warned, you lawyers and notaries! Surely, Susanna fell into great sorrow and pain, as a result of giving false witness, nor is she a solitary example. Theft is involved, here, as well, and it too is expressly contrary to God's command, and both corporeally and spiritually. It is corporeal, for example, if without your neighbor's consent you take his property, whether by force or by some trick, perhaps a false measurement. It is theft, too, if you have your neighbor falsely indicted, just as it is if you borrow and never intend to return. And so on. Spiritual theft is sacrilege, as for example damaging holy objects, or anything sacred to Christ. This involves two distinct manners: first, by the location being holy church, in which any vicious sin is sacrilege, and second, because of falsely depriving holy church of rights which truly belong to it. In clear and universal terms, sacrilege occurs if any holy thing is taken from any holy place, or any unholy thing is taken from a holy place, or any holy thing is taken from an unholy place.

Relief for the sin of Avarice

You must understand that the relief for Avarice is mercy, generously employed. Men may ask why mercy and pity are relief for Avarice. Certainly, an avaricious man shows no pity and gives no mercy to others in need, for he takes great pleasure in holding on to his treasure, and not in rescuing or relieving his fellow Christians. Let me begin with mercy. As the philosopher says, mercy is a virtue by which a man's heart is stirred by the misery of those in distress: mercy follows after pity, in the performance of merciful acts. Surely, such things make a man think of Jesus Christ's mercy, sacrificing himself for our sins, and enduring death out of mercy for us, and forgiveness for our original sin, thereby freeing us from the pains of hell and reducing the pains of purgatory by penance, and giving us the grace with which to accomplish that penance, and, in the end, giving us the bliss of heaven. Mercy operates by lending and giving, forgiving and relieving, with pity and compassion in our hearts for our fellow Christians, and also to discipline and correct them, whenever necessary.

Another method of relief against Avarice is to become generous, but in truth this requires Jesus Christ's grace, as well as some consideration of the worldly goods, and the enduring goods, which have been given by Christ, as well as serious reflection of a man's inevitable death, on a date which no one can know in advance, nor where, nor how. It also requires that a man surrender all his worldly possessions, except what he uses for the performance of good works.

But some people know nothing of moderation, so we need to avoid foolish giving, otherwise known as waste. A prodigal man does not give his property away, but simply loses it. Indeed, whatever he gives, in searching for vainglory—like money spent on musicians, and others, with the purpose of enhancing his worldly renown—is sinful, for this is not almsgiving. Surely, he sinfully loses his property, when all he is thinking about, in making such gifts, is straightforwardly sinful. He is like a horse that prefers to drink muddy or disturbed water than water from a clear, quiet well. And since what they have given ought not to have been given at all, what they deserve is the curse that Christ shall give, on the Day of Judgment, to everyone who is to be damned in hell.

Next comes the discussion of Gluttony

Gluttony is the endless appetite for eating or drinking, and is expressly contrary to God's commandment. This sin has corrupted the entire world, as is easily seen from the sins of Adam and Eve. Here is what Saint Paul says of Gluttony: "There are many, as I have often said to you, and now I say it weeping, who have been enemies of Christ's cross (the result of which is death), and who have made their stomachs their god, and made their glory the ruin and destruction of all those who so cherish worldly things." A man who is accustomed to the sin of Gluttony cannot hold off any sin whatsoever. He is compelled to be in the service of all and every vice, for he seeks his comfort, and takes his rest, in the devil's store and treasure. There are many varieties of this sin; first among them is drunkenness, which is the horrible tomb of a man's reason, and that is a deadly sin. On the other hand, when a man does not ordinarily indulge in strong liquor, and perhaps does not know how strong his drink may be, or is himself somewhat confused at the time, and so drinks even more, and suddenly is caught by drunkenness, there is no deadly sin involved, but only a venial one. Another variety of Gluttony is when drunkenness addles a man's spirit, and his judgment is impaired. Yet another variety of Gluttony is when a man simply devours his food, having no orderly and decent approach to eating. Yet another is when, because of the huge volume of food he consumes, his bodily balance is deranged. And yet another is a forgetfulness, engendered by too much drinking, and which can be so serious that a man may forget, the next day, what he did or said the night before.

Saint Gregory specifies another arrangement for the species of Gluttony. The first, he says, is eating before it is time to eat. The second is when a man becomes a gourmet eater, or drinker. The third is when a man eats too much. The fourth is complexity, when a man is obsessed with the preparation and garnishing of his food. The fifth is to eat too greedily. These are, he says, the five fingers of the devil's hand, by which he draws people into sinning.

Remedy for the sin of Gluttony

Galen says that the remedy against Gluttony is abstinence, but I think he is wrong, if he acts simply with bodily health in mind. Saint Augustine prefers abstinence for the sake of virtue, and performed with patience. "Abstinence," he says, "is worth very little, unless a man really devotes himself to it, and it is reinforced by patience and charity, and men do it for God's sake, and in the hope of heavenly bliss."

What goes along with abstinence are moderation, which involves staying balanced in whatever you do; and also shame, which makes a man avoid all dishonesty; and satisfaction and contentment, that does not long for rich food or drink, and has no particular interest in luxurious preparation of food; also moderation and balance, which apply the power of reason to restrain a foul habit of eating; sobriety, too, which checks extravagant drinking; and frugality, as well, which holds back the voluptuous desire to sit long at the table, leisurely—which is why some people take to eating while standing up, voluntarily choosing, thusly, so that leisurely eating is less feasible.

Now comes the discussion of Lechery

Gluttony and Lechery are so closely related that, often enough, they are in fact inseparable. God knows, this is a sin deeply displeasing to God, for he himself said, "Do not be a lecherous man." And therefore, in the old or Hebraic law, God specified severe punishments for this sin. A slave woman caught being lecherous was to be beaten to death with wooden sticks, and if she was a woman from a good family she would be stoned to death, while a bishop's daughter would be burned to death, all as God has commanded. Moreover, it was because of lechery that God drowned the entire world, in a great flood. And, later, he burned five cities with thunder and lightning, and sank them down into hell.

Let us now speak of that stinking form of Lechery, the sin called adultery, committed by married people. Saint John says that all those guilty of adultery should be in hell, in a pool burning with fire and brimstone—the fire being for their sin of adultery, in brimstone, because of their stinking filth. Surely, breaking the sacrament of marriage is a horrible thing. This was commanded by God himself, high in heaven, and confirmed by Jesus Christ, as Saint Matthew tells us in the gospel: "A man must leave his father and mother, and live with his wife, and they must be two people bound together as if they were one flesh." This sacrament must be understood as parallel to the knitting together of Christ and holy church. Not only did God forbid adultery, as an accomplished fact, he commanded that a man is forbidden to desire his neighbor's wife. "This commandment," says Saint Augustine, "forbids any and every desire to commit all forms of lechery." And hear what Saint Matthew says, in the gospel: "Whoever looks at a woman and desires to have sexual intercourse with her, has already committed lechery with her, in his heart." Whoever commits the cursèd sin of lechery finds it extremely painful, first of all in his or her soul, for he has forced it into sin, and to the suffering of death, which is permanent and everlasting. But it also hurts the body, for it drains him, and saps him, and ruins him; he has sacrificed his blood to the devil in hell. It also ravages his cattle and everything he owns. And surely, if it is a foul thing for a man to ravage his cattle, in order to possess a woman, yet it is even fouler than that for a woman, who in return for such filth, pays the man with her own cattle and other possessions. This sin, as the prophet says, deprives both men and women of their good reputation, and every bit of their honor, and is deeply pleasing to the devil, for this gives him control over the largest part of the world. And just as a merchant is happiest when, after bargaining, he comes off best, so too the devil delights in this foulness.

I spoke of the devil's hand, but here is his other hand, and its five fingers, ready to draw people into his villainy. The first finger is the foolish glance of the foolish woman and the foolish man, deadly in its nature, just as the basilisk kills people who look at him, poisoned by the sight of his venom. The lust of the eyes obeys the lusting of the heart. The second finger is for wicked touching, in wicked ways. Accordingly, Solomon says that "whosoever touches and handles a woman, experiences what happens to a man who picks up a scorpion, who has a deadly sting and a poison that quickly kills." It is like a man who touches hot tar, which burns off his skin. The third finger is foul words, that run like fire, and immediately burn the heart. The fourth finger is for kissing—and truly anyone who would kiss the mouth of a burning oven or a furnace is a great fool, and those who kiss villainously are even greater fools, for then the human mouth is truly the mouth of hell, especially for those old and dotard lechers, who keep on with their illicit kissing, and defile themselves. Certainly, they strongly resemble dogs, who walk by a rosebush, or any other bush, and though he is completely pissed out, will still heave up a leg and pretend to piss.

Many men believe that whatever he does with his wife, no matter how lecherous, it cannot possibly be considered sinful, but that is most certainly wrong. God knows, a man can kill himself with his own knife, and make himself drunk, drinking out of his own barrel. It makes no difference whether he casts his lechery on his wife, or his child, or any worldly thing he loves more than he loves God, he has made that person his living idol, and he has made himself an idolator. A man should love his wife wisely, patiently, and in moderation, and then she becomes more like his sister.

The fifth finger of the devil's hand is the stinking deed of Lechery. Without a doubt, the five fingers of Lechery were put into a man's belly by the devil, and using those five fingers, the fiend grips him by the reins, as a man does with a horse, and thus throws him into hell's furnaces, the fire of which burns forever, and the serpents of which bite forever, and the man goes on weeping and wailing, suffering sharp pangs of hunger and thirst, enduring the grimness of the devil's hordes, which will stamp them into the ground over and over, with no pause, and no end. As I have said, Lechery takes many different forms, as for example fornication, which is when an unmarried man and an unmarried woman have sexual intercourse, this being both against nature and a deadly sin. Indeed, a man's reason tells him that it is a deadly sin, since God has forbidden all lechery. Saint Paul offers men a heavenly kingdom, but makes that offer only to those who refrain from deadly sin. Another sin of lechery is to deprive a virgin of her maidenhead, for a man who does this, for certain, throws her out of the highest degree in this our earthly life, stripping her of that fruit that the book tells us is like a hundred fruit. I cannot phrase it accurately in English, but in Latin it is *Centisimus fructus,* "fructus" signifying far more than merely "fruit," but embracing such meanings as "satisfaction, profit, joy." Again, the man who does this to a virgin causes an immense amount of harm, more than a man knows how to reckon, which is akin to a man trying to assess the damages done by an animal in his fields, breaking the hedge or the fence or the gate beyond repair. Surely, maidenhead cannot be restored any more than an arm cut from the body can ever be put back. The girl may be shown God's mercy, yes, if she does penitence, but she will never again be uncorrupted.

I have already said some things about adulterers, it is useful to display more of its perils, to help keep people from committing this sin. In Latin, adultery signifies going to another man's bed, and bringing it about that someone who was previously as one flesh, one body, with another, having now abandoned their body to someone else is no longer that same flesh, that same body, as the other person in the marriage. As the wise man says, much harm is done by this sin. First, faith is broken, and without any question, faith is the key of all Christendom. And when faith is broken, and lost, truly Christendom stands barren, devoid of fruit. This sin is also a theft, for thievery is based on depriving a man of something against his will. This is surely the foulest of all sins, when a woman steals her body from her husband, and gives it to her lecher so that he may defoul her, stealing her soul from Christ and giving it to the devil. This is a fouler sin than breaking into a church and stealing the chalice, for these lechers break God's spiritual temple and steal the vessel of grace, which is both the body and the soul, for which deed Christ will destroy a lecher, just as Saint Paul says. Truly, Joseph was very afraid of this theft, when his lord's wife tried to entice him into sinning with her; he said, "O, my lady, my lord told me, when he gave me control of all his earthly possessions, nothing that belonged to him was out of power except you, who are his wife. And how should I do this wicked thing, and sin so horribly against both God and my lord? God forbid it!" Alas! all too seldom is such fidelity to be found, in our time.

Another harm caused by this sin is the filthiness by which the two sinners break God's commandment, and defoul the author of matrimony, who is Christ. Surely, the sacrament of marriage is so noble and honorable that, truly, it becomes a still greater sin to break it, for God created marriage in Paradise, in a state of innocence, in order that mankind would multiply and there would be more men doing service to God. Further, breaking this sacrament often interferes with the just distribution of property, by creating false heirs. So Christ keeps them out of heaven's reign, which is to be inherited only by good people. And still further: breaking the sacrament of marriage can and does create situations in which people either marry, or commit sexual sins, with people who are in fact their close relatives, and especially the lechers who frequent houses of prostitution, filled with foolish women who are, in fact, more like a public toilet where men dispose of their dung. What can we say of the pimps who live by this ghastly sin of bodily prostitution, forcing women to give them a specified portion of what they earn—yes, sometimes even the man's own wife or his daughter? These are unquestionably cursèd sins. Be aware that, in the Bible, adultery is most appropriately set between theft and murder, for it is theft of both body and soul. And it is very like killing, for it carves in half and breaks apart those who were once made to be of one flesh. And therefore, under the old Hebraic law of God, they deserve to be killed. Still, under the law of Jesus Christ, which is a law of pity, Christ said to the woman found in adultery, who was supposed to be stoned to death, as the Jews intended, according to their law, "Go," Christ said, "and do not again indulge sin." Indeed, the revenge for adultery is the pains of hell, unless there is repentance and penance.

There are still other varieties of this cursèd sin. For example, when one of the sinners is a cleric, or perhaps both of them, or perhaps they are people admitted into lower orders, like deacons or subdeacons, or Knights Hospitallers. The higher someone may be, in clerical orders, the greater is the sin. What greatly increases their sin is the breaking of their vow of chastity, when they entered into orders. Furthermore, the holy orders are the chief treasures of God, and bear his special sign and mark of chastity, to show that they have been bound to the most precious life that is possible, here on this earth. People in holy orders are God's possessions, his own select household retainers and servants, so that when they commit deadly sins they become special traitors to God, and to his people, who support and sustain them, and for whom they are supposed to pray, but who have become such traitors their prayers cannot be of help to anyone. The honor of their profession makes priests like angels— but as Saint Paul has said, Satan can transform himself into the shape of an angel of light, looking like a genuine angel of light, but truly an angel of darkness. Indeed, a priest who commits deadly sins can be compared to an angel of darkness who assumes the shape of an angel of light. Such priests are the sons of Eli, as we can see in the book of Kings, 1 Samuel, 2:12, and they are the true sons of Belial, the devil. The significance of "belial" is "worthlessness," and that is what they are, thinking they are free, and no one has any authority over them, any more than a wild bull, which takes whatever cow it feels like having. Which is how these men are with women. Just as one wild bull is quite enough for an entire town, so too a wicked priest is sufficient corruption for an entire parish, or even an entire province. Such priests, as the book declares, cannot transmit to the people the true mystery of the priesthood, nor do they know the truths of God. They do not think it sufficient for them to be offered boiled meat, as the book says they should be, but they take raw flesh, and by force. Truly, that is to say, such rascals are not satisfied with the cooked meat they offered, with great reverence, but they want the living flesh of the people's wives and daughters. And women who consent to these rascals' filthy doings are seriously wronging Christ, and holy church, and all the saints, and all souls, for they deprive others of the right to worship Christ, and deprive them of holy church, and of the prayers which should be said for all Christian souls. And so such priests, and their sweethearts who consent to lechery with them, are condemned by all ecclesiastical courts, until they reform themselves.

Yet another form of adultery is sometimes that which takes place between a man and his wife, when all they want is their bodily pleasures, and do not accept the rewards of the spirit, as Saint Jerome has said; they care for nothing except the bare facts of their coupling. Marriage is good enough, in and of itself, or so they believe. But the devil has power over people like this, as the angel said to Tobias, for in their coupling they take no thought of Jesus Christ, putting him out of their hearts, and give themselves up to their fleshly filth.

And yet another form of adultery is sexual activity among people who are bodily related to one another, or related by marriage, or else among people whose fathers, or whose fathers' relatives, had been guilty of sinful sexuality. This sin makes them very like dogs, who pay no attention to who is and who is not related to them. And, without question, kinship occurs in different contexts, either spiritual or fleshly—the spiritual being, for example, someone who is a godfather or a godmother. It is no less adulterous for a woman to have sexual intercourse with a godsibling than with her own fleshly brother.

There are other, and often more horrid, sins of adultery, such as the abominable sin, of which no man can quite manage to speak, or to write about, but which is openly referred to in holy writ. Men and women do this for different reasons, and in different ways, but the fact that holy writ mentions this horrible sin no more befouls holy writ than the sun is befouled by shining down on the manure pile.

Lechery is related to yet another sin, which occurs when someone is asleep, and this comes most especially to virgin girls, and also to those who have been befouled, and men call this pollution. It falls into four different varieties. Firstly, when the body is drooping and weak, for the humors begin to grow rank, that is, strong and offensive, and overabundant; secondly, in illness, when the body is less well able to retain its secretions, as natural science knows; thirdly, when the person has eaten or drunk too much; and sometimes because of the wicked thoughts that linger in a man's mind when he goes to sleep, which are of course sinful, so men must guard against them very carefully, or they will sin most grievously.

Remedy for the sin of Lechery

Chastity and self-restraint are the most common remedies against Lechery: they restrain all the disorderly reactions that stem from fleshly appetites and desires. He who can best restrain the wicked inflammation caused by the ardor of this sin, indeed, earns the higher reward. I speak, here, of chastity in marriage and the chastity of widowhood. You must understand that matrimony is the lawful joining of man and woman, who receive, through the sacrament, the bonding tie that should hold them together, and as one, for the rest of both their lives. This is a very great sacrament indeed. God made it, as I have said, in Paradise, and as Jesus would himself be born of a marriage. And the better to sanctify and purify this sacrament, Jesus went to a wedding and there turned water into wine, which was the first miracle, in his earthly form, he had performed in the presence of his disciples. The sure results of marriage are that it cleanses and purifies fornication, and that it provides proper lineages for holy church, for that is the purpose of marriage; it changes deadly sin to venial sin, as between the two wedded parties, and makes them into one loyal heart as well as one body. This is true marriage, as established by God, before there was any sin here on earth, at a time when natural law was in its correct state, in Paradise, it having been ordained by God that one man should have only one woman, and one woman only one man, as Saint Augustine says, for many reasons.

First: marriage is shaped by God and holy church. And another reason is that the man is set above the woman, being in a sense her head: according to God's command, this must always be the case. If a woman were to have more than one man, she would have more than one head, and that would be a horrible thing for God to see. Furthermore, a woman might not be able to please so many men at once. Nor would there ever be peace and quiet among them, for each person would want different things. And in addition, no man would know which children were truly of his lineage, and who should be his heirs. Also, the woman would be less well beloved, from the moment she was joined to more than one man.

In dealing with his wife, a man should act with consideration and reverence, as Christ indicated when he shaped Eve, the first woman. He did not make her from Adam's head, for she was not to have any claim to lordship. When women are the masters, they create too much disorder. No evidence for this needs to be produced: day by day experience should be proof enough. Also, to be sure, God did not make Eve from Adam's foot, for she ought not to be placed so low, she being unable to bear that. But God made her from Adam's rib, for women should be men's companions. A man should be faithful to his wife, both in his words and in his deeds, as Saint Paul says: a man ought to love his wife as Christ loved holy church, loving it so well that he died for it. So too should a man for his wife, if it was necessary.

Saint Peter says that a woman should be subjected to her husband's governance. First of all, in obedience. Further, says his decree, a married woman, so long as she is married to a man, has no power or authority to swear to anything, or to bear witness about anything, without her husband's permission, he being her lord—as always, according to true reason, he ought to be. She should serve him faithfully, and be moderate in how she dresses. I understand very well that women should try to please their husbands—but not by elaborate clothes and decorations. Saint Jerome says that "wives who are dressed in silk and royal purple can no longer wrap themselves in Jesus Christ." And see what Saint John says of this matter. Saint Gregory says that "no human being seeks precious clothing except in vaingloriousness, in order to arouse more public approbation." It is immensely foolish for a woman to be beautifully dressed, but inside, to be foul. A wife ought to be moderate in how she looks, and how she carries herself, and in how she speaks, discreet in everything she says and does. And above all other worldly things, she should love her husband with her whole heart, and be faithful to him with her body. And the same should be true of a husband, as regards his wife. Since the whole body that a married couple consists of is, in truth, the husband's property, so too should her heart belong to him, or else theirs cannot be a perfect, true marriage.

And it must be understood that a man and woman come together for three reasons. The first is the engendering of children, for service to God, for surely that is the primal reason for matrimony. Another reason is that each of the married pair should give each other, in debt, their bodies, for neither of them has the power to dispose of their own bodies as they themselves may please. And the third reason is to avoid lechery and wickedness. The fourth, indeed, is deadly sin. Engendering children is meritorious, as is the second reason, as well, for as the commandment says, a woman achieves the merit of chastity when she pays her husband the debt of her body, even though she may not want to, and her heart may not desire it. The third reason deals with venial sin—and, truly, virtually none of all this may occur with venial sin, because of our corruption and also because of the fleshly pleasures involved. Deadly sin in marital coupling, it must be understood, occurs when the man and woman are only concerned with amorous love, rather than for any of the other things set out, above; they want only their own burning pleasure, and as much of it as they can get. This is truly deadly sin. But still, I say sorrowfully, there are people who go out of their way to indulge in sexual intercourse, more frequently than is necessary.

To be an honest, pure widow is another way for a married woman to achieve a state of chastity, avoiding men's arms and longing only for the embrace of Jesus Christ. I speak of women who have been wives, but have lost their husbands, or else women who have committed lechery but have been redeemed by penance. Surely, if a woman remains chaste, with her husband's permission, giving him no opportunity for sinning, she earns very high merit indeed. Women who remain chaste, in this way, must be pure in heart as well as in body and in thought, and moderate as to clothing, and also as to her face, and she must also be abstinent in eating and drinking, in speaking, and in her actions. They are the vessels and sacred containers of the blessèd Mary Magdalen, and their perfume spreads itself all over holy church. Of course, virginity is chastity, and requires holiness of heart and purity of body. Such a woman is the spouse of Jesus Christ, and the very life of angels. She embodies the worthiness of this world, and is the equal of all the martyrs. She has inside her that which tongues cannot tell and hearts cannot conceive of. Our Lord Jesus Christ was born of a virgin, and was a virgin himself.

Another remedy against Lechery is to be careful of all things and occasions which might give rise to this sin, as for example comfort, eating, and drinking. Surely, when a pot boils over, the best remedy is to take it off the fire. Sleeping a long time, in utter quiet, is also a great nourisher of Lechery.

Yet another remedy for Lechery is for a man or a woman to avoid the company of those by whom he or she fears to be tempted. Even should the actual deed be shunned, the temptation itself is great. Truly, though a white wall is not burned down, when a lighted candle is stuck against it, yet the wall is blackened by the flame. I have often cautioned that no man should trust in his personal perfection unless he is stronger than Samson, and holier than David, and wiser than Solomon.

Having now explained to you, as best I can, the seven deadly sins, and some of their branches, and some of the remedies for them, I would, if I were truly capable of it, discuss the ten commandments. But that is high, complex theology and must be left to scholarly clerics. Nevertheless, I hope the ten commandments have all of them been in one way or another at least mentioned in my discussion.

THERE FOLLOWS THE SECOND PART OF THE DISCUSSION OF PENANCE

Since the second part of Penance is founded in making confession to a priest, let me say again, as I said at the very beginning, what Saint Augustine has said: "Sin is in every word, and every deed, and every single thing that men desire which is against the law of Jesus Christ, and this is true, as well, for sin in the heart, in the mouth, and in deed, by each and all of your five wits, namely, sight, hearing, smelling, tasting and savoring, and feeling." You must understand the circumstances which powerfully intensify every sin. You must be constantly aware of who and what you are, committing the particular sin, whether you are male or female, young or old, a gentleman or a bond-servant, healthy or sick, married or single, having taken orders or not taken them, a wise man or a fool, a cleric or a secular man, and whether the woman is related to you, either in body or spiritually, or not at all, and if anyone related to you have previously sinned with her, or have not, and many other matters.

Another circumstance is this: whether the sexual act was fornication, or adultery, or not; whether it was incestuous or not; whether she was a virgin or not; whether murder was involved or was not; whether the sins involved were horrible great ones or small; and how long you continued to be thus sinning. Yet another consideration is exactly where the sin was committed—in another man's house or your own; out in a field or in a church or a churchyard; in a church that had been consecrated, or not, for if the church is consecrated, and a man or a woman has spilled their seminal fluids in that place, in the course of committing sin or contemplating one, via temptation, the church has been defiled and cannot be used as a place of holy worship until a bishop has reconsecrated it. Further, if the male sinner is a priest, he must be prohibited from all priestly functions, and never again in all his life be permitted to say a mass, and would commit a deadly sin if he ever again did say a mass.

It must be taken into account, too, who were the mediators, or the messengers, who were employed for enticement, or who went along as friends and companions, for many a wretch will go along with their fellows, even if the road leads directly to the devil in hell. Accordingly, anyone who eggs them on, or consents to their sin, are fully responsible participants in the sin, and deserve and will receive the same damnation.

Yet another consideration is whether he has sinned in this way before, and if so how many times, and whether he has sinned additionally, in his mind. A man who is constantly falling into sin is contemptuous of God's mercy, which makes his sinning more serious, and is offensive to Christ. Such a man becomes more and more unable to refrain from sinning, and becomes a casual and indifferent sinner, more likely to avoid going to confession. People who fall back into their old, sinful ways either completely abandon confession, and their former confessors, or make confession only here and there, and this sort of confession does not deserve that God forgive any sins whatever.

We must inquire into just why a man sins, so that if he has been tempted, and has fallen because of that tempting, what sort of temptation occurred? And did the sinner help arrange the temptation? Or was he tempted while himself engaging in the temptation of others? Did he sin with a woman by the use of force, or was the sinning consensual? Or did the woman attempt to escape him, and do everything she could to avoid sinning, but was not able to stop it? She must be asked whether or not there was a monetary reason, or whether she was too terribly poor to avoid such profitable sins, and whether or not she was an instigator. We need also to investigate the details of their sinning, and whether or not she had previously been thus engaged. And the man must also tell the full story, from his side, and whether or not he had been involved with prostitutes and brothels, and whether sexual intercourse had taken place during religious holidays, and whether he sinned in fasting times, and before or after his most recent confession. In the latter case, he might have broken the penance his confessor had enjoined for him. We need to establish by whose help and advice the sin took place, and whether sorcery or witchcraft was involved. Everything must be told, for all these things, be they large or small, burden a man's conscience. And the priest who is in charge of your case will be better informed, before he passes judgment upon you and, when you have repented, explains the necessary penance you must observe. Understand with great clarity that, once a man has befouled his baptism by sinning, the road to salvation must without any question be penitence, confession, and full compliance, to the satisfaction of his confessor, if he has one, and if the confessor has the authority.

A man must be aware that, if he wants to make a true and worthwhile confession, there are four conditions. First, he must confess in sad bitterness of heart, as King Hezekiah said to God, in Ezekiel, "I will remind myself, for all the years of my life, of the bitterness in my heart." This bitterness has five signs. The first is that confession must be made in shame, neither covering over nor hiding a man's sin, because he has sinned against God and fouled his own soul. About which Saint Augustine says: "The heart struggles, being so shamed by the sin." If a man is deeply ashamed, he is worthy of God's great mercy. That was the confession of the tax-gatherer, who would not lift his eyes toward heaven, for he had offended God, for which acute sense of shame he was quickly granted God's mercy. And Saint Augustine says of this that such thoroughly shamed people are the nearest to forgiveness and remission of their sins. Another sign is the humility shown in confession, of which Saint Peter says, "Humble yourself under God's mightiness." In confession, God's hand is indeed mighty, for that is when God can forgive you for your sins, a power which he alone possesses. This humility, further, must be in your heart, and be visible on the outside, just as a man has humility to God in his heart, so too he should humble his body to the priest who is hearing his confession, seated in God's place. The sinner must not sit as high as his confessor, since Christ is lord of everything, and the priest is a mediator between Christ and the sinner, so the sinner should kneel before him, or at his feet, unless he is physically unable to do so. It is not his business just who is sitting there, but in whose place that person is sitting. If a man had trespassed against a lord, and came to ask for his mercy and settle whatever quarrel had existed, it would be seen as totally outrageous, if he simply walked in and down alongside the lord. This would be so improper as to make remission and mercy highly unlikely, for such a man could not possibly be worthy of grace.

And yet another sign of a proper confession is the tears you shed, if you are capable of tears—and if you are not physically able to weep, you should shed tears in your heart. That was how Saint Peter confessed: when he had forsaken Jesus, he went out and wept very bitterly. Nor should a man try to stop his shame from showing, in confession. That was how Mary Magdalene confessed, suppressing nothing, because those who were present would see her shame; she approached Jesus Christ and told him her sins. And after confession, a man or woman should be dutiful and obedient, when receiving the penance laid upon him or her for their sins, for surely Jesus Christ, not for his sins but for ours, was obedient to the death.

The second condition of true confession is that it be done hurriedly.

Surely, if a man had been mortally wounded, the longer he struggled to heal himself the more would his wound fester, and speed him to his death, and even if he did not die, the wound would be much harder to heal. It is the same with sin that, for a long time, a man has kept hidden. And there are certainly many good reasons for hurriedly showing your sins, as for instance fear of death, which often comes to us suddenly, and we never know when that time will come, nor where. More: keeping a sin alive draws in yet another sin, and the longer this continues, the further the man is from Christ. Should he wait to his last day, a man may barely be able to make a true confession, or recall all the details, or express his repentance, oppressed by the painful sickness of death. He who in all his life has paid no attention to what Jesus Christ told us, he can cry to Christ on his last day on earth, but it is highly unlikely that Christ will hear him.

There are four aspects to this necessary hurriedness. Your confession must be arranged in advance, and carefully considered, for wicked haste earns us nothing. A man must fully confess his sins, whether they are of pride, or of envy, and so forth, making their nature clear, and accompanying that with all the details. And he must have understood, in his mind, the number and weight of his sins, and how long he has remained in sin, and also that he be contrite about having sinned, and is determined, by the grace of God, never to fall into sin again, and will therefore be constantly and fearfully on watch, and will run from the opportunities for sinning toward which he has been inclined. It is very important that you confess yourself to one priest, and to one priest only, not a bit to one and then a bit to another. That is, you must understand, a way of attempting to avoid true confession, for shame or fear, but you are only strangling your soul. Without question, Jesus Christ is entirely good, completely without imperfection, and so he either forgives everything or he forgives nothing at all. I am not speaking of a circumstance in which you have been assigned to a particular penitancer, on account of a particular variety of sin, in which case you are not obliged to tell him all the rest of your sins, unless you feel so inclined, out of sheer humility. This is not to be considered as trying to avoid confession. Nor am I saying, when I thus speak of any subdividing of confessionals, that when you are granted permission to make your confession to a good and honest priest, wherever you please, and with the permission of your parish priest, that you should not make your confession a full and thorough one. But, in any case, do not omit a single sin, let everything be told, so far as your memory will permit. And when you do confess to your parish priest, be sure to tell him all the sins you have committed since the last time you went to confessional. This too does not involve any avoidance of true confession.

True confession requires certain conditions. First, you must confess of your own free will, without having been subjected to any constraint, and you must not be ashamed of what people will think, or any such thing. A man sins because he wants to, and it is only reasonable that he wants to confess what he himself has done, and which no other man can do for him. He must not deny his sin, nor be angry at the priest who hears his confession for warning him that he must stop sinning. There must also be full propriety to your confession: that is, you who make the confession, and the priest who hears that confession, must be truly baptized and confirmed in the faith of holy church, and you must have no doubt of the mercy of Jesus Christ, like Cain or Judas. A man may not accuse anyone of what he himself has done, blaming and admitting his own wickedness, but not that of any other man. On the other hand, if in fact another man has been the cause or the tempter of the sin you committed, or if another person's social standing in some way heightens the sin, or if you cannot truthfully and fully tell your sin without naming the person who also participated in that sin, you may specify that person, since your intention is not to backbite against him or her, but only to truthfully and fully make your confession.

You must tell no lies, in the confessional; for example, humility may perhaps lead you to confess sins that you never committed. Saint Augustine says: "If humility causes you to tell lies about yourself, though you may not have been in sin up to that point, you have then placed yourself in sin, by your lying." The tale of your sin must come out of your own mouth, unless you have been suddenly struck dumb, nor can you make your confession in some writing, for it is you who have sinned, and you who must bear the shame. You must not paint over your confession with eloquent, deceiving words, for by that you cheat yourself and not the priest. You must tell it plainly, no matter how foul or horrible it may be. You must make your confession to a priest who is experienced and wise in giving counsel, nor should you make your confession vaingloriously, nor hypocritically, but for no other reason than fear of Jesus Christ and the healing of your soul. Do not come running to the priest, out of nowhere, to casually tell him your sin, as if you were telling a joke or a story, but advisedly and with great devotion. And confess regularly. If you confess all over again, a sin from which you must be purged, that is to your merit, not your detraction. And, as Saint Augustine says, you will then be more readily freed of sin, and granted God's grace. And certainly you ought to receive communion at least once each year, for every year all things renew themselves.

And now I have told you about true confession, which is the second part of penitence.

NEXT FOLLOWS THE THIRD PART OF PENITENCE

The third part of Penitence is actually performing the meritorious acts, and enduring the various punishments and suffering required by your confessor, in payment for your sin. Alms-giving can be accomplished in three ways: by contrition in the heart, when a man offers himself to God; by having pity on your neighbor's fault and deficiencies; and, thirdly, by giving good counsel and comfort, both spiritual and bodily, when men need such assistance, and especially in ensuring that a man has enough to eat. And be aware that these are things a man always needs: food, clothing, shelter, loving counsel, visitation when sick or in jail, and the burial of his dead body. If you are unable to actually visit a needy person, visit him by means of messages and gifts. These are usually alms given by people with earthly wealth, or experience in the giving of sound advice. These good works will be remembered on the Day of Judgment.

You must give these alms out of your own pocket and store, swiftly and secretly, if at all possible. But if it cannot be done in secret, do not abandon the giving of alms simply because other men see it, as long as you are being charitable for Jesus Christ's thanks, and not that of the world. For as Saint Matthew tells us, in book 5 of his gospel:

"A city that stands on a mountain cannot be hidden, nor can men light a lantern and hide it under a bushel of hay, but you can light a candle, and set it on a candlestick, and it will give light to the people in a house. Just so shall your own light burn in front of other men, so they can see your good works, and glorify your father who is in heaven."

As for bodily pain, in penance: it is part of prayers, vigils, fasting, and virtuously teaching prayers to others. You must understand that prayers are a piteous wish of your heart which rises up to God, expressed by you in outward words; what you ask for may be to remove harms, or to attain things both spiritual and lasting, and sometimes worldly things, all of which Jesus has enclosed and included in the *Pater Noster,* "Our Father." Surely, it has been endowed with the three aspects of his worthiness, and it excels because he himself composed it, and it is short and can be memorized more readily, and can also be kept more easily in a man's heart, and he can more often help himself by saying it, without growing weary in the process, so there is no excuse for not learning it, it being so short and easy, and it takes in itself all good prayers. Any more profound exposition of this holy prayer, so worthy and fine, I will leave to the masters of theology, except that I will say this much: when you pray to God for forgiveness of your sins, as you forgive those who have sinned against you, be keenly aware that you remain in a state of Christian love and right feeling toward your fellow Christians.

This prayer must be said honestly, and in true faith, for men must pray to God methodically, and wisely, and devoutly, and a man must constantly subordinate his own will to the will of God. This prayer must also be said with great humility and purity, and with sincerity, nor to the annoyance of any man or woman. It must also be carried out in charitable works. And it helps against the soul's vices, as Saint Jerome says: "Fasting saves us from the sins of the flesh; prayer saves us from the soul's vices."

Next, you must understand that bodily pain occurs when you leave sleep and, instead, come to prayer, for as Jesus Christ says: "Wake, and pray, so that you do not fall into wicked temptation." You must also understand that fasting involves three things: forsaking bodily meat and drink, forsaking worldly jollity, and forsaking deadly sin, for a man must work with all his might to keep himself free from deadly sin.

And you must understand, too, that God himself commanded us to fast, and that fasting involves more things: alms to poor people; spiritual happiness of heart, neither angry or irritated, nor complaining about fasting; a reasonable time to eat again; and when you do eat, to eat moderately, and not at irregular hours, nor stay at the table and eat longer, because you have been fasting.

And then you must understand that there is bodily pain, too, in learning and teaching, whether by word or by writing, or by example, as there is bodily pain in wearing hair shirts under your normal clothing, or employing only coarse cloth in your apparel, or wearing mail shirts on your bare flesh, for Christ's sake, and similar penances. But be careful that suffering such penances does not make your heart bitter or angry, for it is better to throw away your hair shirts than to discard the sweetness of Jesus Christ. And so Saint Paul says, "Dress yourself, as those who have been chosen by God, in a heart that is merciful and gracious, patient, and clothe yourself in that kind of clothing," by which God is more pleased than by hair shirts, mail shirts, or shirts of chain mail.

You can do penance, too, by beating yourself on the chest, whipping yourself with sticks, in misery and oppression, in patiently suffering wrongs that have been done to you, as also in patient suffering when ill, or suffering from the loss of worldly property, or from the loss of your wife, or child, or other friends.

And you must understand what can interfere with penance, things that take four different pathways: namely, fear, shame, hope, and hopelessness—that is, desperation. Let me first speak of fear, which arises when a man thinks he cannot endure penance. On the other hand, however, there is an available remedy, which is to compare bodily penance, which is short and not terribly serious, to the pain of hell, which is cruel and so long that it lasts forever, without end.

Now the shame a man can feel, when confession is needful—and especially those hypocrites who pretend to be so perfect that they never have any need at all for confession. The remedy to this is to realize that a man who has not been ashamed to do foul things should, most certainly, not be ashamed to do good ones, namely, confession. A man should be thinking that God sees and understands everything he is thinking and everything he does; nothing can be kept hidden from him. Men should also remind themselves at the shame to come, at the Day of Judgment, to those who in this present life have not been penitent and confessed their sins. And on that day, all the creatures in heaven, on earth, and in hell, will see—right out in the open—everything men have hidden, here in this world.

And now to speak of the hope men may have, when they have neglected the confessional. There are two kinds of hope, here: one is for a man to hope he can live long and pile up immense worldly wealth and pleasure, and then go to confession, for that seems to him an appropriate and reasonable time to go about the process. The other is the man who is too confident of Christ's mercy. In the first case, the remedy is to realize that our lives are never secure and safe, and also that all the world's wealth is a matter of luck, and fades away like a shadow on the wall, and as Saint Gregory says, God is perfectly righteous, and if a man will not willingly cease from sinning, then he must endure pain everlasting.

Hopelessness is composed of two pathways: the first concerns God's mercy, and the second is the fear that they are unable to persevere in goodness. In the first case, the man believes that he has sinned so much, and so often, that there is no chance of him being saved. Plainly, the remedy for such despair must be to realize that Christ's suffering, and its consequences for mankind, is far too strong to be undone—infinitely stronger than what it would require to refrain from sin. In the second case, a man must realize that, just as often as he falls, he may rise again, through penitence. No matter how long he may have lain in sin, Christ's mercy is always ready to receive him. And the hopeless man, thinking he cannot persevere in goodness, must think how feeble the devil is, compared to God, and how helpless the devil would be if men did not give him strength. And a man will have the help of God, and all the help of holy church, and the protection of angels, if he chooses to accept these gifts.

And so men must understand the fruits of penance, and according to the words of Jesus Christ those fruits are the endless bliss of heaven, joy without any sadness, or grief, or woe, in which eternal bliss all the harms of this present life will be completely behind them, and they will be forever safe from the pains of hell, and they will have the joyful company of all the others who will be rejoicing eternally, each participating in all the others' joy. Then man's body, once foul and dark, will be brighter and clearer than the sun, and that body, which was formerly sick, frail, and feeble, so completely mortal, will now be immortal, and so strong and healthy that nothing could possibly harm it, there being no hunger, or thirst, nor any cold, but a host of souls replenished by the sight of God's perfect knowledge of them. Men may purchase this blissful realm by spiritual poverty, and this glory by humility, and this plenty of joy by hunger and thirst, and this peace and comfort by hard labor, and this eternal life by death and the slaying of sin.

Here the Maker of This Book Takes His Leave

And now I pray that those who hear this little treatise, or read it, that if there is anything in it that pleases them, they ought to thank our Lord Jesus Christ, from whom comes all intelligence and all goodness. And if there is anything that displeases them, I also beg them to ascribe it to the flaws of my ignorance and ineptitude, and not to my intention, which would have caused me to write better if I had had the skill. As our book says: "Everything that is written is written for and by means of our faith." And so I humbly beseech you, by the mercy of God, that you pray for Christ to have mercy on me, and to forgive me my sins, and especially of my translations and other writings, which deal only with worldly vanities, which I have recalled and withdrawn—as for example the book *Troilus and Criseyde,* and also *The House of Fame,* and *The Legend of Good Women,* and *The Book of the Duchess,* and *The Parliament of Fowls,* and *The Canterbury Tales,* which tend to be sinful, and *The Book of the Lion,* and any other books, if I were able to recall them to mind, and many a song and many a lecherous poem, so that Christ, because of his great mercy, may forgive me my sins.

But for my translation of Boethius' *The Consolation of Philosophy,* and of other books of the lives of saints, and books of prayers and homilies, and morality, and devotion, I thank our Lord Jesus Christ and his blissful Mother, and all the saints in heaven, beseeching them that, from now till my life's end, they send me the grace to sorrow for my sins, and to be solicitous for my soul's eternal salvation, and that they grant me the grace of true penitence, confession, and complete performance of penance, in this present life, by means of the generous grace of him who is king of kings and priest over all priests, and who redeemed us with his heart's precious blood, so that I may be one of those who are saved, at the Day of Judgment. *Qui cum patre et Spiritu Sancto vivit et regnat Deus per omnia secula. Amen.* "He who lives and rules with the Father, and the Holy Ghost, he who is God of the world without end. Amen."

NOTES

TRANSLATOR'S FOREWORD

xxix *Now sing the glory:* "Caedmon's Hymn." *Poems and Prose From the Old English,* trans. by Burton Raffel, ed. by Burton Raffel & Alexandra Olsen. New Haven: Yale University Press, 1995: p. 55.

GENERAL PROLOGUE

3 *God of Winds:* Zephyrus, in truth, god of the west wind only.
   Thomas à Beckett: (1118–70) Archbishop of Canterbury, who opposed Henry II's interference in church self-governance and was assassinated, on the king's orders.
   Southwark: London suburb, roughly sixty miles northwest of Canterbury.
4 *Attalia:* ancient name of Satalye, in southern Anatolia; the battle between Muslim and Christian forces was fought on August 23–24, 1361.
   Tlemcen: a Berber kingdom in northeast Algeria.
   Palatine: Balat, a Muslim emirate; the Christian and Muslim cooperation Chaucer describes seems not to have existed.
6 *centure:* cincture, a belt.
   Stratford on the Bow: name of her convent, near London.
7 *Benedictine Rule:* a set of governing ordinances and procedures for a monastery, established by Saint Benedict (480–c.550).
8 *Friar:* member of a religious organization known as an Order; most orders of friars (as opposed to an order of monks) were mendicants (beggars) and did not own property.
13 *Devonshire:* a county in very far southwest England, located between Somerset (to its eastern side) and Cornwall.
14 *Bath:* southeast of Bristol, between the counties of Gloucester and Somerset.
20 *Saint Veronica's kerchief:* a kerchief on which was represented Saint Veronica's veil. The saint's medals were struck to testify to a pilgrimage to Rome. The saint's veil was said to be imprinted with a portrait of Christ.

22 *Plato:* (427–347 BCE) Greek philosopher, a disciple of Socrates, and founder of "the Academy" in Athens. His most renowned pupil was Aristotle. A brilliant writer (he had started as a poet), his work has been, and remains, profoundly influential.

THE KNIGHT'S TALE

26 *Statius:* Roman poet (c.45–96), author of *Thebaid,* an epic poem about the fierce struggles for the throne of Thebes. Theseus appears late in the poem, as a triumphant warrior and thus a peacemaker.
Theseus: national hero of Athens, son of the king, and later himself king, established his fame by a series of epic, Herculean-type adventures and combats, the most celebrated of which was killing the Minotaur of Crete in the Labyrinth where the bull was kept, in which feat he was aided by Ariadne. Having deserted Ariadne at Naxos, he fought the Amazons, captured and then married their queen, Hippolita.

28 *King Capaneus:* one of the Seven Against Thebes.
Creon: Oedipus' wife, Jocasta, was Creon's sister. In Greek mythology, Creon is both the King of Corinth and friend to Jason and Medea, and sometime ruler of Thebes.

38 *Saturn:* ancient Italian god, adopted by the Romans and blended in with Cronus, Zeus' father. The Saturnalia was a wild festival of celebration in Saturn's name, on the appointed date of December 17 each year.
Juno: Wife of Jupiter, ruler of the Roman pantheon of gods. She was queen both of, and for, all women.

39 *Eros:* the Greek Cupid (whom he closely resembles), son of Aphrodite.
Mercury: Latinized version of Hermes, the messenger god.

42 *Phoebus:* Phoebus Apollo; called "Phoebus" in his sun-god aspects.

43 *Cadmus and Amphion:* Cadmus was the legenday founder of Thebes; Amphion, twin brother of Zetus, with whom he shared the throne. They are the builders of Thebes's great walls.

47 *Diana:* Latin goddess of woodlands and hunting, and protector of women.

49 *Mars:* God of war, identified by the Romans as the father of Romulus, father of Rome. The Romans also gave him the title Ultor, meaning "avenger."

54 *Turnus:* king of the Italian Rutulians, killed by Aeneas in Virgil's *Aeneid.*
Croesus: (c.560–46 BCE) last king of Lydia, of legendary wealth.
Venus: Latin goddess who was identified with the Greek goddess of love, Aphrodite.

57 *Callisto:* nymph who served Diana and was loved by Zeus. When the nymph was made pregnant by Zeus, Diana—deeply virginal—punished her for disloyalty
Meléagra: a hunter who, in a singularly intricate legend, was killed by his mother, after he had killed two of her brothers, who had tried to take away the great boar's skin that Meléagra, who had killed the animal, had given to the virgin huntress, Atalanta, with whom he was in love. The boar had been

sent to ravage the kingdom of which Meléagra's father and mother were king and queen; the king had omitted a sacrifice due to Artemis, who in her anger set the ravaging great boar on him.

Pluto: god of the underworld, Hades.

61 *Adonis:* a beautiful Cyprian youth with whom Venus fell in love, at first sight. A wild boar killed him, and his blood sprouted the rose, and from her tears come the anemone.

63 *Acteon:* Either because he said he was a better hunter than Diana, or because he happened to see her bathing, naked, she changed him into a stag and he was torn to pieces by his own hunting hounds. Chaucer has changed the tale a bit—but an angry goddess is an angry goddess, for all that.

Proserpina and Luna: Proserpina is drawn from Persephone, the young queen of the underworld, who had been kidnapped by Pluto as she picked flowers. Luna is the Roman goddess of the moon.

65 *Thrace:* the rocky, mountainous, most northern part of Greece.

76 *carried his sister:* In Chaucer's time, in-laws were identified, and treated, as if they were blood relatives. This did not, however, change the laws of inheritance.

THE MILLER'S PROLOGUE

86 *who put a cuckoo cap:* "who cuckolded," i.e., slept with his wife.

THE MILLER'S TALE

88 *the Ptólemáic bible, the* Almageste: Claudius Ptolemaeus (fl.127–48 CE) was an astronomer and mathematician, based in Alexandria. Working in good part from his own detailed observation of the heavens, he formulated guides to the movements and positions of both planetary bodies and stars. The ancient theory of the heavens assumed that the earth was at the center of the universe, and everything else either moved or was stationed in terms of the earth's location. Although Ptolemaeus worked on this assumption, his charts and tables became the western world's standard reference for over a thousand years, until superior optical instruments made it possible for Copernicus, Galileo, and Kepler, among others, to supersede the *Almageste* both in fact and, in the sixteenth century, in theory.

89 *Cato's book of maxims: Dicta Catonis,* "The Sayings of Cato," is a collection of moral maxims, most of them in verse. Its author was Marcus Porcius Cato (234–149 BCE), a successful and strongly moralist politician and orator, and a prolific writer. A good many of his surviving works were written for the education of his son. *Dicta Catonis* was a tremendously successful school text throughout the Middle Ages.

92 *Absalom:* a name drawn from biblical accounts of King David, Absalom being his third son. Handsome, aggressive, and rebellious, he tried to overthrow his father. When he failed, and fled, his long hair became entangled

in a tree. Hanging helplessly, he was killed by Jonathan, David's general (2 Samuel: 13–18).

93 *the role of Herod:* Herod was the Roman-appointed governor of Jerusalem, who figures largely in the scriptural Gospels and the execution of Jesus. In biblically based popular dramas known as mystery plays, Herod—appropriately costumed—was one of the favorite characters.

94 *O Fridesweed:* An eighth-century virgin saint, especially popular for her supposed healing powers. An Oxford monastery was named for her.

102 *Don Gerveys:* A then-popular and jocular adaptation of the Spanish title *don,* signifying a knight. The standard English title is "sir," which then and now is taken most seriously, as *don* was not.

103 *that colter, hot:* The colter is a sharp blade, fixed to the frame of a plow, which precedes and aids the ploughshare by cutting into the ground.

THE STEWARD'S PROLOGUE

106 *as far as Deptford:* The distance from Southwark to Deptford is roughly five miles—which is, today, no great distance at all, but seemed much longer in the fourteenth century, with its bad, pock-ridden dirt roads, navigated by plodding horses.
We'll be in Greenwich: roughly the same distance as from Southwark to Deptford.

THE STEWARD'S TALE

107 *At Trumpington:* roughly three or four miles from Cambridge, which latter town is about thirty-five miles due north of London.
a Sheffield knife: Although their knife was probably not made with a steel blade, Sheffield already had a reputation, at least in England, for metalworking. By the seventeenth century this was an international reputation, and by the nineteenth century, Sheffield led the world.

112 *by Saint Cuthbert:* A northern man (d. 687), like the two young men in the tale, Cuthbert had such a reputation for saintliness that, when he refused to accept the post of Bishop of Lindisfarne, King Egfrith personally came to beg him to take the post. Lindisfarne is on the coast, roughly sixty-five miles southeast of Edinburgh.

116 *O Holy cross of Bromholm:* Supposed to be a relic of the true cross on which Jesus was crucified, the Bromholm cross, at Walsingham (in far northeast England, not far from the coast of the North Sea), was an internationally famous holy site, regularly visited by pilgrims.

INTRODUCTORY WORDS TO THE
MAN OF LAW'S TALE

122 *and of Saint John:* In "The First Epistle General of John," known as the Evangelist, we are told the governing strength of truthfulness: "My little children, let us not love in word, neither in tongue; but in deed and in truth. And hereby we know we are of the truth . . ." (1 John 3:18–19).

Seneca claimed: Lucius Annaeus Seneca (c.4 BCE–65 CE), Roman Stoic philosopher, famous for his essays, and also for his distinctly blood-filled tragic plays. He had been tutor to Nero, before he became emperor, but soon lost the ability to control Nero's instabilities. He resigned as tutor in 62 CE; in 65 CE he was ordered to commit suicide. Seneca was powerfully influential in both medieval and Renaissance England.

123 *more than even Ovid:* Publius Ovidius Naso (43 BCE–18 CE), Roman poet, widely read after the eleventh century, and highly influential, as much for his bizarre subject matter as for his intensely dramatic verse. His *Metamorphoses,* brilliantly evocative tales of transformation, was particularly important. Like many other writers, Chaucer drew heavily on these virtuosic, often wonderfully imaginative narratives. Not all of his work has survived.

Lucretia's fatal wounds: She stabbed herself, after being raped by Sextus, of the Tarquinius family, another member of whom was her husband.

Babylonian Thisbee: Two lovers, living next door to one another but not allowed to formally meet, converse through a chink in the wall between their houses. Desperate, they arrange a meeting outside the city, which has fatal consequences for them both. Shakespeare parodies the tale in *A Midsummer Night's Dream.*

the sword that Dido wielded: After fleeing from Troy, Aeneus stops at Carthage, on his way to the god-directed founding of Rome. The queen of Carthage, Dido, falls in love with him, and he with her. But the gods insist on his leaving, and, despite her desperate pleas, he leaves, and she kills herself. The story features prominently in Virgil's *Aeneid.*

Dèmophon, who deserted Phyllis: A son of Theseus and Phaedra, he had been actively involved in post-Homeric Troy. Returning to Greece, he betrothed himself to Phyllis, daughter of the Thracian king, but did not appear for the wedding. Phyllis hanged herself.

And Hermíoné: daughter (and only child) of Menelaeus and Helen. Married to Neoptolemus, Achilles' son, she was claimed by Orestes. When his claim was rejected, Orestes killed Neoptolemus and took her away with him.

Áriádné on Naxos: daughter of Minos, king of Crete. She fell in love with Theseus and gave him indispensable help in fighting with, and killing, the Minotaur. Theseus took her to Naxos and deserted her there.

124 *Leander drowned himself:* Living on one side of the Hellespont (ancient name of the Dardenelles, a strait between Turkey and Bulgaria, west of Constantinople, now known as Istanbul), Leander fell in love with a priestess (Erro,

better known in English as Hero) living in solitude, in a tower on the other side. She lit his way from a lamp atop the tower and he swam over every night—until a storm blew out the light. He lost his way and drowned. Seeing his body on the beach, the next day, Hero threw herself from the top of the tower.

Briséis: Achilles' captive concubine, taken from him by Agamemnon, leader of the Greek expedition against Troy. Achilles withdrew from combat, and the Greeks suffered enormously, until at last, after his dear friend, Patroclus, was killed, he returned and killed Hector, leader of the Trojan forces.

the cruelty of Medea: Married to Jason, after she had enabled him to steal the golden fleece, she is later deserted by him. In revenge, she kills their children and flees.

O my Penèlopé: Odysseus' wife, left alone for twenty years, until (as *The Odyssey* narrates) her husband's spectacular return.

O Alceste: Alcestis is married to Admetus, for whom she feels great love. When he falls mortally ill, the gods will allow him to survive only if someone gives up their life for him. Alcestis does exactly that. (See the powerful play, *Alcestis,* by Euripides.)

wicked Cánacé: A daughter of Aeolus (not a god, but nevertheless given control over the winds, by Zeus himself), who had a madly incestuous relationship with her brother, Macareus. The myth is not clear as to her death, which was either a suicide or an execution performed by her father.

Ápollóniús of Tyre: a picaresque tale of love lost and won, voyages, pirates, separations, reunions, etc. It forms the basis for Shakespeare's *Pericles.*

THE MAN OF LAW'S TALE

131 *Pyrrhus broke the wall:* Pyrrhus is another name for Achilles' son, Neoptolemus ("red-haired"), one of the Greek warriors concealed in the wooden horse. He killed the old Trojan king Priam.

wreaked by Hannibal: Carthaginian prince and leader of Carthage's armies in the second Punic War, which lasted for two decades and which Rome finally won. His name means "master of charm," a description he fully lived up to. He was a brilliant military strategist and tactician (he successfully took African elephants over the Alps and down into Italy) but could not prevail. He committed suicide when the Romans demanded that he be turned over to them.

133 *Semiramis the second:* Babylonian queen, alleged to be ruthless and murderous, and to have insatiable lust.

134 *celebrated by Lucan:* Marcus Annaeus Lucanus (39–65 CE), Roman poet, author of the epic *Pharsalia,* dealing with the civil war between Julius Caesar and Pompey. The title in the manuscripts is *De bello civili, About the civil war;* "Pharsalia" is apparently a later mistranslation. The poem is in ten books, but was not completed. Nero disapproved of Lucan, for no known reason,

and he (as well as his father and his father's two brothers) was obliged to commit suicide.

137   *Saint Mary the Egyptian:* a former prostitute in fifth-century Alexandria, who renounced her former life and, in penance, lived for almost fifty years in the Egyptian desert, eating only grass and weeds.

141   *you saved Susannah:* a story in the Apocrypha (biblical tales not included in the Bible) in which a chaste married woman is maliciously accused, by two elders, of sexual misdeeds—though in fact they were the lustful ones, having come upon her when she was bathing; she had rejected their ardent proposals. But a young Daniel (later to be the prophet who survived the lions' den) intervened and, by separately cross-examining the elders, proved their story to be false. She was exonerated; they were executed.

     Saint Anne: married to Joachim, and the mother of the Virgin Mary; Anne was widely venerated.

150   *who gave Judith:* a beautiful, wealthy Jewish woman, and a widow, who saved the Jewish town of Bethulia from an Assyrian invasion. (The precise location of Bethulia is not known.) The celebrated Assyrian general, Holofernes, had besieged the town. Judith went to his tent, where Holofernes drank himself into a stupor, and after cutting off his head, she went back to Bethulia, taking the head in a food bag. The Assyrians panicked, the Israelites attacked and slaughtered them, and Judith was much praised and admired.

THE WIFE OF BATH'S PROLOGUE

159   *up in Galilee:* a town, and a large lake (also called a "sea"), in northern Israel, where Jesus was born and raised.

     a Samaritan: The Samaritans are a Jewish sect who differ from most Jews by accepting only the first five books of the Old Testament (the Pentateuch) as their bible, and Moses as their only prophet.

160   *Old Lamech:* either descended from Seth, and Noah's father, or else descended from Cain. He had two wives, Adah and Zillah, and three important sons, Jabal, Jubal, and Tubal Cain.

     Abraham seems holy enough: the first patriarch of Judaism (and also of some Arab tribes). He and his wife, Sarah, had a son, Isaac; he and his concubine, Hagar, had a son, Ishmael. Having been born in Ur, in Chaldea, he moved to Hebron, where he died at the age of 175; he is thought to have lived at the beginning of the second millennium BCE.

     And also Jacob: the third patriarch of Judaism (Isaac was the second), born to Isaac and Rebecca as the younger of a pair of twins. Esau was the older twin. Married to his uncle Laban's two daughters, Rachel and Leah, he had twelve sons and one daughter, Dinah. He wrestled with an angel, one night, and defeated him, acquiring thereby the name Israel.

161   *But Paul is not addressing:* Usually the "apostle" mentioned throughout this book (there were twelve original apostles, but Paul was not one of them),

Paul's background and birthplace are not fully clear. He was probably born five or ten years after Jesus, and in Tarsus, in modern Turkey. His family were Hellenistic Jewish; he was educated in both Greek and Hebrew. In a mystical experience, about 35 CE, Paul became a follower of Jesus and quickly evolved into what most scholars of religion call him, "the first Christian." (He had never met Jesus.) He died about 65 CE, probably in Rome, and at the hands of its mad emperor, Nero.

163 *as Mark has written:* The apostle Mark, said to have authored the gospel which bears his name, in the New Testament, which is probably the first of the four gospels to have been written. It may be incomplete—either unfinished or suffering damage at some early point.

164 *In Essex:* county northeast of London, bordering the North Sea.

167 *by the good Saint James:* Saint James of Compostela, in Galicia, Spain; the shrine was one of the most popular sites of medieval pilgrimages.
Almageste: See note to p. 88.

168 *Even if Argus:* Io, daughter of Inachus, first king of Argos, was wanted as a concubine by Zeus. The god's wife, Hera, changed her into a heifer and had a herdsman, Argus, to watch over her; Argus was blessed with eyes all over his body. Hera also sent a gadfly to continually sting Io, so she could not possibly be still enough for Zeus to make love to her. Zeus had Argus killed by Hermes, his son.

170 *what you find in Job:* an Old Testament parable of faith and suffering instigated by God because of Satan's intervention. Despite all the pain and woe, Job remains "perfect and upright," and God ends up giving "Job twice as much as he had had before" all the suffering, and blessing "the latter end of Job more than his beginning."
O by Saint Peter: Simon Peter, usually named by only his last name, was the son of Jonah and one of the twelve apostles. He was a fisherman.

171 *by God and Saint Joducus:* a seventh-century Breton saint, usually known as Joce, or Josse. The owner of the Tabard Inn was the abbot of Hyde Abbey, and the saint's relics were housed there.

172 *the sepulcher of Dárius:* king of Persia from 521 to 486 BCE. He invaded Greece, with a huge army, but was defeated, in 490, at the battle of Marathon.
the famous painter, Ápellés: Known as the greatest painter in all antiquity, he was born in the first half of the fourth century BE. He mostly painted portraits. Alexander the Great chose him as his court painter.

175 *Taurus:* astrological sign of the Bull, which is the second sign of the astrological zodiac, extending from April 20 to May 20.
Ecclesiastes: The Old Testament book declares: "And I find more bitter than death the woman whose heart it snares and nets . . . yet my soul seeketh, but I find not: one man among a thousand have I found, but a woman among all those have I not found" (7: 26, 28).

176 *Valériús and Théophrástus:* Valériús, early-first-century-CE compiler of a collection of anecdotes, extremely popular in medieval times; and one "Théophrástus," who is clearly not the charming Greek writer, 370–c.287

BCE, but the supposed author of a Latin text, *Aureolus liber Theophrasti de nuptis, Theophrastus' Golden Book of Marriage.* This savage denunciation of marriage, which has survived only as quoted in Jerome's attack on Jovinian, *Epistola adversus Jovinianum, Against Joviniam,* is said by Jerome to be a translation from a Greek original, "but the evidence suggests strongly that no such book ever existed in Greek and that it was Jerome who composed it and simply invented the ascription." (Ralph Hanna and Traugott Lawler, *Jankyn's Book of Wicked Wives.* Athens, Ga.: University of Georgia Press, 1997).

Saint Jerome: A Church father (c.347–420 CE) of Italian birth, for the first part of his life he was something of a wandering scholar and hermit, but finally settled in Bethlehem, writing furiously. The Latin translation of the Bible, known as the Vulgate, was one of his most important works. A singularly passionate man, his surviving correspondence is both lively and informative; it includes ten letters from Saint Augustine.

on Jovinián: A monk, Jovinian wrote a small treatise attacking the idea of asceticism. Jerome's harsh attack on the work was not well received. Apologies (though not to Jovinian) had to be made; Jerome preferred, however, the kind of counterassault he made against Donatus, a Roman monk: "Just let him write! Just let him give me the chance of replying to his patter; if he annoys me, it will be about time for me to bite him and to fasten my teeth in his hide!"

Tértulan: Florens Quintus Septimis Tertullianus, or Tertullian (c.160–c.235 CE), is often called the father of Latin theology. He began life as a pagan but converted to Christianity some time before 197. He is (and was) much admired for his richly rhetorical prose.

Crisíppus: perhaps a reference to an antifeminist writer noted in Saint Jerome's attack on Jovinian.

Trótulá: most likely a reference to Trotula di Ruggiero, a female physician of the eleventh century in Salerno. None of her writing has survived, but she seems to have written on gynecology and cosmetics.

Heloíse: The young woman seduced by her tutor, Abelard, after which he was castrated by members of her family; she became a nun and then an abbess, and both of them wrote a good deal. (See Peter Abelard, *The Story of My Misfortunes.* New York: Macmillan, 1972; and D. W. Robertson, Jr., *Abelard and Heloise.* New York: Dial Press, 1972.)

Parables by Solomon: the biblical book of Proverbs.

178 *Phasípha's tale:* Pasipha was the wife of Minos, king of Crete. She was also the mother of the Minotaur, the father of which was a bull.

Clytemnestra's story: wife of Agamemnon, leader of the Greek's war against Troy. He was away for ten years and she took a lover, Ægisthus. To secure his victory, Agamemnon had to sacrifice his daughter, Iphigenia. When Agamemnon came home, Clytemnestra stabbed him to death as he was taking a bath. Her son, Orestes, later killed her.

Amphioráx's wife: She had been bribed, in order to get her to persuade her husband to join in the war of the Seven Against Thebes. Amphiaraus (to correct Chaucer's spelling) was a seer and knew he would die, so he went reluctantly, carefully directing his children to kill their mother. As he fled from the unsuccessful attack, Zeus threw down a thunderbolt, opening the ground, and the fleeing man was swallowed by the earth.

Lívia and Lucíla: Lívia (b. c.13 BCE) was married to Drusus, Emperor Tiberius' son. Her lover, Sejanus (captain of the Imperial Guard), persuaded her to have her husband poisoned. When Sejanus later wanted to marry her, the emperor refused to permit it and, in 31 CE, had her accused of misconduct and executed.

Lucíla, wife of the poet Lucretius (94–55 BCE), author of *De Rerum Natura, On the Nature of Things*. The details are not entirely clear, but it appears that Lucretius was either taking, or else had been given by his wife, an herbal remedy designed to enhance sexual capacity, and ultimately killed himself, allegedly because he felt himself going slowly mad.

Latúmyús: Chaucer appears to have invented the man's name; the story had appeared in several older books, notably the famous *Gesta Romanorum, Tales of the Romans*. Its details varied, especially as to the number of hanging wives.

BEHOLD THE EXCHANGE BETWEEN
THE FRIAR AND THE SUMMONER

181 *Sittingbourne:* a bit less than half the distance between London and Canterbury, and roughly thirty-five to forty miles from Southwark.

THE WIFE OF BATH'S TALE

189 *Dante:* Dante Alighieri (1265–1321), Italian poet and philosopher, author most famous for his *Divina Commedia* (*Divine Comedy*), an epic trilogy. Starting with the *Inferno,* it proceeds to *Purgatorio,* and concludes with *Paradiso.* Woven in a tight and wonderfully melodic, flowing form (the terza rima triplet that uses carry-over rhyme as a binding force), it is one of the greatest poems ever written, rivaling the works of Shakespeare and Homer.

mountains of Caucasus: towering mountain range running down the western edge of southern Russia.

190 *old Valerius:* first-century-CE compiler of a book of highly rhetorical anecdotes about well-known figures. It was very popular all across Europe in the medieval period.

Seneca, and also Boethius: Seneca (c.55BC–c.40 CE), a Roman philosopher and rhetorician, author of many treatises and essays, and of nine plays very popular in Chaucer's time and later; Boethius (c.576–524 CE), philosopher and theologian, best known for *The Consolation of Philosophy,* written in prison as he awaited execution.

Juvenal: Roman poet of the early second century CE, Juvenal is considered to be the greatest of Roman satirists. Indeed, what is described here as "cheerful" seems a good deal more sardonic: the poor can ignore thieves, yes, but only because they have nothing worth stealing.

192 *Now lift the curtain:* Beds were surrounded by heavy curtains, to ensure privacy.

THE FRIAR'S TALE

200 *the case of Job:* See note to p. 170.

Bishop Saint Dunstan: (c. 910–88) Of noble birth and as a youngster a familiar of King Athelstan's court, he was obliged to withdraw, in disfavor. He did not take orders until 934. Always involved in civic life, he was frequently in disfavor; his biographers report that he was able to summon and control devils.

servant to Saint Paul: See note to p. 161.

Witch of Endor . . . Samuel: The story, too long to quote here, can be found in 1 Samuel 7–20.

a living Virgil: In the *Divina Commedia,* Dante's first guide, when he descends to hell, is Virgil, Roman poet (70–19 BCE), most famous for his epic poem, *The Aeneid,* mostly but not completely finished at his death.

THE SUMMONER'S TALE

207 *Yorkshire:* county in middle England, on the North Sea side.

Holderness: rural parish in southeast Yorkshire, housing the office of a clerical dean.

211 *a pure* Te Deum: *Te Deum laudamus,* the first words of an ancient hymn, "We praise thee, O God."

Lazar the beggar, and wealthy Dives: The beggar suffers, eating "crumbs which fell from the rich man's table." He dies, but is "carried by the angels into Abraham's bosom"; the rich man dies, is sent to hell, protests, and is told that this is what he has earned. (Luke 16–31).

Lo! Moses: On Mount Sinai, Moses "was there with the Lord forty days and forty nights; he did neither eat bread, or drink water. And he wrote upon the table[t]s the words of the covenant, the ten commandments" (Exodus 34:28).

212 *And prophet Elijah:* On an angel's instructions, Elijah "did eat and drink, and went [by] the strength of that forty days and forty nights unto Horeb the mount of God" (1 Kings 18:8).

Aaron: Moses' older brother, and his spokesman. "And the Lord spoke unto Aaron, saying: 'Do not drink wine nor strong drink, [neither] thou, nor thy sons with thee, when you go into the tabernacle of the congregation [the temple], lest you die: it shall be a statute [law] throughout your generations' " (Leviticus 10:8–9).

that heretic, Jovinian: See note to p. 176.

214 *The life of Saint Thomas:* Thomas was the "doubting" apostle, saying after the resurrection of Christ, "Except I shall see in his hands the print [hole] of

the nails [used in the Crucifixion] and put my finger into the print of the nails, and thrust my hand into his side [which was pierced by a soldier's spear], I will not believe" (John 20:25). He was said to have preached in India and there converted thousands of people.

215 *Seneca:* See notes to pp. 122 and 190.

Angry Cambises: Son of Cyrus the Great, he held the throne from 530 to 522 BCE. He conquered Egypt in 525. His negative reputation among Greek writers may have followed on Egyptian reactions to his conquest and rule.

216 *angry Cyrus:* Founder and king of the Persian empire, 559–529 BCE. He was a mighty conqueror and had the reputation of being a wise and tolerant ruler. The Greek historian Xenophon regarded Cyrus as an exemplar of the ideal ruler.

217 *old Saint Simon:* possibly the apostle Simon the Canaanite (Mark 3:18).

Elijah, or Elisha: two different prophets, though the older man, Elijah, passed his mantle to the younger Elisha (2 Kings 1–15).

219 *'Rabbi,' it's not what we're called:* Speaking "to the multitudes and to his disciples," Matthew declared: "But be not you called Rabbi, for one is your Master, Christ, and all you are brothers" (Matthew, 23:1, 8).

221 *a convent requires:* A religious community must have twelve members, and a superior, making a total of thirteen.

222 *Euclid or Ptólemy:* famous Greek mathematician (c.300 BCE), father of geometry; Ptolemy (100–c.178 CE), Greek astronomer and mathematician, author of *The Almageste.*

THE CLERIC'S PROLOGUE

223 *Petrarch:* enormously influential Italian poet (1304–74), regarded as the father of Italian humanism, and the most important initiator of classical studies. Chaucer probably met him; he certainly read, and translated, and borrowed from him. Petrarch's rhetoric and his lyrics were poetic models in all of Europe, until roughly the eighteenth century. For English literature, he provided both the model and the inspiration for the writing of sonnets.

224 *Lynyáno did, as well:* Giovanni da Lignano (c.1310–83), Bologna professor of law, who wrote on law, ethics, theology, and astronomy.

THE CLERIC'S TALE

225 *Viso:* an Italian mountain southwest of Turin and even further southwest of Milan.

Lómbardy: Named for the "barbarian" Lombards, who invaded Italy c.500 CE, this northwest portion of Italy, bordering on Switzerland, was a kingdom in Chaucer's time; it is now classified as a region, with about nine million inhabitants in a territory just under ten thousand square miles.

241 *Bologna:* Italian city roughly 120 miles southeast of Milan, Lombardy's capital city.

251 *Job:* See note to p. 170.

CHAUCER'S HAPPY SONG

258 *Echo:* a nymph who angered Hera, Zeus' wife, by chattering with her at a time when Hera was anxious to spy on her husband's behavior with other nymphs. Hera punished the overtalkative nymph by taking away her capacity to speak, except for the very last word in whatever she was saying.

THE MERCHANT'S TALE

262 *Pavia:* an Italian city almost directly due south of Milan, and roughly twenty miles distant.

263 *Theophrastus:* See note to p. 176.

264 *Jacob:* See note to p. 160.

Isaac: See note to p. 160.

Judith: See note to p. 150.

273 *neither Órpheús nor Ámphíon:* A pre-Homeric (and pre-literacy and -writing) poet, his music could charm wild beasts and even trees and rocks. He married Eurydice, a dryad (tree nymph), who died of a snake bite. Orpheus charmed Persephone, goddess of the underworld, into letting him take her back, provided he did not look at her until they had reached the world of the living. They had almost gotten there when he looked back, and she disappeared forever. Orpheus was killed by madly raging women, for reasons not fully clear. His severed head floated, still speaking, until it reached Lesbos, the island home of lyric poetry; it was buried there.

Amphion, one of the builders of Thebes and its famous walls, played the harp so wonderfully that stones were drawn up and into place by his music. *Joab:* "So Joab blew a trumpet, and all the people stood still, . . . neither fought they any more" (2 Samuel 28).

Theódomás the seer: Trumpets were heard at Thebes when he said prayers for the attacking allies of Athens, but they were the Thebans' trumpets, and a counterattack was immediately forthcoming.

274 *Bacchus:* Called Dionysius by the Greeks, Bacchus was his Latin name: god of wine and ecstasy.

Yméneús: Hymen, god of weddings.

Márcian: Martianus Capella (fl. mid-fifth-century CE), author of *De Nuptilis Mercury and Physiológus, The Marriage of Mercury and Philology,* an allegorical poem in which Mercury, the god of eloquence, marries Philologia, which is the love of learning and writing.

Queen Esther . . . Áhasúerus: Esther, a Jew, saved the Jews from persecution, during the Babylonian Captivity (sixth century BCE). She became King

Ahasuerus' queen, and Haman, the Jews' fiercest enemy, was replaced as chief minister by a Jew, Mordechai.

276 *Cónstantíniús, that monk:* Cónstantíniús Africanus, eleventh-century-CE writer and translator into Latin of Arabic medical texts, one of which was *De Coitu, Sexual Intercourse.*

281 Romance of the Rose: thirteenth-century French allegorical romance, the first and most attractive part written by Guillaume de Lorris (d. 1237), the second and longer, and also drier, part by Jean de Meun, about 1275. Chaucer translated the first part.

Príapús: The god not only of gardens, but also of fertility, the symbol of his deity was the male phallus.

283 *Argus:* See note to p. 168.

284 *noble Ovid:* See note to p. 123.

Pyramus and Thisbee: See note to p. 123.

286 *Pluto . . . Prosérpina:* See notes to pp. 57 and 63.

288 Gesta Romanorum: See note to p. 178.

THE SQUIRE'S TALE

294 *Tartary:* the Mongol or Tartar Empire.

Cambéeyuskán: Since Genghis Khan (1162–1227) is Latinized as "Camius Khan," this is probably intended to stand for him—though what we have of the unfinished tale is not historical in nature.

295 *Ides of March:* the fifteenth day of March, in the ancient Roman calendar.

296 *even Gawain:* King Arthur's nephew, most often described as a model knight—courageous, innocent, and courteous. Chaucer may well have known the anonymous *Sir Gawain and the Green Knight,* written in a north-country dialect about 1375. The green knight makes his entrance in very similar style to that of the knight riding the brass horse.

out of Faerie: Fairies were thought to live in a kind of parallel world, invisible to us, though we are completely visible to them. They can cross over and enter or leave our world pretty much as they wish, but most humans never enter their world, and most of those who do, never return.

299 *an Apúlian palfrey:* Apulia was a wild region in southeast Italy (modern Puglia). A palfrey is always a riding horse, rather than a warhorse, and is most often a horse intended to be ridden sidesaddle, by a woman.

Pegasus: one of two winged horses, born of the blood of the Gorgon Medusa, who was pregnant by Poseidon (God of earthquakes and the sea; associated with horses) when she died.

Sinon: He did not invent or construct the Trojan Horse, but was deliberately left behind when the Greeks pretended to be abandoning their war against Troy. He persuaded the Trojans that the horse was meant as an offering to Athena; if brought into the city, it would, he said, make Troy impregnable. See also the note to p. 131.

300 *Álhazén and Wítilo:* Alhazen is the Latinized name of Ibn al-Haitham (965–1039 CE), author of an important treatise on optics. Witilo is a Polish scholar (also known in western Europe as Vitulon or Vitello), who, some time before 1278, wrote on visual perspective, borrowing from Alhazen.

Télephús: Son of Hercules and an Arcadian princess. In fighting against the Greeks, who were on their way to Troy and landed by mistake in the kingdom he ruled, Telephus was wounded by Achilles. When his wound would not heal, he consulted the Delphic Oracle and was told the wound had to be touched by the spear that had caused it. Disguised as a beggar, he went to the Grecian camp at Troy and kidnapped Agamemnon's infant son. To have the child restored, he told the Greeks, they had to have Achilles cure his wound with the spear. The exchange was then made on those terms.

301 *Lancelot:* the greatest, and also the most romantic, of all the knights at King Arthur's court. See Chrétien de Troyes, *Lancelot: the Knight of the Cart*, tr. B. Raffel. New Haven: Yale University Press, 1997.

308 *Argonaut Jason:* See note to p. 124.

Paris of Troy: a son of Priam, king of Troy, and his wife, Hecuba. Sent on a diplomatic mission to Sparta, where Menelaus was king, he fell in love with the king's wife, Helen, and ran off with her. The Trojan War was the Greeks' revenge.

311 *great Théodóra:* unknown.

THE LANDOWNER'S PROLOGUE

313 *Mount Parnassus:* mountain just north of Delphi, in Greece; the mountain and its surroundings were dedicated to the worship of Apollo and the Muses, who divided the body of intellectual pursuits as follows:

Calliopé—epic poetry
Clio—history
Euterpé—flute playing, and the lyric poetry often sung with it
Melpómené—tragedy
Terpsichoré—dancing
Eráto—the lyre, and the lyric poetry often sung with it
Polyhymnia—hymns and pantomimes to the gods
Uránia—astronomy
Thália—comedy and peasant poetry

parsed out Cicero: "deciphered the grammar of Cicero's prose." Marcus Tullius Cicero (106–43 BCE), Roman statesman, orator, philosopher, and perhaps the greatest stylist in all of Latin history (this has made him a perpetual favorite of Latin teachers), was active in politics but too hesitant, too unsure to long survive, nor did he. He was murdered in December 43; famous as he was, his head and hands were displayed in Rome.

Liverpool: seaport (opening out to the Irish Sea) and commercial center in western England.

THE LANDOWNER'S TALE

314 *Armoric . . . Brittany:* Armorica is the ancient name for Brittany; in French the old name is Armorique. The so-called Breton Lays, written in English, are modeled on *le cycle amorican,* the Armorican cycle.

   Brittany is in northwest France and is a peninsula lying between the English Channel and the Bay of Biscay.

319 *like ancient Echo:* See note to p. 258.

322 *Apollo, governor and god:* See note to pp. 42 and 313.

   your sacred sister Lucína: Luna (see note to p. 63). But the transition from Greek mythology to Latin mythology sometimes confuses matters, and Juno, Jupiter's wife in Roman religion, was sometimes known as Lucina, "she who brings to light"—in this case, bringing children to light via the birthing process.

   Neptune, of course: Neptune was more or less the successor to the Greek god Poseidon, but plays a role much inferior to that of Poseidon (see note to p. 299).

323 *ugly Polyphemus . . . sea-nymph Galatéa:* Polyphemus is a Cyclops, or one-eyed giant. In Homer's *Odyssey,* he is blinded by Odysseus. Polyphemus' unsuccessful love for the nymph Galatea is told by both Theocritus and Ovid; in the latter's version, Polyphemus crushes Galatea's accepted love, Acis, by dropping a boulder on his head.

324 *Orléan's halls—The university:* The city of Orleans, roughly sixty miles south-southwest of Paris, boasted one of the oldest and greatest of European universities. In the fourteenth century, its reputation for astrological studies was very high.

325 *Who spoke to them in Latin:* The cleric's nationality was Breton, as was his native language, a Celtic tongue not comprehensible by a native speaker of French. The cleric therefore greets Aurelius in Latin, which was at the time the lingua franca, or universal language, of educated Europeans.

326 *from Gironde to the mouth of the Seine:* roughly sixty-five to seventy miles.

327 *Old Janus, with his double beard:* Old Janus requires two beards, one for each of his two heads, facing in opposite directions. He was the god of gates and doors, and thus of beginnings, and lent his name to the first (beginning) month of the year, January.

   a king in Toledo: Alfonso X, king of Castille, from 1221 to 1284, was consistently devoted to arts and sciences. (Toledo lies roughly sixty miles south-southwest of Madrid; Castille was the largest of the smaller kingdoms into which Spain was divided until 1492, and its language, Castillian, became what we today call Spanish.) The astronomical charts he ordered, known as the Alfonsine tables, were used all over Europe for both astrology and its then less developed cousin, astronomy.

330 *The Thirty Tyrants of Athens:* In 404 BCE, what we would today call an arch-conservative or right-wing revolution took place in Athens. Athenian

democracy was abolished; at least 1,500 citizens were killed until, in 411, a counterrevolution overthrew the tyrants and restored democracy.

Murdered Phidon: Having murdered Phidon, the tyrants ordered his virgin daughters to come to the scene—their father lying dead in pools of blood—and dance lewd dances, naked, in front of the drunken murderers. Well aware of what would happen to them, the girls slipped away and, as one, killed themselves by jumping into a cistern (a "well"), preferring death to dishonor.

the ancient Mycynaeans: once a city-state in the Peloponnesean mountains of northeast Greece, the Myceneans flourished from roughly 1400 BCE to 1200. It is not known just which invading armies destroyed the city; it may have been the Greek-speaking Dorians.

Sparta: Founded by Dorians in the southeast Peloponnese mountains about 1000 BCE, by 700, Sparta was developing into a small but rigidly controlled oligarchy (i.e., rule by the noble upper classes). Sparta became for almost five centuries a legendary militaristic force, warring with and eventually defeating Athens, both larger and wealthier. Sparta contributed remarkably little to what we today call ancient Greek culture.

the tyrant Aristóclidés: tyrant ruler of Orchomenus, in Boetia, a region of central Greece, with Athens to the southeast. When Aristoclides wanted the virgin Stymphalides, and she did not want him, her father supported her refusal. Aristoclides had the father killed, and the girl fled to the temple of Diana. She clung to the statue of the goddess, protectress of women, until the men sent to fetch her realized they could not pry her loose and stabbed her to death. Our only source for this story is Saint Jerome's treatise against Jovinian (see notes to p. 176, and the note immediately following this one).

331 *Hásdrubal's wife:* Married to a Carthaginian general, we are told that she watched his army being defeated by the Romans—but this battle was not, as Jerome says, at the city of Carthage, but in the valley of the river Metaurus, in Italy. The rest of Jerome's story, accordingly, as well as the wife's presence, seems highly unlikely: we are told that she snatched up her children and threw them and herself into the burning ruins of their city, Carthage. Indeed, we know that when Scipio, the Roman general, conquered Carthage, the king's wife threw herself and her children into the burning ruins of her city.

Lucretia: See note to p. 123.

Asian Melétus: Until the fifth century BCE, Meletus was a Greek-colonized city in Asia Minor, a powerful seagoing and trading town, with a good deal of manufacturing. Galatia too was a part of both the Greek and the Roman world. But for the rest of the story we have only Jerome's word. What he tells us might of course have happened; other narratives of a similar sort are abundant. But Jerome's word is simply not to be trusted without other support.

husband of Panthée: Bradates, the husband in question, was king of the Susi, in Asia Minor. Jerome is our source, but we also know he took this story from Xenophon, a Greek historian who was a disciple of Socrates.

Demócion's . . . daughter: The tale is likely; the only source for it is Jerome.

O, Sedásus: A tale from Plutarch: the daughters had been raped, and killed themselves afterward.

332 *Nicánor:* one of Alexander the Great's warriors, at the capture of Thebes (336 BCE).

Nicerátes' wife: He is said to have been killed by the Thirty Tyrants (see note to p. 330); she is said to have thereafter killed herself. The story is likely; the only source for it is Jerome.

Álcibíadés . . . His lover: Her name was Timandra; Plutarch is the source for this story.

Láodámiá: The source is Ovid.

Portia: Plutarch recounts the gradual deterioration of Portia, which continued until, at last, she killed herself by swallowing live coals. Brutus was not dead when this occurred.

Ártemésia: She was both the wife and the sister of King Mausolus of Caria, whose reign was 377 BCE to his death in 353 BCE. But she was not, as Jerome says, the queen of Illyria; he does not mention that she was her husband's sister. The "perfect wifehood" he ascribes to her is evidenced, elsewhere, only to the extent that in her husband's memory she continued the construction of the famous mausoleum which Mausolus had planned and begun, and which neither of them lived to see completed. Jerome must therefore be taken, as before, with a grain of salt.

Teuta: Married to Agron, king of Illyria, she became regent of the kingdom after his death: his son, Pinnes, by a former wife, was too young to rule. She was actively militaristic as the regent and won notable victories, until Rome intervened and called her to a stop. She has been called "the Catherine the Great of Illyria," but only Jerome has anything to say of her "chastity."

Bílyá: wife of Duillius, who in 260 BCE won a naval victory over Carthage. Jerome says she was famous for being able to tolerate her husband's breath; "I thought the mouths of all men smelled like that," Jerome quotes her as having said. We have only his word for it.

Rhódogone: The lady killed her childhood nurse, Jerome reports, for suggesting that, after her husband's death, she ought to marry again. This is Jerome's story; there does not seem to be any supporting evidence.

Valeria: Another woman, says Jerome, who refused to remarry.

THE PHYSICIAN'S TALE

337 *Titus Líviús:* the first and middle names of a man best known by his family name, Titus Livius Livy (19 BCE–17 CE), a fine and famous Roman historian.

Pygmalion: king of Cyprus, who made and then so admired a beautiful statue of a naked woman that he prayed to Aphrodite, goddess of love, to give him a wife who resembled his statue. She brought the statue itself to life, and he married her. See Ovid, *Metamorphoses,* book 10.

Ápellés or Zeuxis: Both famous painters: for Apelles, see note to p. 171; Zeuxis worked in the latter part of the fifth century BCE, something less than a century before Apelles. He was especially noted for his paintings of the female body.

338 *Pallas:* Pallas Athena, both the goddess of wisdom and a goddess of war.
Bacchus: See note to p. 274.

341 *Ápius:* Roman consul in 451 BCE, the judge's full name was Apius Claudius and the girl's name was truly Virginia—and this being told by Livy, not Jerome, the entire story is true. The judge's conduct, indeed, produced a revolution, which led to much more democratic government in Rome. And yes, the judge committed suicide before he could be brought to trial.

INTRODUCTION TO THE
PARDON PEDDLER'S TALE

345 *Saint Ronyán:* This may be Saint Ronan, a Celt (in 1823, Sir Walter Scott published a novel titled *St Ronan's Well*). It may also refer to a Scottish saint with a similar name, often pronounced in widely varying ways, but often referred to in fourteenth-century texts.

346 bel ami: good friend

THE PARDON PEDDLER'S TALE

351 *drunken Lot:* Son of Abraham's brother, Haran, who settled at Sodom. When this immoral city was about to be destroyed by God, Lot was spared. But his two virgin daughters, believing that the whole world had been destroyed, connived to make him drunk, so they could sleep with him and thus begin to repopulate the world. One resulting child was called Moab, founding father of the Moabites; the other child was Benammi, father of the children of Ammon. (See Genesis 19).

Herod: Herod had been afraid of Saint John the Baptist, "knowing that he was a just man, and holy," as Herod, Roman-appointed ruler of the land, was not. Herod married his brother's wife, and John was critical; John was therefore imprisoned. When Herod was drunk one night, his wife's daughter danced for his company, and Herod wanted her. Her asking price was Saint John the Baptist's head. He had it cut off and presented to her. (See also note to p. 93.)

352 *Seneca:* See notes to pp. 122 and 190.

353 *Samson:* Born a Nazarite (a strict Jewish sect), Samson never drank anything but water. See Judges 13:5.

354 *consider Attila:* (d. 453) Chieftain of the Huns, who had been a herding society at the edges of China. They invaded Europe from the east and also invaded India from the north. Most of eastern Europe was under Attila's control at the time of his death: he died of a nosebleed and an apoplectic fit, caused by excessive drinking on the night he married a new wife.

Lamuel: King Lemuel was taught by his mother "It is not for kings, O Lemuel, it is not for kings to drink wine; nor for princes strong drink, lest they drink and forget the law, and pervert the judgment of any of the afflicted" (Proverbs 31: 5–6).

Chilbon: The story is clear, but the identification of Chilbon is not. (Lacedomia is Sparta.) There are at least two candidates. I prefer "Chilon," who in 556 BCE cleaned up the city's politics. He was, by Greek tradition, one of the Seven Sages of Greece, the others being the likes of Solon (c.640–561 BCE), one of the primal reformers of Athens.

355 *King Demetrius:* (187–150 BCE) Probably the second son of emperor Seleucus IV. Having in 162 won back the throne, he proved to be a capable leader, crushing a rebel general and reconquering Palestine. He died in battle, attacked by a pretender to his throne, set on him by the kings of Egypt and a relatively small Hellenic kingdom, Pergamum.

Parthian king: Partia was a west Asian kingdom, semi-nomadic, which began exerting serious military strength in 247 BCE. Their cavalry was daring, and they were famous for their horse archers, who were able to accurately shoot arrows looking backward as they rode.

362 *Avicenna:* (980–1037) Persian-born physician and philosopher, whose Arabic name is Abu Ali al-Husayn ibn Sina. He wrote widely on different scientific topics, but in those matters was best known (and most often consulted) for his *Canon Medicine.* Profiting from a knowledge of Greek that few if any in the West could have rivaled, he brought Greek theosophy into the scriptural tradition.

363 *Saint Helen the holy:* The mother of Constantine the Great (c.285–37), who was emperor of Rome from 306–37, responsible for the fusion of Roman power with the Christian faith. Helena was said to have found the true cross on which Christ was crucified.

THE SHIPMAN'S TALE

366 *Bruges:* The city of Bruges, in northwest Belgium, was connected to the sea, and its Zeebruge port, by a canal. Bruges was a major commercial center.

369 *Saint Martin:* The Bishop of Tours, Saint Martin (d.397) founded the first monastery in what was then known as Gaul, now known as France.

Denys: Also known as Saint Dionysius, Saint Denys (d. 274) was the bishop of Paris and became the patron saint of France.

371 *Saint Yves:* This may have been Saint Ives of Huntingdonshire, known as "a very Persian bishop," who preached in England in the seventh century.

THE PRIORESS'S TALE

381 *Nicholas:* A bishop of the first half of the fourth century, famous both for his precocious learning as a child, and also for the piety he displayed, even as a baby at the breast: he would suckle, it was said, only once on Wednesdays and Fridays. He is the patron saint of all schoolboys. He is said to have provided dowries for poor girls, so they could be married: this may be why the jolly old man who comes bearing presents the night before Christmas is known as "Saint Nicholas."

382 *Herod's People:* See note to pp. 93 and 351.

386 *Hugh of Lincoln:* (?1246–55) One of the many anti-Jewish tales, concocted out of fear and unfamiliarity, this legend declared that a Christian child had been starved, tortured, and crucified by a Jew named either Copin or Joppin, in the city of Lincoln. The body was said to have been found in a well; it was also said to have performed miracles after it was buried at Lincoln Cathedral. The edition of the Middle English text, edited by Larry D. Benson and described in full bibliographical detail in the Translator's Foreword to this book, observes that "Hugh was regularly listed among martyred saints until recent times, though it is clear that the boy was not murdered by Jews."

SIR THOPAS

389 *flowered setwáll:* a gingerlike spice.

391 *Termagaunt:* a fictive invention, supposed to have been a Muslim god.

393 King Horn: the oldest surviving verse romance written in English, dated to about 1225.
  and Ypotis: a verse legend in which a small child teaches the Christian faith to Hadrian, the Roman emperor.
  Beves, Sir Guy and Sir Bevis: characters from other verse romances, *Bevis of Hampton* (late thirteenth or early fourteenth century) and *Guy of Warwick* (about 1340).
  The Fair Unknown: a translation of *Lybeaus Desconus* in modern French ("le beaux inconnu"), a character in Thomas Chester's fourteenth-century romance of that name.
  He Full of Love: called by Chaucer Pleyndamour (modern French, "plein d'amour").

THE TALE OF MELIBEE

397 *what Ovid had said:* See note to p. 123.

398 *Jesus, son of Sirach:* The author of Ecclesiastes is self-identified as "Jesus, son of Eleazar, son of Sirach." There is no known Hebrew title; the Latin title, "Ecclesiastes," probably means "the churchly/ecclesiastical book." The quotation, however, is from not Ecclesiastes, but Proverbs 17:22.

401 *Petrus Alphonus:* a Spanish Jew, converted to Christianity in 1106.

404 *Tobias:* The words quoted are from the *Apocryphal Book of Tobit,* Tobit being the father, and Tobias the son to whom he speaks (Tobit 4:5).

406 *Cicero:* See note to p. 313.

406 *Aesop:* (d. 564 BCE) fabulist and moralist.

407 *Cassiodorus:* Flavius Magnus Aurelius Cassiodorus (c.490–583), Roman statesman, and a Christian; he ended his life as a monk.

408 *Cato:* See note to p. 89.

420 *Pamphilius:* Christian scholar and teacher (b. third century CE), teacher of Eusebius, was martyred in 310. His library provided much of the material Eusebius used in his best-known book, *Ecclesiastical History.*

423 *Judas Maccabeus:* oldest son of the leader of the second-century-BCE Jewish (Hasmonean) revolt against the Syrian king, Antiochus Epiphanes. He became the leader, won many battles, but was killed in 162.

THE PROLOGUE OF THE MONK'S TALE

431 *Madrian:* a saint unknown to us, but perhaps known to Chaucer, or equally likely, a deliberate mangling of some other saint's name.

432 *Rochester:* a town roughly twenty-five miles from Canterbury.

433 *good Saint Edward's:* most likely, Edward the Confessor (1003–66), called to the throne in 1042, and the next-to-last Saxon ruler of England. He was canonized in 1161.

THE MONK'S TALE

436 *Gaza:* ancient Palestine city on the south coastal plain, two miles inland. It is now the chief city of the so-called Gaza Strip, between Israel and Egypt.

437 *Cérberús:* monster dog, guardian of the entrance to Hades, the underworld. There are various accounts of how many heads Cerberus had, but the lowest number is three. Hesiod said the monster had fifty heads.

Búsirús: Egyptian king, son of Poseidon, who killed all foreigners entering Egypt. Hercules killed the king and all his followers.

Áchelós: name of the longest river in Greece, roughly 150 miles.

Cácus: He terrified the Palatine area, near Rome, before making the mistake of stealing from Hercules.

438 *A dying centaur:* Nessus, who ferried travelers over a river. He took Dianira, Hercules' wife, across and then tried to rape her. Hercules killed him with a poisoned arrow.

Nébuckadnézzar: king of Babylon, 605–562 BCE. He conquered everything from the Euphrates River (1,700 miles long, running from eastern Turkey to the Persian Gulf) to the Egyptian border; Judah was among his conquests.

439 *Daniel:* See note to p. 141.

Chaldéan Priests: The Chaldeans were a Semitic tribe; they migrated to southern Babylonia and adopted Babylonian culture. They came to rule the country, losing in a struggle with Persia in 579 BC. Their reputation as astrologers lasted much longer than their empire.

440 *Belshazzar:* Chaucer has taken this version of Babylonian history from the *Apocryphal Book of Daniel.* It has been since established that Belshazzar was not the son of or the successor to Nebuchadnezzar. Nabondinus was the next king; he left the throne three years later, going into the desert to worship the moon god, and making Belshazzar a regent. In 539 the Persians conquered Babylon.

442 *Zenóbiá:* Second wife of the king of Palmyra, she probably murdered both her husband and his son by an earlier marriage, and took the throne as regent for her own young son. When in 271 BCE she proclaimed her son "Augustus," Rome marched against her and captured the queen and her sons. They were taken to Rome and displayed as battle trophies, after which Zenobia was granted a pension and a villa.

445 *Pedro, glory of Spain:* In 1369, the king was assassinated by his illegitimate half brother.

446 *not Charles Oliver:* Charles was a close friend of Roland (in the *Chanson de Roland, Song of Roland,* dating from the early twelfth century), and was a true friend, unlike the Breton Ganelon, who betrayed Roland and caused his death. King Pedro was known at the British court.

Petro, King of Cyprus: Assassinated in 1369, Petro too was known at the British court. However, it was the king's oppressive conduct that led to his death.

Bárnabó, a Viscount from Milan: Imprisoned in May 1385, Barnabo died there in December, most likely after being poisoned. Not only was Barnabo known at and connected to the British court, he was also a personal acquaintance of Geoffrey Chaucer.

Ugilino, Count of Pisa: Ugilino successfully conspired with Bishop Roger to take the throne of Pisa. In 1289, Roger charged him with betrayal of Pisan interests and threw him and his sons into prison, where they all died in 1289.

448 *Nero:* (32–68 CE; emperor of Rome, 54–68) extravagant, vain, fearful, and above all murderous. See also note to p. 122.

450 *Hóloférnes:* See note to p. 150.

451 *Antióchus:* Antióchis IV, king of Syria, 175–163 BCE.

453 *Alexander the Great:* (356–323 BCE) Macedonian king and general, conqueror of Greece, Egypt, Persia, Iran, and in 327–25, northwest India—after which his army refused to follow him any further. We are told that his favorite book was *The Iliad,* Homer's brilliant, intense, but gory tale of the battles at Troy. We do not know whether he died of too much alcohol or poison.

454 *Julius Caesar:* Gaius Julius Caesar (July 12, 100 BCE–March 15, 44 BCE), politician, general, hero. Ordered to disband his armies in 49 BCE, on the other side of the river Rubicon as he headed to Rome, Caesar simply crossed the river and continued on. He was appointed dictator (a tempo-

rary post) and fought many successful battles in many different places—
after one of which, in 47 BCE, he announced, *Veni, vidi, vici,* "I came, I saw, I
conquered." He was approaching the title of "emperor" when Cassius, Bru-
tus et al. assassinated him in the Roman senate.

454 *Pompey the Elder:* Gnaeus Pompeius Magnus (106–48 BCE), politician and
general. In 60 BCE, Pompey joined with Caesar and Crassus and succeeded
in having Caesar elected as one of the ruling consuls. In 55, he and Crassus
were elected consuls; in 53, after Crassus was killed, Pompey became sole
consul. The civil war with Caesar led to Pompey's defeat at the battle of
Pharsalus, and then to his death in Egypt.

455 *Lucan:* See note to p. 134.
Valerius Maximus: See note to p. 190.
Suetonius: Gaius Suetonius Tranquillus (b. c.70 CE), Roman biographer, best
known for his *Lives of the Caesars.*
Croesus: See note to p. 54.

THE NUN'S PRIEST'S TALE

462 *Dionysius Cato:* third- or fourth-century-CE author of *Catonis Disticha, The
Distichs* (rhymed couplets) *of Cato,* usually known simply as *Cato.* This was a
favorite teaching tool until well into the eighteenth century.
cornflower, laurel, fumitory: traditional laxatives.
hellebore: a laxative with other mind-numbing properties.
caper spurge . . . dogwood berries: Caper spurge (better known as euphorbia,
after a Greek physician) has calming effects; dogwood (with other similar
shrubs, like buckthorn: there are more than fifty varieties) seems to have
had pungent flavoring qualities.

463 *ivy leaves:* both a purgative and a poison, depending on the particular vari-
ety, it was often used for cough medicine.

466 *Saint Kenelm's:* (d. 821) Made king of Mercia, in central Britain, at the age of
seven, when his father died, he was raised as a devout Christian; his dream
was that he had climbed a beautiful tree, which was chopped down beneath
him by traitorous hands. At the end of the dream, his soul flew to heaven
like a bird.
Macróbiús: Ambrosius Theodosius Macrobius (fl. 300 CE), Roman writer and
philosopher.
Scípio Áfricánus: (236–183 BCE) Roman general, conqueror of Spain, and suc-
cessful commander of Roman armies in the Second Punic War against
Carthage.

467 *Pharaoh:* See Genesis 40, where Joseph correctly interprets the butler's and
baker's dream, which is about Pharaoh's coming treatment of them, and
then Pharaoh (not knowing of Joseph's predictions) completely vindicates
Joseph's interpretation.
Croesus: See note to p. 54.

Hector's wife: See note to p. 124.

Principio muiler est hominis confusio: The correct translation—Chaucer expected that anyone who could read would know this—is "Woman is the primary cause of man's ruin."

468 *Lancelot of the Lake:* See note to p. 301.

469 *a black coal-fox:* the brant fox, a variety that has more black in its fur.

Gánelón: See note to p. 446

Doctor Áugustíne: In Chaucer's time, the only doctorate anyone ever had was a doctor of theology—a title that Saint Augustine (354–430) well deserved. His *Confessions,* a remarkable autobiography, has never gone out of print. *The City of God* remains a singularly valuable philosophical treatise, motivated by the fall of Rome in 410. (The title was freely used as an honorific, whether it represented an earned degree or not.)

Boéthiús: See note to p. 190.

Bishop Bradwardine: Thomas Bradwardine (c.1290–1349), theologian at Oxford, appointed archbishop of Canterbury just before he died of the plague.

470 *Phísiológus:* Physiologus ("the Naturalist"), an ancient compilation, moral and symbolical, of many fabulous anecdotes, most of them involving animals. Neither its author nor its date is known; it was in use in the fourth century CE.

471 The Mirror of Fools: The *Speculum Stultorum,* written about 1190 by Nigel Wireker (Nigellus Wireker), director of the choir at Christ Church, Canterbury. Its satire is aimed at monks.

a benefice living: an ecclesiastical post with a fixed yearly salary, often requiring virtually no attendance at the site or any churchly responsibilities.

472 *fell on a Friday:* considered to be a day when unlucky things happened. It was also, as Chaucer quickly reminds us, Venus' day.

Geoffroi: Geoffrey of Vinsauf (c.1210), author of *Poetria Nova, The New Poetry,* the standard medieval text on medieval rhetoric and the writing of proper poetry.

Aeneid: See notes to pp. 123 and 200.

Hásdrubal's wife: See note to p. 331.

473 *even Jack Straw:* leader of a huge crowd of angry and oppressed peasants, during the Peasants' Revolt of 1381. The story is powerfully, evocatively told in Simone Zelitch's 1991 novel, *The Confession of Jack Straw.*

THE SECOND NUN'S PROLOGUE

477 *Saint Cecilia:* Martyred between 176 and 180 CE, she became the patron saint of music, apparently because she celebrated God with music as well as words.

PRAYER TO THE VIRGIN MARY

478 *Saint Bérnard:* (c.1090–1153) a monk at Clairvaux famous for his devotion to the Virgin Mary.

479 *daughter of Anne:* See note to p. 141.

COMMENTARY ON THE NAME "CECILIA"

480 The Golden Legend: A fat anthology, in Latin, of the legends and lore of saints' lives, compiled by Jacobus de Voragine (1230–98), an Italian cleric. His own title for the book was *Lives of the Saints.* The editors and translators of a highly readable English translation say all that needs to be said: "From the fact that there are over five hundred [manuscript] copies of the book in existence, and that within the first hundred years of printing it appeared in more than one hundred and fifty editions and translations, it is obvious that [the book] was in extremely wide demand." (*The Golden Legend,* ed. and trans. by Granger Ryan and Helmut Ripperger. New York: Longmans Green, 1941, vii.)

THE SECOND NUN'S TALE

483 *Vía Ápiá:* the Appian Way, in Rome, running from Rome to Capua and Brundisium.
Urban the old: Pope Urban I, so chosen in 222; he was beheaded May 25, 230.

486 *Saint Ambrose:* (c.340–97) Bishop of Milan, who baptized Augustine; he is considered one of the Four Doctors of the Church. He originated the Ambrosian chant and worked at improving church music.

PROLOGUE OF THE CLERIC-MAGICIAN'S SERVANT

495 *Boughton:* roughly five miles from Canterbury.

496 *horse . . . is a hack:* a rented horse, at a time when anyone of elevated status owned rather then rented horses. There is the secondary meaning, not necessarily applicable, here, of a jaded, worn-out animal.

TALE OF THE CLERIC-MAGICIAN'S SERVANT

501 *powdered porphyry:* rock, like marble; more generally crystals made by grinding rocks down.

502 *crucibles:* melting pots.
alembic: transmitting apparatus, used both literally and figuratively.
sal ammoniac: ammonium chloride, used for electroplating and, medically, as an expectorant.
Like agrimony, valerian, and moonwort: common herbs, more usually, in Chaucer's time, employed medicinally than for chemical processes.

furnace of calcification: hardening, using heat to replace other matter by lime.

albumination: using an acid, or other chemical, to alter the structure of albumen (most readily obtained from egg white).

ratsbane: arsenic.

506 *Ninevee:* Nineveh, capitol of the Assyrian Empire, after c.1100 BCE.

518 *Bayard the Blind:* Bayard was a common name for a horse, and "as bold as blind Bayard" was a proverbial comparison.

Arnaldus de Villanova: (c.1235–1314) author of a treatise on alchemy and many other scientific and technical matters.

Hérmes Trísmegéstus: name employed by early Christian-era (but not necessarily Christian) Neoplatonists and mystics when referring to the Egyptian god Thoth (who was said to be Hermes as well). He was thought to be the originator and protector of all knowledge and the author of a collection of Greek and Latin religious and philosophical writings, assembled sometime between the first and third centuries BCE.

Plato: See note to p. 22.

Seniorus Zadith: probably the treatise *Secreta Secretorum, The Secret of Secrets,* attributed to (but certainly not written by) Aristotle.

THE PROVISIONER'S PROLOGUE

520 *Bobbing-up-and-down:* There is an "Up and down field" in Thannington Parish, but most scholars identify Chaucer's "bobbe-up-and-doun" as Harbledown, which can also be spelled "Herbaldown" and "Hebbadonne."

522 *Bacchus:* See note to p. 274.

THE PROVISIONER'S TALE

523 *Ámphión, the king of Thebes:* See notes to pp. 43 and 273.

525 *Plato:* See note to p. 22.

526 *Alexander the Great:* See note to p. 453.

THE PARSON'S PROLOGUE

531 *I am a Southern man:* that is, the south of England, and especially London, where the version of Middle English then spoken is the basis for the English language as we know it. In particular, the Parson (and he of course speaks for Chaucer, here) is casting a mild degree of scorn on alliterative-based poetry, drawing on deep Anglo-Saxon/Old English roots. The prime (but by no means only) surviving exemplars of Middle English alliterative verse are *Sir Gawain and the Green Knight* and *Piers the Plowman,* the former courtly and so much influenced by rhyming poetry that it alternates alliterative and rhyming patterns, the latter blunt and "boorish," but also at times exceedingly beautiful.

THE PARSON'S TALE

Note: Biblical references are not here included.

533 *Saint Ambrose:* See note to p. 486.
Saint Isidore of Seville: (570–636) an immensely prolific and widely ranging author, very popular in the Middle Ages.

534 *Saint Gregory:* (540–604) Pope from 590–604, Gregory was a reformer and a prolific writer; his works were influential for many years.
Saint Augustine: See note to p. 469.
Saint John Christosom: (c.354–407) Bishop of Constantinople; he acquired a huge reputation for his preaching, which explains the name Christosom, meaning "the golden-mouthed."

535 *Saint Bernard:* See note to p. 478

537 *Saint Jerome:* See notes to pp. 176 and 330.
Saint Anselm: (1033–1109) Of Italian birth, he studied in France, and was offered and accepted a post in England. He has been described as the cornerstone of the Augustinian tradition in the Middle Ages, with its emphasis on faith in search of reason.

540 *Saint Basil:* (c.330–79) A Greek by birth, he studied in Constantinople and Athens; he was baptized in 356. In 370 he became bishop of Caesaria (Cappadocia, in Greece). He was a classicist and opposed to solitary asceticism.

552 *Saint Anthony's fire:* ergotism, disease producing blisters and rotting of the skin.

555 *Seneca:* See notes to pp. 122 and 190.

576 *Saint Damasus:* (336–84) Probably born in Rome; he was elected pope in 366. It was Damasus who persuaded Jerome to undertake translation of the Bible into Latin (known now as the Vulgate translation).

579 *Galen:* (?129–199 CE) He began as a gladiator-physician and rose to the position of court physician in Rome during the reign of Marcus Aurelius. He wrote philosophical treatises, but his major and lasting contribution lay in his medical books, which were consulted and widely relied upon for well over a millennium.

ABOUT THE TRANSLATOR

BURTON RAFFEL is Distinguished Professor of Arts and Humanities Emeritus at the University of Louisiana at Lafayette. His many translations include Rabelais's *Gargantua and Pantagruel,* winner of the 1991 French-American Foundation Translation Prize; Chrétien de Troyes's Arthurian romances; Cervantes's *Don Quijote;* and Balzac's *Père Goriot.* His translation of *Beowulf* has sold more than a million copies.

A NOTE ON THE TYPE

The principal text of this Modern Library edition
was set in a digitized version of Janson, a typeface that
dates from about 1690 and was cut by Nicholas Kis,
a Hungarian working in Amsterdam. The original matrices have
survived and are held by the Stempel foundry in Germany.
Hermann Zapf redesigned some of the weights and sizes for
Stempel, basing his revisions on the original design.